T0368407

THE
SOUTHLAND
CONFERENCE

SMALL COLLEGE
FOOTBALL,
BIG DREAMS

GEORGE BECNEL

authorHOUSE°

AuthorHouse™
1663 Liberty Drive
Bloomington, IN 47403
www.authorhouse.com
Phone: 1 (800) 839-8640

Published by AuthorHouse 07/11/2015

ISBN: 978-1-5049-1888-6 (sc)
ISBN: 978-1-5049-1889-3 (hc)
ISBN: 978-1-5049-1887-9 (e)

Library of Congress Control Number: 2015910047

Print information available on the last page.

Also by George Becnel:

*The Wildcats: A History of
St. James High School Football*

*The Bulldogs: A History of
Lutcher High School Football*

*The Cardinals: A History of
E.D. White Catholic High School Football*

*Big Boy: The Life and (Often Hilarious)
Times of Norman Swanner*

*When the Saints Came Marching In:
What the New Orleans NFL franchise did wrong
(and sometimes right) in its expansion years*

To all college football fans, Southern style.

CONTENTS

FOREWORD

The history of Southland Conference football from its birth in 1964 is fully covered in *The Southland Conference: Small College Football, Big Dreams* by George Becnel. In fact, it is almost a year-by-year, game-by-game, play-by-play account. He has written as a sportswriter covering a game with play-by-play action from the time the conference competed as an almost all-Texas league (save one) to its transformation as a conference with teams from throughout the states bordering the Gulf of Mexico.

He carries the reader from the days of the league's station in College Division football to Division II, to Division I and back again to I-AA and to its now domicile in the FCS bracket. Also chronicled are such bowl games as the Pecan Bowl, the Pioneer Bowl and the Independence Bowl to national championship games.

One reads about top game efforts from such players as Leonard Smith (McNeese), Marvin Upshaw (Trinity), John Stephens (Northwestern State) and Roger Carr (Louisiana Tech) who go on to be first round NFL selections and Bill Bergey (Arkansas State), Roger Carr (Louisiana Tech), Larry Centers (SFA), Fred Dean (Louisiana Tech), Terrence McGee (Northwestern State), Rafael Septien (Southwestern Louisiana), John Stephens (Northwestern State), Pat Tilley (Louisiana Tech) and Jeremiah Trotter (SFA) who become pro-bowl selections.

The Southland Conference fan will enjoy this book.

Louis Bonnette
Longtime McNeese State Sports Information Director

PREFACE AND ACKNOWLEDGMENTS

They were not necessarily the biggest, strongest or fastest players. The vast majority were not heavily recruited. Yet, for those involved, the Southland Conference provided an opportunity – and a purpose.

One such player was Billy Stewart, a linebacker at Texas-Arlington from the 1960s.

"I was a three-year starter in high school," said Stewart. "I was a good football player, but analyzing my talent, I shouldn't have gone to the majors or the independents. I would have just been run over or lost. I chose to go to a small college because I felt it fit my talent ability where I could play football, be happy, and get a good education.

"We were inundated with people exactly like me that didn't go major (college) and chose to go to a place where we could play football and have success academically and athletically. In making that choice, our dreams were fulfilled."

The Southland Conference: Small College Football, Big Dreams, chronicles the playing days of Stewart and many others as well as taking a comprehensive historical look at the first fifty years of the league from its inception in 1964.

For the players, coaches and fans of the conference and its teams, *The Southland Conference: Small College Football, Big Dreams* is a chance to relive past glories. It also may help to settle a friendly wager or two on the facts of a specific game as memories start to fade.

For the casual fan, *The Southland Conference: Small College Football, Big Dreams* allows readers to learn about the quality of play in the league, including some of its top teams and star players.

A few readers may discover that some of their favorite NFL players are products of the Southland Conference.

Many may not be aware future NFL receivers such as Roger Carr, Mike Barber, Pat Tilley and Billy Ryckman, for example, were all teammates on Louisiana Tech's Division II national championship team in 1973.

Others may learn such facts as Super Bowl quarterback Stan Humphries of the San Diego Chargers led Northeast Louisiana University to the 1987 Division I-AA national title.

In order to avoid confusion, the university located in Monroe, Louisiana, is referred to as Northeast Louisiana, not by the current name of the University of Louisiana at Monroe. That's because when the school was in the Southland, it was known as the Northeast Louisiana Indians. No teams during the university's tenure in the SLC ever lost or beat a team called the Louisiana-Monroe Warhawks.

Likewise, the school now known as the University of Louisiana at Lafayette is referred to in the book as the University of Southwestern Louisiana.

If a school changed its name during its Southland Conference tenure, then that is reflected. Thus, the Arlington State Rebels become the Texas-Arlington Mavericks and Southwest Texas is later referred to as Texas State University.

The school initials "NSU" are avoided. Both Northwestern State University and Nicholls State University stake a claim to the initials. To avoid confusion, in *The Southland Conference: Small College Football, Big Dreams,* the schools are simply referred to as Northwestern State and Nicholls State.

The author wishes to thank the sports information staffs of the Southland Conference schools, past and present.

Concerning sports information personnel, the author also thanks Louis Bonnette for writing the foreward. The retired longtime sports information director at McNeese State, no one has seen more Southland Conference events than Louis. Plus, it only seemed natural for a SID who can literally see his school's football stadium from his own backyard to write the foreward.

Additional thanks to the staffs of the following libraries for all their help: Albert B. Alkek Library, Texas State University; Ellender Memorial Library, Nicholls State University; Dean B. Ellis Library, Arkansas State University; Jonesboro Public Library, Jonesboro, Arkansas; Lafourche Parish Public Library, Thibodaux, Louisiana, branch; Magale Library, Southern Arkansas University; Middleton Library, Louisiana State University; San Antonio Public Library; State Library of Louisiana, Baton Rouge, Louisiana; and Texas State Library, Austin, Texas.

Source material for *The Southland Conference: Small College Fooball, Big Dreams* includes: *The Arkansas Gazette; Baton Rouge Morning Advocate; Beaumont Enterprize; Dallas Morning News; Fort Worth Star-Telegram; Houma Courier; Houston Chronicle; Houston Post; Jonesboro Evening Sun; Monroe News-Star; The*

Optimist; Abilene Christian University student newspaper; *The Redbird*, Lamar University student newspaper; *San Antonio Express-News*; *Shreveport Times*; and *The Trinitonian*, Trinity University student newspaper.

Special thanks to David Bernard for his editing assistance.

BIRTH OF A CONFERENCE

For four schools that were competing as small college independents and another that was a member of the Lone Star Conference, a National Association of Intercollegiate Athletics league, it was time for a change.

So, at the Baker Hotel in Dallas on March 15,1963, representatives from four Texas schools – Abilene Christian, Arlington State, Lamar Tech and Trinity University – along with Arkansas State, met for form a new league and create a bit of history.

Among those meeting on that fateful day were the presidents of the five schools, Carl R. Reng of Arkansas State, F.L. McDonald of Lamar Tech, J.R. Wolf of Arlington State, Don Morris of Abilene Christian and James W. Laurie of Trinity.

The group bandied together to form a new conference, with the hopes of beginning competition in sports such as football, basketball and track no later than the 1965 season.

"The conference is designed to encourage high academic standards and athletic excellence. Scheduling is to begin with all due speed. It is expected the conference will be in full swing with regard to the required major sports in 1965," Reng said in a press release the day of the announcement.

"We are well satisfied with the new conference and anticipate a long and rewarding relationship with its member schools," offered Jess Carnes, Trinity's athletic board of control chairman.

The officials announced the league would operate within the framework of the National Collegiate Athletic Association.

"The new conference is the best news we've had in a long time. It should stimulate greater interest in varsity sports, not only on campus, but among sportsmen throughout this area who like to see good collegiate football with a championship at stake," said W.C. "Dub" McElhannon, Trinity's football coach.

A.B. Morris, athletic director at Abilene Christian, echoed the sentiments of Reng and McElhannon.

"We in the athletic department are happy to be in the conference and especially associated with these particular schools. All of our coaches feel that it will be beneficial to our department in many ways, such as recruiting. They also feel that the privilege of playing for a championship will give the athletes more incentive," said Morris.

For Abilene Christian and the three other schools besides Lamar Tech that competed as independents, the new league helped to alleviate scheduling problems. The Wildcats had been competing as an independent after the Gulf Coast Conference disbanned following the 1957-58 season.

"I know of past experience that it will be a great help in scheduling as this is quite a problem for independents schools. Being in a good, strong conference, as this one is expected to be, will add prestige to our entire program," Morris said.

Like Abilene Christian, Arkansas State had operated as an independent after leaving the Arkansas Intercollegiate Conference in 1951.

By April 5, 1963, the league had an official name – The Southland Conference.

On the day the new conference got its name, J.W. Roberts of Abilene Christian was voted the Southland's first president. Jack Boon of Arlington State was named vice-president and Carnes secretary treasurer.

The timetable for the start of conference competition was moved up, with the Southland announcing it would determine a basketball champion at the conclusion of the 1963-64 season. Champions in track, golf, tennis and baseball would be determined in the spring of 1964.

Football, the league announced, would not begin to compete for a conference title until 1964. While putting together a conference football schedule would not be difficult for independent schools, Lamar Tech faced a different situation. As a departing member of the Lone Star Conference, Lamar's football schedule was set for two years, so the Southland decided to start league play in 1964.

The move to the Southland Conference meant a major commitment by the schools in the new league. The football scholarship limit in the SLC was set at 50. For a school like Lamar, for example, the institution operated with 55 scholarships for all sports.

"We here at Arlington are real pleased with the set-up. We've wanted to get into a conference for some time. This is the answer," said Claude "Chena" Gilstrap, Arlington State football coach.

Conference officials also stated their desire to achieve major status.

"It was stated in our messages to the school presidents that we would work toward major college status. We're meeting all requirements toward that aim," said Roberts.

IN THE BEGINNING

The first-ever Southland Conference football game featured Lamar Tech hosting Abilene Christian in Beaumont on Sept. 26, 1964 in brand new Cardinal Stadium. It was the second game of the season for the Cardinals, who opened the 1964 campaign with a 21-0 win over East Central of Oklahoma. Abilene Christian, meanwhile, entered the game with two games under its belt. The Wildcats opened with a pair of wins, topping Howard Payne and East Texas State.

The initial points in Southland Conference history came on a 33-yard field goal by Abilene Christian's Roger Youngblood. It would prove to be the only points yielded by a stingy Cardinals defense over the course of their first two games as Lamar went on to post a 14-3 victory over the Wildcats.

Through the first two games, no opponent had driven the length of the field against Lamar as Youngblood's field goal was set up by a Cardinals fumble.

The Cardinals came up with all the points they would need when Dan Yezak raced 5 yards for a touchdown to cap a 72-yard, 17-play drive in the second period for a 7-3 lead.

Lamar looked to put the game away late in the third quarter. A 44-yard run by Yezak advanced the Cardinals deep into Abilene Christian territory, but the Cardinals turned the ball over on downs just short of the goal line.

It proved to be just a momentary delay for the Cardinals. On Abilene Christian's first play following the stop, Jacky Roland fumbled and Lamar defensive tackle Harvey Stuessel recovered in the end zone for the 14-3 final.

Lamar's low-scoring formula continued a week later at Southland Conference foe Trinity.

The Cardinals' streak of not yielding a touchdown ended at eight quarters when Trinity drove 66 yards with the opening kickoff. Quarterback Danny Witwiski scored from a yard out to cap the drive, but like in the Abilene Christian game, Lamar's defense would not allow another score.

Trinity's 7-0 lead held up until the opening drive of the second half. The Cardinals, ranked No. 2 among small college teams, marched 69 yards, tying the game on a 19-yard pass from quarterback Phillip Primm to Frazier Dealy.

The game was still tied when Lamar got the ball back with four minutes left in the game. Needing only a field goal for a win, the Cardinals instead came up with a touchdown on Hal LaFitte's 7-yard scoring run with 56 seconds left in the contest to culminate a 79-yard drive to give Lamar a 14-7 victory.

"Back in those days, the scores were a lot lower than they are today," said Primm. "You didn't have the high-powered offenses. You didn't have the clock that stopped on first downs and you got a lot less plays off."

By being the only Southland team to play – and win - two games, Lamar quickly gained control of the conference race while improving to 3-0 overall. Trinity remained winless at 0-4 after dropping its league opener.

Arkansas State and Arlington College became the final two teams to make their Southland Conference debuts when the Indians visited the Rebels on Oct. 10, 1964. Arkansas State went into the game unbeaten at 3-0 with wins over Tennessee State, North Alabama and Stephen F. Austin. Arlington State, meanwhile, was 1-2 and coming off a 14-0 loss to Southern Methodist of the Southwest Conference.

The only score of the first half between Arkansas State and Arlington State came on a 1-yard run by Kenneth Bowman. The Rebels fullback went on to rush for 123 yards in the game.

Arkansas State marched 78 yards with the second-half kickoff. The big play in the drive was a 34-yard pass from Gary Everett to Tommy Clark. Tommy Reese's 7-yard touchdown run tied the game.

Neither team could produce any more points, resulting in a 7-7 tie. Both teams missed opportunities for more points. The Rebels had four drives end inside the Arkansas State 20-yard line, including two missed field goals by Al Smith. Arkansas State's Dick Famiglietti returned a fumble to the Rebels' 27 but Dan Summers missed an 18-yard field goal attempt.

Bennie Ellender's Indians earned their first Southland Conference victory a week later with a 35-13 domination of Trinity.

Playing at home for the first time since the season opener, Arkansas State turned two blocked punts by Truman Moore into touchdowns on its way to the victory. Moore's first block was recovered by Bob McCuiston in the end zone for a touchdown. Moore's other block eventually led to an 11-yard touchdown pass from Everett to Bill Pagano.

Shelby Lee added two touchdown passes for Arkansas State.

All of Trinity's points came in the fourth quarter on 27-yard touchdown pass by Glenn Obie and a 1-yard run by Bob Eason.

Arkansas State moved to 2-0-1 in the Southland and 5-0-1 overall with a 21-7 win at Abilene Christian.

Instead of blocked punts, Arkansas State turned a pair of fumbles into touchdowns on its way to remaining unbeaten in Southland play with a 21-7 victory at Abilene Christian. Playing a league game for the third week in a row, the Indians used a 17-yard pass from Everett to Pagano following a Wildcats fumble for the only score of the first half. Everett's 6-yard touchdown toss to Reese in the third quarter was set up by an Abilene Christian fumble at the Wildcats' 24.

The Wildcats cut the margin to 14-7 on a 21-yard run by fullback Joe Paty. Abilene Christian recovered the ensuing kickoff but the Wildcats failed to take advantage when Youngblood missed a 25-yard field goal. Arkansas State put the game on ice on an 8-yard run by Billy Joe Bailey with less than three minutes remaining in the fourth quarter.

Halloween in 1964 featured the first time more than one Southland Conference game was played on the same day.

Playing its first Southland game in four weeks, Lamar Tech hosted Arlington State. Following the Cardinals' win over Trinity to move to 2-0 in the SLC, Lamar suffered two non-conference losses for a 3-2 overall record going into the Arlington State encounter. The Rebels entered the contest 2-3-1. After a tie game with Arkansas State in its lone Southland game of the year, Arlington State split two non-conference games.

After giving up a total of 46 points in its two losses, Lamar's defense clamped down once again in Southland Conference play.

A 29-yard Mike Allman field goal broke a scoreless tie to give Lamar a 3-0 lead in the second quarter. Arlington State countered with a 1-yard run by Bowman to give the Rebels a 7-3 edge at halftime.

Following a familiar pattern, the Cardinal defense allowed no more than one score to a Southland opponent, blanking Arlington in the second half. Meanwhile, Lamar put away its third conference win on touchdowns set up by a pair of interceptions. Jake David's interception set up a 3-yard touchdown run by Darrel Johnson and Steve Bailey raced 25 yards after a Burt Allman theft to give the Cardinals a 17-7 triumph.

"It was a good defensive team the time I was there," Primm said of the Cardinals. "It sure made my job a lot easier."

In the other Halloween affair, Trinity defeated visiting Abilene Christian 26-7. The home win in San Antonio was not only the Tigers' first-ever Southland victory, but also their first of the 1964 campaign as Trinity went into the Abilene game 0-7. The Wildcats fell to 4-4 overall after a 4-1 start and dropped to 0-3 in Southland play.

The Wildcats must have thought the footballs were more like hexed pumpkins in the Southland Conference encounter.

Abilene was forced to punt in the first quarter. Jackie Hall returned the kick to the Wildcats' 37. Trinity need 12 plays but eventually scored on a 1-yard sneak by Obie for a 7-0 lead for the Tigers.

A 6-yard punt by the Wildcats early in the third quarter set up Trinity's second score. Taking over at the Abilene Christian 48, the Tigers increased their advantage to 14-0 when Obie hooked up with Obert Logan on a 20-yard touchdown toss.

Another punting miscue set up yet another Tigers touchdown. Abilene Christian punter Mike Love was forced to chase down an errant center snap and was brought down at his own 9-yard line. Logan scored from a yard out two plays later to make it 20-0.

Love scored on a 1-yard run in the fourth quarter as Abilene Christian avoided the shutout in the 26-7 loss.

Something had to give in Abilene Christian's home game with Arlington State. Both teams entered the contest without a win in Southland Conference play. Abilene Christian was 0-3 in the SLC and riding a three-game losing streak. Arlington State managed a tie against Arkansas State to open league play and was 2-4-1heading into the game against the Wildcats.

A 28-yard Youngblood field goal and a 16-yard pass from Ronny Winston to Tommy Walker gave the Wildcats a 10-0 edge.

The Rebels got back in the game when Tony Jackson returned the ensuing kickoff 77 yards for a touchdown. Arlington State kicked off to Dennis Hagaman. Known as "The Menace," Hagaman headed to the sideline before handing the ball off to Bubba Brown. Brown raced 83 yards for a touchdown to put the Wildcats back on top by 10 points.

Abilene Christian scored 20 points in the fourth quarter on touchdown runs by Love and Winston, along with a 43-yard interception return by Jerry Anderson. Pete Estrade closed out the scoring on a 1-yard run for the Rebels to make the final 37-14 as Abilene earned its first SLC victory.

The Southland Conference closed out its inaugural season with a pair of games on Nov. 11, 1964. In a game with no title implications, Trinity defeated Arlington State 23-7. The win allowed Trinity to close out the season with three-consecutive victories to finish the year 3-7 overall and 2-2 in conference play.

Arlington State finished as the league's only team without a win, ending 0-3-1 in the SLC and 3-6-1 overall.

Ever since Lamar Tech defeated Arlington State 17-7 in Week 8 to move to 3-0 in the Southland, the stage was set for a showdown against Arkansas State. Lamar went into the game against the Indians 5-2 overall. After a 21-7 win over Abilene Christian left Arkansas State 2-0-1in the SLC and 5-0-1 overall, the Indians added two non-conference wins to move to 7-0-1 heading into their encounter with Lamar.

Arkansas State and Lamar fought through a scoreless tie in the first half. The Indians missed the best scoring opportunity of the opening half when Summers missed a 37-yard field goal attempt.

The Indians marched 64 yards with the second-half kickoff. Reese was the workhorse of the drive. He had runs of 5 and 10 yards, along with an 11-yard reception. A 16-yard pass from Everett to Pagano advanced the ball to the 7-yard line. Reese added a 2-yard run before Ken Mashburn was knocked out of bounds inside the 1-yard line on a reception. Harold Wallin ran up the middle for the score and Summers kicked the extra point for a 7-0 lead.

Lamar gained possession deep in its own territory early in the fourth quarter following an Everett punt that was downed at the Cardinals' 6-yard line. A face-mask penalty helped keep the drive alive and an 18-yard pass from Primm to Gary Casey advanced the ball to the Arkansas State 42. After a 2-yard run by LaFitte, Primm again handed the ball to LaFitte on a draw. The tailback went up the middle, bounced to the outside and outraced Indian defenders for a 40-yard touchdown.

"Harold was a small running back compared to the other two we had when I was there," Primm said. "He was a tough, quick runner and could cut on a dime. For his size, he was about as tough as anybody running the ball."

Knowing a tie would give his team the conference title, Lamar coach Vernon Glass sent out Mike Allman to kick the extra point. Allman was successful on the conversion and Glass was proven right as neither team scored again.

Lamar captured the inaugural Southland Conference championship with a 3-0-1 mark while moving to 5-2-1. Arkansas State, despite going unbeaten at 7-0-2, had to settle for second place by finishing 2-0-2 in league play.

A 14-7 win at Southwest Missouri State in the regular-season finale gave Lamar a 6-2-1 record. The Cardinals' season, however, was not over. By winning the Southland title, Lamar earned a postseason bid to the inaugural Pecan Bowl against the State College of Iowa.

The Pecan Bowl, played at Shotwell Stadium in Abilene, pitted Lamar, the Southland champion, against State College of Iowa, tri-champions of the North Central Conference, for the NCAA Midwest Regional championship of small colleges.

Lamar struck first on a 27-yard Allman field goal in the first quarter, but that would be the only points the Cardinals would score in the first half.

State College of Iowa (later named the University of Northern Iowa) took a 7-3 lead in the first quarter on a 30-yard pass from Rich Oliphant to Del Hammond. Randy Schultz, a Little All-American and the second-leading rusher among small college running backs, scored on a 3-yard run to increase the Panthers' advantage to 13-3 at halftime.

Lamar quickly put itself back in the game when Primm launched an 80-yard bomb to Dealy to cut the score to 13-10.

An aerial attack or bombs to Dealy were not the norm for the Cardinals in 1964.

"The joke was Dealy could never outrun anybody. He ran such a good pattern. He ran a slant and popped it out and he was well behind the safety. I got the ball to him and he did the rest on his own," said Primm.

Schultz, who rushed for 162 yards, scored on a 1-yard run to make it 19-10.

The Cardinals pulled to within two points at 19-17 with less than three minutes left in the game when Primm hooked up with Casey on a 7-yard touchdown toss.

Lamar missed out on another scoring opportunity in the fourth quarter. A fumble recovery gave the Cardinals the ball at the Panthers' 47. Lamar reached first-and-goal at the 9-yard line but a Tommy Currie pass was intercepted in the end zone to end the threat.

The Cardinals closed the season 6-3-1 and as Southland Conference champs in the first year of the league's existence in 1964.

If Lamar Tech and Arkansas State were to be factors again for the Southland title in 1965, conference fans would find out sooner rather than later. Unlike the 1964 season in which the two teams met to close out league play, they hooked up in Week 4 to kick off the 1965 conference campaign.

Lamar Tech entered 1965 Southland Conference play at home against Arkansas State sporting a 2-1 record. Arkansas State entered Southland Conference play 3-0 and riding a 12-game unbeaten streak dating back to the opening game of the 1964 campaign. The Indians continued their winning ways at the start of 1965 with victories over Tennessee Tech 12-7, North Alabama 33-12 and Stephen F. Austin 3-0.

Perhaps with revenge on their minds, the 10th-ranked Indians jumped out on top 7-0 late in the first quarter on a 1-yard run by fullback Harold Wallin.

The lead held up until the Cardinals scored twice in a span of slightly more than five minutes to close out the first half. A 19-yard pass from Phil Primm to Bernie Aldermann with 5:11 showing in the second quarter and a 3-yard run by Harold LaFitte with 1:20 remaining before the break gave Lamar a 14-7 halftime edge.

Early in the third quarter, Primm was knocked out of the game.

"The first play of the second half I ran a bootleg and didn't throw it. I had about a 10-yard run open for me and I just kept it. I caught three helmets in the back and my back was fractured," Primm recalled.

Tom Smiley's 3-yard run in the second half accounted for Lamar's final score of the game. Arkansas State, meanwhile, squandered an opportunity to rally late in the game when the Indians were unable to convert a pair of Lamar fumbles inside the Cardinals' 30-yard line into points as the Indians went down to defeat 21-7.

Playing without the injured Primm, Lamar moved to 2-0 in Southland Conference play a week later with a 28-18 victory over Abilene Christian.

Smiley, the Cardinal fullback, scored both of Lamar's touchdowns in the first half. His 4-yard run culminated an 85-yard first-quarter drive for a 7-0 lead. A 50-yard run by Dennis Hagaman pulled the Wildcats to within one point. Smiley scored on a 1-yard run in the second quarter to extend the Cardinals' lead at 14-6.

On the same day Lamar was beating Abilene to take early command of the Southland, Trinity and Arlington State opened conference play in San Antonio.

Trinity's Marvin Upshaw, who would go on to play nine years in the NFL as a defensive end and the brother of Hall of Fame offensive lineman Gene Upshaw, kicked a 48-yard field goal for the only points in the first half for either team.

The Tigers were clinging to their scant three-point lead when the Rebels forced Trinity into a third-and-9 situation at its own 20-yard line. Glenn Obie hooked up with Thurman Franks for the needed yardage for a conversion. Not willing to settle for just a first down, Franks, while being tackled at his 40, pitched to Jackie Hall, who was trailing on the play. Hall sprinted 60 yards for a touchdown in a 9-0 triumph for the Tigers.

A week later, a pair of 0-1 teams needing a win to stay in the conference hunt met when Abilene Christian traveled to Arkansas State. After losing to Lamar, Arkansas State bounced back with a non-conference win over The Citadel going into the Abilene game while the Wildcats limped into the contest against the Indians riding a three-game losing streak.

The Wildcats grabbed a 7-0 lead only two plays into the game when quarterback Jacky Roland scrambled 55 yards for a touchdown. Arkansas State immediately responded when quarterback Terry Gwin capped an 84-yard drive with a 3-yard run. Gwin carried the load on the drive, amassing 44 yards on three carries before eventually scoring.

After Gwin's score, the rest of the game belonged to the Indians and Arkansas State's ground game. The Indians rushed for 397 yards with Gwin picking up 121, Tommy Reese 105 and Wallin 83. Gwin scored twice on the ground, while Reese had a 51-yard scoring gallop. Wallin and Billy Joe Bailey both rushed for touchdowns.

The Indians intercepted four passes in the game, three by safety Dick Ritchey, and the Wildcats completed only 5 passes in 15 attempts as Arkansas State dominated Abilene Christian 35-13.

Following a week of non-conference action for all Southland teams, four clubs returned to league play. One contest was a battle of unbeatens between Lamar and Trinity.

Playing at home, Lamar held a narrow 8-3 advantage at halftime. After a 35-yard Upshaw field goal gave Trinity a 3-0 lead, Smiley scored on a 2-yard run and the Cardinals added a two-point conversion to lead by five points at the break.

An interception by Lamar safety Jake David set up the first of two Cardinal touchdowns in the second half. Five plays after David's return to the Trinity 48, Smiley scored from a yard out for a 14-3 lead.

Eugene Washington scampered 85 yards down to the 5-yard line later in the third quarter to set up the game's final score. Primm, who saw his first game action since suffering a back injury against Arkansas State, tossed a 6-yard touchdown pass to Harold LaFitte to make the final 21-3 and clinch no worse than a share of the SLC crown for the Cardinals.

Meanwhile, Roger Youngblood's two extra points and a late defensive play proved to be the difference in Abilene Christian's 14-12 win at Arlington State.

Mike Love scored both of Abilene's touchdowns on runs of 11 and 2 yards, with Youngblood hitting on both conversion attempts.

Mike Baylor, starting at quarterback in place of injured Carl Williams, factored in both touchdowns for Arlington State. Baylor tossed a 5-yard pass to Joe O'Brien and scored on a 3-yard run.

Trailing by two points, the Rebels drove into Abilene Christian territory in the closing moments before Tommy Young intercepted an Arlington State pass at the Wildcats' 10-yard line with 10 seconds left in the game.

Abilene Christian improved to 1-2 in Southland play and 2-5 overall with the win. Arlington State fell to 0-2 in the league and 4-3 overall.

While Lamar was defeating West Texas State in non-conference action, the remaining SLC teams were battling for second place as Arkansas State faced Arlington State and Trinity battled Abilene Christian in Week 9 action.

Arlington State's Keith Luft ran for a pair of second-half touchdowns at Arkansas State to spark the Rebels to their first-ever Southland Conference victory with a 27-12 win over the Indians.

One play after Ronnie Young recovered a fumble at the Arkansas State 8-yard line, Luft scored the first of his two touchdowns for the Rebels. Luft added a 6-yard touchdown run for Arlington State while Faust Parker chipped in a pair of field goals. His two field goals gave Faust seven on the year to establish a new Southland Conference single-season record.

Steve Gankiewicz scored both touchdowns for Arkansas State. He scored the game's first touchdown on a 1-yard run to cap a 68-yard drive and scored on 7-yard run late in the game moments after returning a kickoff 78 yards.

Arlington State's first-ever Southland win moved the Rebels to 1-2 in conference play and 5-3 overall to clinch a winning season. Arkansas State also moved to 1-2 in league play and 6-2 overall.

Abilene Christian's win over Arlington State served as a springboard for the Wildcats down the stretch of the 1965 season. Following the win over the Rebels, Abilene closed the year with a 30-27 Southland Conference home win over Trinity and a 41-12 non-conference triumph at Angelo State to conclude the season 4-5 overall, including 2-2 in the SLC.

The Tigers had their second-highest scoring output of the season but could have used an additional three points against Abilene Christian. Trinity narrowly missed out on the needed additional three points when Upshaw misfired on a 32-yard field goal in the closing seconds.

Trinity trailed most of the game but did manage to take a 19-17 edge on a 13-yard pass from Obie to Franks midway in the third quarter. The Tigers' lead was a short one as Tommy Young returned the ensuing kickoff 55 yards to set up a 2-yard touchdown run by Love and a 23-17 Wildcats lead going into the final quarter.

After Abilene Christian stretched its lead to 30-19, Trinity scored the game's final points on a short touchdown run by Hall and an Obie two-point conversion.

A 49-yard punt return for a touchdown by Young and a 6-yard run by quarterback Roger Youngblood gave Abilene Christian a 14-0 lead. Trinity cut the score to 14-12 at halftime on an 11-yard touchdown reception by Franks and a 3-yard run by Hall.

Trinity slipped to 1-2 in the Southland and 3-5-1 overall.

Looking to avoid a three-game losing streak to close the 1965 season, Trinity found itself trailing 14-0 heading into the fourth quarter of its Southland Conference home game against Arkansas State.

A fourth-quarter comeback seemed rather doubtful, considering Trinity failed to score on three previous trips inside the Indians' 15-yard line.

The Tigers came up with a break early in the fourth quarter when linebacker Billy Woodlee recovered an Indians fumble at the Arkansas State 29-yard line. Obie scored on a 16-yard rollout four plays later to make the score 14-7 with 11:01 left in the contest.

A punt return to the Arkansas State 44 by Hall with three minutes left in the game gave the Tigers one last hope. Eventually facing fourth-and-1 from the 13, Obie got more than enough yards for the conversion by reaching the 4-yard line. Two plays later, Obie hit Clyde Glosson on a 2-yard touchdown pass with 40 seconds left in the game. Obie found Walter Syers in the end zone for the two-point conversion to give Trinity a 15-14 triumph.

Arkansas State built its 14-0 advantage on a 7-yard touchdown pass from Terry Gwin to Bill Pagano and a 1-yard dive by Eddie Rickus.

The win allowed Trinity to conclude the 1965 season 4-5-1 overall and 2-2 in the SLC. Arkansas State finished 6-3 overall and 1-3 in the Southland.

As improbable as Trinity's late comeback may have been over Arkansas State, the big shocker to close Southland Conference play in 1965 took place in Arlington.

At 3-0 going into the season finale, Lamar already had clinched the Southland Conference title for the second year in a row against an Arlington State team that had picked up its first-ever league victory a week earlier against Arkansas State.

A Parker field goal and touchdown passes of 49 yards to Ray Matthews and 44 to Ronny Young by Williams staked the Rebels to a 17-7 halftime lead. Lamar's only points in the first half came on a 4-yard pass from Primm to Steve Bailey.

A 17-yard touchdown pass from Primm to LaFitte in the third quarter narrowed the Cardinals' deficit to three points at 17-14. Any thoughts of a Lamar comeback for another undefeated conference record came to an end on Steve Jackson's 52-yard interception return of a Primm pass for a touchdown as the Rebels built a 24-14 lead on their way to the 31-21 victory.

The loss marked the second-consecutive year that Lamar had a chance to end Southland Conference play with unblemished marks as league champions. A year earlier, Lamar went into the finale 3-0 but had to settle for a 7-7 tie with Arkansas State.

Despite the loss to Arlington State, the Cardinals repeated as SLC champions with a 3-1 record while concluding the season with a 6-4 mark. Arlington State finished 2-2 in the conference and 6-3 overall.

Although the Cardinals were again denied an outright conference championship, they did have a nice consolation prize a day later.

"After the game, we went to see the Cowboys play the Cleveland Browns. It was the end of the season. It was a nice little perk at the end of the season," Primm joyfully recalled.

The game was the final for Chena Gilstrap as Arlington State coach. Gilstrap left the sidelines after guiding the Rebels to an 85-40-3 record in 13 years to concentrate on his duties as the school's athletic director.

"Chena Gilstrap was just a great man," said Billy Stewart, a linebacker at Arlington State from 1964-69. "He was full of humor. He was compassionate. He was competitive. He had a knack for helping young people.

"I came out of West Texas, a poor farm kid. I don't know how he found me. I received a four-year scholarship. China Gilstrap is an absolute role model and a mentor and one of the most positive people in my life."

Seeking to remain the only champion in Southland Conference history, Lamar began defense of its two-time league crown at home against Abilene Christian in 1966. The Cardinals entered the game 1-2 overall. Abilene, meanwhile, went into the game 3-1.

The Wildcats proved no match for Lamar as Cardinals quarterback Phillip Primm tossed four touchdowns passes, including three in the decisive second quarter, in a one-sided 42-16 victory for the defending champs.

A 9-yard run by Tom Smiley gave Lamar a 7-0 advantage that was wiped away seconds later. Kenneth Smith hauled in the ensuing kickoff at the goal line. After running for 10 yards, he pitched to Johnny Hughes. With a host of blockers in front of him, Hughes raced the remaining 90 yards to tie the score.

All that did was set the stage for Primm as the Cardinals scored on three-consecutive possessions. The Lamar quarterback tossed scoring strikes of 45 and 4 yards to Johnny Fuller before hooking up with Steve Bailey from 10 yards out.

"That was a big change," Primm said of the Cardinals' passing attack. "Johnny Fuller was a good, good ball player.

Primm's final touchdown pass came in the third quarter on a 9-yard toss to Bill Kilgore.

Other than the kickoff return for a touchdown, the Wildcats' other nine points came in the fourth quarter against Lamar reserves. Mike Love scored from 2 yards out after Abilene Christian recovered a fumble at the Cardinals' 26 for the touchdown. The other two points came via a safety.

Abilene Christian fared little better a week later at home against an Arkansas State team off to a 4-0 start.

Terry Gwin, who moved from running back after starting at quarterback in 1965, accounted for three touchdowns in a 33-22 victory over the Wildcats. Gwin scored on runs of 5 and 2 yards while hauling in a 17-yard touchdown pass from quarterback Tim Keane.

Abilene Christian, which trailed 20-10 at halftime, was led by quarterback Jacky Roland, who scored on a pair of 7-yard runs.

On the same day Arkansas State defeated Abilene, Burley Bearden was making his Southland Conference debut as Arlington State head coach as his Rebels faced Trinity. Bearden, who had been an assistant at the school since 1946, took over for Chena Gilstrap.

Bearden's Rebels entered the game with Trinity 2-3 on the season but coming off the worst defeat in school history, a 68-21 drubbing at the hands of the Texas Western Miners.

The Tigers were the unfortunate foes to face the wrath of the Rebels following Arlington State's whopping loss. Playing at home, Arlington State's defense rebounded in grand fashion against Trinity.

Arlington State constantly harassed Trinity's Donnie Witwiski. The Tigers' quarterback was dropped behind the line of scrimmage 11 times in the game. The Rebels' defense also intercepted three passes, recovered three fumbles and held Trinity to 30 yards rushing.

Even with all the defensive success, the Rebels only managed a 6-0 halftime lead on a pair of Skipper Butler field goals. Arlington State managed to pull away in the second half after a 66-yard punt return by Ray Matthews down to the 1-yard line in the third quarter set up a Keith Luft touchdown run.

Arlington State's offense took advantage of excellent field position created by the Rebels' defense and special teams. The Rebels' longest scoring drive of the game occurred late in the third quarter. A 5-yard swing pass from Baylor to Jimmy Thomas capped a 23-yard drive that was set up by an 18-yard punt return by Mike Barnes.

Trinity's lone score came on a 7-yard pass from Witwiski to Earl Eason in the fourth quarter as the Southland Conference opener for both teams moved Arlington State to 3-3 while Trinity fell to 2-3.

"On paper, we didn't have a whole lot of chance to win but the offense took care of the ball and didn't cause us to lose," said Arlington State linebacker Billy Stewart. "The defense was in a mode to really step up because we were coming off a shellacking and we knew weren't that bad. We kind of found out maybe how good we really were."

Playing at Arkansas State a week later, the Lamar Cardinals and fifth-ranked Indians both were 1-0 in league play.

A 27-yard John Wiersema field goal accounted for all the first-half scoring as Lamar held a slim 3-0 halftime lead.

Lamar earned the game's first touchdown when the Cardinals scored on their first possession of the second half. Darrell Johnson ran wide right from 13 yards out to cap an 87-yard drive and give the Cardinals a 10-0 lead.

Lee Spears set up the game's final touchdown when he returned an errant Indians pass to the Arkansas State 41. Johnson scampered 31 yards on the ensuing play. Three plays later, Smiley scored from 5 yards out with slightly more than a minute left in the game to give Lamar a 17-0 victory.

The three-game winning streak improved Lamar to 4-2 overall while Arkansas State's first loss of the season dropped the Indians to 5-1.

The win for the Cardinals came despite bulletinboard material inadvertently provided by Primm that dated back an entire year.

"The year before was the game where I got my back fractured," Primm recalled. "I was kind of feeling no pain (because of medication) in the locker room. A (reporter) from Houston asked, 'What happened out there. What about the game?' I saw, 'Awe, we should have beat those guys by 40 points.'

"The joker prints it so when go to Jonesboro and played in 1966, that was the front page of their paper."

Lamar's opponent the following week was Trinity as the Cardinals looked to open Southland play at 3-0 for the third year in a row.

The Cardinals trailed 7-0 at halftime at Trinity on a 4-yard run by the Tigers' Eason in a key SLC showdown.

Unlike the first half, the third quarter provided plenty of action. Eason's second touchdown of the game, this one from a yard out, extended the Tigers' lead. After Lamar put itself back in the game on a 52-yard touchdown sprint by Smiley, Trinity tacked on two more scores in the quarter on a 7-yard pass from Witwiski to Truman Franks and a 29-yard Marvin Upshaw field goal.

A 4-yard pass from Primm to Fuller made the final 23-14.

"We had a game plan and we didn't adjust to it. We didn't make the changes. We didn't execute the game plan and didn't get it done that night," Primm said.

On the same day Trinity defeated Lamar to move to 4-3 overall, Arlington State blanked Abilene Christian 23-0 on the road to become the lone Southland Conference team at 2-0.

Playing the first of three-consecutive SLC games to close the season, the Rebels set the tone against Abilene Christian with their defense as Arlington State had done all season.

Ken Riley's recovery of a fumbled punt at the Abilene Christian 15 set up a 10-yard touchdown pass from Baylor to Matthews. Jim Marcum's 13-yard interception return for a touchdown and a 26-yard Butler field goal made it 17-0 at halftime.

Following a scoreless third quarter, the Rebels added their final score on a 1-yard run by Luft.

Along with Marcum, Barnes had a big game defensively for the Rebels with three interceptions.

The Rebels' quest to move to 3-0 in Southland Conference play for the first time in school history seemed far from assured a week later when Arkansas State marched 75 yards in 18 plays on the opening possession of the game. Arkansas State fullback Steve Gankiewicz capped the drive on a 1-yard run for a 6-0 Indians lead.

Arkansas State's slim lead held up until the closing moments of the first half. After two incomplete passes, Baylor connected with Thomas at the Indians' 45-yard line. The speedy Thomas side-stepped a pair of defenders and sprinted for an 81-yard touchdown to even the game at 6-6.

A 20-yard Butler field goal in the third quarter gave Arlington State its first lead at 9-6. Like they had done throughout the season, the Rebels' defense set up the Arlington State offense to clinch the outcome. Mike Stamps' interception of an Indians pass gave Arlington State the ball at the Arkansas State 29. On the first play from scrimmage, Baylor again hooked up with Thomas on a touchdown strike.

Arlington State defensive tackle Ken Ozee, a contender for Little All-America honors, epitomized the play of the Rebels' defense through the final weeks of the season. Ozee, who was laid up in the school's infirmary until the night before the game with a 104-degree fever, amassed 17 tackles against Arkansas State.

While Arlington State was defeating Arkansas State, Abilene Christian fell to Trinity 37-27 to become the first team in Southland history to go 0-4 in league play.

Trinity and Abilene Christian traded leads six times going into the closing moments of the Tigers' Southland Conference home game against the Wildcats.

A 19-yard pass from Witwiski to Clyde Glosson and a two-point conversion toss to Lemuel Cook gave Trinity a 30-27 edge.

Unlike previous attempts, the Wildcats were unable to counter. Trinity, on the other hand, failed to put the game away when the Tigers were stopped at the Abilene Christian 1-yard line. It proved to be only a momentary setback for Trinity. Mike Speer's recovery of a Wildcats fumble gave the ball back to the Tigers at the 21. Two plays later, Witwiski hooked up with Franks on an 11-yard touchdown to give Trinity a 37-27 victory.

Trinity won the game behind a record-setting performance by Witwiski. The Tigers' quarterback, who passed for four touchdowns and rushed for another, passed for 278 yards in the game. His total set new team and Southland Conference records for most passing yards in a game.

The Tigers improved to 2-1 in the SLC and 5-3 overall. The victory secured Trinity's first winning season since 1958.

Lamar Tech, the winner of the first two Southland Conference titles, was in no mood to hand the 1966 title to the Rebels outright.

Needing to win at home to force a share of the league crown, the Cardinals scored four of the first five times they had to ball in a 27-7 victory over Arlington State.

A 2-yard run by Primm, a 32-yard pass from Primm to Johnny Fuller, a 22-yard run by Johnson and a second touchdown toss to Fuller allowed the Cardinals to put the game away early.

"They (the Rebels) had a small college All-America cornerback that Fuller did all that receiving against," Primm pointed out.

The only score for the Rebels came on an 18-yard pass from Baylor to Ronny Young. Young finished the game with 11 receptions for 123 yards, both single-game school records. His 34 catches for the season also set a new school mark.

Arlington State finished the season as co-champions of the Southland at 3-1 and 6-4 overall. Lamar moved to 6-3 overall but ended the year 6-4 following a 30-26 non-conference loss to the Quantico Marines.

While Lamar and Arlington State were battling for first place, Trinity and Arkansas State were closing out the season in Jonesboro. The Indians won 20-7 as both teams finished 2-2 in league play. Arkansas State concluded the 1966 season 7-2 overall while Trinity ended up 5-4.

Despite being hobbled by injuries, Gankiewicz and Gwin both set new league records. Gankiewicz scored three touchdowns to finish with 76 points while Gwin closed the season with 676 yards rushing.

Arkansas State scored on back-to-back possessions on touchdown runs of 22 and 5 yards by Gankiewicz in the first half. David Walls, playing in place the injured Bill Bergey, blocked a punt in the fourth quarter that was recovered by Thurman Moore at the Tigers' 1-yard line. Gankiewicz scored from a yard out to make it 20-0.

Trinity's lone score came on the ensuing possession on a 1-yard touchdown run by Witwiski.

Sharing the Southland title after winning the crown outright during the first two years of the SLC's existence had the Lamar Cardinals looking to get off to a quick start in conference play in 1967.

Going into Lamar's league opener at Abilene Christian, the Cardinals were riding a three-game winning streak while Abilene was 2-1 on the season.

The Cardinals, who averaged 37.5 points in their previous two outings, were even more potent in the Southland opener, dominating Abilene Christian 54-13 on the road.

Tommie Smiley rushed for 149 yards and scored the game's first touchdown. Kenny Montgomery added a 5-yard scoring run later in the quarter and the Cardinals were off and running as Lamar extended its winning streak to four games.

Abilene Christian was much more competitive a week later, but it still wasn't enough to avert the Wildcats from dropping their sixth Southland Conference game in a row in a 24-14 home loss to Arkansas State. The Indians went into the game 2-2 but on a two-game losing streak after falling to The Citadel and Louisiana Tech.

A 1-yard run by Arkansas State fullback Steve Gankiewicz on fourth down capped a 75-yard drive on the Indians' opening possession of the game. Freshman quarterback Cecil LaGrone's 20-yard touchdown toss to tight end Virgil Peyton staked Arkansas State to a two-touchdown lead.

Quick strikes allowed Abilene Christian to tie the game. The Wildcats had been held without a first down until quarterback David Fuller hooked up with V.T. Smith on a 75-yard bomb with less than four minutes remaining in the second quarter. A partially-blocked Arkansas State punt set up a touchdown reception by Abilene Christian's Steve Bennett to tie the game.

The game remained tied until the final five minutes of the contest. A pass interference call against the Wildcats at the 1-yard line set up tailback Frank

McGuigan's run from a yard out with 4:56 left in the contest. A 42-yard field goal by Mike Everett with 1:33 showing accounted for the 24-14 final.

On the same day Arkansas State was beating Abilene Christian, Arlington College, now called the University of Texas at Arlington, played at Trinity to open Southland Conference play.

With a conference co-championship from the previous year to their liking, the Rebels were off to a rousing start in 1967. Texas-Arlington entered league play with a No. 6 ranking and sporting a 5-0 record.

"We had more maturity and a real good nucleus offensively and defensively and I think we were hungry for the title," said fullback Danny Griffin, a sophomore on the 1967 UT-Arlington squad.

UTA's unbeaten start seemed in jeopardy when the Rebels fell behind 16-15 on a 32-yard field goal by Marvin Upshaw.

The Tigers, however, would not hold the lead for long. Moments after Upshaw's kick, Rebel linebacker Jim Sheridan picked off a Trinity pass in the flat and raced 18 yards for a touchdown to put the Rebels up for good at 22-16.

Texas-Arlington controlled the rest of the game, adding a 34-yard Skipper Butler field goal in the fourth quarter and a 50-yard scoring strike from Mike Baylor to Jimmy Thomas for a 31-16 Rebels triumph.

"We got behind but we had enough firepower with Jimmy Thomas and Baylor could throw the ball well. Jimmy Thomas had speed and nobody could stay with him. He was a game breaker," said Griffin.

UTA led 15-7 at halftime on Baylor touchdown passes of 3 yards to Mike Buchanan and 25 yards to Thomas. Between the two touchdown tosses, the Tigers got on the scoreboard on a 1-yard run by quarterback Ronnie Carpenter.

A 1-yard run by Clyde Glosson and Upshaw's field goal gave the Tigers their momentary 16-15 edge.

Texas-Arlington, which tied a school record for consecutive wins, remained unbeaten at 6-0 by capturing its SLC opener.

Being in no mood to concede anything to Texas-Arlington, the Lamar Cardinals became the first team to move to 2-0 in Southland Conference play a week later with a 28-23 home win over Arkansas State.

Lamar led 14-10 at halftime before Arkansas State took advantage of a fumble by Tom Smiley on the opening possession of the second half. Taking over at the Lamar 28, the Indians lost yards on the first two plays of the drive before scoring on a 32-yard touchdown pass from LaGrone to Peyton.

The Cardinals, ranked No. 9 among small college teams, regained the lead when Smiley scored on a 16-yard run to cap an 89-yard drive to put Lamar on top 21-17.

A 60-yard punt pinned Arkansas State at its own 12-yard line in the middle of the fourth quarter. LaGrone fumbled at his own 1-yard line and Richard Bjerke recovered in the end zone for Lamar to give the Cardinals a 28-17 lead. Gankiewicz scored on a 2-yard run with less than two minutes remaining in the game to make the final 28-23.

Lamar's sixth-consecutive victory improved the Cardinals to 6-1 overall, including 2-0 in the Southland.

The Cardinals' quest for a school-record seventh-consecutive win in a single season seemed in serious doubt as Lamar Tech struggled through a scoreless tie through three quarters in its Southland encounter against Trinity.

Each team threatened only once through the first three quarters. Trinity reached the Cardinals' 31 in the second quarter but came away with no points when Upshaw missed a 49-yard field goal attempt. Lamar advanced to the Trinity 19-yard line in the third quarter but also failed to score when Darryl Henicke misfired on a field-goal attempt.

Taking over at his own 43 early in the fourth quarter following a punt, Lamar quarterback Randy McCollum, who was off target most of the game, hit tight end Wayne Weaver for 12 yards to advance the Cardinals across midfield. A pair of McCollum completions and a short run by Smiley advanced the ball to the 15-yard line and a personal-foul call against the Tigers placed the ball on the 7. McCollum connected with Johnny Fuller for the touchdown.

The 6-0 victory allowed Lamar to stay unbeaten in the SLC at 3-0 as the Cardinals improved to 7-1 on the season.

Looking to remain the only other unbeaten team in Southland Conference play, Texas-Arlington faced Abilene Christian. UTA went into the game 1-0 in league play while the Wildcats were 0-2.

UTA went into the game coming off a 37-27 loss to West Texas State that snapped the Rebels' school-record six-game winning streak.

The Rebels lost to a talented and deep West Texas State team. West Texas State was so deep, future Dallas Cowboys running back Duane Thomas was a blocking back for future Miami Dolphin Mercury Morris.

"We had a good offense, or we wouldn't have scored 27 points on West Texas State. We just couldn't outscore them. They had too many fast guys that ended up in the pros," said Griffin.

Against Abilene, the long ball did the trick for the Rebels as Baylor tossed touchdown passes of 80, 75 and 40 yards in a 34-7 victory.

"They weren't real long passes. Baylor was a really good short- and medium-range passer. He was a pretty good long passer and had excellent field vision and made excellent decisions," Griffin said.

Before the aerial attack began, a turnover helped Abilene Christian take an early 7-0 lead. A fumble by the Rebels at their own 19-yard line set up a 4-yard touchdown run by Fuller.

Baylor put the Rebels on top 14-7 at halftime on touchdown passes of 80 yards to Thomas and 75 yards to Dick Hill. The Rebels quarterback spotted Thomas along the sideline at the UTA 45 before the speedster broke loose. Hill hauled in his catch at midfield on his way to the go-ahead touchdown.

Texas-Arlington pulled away in the second half as the Rebels constantly harassed Fuller and backup quarterback Jim Lindsey. The Rebels forced six interceptions in the last two quarters.

One of the interceptions, by Jim Marcum, eventually set up a 40-yard touchdown toss to Thomas. A Robert Willbacks theft moments later led to a 3-yard scoring run by Baylor.

"We had some excellent defensive backs and linebackers who could run. They were leaner and quick. We had a solid defensive line – not big – but they could put pressure on the quarterback," said Griffin.

While Lamar was suffering its first loss since the season opener to New Mexico in non-conference play to snap its seven-game winning streak, sixth-ranked Texas-Arlington had a chance to match the Cardinals at 3-0 in Southland play at Arkansas State.

Texas-Arlington needed every one of Butler's Southland Conference-record three field goals as the Rebels eked out a 16-14 win to remain unbeaten in league play.

The Rebels led 10-7 at halftime on a 4-yard run by Baylor and Butler's first field goal of the game from 27 yards out in the second quarter. Arkansas State's only score in the opening half came on a 1-yard run by Gankiewicz in the second quarter to tie the game 7-7. The score was set up by a pass interference penalty against the Rebels in the end zone.

Butler, who would go on to kick for the New Orleans Saints and Houston Oilers of the NFL, added two more field goals in the second half, his second coming in the fourth quarter from 42 yards out for what would prove to be the game winner.

At the time of Butler's final field goal, the outcome was hardly secured. Frank McGuigan's 1-yard touchdown run to cap a 64-yard drive with 8:30 remaining in the game rallied the Indians to within two points.

The Indians were moving again on their next drive until Sheridan intercepted an Arkansas State pass at midfield to end the threat. Taking possession with less than four minutes left in the game, the Indians advanced to the UTA 26-yard line but Everett's 46-yard field goal attempt with 27 seconds left in the contest was short, allowing the Rebels to escape with the 16-14 verdict.

"They had a stadium like ours that seated only about 8,000 or 9,000 people. It was close to the field. It was real close quarters. They had some rabid fans that could kind of get on your nerves. They would say things and throw things. I wasn't used to that. They had a home-field advantage," Griffin recalled.

While Texas-Arlington was playing to remain atop the Southland, the Abilene Christian Wildcats were closing out SLC play at home against Trinity hoping to avoid going 0-4 in the conference for the second year in a row.

The reeling Wildcats were held to minus-12 yards rushing in a 20-7 loss that gave the Tigers their first Southland win of the season.

A 1-yard run by A.D. Arnic to culminate a 48-yard drive gave the Tigers a 7-0 lead in the second quarter. The Wildcats tied the game on a 4-yard pass from Lindsey to Bill Lockey.

David Reynolds' 44-yard punt return for a touchdown in the third quarter put Trinity on top 14-7 before the Tigers put the game away on a 3-yard touchdown run by Gary Champion.

The Tigers improved to 1-2 in the SLC and 3-6 overall. Abilene Christian went on to lose to Angelo State in non-conference play a week later to conclude the season 3-6.

In the regular-season finale, Arkansas State took advantage of a pair of Trinity turnovers for a 13-10 victory. The winning score came early in the second half when Arkansas State quarterback Tim Keane, forced to deliver the ball quickly to avoid the Trinity pass rush, found Gankiewicz in the end zone. Gankiewicz managed to leap between two Tiger defenders to pull down the ball for a 13-7 Indians edge.

Arkansas State, which had lost four games by less than a touchdown, ended the 1967 season 4-5 overall and 2-2 in the SLC. Trinity ended 3-7 overall and 1-3 in the conference.

While the Indians were beating Trinity, all eyes focused on the season-ending matchup between defending Southland co-champs Texas-Arlington and Lamar, both 3-0 going into the showdown.

Lamar grabbed the early advantage when a UTA fumble recovered by Ronnie Potts led to a 20-yard Darryl Henicke field goal and a 3-0 Cardinals lead slightly more than four minutes into the game.

The Rebels took the lead at 7-3 on a 10-yard pass from Baylor to Buchanan to cap a 63-yard drive late in the first quarter.

On UTA's next possession, Griffin broke loose on a 57-yard gallop down to the Lamar Tech 15. The Rebels advanced to the 6-yard line before the drive bogged down and Texas-Arlington had to settle on a 32-yard Butler field goal.

Griffin was just getting started. Although the former walk-on failed to score in the game, he rushed for 184 of his Southland Conference single-game record 215 yards in the opening half.

"Our offensive line was making some excellent blocks. Even though they (the Cardinals) had a good team defensively, I think we outmanned them. With had two big guards, Bob Diem was 245 and Greg Bailey was 275. They could pull and could cross block and we had a good center in Richard Norwood and two really good tackles, Ken Riley and Jerry McLaughlin," said Griffin.

Despite Griffin's effort, Lamar managed to tie the game 10-10. A 31-yard pass from McCollum to Johnny Fuller eventually set up a 10-yard touchdown run by Montgomery with 1:12 remaining before halftime.

With time running down in the opening half, Griffin broke a 48-yard gainer to set up a 38-yard Butler field goal with 27 seconds left before intermission to give the Rebels a 13-10 edge.

Neither team could generate much offense in the second half. With the Rebels clinging to their three-point advantage, Butler, also the UTA punter, was brought in to kick the ball away. He dropped the snap from center but managed to scoot around his right end for 19 yards and a first down.

That set up a Butler 25-yard field goal with 5:30 remaining in the game for what would prove to be the game-winning six-point margin. It marked the second game in a row that Butler kicked a Southland Conference-record three field goals in a game.

"Even with all those yards, we didn't score nearly as much as we should have but with Butler, we knew if we got close, more than likely, he was going to kick it through the uprights," said Griffin.

After tying for the SLC title the previous year, Texas-Arlington captured an outright conference crown for the first time in school history. UTA also halted Lamar's three-year reign as either outright or co-champions in the league.

UTA closed the regular season 4-0 in the Southland and 9-1 overall. The Rebels had a knack for winning close games with three, one-point wins in the season. Also, six of their nine victories were by six points are less. Lamar concluded the season 3-1 in the SLC and 7-3 overall.

The Rebels' effort earned Texas-Arlington a postseason berth in the Pecan Bowl against North Dakota State in Abilene for the NCAA small college Midwest regional championship.

With temperatures below freezing and a couple of inches of snow covering the ground in Abilene, the playing conditions seemed much more suited for the Bison than a bunch of Texas Rebels. The frigid temperature limited attendance to approximately 1,500 die-hard fans.

As expected, the conditions led to a low-scoring affair with the only points in the first half coming in the second quarter.

Considering the conditions, a surprising 54-yard toss from Baylor to Hill advanced the Rebels to the North Dakota 23 on a third-and-7 situation. Facing fourth down only inches away from the goal line, Griffin bulled his way into the end zone for a 6-0 UTA lead with only 1:23 remaining before halftime.

"I knew going to the left, with Bob Diem at guard and Jerry McLaughlin at tackle, I knew I had a good chance to score, if I could get good-enough footing. That was the problem all day on that field," recalled Griffin.

The Rebels continued to cling to their six-point advantage throughout the second half until Texas-Arlington came up with a key break late in the contest. A fumble by Bison quarterback Terry Hanson was recovered by Danny Scott at the North Dakota State 18.

UTA's 13-0 margin held up as the Rebels' defense continually turned away North Dakota State advances. The Bison threatened several times in the game but could not score. One drive ended on an interception deep in Rebels territory and another on a missed field goal. UTA forced a turnover on downs twice inside on fourth-and-goal situations.

North Dakota State entered the game with the top rushing offense in small college football, averaging 300 yards per game. The Rebels' defense held the Bison to 106 yards on the ground.

"I had 14 tackles that game and that was just a reflection of the whole team," said Stewart. "We all met the occasion. I know our blitz package was able to get to the quarterback. After they got behind, they pressed a little bit and we were able to get several sacks. We kept the game in check."

The Southland Conference champions closed the 1967 season with a 10-1 record. The 10 wins represented the most ever for Texas-Arlington in a single season.

"Looking back, the win at Abilene (against North Dakota State) was kind of icing on the cake for a 10-1 year and yet even reflecting one year before that going 6-4 and being co-champs," Stewart said.

Change was in the air at Abilene Christian in 1968 though it had a familiar aroma.

When the Wildcats were looking for a replacement for Les Wheeler following the 1967 season, they didn't have far to focus. Named as the 10th head coach in Abilene Christian history was Wally Bullington. Bullington was a star guard for the Wildcats from 1949-52 and was head coach at Abilene High and an assistant with Abilene Christian before getting the head job in 1968.

The Wildcats gave Bullington a win in his first game as head coach when Abilene Christian defeated Northwestern State College 17-16 in the 1968 season opener on the way to a 2-2 record entering the Southland Conference opener at Lamar.

Winning a few non-conference games was one thing, but picking up a Southland victory was quite another. After going 0-4 in league play the previous two years, the Wildcats had not won a league game since 1965.

By contrast, Lamar had been the kingpins of the SLC. The Cardinals won the outright title the first two years of the league's existence and shared the crown in 1966. Lamar went 3-1 in 1967 but lost the league title to unbeaten Texas-Arlington.

Now, the Cardinals were facing hard times. Lamar entered Southland play in 1968 with a 0-4 record, the first time since the inception of the league that the Cardinals went into SLC action winless on the season. Coupled with season-ending losses to Louisiana Tech and Texas-Arlington to conclude the 1967 season, Lamar was mired in a six-game losing streak.

A 40-yard punt and a penalty pinned the Cardinals at their own 3-yard line early in their game against Abilene Christian. Lamar quarterback Lloyd Ricketson was tackled in the end zone to give the Wildcats a 2-0 lead. Abilene's V.T. Smith hauled in the free kick at his own 27. He lateraled to David Wallace, who scooted down the sideline to complete a 73-yard touchdown play to place Lamar in a quick 9-0 hole.

Abilene Christian quarterback Jim Lindsey scored on a 16-yard run in the final minute of the opening quarter and Trent Lancaster added a 7-yard touchdown to give the Wildcats a 22-0 lead at halftime.

Lamar began to rally back late in the third quarter. A 3-yard touchdown by Henry King and a two-point conversion made the score 22-8. Bobby McDowell hooked up with Ronnie Gebauer on a 72-yard scoring strike to make it 22-14 with less than 12 minutes remaining in the game.

Abilene Christian would not let the Cardinals get any closer. Wildcats kicker Bob Bearden booted a 27-yard field goal while Lindsey added touchdown runs of 16 and 4 yards to give Abilene and Bullington a 38-14 Southland Conference victory.

While Bullington and Abilene were in the midst of a long-awaited Southland win, Arkansas State and Trinity opened league play in Little Rock. Arkansas State went into the game with a four-game winning streak after a season-opening loss to Western Michigan. Trinity went into the game 3-1.

Arkansas State's hot start continued into its SLC opener as the Indians built a 21-0 lead only 10 seconds into the second quarter.

Keying on star Frank McGuigan, the Tigers were fooled when the All-America running back took a pitch from freshman quarterback James Hamilton and tossed a halfback pass to Joe Waleszonia down to the 9-yard line. McGuigan followed with a touchdown run for a 7-0 lead on Arkansas State's second possession.

McGuigan's 26-yard run on Arkansas State's next possession set up his 2-yard run one play later for a 14-0 lead.

Trailing by two touchdowns, a fake punt by the Tigers came up short, giving the ball to Arkansas State at the Trinity 33. Another McGuigan halfback pass, this one to Kevin McClelland good for 6 yards and a touchdown made it 21-0 just 10 seconds into the second quarter.

Trinity tried to get back in the game, converting an Indians fumble into a 12-yard halfback pass from Ron Boyette to tight end John Howard.

The Tigers' momentum was momentary as a shanked Boyette punt gave Arkansas State the ball at the Trinity 18. McGuigan's 1-yard touchdown run gave the Indians a 28-7 halftime lead on their way to a 31-14 victory.

The early-season schedule for defending Southland Conference champion Texas-Arlington was a mixed bag for the Rebels. UTA went 3-2 to open the year against non-league competition. Highlights included a record-setting performance by Skipper Butler, quarterback Mike Baylor and Jimmy Thomas in the Rebels' 41-30 win over East Texas.

Butler kicked a 60 yarder and his total of four field goals in the game both established new SLC records. Baylor, meanwhile, had 22 completions in the game for 374 yards and finished with 361 yards of total offense, all UTA career records. Thomas' 54-yard touchdown reception was the 18th of his career, also a career record.

The low point for the Rebels came the week before their Southland opener in the form of a 41-0 shutout loss to West Texas State, the first time Texas-Arlington had been shut out since 1965. The last foe to blank the UTA was Trinity, the Rebels' opponent in their 1968 SLC opener.

Danny Griffin, who rushed for 196 yards, scored on a 1-yard run while Baylor added a 2-yard touchdown run and Butler kicked a 41-yard field goal as the Rebels jumped out to a 17-0 lead and made sure there would not be another shutout to the Tigers.

While there would be no shutout, the game's outcome remained in doubt when a 3-yard run by Trinity quarterback Ronny Carpenter pulled the Tigers to within six points at 20-14 with 3:44 remaining in the game.

An attempted onside kick following Carpenter's touchdown failed when Greg Bailey recovered for the Rebels at the Texas-Arlington 43. Three plays later, Griffin broke loose on a 46-yard gallop to give UTA a 27-14 triumph.

Meanwhile, Arkansas State and Abilene Christian, both 1-0, were looking to stay ahead of Texas-Arlington when the two teams met in Abilene.

An exchange of fumbles saw the Indians trail 7-3 in the first quarter. Arkansas State grabbed a 3-0 lead on a 25-yard Gary Elliott field goal before the Wildcats countered with an 11-yard run by Lancaster for a 7-3 edge.

McGuigan scored on a 4-yard run early in the second quarter to give Arkansas State a 10-7 halftime advantage. McGuigan topped 100 yards rushing in the game to move his season total to 899 to set a new Southland single-season record. He broke the record of Lamar's Ron Smiley, established only a year earlier.

A 30-yard Bearden field goal tied the game 10-10 early in the second quarter and set the stage for a frantic finish.

Jim Lindsey tossed an 18-yard touchdown pass to Bill Lockey for a 17-10 Wildcats lead with 2:40 left in the game. Lockey finished the game with 187 receiving yards. Lindsey was a dual threat, passing for 320 yards and rushing 18 times for 88 yards but threw three costly interceptions in the second half. Two of the interceptions were by Arkansas State linebacker David Walls.

Following Lindsey's touchdown strike to Lockey, Dennis Meyer, who picked off the other errant throw by the Abilene Christian quarterback, returned the ensuing kickoff to the Wildcats' 35-yard line.

Arkansas State converted on fourth down three times in the drive, twice on passes by Hamilton and the other on a roughing-the-passer penalty against the Wildcats. With 56 seconds left in the contest, Hamilton found freshman Tom Johnson on a 19-yard touchdown pass. Elliott kicked the extra point to salvage a tie for the Indians.

The result left both teams 1-0-1 in the Southland Conference while eighth-ranked Arkansas State moved to 5-1-1 overall and Abilene Christian 3-2-1.

As the only Southland game a week later, Arkansas State looked to pick up at least a half game on everyone in the conference when the Indians hosted Lamar.

It took longer than the Indians might ever have expected but Arkansas State finally achieved some payback against Lamar.

Lamar jumped out to a 10-0 lead but Arkansas State scored the next 48 points on the Indians' way to a long-awaited 48-17 victory. The win represented the first time since the start of the Southland Conference in 1964 that Arkansas State defeated Lamar.

A struggling Cardinals team entered the game 0-6 but turned a pair of early Arkansas State fumbles into a 9-yard touchdown pass from Jim Jackson to Patrick Gibbs and a 32-yard Terry Thompson field goal but the Indians scored the next 48 points.

Hamilton accounted for four of the touchdowns on scoring passes of 25 yards to Waleszonia and 17 yards to Virgil Peyton. He also had touchdown runs of 4 and 11 yards.

McGuigan, who scored on a 1-yard run, rushed for 124 yards to become the first runner in Southland Conference history to top 1,000 yards in a season.

Defensively, Terry Whiting returned an interception 70 yards for a touchdown and the Arkansas State defense dropped Lamar runners for a total of 109 yards in losses.

Arkansas State improved to 2-0-1 in the SLC and 6-1-1 overall. Lamar fell to 0-7.

With Arkansas State playing a non-conference game against Southwestern Louisiana the following week, it was Texas-Arlington's turn to try and pick up win No. 2 in Southland Conference play at Abilene Christian. The game turned into an air show between the top two quarterbacks in the league.

Lindsey, the leading passer in the league, tossed for 342 yards while UTA's Baylor passed for 317 as the duo combined to put the ball in the air a total of 91 times. Baylor tossed two touchdown passes in the game while Lindsey had one. Lindsey was intercepted four times in the contest.

Butler kicked a 27-yard field goal in the closing seconds of the first half to give the Rebels a 17-13 halftime edge. It was Butler's 12th field goal of the year, tying the NCAA College Division record for most field goals in a single season.

Clinging to its four-point advantage, Texas-Arlington put the game away in the third quarter when Baylor tossed both of his touchdown passes. A 20-yard strike to Thomas and a 34-yard toss to Ronnie Lucas made the score 30-13. Lindsey's lone touchdown pass of the game, a 38-yard toss to Wallace with 3:36 remaining made the final 30-20.

While Texas-Arlington was beating Abilene, Lamar and Trinity met in a game to avoid the Southland cellar.. Both teams we 0-2 in the league entering the game, with the Cardinals 0-7 overall and the Tigers 3-4.

Neither team seemed eager for the last-place distinction with several lead changes in the first half.

Lamar scored on the game's opening possession when Ricketson ran in from a yard out to cap a 63-yard drive.

Trinity countered with the next 10 points on a 35-yard Tommy Chenault field goal and a 2-yard run by Gerry Steffano.

The Cardinals regained the lead at 14-10 on a tackle-breaking 24-yard run by fullback Robert Fonto and stretched the advantage to seven points at halftime on a 36-yard Thompson field goal.

After Lamar built a 20-10 lead in the third quarter on another Thompson field goal, the Tigers rallied.

A 48-yard touchdown strike from quarterback Lionel Garza to Terry McCarthy made the score 20-17 in the third quarter. Down by three points and facing fourth down at his own 30, Garza hooked up with Howard for a 63-yard gain down to the 7-yard line. Garza's 3-yard touchdown run with two minutes left in the game put Trinity on top 24-20.

Lamar reached the Trinity 14-yard line in the closing moments but after four incomplete passes by McDowell, the Tigers were able to run out the clock and preserve the four-point triumph.

Since early in the season, it appeared Arkansas State and Texas-Arlington were destined to meet late in the year to determine the Southland Conference championship. The Rebels, who shared the league crown in 1966 and won it outright in 1967, were looking for another title and entered the Arkansas State game 2-1 in the SLC. The Indians went into the game 2-0-1 in the conference.

With the school's first-ever Southland championship on the line, Arkansas State turned to its star player when the Indians needed him most.

Trailing 21-14 in the middle of the fourth quarter, the Indians faced fourth-and-2 at their own 28. McGuigan, the All-America running back got the call. He got the much-needed 2 yards and 23 more for a first down at the UTA 47.

Three more McGuigan carries and a pass from Hamilton to Waleszonia advanced the ball to the UTA 14. A 7-yard pass reception by Waleszonia on third down left the Indians facing fourth down from the Rebels' 7. Again, McGuigan got the call. He barreled through the Rebel defense into the end zone to make the score 21-20. McGuigan ran for a two-point conversion to put Arkansas State on top 22-21.

An interception by Meyer gave the ball back to the Indians with 2:29 left in the game. Texas-Arlington eventually got the ball back with a few seconds remaining. An incomplete pass secured the outcome for the Indians.

Arkansas State moved to 3-0-1 to capture its first-ever SLC championship as the Indians improved to 7-2-1 overall. Texas-Arlington dropped to 2-1 in the conference with a league game remaining versus Lamar. The loss snapped a 15-game winning streak for the Rebels at Arlington Memorial Stadium.

A 4-yard run by Griffin and a 2-yard touchdown by McGuigan to cap an 80-yard drive provided the only scoring in the first half for a 7-7 tie at the break.

McGuigan tossed a 7-yard halfback pass to Johnson for a touchdown and a 14-7 Arkansas State lead in the third quarter on a drive set up by a blocked Butler field goal. The field goal was blocked by Bill Bergey, the future Philadelphia Eagles and Cincinnati Bengals linebacker.

Butler made amends when he kicked a field goal late in the third quarter to make the score 14-10. The kick was No. 13 on the season for Butler, establishing a new NCAA single-season record. He later added a 54-yard field goal to narrow the score to 14-13 less than two minutes into the fourth quarter.

A fumble gave the Rebels the ball at the Arkansas State 27. Backup quarterback Ronnie Faulkner tossed 20 yards to Thomas to set up Griffin's 7-yard touchdown run. Baylor hit Mike Buchanan on a two-point conversion pass to give UTA a 21-14 lead with 11:52 left in the game to set the stage for the Indians' conference title-clinching drive.

On the same day, Trinity defeated Abilene Christian 13-7, allowing the Tigers to finish the season 2-2 in the Southland Conference and 5-4 overall. The Wildcats ended the year 1-2-1 in the conference and 4-5-1 overall. The following week, Texas-Arlington beat Lamar 37-20 to finish 3-1 in the SLC and 6-4 overall. Lamar went winless in 10 games, including 0-4 in the Southland, and extended its losing streak to 12 games.

Arkansas State's regular-season success earned the Indians a postseason berth in the Pecan Bowl against North Dakota State, the top-ranked team in small college football. With Arlington being the site of the bowl game, the Indians were in familiar surroundings but it was the Bison who felt at home, especially in the first half.

The Bison dominated from the start. A fumble by a scrambling Hamilton was recovered by North Dakota State's Dan Olson at the Arkansas State 16. An 11-yard touchdown pass from quarterback Bruce Grasamke to fullback Joe Roller saw the Indians fall behind 7-0 less than three minutes into the game.

An 18-yard run by All-America running back Paul Hatchett to cap a 70-yard drive, a 30-yard Ken Blazei field goal and a 4-yard run by Grasamke gave North Dakota State a 23-0 halftime lead.

Contributing to the Indians' first-half woes was the loss of McGuigan. An All-America in his own right, McGuigan left the game in the second quarter with only 3 yards on seven carries after suffering a sprained ankle.

Without McGuigan, the Bison knew the Indians would be forced to pass. Although Waleszonia had nine catches for 111 yards, Hamilton was dropped 10 times for losses by North Dakota State's defense.

The lack of offense overshadowed the play of Bill Bergey. The future NFL linebacker was in on 21 tackles and had two interceptions. He returned one of the interceptions 42 yards to the North Dakota 6 early in the third quarter, but typical of Arkansas State's day, the Indians turned the ball over at the 10 four plays later.

Arkansas State finally scored on a 10-yard run by Hamilton early in the final quarter. A two-point conversion pass by Cecil LaGrone made it 23-8. The Indians' final score came on a 1-yard run by Hamilton.

The Pecan Bowl loss ended Arkansas State's season at 7-3-1 while North Dakota State's slate remained unblemished at 10-0.

The opening Southland Conference game of 1969 featured a pair of teams that seemed to be turning their gridiron fortunes around from the previous year.

Lamar, which had gone 0-10 in 1968, used a 13-7 season-opening win over McNeese State as a springboard to a 3-1 start going into conference play. Abilene Christian, which sported a 4-5-1 record a year earlier, was off to a rousing 4-0 start.

The Wildcats scored off the opening kickoff against Lamar on a 2-yard run by David Wallace to cap an 80-yard drive. Lamar countered with a 36-yard Ronnie Baird field goal on its first possession and added a 5-yard run by freshman Glenn Hill in the second quarter to take a 9-7 halftime edge.

Abilene Christian regained the lead at 10-9 with the only points of the third quarter on a 36-yard Mike Melton field goal.

The defensive-oriented second half continued until the Wildcats struck for two touchdowns with less than seven minutes left in the game.

An 11-yard pass from quarterback Jim Lindsey to Ronnie Vinson at the 6:59 mark of the fourth quarter and a 4-yard toss from Lindsey to Pat Holder allowed Abilene to pull away for a 22-9 triumph.

The loss proved especially devastating for the Cardinals, who would go on to lose their final six games of the season.

Abilene Christian put its 5-0 start on the line a week later against defending Southland Conference champion Arkansas State, which was off to a 3-1 start.

Lindsey, the college division's leading passer, tossed for 327 yards against Arkansas State but four interceptions, three of which led to Indians scores, sank the Wildcats.

An 11-yard run by Calvin Harrell, who rushed for 161 yards, staked the Indians to a 6-0 lead before Lindsey and company countered on the ensuing possession. Two Lindsey passes quickly advanced Abilene Christian to midfield. Lindsey connected with Holder at the Arkansas State 35, who raced past the Indian secondary for a 7-6 lead for the Wildcats.

Arkansas State managed a 13-7 halftime lead when Marshall Walls scored on a 5-yard run to cap a 55-yard drive that was set up by Donnie Beshears' interception on the first of Lindsey's errant throws.

Abilene Christian regained the lead on the opening possession of the second half, capping an 80-yard drive on a 29-yard run by Ronnie Green before the Indians' defense came up big once again. Orley Massena hauled in an overthrown ball and Lindsey scampered 35 yards for a touchdown to put Arkansas State on top 19-14.

Arkansas State increased its lead on the first play of the fourth quarter on a sneak by James Hamilton and the quarterback's two-point conversion pass to Walls.

Two long pass plays quickly ate up yardage for the Wildcats but an interception by Arkansas State's Terry Whiting at the Indians' 20 ended the threat. Later in the fourth quarter, an interception by linebacker Gary Cleve set up a 5-yard touchdown run by Harrell to give Arkansas State a 34-14 lead on its way to a 34-22 victory.

While Arkansas State was bringing the Wildcats' undefeated season to an end, Texas-Arlington and Trinity were making their 1969 Southland Conference debuts in San Antonio. The Rebels entered the game 3-2 while Trinity sported a 1-3 mark.

Texas-Arlington's Skipper Butler kicked a field goal on the Rebels' opening possession of the game. Earlier in the season Butler established new NCAA College Division career records for field goals and points.

Following Butler's field goal, UT-Arlington added a 17-yard touchdown pass from Ronnie Faulkner to Mike Buchanan and a 1-yard run by Mark Griffin. The Rebels added to their lead on runs of 25 yards by Tim Christy and 4 yards by Robert Hill in the 34-7 victory.

Texas-Arlington's ball-hawking secondary was in top form for the second week in a row. The Rebels picked off four errant throws by Trinity a week after Robert Evans intercepted four passes in UTA's 27-10 loss to San Diego State.

The Rebels improved to 4-2 on the season with all four victories coming on the road.

In the only Southland game the next week, Arkansas State blanked Lamar 20-0 as Hamilton accounted for all three of the Indians' touchdowns.

The Indians marched 80 yards on the opening drive of the game, scoring on a touchdown pass from Hamilton to tight end Steve Lockhart for a 7-0 lead but Arkansas State would not score again until the fourth quarter.

Hamilton scored on a 1-yard run to make it 13-0 before Charley Hinrichs' recovery of a Cardinals fumble at the Lamar 6-yard line set up the quarterback's 6-yard touchdown toss to Walls one play later for the 20-0 final.

Hinrichs' recovery of a Lamar fumble was typical of Arkansas State's defensive effort against the Cardinals. The Indians intercepted five passes and forced three fumbles. Defensive tackle Clovis Swinney had 12 tackles, dropped Lamar quarterbacks three times for losses and forced a fumble in the shutout.

The effort of Hamilton and the defense helped the Indians overcome the loss of Harrell. The Southland Conference's leading rusher left the game in the first quarter with an ankle sprain and did not return.

With Arkansas State involved in a 21-21 tie with Drake in non-conference action a week later, Texas-Arlington missed out on its chance to join the Indians as the only other 2-0 team in Southland play with the Rebels' 28-24 loss at home to Abilene Christian.

Faulkner connected with Arthur Hobbs on a 54-yard touchdown strike with 28 seconds remaining in the first half to give UTA a 24-10 halftime lead. The touchdown connection would prove to be the final points of the game for the Rebels.

A pair of touchdown runs by Jim Lindsey in the fourth quarter put the Wildcats on top 28-24.

Texas-Arlington got the ball back at its own 48 late in the game. The final opportunity for the Rebels to win the game came via a fumble recovery by Mickey Eddleman. The UTA safety also intercepted three passes in the game to give him eight on the season, a new school single-season mark.

Facing fourth-and-4 with less than two minutes left in the game, Faulkner found Ronnie Lucas for a first down at the Wildcats' 25-yard line. The play was nullified, however, on a holding penalty against the Rebels. The resulting infraction left UTA in a fourth-and-33 situation. An incomplete pass allowed Abilene Christian to hold on for the four-point triumph as the Wildcats improved to 2-1 in the Southland.

The loss to Abilene continued a disturbing trend for UT-Arlington. It marked in the fifth-consecutive home loss for Rebels. Prior to the start of the 1969 season, UTA had won 14 of its previous 15 home games.

Meanwhile, Lamar's woes continued as the Cardinals were blanked at home by Trinity 22-0 to drop to 0-3 in Southland play. The win evened the Tigers' SLC mark at 1-1.

The Tigers turned a fumble by the Cardinals on Lamar's opening possession into a 6-0 lead on a 3-yard run by David Steffano. The turnover was the first of five lost fumbles for the Cardinals in the game.

Trinity made it 16-0 at halftime when the Tigers converted Lamar's fourth fumble in the first half into a 37-yard Ron Boyette field goal before Shawn Meagher turned a short pass from quarterback Leonel Garza into a 70-yard touchdown.

The only score of the second half came late in the third quarter on a 20-yard pass from Garza to Walter Huntley.

If the Rebels were to stay in the Southland Conference race, they needed to win the following week at Arkansas State.

Texas-Arlington finally broke through a scoreless defensive struggle to take a 3-0 lead but with the SLC title on the line, the No. 7 Indians responded thanks to a pair of Rebel miscues.

Craig Johnson partially blocked a Butler punt, allowing the Indians to take possession at the Texas-Arlington 39 in the fourth quarter. It took eleven plays, but Arkansas State finally grabbed a 7-3 lead on a 1-yard run by Hamilton.

Arkansas State put the game away on a 2-yard Hamilton run to wrap up the Southland Conference title with a 13-3 victory. Hamilton's touchdown was set up on an interception by Walls, the sixth interception by the opportunistic Indians defense.

The Indians improved to 3-0 in the SLC to secure no worse than a tie for the Southland title while moving to 6-1-1 overall. Texas-Arlington dropped to 1-2 in the conference and 4-5 overall.

Trinity made it two Southland wins in a row with a 16-13 triumph at Abilene.

A 25-yard touchdown pass from Garza to Meagher following the opening kickoff proved to be the only scoring of the first half as Trinity took a slim 6-0 lead to the locker room.

The Wildcats moved ahead 7-6 in the third quarter on a 23-yard pass from Lindsey to Jim Williams. Trinity regained the lead for good with nine minutes left in the game on a 25-yard Ken Cooper field goal.

Trinity extended its lead less than two minutes later on a 48-yard touchdown reception by Bill Hodge.

After an Abilene Christian touchdown made it 16-13, the Wildcats managed to reach the Trinity 24-yard line in the closing moments but back-to-back sacks of Lindsey allowed the clock to run out and the Tigers to preserve the three-point triumph to drop the Wildcats to 2-2 in the Southland.

The win moved Trinity to 3-5 overall and 2-1 in the SLC and gave the Tigers an opportunity to tie for the conference title with a win over Arkansas State.

In the final week of Southland Conference play, Texas-Arlington beat up on hapless Lamar 53-16. The Rebels finished the season 5-5 overall and 2-2 in the SLC. The loss was the sixth-straight to close the year for Lamar, which finished 3-7 overall and 0-4 in the league for a second year in a row. The Cardinals ended the season having lost their last nine league games, a Southland record.

The game saw a pair of record-setting UTA seniors go out in style.

Butler kicked two field goals in the game and added five extra points to finish his career with 216 points and 44 field goals, both NCAA College Division career marks.

Griffin set a new single-game school record by scoring four touchdowns. Griffin, who entered the game without a touchdown reception on the season, scored three times on passes and added a rushing touchdown.

UTA also established a single-season Southland Conference and team record. The Rebels picked off five passes in the game, giving them 32 for the year.

The focus the final weekend of the Southland season, however, was on Trinity's game against defending champion Arkansas State.

Arkansas State showed it was not ready to relinquish the crown, jumping out to a 20-3 halftime lead. Harrell, who rushed for 127 yards in the game to finish with 824 on the season as the SLC's leading rusher, carried the ball on an early Indians drive seven-consecutive times, the final going for 2 yards and a touchdown.

Trinity countered with a 36-yard Cooper field goal on the ensuing drive to make it 7-3.

A 27-yard interception return for a touchdown by Johnson moved the score to 13-3. Later, a fumble on a punt return by the Tigers gave Arkansas State the ball at the Trinity 45 to set up a touchdown toss from Hamilton to Chet Douthit with 50 seconds left in the second quarter to give the Indians their 20-3 halftime lead. Hamilton played despite being released from the hospital the morning of the game with an undetermined ailment.

An exchange of fumbles led to two, third-quarter scores. The first led to a 5-yard run by Trinity's Garza before Harrell scored on a 3-yard run to make it 27-10. A Joe Steffano run from a yard out with 13:20 in the fourth quarter accounted for the 27-17 final.

The Indians finished 4-0 in the SLC and concluded the regular season 7-1-1. Trinity ended 2-2 in the Southland and went on to defeat the University of Mexico 49-6 a week later to conclude its season 4-6 overall.

It was with a sense of familiarity that Arkansas State took on Drake in the Pecan Bowl. Another Southland Conference title put the Indians in the bowl game for the second year in a row against a team Arkansas State faced earlier in the 1969 season.

The friendly confines of Arlington proved to the Indians' liking as Arkansas State jumped out to a 22-0 halftime lead. The Indians built their seemingly comfortable halftime advantage despite losing Hamilton because of a sprained ankle on Arkansas State's first possession of the game.

Hamilton's injury pressed seldom-used Wayne "Bubba" Crocker into action. The senior went into the game having completed only 1 of 7 passes for 15 yards and had six rushing attempts for 64 yards.

On his first pass attempt in the Pecan Bowl, Crocker connected with Steve Lockhart on a 75-yard touchdown bomb for a 7-0 Arkansas State lead.

The score remained the same until the middle of the second quarter. An interception of a Drake pass by Whiting gave the Indians the ball at their own 41 and set up an 8-yard touchdown strike from Crocker to Virgil Peyton. Crocker finished the game 6 of 11 passing for 126 yards and two touchdowns. The extra-point attempt following Peyton's score was blocked but the Bulldogs were offside on the play. Going for a 2-point conversion, Crocker called his own number and scampered into the end zone for a 15-0 Arkansas State lead.

Drake fumbled the ensuing kickoff, with Butch Murray's recovery giving the ball back to Arkansas State at the Bulldogs' 28. Harrell, who rushed for 180 yards in the game, scooted down to the 8-yard line to set up Crocker's touchdown run one play later for a 22-0 Indians lead with 2:47 remaining before halftime.

Drake quarterback Mike Grejbowski, who suffered through a 4 of 18 passing performance in the first half, got hot in the second half. He directed a 77-yard scoring drive on the Bulldogs' initial possession of the second half, leading to a 2-yard touchdown run by fullback Scott Sharpe to make the score 22-6.

The Bulldogs' defense forced a three-and-out on the ensuing possession, getting the ball back at their own 22 following a punt. Grejbowski tossed to Duane Miller, who fought off Indians defender Dennis Meyer at the 6-yard line and fell into the end zone to complete a 51-yard pass to make the score 22-13 at the 4:12 mark of the third quarter.

Minutes later, a 30-yard field goal attempt by Arkansas State's Mike Everett was blocked and Drake's Bill McClintock rambled with the ball to the Indians'

41. Arkansas State avoided damage when Meyer intercepted a pass in the end zone intended for Miller on the very next play.

Arkansas State followed with an 80-yard march. Harrell capped the drive on a 3-yard run to make the score 29-13 at the 9:28 mark of the fourth quarter. Drake answered with a 59-yard scoring drive, culminated on a 1-yard pass to Bob Rogers to make it 29-21 with 2:11 remaining in the game. The Indians recovered an onside kick attempt and ran out the clock for the win to close out an 8-1-1 season.

Two-time defending Southland Conference champion Arkansas State showed the success of the previous two seasons was no fluke. Picking up where they left off in 1969, the Indians won their first three games of the 1970 season to stretch their unbeaten streak to 11 games while earning the No. 1 ranking among College Division teams. Arkansas State opened conference play at home against 2-2 Trinity.

The rapport between the Indians' coaching staff and the Arkansas State players created an air of loyalty and confidence among the team, according to Chet Douthit, a senior receiver on the 1970 squad.

"Benny Ellender was a fundamentalist and he was a head coach. Our line coaches, our backfield coaches, our defensive coaches, were the heart of the team," Douthit said. "Those coaches, we would do anything in the world for. They made you want to play. We loved those coaches even though they would get on your fannies sometimes."

The Indians were off and running to open Southland play in 1970 as Kearney Blalack returned the opening kickoff against Trinity 95 yards for a touchdown to stake the nation's top-ranked team to a quick 7-0 lead.

The Tigers shook off Blalack's touchdown with a score of their own on a 38-yard touchdown pass from quarterback Mike Curry to Bill Hodge to trail by one point after the first quarter. Arkansas State took a 14-6 lead at halftime when Johnny Carr tossed a halfback pass to Douthit, good for 74 yards and a touchdown with less than two minutes remaining in the second quarter.

"My junior year, I was the fastest guy on the team. We traditionally were a running team but when I got there they kind of changed the sergeant at the door a little bit. We were still a rushing team but I added a new dimension they never had before," Douthit said.

Trinity tied the game early in the third quarter on a 3-yard run by Curry and a two-point conversion by Ralph LeFlore. Curry's touchdown capped a 76-yard drive.

The Tigers appeared on their way to grabbing the lead until Curry fumbled at the Trinity 1-yard line on fourth-and-goal. It was the second untimely turnover for the Tigers in Arkansas State territory. In the first half, Costley fumbled inside the Indians' 30-yard line.

Arkansas State marched 76 yards early in the fourth quarter with quarterback James Hamilton scoring on a 3-yard run to lift the Indians to a 21-14 triumph.

The Abilene Christian Wildcats and Lamar Cardinals made their 1970 Southland debut a week later when the two teams met in Beaumont. Winners of four-consecutive games after a season-opening loss to Howard Payne, ninth-ranked Abilene was 4-1 on the year. The Cardinals, losers of their last six games in 1969, opened the 1970 season with a 2-2 mark.

Back on a two-game losing streak, Lamar would drop its third game in a row as the Cardinals simply could not stop Jim Lindsey. The prolific Abilene Christian quarterback passed for 372 yards and four touchdowns in a 42-27 victory as the Wildcats quarterback became the all-time leading passer in College Division history. Lindsey's effort against Lamar gave him 7,479 for his career. He needed only 39 yards going into the game to top the mark of 7,116, previously held by Bob Caress of Bradley.

It was hardly as one-man show for Abilene Christian as the Wildcats amassed 629 yards of offense.

Ironically, it was the Cardinals who scored first when Donald Krushall returned a Lindsey pass attempt 36 yards for a touchdown.

Lindsey made quick amends for his interception, tossing a touchdown pass to David Wallace on Abilene's next possession to tie the game. His touchdown toss to Ronnie Vinson with less than two minutes left in the first half gave the Wildcats a 14-7 halftime lead.

Abilene Christian's lead could have been much larger. On five other occasions in the first half, the Wildcats drove into Lamar territory but failed to come away with points.

The Wildcats turned that around in the second half by scoring on their first two possessions of the third quarter. A 1-yard touchdown run by Lindsey and the quarterback's touchdown pass to Vinson gave Abilene a 28-7 edge.

Lamar answered Vinson's touchdown on the ensuing drive when quarterback Bruce Allen ran in for a score of his own. The touchdown proved costly as Allen was injured on the play.

The teams traded a pair of touchdowns but Lamar could never manage to get closer than 14 points in eventually falling 42-27.

The win over Lamar set up a showdown between teams ranked in the Top 10 in Abilene Christian's Southland Conference home game against Arkansas State.

The Wildcats moved up to No. 8 following the victory over the Cardinals while Arkansas State, despite a 38-17 non-conference win over Louisiana Tech, slipped to No. 2 in the nation.

Arkansas State built a 14-10 halftime lead. Carr scored on a 3-yard run and Calvin Harrell on a 2-yard scamper to produce the two scores for the Indians. Abilene Christian countered with a 32-yard Sonny Kennedy field goal and a 24-yard pass from Lindsey to Vinson.

Following a scoreless third quarter, the Indians extended their lead on scoring runs of 1 and 11 yards by Hamilton.

Lindsey rallied Abilene Christian with a pair of touchdown passes to Vinson but it wasn't enough as Arkansas State held on for a 28-23 victory.

In a losing effort, Lindsey was 33 of 63 passing for 414 yards, all Southland Conference single-game records. Vinson finished with 13 catches for 193 yards and three touchdowns.

Arkansas State's win over the Wildcats gave the Indians early command in the Southland race. On the same day the Indians toppled Abilene, 0-5 Texas-Arlington, making its 1970 conference debut, lost 24-0 to Trinity, leaving Arkansas State as the only unbeaten team in the league.

The Rebels only trailed 7-0 at halftime on a 15-yard pass from Curry to wingback Shawn Meagher. UTA missed on a chance to tie the game at halftime when Calvin Whitmire missed a 35-yard field goal attempt. Whitmire's attempt came after the Texas-Arlington drive bogged down after the Rebels reached the Trinity 7-yard line.

Trinity's lone score of first half would have held up but the Tigers added insurance scores in the second half. A fumble by Robert Hill on the opening play of the second half set up a touchdown toss from Curry to Hodge. Ken Cooper added a 26-yard field goal and a 1-yard run by Greg Oliver with 5:10 left in the contest accounted for the game's 24-0 final score.

Ellender's squad showed why they had the No. 1 ranking among College Division schools. The Indians raced out to a 48-7 lead at halftime against struggling Lamar on their way to a 69-7 domination of the Cardinals. The win, the seventh straight in 1970 and 10th overall, gave Arkansas State a 3-0 SLC mark and allowed the Indians to clinch at least a share of the conference title for the third-consecutive season.

Harrell rushed for three touchdowns in the first half. Carr added two scoring runs and Hamilton tossed to Douthit on a 98-yard scoring play. Even the Arkansas State defense got into the scoring act in the opening half when safety Terry Whiting returned an interception 49 yards for a touchdown.

Douthit's touchdown reception still stands as a school record some 40 years later.

"It was right before the half. The coaches just called a post pattern," recalled Douthit. "I took off. It was a night game. I knew their defensive back was supposed to run a 9.6 or 9.8 hundred. I made my cut and caught it and I could see his shadow (from the stadium lights) behind me. I was running as hard as I can run. I going, 'Please, Lord, get me to there (the end zone).' He (the defensive back) never caught me."

The Indians ground game was crushing, amassing 400 of the team's 667 yards of total offense.

A fumble by Arkansas State at its own 14 on the Indians' opening possession set up an early 7-0 Lamar lead on a 1-yard run by Doug Matthews. That would prove to be the Cardinals' only score as Lamar was limited to 169 yards of total offense, including only 57 on the ground.

Another struggling team, winless Texas-Arlington, faced the unenviable task a week later of facing Lindsey and 10th-ranked Abilene Christian's potent passing attack. The Wildcats' quarterback was coming off a game in which he was 27 of 57 passing for 402 yards in a victory over Drake that allowed him to break the national record for passes attempted and completed. The effort gave Lindsey career totals of 1,201 attempts and 621 completions.

At home against Texas-Arlington, Lindsey tossed for 256 yards and a touchdown before suffering a broken arm in Abilene Christian's 21-7 victory to bring the prolific passer's career to a premature end by two games.

The Rebels scored in the opening quarter for the first time all season on a 10-yard run by quarterback Steve Cox at the 5:10 mark.

Abilene tied the game early in the second quarter on a 2-yard run by Pat Holder. The Wildcats pulled ahead 14-7 on a 3-yard pass from Lindsey to Nicky Pruitt.

UTA appeared to tie the game on a long touchdown pass from Cox to Ronnie Lucas but the play was called back when the flanker was judged guilty of offensive pass interference.

On Lindsey's final scoring drive of his career, the quarterback passed for 64 yards to set up a 1-yard run by Don Harr. Lindsey earned All-America honors his senior year and finished his career as the NCAA College Division's all-time leader in passing yards with 8,521, and in completions with 642 and attempts with 1,237.

Abilene Christian improved to 2-1 in the Southland and 7-2 overall. UTA remained winless at 0-2 in the league and 0-8 overall.

On the same day, Lamar fared little better than the Rebels as the Cardinals' defense allowed three different Trinity running backs to rush for at least 99 yards in a 37-31 road loss to the Tigers.

LeFore led the way with 115 yards rushing for the Tigers while Oliver and Costley added 99 yards each.

Despite falling to 0-3 in the SLC while losing on the road for the 15th time in their last 16 outings, the Cardinals had a few bright spots. With Tommy Tomlin back at quarterback after recovering from a shoulder injury and the debut of the "I" formation, Lamar had one of its best offensive showings of the season. The 31 points for Lamar was the most points scored by the Cardinals in 1970 since their season-opening 33-28 victory over West Texas State.

The first of two touchdown passes from Tomlin to Pat Gibbs gave the Cardinals a 10-7 lead. Trinity countered on the ensuing drive, capping a 74-yard march on a 26-yard pass from Curry to Hodge to give the Tigers a 14-10 halftime edge.

Lamar and Trinity, which improved to 2-1 in the SLC, continually traded scores in the second half. Costley ran for two touchdowns in the third quarter while Archie Bennett countered with a 26-yard scoring run for the Cardinals. An 8-yard touchdown run by Lamar's Clinton Hill on the final play of the third quarter pulled the Cardinals to within 27-24 heading to the fourth period.

A field goal and a 23-yard run by Oliver extended Trinity's lead to 37-24 before Lamar scored the game's final points on a 27-yard touchdown pass from Tomlin to Gibbs.

Tomlin passed for 230 yards in his return while Ronnie Baird kicked a school-record 46-yard field goal for the Tigers.

If Abilene Christian had any hope of earning a Southland Conference co-championship the following week, the Wildcats would need a lot of help. Not only was Abilene without Lindsey in its game against Trinity, the Wildcats would need winless Texas-Arlington to upset top-ranked Arkansas State.

Harr picked up the slack for the injured Lindsey, rushing for two touchdowns to lead Abilene Christian to a 20-15 win at Trinity. The tailback, who rushed for 171 yards, scored on a 26-yard run in the first quarter and added a 1-yard touchdown run in the third quarter to spark the Wildcats.

Trinity's two touchdowns came on short runs by Curry and Oliver.

Facing a biting north wind, the Wildcats kept the ball on the ground for all 12 plays of an 80-yard opening drive to take a 6-0 lead on Harr's 26-yard touchdown run. Abilene Christian began another first-quarter possession at its own 1-yard line following a punt but managed to travel the length of the field behind

Ron Lauterbach, who was subbing at quarterback for Lindsey. Lauterbach scored on a 1-yard run to give the Wildcats a 12-0 halftime lead.

Trinity cut the deficit to five points at halftime on a 3-yard keeper by Curry with less than two minutes remaining in the second quarter.

The Tigers concluded Southland play 2-2, while the victory gave Abilene Christian momentary hope of a conference co-championship.

Arkansas State, however, had no plans to help out Abilene Christian as Texas-Arlington proved to be a mere speed bump on the Indians' way to another Southland Conference title in the final home game of the season for the Rebels.

The teams battled through a scoreless opening period before the Indians erupted for 17 points in the second quarter. Harrell, who rushed for 161 yards in the game, scored on a 12-yard run on the first play of the second quarter to get Arkansas State going. A 30-yard Bobby Gentry field goal and a 32-yard interception return for a touchdown by Dennis Meyer a mere 29 seconds later made it 17-0 at halftime.

With the Indians leading 20-0 in the third quarter, it was time for the Rebels to get what seemed like their obligatory lone touchdown of the game. Like in six of its previous eight games, UTA scored for its only time in a contest, this time on a 1-yard run by Sid Sims late in the third quarter. Sims ended the game with 101 yards to become the only Rebels runner to top 100 yards in a game during the 1970 season.

Carr's 6-yard touchdown run in the fourth quarter wrapped up a 27-7 win for Arkansas State as well as the Southland Conference title for the Indians.

While Arkansas State was closing out a perfect season with a 27-3 non-conference win over Southern Illinois and Abilene Christian was beating McMurry 43-26 to finish the season 9-2, the Southland's bottom teams met to avoid the league cellar in the 1970 finale.

Considering the way the 1970 season had gone; it seemed somehow fitting that the Rebels ended the season by being unable to score in a 24-0 loss at equally-struggling Lamar Tech.

Texas-Arlington put up a gallant effort early, but like the Rebels had done throughout the season, they blew numerous scoring opportunities. UTA advanced inside the Cardinals' 30-yard line three times in the opening quarter but came away with no points.

The Cardinals broke a scoreless first half with a 26-yard Baird field goal with only 30 seconds remaining in the second quarter.

Lamar added fourth-quarter touchdowns on a 1-yard dive by Matthews, while Gibbs hauled in touchdown catches of 56 yards from Glenn Hill and 11 yards from Tomlin for the 24-0 final that allowed the Cardinals to end the season 3-7 overall, 1-3 in the Southland.

Texas-Arlington, which managed more than one score in only one game all season while being shut out twice, ended its worst season in history at 0-10.

The top-ranked Indians' opponent in the Pecan Bowl was Central Missouri State, champions of the Missouri Intercollegiate Athletic Association.

Arkansas State grabbed a 3-0 lead on a 37-yard Gentry field goal. The Indians extended the advantage to 10-0 when Hamilton hooked up with Douthit along the left sideline on a 49-yard scoring pass.

Hard work led to the combination of Hamilton-Douthit to become almost instinctive, according to Douthit.

"I stayed with Hamilton after every practice for almost an hour and run patterns," Douthit said. "My favorite pattern was a comeback pattern. We ran it so much, when I made my cut, the ball was always right there.

"When I would get that defensive back running with me, he'd have to turn to run with me because of the threat of a deep pattern, I made the cut and Hamilton always had the ball right there on my shoulder pad."

Central Missouri put itself back in the game, capping a 68-yard drive on a 12-yard touchdown pass from quarterback Steve Eckinger to Reggie James to make it 10-7.

Hamilton and Douthit connected once again, this time on a 42-yard touchdown strike with 1:28 left in the first half to give Arkansas State a 17-7 halftime lead.

"It was a big boost for us. It gave us a big shot in the arm," Douthit said of his touchdown reception right before halftime.

The 10-point margin hardly demonstrated just how dominant the Indians were in the first half. Hamilton was 12 of 21 passing for 274 yards in the opening half and Harrell ran for 121 of his game-high 135 rushing yards as Arkansas State rolled up 408 yards of total offense. Arkansas State's halftime lead could have been much larger if not for two drives stalling inside the Mules' 10-yard line.

A short scoring pass to tight end Steve Lockhart, the only third-quarter touchdown allowed by the Mules all season, extended the score to 24-7.

The Mules were forced to punt from their end zone less than a minute into the fourth quarter. Arkansas State's Cleve Barfield blocked the punt and Ricky Bone recovered in the end zone to make it 31-7. Harrell added a short touchdown run with 11:50 left in the game go give the Indians their biggest lead of the game at 38-7.

Arkansas State reserves turned the ball over three times late in the game, allowing Central Missouri to add two touchdowns on a pass to Ron Culp and a 3-yard run by Ira Clemmons with less than two minutes left in the game to make the final score 38-21.

The win allowed Arkansas State to capture the College Division National Championship. The Indians closed a perfect season with a 14-game winning streak while extending their unbeaten mark to 19 games.

"We knew we could win the game," Douthit said. "The confidence was never a doubt on that team. Nobody was going to take it away from us."

NEWCOMER LOUISIANA
TECH DOMINATES SLC

The 1971 season was a year of major change for the Southland Conference. For the first time in history, the league expanded, adding Southwestern Louisiana and Louisiana Tech. Also, two holdover teams, Arkansas State and Texas-Arlington, featured new head coaches.

Southwestern Louisiana and Louisiana Tech both departed the Gulf States Conference. USL was coming off a league title in 1970, while Louisiana Tech struggled through a 2-8 season a year after winning the Gulf States crown during quarterback Terry Bradshaw's senior season.

On the coaching front, Bennie Ellender left Arkansas State for Tulane, his alma mater. Ellender was replaced by Bill Davidson, Arkansas State's offensive coordinator and a former Indians player.

After Texas-Arlington's winless season in 1970, Burley Bearden was replaced by John Symank. Symank, a former NFL player, was head coach at Northern Arizona for two years prior to being named coach at UTA. UT-Arlington went through another change as well, switching from Rebels to Mavericks as the new nickname for the school's athletic teams. Following UTA's example, Lamar Tech went through a bit of a name change as well in 1971, becoming Lamar University.

Also, expansion played havoc with the league schedule. Not all teams in the Southland were able to play each other in 1971, causing some non-conference games to be declared "wild card" league contests so that each team would have at least five "conference" games. For those teams playing all six conference opponents, one game was designated as a non-league affair.

It didn't take long for Louisiana Tech to make its Southland debut or for the Bulldogs to show they planned to be a major force in the conference.

Charles "Quick Six" McDaniel scored three times on a pair of runs and a touchdown reception as the Bulldogs defeated Lamar 26-7 in Ruston in Louisiana

Tech's first-ever Southland Conference game on September 25. The league contest took place only two games into the Bulldogs' 1971 season.

McDaniel rushed for 114 yards and added another 110 reception yards. That came a week after the freshman rushed for 117 yards and had 99 yards on kick returns in his first-ever collegiate game as Louisiana Tech upset the nationally-ranked University of Tampa 28-20.

The ninth-ranked Bulldogs set the tone on their opening drive against Lamar, keeping the ball on the ground for the entire 76-yard touchdown march that used up 6:21. McDaniel capped the drive on a four-yard touchdown run.

A 5-yard run by quarterback Ken Lantrip gave the Bulldogs a 13-0 lead after one quarter. Lantrip and McDaniel hooked up on a 26-yard touchdown pass to make it 20-0 at halftime. McDaniel rounded out the scoring on a 7-yard run in the third quarter.

Tech's defense was just as dominant, holding the Cardinals to 74 yards rushing as a team and not allowing a Lamar score until 8:24 remaining in the contest. The only points Lamar could muster came on an 11-yard pass from Russ Rogers to Joe Bowser in the fourth quarter as the Cardinals dropped to 0-3.

Southwestern Louisiana made its Southland debut a week later against Trinity in Lafayette. The Ragin' Cajuns entered the game 2-0 on the season with wins over Southeastern Louisiana and Santa Clara. The 21-0 win over Santa Clara took place as USL played its first-ever game at new Cajun Field before an estimated crowd of 21,000. The victory over Santa Clara also made Russ Faulkinberry the winningest coach in USL history with 58 wins. Going into the game, he had been tied with T. Ray Mobley.

Playing at home in their first-ever Southland Conference game, the Ragin' Cajuns found themselves trailing 20-7 before mounting a rally against Trinity.

Trinity held a 13-7 halftime lead when the Tigers marched 57 yards with the opening kickoff to extend their lead. Greg Oliver's 1-yard run gave Trinity its biggest lead of the game at 20-7.

USL responded on the ensuing possession. Robbie Juul's 3-yard run capped an 86-yard drive that pulled the Cajuns to within six points at 20-14.

The Cajuns came up with a break later in the quarter when linebacker Larry Sikes recovered a Tigers fumble at the Trinity 41. Juul's quarterback sneak nine plays later gave USL a one-point edge at 21-20.

Down by one point, the Tigers mounted a 16-play, 58-yard drive early in the fourth quarter. Oliver's 2-yard run with nine minutes left in the game put Trinity back on top at 27-21.

The Cajuns marched from their own 22-yard line down to the Trinity 6 with less than two minutes remaining. Facing third-and-1, Robert Gill was stopped for no gain. On fourth down, Juul slipped in the backfield and lost 2 yards, allowing Trinity to hold on for the win and spoiling USL's Southland Conference debut as both teams moved to 2-1 overall.

Southwestern Louisiana and Louisiana Tech, the two old Gulf States rivals, met the following week for the first time as Southland Conference foes and an injury-depleted Cajuns defense was no match for the Bulldogs in USL's 35-15 road loss. USL, playing without five defensive starters due to injury, started seven freshmen on defense.

Louisiana Tech took early advantage of the inexperienced Cajuns, scoring two quick touchdowns. Lantrip scored on a 5-yard run only three plays into the game. A 54-yard pass from Lantrip to Eric Johnson set up the score. Tech made it 14-0 less than four minutes into the game on Glen Berteau's 22-yard halfback pass to Roger Carr.

Trailing 21-0, USL cut the deficit to two touchdowns on a 1-yard run by Juul with seven minutes remaining in the opening half. Tech put the game away by halftime when freshman McDaniel scored on a 3-yard run with 38 seconds showing before the break for a 28-7 lead. McDaniel, who ended the game with 110 yards, topped the 100-yard mark for the third time in four games.

An early-season marquee matchup in the Southland Conference took place the following week as newcomer Louisiana Tech hosted Arkansas State.

Already 2-0 in the Southland, the Bulldogs had the early momentum in the conference. Louisiana Tech entered the game 3-1 on the season, its only blemish a 29-22 non-conference loss to McNeese State. Arkansas State, the defending national champions went into the game 2-1 on the year, coming off a 21-14 loss to Southern Illinois. The loss was the first for Davidson as Arkansas State head coach and snapped the Indians' 16-game winning streak and 21-game unbeaten mark dating back to the 1969 season.

Like the Southwestern Louisiana game, the Bulldogs jumped out to quick lead against Arkansas State. A 44-yard pass from Lantrip to Roger Carr gave Tech a 7-0 edge. On Arkansas State's ensuing possession, the Bulldogs recovered the first of five lost fumbles by the Indians, giving Louisiana Tech the ball at the Arkansas State 21. On the first play from scrimmage, Lantrip hooked up with Johnson for a 14-0 Louisiana Tech lead.

Unlike the USL game, the early scores didn't lead to a cakewalk for the Bulldogs. Arkansas State exploded for 24 points to take a 24-14 halftime lead. James Hamilton and Johnnie Carr had touchdown runs while Joe Duren kicked a

40-yard field goal. The Indians added a defensive touchdown when Craig Johnson returned an interception 35 yards for a touchdown.

On fourth-and-3 from the Indians' 7, Lantrip eluded an oncoming defender before scampering for the only score of the third quarter. A 48-yard Duren field goal gave Arkansas State a 27-21 lead.

Again facing a fourth down deep in Arkansas State territory, the Bulldogs pulled ahead 28-27 when McDaniel scooted in from 5 yards out on a pitchout from Lantrip with 9:19 left in the game.

The Indians marched into possible field goal position in the closing moments of the game. A 15-yard clipping penalty against Arkansas State with 44 seconds remaining pushed back the Indians. Short passes by Hamilton advanced the ball to the Louisiana Tech 37. Duren's 55-yard field goal attempt as time expired fell short, allowing the Bulldogs to escape with the one-point win while remaining unbeaten in the SLC. The defeat marked the first conference loss for Arkansas State since 1967.

As Louisiana Tech jumped out to a commanding 3-0 Southland Conference mark, USL also was back in action, hosting Texas-Arlington. The newly-named Mavericks entered their league opener 1-3. After dropping their first three games, the Mavericks defeated West Texas 13-0 to give Symank his first win as coach and halt UT-Arlington's losing streak at 13 games.

A stifling defense and an opportunistic offense allowed the Cajuns to pick up their first Southland Conference win with a 16-0 victory.

Southwestern Louisiana's defense held the Mavericks to 62 yards total offense, including minus-6 rushing. The Cajuns' defense also helped to set up USL's first two scores.

USL took a 3-0 lead six minutes into the game when a Mavericks' fumble at the UTA 6 set up a 21-yard Richard Azios field goal. Six plays after UTA punter Randy Hooten fumbled the ball at his own 32, Dickie Haik's 26-yard burst gave the Cajuns a 10-0 lead they would take to the locker room at halftime. Juul scored on a 10-yard run early in the fourth quarter to round out the scoring.

Arkansas State bounced back from its loss to Louisiana Tech with a 36-9 victory over Abilene Christian. The Wildcats went into their Southland opener 4-1.

The Indians used four bombs from Hamilton to get back on track. The Arkansas State quarterback fired a first-half touchdown strike of 70 yards to Steve Lockhart, while Kearney Blalack had scoring receptions of 76 and 69 yards as the Indians built a 22-3 halftime lead on a wet and slippery War Memorial Stadium turf in Little Rock.

Hamilton's fourth touchdown toss was a 39-yard hookup with Steve Burks in the third quarter.

The defense had a big hand in the victory as well as Terry Whiting returned an interception a Southland-record 87 yards for a touchdown. Dennis Meyer also picked off a pass, the 28th of his career.

Abilene's scores came on a first-half field goal by Sonny Kennedy and a short touchdown run by tailback Don Harr with 7:30 left in the game.

When Southwestern Louisiana played at Lamar, it was the fourth-consecutive Southland game for the Ragin' Cajuns. The game, however, was not a league contest for the Cardinals because of a scheduling formula created to allow USL to compete for the conference title in its first year in the league.

Looking to even their conference record at 2-2, the Cajuns trailed in the fourth quarter before getting a key break on Ken Williams' recovery of a fumble by Lamar quarterback Glen Hill at the Cardinals' 12-yard line. Gill scored from 4 yards out two plays later to give USL a 21-14 lead.

Lamar was forced to punt on its ensuing possession but Mike McDonald fumbled after making a fair catch. Bowser was on the spot for the recovery at the USL 30. The Cardinals faced two, fourth-down situations in the drive. On the second occasion, Doug Matthews ran wide right from 2 yards out for the touchdown.

Going for the win with a two-point conversion attempt, Hill was brought down by USL's Charles Fox and Leroy Booker, allowing the Ragin' Cajuns to hold on for a 21-20 triumph.

The two fourth-quarter touchdowns were the only scores of the second half after the game had been tied 14-14 at the break.

USL, which improved to 4-2, scored in the first half on a 29-yard touchdown pass from Juul to Reggie Dupre in the first quarter and on a 26-yard connection by the duo in the second quarter.

Lamar scored twice on a pair of Matthews touchdown runs that were sandwiched between the two Juul-to-Dupre scoring tosses.

The Cardinals, whose only win on the season was a 35-6 non-conference game against Central Missouri, dropped to 1-6 with the loss to USL.

Louisiana Tech improved to 6-1 overall and 4-0 in the Southland with a 24-9 win in a designated conference game against Southeastern Louisiana in Hammond.

Despite having lost its previous eight games over the course of two seasons, SLU's defense entered the game only allowing 84 yards through the air. Lantrip threw for 84 yards, and managed 100 more, along with two touchdown passes against the Lions' pass defense.

Even with those numbers, Lantrip and his Tech teammates held a scant 6-3 lead at halftime. Southeastern marched 66 yards to open the second half, with quarterback Mark Varisco's 1-yard run giving the Lions a 9-6 lead.

Tech answered on its next drive as Lantrip hooked up with Berteau on a 33-yard scoring strike. The duo connected again on a two-point conversion to give the Bulldogs a 14-9 lead.

A third-quarter field goal of 23 yards by freshman Danny Norris made it 17-9. Louisiana Tech took advantage of excellent field position moments later after the Lions failed to convert on fourth-and-1 at the SLU 30. On the first play after the turnover on downs, Lantrip found an open Carr in the end zone for the touchdown as the Bulldogs put the game away early in the fourth quarter.

With Tech coming off a losing season a year after the departure of Bradshaw, the No. 1 overall pick in the 1970 NFL draft, the Bulldogs had no inkling how good they might be going into their first year in the Southland, according to Carr.

"We were a bunch of young kids. Terry Bradshaw had graduated and we had some good teams in those eras and we were struggling. There was talent there and I don't think any of us had any idea how much it was and what we could accomplish," said Carr, a sophomore on the 1971 squad.

As the season progressed, however, Carr noticed a change in the team.

"There were some neat things that happened," Carr said. "We had a couple of players, Denny Duron ended up being the quarterback. There was a Christian influence that really developed in that team. There were several young men, Huey Kirby was another one, Randy Crouch and there was a Christian influence that began to surface and players began to change, coaches began to change, the atmosphere a little bit began to change. I think that was the bedrock of what kind of propelled us into the Southland Conference. Of course, who knew we would have the success we had. It all seemed like there was a timing there involved that none of us were quite aware of."

Lamar's switch to the wishbone earlier in the season began to pay dividends in the Cardinals' Southland Conference road game at Abilene Christian.

The Cardinals amassed 290 yards on the ground, including 64 on a first-quarter touchdown run by Clinton Hill, to spark Lamar to a 30-28 victory over the Wildcats.

After a 4-yard run by Matthews gave Lamar a 13-0 lead in the first quarter, a 1-yard touchdown run by Abilene Christian's Nicky Pruitt was matched by a Mike Drake run to give the Cardinals a 20-7 halftime lead.

The Cardinals fought off an Abilene rally as the Wildcats outscored Lamar 21-10 in the second half. Pruitt added two more scoring runs from a yard out and hauled in an 11-yard touchdown pass from quarterback Clint Longley. Glen Hill's 22-yard field goal in the fourth quarter – his first successful kick in six attempts on the season – proved to be the difference for the Cardinals.

Lamar snapped a 13-game road losing streak in improving to 2-6 overall, including 1-1 in Southland play. The Wildcats dropped to 4-3 overall and 0-2 in the SLC.

On the same day the Cardinals were celebrating the end of their long losing streak, the Trinity Tigers were dealing with a different set of emotions heading into their Southland Conference game with Texas-Arlington. A week earlier, the Tigers learned Trinity officials planned to no longer award athletic scholarships in the future except in tennis. Starting with their game against Northern Arizona prior to the UTA game, Tiger players covered up the "TU" logo on their helmets as a form of protest.

"A lot of people wanted to transfer out at that time," recalled Costley. "We felt like we had a pretty decent ball club."

Costley credited Trinity head coach Warren Woodson with keeping the team together. A longtime coach at New Mexico State and an early user of the Wing-T offense, Woodson was forced to retire from New Mexico State at age 65 in 1967. After serving a few years as athletic director at Trinity, he became the Tigers' head coach.

"The leadership came from Coach Woodson. Everybody wanted to leave but he did a good job of selling everybody on wanting to stay," said Costley.

Still, it was hard to get players motived going into the UT-Arlington contest, according to Costley.

"Practice that week was horrible because nobody showed up. Our offensive line - that was the group that didn't show up. They were a senior group and they felt like they had been betrayed," Costley said.

Tiger players felt another indignity on their way to play the Mavericks.

"We rode the bus all the way to Arlington. It was a big game. We hadn't had a chance to speak to the school president at that time so it was kind of us against the world," said Costley, noting that Trinity normally traveled by airplane on long trips.

The homestanding Mavericks were the first unlucky Southland foes to face Trinity after the announcement and fell victim to an emotional Tigers team in a 28-7 loss for UTA. Leading the way for the Tigers, who were on a four-game winning streak, were Greg Oliver and Costley as each rushed for more than 100 yards against the Mavs.

Costley, who rushed for 134 yards, scored on a 34-yard run late in the first quarter to give the Tigers a 6-0 lead. He scored on a 14-yard run early in the third quarter to give Trinity a 22-0 lead.

After Costley's first touchdown, Steve Majka recovered a mid-air fumble and scooted 5 yards for a touchdown to make the score 13-0. Following Costley's second touchdown, Oliver, who ran for 104 yards, scored on a 20-yard run for a 28-0 Trinity lead.

Texas-Arlington's only score came on a 17-yard pass from Lanny Fleming to Billy Wray with 1:38 left in the contest.

Having one of their best seasons ever, the Tigers improved to 2-0 in the Southland and 6-1 overall. UTA dropped to 1-6 in losing its conference opener.

Trinity's five-game winning streak was snapped with a 27-15 Southland loss to Lamar. The loss left the Tigers' league record at 2-1 as Trinity slipped to 6-2 overall. Lamar also moved to 2-1 in SLC play while improving to 3-6 overall.

The Tigers held a 15-14 edge at halftime, scoring all of their points in the second quarter. A 70-yard sprint down to the Cardinal 14-yard line by Costley eventually set up the running back's 2-yard touchdown run. The Tigers turned a bad snap on the conversion attempt into two points when Mike Scott, the Trinity kicker, tossed to Bill Hodge for an 8-6 lead.

Costley's fumble later in the quarter set up a 5-yard run by Matthews on an option pitch to put Lamar on top 14-8 before Oliver scored on a 1-yard run in the closing seconds of the first half for Trinity's 15-14 halftime lead.

Trinity would not score the remainder of the game. Lamar, meanwhile, pulled away with two second-half touchdowns, both set up by the Cardinals' defense. Richard Kubiak's interception of a Tiger pass set up a 10-yard touchdown run by Matthews. Matthews rushed for 105 yards for a Cardinals team that amassed 288 yards on the ground with their wishbone offense.

Bruce Taylor's return of another errant Tigers pass to the Trinity 9-yard line led to an 8-yard touchdown run by Glen Hill in the fourth quarter for Lamar's 27-15 victory.

"We were a second-half team," Costly remembered. "The coaches made good second-half adjustments. Normally, throughout my career, we were a second-half team. For us to lose the lead that was a rarity."

Riding a three-game winning streak, Southwestern Louisiana returned to Southland Conference play at 10th-ranked Arkansas State – the Ragin' Cajuns' final league game of the season.

USL jumped out to a 10-0 halftime lead on a 28-yard Azios field goal and a 15-yard run by Juul. Arkansas State got back in the contest in the third quarter on a 30-yard Duren field goal. The Indians tied the game with 12:57 remaining in the fourth quarter on a 52-yard scoring strike from James Hamilton to Steve Burks.

Late in the game, Rocky Self was stopped at the Arkansas State 2-yard line for what appeared to be the final play of the game. Off-setting penalties on the play gave the Cajuns an untimed down. Attempting a possible game-winning field goal from the 7-yard line, Azios pushed the ball slightly to the right of the upright, resulting in a tie game.

The tie was costly for Arkansas State, which was seeking its fourth-straight conference championship. The result left the Indians 1-1-1 in the league and 3-2-1 overall. USL moved to 5-2-1 overall and concluded conference play at 2-2-1.

A non-conference win over Tennessee-Chattanooga stretched Louisiana Tech's winning streak to five games as the Bulldogs moved up to No. 5 in the polls.

Being nationally-ranked, riding a five-game winning streak while sporting a 7-1 overall record and undefeated in SLC play at 4-0, things set up nicely for the Bulldogs in their first season in the league. A win in its next game – at home – would give Tech the outright conference title.

The opponent for the contest was Southern Mississippi in another "designated" conference game. While much was working in Louisiana's Tech's favor, one fact nagged at the Bulldogs. In the previous four contests between the two teams, the road team spoiled the home team's Homecoming. For Tech to capture the outright SLC title, the Bulldogs would have to end the trend.

Louisiana Tech seemed on its way to ending the jinx; holding leads of 14-0, 14-7 and 20-7, but the Bulldogs couldn't seem to put Southern Miss away. A 2-yard run by Doyle Orange and a 39-yard field goal by future Pro Football Hall of Fame punter Ray Guy allowed USM to only trail 20-17 in the fourth quarter.

Southern Mississippi took possession at its own 25 with 3:26 remaining in the game. Southern Miss converted on fourth down from within its own territory when quarterback Rick Donegan connected with fullback Billy Foley on a 27-yard gain to the Tech 39. A 25-yard pass to Steve Broussard and a 13-yard run by Orange brought the ball to the Bulldogs' 1-yard line. Orange dove in for his third touchdown of the game, giving USM a 24-20 lead with 1:38 remaining in the contest.

The Bulldogs managed to reach the Southern Mississippi 32-yard line in the closing moments. After three-straight incomplete passes, a Lantrip pass was intercepted by Eugene Bird, sealing Louisiana Tech's fate.

Louisiana Tech finished conference play 4-1 but the loss to Southern Miss left the door open for Trinity and Lamar.

Alert defensive plays by Costley set up three of Trinity's touchdowns as the Tigers rebounded from their loss to Lamar with a 27-14 victory at Abilene Christian.

Trinity trailed 7-0 going into the second half on a 14-yard first-quarter touchdown pass from Clint Longley to Travis Horn.

Costley's recovery of a Trinity fumble at the Wildcats' 48 led to a 10-yard run by Oliver to tie the game. Two plays into Abilene Christian's next drive, Costley picked off a Tigers pass at the Wildcat 19, setting up an eventual 5-yard touchdown pass from Mike Curry to Shawn Meagher to give Trinity the lead. Costley returned another interception to the Wildcats' 27 to set up yet another score. Oliver, who rushed for 162 yards, picked up 26 on first down and scored one play later to increase Trinity's lead.

Trinity's other score came on a Southland Conference-record 91-yard punt return for a touchdown by Richard Ramirez.

Longley and Horn hooked up again for a 13-yard touchdown in the fourth quarter for the 27-14 final.

Trinity improved to 3-1 in the Southland and set the stage for a possible conference co-championship with a win over Arkansas State in the Tigers' regular-season finale.

Prior to the Abilene Christian game, Costley saw only limited action on the defense. The use of Costley and other offensive players was a strategy used to try and contain Longley.

"Longley was pretty good and we prepared for him all week and we were going to put in our better players to do whatever we could to shut him down. We were just trying to put athletes on the field for that particular game," said Costley.

Playing at home, Arkansas State scored a touchdown in each quarter while Texas-Arlington repeated a season-long pattern of not scoring until the fourth period in the Indians' 28-7 victory.

Johnnie Carr's 25-yard pass to Kearney Blalack gave the Indians their first touchdown of the game. Calvin Harrell scored twice on runs of 12 and 1 yard, while Hamilton edged in from a yard out to produce Arkansas State's 28 points.

A 38-yard pass from David Taylor to Royce West in the fourth quarter accounted for the only touchdown for the Mavericks.

In an ironic twist of fate, Trinity, which had never won a Southland title, went into its 1971 season finale at home against Arkansas State with a chance to capture a share of the title with a win over the defending national champs.

"Earlier in the year, Texas A&I had been the defending NAIA champions an we beat them and we had a chance to defeat two national champions and we were real excited about that," Costley said.

Looking to go out as a champion before dropping down to non-scholarship status, the Tigers found themselves trailing 3-0 on a Duren field goal on Arkansas State's opening possession, but the rest of the first half was all Trinity.

On the Tigers' first play from scrimmage following Duren's field goal, freshman Billy Lynch, a third unit tailback, tossed a 57-yard halfback pass to Hodge down to the Indians' 4-yard line. After being pushed back, Curry hooked up with Hodge on an 8-yard touchdown to give Trinity a lead it would never relinquish.

A 1-yard touchdown run by Oliver to cap an 80-yard drive extended the Tigers' lead. An interception by Scott set up a 1-yard scoring run by Curry with eight seconds left in the first half to give Trinity a 21-3 halftime advantage.

Curry ran out of the end zone for an intentional safety when Trinity faced third down from its 4-yard line in the third quarter. An 11-yard run by Arkansas State's David Mitchell in the fourth quarter made the score 21-11.

Trinity put the wrappings on its Southland Conference co-championship on a 16-yard touchdown pass from Curry to Costley with less than three minutes left in the game to make the final 28-11.

"Curry and Hodge, they were our team leaders and they had really emphasized that all week – the fact they were defending national champs and we wanted to close out Trinity in Division I with a victory," Costley said.

For Lamar to thrust its way into a possible tri-championship in the Southland, the Cardinals needed to beat both Texas-Arlington and Arkansas State to close out the season.

The switch to the wishbone continued to provide positive results for the Cardinals as Lamar won its third-straight Southland Conference game since the move with a 23-14 victory at UT-Arlington.

The Cardinals jumped out to a 10-0 lead on a 31-yard Drake field goal and a 2-yard run by Matthews in the second quarter. Matthews' touchdown was set up by a Tommy Kizer interception of a Mavericks pass. Jerry Harvey picked off two passes for Lamar as well to give the Cardinals 25 on the year for a new single-season school record.

Lamar rushed for 215 yards in the game and led 16-0 before UTA cut the gap to 16-14 on a pair of touchdown passes by Taylor.

Clinging to a two-point lead, Lamar pinned the Mavericks deep in UTA territory late in the game on a 50-yard punt. The Cardinals got the ball back at their own 43 on a punt exchange to set up a 2-yard touchdown run by George Toal.

The backup quarterback was in the game for Hill, the Lamar starter, who suffered a knee injury earlier in the drive to help make the final 23-14.

Lamar improved its SLC record to 3-1 while improving to 4-6 overall. Texas-Arlington dropped to 1-9 overall and 0-4 in conference play.

UTA snapped a six-game losing streak to close the season the following week in a 21-17 victory over Abilene Christian. The Mavericks closed the year 2-9 overall and 1-4 in the Southland. Abilene Christian finished the season 5-5 overall, including 0-4 in SLC play.

Lamar went into its season finale at home needing a win over Arkansas State to secure a tri-championship. With Hill not available for the game with an injury, things seemed bleak for the Cardinal offense, so Lamar turned to its ball-hawking secondary.

Patrick Gibbs intercepted a pass by Hamilton in the first quarter to set up Lamar's initial score. Two plays after Gibbs' theft, Drake galloped 22 yards for a touchdown and a 7-0 Cardinals lead. Gibbs picked off Hamilton again early in the second quarter to set up a short touchdown run by Matthews for a 14-0 Lamar edge.

The Cardinals picked off four passes in the game to increase their single-season school mark for interceptions to 29.

After the second Lamar score, freshman James Flynn took over at quarterback for Arkansas State and promptly led the Indians to a touchdown. Flynn tossed to Tom Johnson, who made the catch at the 3-yard line and fell into the end zone to complete a 28-yard scoring play to make it 14-7 at halftime.

A personal foul against the Indians on the opening kickoff of the second half gave Lamar excellent field position to open the third quarter at the Cardinals' 48. A 19-yard halfback pass from Clinton Hill to Jay Verde down to the 10 eventually set up a 3-yard touchdown by Matthews as Lamar rebuilt its lead to two touchdowns at 21-7.

An Arkansas State drive ended on downs at the Lamar 5-yard line. The Cardinals answered with a drive of their own as a Matthews field goal made it 24-7 late in the third quarter.

Harrell scored on a 22-yard draw play with less than a minute remaining to make the final 24-13.

The win allowed Lamar to finish in a three-way tie atop the Southland Conference along with newcomer Louisiana Tech and departing Trinity, all with 4-1 league marks. The Cardinals ended the season 5-6 by winning four of their final six games. Arkansas State ended the season 4-4-1 overall and 1-3 in the SLC

It may have been a three-way tie atop the Southland, but Louisiana Tech's 8-2 overall mark helped the Bulldogs earn a postseason berth to take on Eastern Michigan in the first-ever Pioneer Bowl in Wichita Falls, Texas.

Lantrip managed to pass for 170 yards despite winds gusting up to 26 miles per hour to garner top offensive player honors in Louisiana Tech's 14-3 win over Eastern Michigan to claim the Midwest Regional College Division Championship. The lefthander's 17-yard touchdown pass to Berteau late in the first quarter staked the Bulldogs a lead they would never relinquish.

Meanwhile, freshman defensive tackle Fred Dean and his teammates came up with several key defensive stops to hold off Eastern Michigan. The future Pro Football Hall of Famer led Louisiana Tech with eight tackles to earn top defensive player recognition.

Tech cornerback Rob Carter came up with a pair of tackles for losses in the second half to stymie Eastern Michigan drives. Dean came up with a defensive stop at the Louisiana Tech 4-yard line on a fourth-quarter Huron drive. A fumble gave the ball back to Eastern Michigan deep in Tech territory, but David Brookings' fumble recovery ended that threat at the Bulldogs' 18.

The Bulldogs held a scant 7-3 edge until Wenford Wilborn returned a punt 91 yards for a touchdown in the third quarter to stretch the Tech lead.

TRINITY DEPARTS,
MCNEESE JOINS SLC

Trinity's departure was accompanied with the arrival of McNeese State, meaning membership in the Southland Conference for 1972 remained at seven. McNeese joined the SLC after one year as an independent. Prior to that time, since 1952, the school was a member of the Gulf States Conference, along with the likes of Louisiana Tech and Southwestern Louisiana.

It didn't take long for the incumbent schools to learn all about McNeese as the Cowboys played at Arkansas State on Sept. 9, 1972, Week 1 of the 1972 season, to open Southland action.

Arkansas State jumped out to the early lead when David Hines returned an interception 39 yards for a touchdown. Arkansas State added a 32-yard Joe Duren field goal and a 5-yard touchdown run by Stan Winfrey.

The Cowboys of third-year coach Jack Doland overcame the early interception as quarterback Greg Davis rushed for two short touchdowns and hooked up with split end Mick Crockett on an 11-yard touchdown pass. Allen Dennis, alternating with Davis a quarterback, scored the game-winning touchdown on a 4-yard run with four minutes left in the contest to give McNeese a 24-17 triumph.

Also kicking off Southland play the opening week of the 1972 season were McNeese's old Gulf States rivals, Louisiana Tech and Southwestern Louisiana.

The Bulldogs would know exactly where they stood in conference play early in the season as the schedule called for Louisiana Tech to play all five of its SLC games over the first six weeks of the 1972 gridiron campaign.

Scoreless at halftime, the visiting Bulldogs came up with the only points of the game midway in the third period. Bobby Bernard, who grew up in the shadows of USL's Cajun Field, guided Louisiana Tech on the game's lone scoring drive in place of ineffective starting quarterback Denny Duron. Bernard marched the Bulldogs 88 yards in nine plays. On six occasions in the drive, the ball went to Glen Berteau. Berteau rushed for 73 yards on the drive, including a 54-yard romp down to the Ragin' Cajun 2-yard line. Berteau's touchdown run from 2 yards out gave the Bulldogs all the points they would need.

"We called him 'Boom Boom,'" Carr said of Berteau. "He was from a little Baton Rouge high school. They had a cannon and every time Glen would score, they would set that cannon off."

The Cajuns had costly turnovers in their new offense. USL switched from the Veer to the Wishbone for the 1972 season and fumbled the ball seven times, including four lost fumbles, in the season opener. Only two plays after USL's Lafayette Mitchell returned the opening kickoff 63 yards to the Tech 33, the Cajuns coughed up the ball for the first time. Late in the game, a potential game-tying drive for USL was halted deep in Louisiana Tech territory by another lost fumble.

Following a week of non-conference action for all the teams in the Southland, Louisiana Tech was back to league play against McNeese State in a battle of teams ranked in the Top 5. Both teams were 2-0 and coming off non-conference victories. Louisiana Tech defeated Southern Mississippi while McNeese blanked Sam Houston State.

A 42-yard halfback pass from Berteau to Roger Carr, who ended up with 222 reception yards, gave the Bulldogs a 7-0 lead three minutes into the game. Carlos Medrano's field goal cut the McNeese deficit to 7-3.

"I guess you could say I had a career day. It was a good game and a great experience," Carr recalled of his effort against McNeese State.

With McNeese trailing 13-3, Dennis hit tight end James Moore on a 4-yard touchdown pass to pull the Cowboys to within three points at 13-10 with two minutes remaining in the opening half. Tech answered when Duron connected with Eric Johnson on a 7-yard strike with 24 seconds showing before halftime to stretch the Bulldogs' lead to 20-10.

Charles McDaniel came up with touchdown runs of 3 yards in the third quarter and 16 yards in the fourth. The only touchdown McNeese could manage in the second half was an 8-yard run by fullback Don Soilleau with 12 minutes left in the game as Louisiana Tech took a 34-17 decision.

The second of four-consecutive Southland games for Louisiana Tech continued with the Bulldogs hosting Abilene Christian. The Wildcats entered their conference opener at now second-ranked Tech with a 1-2 record.

Louisiana Tech got off to another quick start as the Bulldogs built a 28-0 halftime lead on their way to a 35-12 win over Abilene Christian to remain unbeaten.

The Bulldogs spread the ball around as four different Tech players scored in the opening half. Roland Harper hauled in a 9-yard scoring toss for the only points of the first quarter. Louisiana Tech added three touchdowns in the second quarter. The first came on a 24-yard scamper by Duron with the other via short runs by McDaniel and Berteau.

All of Abilene Christian's points came in the fourth quarter on 1-yard run by Wolfgang Halbig and Halbig's 66-yard touchdown reception.

On the same day Louisiana Tech was defeating Abilene, Arkansas State and Southwestern Louisiana squared off. With the Bulldogs already off to a 3-0 Southland start, the Indians and Ragin' Cajuns, both 0-1, could not afford another conference defeat.

Arkansas State's Steve Burks was a near one-man show, rushing for 96 yards on an eye-popping 35 carries in the Indians' 21-18 victory at Southwestern Louisiana.

The sophomore quarterback staked the Indians to a 7-0 lead when he scored on a 4-yard run to cap a game-opening 84-yard drive. USL countered with a 38-yard Richard Azios field goal.

Clinging to a four-point lead to open the third quarter, the Indians gained possession at the USL 46 on a Craig Johnson interception. Joe Hollimon capped a 10-play drive with a 4-yard run to give Arkansas State a 14-3 lead.

After USL moved to 14-10 on a 4-yard run by Mitchell, Burks' second touchdown run of the game, this one from 2 yards out, made it 21-10. Rolando Surita's 2-yard run with four minutes in the game made the final 21-18 – the second-straight three-point loss for the Cajuns, who fell 13-10 to Trinity the previous week.

After opening the 1972 season with a brutal schedule that included four road games against several heavyweights, the reward for Texas-Arlington's home opener was a Southland Conference encounter with powerhouse Louisiana Tech.

The Mavericks were off to an 0-4 start. After opening with a loss to Southern Mississippi, Texas-Arlington lost to Oklahoma State. It was the first time for the Mavs to face a team from the Big Eight or to play on artificial turf. The following week, UTA had the task of taking on a Toledo team that was coming off a loss a week earlier that snapped a 35-game winning streak, the longest in the nation. UT-Arlington remained winless with a loss to Texas Christian.

The Bulldogs intercepted a whopping nine passes – two short of the national record – as Louisiana Tech cruised to another Southland Conference win with a 35-14 road victory.

John Causey led the way for the Tech defense as the safety intercepted four passes. Larry Griffin picked off three errant Maverick throws as UTA fell to 0-5 on the season.

"You look back at a lot of that offense we had; we had a mighty good defense," said Carr.

Berteau scored on a pair of short runs and on a 15-yard pass from Duron. Carr continued to show his big-play ability, hauling in four catches for 115 yards, including a 27-yard touchdown.

"We were starting to get our timing down," Carr said. "Denny Duron had been a quarterback in high school and he was a receiver for a year or so while Lantrip was the quarterback and then he began to make his mark."

At the same time Louisiana Tech was moving to 4-0 in Southland play and only one win away from going undefeated in conference action, 3-1Lamar was finally playing its league opener against McNeese State. At 2-1 overall, including 1-1 in SLC play, the Cowboys were ranked No. 8 in the nation and coming off an open date.

The well-rested Cowboys scored all of their points against Lamar in the second quarter to earn a 17-7 victory.

McNeese culminated its first scoring drive of the game when Davis, facing fourth down at the Lamar 2-yard line, sprinted to his right before tossing to slotback Lee Duplichan in the end zone for a 7-0 lead.

A 9-yard run by Barry Boudreaux and an 18-yard Medrano field goal gave McNeese a 17-0 halftime lead.

Lamar's only score came on a 3-yard pass from Glen Hill to Rusty Brittain in the third quarter. The Cardinals advanced inside the McNeese 35-yard line four times in the fourth quarter but were unable to score against a stingy Cowboys defense.

The Ragin' Cajuns offense, meanwhile, had one of their best outings in the season in a 35-14 home win over Abilene Christian. USL rushed for 335 yards, with quarterback Mark Speyrer leading the way with 101 yards and four touchdowns.

Speyrer's first touchdown, a 9-yard run in the first quarter, gave the Cajuns the early lead. On the ensuing kickoff following the sophomore quarterback's touchdown, the Wildcats were unable to handle the football, with Bill Hairston recovering at the Abilene Christian 20. Speyrer broke loose on the very next play, giving USL a 14-0 lead.

Short touchdown runs by Speyrer and Robbie Juul gave Southwestern Louisiana a 28-7 halftime lead.

Abilene Christian's only score in the first half came on a 47-yard touchdown reception by Churchill on a pass from Clint Longley. Each team added a touchdown to account for the final margin as USL improved to 2-3 on the season while Abilene Christian fell to 1-4.

Longley is best remembered for coming off the bench in place of an injured Roger Staubach as a rookie in 1974 to lead the Dallas Cowboys to a come-from-behind 24-23 win over the rival Washington Redskins on Thanksgiving Day. In a nationally-televised game, Longley entered the contest in the third quarter with the Cowboys trailing 16-3. Longley threw a 50-yard touchdown pass with 28 seconds left in the game to give Dallas the victory.

Louisiana Tech needed little motivation for its Week 6 encounter against Arkansas State in Little Rock. All Tech needed was a win over the Indians to capture its second-straight Southland Conference championship. Needed or not, additional motivation came Louisiana Tech's way in the week leading up to the game when the Bulldogs moved up to the top spot in the nation.

Like they had done in their three previous games, the Bulldogs jumped out to a big halftime edge, leading 24-10 at the break. Despite the advantage, Louisiana Tech had to come from behind for the first time in the 1972 – albeit while trailing only 3-0 following a 28-yard field goal by Duren, the Arkansas State kicker.

The early 3-0 deficit proved to be just another motivational factor for the Bulldogs, who went on to score on four-straight possessions in building their halftime lead. McDaniel put Tech ahead for good with a 3-yard scoring run in the first quarter. Duron added a 10-yard touchdown run, while Danny Norris booted a 41-yard field goal and Robert Sheppard had a 41-yard scoring reception. Norris' field goal was the longest in Louisiana Tech history as the Bulldogs went on to win 38-17.

Only six weeks into the season, the top-ranked Bulldogs were undefeated at 6-0, but more important to Louisiana Tech was one of the earliest clinchings of a conference title in the annals of college football.

As Louisiana Tech was wrapping up Southland Conference play, the Lamar Cardinals were in league action for only the second time all season, hosting Abilene Christian.

The Cardinals allowed Abilene Christian to score the first and final points but the rest of the game belonged to Lamar. A 22-yard Sonny Kennedy field goal led to the only points of the first quarter but the Wildcats would not score again until a 35-yard pass from Tony York to Kelly McCarthy in the fourth quarter in Lamar's 31-10 victory on Cardinal coach Vernon Glass' 44th birthday.

Glass named Hill his starting quarterback for the Abilene Christian game after the senior and Mike Drake alternated at the position to open the season. With Hill named the fulltime starter, Drake moved to fullback in the Cardinals' wishbone offense.

The move paid quick dividends as Hill scored on a 1-yard run in the second quarter to put Lamar on top of the Wildcats 7-3. Doug Matthews added a 4-yard touchdown run to give the Cardinals a 14-3 halftime edge.

Matthews, who rushed for 92 yards, added a 28-yard touchdown run in the third quarter and backup quarterback George Toal scored from 7 yards out for a 28-7 Cardinals lead. Lamar added its final points on a 28-yard Jabo Leonard field goal in the fourth quarter.

Lamar evened its Southland record at 1-1 while improving to 4-2 overall. Abilene Christian fell to 0-3 in the SLC and 1-5 overall.

As Louisiana Tech was closing out the regular season with a string of five non-conference games, starting with Northwestern State, the rest of the Southland Conference was vying for second place.

With still a number of Southland games remaining for most league teams, only three teams other than Louisiana Tech were limited to one loss midway in the season. Like, Louisiana Tech, McNeese State, which lost to the Bulldogs earlier in the season, faced non-conference opponent Nicholls State. Lamar was 1-1 at this point and didn't have Louisiana Tech on its schedule. Texas-Arlington only had one conference game under its belt and that was a loss to the Bulldogs, and like McNeese, faced a non-league opponent in New Mexico State.

Lamar looked to equal McNeese's 2-1 mark at Southwestern Louisiana.

In a defensive struggle against USL, Lamar drove down to the Ragin' Cajuns' 21-yard line on its opening possession of the game but failed to come away with points when Drake fumbled on fourth-and-1. A short punt gave the ball right back to the Cardinals at the USL 40. That led to Matthews' field goal and a 3-0 lead for Lamar.

USL threatened in the fourth quarter. One drive ended on an interception by Donald Hill, the second theft of the game for the Cardinal defender. A fourth-down pass with less than three minutes left in the game to a wide-open Doug Abel was off target by Spreyer, allowing the Lamar defense to record its second shutout of the season with a 3-0 triumph.

Lamar improved to 2-1 in the Southland and 5-2 overall. USL remained winless in conference play through three games while falling to 3-4 overall.

At the bottom of the league standings, 0-3 Abilene Christian hosted 1-2 Arkansas State.

At home for the first time in four games, the Wildcats snapped a five-game losing streak with a 3-0 triumph over Arkansas State.

Kennedy's 27-yard field goal with eight second remaining in the first half held up the entire game to give Abilene Christian its first Southland Conference win of the season.

The results left both teams 1-3 in the conference and 2-5 overall.

Because of scheduling quirk with the addition of McNeese State to the league, Lamar's game at Arkansas State counted in the Southland standings for the Cardinals but not the Indians.

Official league game or not, the Cardinals found themselves trailing 24-12 in the second half.

After Arkansas State increased a 17-12 halftime lead on a 1-yard run by Indians freshman quarterback Greg Hill to cap a 71-yard drive, Lamar quickly responded.

Glen Hill hit Brittain with a 1-yard pass to culminate an 81-yard, 14-play drive. In the fourth quarter, a pass interference call against the Indians at the Arkansas State 4-yard line set up the go-ahead score. Following a 3-yard run by Matthews, Glen Hill scored from a yard out for a 26-24 Lamar lead with slightly more than six minutes remaining in the game.

The Indians reached the Lamar 41 in the closing moments but a 48-yard field goal attempt by Duren was partially blocked by Thomas Gage with 30 seconds remaining to secure the two-point victory for the Cardinals.

A pair of touchdown runs by Greg Hill and a 32-yard Duren field goal helped Arkansas State build its 17-12 halftime lead. Playing on occasion out of a Wing-T offense, the Cardinals showed some ability to throw the ball. Glen Hill, who was 10 of 13 passing for 136 yards, tossed a 23-yard strike to split end Joe Bowser in the second quarter that pulled Lamar to within four points at the break.

Lamar moved to 3-1 in the SLC and 6-2 overall. Arkansas State dropped to 2-6.

In Southland play for only the second time all season, the Texas-Arlington defense saved the day for the Mavericks against visiting Southwestern Louisiana.

Ernest Baptist's interception of a Juul pass gave the Mavs the ball at the Ragin' Cajuns' 47-yard line. Baptist's theft set up a 6-yard touchdown run by Dexter Bussey, a future Detriot Lions running back, to give UTA a 7-0 lead that would hold up through halftime.

USL reached the Texas-Arlington 2-yard line early in the second half but the Mavericks turned back the Cajuns when Baptist and linebacker Hiram Burleson stopped Juul short of the goal line.

It was just the first of several key defensive stops for the Mavericks' defense in the second half. On one occasion, Baptist knocked away what appeared to be a sure touchdown at the Texas-Arlington 5-yard line. USL failed to take advantage of a Mavs fumble early in the fourth quarter when Thomas Younkin missed a 50-yard field goal.

Finally, the Cajuns reached the UTA 6-yard line before Mike Shiflett stripped the ball from Speyrer with Eugene Ayer recovering to preserve the win for the Mavericks.

In snapping a six-game losing streak, the Mavericks moved to 1-1 in the Southland and 1-6 overall.

In the only Southland game the next week, Texas-Arlington played at Abilene Christian. While UTA was coming off its first win of the season, Abilene defeated Eastern New Mexico in non-conference action to bring a 3-5 record into its game against the Mavericks.

Winning a football game seemed to be to the Mavericks' liking as Texas-Arlington scored on its first four possessions to take a 36-22 home triumph over Abilene.

UTA scored on its opening possession on a 24-yard Coppedge field goal. The kick was the first of five field goals in the game for Coppedge, setting a new team and Southland Conference mark for most field goals in a game. His effort broke the records of Skipper Butler, set in 1968.

A Wildcats' fumble on the ensuing possession set up a 9-yard touchdown run by Bussey. It also was a record-setting game for Bussey. The UTA running back rushed for 225 yards in the game, breaking the single-game school record of 215 set by Danny Griffin in 1969.

Another Abilene fumble set up a 2-yard touchdown run by Vic Morriss. Bussey raced 73 yards to set up his touchdown run from a yard out one play later and Coppedge added a 43-yard field goal to give UTA a 27-0 lead.

Abilene Christian avoided a first-half shutout on a 1-yard run by Longley.

The Mavericks won back-to-back games for the first time since 1969. Texas-Arlington moved to 2-1 in the SLC and 2-6 overall. Abilene Christian fell to 1-3 in the league and 3-6 overall.

Following a week of non-conference action for all Southland teams, league play resumed the following week. In the key game, 3-1 Lamar had a chance to wrap up second place at home against 2-1 Texas-Arlington. The Cardinals went into the game coming off back-to-back non-conference wins over New Mexico State and Nicholls State to stretch their winning streak to five games. UTA was seeking its fourth-straight victory, and with a bit of luck, a potential second-place Southland finish after a 0-6 start.

A stiff wind played a factor in the game's only touchdown when a first-quarter punt by Drake from deep in Cardinals territory traveled only 13 yards to the Lamar 21. Following a loss, a 22-yard pass from Morriss to Royce West down to the 1-yard line set up Bussey's touchdown run and a 7-0 Mavericks lead.

The score held up until Leonard connected on a 29-yard field goal in the third quarter to rally the Cardinals to within four points.

Thomas McClendon's recovery of a Mavericks fumble gave Lamar the ball at the Texas-Arlington 19 early in the fourth quarter. Toal tossed to Bowser in the end zone on fourth down from the 5-yard line but a hit by UTA's Baptist jarred the ball loose from the Lamar split end.

Lamar forced a punt late in the game but Larry Neumann, the Cardinal return man, fumbled at his own 11. Coppedge kicked a 22-yard field goal with less than two minutes remaining to give the Mavericks a 10-3 triumph.

The Cardinals ended their season 8-3 overall and 3-2 in the Southland. Texas-Arlington improved to 4-6 overall and 3-1 in the SLC.

Playing its first Southland Conference contest since the fourth game of the season, the Cowboys used a strong running game and stout defense to take a 22-0 home win over Abilene Christian.

Enos Hicks rushed for 187 yards to lead the McNeese offense. The Cowboys' defense held Longley, the leading passer in the SLC, to only 109 yards and picked off three of the Wildcat quarterback's passes.

Scoreless after one quarter, the Cowboys took a 9-0 lead at halftime on a 33-yard Medrano field goal and a 4-yard pass from Davis to Moore. The score remained the same until the fourth quarter when Marshall Higginbotham scored on a 3-yard run and Tommy Leger raced in from 30 yards out.

McNeese improved to 3-1 in the Southland and 8-2 overall. Abilene Christian ended its season 3-8 overall and 1-4 in the SLC.

The Cowboys and Texas-Arlington each went into the final week of the 1972 season with a shot at second place. Both teams were 3-1 in league play as McNeese closed the year at home against a Southwestern Louisiana team that was winless in Southland play while Texas-Arlington was at home against 1-3 Arkansas State.

In a defensive struggle, neither team could generate as much as 270 yards of offense in the season finale between McNeese and USL.

Charlie Fox's interception of a Dennis pass gave USL the ball at the McNeese 22-yard line early in the second quarter. On fourth down from the

6-yard line, the Ragin' Cajuns settled on a 22-yard Azios field that held up through halftime.

Another interception, this one by Leroy Johns, gave USL the ball at its own 47. The Bulldogs turned the Cowboys miscue into a touchdown when Juul hooked up with Abel from 14 yards out to give USL a 10-0 triumph.

The lone bright spot for the Cowboys were two pass receptions by Moore. The catches gave him 75, breaking the McNeese State career mark of 74 set by R.C. Slocum, the future head coach at Texas A&M.

McNeese finished the season 3-2 in the Southland and 8-3 overall. The lone conference win allowed Southwestern Louisiana to finish 1-4 in the league and 5-6 overall.

With McNeese's loss to USL, Texas-Arlington could finish no worse than second place in the Southland, but a win over Arkansas State would give the Mavericks sole possession of the runner-up spot.

The Mavericks faced a third-and-10 at their own 34 early in the game when Sid Sims gained the exact yards needed to keep the drive alive. Bussey capped the 17-play, 66-yard drive on a 5-yard touchdown run for a 7-0 UTA lead at the 7:25 mark of the first quarter.

Bussey ended the game with 105 yards rushing to finish the season with 862 yards to set a new UTA single-season mark.

The 7-0 lead held up going into the final period. A 57-yard run by Hollimon early in the fourth quarter appeared to be a potential game-tying touchdown. The play was called back, however, on a clipping call against the Indians.

Texas-Arlington avoided disaster later in the quarter. A snap over the head of Joe Whitney rolled into the Mavericks' end zone. The alert UTA punter recovered the ball and managed to get off a punt that rolled to the Arkansas State 45 to dodge a bullet.

The Indians had one bullet left in the closing seconds. Arkansas State marched 80 yards in 14 plays, finally scoring on a 27-yard end-around by Kearney Blalack. Going for two points and the win with 47 seconds remaining, Winfrey, the Arkansas State fullback, got the ball. Like he had done in the Southwestern Louisiana game to get the five-game winning streak started, Burleson stopped Winfrey short of the end zone to preserve the win for the Mavs.

After losing its first six games, Texas-Arlington won its final five and finished 4-1 in the Southland Conference. The winning streak was the longest for UTA since the Mavericks won their first six games of a 10-1 1967 season. Arkansas State closed the season 1-5 in the league and 3-8 overall.

Louisiana Tech wrapped up the 1972 Southland Conference title only six weeks into the season and went on to take non-conference wins over Northwestern State, Southeastern Louisiana, Northern Arizona, Eastern Michigan and Northeast Louisiana to finish 11-0 and extended its winning streak to 13 games over two years.

Although the outcome wouldn't necessarily change things, the Bulldogs wanted to make the Grantland Rice Bowl at Memorial Stadium in Baton Rouge a statement. That statement was that Louisiana Tech may very well be the best College Division team in the land.

Tech put an exclamation point on that theory with a whopping 35-0 thrashing of Ohio Valley Conference champion Tennessee Tech. The Bulldogs entered the battle for the NCAA Mideast region title ranked No. 2 in the country. Delaware ended the regular season as the top-ranked team but declined a postseason invitation. Without some sort of playoff system there was no way to settle the argument of who was really No. 1.

Louisiana Tech left no doubt who the Eagles thought was the best team in the country. Duron riddled the Tennessee Tech defense for 275 yards and two touchdowns on his way to being named the game's top offensive player. Carr, the All-American flanker who ended the season with 1,000 reception yards, continued to show his big-play ability by hauling in six passes for 141 yards and a touchdown. Duron's other touchdown toss, a 23-yard strike to Johnson, staked the Bulldogs to a 7-0 lead. Berteau added two touchdown runs.

The Louisiana Tech defense was in dominating form. Led by the likes of Joe McNeely, Fred Dean, Mike Myers, Lewis Frost, Danny Curtis, Ricky Shirley, Craig Springmeyer and Charles New, the Bulldogs held Tennessee Tech to 94 yards total offense and four first downs. McNeely, named the top defensive player in the game, returned a 31-yard interception for a touchdown that gave the Bulldogs a 14-0 lead at the time and set the stage for a perfect 12-0 season.

"We were pretty solid on both sides of the ball and had a good kicking game. Anytime you go undefeated, you've got to be pretty good. I think we had kind of arrived back then," Carr said of the undefeated season.

LOUISIANA TECH, DIVISION II NATIONAL CHAMPS

The College Division was renamed NCAA Division II in 1973. Abilene Christian departed the league in favor of the Lone Star Conference and the Wildcats went on to win the NAIA Division I national championship their first year in the new classification. With the departure of Abilene Christian, Southland membership was reduced to six teams.

Arkansas State hosted Southwestern Louisiana to open up Southland play in 1973. It was the first game of the year for the Ragin' Cajuns, while the Indians entered the game 1-0 with a wild 56-46 victory over Abilene Christian.

Southwestern Louisiana had trouble keeping the Indians off the field in the second half after trailing 14-6 at halftime. USL scored off the opening drive of the game for a quick 6-0 lead on a 4-yard run by quarterback Rolando Surita before eventually trailing at the break.

Arkansas State managed drives of 65 and 57 yards in the third quarter and held onto the ball for more than 12 minutes in the period. Indians quarterback Steve Burks capped both drives on touchdown runs.

The Cajuns drove deep into Arkansas State territory three times in the final quarter but failed to produce any points. Two of the drives ended with interceptions at the 1-yard line.

After USL took its 6-0 lead, the Indians responded with touchdown runs by David Mitchell and Burks to take the lead on its way to a 27-13 victory.

The Ragin' Cajuns were back in Southland action a week later at Louisiana Tech. The Bulldogs entered the game 0-1 on the season after opening with a 21-19 loss at Eastern Michigan in a rematch of the 1971 Pioneer Bowl. The loss snapped Louisiana Tech's winning streak at 15 games, which had been the third-longest in the nation.

"There was some crying in the locker room after that game," said Roger Carr, a Louisiana Tech receiver from 1970-73. "We missed a field goal. I got hurt in the first quarter. I separated my shoulder and didn't play for three quarters of the game. We made up our minds we would continue on and come back strong."

The season-opening loss for Louisiana Tech featured three interceptions, three lost fumbles and 130 yards in penalties. The inability to hold onto the football showed up again for Tech as the Bulldogs lost four fumbles against USL.

Louisiana Tech overcame the mistakes as the Bulldog defense showed a sign of things to come for the 1973 season. USL marched inside the Louisiana Tech 10-yard line three times but came away with no points, enabling Tech to take a 23-0 win. Along with the key defensive stops, the swarming Tech unit held the Ragin' Cajuns to totals of 81 yards rushing and 58 passing in tossing the shutout.

A 34-yard field goal by freshman John Pope and a 5-yard touchdown run by Glen Berteau gave the Bulldogs a 10-0 lead at halftime. The score remained the same until a 1-yard run by Charles McDaniel in the fourth quarter made it 16-0.

Tech closed out the scoring in record-breaking fashion. Denny Duron went back to pass from his own 6-yard line. The quarterback spotted receiver Mike Barber, who slipped past the Cajun secondary. Barber hauled in Duron's throw and scooted 94 yards for the longest passing touchdown in Louisiana Tech history.

Lamar and McNeese State, meanwhile, opened Southland Conference play in Lake Charles. The Cardinals went into the game 1-1 on the year after splitting with New Mexico State and Howard Payne. The Cowboys were 1-0 with a 40-10 win over Southeastern Louisiana.

Things didn't look good for the Cowboys late in their conference opener.

The Cowboys came up with a 21-yard run by Lee Duplichan but a missed extra point left McNeese down by four points at 17-13. McNeese reached the Lamar 2-yard line on its next drive, only to be turned away by the Cardinals' defense.

Needing a big break, the Cowboys got it three plays later when Jim Miller recovered a Cardinals fumble at the Lamar 21. It took six plays but McNeese finally scored the game-winner with 18 seconds left in the game on tailback Barry Boudreaux's run from a yard out for a 20-17 come-from-behind win for the Cowboys.

A 5-yard Boudreaux run on McNeese's first possession gave the Cowboys a 7-0 lead. McNeese would not score for the remainder of the half as Lamar went on to build a 17-7 lead at the break.

Scoring all of their points in the second quarter, the Cardinals came up with a pair of short Richard Rafes runs and a 29-yard Jabo Leonard field goal to take a 10-point advantage at halftime.

McNeese again was at home the following week against Louisiana Tech.

After combining for four missed field goals, McNeese State's game against No. 9 Louisiana Tech seemed fated to end with a kick.

Louisiana Tech's Pope missed field goals of 44 and 52 yards. His Cowboys counterpart, Ted Hill, was off-target from 41 and 35 yards out.

That led to a 7-7 tie going into the closing seconds. An interference call against the Cowboys on a fair catch gave Louisiana Tech the ball at the McNeese 40. That set up a touchdown strike from Duron to tight end Huey Kirby to give the Bulldogs a 7-0 lead at the 7:57 mark of the second quarter.

The Cowboys responded by moving 63 yards on the ensuing possession, with Boudreaux capping the drive on a 2-yard run to tie the game.

With the 7-7 tie holding up until the closing seconds, Pope booted a 42 yarder with three seconds left in the game to give the Bulldogs a 10-7 triumph as the Louisiana Tech kicker made amends for his miss in the season opener against Eastern Michigan that snapped Tech's 15-game winning streak.

Playing a Southland game for the third week in a row, McNeese played at Texas-Arlington in the Mavericks' conference opener.

The Mavericks went into the game 1-2 on the season. UTA spoiled the home debut of North Texas coach Hayden Fry in a 31-7 season-opening win over the Mean Green. UT-Arlington lost 56-7 to Oklahoma State to snap a six-game winning streak and followed that up with a 49-13 loss to Texas Christian. The Mavs went into the McNeese game well rested with an open date following the TCU contest.

After trading leads throughout the first half, McNeese gained a 24-23 lead on a 15-yard touchdown pass from Johnnie Thibodeaux to Pat Victor in the fourth quarter.

Dexter Bussey returned the ensuing kickoff 27 yards and a face-mask penalty against the Cowboys gave Texas-Arlington great starting position at its own 49. The Mavericks advanced to the McNeese 30 before the drive stalled. R.A. Coppedge drilled a 47-yard field goal – his fourth of the game – for what proved to be the game-winning points in a 26-24 victory with 4:21 remaining in the contest.

Coppedge opened the scoring with a 28-yard field goal for the only points of the first quarter. McNeese took its first lead of the game on a 7-yard pass from Thibodeaux to tight end Nathanial Allen in the second quarter. A 2-yard touchdown run by Bussey and a 43-yard Coppedge field goal gave UTA a 13-7 halftime edge.

In the only Southland game the following week, Louisiana Tech hosted Arkansas State.

Louisiana Tech was in the midst of building another winning streak. After the wins over USL and McNeese State, the Bulldogs beat Northern Arizona in non-conference play for their third-consecutive win and sported a 3-1 overall mark. Following Arkansas State's win over USL, the Indians lost to Wichita State and defeated Indiana State. The 3-1 Indians had an open date to prepare for Tech.

The extra preparation time didn't help the Indians much as a confident Pope kicked three field goals, including a school-record 51 yarder, to ease Louisiana Tech past Arkansas State 23-7 and the Bulldogs were off to another 3-0 conference start. Along with Pope's mark, Roger Carr also established a new school record. His 19-yard scoring reception in the second quarter gave him 16 scoring touchdown catches in his career.

"Denny was throwing the football well. We had a good offensive line. When we got within striking distance, I'd get an opportunity to catch a long ball," said Carr.

Arkansas State actually led 7-3 on a 1-yard sneak by Burks to cap a 74-yard drive to counter Pope's first field goal, a 26-yard kick.

A pair of struggling teams met a week later when Southwestern Louisiana visited Lamar. USL was winless through five games, including 0-2 in Southland competition. Lamar was 2-4, including 0-1 in SLC play.

Special teams and a stout defense set up the Cardinals' 31-0 blanking of Southwestern Louisiana in the first of four-consecutive Southland Conference games to close the season for Lamar. Playing at home, Lamar's offensive numbers were strikingly similar to that of USL. Both teams rushed for 69 yards while the Cardinals passed for 215 yards and the Ragin' Cajuns 208.

Lamar's special teams set the tone early in the game. A 51-yard punt by Lynn Bock pinned USL deep in its own territory. Forced to punt from the 9-yard line, the Cajuns' kick was blocked by Lamar's Leon Babineaux. Four plays later, fullback James Chambers scored from 2 yards out for a 7-0 Cardinals first-quarter lead.

Another Bock punt, this one traveling 80 yards, pinned the Ragin' Cajuns once again in the second quarter. A short USL punt gave Lamar the ball at the Cajuns' 34. Lamar freshman quarterback Bobby Flores hit Joe Bowser on a 10-yard touchdown strike. A 77-yard punt return for a touchdown by Randy Colbert and a 27-yard Leonard field goal gave Lamar a 24-0 lead as the Cardinals put the game away by halftime.

The same week Louisiana Tech was defeating Southeastern Louisiana 26-7 in non-conference action, several league foes were looking for a chance to gain a little ground on the Bulldogs.

Texas-Arlington went into its road game at winless Southwestern Louisiana looking to move to 2-0 in Southland action while the winner of the Arkansas State-Lamar contest would improve to 2-1 in the conference.

A week earlier, the Mavericks led 14-13 at halftime against Southern Mississippi but could not score in the second half in an eventual 41-14 loss. Against the Ragin' Cajuns, UTA was tied at the half 14-14 before dominating the final two quarters.

A pair of Elmo Simmons touchdowns led to Texas-Arlington's tie with USL at the half. Coppedge broke the tie on a 26-yard field goal in the third quarter. A Cajuns fumble on the ensuing possession gave the ball back to UTA at the USL 21. A 1-yard dive by Bussey put the Mavs on top 24-14 with 2:53 remaining in the third quarter.

Ron Barnett raced 64 yards with a toss from Craig Holland early in the fourth quarter to make it 31-14 before USL added a late touchdown and two-point conversion for the 31-22 final.

A 30-yard interception return for a touchdown by David Neustrom and a 10-yard touchdown pass from Ken Boynick to Oliver Mitchell accounted for USL's first-half points.

In Beaumont, a string of six scoreless quarters for the Lamar defense came to a quick end as the Indians marched 69 yards in 12 plays to open the game. Mitchell, who rushed for 127 yards, scored from a yard out to give Arkansas State a 7-0 lead.

Lamar's defense, with the aid of the Cardinals' special teams unit, would not allow another point the remainder of the contest.

A 27-yard Leonard field goal made the score 7-3 but the Cardinals continued to trail by four points going into closing minutes of the game.

Lamar journeyed 67 yards in 12 plays, capping the drive on an 11-yard pass from Flores to tailback Larry Spears, a fellow freshman, with slightly more than two minutes left in the fourth quarter. Leonard added the extra point, his 17th successful attempt in a row, to set a new school record.

Now trailing 10-7, the Indians quickly put themselves into field-goal range. Joe Duren's 51-yard attempt was blocked by Lamar's Audwin Samuel with 51 seconds left in the game, allowing the Cardinals to hold on for the victory. It was Duren's second blocked kick of the game. Earlier in the contest, he also missed a 47-yard field goal.

Gaining ground on Louisiana Tech was one thing but Texas-Arlington and Lamar found out in successive order that beating the Bulldogs head-to-head was something else.

Louisiana Tech secured at least a share of the SLC title for the third-straight year and Maxie Lambright picked up his 50th win as Tech coach in a 44-0 thrashing of the Mavericks.

In what seemed like just another day at the office for the Bulldogs, Duron threw three touchdown passes. Two of the tosses – a 46 yarder to Carr and a 42-yard connection with Barber – were part of a 31-point scoring barrage in the first half. Other first-half scores came on a 32-yard gallop by McDaniel, a 3-yard Arry Moody run, and a Pope field goal. There would be no late score to spoil the shutout as the Mavericks were held to 156 total yards, including only 43 passing.

"He wasn't an up-and-down coach. He was very methodical and steady. We just played week-to-week and a lot of the consistency we had was because of his personality," Carr said of the reason for Lambright's success.

Lamar, sporting a 2-1 Southland record, hosted Louisiana Tech and needed a win over the undefeated Bulldogs for a chance at a potential conference co-championship.

Louisiana Tech found Lamar's defense surprisingly tough as the Bulldogs were unable to cross midfield until the latter portions of the second quarter. Meanwhile, the Cardinals broke a scoreless tie earlier in the quarter on a 28-yard Leonard field goal.

The Bulldogs managed to take a 7-3 lead right before halftime on a 2-yard run by McDaniel with 1:08 left in the first half.

Lamar seemed poised to take the lead in the third quarter when a muffed punt gave the Cardinals the ball at the Louisiana Tech 11-yard line. The Cardinals failed to take advantage when Bulldogs defender Larry Griffin picked off a Flores pass at the 4-yard line and raced 69 yards. That set up a 26-yard Pope field goal to give Tech a 10-3 lead.

A Lamar fumble on a pitchout led to a 6-yard touchdown run by McDaniel in the fourth quarter to give the Bulldogs a 17-3 victory.

Louisiana Tech moved to 5-0 in the SLC to win the conference title. Lamar dropped to 2-2 in the league and 4-5 overall.

The Tech defense set a new Southland Conference record for fewest points allowed in league play. Louisiana Tech's five conference foes were held to a total of 17 points. Lamar held the previous mark at 24 points allowed.

A two-week span was all it took for Texas-Arlington to go from Southland Conference title contender to an also-ran. Following the 44-0 drubbing by Louisiana Tech, the Mavericks were unable to overcome an early 14-0 deficit in falling 30-14 at Arkansas State.

A Dexter Bussey fumble at his own 35 three plays into the game gave the Indians their first break. Two plays later, Willie Harris scored on a 31-yard scamper to give Arkansas State an early 7-0 lead.

Arkansas State was forced to punt on its next possession at the UTA 42 on fourth-and-13. Burks, the Indians' quarterback, dropped back to kick the ball away. As the Mavericks pealed back to set up a return, Burks took off in search of a first down. He didn't stop running until he found the end zone and a 14-0 Arkansas State lead.

After rallying to within 21-14, the Mavericks advanced to the Arkansas State 32-yard line or deeper three times in the third quarter but came away with no points.

A fumble by D. J. Williams at his own 30 while attempting to haul in a punt proved to be the killing blow for the Mavericks. Burks scored on a 23-yard run and the Indians came up with a safety in the closing seconds to give Arkansas State the 30-14 victory.

Arkansas State closed out its season a week later with a 26-23 win at McNeese State.

The Cowboys built what seemed like a comfortable 23-7 lead going into the fourth quarter, before the Indians, the top-rushing team in the Southland Conference, went to the air in their comeback bid.

After a 4-yard run by Thibodeaux with 3:01 remaining in the third quarter gave McNeese its 23-7 advantage, a personal-foul penalty against the Cowboys on the ensuing kickoff allowed the Indians to begin possession at the at their own 44. Burks hit David Mitchell for a 12-yard touchdown and the duo hooked up on a two-point conversion toss to make the score 23-15.

A 37-yard Duren field goal left Arkansas State behind by only five points at 23-18. On the following kickoff, Pat Victor bobbled the ball out of bounds at the 1-yard line on his attempted return. A subsequent punt gave the Indians the ball back near midfield.

After advancing to the 25-yard line, the Indians inserted backup quarterback James Flynn into the game at setback. Burks tossed a lateral to Flynn. Flynn passed to Burks, who raced in for the game-winning score with 1:17 left in the game to give Arkansas State a dramatic 26-23 victory.

McNeese built its 23-7 lead on three Conley Hathorn field goals, a 17-yard touchdown reception by Victor and a 4-yard Thibodeaux run. Hathorn's three field goals in the game set a new single-game record for the Cowboys.

The Cowboys fell to 1-3 in the Southland and 6-3 overall. Arkansas State improved to 7-3 in its season finale and 3-2 in the conference.

In order to avoid a winless season, the Cajuns would have to topple McNeese in the season finale. Prowling the sidelines of Cajun Field for the game would be a new head coach. Russ Faulkinberry had been dismissed by USL, with assistant Dan Roy named interim coach.

The change in coaches provided no spark as the Ragin' Cajuns fell to McNeese 37-0. USL's 10th loss of the season marked the fifth time the Cajuns were shut out in 1973.

USL was unable to stop Higginbotham. The Cowboys' junior quarterback rushed for four touchdowns. He scored on a pair of 4-yard runs, with the other two coming on runs of 14 and 17 yards. Hathorn rounded out the scoring for McNeese, hitting on a 27-yard field goal and a pair of 31 yarders to go along with four extra points. Hathorn's three field goals gave him seven on the season, tying a school record.

McNeese led 16-0 at halftime. The Cowboys' defense limited USL to 154 total yards. Richard Azios and Boynick, the Cajuns' quarterbacks, were a combined 6 of 24 passing for 55 yards.

The loss left Southwestern Louisiana 0-5 in the Southland. McNeese finished its season at 7-3 overall, 2-3 in the conference.

In one final Southland game, Lamar managed to finish 5-5 overall and 3-2 in the SLC with a 10-3 victory at Texas-Arlington. The Mavericks ended the season 2-3 in the Southland and 4-6 overall.

Louisiana Tech went into the 1973 Division II playoffs at the top of its game. The Bulldogs closed the season with a 40-0 thrashing of rival Northeast Louisiana to finish 9-1 in the regular season and on a nine-game winning streak.

Against NLU, Carr hauled in the 19th touchdown catch of his career to establish a new Louisiana collegiate mark. Carr, who would go on to play 10 years in the NFL, mostly with the Baltimore Colts, entered the game tied for the all-time lead with LSU's Andy Hamilton and Bernie Callendar of Louisiana College.

Also, McDaniel rushed for 167 yards and scored a touchdown. The touchdown gave McDaniel 218 points, allowing him to establish a new SLC record for career points.

The Bulldogs found out things would not be so easy in the opening round of the NCAA Division II championship playoffs in Ruston against the Western Illinois Lumberjacks.

Gary Birch field goals of 27 and 22 yards gave Western Illinois a 6-0 lead in the first quarter before Tech countered with a pair of 1-yard touchdown runs by Duron and McDaniel to lead 12-6 at intermission.

A 68-yard strike from Duron to Barber, a future NFL tight end, gave Louisiana Tech an 18-6 lead in the third quarter. The Lumberjacks, who managed a season-high 364 yards against the Tech defense, closed the gap in the fourth quarter. Steve Mikez's 8-yard touchdown toss to Tom Kevin made it 18-13 with 13:21 left in the game.

Despite the amount of yards allowed, the Bulldogs' defense came up big when needed. The Lumberjacks were driving midway in the fourth quarter when Wenford Wilborn picked off a Western Illinois pass in the end zone. It was Wilborn's third interception of the game. Louisiana Tech managed to pick up three first downs in the final three minutes of the game to run out the clock and post the five-point victory.

"They had a good football team and we didn't play particularly well on offense that game. I had a hamstring that was bothering me and I couldn't run very well," Carr said of the narrow win over Western Illinois.

Things didn't look good in the early stages of Louisiana Tech's Pioneer Bowl game against Boise State in the Division II semifinal game in Wichita Falls, Texas.

Touchdown runs of 7 and 8 yards by Boise State quarterback Jim McMillan gave the Broncos a quick two-touchdown lead in the first quarter. Settling down after the early Boise scoring barrage, the Bulldogs rallied back. A 49-yard gallop by McDaniel made it 14-7 after one quarter. A 26-yard Pope field goal and a 2-yard run by McDaniel gave Tech a 17-14 halftime lead and it was apparent a shootout was in progress.

"We knew we were in for a football game all four quarters. We played long enough to know that when we got down, if we got down, we had the capability to come back. We had some confidence and we knew it was a four-quarter game," Carr said of the Bulldogs being able to overcome an early deficit against Boise State.

The teams traded scores throughout the second half. McMillan's third touchdown pass of the game, a 31-yard connection with Don Hutt, gave Boise State a 34-31 lead with less than four minutes remaining in the game.

Louisiana Tech got the ball back needing to travel 65 yards for a potential game-winning touchdown to send the Bulldogs to the national championship game. A quarterback sneak by Duron on fourth down at the Boise 32 kept the drive alive. Later, a catch down to the Boise 22-yard line by Carr set up another fourth-and-one situation.

Like he had done before, Duron called his own number. He managed to barely squeeze through for the necessary inches to give the Bulldogs a first down with time running out. On the next play, Duron spotted Carr. The fleet-footed

Tech receiver beat single coverage and hauled in Duron's toss with 12 seconds left in the game for a thrilling 38-34 win.

Carr beat Boise State defensive back Rolly Woolsey, who was in the game in place of Ron Neal after the starting cornerback was forced to leave the game with a concussion sustained earlier in the contest.

"I ran a corner route at the end. It was just a great call. How I got one-on-one coverage was they blitzed and Roland Harper, our fullback, picked up the linebacker and gave Denny time to throw the football," Carr explained.

One more victory and Louisiana Tech would be the Division II national champions. In 1972, the Bulldogs went undefeated in 12 games but finished behind Delaware in the polls. Louisiana Tech had to settle for the NCAA Mideast regional title following its 35-0 demolition of Tennessee Tech. That would not be the case in 1973 with the new playoff system in place, yet coming away with the national championship would be no easy task for the Bulldogs.

Louisiana Tech featured one of the most prolific offenses in the country and a stingy, record-setting defense. But to claim a national title, the Bulldogs would have to defeat a 12-0 Western Kentucky squad that entered the Camellia Bowl in Sacramento, California, boasting an offense averaging more than 400 yards and 37.7 points per game.

As they had done throughout the season, the Bulldogs' offensive, defensive and special teams units worked hand-in-hand to help Tech establish a big, early lead in the championship game.

A 33-yard field goal by Pope gave Louisiana Tech a quick 3-0 advantage. Wilborn's 41-yard punt return set up a 1-yard McDaniel touchdown to give the Bulldogs a 10-0 lead after one quarter. The defense contributed mightily to the next two Tech scores. Defensive end Danny Curtis returned an interception back 11 yards for one touchdown and Wilborn's 17-yard interception return set up a 36-yard touchdown pass from Duron to Carr that gave the Bulldogs a surprising 24-0 halftime lead.

About the only thing that could slow down the Bulldogs was an injury to Duron. The quarterback suffered a shoulder injury in a scoreless third quarter. All that did was slow Tech down, but nothing would stop Louisiana Tech on this day. After a 31-yard field goal by Pope, freshman quarterback Steve Haynes hooked up with Tilley on a 28-yard touchdown pass with 5:07 left in the game to secure a 34-0 Tech win and a national championship.

McDaniel rushed for 116 yards – producing more yards on the ground than Western Kentucky could manage in total offense in a game played on a muddy, grassless field. While Tech went on to amass 336 yards total offense, the stout

Bulldog defense limited Western Kentucky to 76. The Hilltoppers were held to 88 yards passing and minus-12 rushing. Louisiana Tech's defense also picked off four passes and recovered a fumble.

"Looking back, the week before was probably the national championship game," Carr said. "I just think Boise State was that good. I think Boise State was the best team we played all year.

"Things went our way in the national championship game, obviously, but the Boise State game was the big game for us. The game afterward wasn't as interesting as that one was when you look at it going down to the wire. Probably us and Boise State, in my mind, had the two best teams."

Louisiana Tech's stretch of success, ultimately leading to a national championship, harkened back to the togetherness and faith the team had in the early 1970s, according to Carr. Along with Carr, almost a dozen members of the national championship Bulldogs went on to become preachers.

"There was Christian underlay and foundation to that thing," Carr said. "God does what only God can do. He put us all together.

"Who was to say we could go 24-1 and win a national championship with Denny Duron at quarterback. We don't go 24-1 without Duron. We just don't do it. Not only was his play on the field wonderful but off field. He grew up and his dad was a minister, and all of sudden, all of that began to come on. Lives were changed and bonded. We had a saying that "unity is our strength," and that's what it was. We were a unified team."

New Texas-Arlington coach Harold "Bud" Elliott faced the unenviable task of making his Southland debut in 1974 against Louisiana Tech, the defending conference and Division II national champion. Replacing John Symank, Elliott took over as Mavericks coach after serving three years as head coach at Emporia State, leading the team to the Great Plains Athletic Conference title in 1972 and 1973. Prior to Emporia State, Elliott served as head coach at Southwestern College and Washburn.

UTA went into the Louisiana Tech game 0-2 while Tech was 1-0 with a 16-7 season-opening victory over Illinois State.

Charles McDaniel was held to 21 yards by Illinois State and an open date gave Louisiana Tech's all-time leading rusher extra time to stew over his performance. Anxious to show his form of previous years, McDaniel ran for four touchdowns in a 42-15 win in the Bulldogs' conference opener played at the Cotton Bowl in Dallas. The win extended second-ranked Tech's winning streak to 14 games – the longest in the nation.

The Mavericks didn't do themselves any favors, turning the ball over on their first two possessions, which Louisiana Tech quickly converted into touchdowns. The two touchdowns, both on short runs by McDaniel, allowed the Bulldogs to build a 20-7 lead at halftime. Tech put the game away with a 15-point third quarter that included the third of McDaniel's school record-tying four rushing touchdowns.

Opening Southland Conference play the same day as Elliott and Texas-Arlington was new Southwestern Louisiana coach Augie Tammariello. Tammariello, a former Colorado University offensive line coach, replaced Russ Faulkinberry following USL's 0-10 season in 1973. The Ragin' Cajuns went into their league opener at McNeese State 0-1 following a 17-16 loss to Tulane in the closing seconds that stretched USL's losing streak to 11 games. The Cajuns were slated to make their debut a week earlier, but their home game against Arkansas State had to be postponed because of a hurricane.

The Ragin' Cajuns were unable to replicate the Tulane effort against seventh-ranked McNeese State as USL, featuring a veer offense, failed to pick up a first down or complete a pass until the third quarter. By that point, the Cajuns already trailed 24-0.

McNeese, which went into the game 1-0, led USL 17-0 at halftime as Marshall Higginbotham scored on touchdown runs of 10 and 1 yard. His second touchdown was set up by a Doug Dutt interception moments after Higginbotham's initial score. Conley Hathorn booted a 42-yard field goal to round out the first-half scoring.

The 38-point win was the largest margin of victory for the Cowboys in the series, topping the 37-point spread a year earlier in McNeese's 37-0 victory.

After McDaniel's four-touchdown performance a week earlier against UTA, the now top-ranked Bulldogs switched to their aerial show to take a 20-7 Southland win over Arkansas State, which was making its 1974 debut. Steve Haynes connected on 13 of 20 passes while tossing a pair of touchdown strikes to Mike Barber. John Pope added a pair of field goals for the Bulldogs.

The Indians' season got off to a late start because their original season-opener at Southwestern Louisiana was postponed because of a hurricane. Two open weeks followed, leading to Arkansas State not playing a game until the final weekend of September.

Arkansas State avoided the shutout on a 1-yard run by Stan Winfrey that was set up by a Bulldogs fumble deep in Louisiana Tech territory.

Off to a 2-0 start, Lamar was the final team to make its Southland Conference debut when the Cardinals traveled to Southwestern Louisiana.

Fullback Dale Spence scored on a 22-yard run to cap an 81-yard drive and quarterback Bobby Flores added a scoring run from a yard out to give Lamar a 14-0 lead after its first two possessions on the Cardinals' way to a 38-13 victory. USL kicker Rafael Septien booted field goals of 57 and 52 yards to cut the margin to 14-6 before the Cardinals scored the final 10 points of the half on a 23-yard Jabo Leonard field goal and a 60-yard interception return for a touchdown by Lamar's ball-hawking cornerback Audwin Samuel.

The highlight of the second half was a 58-yard halfback pass for a touchdown from Lamar split end Larry Spears to tight end Rusty Brittain in the fourth quarter.

Lamar's defense, ranked No. 2 in the nation, held the Cajuns to 93 yards rushing and 105 passing.

Teams with streaks from opposite spectrums met a week later when top-ranked Louisiana Tech put its unbeaten record on the line at Southwestern Louisiana. Not only were the Bulldogs 3-0 and ranked No. 1 in the nation, Tech entered the game with a 15-game Southland Conference winning streak. Winless USL, meanwhile, was in the midst of a 13-game losing streak.

By the time the game was over, both steaks remained as the Bulldogs took a 35-20 verdict over the Cajuns.

Louisiana Tech left little doubt of the outcome as McDaniel returned the opening kickoff a Southland Conference-record 100 yards for a touchdown. Shortly after McDaniel's kickoff return, the Bulldogs recovered a USL fumble to set up a 1-yard run by the Tech running back for a 14-0 lead. The Bulldogs took a commanding 21-point lead after one quarter following Arry Moody's 76-yard touchdown jaunt.

USL's first touchdown came on a Raymond Lation 1-yard run on a drive set up by a Bulldogs fumble to make it 21-7. After Tech built a 35-7 halftime lead, the Cajuns came up with the only two scores of the second half on a 1-yard run by Bruno Parker and a 12-yard pass from Barry Pollard to Oliver Mitchell.

Top-ranked Tech moved to 4-0 overall and 3-0 in the Southland. USL remained winless through four games, including 0-3 in conference action.

After losing their first game of the year in a 37-21 defeat at Mississippi State of the Southeastern Conference, the Cardinals returned to Southland action at Arkansas State.

Lamar's offense struggled against the Indians as the Cardinals were limited to 53 yards rushing and 93 passing. Field goals produced the only points of the game until the closing moments. A 36-yard Leonard field goal was sandwiched around a pair of kicks by Arkansas State's Joe Duren. Duren's kicks were from 45 and 51 yards, the latter setting a new school record for the Indians.

A struggling Lamar offense was down to its third quarterback in the closing moments of the game. Flores reinjured a foot injury sustained a week earlier against Mississippi State and backup David Silvas proved to be ineffective. That left the game in the hands of Al Rabb.

Lamar took possession of the football at its own 35 down by three points with 2:22 remaining in the contest. Rabb promptly rolled to his left and spotted tailback Anthony Pendland along the sideline. Pendland pulled away from the Indians' secondary on his way to a 65-yard touchdown and a 10-6 Cardinals lead with 2:11 left in the fourth quarter.

The Cardinals sealed the victory when middle linebacker David Halbrook intercepted a James Flynn pass with 32 seconds remaining in the game.

Lamar moved to 2-0 in the Southland and 4-1 overall. Arkansas State dropped to 0-2 in the SLC and 2-2 overall.

A 29-24 loss to Delaware in a battle of Top 10 teams and a 6-6 tie with Eastern Michigan dropped McNeese State to 3-1-1 on the season but the Cowboys still had the opportunity to join Lamar at 2-0 in the Southland Conference and stay in striking distance of Louisiana Tech with a home win against Texas-Arlington.

McNeese took its frustrations out on Texas-Arlington by pounding the Mavericks 43-0. The Cowboys led 16-0 at halftime before pulling away with two touchdowns in less than 30 seconds early in the second half.

The Cowboys forced a Mavericks punt on the opening possession of the third quarter. An interference call against Texas-Arlington on a fair-catch attempt by Victor gave the Cowboys the ball at the UTA 30. Thibodeaux scored on a quarterback sneak four plays later to give McNeese a 23-0 lead.

Chester Clark picked off a Mavericks pass at the UTA 29 on the ensuing possession, with Thibodeaux quickly tossing a touchdown strike to Victor to make the score 29-0.

Touchdown runs of 9 and 4 yards by Higginbotham, along with a safety, gave the Cowboys their 16-0 halftime lead. On Higginbotham's 4-yard score, he fumbled at the 3-yard line but the ball bounced right back to the running back on his way into the end zone.

For the second time in the 1974 season, McNeese State found itself in a battle of Top 10 teams when the Cowboys played at top-ranked Louisiana Tech in a Southland Conference showdown.

Like McNeese had done in the Delaware game, the Cowboys built an early lead against the Bulldogs, scoring the first two times they touched the ball.

Thibodeaux touchdown passes of 31 yards to Jim Gonsulin and 26 yards to Tommy Thomason staked the Cowboys to a 14-0 first-quarter lead.

Trailing 17-10, Louisiana Tech tied the score when Randy Robertson, subbing for an injured Haynes, hit Mike Barber with a 28-yard scoring strike at the 8:05 mark of the third quarter.

Later in the quarter, a Thibodeaux interception gave Tech the ball at the McNeese 40. Robertson hooked up with Billy Ryckman on a 13-yard strike to put the Bulldogs on top 24-17.

The Cowboys threatened twice down the stretch. The first time the drive ended at the Louisiana Tech 4-yard line on an incomplete pass on fourth down. The final attempt ended in Gary Griffin's interception of a Thibodeaux pass with 1:28 remaining in the game.

McNeese fell to 4-2-1 overall and 2-1 in the Southland Conference.

Louisiana Tech, unbeaten in SLC play since joining the league in 1971, won its 17th-straight conference game.

Following a week of non-league games for all teams in the Southland, Lamar played at Louisiana Tech as the last SLC team with a chance to possibly knock the Bulldogs from atop the conference mountaintop.

Pat Tilley showed the Cardinals that Louisiana Tech was not about to end its reign of domination in the Southland as the Bulldogs receiver and future St. Louis Cardinal caught three touchdown passes in Tech's 28-0 victory.

The win gave Louisiana Tech, the top-ranked team in the nation, its fourth-consecutive SLC crown since joining the league. Along with moving to 8-0 overall and clinching the conference title with a 5-0 mark, the Bulldogs stretched their winning streak to 20 games. The victory gave Tech a perfect 18-0 SLC record since becoming a league member in 1971.

Lamar dropped to 2-1 in the Southland and 6-2 overall.

McDaniel gave Tech a 7-0 lead with a 4-yard touchdown run in the first quarter before leaving the game later in the second quarter with a knee injury.

Tilley more than compensated for McDaniel's loss with his three-touchdown effort. The split end had scoring receptions of 25 and 41 yards from Robertson. Tilley hauled in an 11-yard touchdown pass from Don Dean in the fourth quarter to round out the scoring.

Louisiana Tech's defense held the Cardinals to 75 yards rushing and 57 passing. Lamar's deepest penetration into Bulldogs territory was the Tech 37. The Cardinals lost four fumbles and had three passes intercepted.

The Bulldogs' balanced offensive attack produced 202 yards rushing and 207 passing. Tilley had 122 reception yards while Robertson passed for 196.

While Louisiana Tech was securing another Southland title, a pair of teams with a combined one win met as Southwestern Louisiana played at Texas-Arlington with each team looking to pick up its first conference victory of the season.

USL went into the game 0-3 in the Southland and 1-6 overall. The Ragin' Cajuns' lone win was a 21-20 victory over Tennessee-Chattanooga that gave Tammariello his initial win as coach while snapping a 15-game losing streak. UT-Arlington entered the contest 0-2 in the Southland and winless through eight games.

Mike Wecker's 87-yard return of the opening kickoff gave the Mavericks a quick 7-0 lead. The Cajuns advanced 87 yards the first time they had the ball, but instead of a quick strike, it took 17 plays before Lation scored on a 7-yard run. Septien's rare conversion miss left USL behind by a point.

The Ragin' Cajuns grabbed the lead when a short punt out of the Mavericks end zone was returned 12 yards for a touchdown by Steve Hardin. A two-point conversion gave USL a 14-7 lead.

Texas-Arlington tied the game 14-14 on a 73-yard strike from Vic Morriss to Ronnie Barnett.

A slight rain and cool temperatures created sloppy field conditions and led to turnovers. One such turnover came midway in the second quarter when a Cajun fumble gave the ball to UTA at the Southwestern Louisiana 41-yard line. Eight plays later, Derrick Jensen scored on a 1-yard run to put the Mavericks on top 21-14.

With field conditions deteriorating in the second half, the turnovers mounted. The Cajuns lost five of eight fumbles in the mud while the Mavericks had five fumbles, losing three.

As a result, the only points produced in the second half came on a 47-yard Septien field goal. Prior to his 47 yarder, the normally sure-footed kicker missed on two attempts.

The 21-17 decision allowed Texas-Arlington to pick up its first conference win of the season and snap a nine-game losing streak. USL fell to 0-4 in league play and 1-7 overall.

Lamar bounced back from the Louisiana Tech loss with a 17-3 home win over McNeese State.

Flores scored on a 1-yard run to cap an 80-yard drive to give Lamar a 7-0 lead. The opening touchdown ended a streak of 11-consecutive scoreless quarters for the Cardinals. Lamar caught McNeese off-guard on the drive as the Cardinals switched from the Wing-T offense to the Slot-I Lamar employed in 1973. The switch proved productive as the Cardinals amassed 251 yards rushing and 112 passing.

Lamar's other points came on a Leonard field goal and a 1-yard touchdown run in the fourth quarter by Ronnie Melancon, who topped 100 yards in the contest.

McNeese's only score came on a 34-yard Hathorn field goal in the second quarter.

Following its loss to Lamar, Arkansas State went 1-2 against non-league competition before picking up its first Southland win of the season with a 42-12 road domination of Texas-Arlington.

Arkansas State took advantage of five Mavericks fumbles and intercepted two passes in the rout. Winfrey rushed for 159 yards and three touchdowns. Of his total, 120 came in the first half as the Indians built a 28-0 lead at the break. Arkansas State held the Mavs to 56 total yards in the opening half of play.

UTA's scores came long after the game was decided and against Indian reserves. Elmo Simmons had a 7-yard touchdown run and Morriss connected with Barnett on a 10-yard pass to account for the Mavericks' scoring.

The Texas-Arlington game was the start of a roll for Arkansas State, which closed the 1974 season with three-consecutive Southland wins. The Indians, however, needed a dramatic finish to make it two-in-a-row in Arkansas State's home game against McNeese State.

Duren booted a 56-yard field goal as time expired in a 22-20 Arkansas State victory. That was only the final achievement of a record-setting day for Duren. A former walk-on, Duren kicked a 63-yard field goal earlier in the game to set a new NCAA record.

Duren's 63 yarder broke the mark of 62 yards set by Mike Flater of Colorado Mines in 1973. The kick also broke the Southland Conference record of 60 yards set by Skip Butler of Texas-Arlington in 1968. He even added a 43-yard field goal to give him a single-game school record for UTA.

Three McNeese miscues in the first half inside its own 40-yard line turned into 13 points for Arkansas State.

Glen Moreau's fumble at the 29 set up a 3-yard Winfrey touchdown. The Indians turned a Moreau interception and a poor McNeese punt into six more points on two Duren field goals. The second one, which gave Arkansas State a 13-0 lead at the 1:35 mark of the opening quarter, was the record-setter.

Mike Ratcliff's 43-yard interception return for a touchdown provided the only points for McNeese at halftime as the Cowboys inched closer at 13-7.

McNeese opened the second half with a 60-yard drive to take a 14-13 lead on Bobby Wilson's 1-yard run.

The Indians regained the lead at 19-14 on a 1-yard dive by Willie Harris with 11:17 left in the game to cap an 80-yard drive.

A partially-blocked punt gave McNeese favorable field position at the Arkansas State 46 late in the game. A fourth-down pass fell incomplete, but an offside penalty against the Indians gave the Cowboys new hope. Johnnie Thibodeaux promptly tossed a 7-yard bullet to Nathaniel Allen for a touchdown. A two-point conversion attempt failed, leaving McNeese with a 20-19 edge.

Only 15 seconds remained when Flynn hurled a 39-yard pass to Jamie Klipsch up to the McNeese 38. Duren then connected on his dramatic 56-yard game-winner.

McNeese ended its season at 6-4-1 overall and 2-3 in the Southland.

Arkansas State won at Southwestern Louisiana 28-6 in a game that had been postponed earlier in the season because of a hurricane. USL concluded the season 2-9 overall and 0-5 in the Southland Conference. The win allowed the Indians to conclude the season 7-3 overall, including 3-2 in the Southland.

The Indians' 3-2 SLC mark was good enough for a third-place finish in the league. The week Arkansas State was defeating McNeese, Lamar blanked Texas-Arlington to finish 4-1 in the conference.

One play after Melancon fumbled at the UTA 1-yard line, Cardinal defensive tackle Garry Wright tackled Jensen, the Mavericks fullback, in the end zone for a safety and a 2-0 lead in the first quarter. Field goals by Robert Murphy in the second quarter and Leonard in the final quarter accounted for Lamar's other points.

UTA missed out on several scoring opportunities. A field goal attempt by Gary Briscoe in the third quarter was blocked by Samuel.

With less than two minutes remaining in the game a fourth-down pass from Morris was caught by Barnett but the Mavericks' split end was out of bounds when he made the grab.

At 8-2 overall, Lamar recorded its second-best season in the school's senior college history. Lamar went 8-0-2 in 1957.

UTA finished the season 1-4 in the Southland and 1-10 overall.

On the same day Arkansas State and USL were bringing their regular-season to a close, defending national champion Louisiana Tech was opening the Division II playoffs.

Roland Harper's 54-yard touchdown run on Louisiana Tech's first offensive play of the game gave the Bulldogs a quick 7-0 lead against Western Carolina. Little did the fans gathered for the opening round of the Division II playoffs in Ruston know that it would be the only touchdown Tech would score that day.

Cold weather, strong winds and a sloppy field were hardly conducive to a high-scoring affair. The conditions helped to contribute to seven lost fumbles and an interception by the Bulldogs. The Catamounts had equal trouble holding onto the football with three lost fumbles and five interceptions.

Louisiana Tech's normally prolific aerial attack didn't complete a pass until the second half. The first completed pass actually worked against the Bulldogs when Ryckman fumbled after the catch at the Tech 49. Several plays later, Herb Cole scored on a 3-yard run to tie the game.

The Bulldogs mounted a 69-yard drive in the fourth quarter for a possible tie-breaking score when Moody fumbled at the Western Carolina 3. A Catamount fumble a few plays later proved even more costly to Western Carolina.

Tech's Rod Bagley, named the game's "Outstanding Defensive Player," stripped the ball away from WCU runner Jeff Kirwin at the Catamounts' 9-yard line with 3:40 left in the game. Taking no chances, the Bulldogs ran the ball three straight times to set up a field goal attempt by Pope.

Pope, who had one kick partially blocked and missed from 42 yards out earlier in the game while facing a strong wind, now had the wind at his back for a 22-yard attempt.

This time, his kick was good. Then, in fitting fashion, Louisiana Tech freshman safety Donnie Perry intercepted his third pass of the game to preserve the 10-7 win and send the Bulldogs to the Pioneer Bowl for the second year in a row.

For the Louisiana Tech fans that made the journey to Wichita Falls, Texas, for the 1974 Pioneer Bowl, about the only thing on their minds that could keep the defending champion Bulldogs from advancing to another national championship game was a complete reversal of form. Unfortunately, for Tech partisans, that's exactly what they witnessed.

The Bulldogs became the victim of what they had perpetrated on most of 23-straight foes – jump out to an early lead and overwhelm the opposition. After a scoreless opening quarter, Central Michigan scored 14 points in a span of four minutes in the second quarter. The Chippewas eventually built a lead of 35-0 before Louisiana Tech scored two late touchdowns for a 35-14 loss that ended the Bulldogs' dream of a second-straight national title.

Dooming the Bulldogs' quest to repeat as national champions were six Tech interceptions – one shy of the NCAA College Division postseason single-game record.

After the scoreless first quarter, Central Michigan tailback Walt Hodges managed to gain control of a bad option pitch by quarterback Mike Franckowiak and rambled 55 yards down to the Louisiana Tech 2-yard line. Hodges scored from a yard out two plays later for a 7-0 CMU lead with 14:09 remaining in the second quarter.

On the ensuing drive, Central Michigan linebacker Bill Schmidt returned a Haynes interception 31 yards down to the Tech 14. A 13-yard completion by Franckowiak down to the 1-yard line set up a quarterback sneak for a touchdown to give the Chippewas a 14-0 lead.

A pair of short scoring runs by Dick Dunham and a 5-yard touchdown reception by Matt Means gave Central Michigan its 35-0 lead. Moody allowed Louisiana Tech to avoid a shut out by scoring the game's final two touchdowns. The first came on a short pass from Haynes, with the final score coming on a 1-yard run.

Louisiana Tech finished the season 11-1 and the Bulldogs' winning streak, the longest in the nation, came to an end at 23 games.

Despite losing to Central Michigan, Louisiana Tech was voted College Division National Champion by the United Press International wire service.

DIVISION I STATUS FOR SOUTHLAND

Louisiana Tech would find out rather quickly if it was a serious contender for a fifth-straight league title in the now-reclassified Division I Southland Conference. The Bulldogs opened the 1975 season with four SLC games. Those games preceded five non-league contests before closing the regular season against conference foe Arkansas State.

The Bulldogs got off to a slow start in the season opener, facing a 7-7 tie at halftime against McNeese State in Lake Charles. A 12-yard touchdown pass from Steve Haynes to Pat Tilley managed to give Louisiana Tech its halftime tie, but other than that, the Bulldogs struggled on offense. To demonstrate Tech's first-half woes, the Haynes-to-Tilley connection was set up on a 43-yard punt return by freshman George Pree.

Louisiana Tech then took advantage of Cowboy mistakes to build a 21-7 lead in the second half. A roughing-the-kicker penalty kept a Bulldogs drive alive at the Tech 46 early in the third quarter. That helped to set up a 3-yard touchdown run by Arry Moody and a 14-7 Louisiana Tech lead.

Another mistake by the Cowboys, this one on Terry Slack's interception of a Johnnie Thibodeaux pass, set up Tech at the McNeese 28. A 1-yard sneak by backup quarterback Randy Robertson gave the Bulldogs a 21-7 lead. McNeese countered with an 80-yard touchdown drive, culminated on an 8-yard run by Mike McArthur to make it 21-14 for the game's final score.

Playing in Lake Charles, it took Arkansas State only 20 seconds to set one of two Cowboy Stadium records. A 72-yard bomb from David Hines to Jimmy Wicks set the mark for longest pass play at the stadium and gave the Indians a 6-0 lead.

McNeese shrugged off the early score when Preston Lanier picked off a tipped Hines pass, giving the Cowboys the ball at the Arkansas State 13. Thibodeaux's sneak from a yard out and Conley Hathorn's conversion gave McNeese a 7-6 edge at the 2:08 mark of the first quarter.

The lead would not last long as Roy Painter's recovery of a fumbled punt by McArthur gave the Indians the ball at the McNeese 22 to set up a 16-yard Dennis Bolden run for a 12-7 Arkansas State lead at halftime.

Bolden, a third-team running back, added touchdown runs in each of the final two quarters to amass another Cowboy Stadium record – 259 yards rushing – in Arkansas State's 24-7 victory.

While McNeese fell to 0-2 both overall and in Southland, Arkansas State won its league opener to remain unbeaten at 3-0 overall.

Along with opening the season with four-consecutive conference games, another quirk in the schedule provided Louisiana Tech with an open date only one week into the season. Despite having played only one game, when Tech returned to action, it was for the Bulldogs' Homecoming against 1-1 Texas-Arlington.

The week off did wonders for Haynes. After he and the Louisiana Tech offense struggled in a season-opening win against McNeese, the quarterback bounced back with a record performance against the Mavericks.

Haynes connected on 12 of 13 passes for 302 yards and three touchdowns. His 92.3 completion percentage set a new school record. The junior signal caller's completion percentage topped the 9 of 10 performance set in 1969 by future NFL Hall of Fame quarterback Terry Bradshaw.

Haynes completed all six of his passes in the first quarter, including touchdown tosses of 4 yards to Moody and 33 yards to Tilley as the Bulldogs went on to build a 30-0 halftime lead. An 84-yard pass play to tight end Mike Barber in the third quarter accounted for Hayes' other touchdown pass. Tech led 37-0 before UTA came up with the game's last score to make the final 37-8.

Louisiana Tech made it three-for-three with a 24-10 road win over Lamar. The Cardinals entered their league opener 0-3. Lamar hung tough with Houston in its opening game of the season, eventually falling to the Cougars 20-3. Playing in the Houston Astrodome, the game marked the first time in history for the Cardinals to face a team from the Southwest Conference.

Extra time to prepare in the form of an open date did little to help the Cardinals against Louisiana Tech in Lamar's 24-10 home loss. It was the Bulldogs' defense that sparked the win, holding the Cardinals to 21 yards of total offense at halftime and 164 for the game. Nose guard Ron Bagley spearheaded the effort with 10 tackles as the Louisiana Tech defense recovered four fumbles and intercepted two passes.

The Bulldogs' offense took advantage of excellent field position provided by the defense's stellar effort to build a 17-3 halftime lead. Jerry Pope kicked a 19-yard field goal while Ricky Herren scored on a pair of short runs.

Arkansas State joined Louisiana Tech as the only unbeaten teams in the Southland Conference with the Indians' 39-17 home victory over Southwestern Louisiana. The Indians went into the game 4-0, following up their win over McNeese with a 29-10 non-conference triumph over Memphis State.

Southwestern Louisiana went into its conference opener 3-0. The Ragin' Cajuns started the season with a 22-17 victory over Long Beach State for USL's first season-opening win since 1971. USL defeated Southern Illinois and New Mexico State to set up a contest of unbeaten teams.

USL jumped out to a 17-6 lead at Arkansas State, but the winning ways for the Cajuns would not extend into Southland Conference play.

Down by 11 points at halftime, the Indians scored 18 points in the third quarter on their way to the victory

Jimmy Lisko's block of a Cajuns punt got the scoring started for Arkansas State in the second half. A 1-yard run by Hines pulled the Indians to within three points at 17-14.

Arkansas State, which rushed for 464 yards - 207 by Leroy Harris - took the lead for good at 21-17 on a 9-yard run by Hines. Bobby Watson added a 40-yard field goal to put the Indians on top 24-17 after three quarters.

Hines, who ran for 125 yards, added a third rushing touchdown in the fourth quarter and passed for a two-point conversion. Arkansas State rounded out the scoring on a 5-yard run by Larry Harkless.

USL built its 17-6 halftime edge on a 25-yard Rafael Septien field goal, a 2-yard run by Raymond Lation and a 42-yard interception return for a touchdown by Ed Davis.

Trying to bounce back from their first loss of the season would be a tough task for the Ragin' Cajuns, considering the opponent was a Louisiana Tech team that had never lost a Southland Conference game since entering the league in 1971.

The home-standing Bulldogs seemed well on their way to another victory, leading 17-0 going into the fourth quarter.

A determined Cajuns squad could not make up any ground on Tech in the third quarter. That was not unexpected since no conference opponent had ever scored on the Bulldogs in the third quarter.

So, it came down to the fourth quarter for the Cajuns. A 32-yard strike from Henry to David Oliver made the score 17-7. USL got the ball back moments later when a fumble by Robertson was recovered by Sidney Venerable at the Bulldogs' 34. Three plays later, Roy Henry connected with Walt Slattery on a 23-yard strike to pull USL to within three points with 7:53 remaining in the game.

The Bulldogs would strike back on a 15-yard touchdown toss from Robertson to Barber, the future Houston Oiler, to put the game out of reach with a 24-14 victory.

Louisiana Tech moved to 4-0, both overall and in the Southland and would not face another conference team until hosting Arkansas State in the regular-season finale. Still above .500 at 3-2, the Cajuns fell to 0-2 in conference play.

McNeese State went into its Southland Conference game at Texas-Arlington coming off its first victory of the season. After falling to Louisiana Tech and Arkansas State, the Cowboys lost 20-9 at Eastern Michigan before taking out their frustrations with a 33-3 road thumping of Marshall.

The Cowboys took better advantage of second-half special teams mistakes by both teams to win their second-straight game with a 28-24 victory over the Mavericks.

Trailing 14-6 early in the third quarter, it actually was the Mavericks who took advantage of the first special teams miscue. A bad center snap led to a 15-yard McNeese punt, giving UTA the ball at the Cowboys' 46. Texas-Arlington quarterback Doug Dobbins scored on an 11-yard run five plays later and a two-point conversion pass to Al Benson tied the game at 14-14.

It became the Cowboys' turn to take advantage of a special teams mistake after a fumbled punt by Gene Ayers was recovered by Carl White at the Texas-Arlington 7-yard line. McArthur scored on a 4-yard run three plays later for a 21-14 McNeese lead.

After a 36-yard Chris Walker field goal cut the UTA deficit to four points at 21-17, Walker was brought down at his own 34 while in punt formation because of a bad center snap. Bobby Wilson eventually scored on a 1-yard run for a 28-17 lead with 8:14 remaining in the game.

A flea-flicker reverse ended with Ronnie Barnett tossing 30 yards to Benson to make the score 28-24 with 4:01 left in the game.

The Mavericks got the ball back at their own 30 with 53 seconds left in the game. UTA reached the McNeese 36 before a desperation pass was intercepted by Ralph Phillips in the end zone as time expired, allowing the Cowboys to hold on for the four-point victory.

The result left both teams at 2-3 overall. McNeese moved to 1-2 in the Southland while Texas-Arlington dropped to 0-2 in conference play.

The only Southland game a week later was hardly a showcase for the league in a game featuring two winless teams but Southwestern Louisiana's home contest versus Lamar provided an interesting plot twist to the 1975 season. In order to avoid setting a new futility record for consecutive conference losses, the Cajuns would have to beat Lamar. Ironically, the winless Cardinals had originally set the mark with 12-straight losses. They would have liked nothing better than to stick No. 13 on the Cajuns.

Two field goals by Lamar's Jabo Leonard were countered by an 8-yard pass from Barry Pollard to Walt Slattery as the Cajuns took a 7-6 lead at halftime.

Lamar, winless through five games and 0-1 in Southland play, gained the lead in the fourth quarter on a 15-yard pass from Bobby Flores to Larry Spears.

Trailing 12-7, the Cajuns came up with two quick touchdowns to put the game away. The first score, a 6-yard run by quarterback Rick Young, put Southwestern Louisiana on top 14-12. Moments later, Bobby Johnson returned an interception 46 yards for a touchdown to give USL a 21-14 victory – the first Southland win for the Cajuns since 1972.

USL moved to 4-2 by ending a two-game skid and improved to 1-2 in conference action.

The Cardinals must have figured even the elements were against them as Lamar sought again to win its first game of the season the following week versus 2-0 Arkansas State when a strong rainstorm in Beaumont led to a combined six lost fumbles.

As luck would have it, the Cardinals only lost one fumble but the Indians were opportunistic on special teams. Following a scoreless first half, Lisko blocked a Lamar punt in the third quarter to set up 36-yard Watson field goal. Steve Stinnett blocked another Cardinal punt in the fourth quarter, giving Arkansas State the ball at the 1-yard line. Hines scored to give Arkansas State a 10-0 lead. The Indians' other score came on a 39-yard run by Bolden in the fourth quarter.

Lamar dropped to 0-3 in the SLC and 0-7 overall. Arkansas State remained unbeaten at 3-0 in the league and 7-0 overall.

Although things were not quite as bleak for Texas-Arlington as they were for Lamar, the Mavericks were still seeking their first Southland Conference win of the season when they visited Southwestern Louisiana.

The Cajuns built a halftime lead of 28-6 in front of a Cajun Field-record crowd of 25,280 before having to hold off a furious third-quarter rally in a 35-32 win over the Mavericks.

A 59-yard touchdown pass from Dobbins to Barnett, a 17-yard run by Elmo Simmons and an 11-yard run by Dobbins closed the Mavericks' deficit to only two points at 28-26.

Mike Northcutt made sure UTA would get no closer, galloping 80 yards following Dobbins' score to build the Cajuns' lead back up to 35-26 late in the third quarter. Northcutt finished with 129 yards rushing.

Dobbins and Barnett hooked up again in the fourth quarter on a 31-yard touchdown pass for the 35-32 final.

USL built its 28-6 halftime lead on two Septien field goals, two Roy Williams touchdown runs and a 1-yard pass from Henry to Doug Hundley. Henry's short touchdown toss came with only three seconds remaining before intermission.

The Cajuns improved to 5-3 overall and 2-2 in the SLC. Texas-Arlington dropped to 2-6 overall and 0-3 in conference action.

In another case of someone was bound to win, Lamar, at 0-8, played at Texas-Arlington. Along with being winless through eight games, the Cardinals also were 0-3 in Southland Conference play. The Mavericks also entered the game 0-3 in league play and 2-6 overall.

The Cardinals took an early 7-0 lead when Roy Hudson raced 48 yards for a touchdown after pulling the ball away from Barnett following a reception by the Maverick split end.

Lamar went on to lead 10-9 after one quarter before UTA pulled ahead on a 1-yard dive by Derrick Jensen in the middle of the second quarter before the Mavericks eventually pulled away.

Barnett made up for the earlier miscue with an 80-yard touchdown reception from Dobbins. Dobbins also tossed a 5-yard touchdown pass to Jimmy Bailey.

Lamar dropped to 0-4 in the Southland and 0-9 overall. Texas-Arlington improved to 1-3 in the league and 3-6 overall.

Texas-Arlington's chances of making it two-in-a-row didn't seem bright as the Mavericks' next opponent was an unbeaten Arkansas State team looking to move to 4-0 in the Southland Conference to force a showdown with Louisiana Tech.

The Indians took no chances, jumping out to a 34-0 halftime lead on their way to a 54-7 thrashing of the Mavericks. The early cushion helped ease the pain of Arkansas State coach Bill Davidson. Davidson had been in traction much of the week leading up to the game with a slipped disc. He was in the hospital from Wednesday of game week until early on game day.

A fumble and a pair of blocked punts helped to give the Indians a 20-0 lead by the first play of the second quarter. Doyle Cross' recovery of a Dobbins fumble led to a 2-yard run by Bolden and a 7-0 Arkansas State lead. Sylvester Loving's block of a Chris Walker punt was recovered by Ron Meeks, who scooted 39 yards for a touchdown and a 14-0 lead for the Indians. Forced to punt from its own end zone, a UTA punt was blocked by Lisko. Lisko recovered at the Mavs' 3-yard line, setting up Hines' touchdown run one play later on the initial play of the second quarter and the rout was on.

Playing in Ruston, Arkansas State faced a Louisiana Tech team that also was 4-0 in Southland action but hadn't played a conference game in six weeks. After Tech's 24-14 win over Southwestern Louisiana, the Bulldogs played five-consecutive non-league opponents.

Louisiana Tech defeated Northwestern State 41-14 before being beaten at home by Southern Mississippi 24-14. The Bulldogs rallied from a 10-0 deficit to lead 14-10 before USM took control. The loss ended a 24-game regular-season winning streak for Louisiana Tech that stretched back to the 1973 season. It also was the Bulldogs' first home loss in 18 games. The last time Tech lost at home was to Southern Mississippi in 1971.

The Bulldogs bounced back from the Southern Miss loss with wins over Southeastern Louisiana, Northeast Louisiana and Tennessee-Chattanooga to run their record to 8-1 going into the Arkansas State game.

Early mistakes put the Bulldogs in a quick hole. Louisiana Tech fumbled the ball away on the first offense play of the game and although the Indians didn't score, an early tone was set. After a 25-yard Watson field goal later in the first quarter, a fumble on the ensuing kickoff eventually led to a 1-yard touchdown run by Bolden and a 9-0 Arkansas State lead. The Indians made it 16-0 at halftime on a 5-yard run by Harris late in the second quarter.

Arkansas State made it 23-0 four minutes into the second half on an 11-yard option keeper by Hines. The touchdown marked the first score ever by a Bulldogs league foe in the third quarter since Louisiana Tech joined the SLC in 1971.

The running game played a major role in the contest. The Indians shredded the Tech defense for 376 yards. Arkansas State's defense, meanwhile, held the Bulldogs to minus-7 rushing.

Robertson entered the game in place of Haynes and tossed for 240 yards in the second half in a case of too little, too late for Tech. He led the Bulldogs to two late touchdowns. The first came on a pass tipped by Moody, the intended receiver, into the hands of Barber. The final touchdown came on a 64-yard bomb to Tilley with 3:52 left in the game as Arkansas State ended the Bulldogs' reign with a 30-13 victory.

It was a particularly sweet triumph for the Indians. Arkansas State had dominated the Southland from 1968 through 1970 before Louisiana Tech's 28-27 win over the Indians in 1971 served as a changing of the guard. Now, the Indians were back atop the SLC.

The 30-13 loss ended 8-2 Louisiana Tech's four-year reign as Southland Conference champions. It also was the Bulldogs' first-ever league loss after 23-straight conference triumphs.

Arkansas State finished the season 11-0 and with the nation's longest winning streak at 14 games. Alas, in their first year as a Division I program, there would be no postseason game for the Indians. Although there had been talk of a potential Tangerine Bowl bid, Arkansas State received no bowl invitation. Instead, the Indians had to take solace in again being atop the Southland Conference.

The Arkansas State-Louisiana Tech clash was the showcase of the Southland but there was still a bit of unfinished business in the conference.

On the same day of the Arkansas State-Louisiana Tech battle, McNeese faced Southwestern Louisiana.

The Cowboys spotted USL two touchdowns in the first quarter before rallying for 20 points in the second quarter on their way to a 33-21 victory over the Cajuns.

Southwestern Louisiana ended its season 6-5 overall, including 2-3 in Southland play. McNeese improved to 6-4 overall and 2-2 in conference play with one game remaining in the 1975 season at home against Lamar.

After opening the season by losing its first nine games, Lamar defeated Southern Illinois 30-10 entering the McNeese State contest.

Like the USL game, the Cowboys had to rally from an early deficit on their way to a 20-10 victory. McArthur and Joe Crawford each topped 100 yards rushing and Thibodeaux became McNeese's all-time leader in career pass completions in the Cowboys' 20-10 Southland Conference win to conclude the 1975 season.

Crawford ran for 120 yards in place of an injured Wilson, while McArthur added 117 yards on the ground. Meanwhile, Thibodeaux completed only three passes but that was exactly what he needed to set the new mark. Thibodeaux's 207 completions topped the previous record set by Greg Davis.

McNeese won seven of its final eight games to finish the season at 7-4 overall and 3-2 in the Southland Conference. Lamar ended the season 1-10, its worst record since a 0-10 finish in 1968.

THE INDEPENDENCE BOWL
AND THE SLC

There was no postseason berth for Arkansas State in 1975 despite the Indians' undefeated season and the nation's longest winning streak but that would not happen again to the Southland Conference champion in 1976.

In 1975, the Shreveport-Bossier City Sports Foundation came up with the idea of starting a postseason bowl game. After receiving approval from the National Collegiate Athletic Association, the inaugural game would be played in 1976 with the winner of the Southland Conference receiving an automatic bid to the game against an at-large opponent. With the first game taking place in 1976 – the year of America's bicentennial – in an area with a strong military presence, the game was dubbed the "Independence Bowl."

The quest for a spot in the first-ever Independence Bowl began with a contest between Louisiana Tech and McNeese State to open Southland Conference play in 1976. Each team entered the encounter with a game on its belt. McNeese opened the season with a 38-0 blanking of Southern Illinois while Louisiana Tech was coming off 41-28 loss to Ball State and looking to avoid an 0-2 start for the first time since 1966.

John Henry White broke loose for 62 yards down to the McNeese 20 on the opening play from scrimmage. Five plays later, Arry Moody scored from a yard out for a 7-0 Bulldogs lead less than three minutes into the contest.

Tech's 7-0 lead would hold up until the third quarter. Bobby Wilson capped a 78-yard McNeese drive with a 6-yard touchdown run but Conley Hathorn missed the conversion, allowing Louisiana Tech to maintain the lead.

That changed on the Cowboys' next possession. Jimmy Morvant, who replaced Terry McFarland at quarterback after the starter was injured on an 18-yard run earlier in the drive, scored on a 4-yard run. A two-point conversion attempt failed, leaving McNeese with a 12-7 lead.

Doug Fruge returned an errant Steven Haynes pass to the Louisiana Tech 24 two plays into the Bulldogs' next possession. Hathorn's 31-yard field goal extended the Cowboys' lead to eight points at 15-7 with 29 seconds remaining in the third quarter.

A 71-yard bomb from Randy Robertson to Larry McCartney advanced Tech to the McNeese 18 early in the fourth quarter. Moody scored on a 3-yard run to tie the game. Robertson hit Moody with a two-point conversion but McCartney was penalized for offensive interference, erasing the score and leaving the Bulldogs with a 15-13 deficit.

Louisiana Tech got the ball back at its own 46 with 1:42 left in the game. A 26-yard pass from Robertson to Rod Foppe put the Bulldogs in field-goal range. Tech ran two plays to get the ball in position for Jerry Pope. Pope, who hit a 42-yard field goal with six seconds left in the game to beat McNeese 10-7 in 1973, was wide left from 37 yards away, enabling the Cowboys to hold on for the two-point triumph.

Tech's game the following week had a double purpose for the Bulldogs. A win at Arkansas State would avoid Louisiana Tech's worst start in 11 years. Also, a victory would be payback for the Indians' win the previous year that ended the Bulldogs' four-year reign atop the SLC.

Defending Southland champion Arkansas State, meanwhile, was struggling entering its conference opener. After opening the season with a 31-13 victory over Northeast Louisiana to stretch the nation's longest winning streak to 15 games, the Indians lost to San Diego State and Indiana State.

Looking like the Bulldogs of previous years, Louisiana Tech scored 21 first-quarter points on its way to a 27-13 triumph. A 67-yard halfback pass for a touchdown from Moody to McCartney kick-started the Bulldogs' offense less than two minutes into the game. A 10-yard touchdown reception by Foppe and a 1-yard run by White gave Tech it's three-touchdown edge after one quarter of play. A Pope field goal less than three minutes into the second quarter gave Louisiana Tech a 24-0 halftime lead.

Arkansas State's only scores came on a pair of 1-yard touchdown runs by sophomore quarterback Bucky Lane but the loss gave the Indians their worst start since 1959.

Louisiana Tech's game the following week was at a Southwest Louisiana team that had been off to a 2-0 start with wins over Fresno State and Cincinnati. During an open week prior to the Tech game, however, the Southland ruled Southwestern Louisiana had used an ineligible player in the first two games and the Cajuns had to forfeit the two wins. In addition, USL would be ineligible for the conference championship or a postseason bowl bid.

Perhaps showing their disappointment, the Cajuns, who were playing their third-straight game at home, fell behind Louisiana Tech by 16 points at halftime.

Robertson tossed a pair of touchdown passes in the opening quarter; the first was 31 yards to Rod Foppe and the second 33 yards to Billy Ryckman, the future Atlanta Falcons receiver. Rafael Septien kicked a 25-yard field goal to make it 14-3 after the first quarter.

Playing before a Southland Conference-record crowd of 26,640, USL put itself back in the game on a 12-yard touchdown pass from Roy Henry to Walt Slattery to trail 14-10. The Bulldogs, however, countered with a 5-yard scoring run by Moody and another Robertson-Ryckman hookup as Tech built a 26-10 halftime lead.

The Cajuns marched 80 yards with the opening kickoff of the second half to inch a bit closer. A pass interference call against the Bulldogs placed the ball at the Tech 1-yard line. Raymond Lation's touchdown made the score 26-17.

USL moved to within two points at 26-24 on a 9-yard screen pass to Emanuel Guidry with 6:42 remaining in the game.

A Ron Irving interception gave the ball back to the Cajuns at their own 18 late in the game. Henry's 37-yard toss to Ulysses Abadie was the big gainer in the drive. A 9-yard run by Ray Williams advanced the ball to the 3. Three plays later, Guidry scored from a yard out with 1:22 left in the game.

Although the Cajuns had not been beaten on the field of play, the victory over Louisiana Tech was officially Southwestern Louisiana's first win of the season and gave USL a 1-2 overall record. Tech fell to 0-2 in Southland Conference play and 1-3-1 overall.

A week later, the Bulldogs could have only hoped for a game that went down to the closing minutes. Unable to stop Texas-Arlington's wishbone offense, the Tech defense saw the Mavericks score on seven of their first nine possessions in taking a whopping 56-35 win in Arlington, Texas.

Leading the way for the Mavericks was fullback Derrick Jensen, who rushed for two touchdowns and 152 of the 485 yards UTA amassed on the ground. The Mavericks' ground dominance completely overshadowed four touchdown passes by Haynes.

The 56 points scored by Texas-Arlington was the most surrendered by a Tech defense since a 58-7 loss to Southern Mississippi in 1967.

Along with winning its Southland Conference opener, UT-Arlington improved to 3-3 overall to overcome a 1-3 start.

On the same day Louisiana Tech was dropping to an uncharacteristic 1-3, Bob Frederick was making his Southland Conference debut as Lamar's head coach in the Cardinals' home game against Southwestern Louisiana. Following Lamar's 1-10 season in 1975, veteran coach Vernon Glass was replaced by Frederick, an assistant on the Cardinal coaching staff.

Lamar went into the game 2-2 on the year, including a 17-6 season-opening victory over Northwestern State that gave Frederick his first win as Cardinals coach.

Lamar battled toe-to-toe against USL until a pair of turnovers early in the second half allowed the Ragin' Cajuns to pull away.

An Ed Perkins interception early in the third quarter eventually led to an 11-yard touchdown run by Southwestern Louisiana's Allen Strambler. Moments later, Barry Johnson picked off an errant Bobby Flores throw to set up a 20-yard touchdown pass from Roy Henry to Roy Oliver. Henry and Oliver later hooked up on a 5-yard touchdown pass and Lation scored on a pair of 1-yard runs for the Cajuns in USL's 34-9 victory.

The only touchdown for Lamar was an 18-yard run by James Rollins in the first half.

Lamar fell to 2-3 overall in dropping its Southland opener. USL picked up its second conference win.

Texas-Arlington and McNeese State each put their 1-0 Southland Conference records on the line when the teams met the following week in Lake Charles. While the Mavericks were fresh off a league win over Louisiana Tech, McNeese won three non-conference games to run its record to 5-0 heading into the game with UTA.

McNeese State's unbeaten record was in jeopardy in the third quarter against Texas-Arlington. After leading 3-0 at halftime on a Hathorn field goal, McNeese surrendered the lead on a 1-yard run by Jensen early in the third quarter to trail 6-3.

With 45 seconds remaining in the third quarter, Mike McArthur broke loose on a 35-yard gallop to put McNeese on top 10-6.

The lead would not last long. UTA responded with a 35-yard touchdown run of its own by quarterback Doug Dobbins to give the Mavericks a 13-10 lead early in the fourth quarter. Jensen, the Southland's leading rusher, broke off a 53-yard run to set up a Dobbins 11-yard run to extend the Texas-Arlington lead to 20-10. Jensen finished the game with 192 yards on the ground.

There would be no Cowboys rally this time as UTA added a 7-yard run by Ricky Kelly with 24 seconds left in the game to give the Mavericks a 27-10 victory.

The loss snapped a nine-game winning streak stretching over two seasons for the Cowboys, which tied for fourth-longest in the nation. McNeese evened its Southland mark at 1-1 in falling to 5-1 overall. UTA moved to 2-0 in the conference and 4-3 overall.

Although it was only midseason, Louisiana Tech closed out the conference portion of its schedule with a 37-7 home win over Lamar. Haynes threw a pair of touchdown passes to Foppe and another to Ryckman as Tech scored 23 points in the opening half. Moody paced the ground attack with 114 yards.

Lamar's only score came in the fourth quarter on a 2-yard run by Kevin Bell.

The win allowed Louisiana Tech to move to 2-4 overall. The 2-3 league record represented the first time in the Bulldogs' tenure in the SLC that they finished with a losing record in conference play. A third-consecutive loss dropped Lamar to 2-4 overall and 0-2 in the Southland.

Seeking to bounce back from its loss to Texas-Arlington, McNeese State found itself trailing again in the second half a week later at Arkansas State.

Down 21-10, McNeese took advantage of a pair of Indians fumbles to take the lead. Mitch Tyson's recovery of an Arkansas State fumble at the Indians' 36 in the third quarter set up a 28-yard touchdown pass from Morvant to Richard Ellender to make the score 21-16.

A mishandled center snap by Joe Slayton on a punt attempt in the fourth quarter gave the ball to McNeese at the Arkansas State 10-yard line. Morvant scored on a 1-yard run before hitting tight end Alan Heisser with a two-point conversion pass to give the Cowboys a 24-21 triumph.

Playing on a wet field from an all-day rain and with a swirling wind, Arkansas State built its 21-10 lead early in the second quarter. A 55-yard reception by fullback Leroy Harris down to the McNeese 5-yard line set up a 4-yard touchdown toss from Lane to Orna Middlebrook for a 6-0 Indians lead. After a touchdown put the Cowboys on top 7-6, Harris broke loose on a school-record 85-yard touchdown run.

Harris, who rushed for 130 yards on eight attempts, carried the load on Arkansas State's final scoring drive early in the second quarter. He wasn't in the game by the end of the possession, however, as he suffered a hip pointer injury during the drive and did not return. Already without Dennis Bolden, the Southland's leading rusher who suffered a thigh bruise a week earlier against Southern Illinois, the Indians turned to tailback Tommy Foulks. Foulks capped the drive from 4 yards out for Arkansas State's 21-10 advantage.

McNeese improved to 2-1 in the Southland and 6-1 overall. Arkansas State dropped to 0-2 in the SLC and 3-5 overall.

Southwestern Louisiana may not have been eligible for a spot in the inaugural Independence Bowl because of the ruling by the Southland Conference but the Ragin' Cajuns sure seemed like they wanted to prove they were the best team in the league going into their game at Texas-Arlington, the only other 2-0 team in the SLC.

USL trailed 10-7 at halftime and seemed poised to add more points early in the second half. That changed when a Southwestern Louisiana field-goal attempt was blocked and UTA's Bill Bradshaw raced 86 yards for a touchdown. Instead of a possible 10-10 tie, the Ragin' Cajuns now trailed 17-7.

The Cajuns marched once again, this time scoring on a 1-yard pass from Henry to Oliver to narrow the gap to 17-14. The Mavericks showed they weren't about to wilt as Elmo Simmons returned the ensuing kick 95 yards for a touchdown to put UTA back on top by 10 points.

Two quick scores turned the tide for the Cajuns. Only 11 seconds after Williams scored on a 45-yard run, Irving stole a mid-air Wishbone option pitch and scooted 20 yards for a touchdown and a 28-24 USL lead with 10:59 left in the game. Septien, a future NFL kicker who played mostly with the Dallas Cowboys, added a 36-yard field goal with slightly more than two minutes remaining in the 31-24 triumph.

The win moved USL to 5-2 overall and 3-0 in the Southland. Texas-Arlington fell to 4-4 after dropping its first conference game of the season.

While Texas-Arlington and USL battled to become the only 3-0 team in the Southland, Arkansas State and Lamar squared off to avoid being the only 0-3 team in the league.

A Cardinals' fumble in the first quarter set up a 2-yard touchdown run by Harris and served as an omen for Lamar in a 31-0 loss. The Indians fullback, who would go on to rush for 157 yards, added two additional short touchdown runs in the rout of Lamar. Arkansas State's other scores came on a Bobby Watson field goal in the second quarter and a 5-yard touchdown by backup quarterback Gene Bradley in the fourth quarter.

Lamar remained winless in the Southland at 0-3 while falling to 2-6 overall. Arkansas State improved to 1-2 in the SLC and 4-5 overall.

For the sixth game in a row, Southwestern Louisiana fell behind an opponent early but managed to trail by a few points going into the second half. This time, it was Arkansas State that grabbed an early lead before a Cajun Field crowd of 30,176.

USL spotted the Indians a 14-10 halftime lead. The Cajuns actually struck first on a 53-yard Septien field goal in the first quarter. Arkansas State went on top 7-3 later in the first quarter on a 1-yard run by Layne. The Indians extended their lead to 14-3 in the second quarter on a 1-yard run by Harris.

The Cajuns managed to trail by only four points at halftime when Henry hit Slattery with a 10-yard scoring toss on fourth-and-10 with 10 seconds remaining before the break. The touchdown was set up by Frank Bartley's recovery of an Indians fumble at the Arkansas State 37.

Like most of the season, the second half belonged to the Cajuns. The USL defense blanked the Indians over the final two quarters while the offense went on to score three times in the final 30 minutes.

As in previous games, special teams contributed mightily to the Cajuns' comeback. Early in the second half, Brady Muth blocked an Indians punt, with Bartley recovering at the Arkansas State 21. Three plays later, Henry connected with Slattery on an 8-yard touchdown strike to put USL on top 17-14 at the 10:58 mark of the third quarter.

Septien added a 52-yard field goal later in the third quarter and a 23 yarder in the fourth to give USL a 23-14 victory.

Another rally allowed the Cajuns to improve to 4-0 in the Southland and 8-2 overall. Arkansas State fell to 1-3 in the conference and 4-6 overall.

With Southwestern Louisiana ineligible for a berth in the Independence Bowl, McNeese State and Texas-Arlington, both 2-1, each had a chance to take a step up in the Southland race. The Cowboys seemingly had the easier task, playing at a 2-7 Lamar team that was 0-3 in the SLC and the owner of a six-game losing streak. UT-Arlington hosted an Arkansas State team that was playing its season finale sporting a 1-3 Southland mark and 4-6 overall.

Playing its final road game of the regular season on a cold, rainy day, the McNeese State defense held Lamar to a school-record low of 29 yards total offense as the Cowboys handed coach Jack Doland win No. 50.

The Cowboys led only 6-0 at halftime on Hathorn field goals of 26 and 47 yards. The two field goals gave Hathorn 11 on the season, a new single-season McNeese record.

McNeese added a 6-yard run by Wilson and a 40-yard punt return by Ellender to give the Cowboys a 21-0 lead after three quarters. Gerald Polaski scored the final points of the game on a 9-yard run in the fourth quarter for a 27-0 victory for McNeese that improved the Cowboys to 8-2 on the season.

Needing a win to keep pace with the Cowboys, Texas-Arlington broke a scoreless tie against Arkansas State in the second quarter in a game that featured several inches of wet snow on the field.

Field conditions played a role in the first score when Slayton, the Indians punter, dropped a snap from center at his own 44-yard line. That set up a 1-yard touchdown run by Jensen to give UTA a 7-0 lead less than three minutes into the second quarter. Jensen, the Southland Conference's leading rusher, finished with 139 yards on the ground.

John Lorick's interception of a Dobbs pass stopped a UTA drive at the Arkansas State 27 and led to the game-tying score on a 3-yard run by Harris with 2:39 remaining in the second quarter to send the teams to the locker room in a 7-7 deadlock.

Harris, who rushed for 196 yards, put the Indians on top 14-7 on an 80-yard jaunt in the third quarter.

Kelly capped a 45-yard drive early in the fourth quarter on a 3-yard run. Chris Walker missed the extra point, leaving the Mavericks down by a point at 14-13.

The Mavs drove in the closing moments before the drive stalled at the Arkansas State 31. Walker was sent in to try a game-winning kick from 49 yards out in unfavorable conditions. His attempt was partially blocked with five seconds left in the game, handing the Mavericks a heart-wrenching one-point defeat.

For Texas-Arlington to have any chance at a potential Southland Conference co-championship, the Mavericks had to win over Lamar on the same day they needed USL to defeat McNeese State.

Dobbins did his part for the Mavericks, accounting for three touchdowns in Texas-Arlington's 34-14 win at Lamar. Dobbins rushed for a pair of scores and tossed a touchdown pass as Texas-Arlington scored 20 fourth-quarter points on its way to the triumph.

The win allowed UTA to finish 3-2 in the Southland and 5-6 overall. Lamar concluded the 1976 season 0-5 in the SLC and 2-9 overall.

USL's Ragin' Cajuns were more than happy to try and help out the Mavericks. Southwestern Louisiana went into the McNeese State game coming off a 7-3 non-conference loss to Northwestern State. It was the first loss of the season on the field for USL. The Cajuns were forced to forfeit their first two wins of the season because of the use of an ineligible player. Officially, that made USL's record 6-3. More significantly, the Ragin' Cajuns were 4-0 in the Southland and a win over the Cowboys would allow USL to finish alone atop the conference, although the Cajuns were ineligible for postseason play.

The Ragin' Cajuns were playing the role of spoilers, leading 19-7 in the fourth quarter. USL built its lead on a 1-yard run by Lation in the first quarter, a 70-yard pass from Henry to Oliver in the second quarter and a 41-yard toss from Henry to Oliver in the fourth quarter. The only points McNeese was able to produce came on a 1-yard run by Wilson in the second quarter that made the score 12-7 at halftime.

Wilson's second 1-yard touchdown run capped a 69-yard drive with 7:50 left in the game. Hathorn's conversion attempt was blocked as the Cowboys trailed 19-13.

The McNeese defense held on Southwestern Louisiana's ensuing possession, getting the ball back to the Cowboys' offense at midfield. A pass interference call against the Cajuns moved the ball to the USL 31. Feeding the ball to Wilson and McArthur, McNeese eventually faced fourth down from the 1-yard line. Morvant scored on an option play to tie the game. Hathorn booted the extra point for a 20-19 Cowboys win for a 4-1 conference mark, 9-2 record overall and a berth in the Independence Bowl.

Southwestern Louisiana went on to defeat Northeast Louisiana 7-5 in non-conference action a week later to finish 7-4.

The Cowboys went into the first-ever Independence Bowl against Tulsa, played on Dec. 13, 1976, a Monday night, at a distinct disadvantage.

"During that time, fifth-year seniors were not allowed to play in bowl games," explained Tommy Tate, a sophomore defensive back on the 1976 McNeese squad. "We only had one senior who was eligible for the bowl game so they kind of made fun of us and kind of called us a jayvee team. We were up against a really good Tulsa team and the odds against us were pretty dim."

Compounding matters was the loss of Morvant, the team's starting quarterback, with an injury on the Cowboys' opening possession.

Tulsa drove to the McNeese 27 on the Hurricane's first possession of the game but came away with no points when kicker Steve Cox missed the first of three field goals in the contest.

The Hurricane forced the Cowboys to punt on its next possession. Tulsa moved 65 yards, mostly on passes by quarterback Ron Hickerson. From the 7-yard line, Tom Bailey got the call on three-straight runs. His final carry from a yard out gave the Hurricane a 7-0 lead at the 4:56 mark of the first quarter.

Jan Peebles, making his debut as the McNeese kicker, hit a 42-yard field goal late in the first quarter to make the score 7-3. He added a 34-yard kick with 30 seconds remaining in the second quarter and the Cowboys trailed 7-6 at halftime.

Peebles' second field goal was set up on Bob Howell's recovery of a Hickerson fumble at the Tulsa 33.

McNeese drove to the Tulsa 4-yard line early in the second half. Three-straight offside penalties on the Hurricane moved the ball inside the 1-yard line. Tulsa's defense held for two plays before McArthur finally scored on a pitch to his left. Rolling out on an attempted two-point conversion, McFarland tucked the ball away and scored to give the Cowboys a 14-7 lead.

Later in the third quarter the Cowboys were looking to pad their lead with a 41-yard field goal attempt by Peebles. His kick was blocked by Anthony Field and Tulsa's Mel McCowen scooped up the loose ball and raced 66 yards for a touchdown. The extra point by Cox was blocked by David Adams, allowing McNeese to maintain a one-point edge at 14-13.

Cox, who missed a 34-yard field goal with nine seconds left in the first half that would have given Tulsa a 9-7 halftime lead, was given another chance. This time, he connected from 38 yards away with 4:22 left in the game to put the Hurricane on top 16-14.

The Tulsa kicker missed a 42-yard field goal with two minutes remaining that could have extended the Hurricane's lead.

Given one last chance, a 28-yard halfback pass from McArthur to Heisser got the Cowboys moving. Tulsa picked off a McFarland pass but a holding penalty against the Hurricane allowed McNeese to retain possession.

Oliver Hadnot, playing in place of the ineligible Wilson, picked up 9 yards. Hadnot got the ball again, this time bursting 25 yards for a touchdown with 37 seconds left in the game to give McNeese State a 20-16 bowl victory and a 10-2 season.

"We were just trying to make a first down and he broke it for a touchdown," said Ernie Duplechin, an assistant coach on the 1976 McNeese squad.

"We competed so hard and the coaches did such a good job. It was a great win for McNeese State and a big point in McNeese history to win the inaugural Independence Bowl against a really good Tulsa football team," said Tate.

Impressive home wins of 48-21 over Tulsa and 34-13 over Fresno State had Southwestern Louisiana off to a 2-0 start in 1977 as the Ragin' Cajuns hit the road for the first time in the season to open Southland Conference play at Lamar. The Cardinals went into their SLC opener feeling good about themselves, opening the year with a 21-7 win over Northeast Louisiana to snap an eight-game losing streak.

After the two home wins, the Cajuns found themselves in a struggle in their first road test of the season.

The Cajuns took advantage of a pair of Cardinal turnovers to take a 10-0 halftime lead. A Lamar fumble at the Cardinals' 20 set up a 23-yard John Roveto field goal in the first quarter. Mike Pentecost's interception return to the Lamar 15 led to a 6-yard touchdown pass from Roy Henry to Nat Durant.

After failing to move the ball with J.S. Johnson at quarterback, the Cardinals switched to Bruce Turner in the second half. Lamar turned the tables on USL in the fourth quarter, turning a Cajuns miscue into a touchdown. A blocked punt in USL territory set up a 28-yard run by Weldon Cartwright for the Cardinals' only score in USL's 10-7 victory.

Southwestern Louisiana had an early opportunity to jump out to the lead in the SLC with the Cajuns again playing a league game the following week against visiting Texas-Arlington that was 1-1 on the new season.

Something about playing Texas-Arlington always seemed to bring out the best in USL's Ron Irving. A year earlier in the matchup between the two teams at UTA, the Cajuns defensive back stole an option pitch and raced for a touchdown in Southwestern Louisiana's 31-24 triumph.

Irving was in similar form this time around. After USL took a 23-20 lead on a 39-yard Roveto field goal in the fourth quarter, the Mavericks marched down to the Cajuns' 3-yard line. On first-and-goal, halfback Kent Sharp fumbled in midair. Irving came up with the loose ball and scampered 95 yards to put the game out of reach in a 30-20 Cajuns victory.

UTA built a 20-10 halftime lead on a 5-yard run by Sharp, a 14-yard pass from Roy DeWalt to Jerry Woodard and two Tom Skoruppa field goals.

Southwestern Louisiana was able to rally back thanks to a Cajuns defense that shut out the Mavericks in the second half. A Derrick Jensen fumble set up a 39-yard Roveto field goal to make the score 20-10 to begin the USL comeback. The Cajuns got the ball back after forcing a three-and-out and tied the game on a 15-yard pass from Henry to Dennis Reidmiller. Roveto's go-ahead field goal came with 13:30 remaining in the game.

Louisiana Tech went into its Southland Conference opener at McNeese State 1-0-1 and looking to prove 1976's sub-.500 SLC record was an aberration and not a trend. McNeese, the defending Southland Conference champions, went into its league opener 2-1.

Cowboy linebacker Billy Joe Davenport intercepted a Keith Thibodeaux pass on Tech's second possession of the game, giving McNeese the ball at the Bulldogs' 49-yard line. On third down from the 14, Preston Lanier broke loose for a touchdown to give the Cowboys a 7-0 lead at the 7:49 mark of the first quarter. Larry Anderson tied the game 7-7 when he returned a punt 73 yards for a touchdown moments later - his third return for a touchdown on the season – to tie the game.

Each team missed scoring opportunities later in the first half. Jan Peebles missed a 36-yard field goal and a blocked punt by Louisiana Tech was nullified by off-setting penalties. A 41-yard pass from Thibodeaux to Rob Foppe allowed the Bulldogs to reach the 2-yard line before losing the ball on a fumble.

A 57-yard bomb from Thibodeaux to Foppe set up a 37-yard touchdown strike by the duo in the third quarter to give Louisiana Tech a 14-7 lead.

McNeese threatened twice later in the fourth quarter. The Cowboys had first-and-goal at the 8-yard line following a Tommy Murphy interception but came away empty after a 2-yard loss by Lanier and three incomplete passes. The Cowboys reached the Louisiana Tech 33 in the closing seconds but a pair of sacks, two of nine recorded by the Bulldogs in the game, allowed Tech to gain possession and run out the clock.

Louisiana Tech's game the following week at home was against a Southwestern Louisiana team coming off a loss but could still claim to be unbeaten in the continental United States. USL, 2-0 in the Southland Conference, went into its game with the Bulldogs coming off a 20-6 loss at Hawaii.

Back on the mainland, the Ragin' Cajuns traded scores throughout the game with the Bulldogs.

A 14-14 tie at halftime stood up until the fourth quarter. USL took a 21-14 lead with 12:31 left in the game as the Cajuns took advantage of one of six Bulldogs turnovers. Keith Walker's recovery of a fumble, one of four in the game for Louisiana Tech, set up USL at the Tech 28. Five plays later, Henry's 17-yard strike to Calvin James put the Cajuns on top by seven points.

From the Tech 35, Thibodeaux threw the ball in the direction of George Pree. The ball was a bit underthrown, with USL coming up for an interception bid. The ball went through the defensive back's hands. Pree caught the ball at about the USL 35 and scampered the remaining yards for a 21-21 tie with 7:42 left in the game.

An interception by Anderson of a Henry pass with 26 seconds left in the game gave the ball to the Bulldogs at the USL 37. Tech missed out on a chance to win the game when Keith Swilley missed a field goal attempt, resulting in a tie.

The Cajuns, who committed five turnovers, including four interceptions, got all of their points on three Henry-to-James touchdown passes. The duo connected twice in the first half for scores of 19 and 4 yards. Tech's two first-half touchdowns came on a 1-yard sneak by Thibodeaux and a 5-yard run by Ricky Herren.

USL moved to 2-0-1 in the Southland and 4-1-1 as a result of the tie. Louisiana Tech's mark became 2-0-2 with its second tie of the season, 1-0-1 in conference play.

As Louisiana Tech and USL were settling for a tie, McNeese State was looking to bounce back from its loss to the Bulldogs at a Texas-Arlington team that also was 0-1 in Southland play.

Points continued to be hard to come by for McNeese State in the Cowboys' 24-7 loss to Texas-Arlington. The game was the third straight in which McNeese could muster no more than a single touchdown.

The Cowboys gained the early lead when Davenport's recovery of a Jensen fumble gave McNeese the ball at the UTA 25. Oliver Hadnot scored three plays later on a 3-yard run for a 7-0 lead at the 7:12 mark of the first quarter.

Texas-Arlington inched to 7-3 after one quarter on a 19-yard Skoruppa field goal. The Mavericks pulled ahead 10-7 on a 3-yard DeWalt run midway in the second quarter on a drive set up on Dwight Carey's recovery of a Russ Jackson fumble. Mike Guadagnolo's 42-yard punt return led to a 9-yard DeWalt run less than five minutes later to give the Mavs a 17-7 halftime lead.

The only other points of the game came early in the third quarter on an 11-yard run by James Bailey.

Arkansas State was the final team to make its 1977 Southland Conference debut when the Indians played at Lamar. Arkansas State went into the game 3-1 on the season. Lamar went into the contest 1-3 on the year and on a three-game losing streak following a season-opening win over Northeast Louisiana.

The Indians grabbed an early lead on their way to a 10-6 victory. A Lamar fumble midway in the first quarter set up a touchdown pass from Kennon Taylor to tight end Danny Garrison. A Doug Dobbs field goal in the second quarter gave the Indians a 10-0 advantage at halftime.

Lamar's only score came in the third quarter on a 1-yard run by Turner on a drive that was set up by an Indians fumble at the Arkansas State 33.

Arkansas State didn't have to wait long to take on its second Southland opponent, hosting a Louisiana Tech team looking to match Southwestern Louisiana's 2-0-1 conference start with a win over the Indians.

The Indians were unable to stop Louisiana Tech running back John Henry White, who rushed for 223 yards in the Bulldogs' 20-7 victory. White made his presence felt early in the game, racing 65 yards down to the 1-yard line two plays into the game to set up Herren's touchdown run to give Tech an early 7-0 lead.

Louisiana Tech added a pair of Swilley field goals to give the Bulldogs a 13-0 halftime lead. Swilley's first field goal from 30 yards out was his first successful kick in nine tries.

Missed field goals hurt Arkansas State. Dobbs, the Indians' usual kicker, suffered a foot injury in the week leading up to the game and missed the Louisiana Tech contest. Bobby Watson, kicking in place of Dobbs, missed two field goals. The kicks came as part of six penetrations inside the Tech 30-yard line but the Indians managed to score on only one occasion.

Arkansas State's lone score came on a 1-yard run by Larry Lawrence. Lawrence finished with 111 yards rushing. Helping to set up the score were pass receptions of 7, 15 and 17 yards by Dikki Dyson. Dyson established a new single-game school record with 196 yards on seven catches.

The Indians faced their third Southland opponent in a row when Arkansas State played at a 3-3 McNeese State team seeking its first SLC triumph.

McNeese State struck first for the fourth-straight game when Artie Shankle scooted 40 yards to set up James Galloway's 16-yard gallop for a 7-0 lead less than four minutes into the first quarter. Field goals of 44 and 46 yards by a healthy Dobbs narrowed the margin to 7-6.

Charles Jefferson's interception of a Taylor pass only five plays into the second half led to a Shankle touchdown to extend the Cowboys' lead to 14-6. A Joe Griffin fumble on the first play of the ensuing possession gave the ball right back to McNeese at the Arkansas State 14. The Indians held, limiting the Cowboys to a 22-yard Peebles field goal as the score moved to 17-6.

A Tommy Foulks touchdown and a two-point conversion pass from Taylor to Dyson pulled Arkansas State to within three points at 17-14 with 8:12 left in the game.

Although McNeese failed to score after that point, it did go on a drive that used up six minutes on the clock.

Arkansas State reached the McNeese 30 late in the game before losing possession on a fumble. In the closing moments, Tim Harris intercepted a pass with 22 seconds remaining as the Cowboys held on for the three-point triumph.

The result left both teams 1-2 in the Southland and 4-3 overall.

Looking for a win to take sole possession of first place in the Southland Conference, Louisiana Tech's run defense seemed non-existent at home against Texas-Arlington. The Tech defense, which had been yielding 62 yards per game on the ground, was shredded for 176 yards by UTA's Jensen but the Bulldogs' defense came up big when it needed to.

Tech was clinging to a 17-7 lead with the Mavericks threatening in the third quarter. The Bulldogs' defense stiffened, holding UTA to a field goal. That sparked the Louisiana Tech offense. Thibodeaux, who threw for 311 yards in the game, drove the Bulldogs on a scoring drive culminating in a touchdown run by White. Thibodeaux later scored on a 1-yard run and Swilley contributed a 27-yard field goal as Tech took a 34-12 win to improve to 3-0-1 in the SLC.

Following its tie with Louisiana Tech, Southwestern Louisiana went 2-1 over non-conference opponents with to move to 6-2-1. In that span, the Ragin' Cajuns saw the Bulldogs move to 3-0-1 in the Southland. At 2-0-1, the Cajuns returned to Southland play looking for a win over Arkansas State while hoping for Lamar to upset Tech so they could surpass the Bulldogs.

Neither scenario played out in Southwestern Louisiana's favor.

The Ragin' Cajuns went into their game at Arkansas State feeling pretty confident as USL was coming off a 9-7 road win over an East Carolina team that won 29 of its previous 30 games at home.

Southwestern Louisiana fell behind Arkansas State 3-0 on a career-best 46-yard field goal by Dobbs in a game in which the Cajuns played most of the contest without Henry because of ankle injuries. Without its starting quarterback, USL still managed a 13-3 halftime lead despite no offensive touchdowns. Roveto connected on a pair of field goals and Irving returned an interception 90 yards for a touchdown to give the Cajuns a 10-point halftime advantage.

USL seemed well on its way to a third Southland win of the season when a safety extended the Cajuns' lead to 15-3. The safety occurred when Taylor was sacked in the end zone by Southwestern Louisiana defensive lineman Kenny Chenier while attempting to pass.

The Indians howled back late in the second half. Arkansas State pulled to within five points at 15-10 on a pass from Gene Bradley to Jimmy Wicks with 3:50 remaining in the game. The scoring play came when Taylor pitched to Bradley. Bradley looked to toss the ball back to Taylor. With Taylor covered, the Indians halfback found Wicks, the Arkansas State flanker, open in the end zone for the touchdown.

Arkansas State failed on an onside kick attempt but the Indians' defense held, giving the ball back to the offense at their own 34. Eight plays later, Taylor connected with Bradley on a 23-yard strike with 59 seconds remaining for a 17-15 Arkansas State triumph.

Lamar didn't give the Cajuns any help as the Cardinals lost 23-6 at home to Louisiana Tech to fall to 0-3 in the Southland in handing the conference title and an Independence Bowl berth to the Bulldogs.

Despite rolling up 218 yards of offense in the first half, Louisiana Tech trailed 6-3 before Thibodeaux capped a 97-yard drive with a 17-yard run in the closing moments of the second quarter. A blocked punt by Tech's Jackie James set up a quarterback sneak by Thibodeaux for a touchdown and Anderson later returned a punt for a touchdown to give the Bulldogs the 23-6 win that improved Louisiana Tech to 6-0-2 overall and 4-0-1 in conference. The Bulldogs captured their fifth SLC title in seven years.

With another title in the Bulldogs' hands, the remaining Southland teams were playing out the string to the 1977 season.

Arkansas State was unable to built off its momentum with the win over USL as the Indians lost 44-14 at home a week later to Texas-Arlington.

Jensen rushed for 109 yards to top 1,000 for the season and UTA's wishbone attack amassed 297 yards on the ground but an efficient Mavericks' passing game surprised the Indians. Dewalt, the UT-Arlington quarterback, was 5 of 6 passing for 181yards and three touchdowns in the Mavs' triumph.

All three of Dewalt's touchdown passes came in the first half. He tossed 24 yards to Jensen five plays into the game and hit Scott Burt on a 46-yard pass play with 3:47 remaining in the second quarter to give UTA a 21-14 edge. The first touchdown pass came one play after Joe Slayton, the Indians' punter, dropped a snap from center. Burt's go-ahead touchdown took place three plays after Arkansas State had managed to tie the game.

Arkansas State's first-half scores came in the second quarter on a 1-yard run by fullback Larry Harkless and a 7-yard strike from Taylor to Wicks.

After Arkansas State failed to convert on fourth down at the UT-Arlington 36 in the closing moments of the first half, Tony Felder turned a short pass from DeWalt into a 51-yard touchdown for a 28-14 lead with 39 seconds remaining in the half as the Mavericks pulled away for the 44-14 victory.

Big plays highlighted the start of McNeese State's home finale against Southland Conference foe Lamar.

Four plays into the game, Lamar's Kevin Bell rambled 74 yards to give the Cardinals a 7-0 lead. McNeese tied the game on a school-record 69-yard pass from Tommy McFarland to Tony Burlingame. Lamar regained the lead at 14-7 when Johnny Ray Smith returned and errant McFarland pass 69 yards for a touchdown.

There would be no more big plays for McNeese State as Lamar held the Cowboys to 42 yards rushing in the game, the lowest total for McNeese since 1967.

Lamar stretched its lead to 21-7 late in the first half on a 21-yard run by Jeff Bergeron on a short drive set up by a Cowboys turnover. The Cardinals added a 53-yard touchdown pass from Chris Fredrich to Mark Teichman and a 35-yard Bergeron run in the second half for Lamar's surprising 35-7 pounding of McNeese.

The victory for the Cardinals was Lamar's first SLC win in three years. Lamar moved to 2-8 overall in a game in which Bell rushed for 127 yards to become the first Cardinal to top 100 yards in a game since 1974.

McNeese fell to 1-3 in the Southland and 5-5 overall.

Lamar was unable to follow up on the McNeese upset, falling 14-7 at Texas-Arlington. The victory allowed the Mavericks to finish in third place in the Southland Conference at 3-2 and 5-6 overall. The Cardinals concluded the year 1-4 in the SLC and 2-9 overall.

DeWalt scored both touchdowns for UTA. His 77-yard run with 3:27 remaining in the second quarter gave the Mavericks a 7-0 halftime edge. His 4-yard run in the third quarter made it 14-0.

Lamar's lone score came in the fourth quarter. Jensen, who rushed for 110 yards in his final collegiate game, fumbled at the UT-Arlington 30 with 8:36 left in the game to eventually set up a 5-yard touchdown run by Bell.

A 9-9 tie at home against McNeese State allowed Southwestern Louisiana to finish second in the Southland Conference with an unusual 2-1-2 mark. The Ragin' Cajuns concluded the season 6-4-2 overall. McNeese, meanwhile, ended 1-3-1 in the SLC and 5-5-1 overall.

Roveto kicked three field goals in the game, including a career-long 49 yarder in the first quarter, that was set up by an 18-yard Cowboys punt to give the Ragin' Cajuns a 3-0 lead. Peebles hit a 22-yard field goal for McNeese in the second quarter for a 3-3 tie that held up until the fourth quarter.

The score remained tied late in the first half due to missed opportunities by both teams. After Peebles' game-tying field goal, a USL fumble gave the ball right back to the Cowboys. McNeese failed to take advantage when Peebles missed on a 37-yard attempt. The Cajuns fumbled the ball away again on their next possession, this time at the 23. Again, the Cowboys failed to take advantage when they came up short on a fourth-down conversion try. Near the end of the half, Roveto missed a 39-yard field goal attempt.

Roveto connected on field goals of 30 and 47 yards in the fourth quarter to give USL a 9-3 edge.

The Cowboys marched 77 yards in the closing minutes. Jim Morvant's 7-yard touchdown pass to Alan Heisser with 19 seconds left in the game knotted up the affair 9-9. Peebles pushed the conversion attempt wide left, resulting in a tie to close the season.

USL finished the year 6-4-2 overall and 2-1-2 in the Southland. McNeese ended its season at 5-5-1, including 1-3-1 in conference play.

After Louisiana Tech wrapped up the Southland Conference title with its 23-6 win over Lamar, the Bulldogs had to face three non-conference opponents before they could go bowling.

After defeating Southern Mississippi 28-10, the Bulldogs suffered their only loss of the season with a 41-14 drubbing at the hands of North Texas State in a game played in Shreveport. Tech got back on track with a 20-0 blanking of Northeast Louisiana.

Playing at the site of Louisiana Tech's only defeat of the season, the Bulldogs faced Louisville in the second-annual Independence Bowl in Shreveport.

Kevin Miller's 60-yard punt return for a touchdown made an early decision by Cardinals coach Vince Gibson look like a smart one in the early stages of the Independence Bowl. When Louisiana Tech won the opening coin toss and elected to receive, Gibson decided to let the Bulldogs have the wind at their backs for the opening quarter.

Miller's score against a wind gusting as much as 32 miles per hour seemed to validate Gibson's strategy – until Thibodeaux went to work. The Tech quarterback countered by guiding the Bulldogs to three-straight touchdowns after Miller's punt return for a 21-7 lead Louisiana Tech would never relinquish in a 24-14 triumph.

Of the three first-quarter touchdowns, two were passes. One was a 41-yard bomb to Pree and the other an 8-yard strike to Larry McCartney as Thibodeaux went on to pass for 287 yards.

The only other score in the game for Tech was a 21-yard Swilley field goal late in the second quarter as the game turned into a defensive battle in the second half. Thibodeaux's early passing yards were needed as a Louisville defense, led by linebacker Otis Wilson, limited the Bulldogs to 48 yards rushing, including two in the second half. Wilson would go on to be a key member of a record-setting Chicago Bears defense that would win the Super Bowl following the 1986 season.

Tech, the Southland Conference champions, concluded the 1977 season, 9-1-2.

Louisiana Tech began defense of its Southland Conference title at Texas-Arlington 0-1 following a 12-7 non-conference loss at home to Tennessee-Chattanooga to open the 1978 season.

The Mavericks went into their SLC opener 0-3 on the season with losses to Drake, West Texas State and North Texas State.

Trailing 14-7 at halftime, a 2-yard touchdown run by John Johnson in the third quarter and a 7-yard run by UTA quarterback Roy Dewalt gave the Mavericks a 21-14 lead early in the final period. Tech countered with a 26-yard touchdown pass from Keith Thibodeaux to Scooter Spruiell to tie the game with 8:58 left in the game. Louisiana Tech pulled out a 28-21 win when defensive back Jean Dornier stepped in front of a Dewalt pass and raced 34 yards for a touchdown with 4:10 left in the game. Dornier closed out the first half with 70-yard interception return but failed to score when tackled at the UTA 5-yard line as time expired.

Playing a Southland game for the second week in a row, Louisiana Tech had a chance to put early pressure on the rest of the league with a win at home over McNeese State.

Louisiana Tech seemed destined for a tie with a SLC opponent for the second year in a row when the score was knotted 20-20 in the late stages of the fourth quarter until Thibodeaux hit Bryan Leviston with a 41-yard touchdown strike with 52 seconds remaining to give the Bulldogs a 27-20 lead.

Now needing a quick score to avoid a loss, a forced Wendell LeJeune pass was intercepted by Max Ray Davenport and returned 27 yards for a touchdown with five seconds left to give Tech a misleading 14-point final margin at 34-20.

McNeese built a 17-10 halftime lead on a 5-yard Harry Price run, a 93-yard punt return by Richard Ellender and a 35-yard Don Stump field goal. Louisiana Tech's first-half points came on a Keith Swilley field goal and 48-yard pass from Thibodeaux to Sammy Willis with 31 seconds left before intermission.

While Louisiana Tech was moving to 2-0 in Southland play, Lamar played at Southwestern Louisiana in the league opener for both teams. Lamar went into the game 1-2, with its only win being a 23-16 victory over Stephen F. Austin, while USL was winless through three games.

Off to their worst start in four years, the Ragin' Cajuns spotted Lamar 16 first-quarter points. By failing to score in the first quarter, the Cajuns stretched their drought of no touchdowns to open the season to 13 quarters. That all changed as USL produced a 16-point quarter in the second period for a 16-16 halftime tie.

The Ragin' Cajuns ended the touchdown drought with several big plays. An interception by USL linebacker Clarence Hannah at the Cajuns' 47 set up the team's first touchdown of the season. David Guidry, in relief of David Pingston at quarterback, raced 53 yards on an option keeper on his first play of the game for a touchdown. His two-point conversion run made it 16-8.

Lamar marched to the USL 11 on its next drive but turned the ball over on a fumble by quarterback Larry Haynes. Two plays later, Guidry hit Rodney Smith with an 83-yard touchdown toss. The quarterback then connected with Dennis Riedmiller on a two-point conversion, and all of a sudden, the game was tied.

The score remained the same until the middle of the fourth quarter. The Cardinals attempted to pick up a first down when facing fourth-and-inches from the USL 43. A quarterback sneak failed to produce the needed few inches, giving the ball to the Cajuns.

Guidry, who sparked the first-half comeback, was out of the game with bruised ribs. Pingston returned to the game and promptly picked up 22 and 15 yards on a pair of runs. The freshman quarterback raced around right end from 4 yards out with 8:10 left in the game to pull out a 23-16 triumph.

Lamar built its 16-0 first-quarter lead on a 36-yard Mike Marlow field goal and a pair of short touchdown runs by Haynes. The second touchdown for the quarterback was set up on an interception of a Pingston pass by Danny Hanson.

While USL won its first game of the season, Lamar fell to 1-3 in losing its Southland Conference opener for the fourth year in a row.

After failing to score a touchdown in 13 quarters to open the season, the Cajuns suddenly found themselves in Southland Conference title contention a week later after a 24-6 home win over Louisiana Tech.

Guidry, still suffering from rib injuries, didn't get the start against Louisiana Tech. He made his presence felt when he did enter the game, tossing three touchdowns to spark the Cajuns.

The Bulldogs failed to take early advantage of a pair of Cajun turnovers deep in USL territory. Tech finally put points on the board when freshman Eric Barkley, subbing for a banged up Thibodeaux at quarterback, hooked up with Spruiell on a 7-yard touchdown pass for a 6-0 lead with 3:20 showing in the initial quarter.

USL exploded for 17 points in the second quarter. Roveto started the scoring with a 33-yard field goal. Guidry tossed 13 yards to Riedmiller to put the Cajuns on top 10-6.

Tech looked to bounce back right before the end of the first half, advancing into Cajuns territory. Thibodeaux fumbled while being sacked by linebacker Frank Barkley, with Joe Kelly recovering. On the first play from scrimmage, Guidry and Smith teamed up on a 60-yard touchdown to give USL a 17-6 lead with 57 seconds remaining before intermission.

In the second half, Ron Irving returned an interception 75 yards for an apparent touchdown. The officials ruled he had been illegally aided by a teammate on the return, placing the ball at the Tech 17. It mattered little to the Cajuns as Guidry tossed to Curt Calhoun for the touchdown as USL put the game away with the 24-6 verdict.

USL moved into sole possession of first place in the Southland at 2-0, despite being 2-3 overall. Louisiana Tech was held to its lowest point total in 89 games in suffering its first conference defeat of the season.

The Cajuns were unable to solidify their spot atop the Southland Conference standings a week later, falling at Texas-Arlington 24-3 and reverting to a team struggling to score offensive touchdowns.

A fumble by Pingston at his own 7-yard line in the first quarter set up a 22-yard Tom Skorrupa field goal for a quick 3-0 Mavericks lead. After a missed Roveto field goal, the Mavs marched for the only touchdown of the first half when Dewalt scored on a 6-yard run to give UTA a 10-0 lead at the break.

Dewalt hooked up with Jerry Woodard on a 2-yard touchdown pass in the third quarter to make it 17-3. A second Roveto field goal made it 17-6 but Bill McClesky, who rushed for 146 yards, scored on a 4-yard run with 1:02 left in the game to give the Mavericks a 24-3 victory.

USL, which was limited to 182 yards, including only 47 passing, suffered its first Southland loss and dropped to 2-1 in the league and 2-4 overall. Texas-Arlington moved to 1-1 in conference action and improved to 2-5 overall after an 0-5 start.

Despite the poor start to the season, the win over Southwestern Louisiana put UT-Arlington into the position of possible conference contender if the Mavericks could follow up a week later with a win at Lamar.

The Mavericks quickly fell behind Lamar on a 59-yard touchdown pass from Haynes to Howard Robinson but the Cardinals would add only 10 points the remainder of the contest in Texas-Arlington's 37-17 victory.

DeWalt, who rushed for 162 yards, scored on a 13-yard run later in the first quarter to tie the game. Tony Felder rushed for three touchdowns and McClesky gained 126 yards as UTA amassed 436 on the ground to run past the Cardinals.

Lamar fell to 0-2 in the Southland and 1-5-1 overall. UTA evened its league record at 1-1 while improving to 3-5 overall.

Meanwhile, 4-2 Arkansas State became the final team to start Southland Conference play as the Indians hosted McNeese State.

With McNeese running back Artie Shankle being held to only 21 yards after three-consecutive games of 100-yard efforts, the Cowboys found themselves in a low-scoring battle against Arkansas State.

Larry Lawrence, who rushed for 105 yards for Arkansas State, helped provide the Indians with the only points of the first half. Gaining 40 of his team's 77 yards on a drive that began late in the first quarter, the running back's effort set up a 24-yard Doug Dobbs field goal for a 3-0 Arkansas State lead mere seconds into the second quarter.

Davenport's interception of a Kennon Taylor pass, plus a personal-foul penalty against the Indians, gave McNeese the ball at the Arkansas State 26. The Cowboys could advance no farther than the 14 and had to settle on a 31-yard Stump field goal and a 3-3 tie at the 3:14 mark of the third quarter.

Early in the fourth quarter, McNeese got the ball at the Arkansas State 30 following a short punt. On fourth down from the 1-yard line, Price was stopped by the Indians' Glen Keenig to turn away the Cowboys.

McNeese held and got the ball back at its own 47. Able to advance no closer than the 32, Stump was sent in to try a 49-yard field goal to tie the game. His kick fell short with 5:58 left in the game.

With Lawrence and Joe Griffin doing the bulk of the work, the Indians marched to the McNeese 10-yard line. Dodds set up for a field goal with 11 seconds left, but a bad snap forced Jerry McKenna, the holder, to toss a pass that sailed through the end zone.

The Indians were guilty of having an illegal receiver downfield on the play. That backed up Dobbs but gave him one more chance. This time, he booted a 42-yard field goal with no time left on the clock as Arkansas State edged McNeese 6-3.

McNeese suffered a similar fate against the Indians in 1974 when Joe Duren kicked a 57-yard field goal as time expired to give Arkansas State a 22-20 victory.

The result left both teams 4-3 on the season. McNeese fell to 0-2 in the Southland while Arkansas State won its league opener.

With Louisiana Tech and Southwestern Louisiana both 2-1 in the Southland and facing non-conference opponents a week later, the winner of the Arkansas State at Texas-Arlington matchup would have a chance to gain a temporary lead in the league. An Arkansas State win would leave the Indians as the SLC's only unbeaten team at 2-0, while a victory by UTA would make the Mavericks the only 3-1 team in the conference.

The Indians took advantage of good field position and UT-Arlington mistakes to win their fifth game in a row with a 27-7 decision over the Mavs.

Favorable field position was provided by Joe Slayton. The Arkansas State punter pinned the Mavericks inside the UTA 15-yard line six times in the game. Arkansas State was leading 10-7 early in the second half when one of Slayton's punts hit a Mavericks player, giving the ball to the Indians at the UT-Arlington 12-yard line to set up a Lawrence touchdown. Lawrence rushed for 127 yards for his fourth-consecutive 100-yard effort.

Arkansas State drove 90 yards for its opening score, capping the drive on an option keeper by Taylor. UTA's first fumble of the game set up a 40-yard Dobbs field goal to make the score 10-0.

UTA's lone score came on a 1-yard run by Phillip Jessie with 22 seconds left in the second quarter to narrow the score to 10-7 at halftime. After Lawrence's touchdown run early in the third quarter, a touchdown reception by tight end Paul Gilbow and a 32-yard field goal by Dobbs allowed the Indians to pull away.

A week later at Southwestern Louisiana, Dobbs and the surging Indians got the best of Roveto, his USL kicking counterpart, and the Ragin' Cajuns. Dobbs booted second-quarter field goals of 43, 32 and 27 yards to give Arkansas State a 9-3 halftime lead. Roveto booted a 20 yarder in the second quarter for the Cajuns' only points of the opening half.

USL only trailed 6-3 late in the second quarter. With time running out in the opening half, Taylor tossed a pass intended for Gerald Joseph that was intercepted as time expired. Officials ruled defensive pass interference against the Cajuns, giving Arkansas State an untimed down. Dobbs hit his 27 yarder to put the Indians up by six points.

Roveto kicked a 45-yard field goal in the fourth quarter to make it a 9-6 game but failed to tie the game with 6:32 remaining when he was wide right on a 48-yard attempt.

Trailing by three points, USL was forced to punt in the fourth quarter from its own 7-yard line. Indians backup fullback Donald Barnett then barreled 49 yards for a touchdown to give Arkansas State a 16-6 victory.

USL, which was held to 95 yards total offense, including 18 rushing, fell to 2-6 overall while falling out of Southland contention at 2-2.

While Arkansas State improved to 3-0 in the Southland, Louisiana Tech walloped Lamar 40-3 to move to 3-1 in the SLC to set up a conference showdown the following week.

Following their loss to USL, the Bulldogs defeated Ball State and Northwestern State before losing to North Texas State for a 4-3 record going into the Lamar game.

Thibodeaux and tailback George Yates each scored twice for Louisiana Tech against Lamar. Leading 28-3 at halftime, Zack Jones returned the second-half kickoff 97 yards to increase Tech's advantage.

The Bulldogs, who sacked Haynes 10 times, only allowed a 37-yard Marlow field goal in the second quarter.

Lamar fell to 0-3 in the Southland and 1-6-1 overall.

With the Southland crown on the line at home against Arkansas State, Thibodeaux passed for 130 of his 194 yards in the opening half against the nation's third-best passing defense, but it was Yates who crossed the goal line three times to give Louisiana Tech a 24-10 win and its sixth conference title.

A pair of short touchdown runs by Yates gave the Bulldogs a 14-0 lead after one quarter. Yates, who rushed for 138 yards, broke loose on a 66-yard gallop in the second quarter as Tech built a 24-7 halftime lead.

Arkansas State, which dropped to 6-4 overall, scored its only touchdown of the game in the first half when Jerome Miller fought off Bulldogs defender Lavon James on an underthrown ball by Taylor for an 80-yard touchdown. Dobbs connected on a 37-yard field goal in the second half for the Indians' final points of the contest.

While Louisiana Tech and Arkansas State were battling for the top spot in the Southland, Lamar and McNeese State, both winless in the SLC, were looking to avoid the conference cellar.

Following an open date, the Cowboys found themselves in a role reversal. A week earlier, McNeese, taking advantage of 25 suspended Tennessee-Chattanooga players, ended the Moccasins' unbeaten streak – the longest in the nation at 15 games – with a 28-24 victory. Playing at Lamar, the Cowboys were hoping to avoid the ignominy of losing to a Cardinals team that only had one win all season long.

McNeese seemed to put any fears to rest by building a 24-9 lead early in the fourth quarter.

It was close in the early going, however, as the Cowboys only managed a 10-8 halftime edge. After Lamar took a 6-0 lead on a 4-yard run by Keith Gilchrist, McNeese countered with an 8-yard Shankle run and a 22-yard Stump field goal. Lamar answered with a 29-yard Marlow field goal for the two-point margin at halftime.

A 15-yard pass from Chad Millet to Ellender provided the only points of the third quarter. Millet's 8-yard run in the fourth quarter gave the Cowboys their 24-9 lead.

The Cardinals were not about to surrender quietly. A 6-yard pass from Haynes to Rick Casey made the score 24-15. Haynes hooked up with Robinson with an 11-yard strike later in the quarter and the Lamar quarterback connected with Eddie Horn on a two-point conversion pass to pull to within 24-23 but the Cowboys held off the late Cardinal charge to secure the one-point triumph.

McNeese improved to 1-2 in the Southland Conference and 6-3 overall. Lamar fell to 0-4 in the conference and 1-7-1 overall.

Lamar secured the bottom spot in the conference a week later while handing second place to Arkansas State with a 6-3 loss to the Indians.

A 32-yard Marlow field goal broke a scoreless tie in the third quarter before the Indians won the game on a 2-yard run by Lawrence with 7:46 remaining in the game.

Arkansas State finished 4-1 in the Southland and 7-4 overall. The Cardinals ended the 1978 season on a positive note, topping Long Beach State to finish 2-7-1 on the year.

McNeese State split its final two games to finish 2-3 in the Southland and 7-4 overall. The Cowboys lost to UT-Arlington 20-17 before ending with a 44-15 victory over Southwestern Louisiana. The results allowed the Mavericks to finish 3-2 in the SLC and 5-6 overall. USL ended 2-3 in the conference and 3-8 overall.

The Cowboys and Texas-Arlington matched scores in the first half, leading to a 10-10 halftime tie.

Texas-Arlington fumbled on its first two offensive series of the game. The Cowboys took advantage of the second miscue on a 5-yard touchdown run by Theron McClendon. The score was set up on a fumble by Dewalt at the UTA 27-yard line.

Dewalt made up for the mistake moments later on a 13-yard touchdown pass to Gary Lewis. Stump and Skoruppa exchanged field goals in the second quarter for the 10-10 tie at intermission.

UTA marched 72 yards with the opening drive of the second half to gain the lead. The big gainer of the possession was a 44-yard run by Dewalt. The UTA quarterback capped the drive on a 3-yard run to give the Mavericks a 17-10 edge.

A Shankle fumble on the first play of the ensuing drive gave the ball back to the Mavs at the McNeese 26. The Cowboys' defense held but Skoruppa's 25-yard field goal stretched Texas-Arlington's lead to 20-10 at the 8:33 mark of the third quarter.

McNeese drove on its next possession but came away with no points when Stump missed a field goal attempt.

The Cowboys shook off the miss to add a 4-yard touchdown pass from LeJeune to Ellender only seconds into the fourth quarter to pull to within three points at 20-17 but the Mavs held on for the win.

Closing the season at home against rival Southwestern Louisiana, the Cowboys spotted the Ragin' Cajuns a 3-0 lead on a 39-yard Roveto field goal before going on to score on six-straight possessions in the second and third quarters to build a 38-3 lead on their way to the 44-18 rout.

Turnovers plagued Louisiana Tech in a 35-13 loss to East Carolina in the third-annual Independence Bowl. The Pirates' defense set up ECU's first three scores as Barkley had a tough first half for the Bulldogs.

A 3-yard run by Anthony Collins and a 1-yard run by quarterback Leander Green gave East Carolina a 14-0 first-quarter lead. The first touchdown was set up on a bad pitch by Barkley and the second on a Barkley fumble at the Tech 49. The Pirates made it 21-0 early in the second quarter when Ruffin McNeill intercepted a Barkley pass to set up another 1-yard run by Collins.

Louisiana Tech made it 21-10 at halftime on a 32-yard touchdown pass from Thibodeaux to Spruiell and a 36-yard Swilley field goal. Swilley added another 32-yard kick in the third quarter to make it 21-13 but that was as close as the Bulldogs would get as the Southland champions ended their season with a 6-5 record.

COACHING UPHEAVAL

The 1979 season saw unprecedented coaching changes in the Southland Conference as four of the six schools had new head coaches. All of the changes left Southwestern Louisiana's Augie Tammariello and Texas-Arlington's Bud Elliott as the deans of SLC coaches. Both were entering their sixth year at their respective schools.

Among the changes, Larry Beightol was named the new head coach at Louisiana Tech following the retirement of Maxie Lambright, citing health reasons. Lambright coached the Bulldogs from 1967-78, posting a 95-36-2 record. Beightol took over at Tech after a two-year stint as offensive line coach at the University of Arkansas. He was offensive line coach at William and Mary, North Carolina State and Auburn before going to Arkansas.

Also, Bill Davidson retired as head coach of Arkansas State after the 1978 season and was replaced by Larry Lacewell. A former defensive coordinator at the University of Oklahoma, Lacewell was a consultant for the Arkansas State program in 1978 before being named Davidson's successor.

Prior to the start of the 1979 season, Jack Doland was named the new president at McNeese State, with Ernie Duplechin elevated to head coach after serving as an assistant at the Lake Charles school for 14 years. Doland compiled a record of 64-32-3 as McNeese coach.

"I had been here forever so they might as well give me a chance," joked Duplechin.

After a three-year stint in which Lamar went 6-26-1 and never won more than two games in a season, Bob Frederick was replaced as Cardinals coach by Larry Kennan. Kennan took over at Lamar after serving as offensive coordinator at Southern Methodist from 1976-78. Prior to SMU, Kennan was offensive coordinator at the University of Nevada at Las Vegas from 1973-75.

Beightol and Kennan were the first of the new Southland coaches to make their conference debuts when Louisiana Tech visited Lamar. Tech went into the

SLC opener struggling under Beightol as the Bulldogs' new veer offense produced a total of seven points in their first two games. Lamar lost its first game under Kennan, falling 20-7 at Baylor before defeating Western Kentucky 58-27.

Louisiana Tech held a 7-0 lead over Lamar when Mark Buchanan, the newly-named starting quarterback for the Bulldogs, hooked up with John Rodgers on a 44-yard scoring strike. Buchanan left the game in the third quarter with a severely sprained ankle and Tech would fail to score again in the contest. Meanwhile, Lamar quarterback Larry Haynes factored in all three of the Cardinals' scores. He scored on two short runs and tossed a 14-yard pass to Howard Robinson for the other as Lamar snapped a seven-game losing streak to the Bulldogs and won its first SLC game since 1977.

A week later, Lacewell made his Southland coaching debut at home against Southwestern Louisiana. Arkansas State went into the game 2-1, including a season-opening victory over East Texas for Lacewell's first win. The Ragin' Cajuns, meanwhile, were 2-2.

The Cajuns amassed a season-high 391 yards against Arkansas State but couldn't crack the scoreboard – until the middle of the fourth quarter.

Shortly after Southwestern Louisiana scored to pull to within 9-7, Ragin' Cajuns cornerback Mack Scott picked off a Gene Bradley pass, giving the ball back to USL at its own 45. Facing a second-and-23, freshman quarterback Dwight Prudhomme tossed 26 yards to Mike Hoffman to keep the drive alive. That eventually set up a 42-yard field goal by John Roveto to put the Cajuns on top by a point.

The Indians' fifth fumble of the game gave the ball to USL once again. Roveto booted another field goal to give the Cajuns a 13-9 win.

Arkansas State led 6-0 at halftime on a pair of Doug Dobbs field goals. He added a 35-yard kick early in the fourth quarter to make it 9-0 before the Cajuns began their rally.

The final newcomer to make his Southland coaching debut was Duplechin when his McNeese State Cowboys visited Texas-Arlington. The Cowboys were off to a 4-0 start, with a season-opening victory over Tulasa giving Duplechin his initial win as Cowboys coach. UTA entered the game 3-1, with its lone loss coming against North Texas.

Special teams provided the first score for McNeese against UT-Arlington. A 54-yard punt by Stump was downed at the UTA 3-yard line. Forced to punt from his own end zone, Odes Mitchell fumbled the ball while facing a heavy rush. Craig Cryer fell on the ball in the end zone, giving the Cowboys a 7-0 lead early in the second quarter.

Texas-Arlington responded with a 66-yard drive and tied the game on a 22-yard run by Roy Dewalt. After a 1-yard run by Artie Shankle capped an 80-yard drive, Brian Happel kicked a 31-yard field goal at the 4:38 mark of the second quarter to make it 14-10 at halftime.

The score stood up until early in the fourth quarter when a 22-yard Happel field goal made it a one-point game at 14-13 but the Mavericks could get no closer.

A fourth-consecutive road defeat, this time a 6-0 loss to Miami, kept Louisiana Tech winless through four games going into the Bulldogs' first home game of the year against Southwestern Louisiana.

In USL, the Bulldogs found themselves taking on an offense even more error prone than their own. Jean Dornier tied a school record with four interceptions and the Tech defense picked off a total of seven passes in a 17-0 win. USL quarterbacks combined to only complete 2 of 19 passes as the Ragin' Cajuns finished with 65 yards of total offense.

With the defense providing good field position, Louisiana Tech's offense scored three points more against the Cajuns than the Bulldogs had mustered in their previous four games combined. Dornier's first interception set up a 6-yard George Yates run. Tech's other scores came on a 31-yard touchdown pass from freshman quarterback Matt Dunigan to Scott Coates that was set up by a 33-yard punt return by Michael Conant and a 39-yard Keith Swilley field goal.

The win, the first for Beightol as coach, allowed Louisiana Tech to even its Southland Conference record at 1-1.

Any notions of Louisiana Tech becoming a contender in the SLC race came to a halt a week later when the Bulldogs returned to form in a 14-7 home loss against Arkansas State.

Mistakes contributed to a 7-7 tie at halftime. Arkansas State fumbled the ball away at its own 21 on the opening play from scrimmage. That set up a 3-yard run by Dunigan for a 7-0 Louisiana Tech lead. The Indians tied the game in the second quarter on a botched punt attempt by the Bulldogs that led to a blocked punt recovered by Arkansas State at the Tech 32. On the very next play, Bradley hooked up with Curtis Clay with the game-tying score.

Arkansas State pulled the game out on a 76-yard march in the third quarter. Anthony Williams, who rushed for 90 yards in the game, carried the ball eight times in the drive that was culminated on a 6-yard run by Bradley.

While the Bulldogs were losing to Arkansas State, McNeese State was beating Lamar 34-25 on the road to remain the Southland's only unbeaten team at 2-0 in the conference and 6-0 overall. The loss dropped the Cardinals to 1-2 in league play.

Based on his performance at Lamar, if Rusty Guilbeau had been a baseball player, he likely would have been a great set-up man. The McNeese State defender intercepted a pass and recovered two fumbles to set up scores in the Cowboys' win over the Cardinals.

It seemed whenever he set up a score, Shankle was there as the closer. That's what happened on McNeese's first score when Guilbeau's recovery of a Ron Booker fumble set up a 4-yard Shankle run to give the Cowboys a 7-0 lead.

Shankle later added a 9-yard run and Chad Millet hit Harry Price with a 38-yard touchdown pass to give the Cowboys a 21-12 halftime lead. Haynes, the Lamar quarterback, kept the Cardinals in the game with a 13-yard touchdown toss to Alfred Mask and a 1-yard run.

McNeese seemed to take a commanding 27-12 lead at the start of the third quarter on a touchdown run by Millet to cap an 82-yard drive to open the second half.

Again, Haynes kept Lamar in the game as touchdown passes of 9 yards to Mask and 13 yards to Percy Bruce cut the Cardinal deficit to two points at 27-25 with 13:56 remaining in the game.

With an unbeaten season perhaps in the balance, Guilbeau and Shankle did it one more time. Guilbeau's recovery of a Floyd Dorsey fumble gave McNeese the ball at the Lamar 32. Shankle got the call seven times in the drive, with the final carry from 2 yards out to give the Cowboys a 34-25 victory.

McNeese State had a scare in maintaining its unbeaten record with a narrow 10-7 win at home over Arkansas State.

The Cowboys only managed a 3-0 lead at home against Arkansas State when the Indians made a decision that would prove to be an omen for later in the game.

When Shankle was unable to handle a poor pitch from Millet, Ron Norman's recovery for Arkansas State gave the ball to the Indians at the McNeese State 27. Three plays produced 6 yards but instead of attempting a game-tying field goal, the Indians elected to throw on fourth down. Bernard Bell's well-timed hit on Gary Hinton's attempt to haul in a Gene Bradley pass at the 5-yard line led to an incompletion and allowed the Cowboys to take over on downs.

Arkansas State eventually took the lead 7-3 later in the third quarter. A Bradley run of 13 yards, plus a facemask penalty against the Cowboys, moved the ball to the McNeese 11. Bradley tossed to Jerry Mack for the touchdown and a four-point advantage for the Indians with 1:03 remaining in the third quarter.

McNeese rallied in the fourth quarter on a drive that was set up by a punt by Arkansas State's Joe Slayton that went straight in the air and came down at the

Indians' 48-yard line. Shankle, who rushed for 161 yards, dove over from 4 yards out to give the Cowboys a 10-7 edge.

Needing a break in the closing moments of the game, Thomas Johnson gave it to the Indians when he blocked Stump's punt to give Arkansas State possession at the McNeese 19 with seven seconds remaining in the game. Instead of a potential game-tying field goal, the Indians went for the win. Bradley's pass was knocked away at the goal line by Tim Harris to seal the three-point win for the Cowboys.

The Cowboys surprised Arkansas State on their opening drive with a four-receiver set. Despite the alignment, McNeese fed the ball to Shankle. The running back ran the ball 11 times for 66 yards before the drive finally stalled and Stump's 24-yard field goal gave the Cowboys a 3-0 lead. Stump's kick proved to be the only points of the first half.

Lamar bounced back from its loss to McNeese State and managed to stay within a game of the Cowboys with a 21-17 home win over Southwestern Louisiana.

The Cardinals' offense was held to a pair of Mike Marlow field goals before Haynes got a hot hand in the fourth quarter against Southwestern Louisiana.

Trailing 17-6, Haynes hooked up with Robinson on a 6-yard touchdown pass and added a two-point conversion toss to Ben Booker to make the score 17-14. Haynes connected with Mask from 36 yards out to give the Cardinals a 21-17 triumph as Lamar improved to 2-1 in the SLC and 3-2-1 overall.

USL, 1-2 in the Southland and 3-5 overall, built its lead on a 17-yard run by Ed Blanco, a 43-yard Roveto field goal and a 3-yard sprint by Rodney Smith. The three wins for Lamar were the most for the Cardinals in four years.

While McNeese State was moving to 8-0 with a 24-17 non-conference win at Tennessee-Chattanooga, Lamar remained the only other Southland team with a winning conference record following the Cardinals' 20-10 triumph at Arkansas State.

It was no easy task for the Cardinals who found themselves down by 10 points only two possessions into their encounter at Arkansas State.

Bobby Young scored on a 1-yard run to cap the Indians' opening drive and Dobbs kicked a 20-yard field goal to give Arkansas State its lead.

The two scores, however, would prove to be the only points of the game for the Indians as Lamar rallied for 17 points in the second quarter to lead by a touchdown at halftime.

A 16-yard pass from Haynes to Robinson and a school-record 53-yard field goal by Marlow with the aid of a strong wind tied the game. Haynes connected with Robinson from 3 yards out to give Lamar a 17-10 halftime edge. Marlow added a 45-yard field goal in the third quarter to give the Cardinals a 20-10 victory.

Lamar stayed in Southland contention at 3-1 in the league along with moving to 4-2-1 overall. Arkansas State dropped to 1-3 in the conference and 4-4 overall.

Texas-Arlington, playing only its second Southland game of the season, earned its initial conference victory with a 30-16 triumph at struggling Louisiana Tech. A 25-21 non-conference loss to Northwestern State in the annual State Fair Classic in Shreveport a week earlier snapped Louisiana Tech's eight-game winning streak over the Demons and dropped Tech to 1-6 – guaranteeing the Bulldogs a rare losing season.

Things started off well enough for the Bulldogs against UTA. A Swilley field goal and a pair of touchdown passes by Buchanan allowed Louisiana Tech to take a 16-13 halftime lead. The 16 points were all the Bulldogs would manage, but the Mavericks were just getting started in the second half. A 4-yard run by Phillip Jessie, a 38-yard Brian Happel field goal, and an 11-yard run by Kent Sharp allowed the Mavs to take a 30-16 win to drop Tech to 1-7 overall and 1-3 in conference play.

UT-Arlington made it two conference wins in a row with a whopping 56-18 road domination of Arkansas State.

The Mavericks turned the ball over on their first two possessions of the game but Arkansas State could manage only a Dobbs field goal. UTA traveled 85 yards following Dobbs' field goal, capping the drive on a 28-yard Jessie run.

UT-Arlington led 14-3 before the Indians tightened things up on a 5-yard run by Bradley to make it 14-10 before the Mavs scored the final three touchdowns of the opening half on runs of 3 and 1 yard by Mike Piwonka and an 11-yard run by Tony Felder to lead 35-10 at the break.

The Mavericks, who rushed for 456 yards, added three more touchdowns in the third quarter for the lopsided victory.

Following the loss to UTA, which left Arkansas State with a 1-4 league mark, the Indians dropped non-conference games to Wyoming and Southern Mississippi to end the 1979 season on a five-game losing streak and a 4-7 overall record.

If UTA had any chance at a Southland title, the Mavericks needed a win versus Southwestern Louisiana and a bit of help down the stretch of the 1979 season.

Things looked a bit dicey for the Mavericks at halftime. Despite being limited to 155 yards of total offense in the game, the Cajuns managed to hold a 10-3 lead over Texas-Arlington in the middle of the third quarter thanks to the USL defense. Evidence of that was Rodney Breaux's 59-yard interception return to the UTA 4-yard line to set up Rusty Miller's touchdown run to break a 3-3 tie.

The Cajuns found out a defense can only do so much as the Mavericks rallied for 21 points in the fourth quarter to take a 24-20 victory.

A tired USL defense allowed the Mavericks' wishbone offense to rush for 219 of their 300 yards in the second half. UTA mounted scoring drives of 62, 57 and 53 yards in the fourth quarter. Sharp capped the first drive on a 3-yard run to tie the game. Piwonka scored on runs of 2 and 24 yards to put the game away for the Mavericks.

Texas-Arlington improved to 3-1 in the conference and 7-2 overall. The seven wins were the most for the Mavericks in 12 years. USL fell to 1-3 in the Southland and 4-6 overall.

The help the Mavericks were looking for included a Louisiana Tech upset over McNeese State and a loss by the Cowboys the following week against Southwestern Louisiana.

During most of Louisiana Tech's tenure in the Southland Conference, the final league game of the season either meant the Bulldogs were playing for the conference title or already had the crown secured. It was the complete opposite this time around when Beightol, the embattled Tech coach, and his Bulldogs traveled to Lake Charles to take on unbeaten McNeese State. A narrow 19-17 non-conference loss to North Texas dropped the Bulldogs to 1-8 and extended Tech's losing streak to four games going into the McNeese encounter. The Cowboys went into the game 9-0 after non-league victories over Tennessee-Chattanooga and Northwestern State.

The Bulldogs proved little more than a speed bump to the Cowboys, falling 41-7. Theron McClendon rushed for 212 yards on a SLC-record 46 carries and scored three touchdowns. He proved to be more than an adequate replacement for Shankle, the Southland's leading rusher, who missed the game with an injury. Besides McClendon's effort, other McNeese scores came on a touchdown pass from Millet to Price, a 22-yard run by Gerald Polaski and a pair of Strump field goals. Tech's lone score came with four seconds left in the game on a 28-yard pass from Dunigan to Leland Padgett.

Beightol was not around for Louisiana Tech's season finale against non-conference rival Northeast Louisiana. His 1-9 record caused the powers that be at Tech to dismiss Beightol two days after the loss to McNeese and replace him with interim coach Pat Patterson. In Patterson's only game as head coach, the Bulldogs defeated NLU 13-10 to end the season 2-9. Louisiana Tech's official record would go on to become 3-8 when New Mexico State was forced for forfeit its 34-0 win in the Bulldogs' 1979 season opener.

McNeese's win clinched no worse than a tie for the Southland title for the Cowboys with one game remaining against Southwestern Louisiana. For UTA, the best the Mavericks could now hope for was to capture a piece of the league crown with a win over Lamar and a USL upset of McNeese.

UT-Arlington again did its part, taking a high-scoring 47-37 win at home over the Cardinals.

UTA, which entered the game with the nation's seventh-best rushing offense, amassed 338 yards on the ground. Lamar, boasting the No. 7 passing offense in the country, got 402 yards from Haynes but it was not enough to overcome the Mavericks' ground game.

Leading the way for UTA was Dewalt, the Mavericks' quarterback who rushed for 102 yards and a touchdown. He also threw two touchdown passes.

Texas-Arlington scored in a variety of ways to take a 19-0 lead in the first quarter. Brian Happel kicked a pair of field goals, split end Don DeLeo tossed a 25-yard touchdown pass to tight end Gary Lewis, and Chris Middleton returned an interception 99 yards for a touchdown.

After a 1-yard touchdown pass from Haynes to Booker in the second quarter, Dewalt hit Lewis and Tony Felder with touchdown tosses. A 12-yard touchdown pass by Haynes made it 33-13 at halftime.

The Mavericks finished 4-1 in the Southland and improved to 8-2 overall. UTA went on to finish the year with nine victories on the season following a 48-8 home domination of Idaho State. Lamar closed SLC play at 3-2 while moving to 6-3-1 overall. The Cardinals closed the season with a 24-24 tie against the University of Nevada at Las Vegas to conclude the season 6-3-2.

Having sewn up the Southland Conference title and a postseason bid to the Independence Bowl, the last remaining hurdle of the 1979 regular season for McNeese State was a win at league rival Southwestern Louisiana to record an undefeated season.

Things looked a bit bleak with the Cowboys trailing 6-0 early in the fourth quarter. While McNeese had been blanked for three quarters, USL's early touchdown held up at the start of the final period.

The Ragin' Cajuns were no offensive juggernaut themselves, getting their only points on a 1-yard drive. McNeese's Robert Davenport touched a rolling punt at his own 3 and David Foret recovered for USL at the 1-yard line. A procedure penalty backed up the Ragin' Cajuns, but Dwight Prudhomme, the USL quarterback, eventually scored from a yard out for the Cajuns' 6-0 advantage.

Clinging to its six-point edge, USL lost the ball when a bad pitch by Prudhomme was recovered by Bryan Hicks at the Ragin' Cajun 14. Oliver Hadnot got the call on two-straight carries; the second from 8 yards out tied the game. Stump's conversion gave McNeese a 7-6 lead with 10:11 left in the game.

Moments later, Hicks intercepted a Cajun pass at the USL 21. With 7:28 remaining in the game, the Cowboys had to settle on a 30-yard Stump field goal but the four-point victory was good enough to complete an undefeated regular season for McNeese.

By finishing 11-0, the Cowboys recorded their first unbeaten, untied season since going 8-0 in 1963. McNeese finished Southland play with a perfect 5-0 mark.

Southwestern Louisiana ended its season 4-7 overall, including 1-4 in the SLC.

Played on a Saturday night, McNeese State faced Syracuse in the fourth-annual Independence Bowl in Shreveport. The Orangemen entered the game with a 6-5 record, having played the likes of Eastern powers such as Pittsburgh and Penn State, among others.

While the unbeaten Cowboys may not have faced the type of schedule Syracuse played, McNeese stayed with the Orangemen for most of the contest.

Syracuse only held a 3-0 halftime lead and was up 10-7 before exploding for 21 points in the fourth quarter for a 31-7 victory.

The Orangemen's veer offense eventually took its toll on the Cowboys. Syracuse running back Joe Morris, the future New York Giant, rushed for an Independence Bowl-record 155 yards as the Orangemen amassed 276 yards on the ground and 23 first downs. Syracuse set a new team record with 73 rushing attempts.

Going into the game, Duplechin said, the Cowboys had some experience defending the veer, but it didn't help much.

"We had seen it against Arlington. That wasn't the problem," said Duplechin. "They were more physical than we were. They were a big, strong, physical football team. They ran the option exceptionally well and we had trouble defending it."

McNeese finished the season 11-1, with the defeat at the hands of the Orangemen representing Duplechin's first loss as Cowboys coach.

The two newest Southland coaches seemingly had their teams going in opposite directions when each made their conference debuts in 1980.

Louisiana Tech's Billy Brewer had his Bulldogs 2-2 on the season and riding a two-game winning streak going into Tech's Southland Conference opener at home against Lamar. Brewer took over the Louisiana Tech program after a six-year stint at Southeastern Louisiana, where he posted a record of 38-24-2.

Brewer lost his debut as Louisiana Tech coach as the Bulldogs fell 31-11 to Mississippi State. Following a 38-11 loss to Southern Mississippi, Tech defeated

Western Illinois and East Tennessee State to reach the .500 mark going into the SLC opener.

The league's other new coach, Southwestern Louisiana's Sam Robertson, had his Ragin' Cajuns off to a 3-2 start but on a three-game losing streak going into USL's league opener at home against Arkansas State. Robertson, a former Texas Tech assistant, won his first two games at USL with victories over New Mexico State and East Carolina before the Cajuns dropped three in a row to Fresno State, Northeast Louisiana and North Texas State.

Gaining confidence after splitting their first four non-conference games – three of which came on the road – Brewer's Bulldogs returned home to take on Lamar in Louisiana Tech's Southland opener. A 19-yard touchdown pass from Matt Dunigan to James Greer countered an earlier touchdown pass from Lamar's Ray Campbell to Ben Booker to give Tech a 7-6 halftime lead.

While the Louisiana Tech defense was busy intercepting three passes and limiting the Cardinals to 87 passing yards, the offense was putting the game away in the second half. Tech drove 77 yards with the second-half kickoff, culminating in Leland Padgett's 14-yard touchdown reception. Roberto Dager added a 37-yard field goal in the fourth quarter to make the final 16-7 and improve the Bulldogs to 3-2 overall and 1-0 in league play.

The loss in Lamar's Southland opener dropped the Cardinals to 2-3 overall.

On the same day Brewer was winning his debut game as a Southland coach, Robertson was doing the same at Southwestern Louisiana.

Like Louisiana Tech, the Cajuns finally returned home to open Southland play. The game against Arkansas State was USL's first home game after four straight on the road.

Southwestern Louisiana scored less than five minutes into the game on a 35-yard Larry Trussell field goal. While the kick would be the only points USL would score in the game – it proved to be enough. The Cajuns defense held Arkansas State to 26 yards passing and 136 total yards to gain the shutout victory.

USL was able to win despite four interceptions and a lost fumble in a game with more missed opportunities than scoring.

The Trussell field goal came as the Cajuns took advantage of an Indians mistake. Arkansas State fullback Erven Beasley was stripped of the ball by USL defensive end Andy Martin, with Jeff Holm recovering at the 19.

USL missed out on other scoring opportunities. One such occasion was when an apparent 3-yard touchdown pass from Phillip Reynolds to Barry Herbert was called back because the Cajuns had an illegal man downfield. Reynolds threw an interception to kill the drive. The game's hero, Trussell, missed on a pair of field goals that would have extended the USL lead.

Mark Stadler came up short on a 57-yard field goal to force a tie on the final play of the game.

USL snapped a three-game losing streak to even its record at 3-3 in its conference opener. Arkansas State fell to 1-4. The loss was the fourth in a row for the Indians.

Arkansas State got the 1980 season off to a winning note with a 29-9 victory over Tennessee-Martin but the Indians lost their following three games going into their Southland Conference opener at Southwestern Louisiana.

After a week that featured a mixture of open dates and non-conference games, all six teams were involved in Southland play the following Saturday.

The Cajuns had an extra week to savor the win in their conference opener as one of the two league teams coming off an open date. Returning to action to face Southland foe Lamar at home, USL came up with a big third quarter to beat the Cardinals 38-10 for its largest victory margin ever in an SLC game. The 28-point spread topped the 25-point margin the Cajuns had in a 34-9 victory over Lamar in 1976.

USL led 10-3 at halftime before a 9-yard touchdown pass from Reynolds to Chris Calhoun early in the second half kick-started a 28-point third quarter for the Cajuns. After Rodney Smith broke loose on a 48-yard punt return for a touchdown, Southwestern Louisiana added two more scores in the quarter on a 34-yard touchdown pass from Dwight Prudhomme to Herbert and a 20-yard reverse by Herbert.

Southwestern Louisiana moved to 2-0 in Southland play and 4-3 overall while Lamar fell to 0-2 in the league and 2-5 overall.

Louisiana Tech was unable to match USL's 2-0 league start when the Bulldogs were nipped 21-20 at home against Texas-Arlington a week after Tech's 27-23 non-conference triumph over Northwestern State.

Riding a four-game winning streak while sporting a 4-2 overall record and 1-0 in the Southland, the Bulldogs seemed to be on track for a winning season, especially after building a 17-0 second-quarter lead at home against Texas-Arlington. A touchdown run by Greer, a Dager field goal, and a Dunigan touchdown pass produced the lead, but Tech would only add a third-quarter Dager field goal the remainder of the game.

UTA, meanwhile, rallied to within 20-15 in the fourth quarter. Clinging to a five-point advantage, Greer fumbled at the Tech 44, setting up a 22-yard field goal by Brian Happel with slightly more than eleven minutes left in the game. Another

Bulldogs fumble, this one by George Yates, gave the ball back to the Mavericks at the Louisiana Tech 43. UTA moved the ball down to the 1-yard line to set up Happel's game-winning kick with 5:22 left in the game to give the previously winless Mavs their first victory of the season.

Few might have seen UTA's one-point victory coming. Going into the Louisiana Tech game, the Mavericks lost all six of their non-conference contests. Except for a 38-31 loss to Northwestern State, all of the Mavs' losses were by 10 points or more.

McNeese State was the last Southland team to make its conference debut in 1980. The Cowboys won their first three games of 1980 to stretch McNeese's regular-season winning streak to 15 games, dating back to the final game of the 1978 season.

The streak came to an end when Northwestern State kicker Dale Quickel booted a 19-yard field goal with one second left in the game to knock off the Cowboys 13-10. The defeat was the first-ever regular-season loss for Cowboys coach Ernie Duplechin.

McNeese bounced back with wins over Ball State and Northeast Louisiana to improve to 5-1 going into its Southland opener against 1-5 Arkansas State, the loser of five-consecutive games.

Maybe it was the layoff from an open date or perhaps it was the shock of giving up a touchdown, but the Cowboys needed a bit of time to get started at struggling Arkansas State.

A mishandled punt by Derrick Batiste was recovered by Arkansas State's Mike Morris at the McNeese 40 early in the game. Seven plays later, Tim Langford scored on a 3-yard run to give the Indians a 7-0 lead at the 10:21 mark of the opening quarter. The touchdown was the first in four games for the Indians.

McNeese quarterback Stephen Starring, who would go on to play as a receiver and kick returner with the New England Patriots, capped a 75-yard drive with a 1-yard run and Rusty Guilbeau returned a blocked punt 7 yards for a touchdown to put the Cowboys on top 14-7.

Just as it looked like McNeese had regrouped, the Indians came up with a series of big plays to stretch their advantage to 28-14 late in the second quarter. Langford hooked up with Jerry Mack on an 80-yard bomb to tie the score. Tim Allison returned an errant Starring pass 38 yards for a touchdown to give the lead back to Arkansas State and Beasley galloped 61 yards to give the Indians a two-touchdown lead.

McNeese pulled to within seven points at halftime on a 17-yard pass from Starring to Dwayne Dartez with 1:57 left before intermission.

The big plays stopped for Arkansas State and the second half belonged to the Cowboys. McNeese mounted an 80-yard drive to open the second half, with Theron McClendon scoring on a 1-yard run to pull McNeese to within one point at 28-27. A 12-yard run by Starring ended a 71-yard drive to give the Cowboys a 33-27 lead with 6:13 left in the game before Don Stump kicked a 29-yard field goal to put the game out of reach at 36-28.

"Stump was almost automatic kicking field goals," said Duplechin. "We got to the point where we played a lot for a field goal because we knew we had it in our pocket because he didn't miss any."

While Southwestern Louisiana was defeating Southern Illinois in non-conference action, McNeese State matched the Ragin' Cajuns at 2-0 in the Southland with a 31-17 home win over Texas-Arlington.

McNeese State was tied 10-10 with Texas-Arlington before another fourth-quarter rally allowed the Cowboys to pull away for a 31-17 victory.

The Cowboys' Blue Wall defense forced four Mavericks turnovers, turning three into points. One of the miscues, a fumble by Tony Felder was recovered at the McNeese 28 early in the third quarter. The Cowboys took advantage when Stump kicked a 19-yard field goal to give McNeese a 10-7 lead.

McNeese returned the favor when a Starring fumble led to a 34-yard Happel field goal to tie the game going into the fourth quarter.

One play after Texas-Arlington tied the game, Starring made up for his fumble when he connected with Louis Landry on a 79-yard strike for a 17-10 McNeese edge. Another Mavs fumble, this one recovered by LeRoy Gedward at the UTA 30, set up another score. Starring connected with Mark Barousse on a touchdown toss for a 24-10 lead for the Cowboys with 11:05 showing on the scoreboard clock.

After UTA made it 24-17, the Cowboys put the game away with 6:07 remaining on a 59-yard gallop by Buford Jordan.

A freshman out of Iota, Louisiana, Jordan was a 190-pound running back when he was recruited by Duplechin, then an assistant coach at McNeese.

"His momma was Miss Clara and his daddy weighed about 125 pounds," recalled Duplechin. "I went up there to visit with him and he was outside cooking barbeque, so I ended up having barbeque supper with him."

Jordan, Duplechin said, was always up front with him about his desire to play college football.

"He was big and strong and ran over everybody," recalled Duplechin. "Of course, they played in a Class B classification, which was the smallest classification back in those days but he was big enough to play for anybody.

"He also told me while I was recruiting him that he really wanted to go to LSU but they didn't offer him. He kept telling me, 'If they don't offer me, I'm coming to McNeese.' That's the way it ended up."

By the time his career at McNeese was over, Jordan was the leading rusher in McNeese and Louisiana collegiate history, amassing more than 4,000 yards.

McNeese improved to 2-0 in the SLC and 7-1 overall. Texas-Arlington fell to 1-1 in the league and 1-7 overall.

Louisiana Tech, meanwhile, used a strong ground game to quickly bounce back from its loss to Texas-Arlington with a 28-0 win at Arkansas State. Tech rolled up 274 rushing yards with all four touchdowns coming on the ground. Dunigan and Greer each had a pair of short rushing touchdowns. Greer paced the ground game with 103 yards on 25 carries. The Louisiana Tech defense also made its presence felt, limiting the Indians to three first downs and 82 yards of total offense as Arkansas State's losing streak reached seven games.

The Bulldogs' win moved Louisiana Tech to 2-1 to set up a showdown at home against 2-0 McNeese State.

The Cowboys intercepted Dunigan on the opening play from scrimmage as the Southland Conference's defending champions send a quick message. Eight plays after Leonard Smith's interception, Starring scored on a 7-yard run for a quick lead for the Cowboys.

That set the tone for the regionally-televised game in which the Cowboys scored 35 first-half points on their way to a 45-8 thrashing of Louisiana Tech. The Cowboys' defense held the Bulldogs to 1 net yard rushing and 205 passing in Tech's worst defeat in 12 years at Joe Aillet Stadium.

A 3-yard run by Jordan gave McNeese a 13-0 lead going into the second quarter. The Cowboys added touchdowns runs of 3 yards by McClendon and 5 yards by Starring, plus a 1-yard interception return for a touchdown by Clay Carroll to lead 35-0 at halftime. By contrast, the Bulldogs crossed midfield only once in the opening half.

Tech's only score came in the third quarter on a 9-yard pass from Dunigan to Earl Greer before the Cowboys added the game's final 10 points on a 46-yard Stump field goal and a 2-yard run by Tony Burlingame.

McNeese moved to 3-0 in the SLC with the win and 8-1 overall while Tech fell to 2-2 in the league and 5-4 overall.

Following a non-conference win over Southern Illinois, Southwestern Louisiana returned to Southland play at Texas-Arlington with a chance to match McNeese at 3-0 in the league.

The Cajuns used a pair of touchdown runs by Ed Blanco, a 43-yard Oscar Speer field goal, and a 10-yard touchdown pass from Reynolds to Kevin Sigue to build a 24-0 halftime lead.

The Cajuns were still in solid shape after surrendering a 1-yard run by Mavericks quarterback Scott Logan that made the score 24-6. After a 2-yard touchdown run by Ricky Johnson on the first play of the fourth quarter, things got a bit tighter at 24-13.

Clarence Verdin, who would go on to play in the NFL, mostly with the Indianapolis Colts, helped ease the tension with a 55-yard return to the UTA 40 on the ensuing kickoff following Johnson's touchdown. The Cajuns made sure to make good use of the advantageous field position provide by Verdin as Smith scored on a 4-yard run nine plays later for a 30-13 victory.

The outcome left only USL and McNeese with 3-0 records in the Southland Conference as the Cajuns moved to 6-3 overall. Texas-Arlington fell to 1-8 overall and 1-2 in the conference.

While Southwestern Louisiana and McNeese were alone atop the Southland, Arkansas State was hoping to avoid a loss at Lamar to avoid being the only 0-4 team in the league. Following a 36-10 non-conference loss to Southern Mississippi, the Cardinals went into the Arkansas State game 0-2 in the SLC and 2-6 overall.

Showing off a rarely-used passing game, Arkansas State built a 20-16 halftime edge thanks to a pair of touchdown receptions by Mack, the Indians' tight end. One of his scoring catches was a halfback pass from Waddell Kelly and the other from quarterback Rick Spivey.

A 15-yard run by Booker allowed Lamar to take a 23-20 lead less than 30 seconds into the fourth quarter. The Indians responded with an 81-yard drive but came away with no points when Spivey was picked off in the end zone by Lamar's Demarcus Baxter.

The Arkansas State defense forced a quick punt that was blocked by Elroy Brown for a safety to make it a one-point game. The Indians moved 36 yards following the free kick but a Spivey fumble was recovered by Lamar's Ed Anderson to secure a 23-22 triumph for the Cardinals.

Southwestern Louisiana and McNeese State both were looking for wins the next week to set up a battle of unbeatens in the 1980 Southland season finale. For that to happen, the Ragin' Cajuns needed a win over 2-2 Louisiana Tech while the Cowboys sought a victory over 1-2 Lamar.

The Cajuns wasted little time in trying to dispose of Louisiana Tech at home to set up a showdown against McNeese, jumping out to a 14-0 lead only two minutes into the game. Tech's Austin Kattenbraker fumbled on the opening kickoff, with the ball popping into the arms of Mike Selver. Selver rambled 11 yards for the touchdown and quick 7-0 USL lead.

Tech fumbled early in the ensuing possession, giving the ball right back to the Cajuns at the Bulldogs' 22. Reynolds hooked up with Calhoun on a 13-yard scoring strike and USL was up by 14 points.

The Cajuns were never seriously threatened from that point. All Tech could muster was a first-quarter field goal and a 31-yard pass from Kyle Gandy to Johnny Giordano late in the fourth quarter. USL added a 40-yard run by Blanco and a 17-yard pass from Reynolds to Herbert for a 27-9 victory.

Along with being an all-important 4-0 in the Southland Conference, the Cajuns improved to 7-3 with their fifth-straight triumph. Tech would go on to drop a 19-14 non-conference decision the following week to end the season 5-6 overall and 2-3 in the SLC.

McNeese, meanwhile, spotted Lamar a 3-0 lead but that was all the points the visitors from Beaumont could generate as the Cowboys held up their end of the bargain by cruising to a 35-3 home win over the Cardinals.

Lamar's 3-0 lead came on a 40-yard Jamie Harvey field goal after Starring's first pass of the game was intercepted by Justin Eicher.

Jordan, who rushed for 122 yards in the game, put the Cowboys on top 14-3 at halftime on touchdown runs of 10 and 49 yards in the second quarter. Following a scoreless third quarter, McNeese scored the final 21 points of the game on an 87-yard run by McClendon, a 4-yard run by Burlingame and an 85-yard interception return by Carlton Briscoe. McClendon finished with 164 yards rushing.

McNeese improved to 9-1 on the season while Lamar fell to 3-7.

In the final week of the 1980 regular season, UT-Arlington defeated Lamar 44-27 as both teams finished 3-8 overall. UTA concluded league play 3-2 and Lamar 1-4. Arkansas State defeated Austin Peay 14-9 in non-conference play to snap a nine-game losing streak. The Indians concluded the season 2-9 overall and 0-5 in the SLC.

All eyes, however, were focused on the showdown in Lake Charles.

A constant rain greeted McNeese and Southwestern Louisiana with the Southland Conference title on the line.

Fumbles ended McNeese's first two drives and USL missed out on a scoring opportunity when Trussell's 41-yard field-goal attempt was wide right as neither team could produce points in the early going.

McNeese finally broke a scoreless first half by mounting a 75-yard drive that consumed 12 plays. Runs of 14 yards by McClendon, 10 yards by Jordan and 16 by Starring set up a 27-yard touchdown strike from Starring to Mike Kysar to give the Cowboys a 7-0 lead at the 9:29 mark of the second quarter.

The Cowboys missed an opportunity to stretch their lead late in the third quarter. After Stump pinned the Ragin' Cajuns at the 2-yard line, USL's return punt four plays later by Trussel reached only the 29 and was returned 10 yards by Robert Davenport. The Cajuns held and Stump missed a short field goal with 1:16 left in the quarter.

It remained a one-score game until early in the fourth quarter. Taking over at the USL 48 following a punt, the Cowboys used runs by Jordan and Gerald Polaski to advance down the field. After a penalty against USL moved the ball to the 4-yard line, Jordan powered his way in for a touchdown and a 14-0 win to send McNeese back to the Independence Bowl.

The Cowboys' defense limited USL to only 40 yards rushing. Reynolds completed only 10 passes in 29 attempts for 124 yards and tossed three interceptions. Meanwhile, McNeese got 83 yards rushing from Jordan, 71 from Polaski and 70 from Starring to finish with 292 yards on the ground.

"He could not outrun me. He was slow but he was tough," Duplechin said of Polaski.

Along with finishing the regular season at 10-1, McNeese ended 5-0 in Southland Conference play to claim the league title for the second year in a row.

Although Southwestern Louisiana failed in its quest for the conference championship, the team did finish 7-4 overall in Robertson's first year as Ragin' Cajuns coach.

McNeese fell behind early to Southern Mississippi in its third trip to the Independence Bowl. A 37-yard Winston Walker field goal on USM's second possession of the game and a 14-yard run by Clemon Terrell after a Cowboys fumble at the McNeese 25 gave the Golden Eagles a 10-0 lead late in the first quarter.

The Cowboys cut the deficit to 10-7 with 44 seconds left in the first half. Two Starring pass completions, including an Independence Bowl-record 52-yard strike to Barousse helped to set up a 1-yard touchdown run by Jordan.

Picking up where they left off to close the opening half, the Cowboys drove 80 yards in 13 plays to begin the third quarter. On fourth-and-2 from the USM 11, Jordan appeared to be stopped short of the first down. The Golden Eagles were penalized for being offside, giving new life to McNeese. Two plays later, Starring scored from 2 yards out to give the Cowboys a 14-10 edge.

A 45-yard punt by Southern Mississippi's Bruce Thompson pinned McNeese at its 4-yard line. The Cowboys marched from the shadow of their own end zone and eventually faced fourth-and-2 from the 14-yard line. After Stump had missed two field goals earlier in the game, the Cowboys opted to try and pick up the first down. Jordan was stopped inches short, allowing USM to stay within four points with 9:22 remaining in the contest.

Thompson pinned the Cowboys once again, this time at the 2-yard line with 2:24 left in the game. The helmet of a Southern Miss defender knocked the ball loose from Polaski, with Ron Brown recovering for USM. Mike Woodard scored from a yard out to give the Golden Eagles a 16-14 triumph.

Polaski's fumble was one of four by the Cowboys, two of which the Golden Eagles turned into touchdowns.

The McNeese defense played well enough to win, holding Sammy Winder, the nation's scoring leader to 48 yards. Multi-threat USM quarterback Reggie Collier was limited to 63 yards rushing and 68 passing as the Golden Eagles were held to 250 yards of total offense.

McNeese ended its season 10-2.

NOWHERE TO GO

A pair of teams coming off of demanding early-season schedules met in Texas, as Louisiana Tech visited Texas-Arlington in the 1981 Southland Conference opener for both teams. Tech and UTA, both 1-4, each had a pair of losses against teams from the Southwest Conference. Tech lost to Baylor and Texas A&M, while the Mavericks fell to Texas Christian and Southern Methodist.

Facing such similar backdrops, it seemed as though a hotly-contested game was about to take place. Louisiana Tech struck first when Ronnie Williams scored on a 9-yard run. It was all Mavericks, however, from that point on.

UTA quarterback Scott Logan rushed for 82 yards and passed for 115 more. He scored two rushing touchdowns on runs of 9 and 31 yards. Logan also threw touchdown strikes of 53 yards to Gilbert Smith and 31 yards to Andre Gray. Brian Happel added a 50-yard field goal, all adding up to a 31-14 win for the Mavericks.

After losing its first three games of the regular season, an open date gave Southwestern Louisiana an extra week to savor its first victory of the year – a 31-14 decision over North Texas – before opening Southland play at home against Arkansas State. The Indians went into the game 2-2 on the season.

Arkansas State was leading by a touchdown when the Ragin' Cajuns forced a punt early in the fourth quarter. USL return man Mack Scott awaited the punt. Scott was belted by Joe Fishback as he tried to field the kick. Scott was unable to hold onto the ball, with the Arkansas State defensive back recovering at the Cajuns' 23. Waddell Kelly's 1-yard touchdown gave the Indians a 14-0 lead with 12:18 remaining in the game.

USL followed with a 22-yard Oscar Speer field goal but the Cajuns could get no closer in falling to 1-4 in their conference opener.

Arkansas State moved to 3-2 on the season, the first time the Indians had been over .500 since getting off to a 4-2 start in 1979. Arkansas State went on to drop its final five games that season to finish 4-7.

USL and Arkansas State both missed out on several scoring opportunities.

Arkansas State freshman kicker Scott McDonald, ranked No. 3 in the nation in field goal accuracy, missed two kicks and had a third blocked. The Indians also had a touchdown called back because of an ineligible receiver.

USL, meanwhile, advanced into Indians territory five times in the second half and came up with only the one field goal by Speer.

Looking to bounce back from its loss to UTA, Louisiana Tech hosted Lamar. The Cardinals went into their first Southland Conference game of the season at 3-2. Included in the three wins was a shocking 18-17 victory over Baylor, the defending Southwest Conference champions, in the 1981 season opener when Mike Marlow kicked a 42-yard field goal with three seconds remaining in the game. Lamar's defense held star Bears running Walter Abercrombie to 50 yards on 16 carries.

In the Bulldogs' most balanced offensive output of the season, Louisiana Tech amassed a season-high 484 yards on 268 rushing yards and 216 passing in a 16-7 triumph.

A 25-yard Roberto Dager field goal, set up by a Cardinal turnover at the Lamar 15, gave the Bulldogs a 3-0 lead. Louisiana Tech made it 10-0 on a 25-yard touchdown connection with Chris Tilley. Tilley, the younger brother of former Bulldogs great, Pat, hauled in five catches for 104 yards.

The 10-point advantage stood up until a Lamar touchdown late in the third quarter. Cardinals quarterback Fred Hessen tossed in the direction of his split end. Tech cornerback James Thaxton tipped the ball twice, with Herbert Harris finally coming down with the ball to make it 10-7. Tech's final touchdown came on a 1-yard run by Dunigan with 9:44 left in the game to cap a 69-yard drive.

In the only SLC matchup a week later, McNeese State opened league play at home with a 21-7 home victory over Arkansas State. The Cowboys went into the game 4-2. McNeese lost 24-21 to Ball State in its second game of the season, suffering only its second regular-season loss since Ernie Duplechin became Cowboys coach prior to the start of the 1978 season. The loss snapped an eight-game regular-season winning streak.

Although the Cowboys allowed Arkansas State's wishbone offense to amass 365 yards on the ground, the defense forced the Indians out of their comfort zone.

Arkansas State's Erven Beasley ran for a game-high 188 yards but the Cowboys held the Indians to a net minus-1 yard passing.

McNeese drove 62 yards on its opening possession of the game. Stephen Starring fumbled at the goal line on an attempted 3-yard run for a touchdown but fumbled. Luckily for the Cowboys, Lonnie Collins recovered in the end zone as McNeese took a quick 6-0 lead.

The Cowboys made it 14-0 at halftime on a 40-yard pass from Starring to Mark Barousse and a two-point conversion run by the McNeese quarterback in the second quarter. Buford Jordan, who rushed for 157 yards, scored on a 10-yard run in the third quarter for a 21-0 Cowboys lead.

Arkansas State avoided the shutout when Tim Langford scored on a 26-yard run in the fourth quarter to make the final 21-7 as the Indians fell to 1-1 in the league and 3-4 overall.

Halloween is known as a night of the living dead, so it may have been appropriate that two of the Southland's three conference games that day in 1981 ended in deadlocks, leaving four of the six league teams with ties on their records.

In the case of Louisiana Tech-Southwestern Louisiana game in Ruston, it was a matter of missed opportunities for both teams down the stretch. The score was tied 17-17 when Speer missed from 35 yards out for USL with 3:13 left in the game while Dager's 36-yard attempt as time expired missed to the right.

Trailing 10-7 at halftime, the Bulldogs came up with a break to open the second half when a fumble by USL return man Rennick Tuck was recovered by Aldon Kelly. That led to a 37-yard Dager field goal to tie the game. A pair of long touchdown passes by each team led to the 17-17 tie. Curt Caldarera's 50-yard touchdown pass to Claude Charles gave the Ragin' Cajuns a temporary 17-10 lead until the Bulldogs tied the game on Dunigan's 57-yard strike to Freddie Brown.

On a rainy Saturday night at Lamar, a tie hardly seeming in the offing as the Cowboys trailed the Cardinals 17-3 entering the fourth quarter.

McNeese's lone points came on a 29-yard Stump field goal on the Cowboys' opening possession. The big play in the drive was a 68-yard toss from Starring to Barousse on the second play of the game.

After Lamar tied the game on a 19-yard Marlow field goal, the Cowboys missed out on an opportunity to regain the lead on a 54-yard Stump field-goal attempt. Instead, the kick was blocked and a 42-yard return by Wesley Bryant gave the Cardinals possession at the McNeese 21. Hessen scored on a 1-yard run with less than two minutes remaining in the first half to give Lamar a 10-3 halftime edge.

Lamar built its lead to 17-3 on a 1-yard run by Ben Booker to cap an 82-yard drive in the third quarter before the Cowboys began to rally.

Bill Kingery's recovery of a Cardinal fumble gave McNeese the ball at the Lamar 22. The Cowboys took advantage of the turnover when Jordan scored from a yard out on the first play of the fourth quarter to make the score 17-10.

The Cowboys' deficit grew to 10 points following a 46-yard Marlow field goal.

A second block of a Stump field goal kept the margin at 10 points before the kicker eventually hit from 23 yards out to cut the deficit to seven points.

Moving 52 yards in the game's final two minutes, Jordan, who rushed for 114 yards, scored on a 6-yard run with 16 seconds left in the game to make the score 20-19. Stump's extra point made the final a 20-20 tie.

Despite the blocked field goals, Stump had two field goals and two extra points to become the all-time Louisiana collegiate kick-scoring leader.

McNeese moved to 1-0-1 in the Southland and 5-2-1 overall. The tie left Lamar 0-1-1 in the conference and 3-4-1 overall.

Meanwhile, Arkansas State's game at Texas-Arlington easily could have resulted in another tie as a heavy downpour took place in the second half.

Stacy Price's block of a Mavericks punt early in the third quarter led to a 32-yard McDonald field goal to cut Arkansas State's deficit to 7-3. In the middle of the fourth quarter, Price blocked another punt. That one was returned 3 yards for a touchdown by Melvin Taylor to give the Indians a 10-7 lead.

UT-Arlington reached the Arkansas State 13-yard line late in the game before Mike Morris came up with a fumble recovery to preserve the win for the Indians.

A penchant for low-scoring games suddenly started to work into Arkansas State's favor and helped to put the Indians in Southland title contention. After a 14-3 win over USL, the Indians lost a 3-2 non-conference game to Tennessee-Chattanooga and 21-7 to McNeese, but the 10-7 win over UTA left Arkansas State 2-1 in SLC play.

The lone score of the first half was set up when Tracy Bullard, a UTA defensive back, was inserted into the game at wide receiver and tossed a 39-yard pass to Darryl Lewis to set up a 13-yard touchdown run by Randy Johnson with 59 seconds left in the second quarter.

UTA recovered five of seven Arkansas State fumbles and partially blocked a kick in the first half but only had one touchdown to show for its effort as the Mavericks dropped to 1-1 in the Southland.

Unable to score in the first half against Lamar a week later, Arkansas State only had a total of 19 points over its last 14 quarters. By keeping Lamar's passing game in check, however, the Indians limited the Cardinals to two Marlow field goals to trail only 6-0 at halftime.

Arkansas State's status as a Southland contender seemed in a bit more jeopardy when Marlow connected on a 42-yard field goal early in the third quarter before the Indians began to rally.

An 11-yard run by Arkansas State fullback Maurice Carthon, who would go on to play in the USFL and the NFL, and a 41-yard McDonald field goal on the first play of the fourth quarter gave the Indians a 10-9 lead.

Langford scored on a 4-yard run to give the Indians a 16-9 triumph. The Arkansas State quarterback rushed for a game-high 137 yards in the Indians' wishbone offense.

The Indians, who intercepted four Cardinals passes, improved to 3-1 in the SLC and 5-4 overall. Lamar fell to 0-2-1 in the Southland and 3-4-1 overall.

Carrying over the theme of deadlocked games from the previous week, McNeese State and Louisiana Tech were involved in a 20-20 tie but the home-standing Cowboys were determined not to let that be the final outcome in its Southland Conference encounter against the Bulldogs.

A 17-13 McNeese lead going into the fourth quarter disappeared on a 3-yard run by Carlton Jacobs. Stump tied the game at 20-20 on a 27-yard field goal.

Jordan, who rushed for 118 yards in the game to top the 1,000-yard mark, scored on a 1-yard run with 1:58 left for a 27-20 victory.

Along with Jordan topping 1,000 yards, a couple of other Cowboys reached milestones as well. McClendon rushed for 59 yards to become McNeese State's all-time rusher. He finished the game with 2,797 yards, moving past Larry Grissom into the top spot. Barousse had 62 reception yards to give him 512, a new team single-season mark.

Tech drove on its opening drive to take the early lead on a 1-yard pass from Dunigan to Johnny Rodgers before McNeese countered with touchdown runs of 6 yards by James Galloway and 12 yards by McClendon to lead 14-7 after one quarter.

The Bulldogs made it 14-10 at the half on a 41-yard Dager field goal.

McNeese remained the only unbeaten team in the SLC with a 2-0-1 league mark while improving to 6-2-1 overall. Louisiana Tech dropped to 1-2-1 in the conference and 3-6-1 overall.

In the other game that same day, UT-Arlington, despite the loss to Arkansas State a week earlier, looked to quietly join the Southland Conference race as the Mavericks hosted Southwestern Louisiana.

The Mavericks' ground game proved to be too much for USL as Randy Johnson rushed for 127 yards and Robert Johnson 101 as UTA amassed 383 yards on the ground in a 23-7 victory.

Despite all the rushing yards, the Mavericks only led 10-7 at halftime on a 47-yard run by Logan and a 21-yard Happel field goal. USL's only score came on a 4-yard run by David Chatman that gave the Cajuns a momentary 7-0 lead.

Randy Johnson capped the big rushing effort for the Mavericks with second-half touchdown runs of 8 and 6 yards. USL fell to 0-2-1 in conference play and 1-7-1 overall.

The win improved Texas-Arlington to 2-1 in the Southland and 4-5 overall and set up a key matchup with McNeese State. A victory at home over the 2-1-1 Cowboys would give the Mavericks a half-game lead over McNeese. That, coupled with a Louisiana Tech defeat of Arkansas State, would put the Mavs all alone in first place.

The theme of the 1981 Southland Conference race continued as Texas-Arlington and McNeese were tied 14-14 early in the fourth quarter of their Week 10 encounter.

John Johnson ran wide to his right for a 6-yard touchdown to give the Mavericks a 21-14 lead at the 9:54 mark of the third quarter. The Cowboys responded quickly when Starring scored on a 3-yard run to cap an 80-yard drive, but when Stump suffered his first blocked extra point in 117 attempts, McNeese trailed 21-20.

McNeese got one final chance, reaching the UTA 10 in the final moments. Stump missed a 27-yard field-goal attempt with 21 seconds remaining, dropping the Cowboys from Southland title contention.

The Mavs had a chance to break a 7-7 tie late in the first half but Happel's 19-yard field-goal attempt was blocked by Leonard Smith as time expired. It was Smith's third blocked field goal of the season.

McNeese fell to 2-1-1 in the Southland and 6-3-1 overall. With one conference game remaining, Texas-Arlington moved to 3-1 in the SLC and 5-5 overall.

Louisiana Tech found itself in the role of spoiler and played it to perfection, dominating the Indians 32-0. A pair of touchdown runs by Williams and two Dager field goals helped the Bulldogs put the game away early. A 54-yard bomb from halfback Doyle Adams to Brown on a flea-flicker provided the most exciting score of the night. Backup quarterback John Lee led Louisiana Tech to its final score on a 4-yard pass to tight end Johnny Rodgers with 1:05 left in the game.

Louisiana Tech senior safety Andre Young ended his career on a memorable note, intercepting three passes.

The Bulldogs finished 4-6-1 overall and 2-2-1 in the Southland.

As UTA was moving into first place in the Southland, a pair of 0-2-1 teams squared off to try and avoid the conference cellar as Lamar hosted Southwestern Louisiana.

Taking advantage of a depleted Southwestern Louisiana squad, the Cardinals built a 14-0 lead in the third quarter against the Ragin' Cajuns. USL had suspended 38 players because of team curfew violations and played the game with a host of freshmen.

A 13-yard pass from Hessen to Harris in the second quarter and Larry Hill's 60-yard return of an errant pass by Calderera, the USL quarterback, in the third quarter gave Lamar its 14-0 lead.

Trinion Smith's 13-yard touchdown run in the fourth quarter made the score 14-6. Calderera made amends for the earlier interception when he connected with Smith on a 12-yard touchdown pass but a failed two-point conversion allowed Lamar to hold on for a 14-12 triumph.

On the final week of the regular season, Arkansas State defeated Tulsa 31-7 in a non-conference game to finish the year with a winning season at 6-5 while McNeese State edged Southwestern Louisiana 14-7 to finish 7-3-1 overall and 3-1-1 in the SLC, good enough for second place in the league. USL ended the year 1-9-1 overall, including 0-4-1 in the Southland.

Jordan, the record-setting running back for McNeese State, provided all the offense his team would need in the win at Southwestern Louisiana.

The McNeese running back gained 84 yards to finish the season with 1,276 yards. That set a new Southland Conference single-season mark, topping the old record of 1,266 set by Texas-Arlington's Derrick Jensen in 1977.

Jordan scored both McNeese touchdowns, giving him 18 on the year to set the conference record for most touchdowns in a season.

McNeese built a 14-0 halftime lead behind short touchdown runs by Jordan in each of the first two quarters. Jordan scored on a 6-yard run to cap a 76-yard Cowboys drive to open the game. His second touchdown, from 2 yards out, capped an 80-yard drive. Each scoring possession for McNeese used up more than seven minutes on the clock.

USL made it 14-7 with 4:21 remaining in the third quarter on an 8-yard run by freshman quarterback Don Wallace.

Caldarera, the senior who started the game at quarterback for the Ragin' Cajuns, guided USL on one last drive. Facing fourth-and-16, Caldarera connected with Charles for 22 yards to the McNeese 44. Facing another fourth down from the McNeese 34 with less than a minute remaining, Caldarera was sacked by defensive end Rusty Guilbeau, enabling the Cowboys to end the season with a seven-point squeaker.

McNeese's 3-1-1 mark led to a second-place finish because UT-Arlington made sure to take care of business at home against Lamar as the Cardinals were no match for a UTA team on a mission.

Lamar led 7-3 on an 18-yard touchdown pass from Hessen to fullback Tim Johnson but the Cardinals would not score again for the remainder of the contest. Logan tossed a touchdown pass to Gilbert Smith and rushed for a touchdown while Randy Johnson added a 37-yard scoring run to give the Mavericks a 24-7 halftime lead. Johnson scored on a 3-yard run in the closing minutes for the 31-7 final.

The Cardinals closed the season a week later with a 45-13 loss at Southern Mississippi to conclude the year 4-6-1, 1-3-1 in the Southland.

UTA won the Southland title, it's first since 1967, but eighth-year coach Bud Elliott, the dean of SLC coaches, and his Mavericks, had no place to go. The Independence Bowl, which was created to give the Southland champion a host spot in the postseason game, ended its association with the conference in favor of inviting two at-large opponents.

The Mavericks had to settle for the satisfaction of a 4-1 SLC record, 6-5 overall mark – and a conference championship.

SOUTHLAND DESIGNATED AS DIVISION I-AA LEAGUE

Texas-Arlington's fate would not be repeated in light of the changing landscape of college football in 1982.

The Southland Conference was designated a Division I-AA conference. Instead of playing for a possible bid to the Independence Bowl as in the recent past, the winner of the SLC would now play for a chance to qualify for the Division I-AA playoffs.

Some schools, such as Southwestern Louisiana, elected to play in the larger-school Division I-A. The departure of USL led the Southland to add Northeast Louisiana and North Texas to its ranks, although North Texas would not play a league schedule until 1983 while dropping down in classification. For the 1982 season, the Southland remained a six-team football league.

Along with the addition of Northeast Louisiana, the 1982 season featured a few more changes with the arrival of two new coaches.

McNeese's Ernie Duplechin departed after three highly-successful seasons and Hubert Boales, the Cowboys' defensive coordinator, was elevated to head coach. Duplechin's overall record was 28-6-1, including 13-1-1 in the Southland Conference. His .814 overall winning percentage and .900 mark in the Southland were the highest of any SLC coach.

After three years and a 13-16-2 record, Lamar's Larry Kennan was replaced by Ken Stephens. Stephens took over as head coach of the Cardinals after guiding Central Arkansas to a 67-35-6 record in 10 years.

Northeast Louisiana didn't have to wait very long to make its debut in the Southland Conference on September 25, 1982, hosting defending league champion Texas-Arlington only four weeks into the season. The Indians were guided by second-year coach Pat Collins, formerly a longtime assistant at Louisiana Tech, who was quite familiar with the league.

NLU entered the game against the Mavericks 2-1 on the season after opening with three games on the road. UTA went into the contest 1-1.

A 26-yard touchdown pass from quarterback John Holman to Joey Evans, along with a 1-yard Dwayne Robinson touchdown and a 41-yard Ben Simmons field goal, the latter two set up by Maverick turnovers, gave NLU a 17-0 lead. Scott Caldwell's 22-yard run and a 37-yard Scott Tennison field goal made it 17-9 before Simmons tied his own school record with a 52-yard kick to give the Indians a 20-9 halftime lead.

NLU's defense, which limited Division I-AA's top-scoring offense to only a fourth-quarter touchdown the remainder of the game, came up with a big play early in the third quarter on a 51-yard interception for a touchdown by Bruce Daigle to make the score 27-9. Each team added a touchdown pass as the 33-16 final made the Indians' SLC debut a successful one. The contest in Monroe was played before a Malone Stadium-record crowd of 18,250.

Next for Northeast Louisiana was an encounter with McNeese State. The Cowboys totally dominated the series between the two teams but the Indians set their sights on changing the trend now that Northeast was a member of the Southland Conference. The site of the 1982 McNeese-NLU clash was in Monroe, a place where the Indians had never beaten the Cowboys.

McNeese entered the game 1-3. Boales won his debut as McNeese head coach with a 42-21 victory over Texas A&I but dropped the next three games.

The teams were tied 21-21 when Northeast drove 71 yards, capping the drive on a 2-yard Greg Huskey run to give the Indians a 28-21 lead with 3:05 left in the game. Not wanting to leave the outcome to chance after getting the ball back on a Mike Howard interception of a Stephen Starring pass, Holman fell on the ball for three downs before tossing to Bobby Lewis for 28 yards for a touchdown and a 35-21 Indians victory.

Northeast snapped a 13-game losing streak to McNeese with the win. The Indians improved to 2-0 in the Southland and 4-1 on the season. McNeese fell to 1-4 on the season in dropping its conference opener. The loss represented the first time since 1968 that the Cowboys had lost four games in a row in a season.

While newcomer Northeast Louisiana was getting off to a fast start in the Southland Conference, defending champion UT-Arlington quickly dropped to 0-2 with a 17-14 home loss to Louisiana Tech.

Louisiana Tech entered the game 2-1 on the season. The Bulldogs' lone loss was to Texas A&M after opening with a pair of wins. In the week leading up to the game against the Aggies, Louisiana Tech learned its football program had been placed on two-year probation by the Southland Conference for allegedly offering cash performance bonuses to players in 1980. Tech coach Billy Brewer was not allowed to take part in recruiting for the first year of the probationary period and three scholarships were taken away from 1983-84.

Louisiana Tech grabbed a 7-0 lead less than two minutes into its game against UTA on a 2-yard run by fullback Steve Hartley. The score was set up when Tech's Douglas "Tank" Landry recovered a game-opening fumble. UTA countered with a short Danny Jackson touchdown pass and a 2-yard run by Caldwell to lead 14-7 at halftime.

An 89-yard bomb from Matt Dunigan to Mike Sherman tied the game only seconds into the fourth quarter. The Mavericks squandered an opportunity to take the lead when Tennison missed a 36-yard field goal attempt. Following the miss, Tech drove to the Texas-Arlington 17. Roberto Dager, who had hit on only one of five field-goal attempts, booted a 34 yarder with 11 seconds remaining to give the Bulldogs a 17-14 triumph.

A week later, longtime rivals Louisiana Tech and Northeast Louisiana met for the first time as members of the Southland Conference. Played in Monroe, a home-record crowd as 23,950 packed Malone Stadium to witness two Top 10 teams. It was the second time during the 1982 season that NLU set a single-game attendance record.

The game was as closely contested as expected with the only points of the first half coming on a 10-yard run by Ronnie Williams for No. 10 Louisiana Tech on the Bulldogs' opening drive of the game. Seventh-ranked NLU tied the game 7-7 in the middle of the third quarter when Feotis Moore's 1-yard run capped an 81-yard drive. The Indians took their first lead of the game at 10-7 on a 47-yard Simmons field goal with 1:07 left in the third quarter.

Tech came up with two quick scores in the fourth quarter. A 2-yard touchdown pass from Dunigan to tight end Bobby Fowler put the Bulldogs on top 14-10. Doyle Adams' interception of a Holman pass on the first play of the ensuing drive led to a 20-yard Dager field goal and a 17-10 Louisiana Tech lead.

Now down by seven points, Northeast Louisiana, behind the passing of Holman, had one last chance. Going exclusively with the passing game, the Indians eventually had first-and-goal from the Tech 2-yard line. Robinson carried across the goal line, but NLU was penalized for illegal motion, wiping out the score. The call pushed back the Indians to the 7, where Holman was tackled for a 1-yard loss on first down. After an incomplete pass on second down, Holman tried to get the ball to Tag Rome. James Thaxton intercepted the pass in the end zone with 30 seconds remaining, handing the Indians their first-ever loss in the Southland Conference.

Northeast lost the game despite a record-setting performance by Holman. His 32 completions in 66 attempts were both new school records. He also passed former Tulane quarterback Roch Hontas and Grambling's Doug Williams to become the all-time completions leader in Louisiana collegiate history.

After a pair of close games that came down to the closing seconds, Louisiana Tech changed the script a bit against a 3-2 Lamar team, which was playing its first Southland Conference game of the season under Stephens, the new Cardinals coach

Although Louisiana Tech dominated most of its game against the Cardinals, a pair of costly turnovers by the Bulldogs allowed Lamar to stay within 21-13 mere seconds into the second half. Tech then scored 19-unanswered points, including 16 in the final quarter, to post a 40-13 victory.

Dunigan tossed three touchdowns in the game, including two in the first half. Tech led 21-7 at halftime, with Lamar's lone score of the period being a 7-yard run by Parnell Lykes that was set up on a Roderick Arterberry fumble at the Louisiana Tech 5-yard line. A fumble by Dunigan when he was blindsided in the end zone was recovered by the Cardinals for a touchdown only 50 seconds in the second half to make the score 21-13.

The Bulldogs would not let this game come down to the final seconds. A Dager field goal, a short Dunigan touchdown pass and a safety helped to contribute to the final score. Louisiana Tech moved to 3-0 in the Southland Conference with the win. At 5-1 overall, the Bulldogs won more games through six games than they did during the entire 1981 season.

On the same day Lamar was playing its initial Southland game of the season, Arkansas State also was making its conference debut at home against Northeast Louisiana. Arkansas State went into the game 3-2, its two losses coming to a pair of Southeastern Conference schools, Mississippi State and Alabama.

Another record crowd - this time 18,828 in Jonesboro - showed up to watch the battle of the Indians. A 3-yard run by Robinson and a 13-yard pass from Holman to Lewis gave Northeast Louisiana a 14-0 lead. Arkansas State rallied for the final 13 points of the first half on a 58-yard Maurice Carthon run and a 1-yard touchdown by Waddell Kelly to trail 14-13 at intermission.

Northeast Louisiana held a slim 17-13 lead when NLU came up with two quick scores in the fourth quarter. A 37-yard touchdown pass from Holman to tight end Bobby Craighead put Northeast on top 24-13. Keith Weaver fumbled on the ensuing kickoff, with Jerry Thurman recovering at the Arkansas State 13. Moore galloped the needed yardage on the next play for the touchdown, giving Northeast 14 points in the span of nine seconds to turn a close game into an eventual 31-21 victory.

Arkansas State fell to 0-2 in Southland play a week later with a 21-10 home loss to McNeese State.

Needing a win to even its Southland mark at 1-1, McNeese got the ball back at its own 18-yard line in the closing moments of the first half while trailing 10-0 at Arkansas State.

The Cowboys managed to pull to within three points at halftime when Flip Johnson scored on a 12-yard run with 11 seconds remaining in the second quarter to make it 10-7.

Arkansas State, which lost five fumbles, came up with a costly turnover in the third quarter when a fumble gave McNeese the ball at the Indians' 49-yard line. Johnson made Arkansas State pay dearly when he scored on a 4-yard run to put the Cowboys on top 14-7. Buford Jordan put the game away with 1:18 remaining on a 14-yard run for a 21-10 McNeese victory.

Along with the five fumbles, the Cowboys also forced an Arkansas State interception and cornerback Leonard Smith, who would go on to play with the NFL's Cardinals, blocked the 14th kick of his career. After allowing the Indians 214 yards rushing, the McNeese defense held Arkansas State's ground game to 92 yards in the second half.

Arkansas State took a 10-0 lead on a 44-yard Scott McDonald field goal in the first quarter and a 1-yard touchdown run by quarterback Rick Spivey in the second quarter.

A tough stretch of Southland Conference games continued for Arkansas State when the Indians hosted second-ranked Louisiana Tech.

Coming off a 33-0 blanking of Northwestern State in the State Fair Classic to secure the Bulldogs' first winning season since 1978, Dunigan passed for two touchdowns and rushed for another against Arkansas State. Dunigan's 3-yard scoring run, along with touchdown passes of 64 yards to Sherman and 31 yards to Austin Kattenbraker helped Tech take a 21-7 lead. Weaver's 5-yard touchdown pass from quarterback Tim Langford made it 21-14 with 7:20 left in the game.

Nursing a seven-point lead, Dunigan tried to recover a fumbled pitch to Carlton Jacobs. A personal foul call for a late hit on Dunigan was called against the Indians. Arkansas State coach Larry Lacewell ran on the field to protest the call. Another personal foul penalty was called against the Indians. The infractions moved the ball to the Arkansas State 33 and eventually led to a 41-yard Dager field goal with 3:56 remaining to ice the game at 24-14 for the Bulldogs.

The win improved Tech to 4-0 in league play and clinched no worse than a tie for the conference title. Arkansas State fell to 0-3 in the Southland and 3-5 overall.

Looking to keep pressure on Louisiana Tech, Northeast Louisiana's defense was imposing at Lamar – and it needed to be. That's because Northeast had its own problems on offense. The only points the Indians could muster were two first-half touchdown passes from Holman to Alfred Kinney.

Lamar had first-and-goal at the Northeast Louisiana 8-yard line late in the third quarter. After a penalty moved the Cardinals back to the 13, running back George Landry was brought down for a 2-yard loss. Bruce Daigle's sack of Lamar quarterback Dale Brannan pushed Lamar back to the 30. Facing fourth down from the 11, Brannan's pass intended for Herbert Harris was tipped away by Howard in the end zone.

The Cardinals reached the NLU 24 later in the game but the drive ended when Indian defensive end Barry Broussard tugged the ball away from Brannan. Brannan was sacked six times in the game while the Northeast defense, which posted back-to-back shutouts, also forced a fumble and picked up a sack.

Northeast finished the SLC portion of its schedule 4-1. NLU went on to split its final two non-conference games with a loss to Southwestern Louisiana and a victory over Northwestern State to conclude the season at 8-3.

Despite a 1-4 start, McNeese State put itself in the thick of the Southland Conference race with a 38-12 home win over Texas-Arlington to move to 2-1 in league play and set up a showdown with No. 2 Louisiana Tech.

McNeese jumped out to a 20-0 halftime lead against UTA on a 20-yard run by Starring and a pair of short touchdown runs by Jordan. The tailback scored on a 1-yard run in the third quarter to make it 28-0. Jordan ran for 135 yards in the game to become the school's all-time rusher with 2,966 yards.

UTA scored twice in the second half on an 8-yard run by Randy Johnson in the third quarter and an 8-yard pass from Danny Jackson to Byron Williams with two minutes left in the game.

With Louisiana Tech already having clinched a share of the Southland Conference title, the best the visiting 2-1 Cowboys could do was force a potential tie for the league crown.

Dunigan made sure that didn't happen, passing for four touchdowns and rushing for another in the Bulldogs' 35-14 romp over the Cowboys.

McNeese grabbed a 7-0 lead when Starring scored on a 1-yard run on the game's opening drive. Dunigan, who completed his first 10 passes, hooked up with Williams on a 6-yard toss to make it 7-6.

A fumble at the McNeese 13 set up Dunigan's second touchdown pass, this one to Jerry Jones to give Tech a 12-7 edge. After Starring was tackled in the end zone for a safety by Trey Junkin, Dunigan hit Williams with a 5-yard strike following the free kick to make it 21-7. McNeeese missed out on a chance at points early in the second quarter when Johnson fumbled at the Bulldogs' 1-yard line. Junkin would go on to play for six NFL teams over a 19-year career.

McNeese made it 28-14 early in the fourth quarter on a 39-yard scramble by Starring before the Bulldogs countered on a 7-yard pass from Dunigan to Kattenbraker.

The Cowboys, who fell to 2-2 in the Southland and 4-5 overall, lost Jordan on the second series of the game with a shoulder injury.

With the Southland title secure, the Bulldogs split two non-conference games, falling to Southwestern Louisiana 29-19 to snap a six-game winning streak before edging Southern Mississippi 13-6 to close the regular season at 9-2 in a tune-up for the first-ever Division I-AA playoffs.

Louisiana Tech's win and Northeast Louisiana's 4-1 Southland mark meant the rest of the conference was closing out the season trying to avoid the league cellar.

With Lamar 0-2 going into its home game against 0-3 Arkansas State, the loser of the game seemed a pretty sure bet to finish at the bottom of the league standings.

After going two games without scoring a point in losses of 24-0 to Southwestern Louisiana and 14-0 to Northeast Louisiana, the Cardinals took an early 7-0 lead against Arkansas State on a first-quarter touchdown pass from Brannan to Harris.

When Indians return man Harold Mason stepped back into the end zone on the ensuing kickoff, the resulting safety put Lamar on top 9-0. The lead didn't last as touchdown runs of 15 and 10 yards by Langford gave the Indians a 14-9 edge. Lamar went on to lead 16-14 at halftime on a 5-yard run by Brannan.

Jamie Harvey's 43-yard field goal extended the Cardinals' lead to five points at 19-14 until the closing moments. On fourth-and-15 from his own 11, Kelly broke loose after hauling in a shovel pass from Langford and sprinting 89 yards for a touchdown to give the Indians a 20-19 triumph.

Arkansas State improved to 4-5 overall in snapping a three-game losing streak. Lamar dipped to 3-6 as its losing skid was extended to four games.

Lamar showed it wasn't quite ready for the conference cellar a week later at McNeese State. Reeling from their loss to Louisiana Tech, the Cowboys could produce only three points in a 12-3 loss to Lamar. Both teams moved to 4-6 overall in the Cardinals' first Southland Conference win of the season while McNeese State was guaranteed its first losing season since 1970.

An exchange of field goals led to a 3-3 tie at halftime. Lamar's Ricky Hernandez booted his first collegiate field goal from 49 yards while Tony Whittington hit from 22 yards with 37 seconds remaining in the second quarter.

Lamar took a 9-3 lead on a 39-yard pass from backup quarterback Fred Hessen to Harris. Hessen entered the game in place of Brannan, the injured starter. The Cardinals put the game away on a 25-yard Fernandez field goal.

McNeese ended its season with a 10-10 tie with Southwestern Louisiana to end the season 4-6-1.

Arkansas State edged Texas-Arlington 20-17 to finish 2-3 in the Southland while reaching the .500 mark overall at 5-5. The Indians concluded the season with a losing record, however, with a 12-0 loss to Memphis. The result of the Arkansas State-UTA game meant the final week of the regular season would decide last place in the conference between the Mavericks and Lamar.

Lamar went into its home game against Texas-Arlington 1-3 in the Southland while the Mavericks were 0-4.

The score was tied 17-17 at halftime before Caldwell scored on a 2-yard run in the third quarter for Texas-Arlington. He added a 66-yard scoring romp in the fourth quarter on his way to a three-touchdown, 136-yard effort.

Both teams concluded the season 1-4 in the Southland. Lamar ended its season 4-7 overall and UTA 3-8.

Louisiana Tech was able to host its first-ever Division I-AA playoff game, taking on South Carolina State. Spotting S.C. State a 3-0 lead, the Bulldogs barked back with a Dager field goal and two long scoring drives. The first one, which covered 80 yards, ended on a 3-yard Dunigan toss to Gerald McDaniel. The other drive, consisting of 95 yards, culminated on a 1-yard quarterback sneak. The big play of the drive was a 59-yard Freddie Brown reception down to the South Carolina State 5-yard line as the Bulldogs took a 17-3 halftime lead.

The Bulldogs just added on from there, with two second-half touchdowns being set up by the Tech defense. A 46-yard interception return by Steve Fisher helped to set up a 3-yard touchdown reception by Jacobs. A 65-yard rumble by defensive end Jimmy Hand of another interception by backup quarterback Lamont Green, set up a 1-yard Dunigan sneak as Louisiana Tech went on to take a 38-3 win.

South Carolina State went into the game limiting opponents to 191 total yards. Tech rolled up 474 yards with Dunigan throwing for 211. S.C. State entered the game with I-AA's fifth-best rushing offense, averaging 246.7 yards per outing. The Bulldogs held their playoff opponent to 50 rushing yards on 43 carries.

Louisiana Tech was playing in Ruston but the University of Delaware seemed more at home in the Division I-AA semifinals. Poor weather conditions and a tough defense stifled the normally-potent Bulldogs passing attack. The Blue Hens' defense also helped to set up an opportunistic Delaware offense in a 17-0 win to eliminate Tech.

Dunigan, the future Canadian Football League Hall of Fame quarterback, playing his last game for Louisiana Tech, passed for 285 yards while completing less than 50 percent of his passes on a sloppy field. The Delaware defense also picked off three passes and limited the Bulldogs to 46 yards rushing.

With Louisiana Tech attempting to punt, Lou Reda blocked and then recovered a punt by Bulldogs punter Brett Brewer at the Louisiana Tech 24. Five plays later, quarterback Rick Scully scored from 2 yards out to give Delaware a 7-0 lead with 5:47 remaining in the opening quarter.

The lone touchdown held up until early in the fourth quarter when a 19-yard punt by Brewer gave the Blue Hens excellent field position at the Tech 31. A 2-yard sweep by Kevin Phelan six plays later made it 14-0. An interception return down to the Tech 46 by Delaware safety Jim Pawloski set up the game's final score, a 22-yard K.C. Knobloch field goal with 6:55 left in the game.

Louisiana Tech, which ended its season at 10-3, missed out on several scoring opportunities. The first came on the game's opening drive when Sherman raced to the Blue Hens' 26-yard line but fumbled after a 35-yard reception. Later in the first half, the Bulldogs reached the Delaware 13 with 21 seconds left, but a fumbled snap on third down cost valuable seconds before the clock ran out on a fourth-down pass to Kattenbraker. A long pass by Dunigan to a wide-open Brown at the Blue Hens' 5-yard line glanced off the fingertips of the Tech receiver.

With North Texas State competing for Southland honors in 1983, the SLC had a six-game league schedule for the first time in conference history.

Along with the addition of North Texas, other changes in the Southland Conference for 1983 included a pair of coaching changes.

The last time Louisiana Tech went looking for a head football coach in 1980, it traveled no farther than south Louisiana to pluck Billy Brewer away from Southeastern Louisiana University. Brewer parlayed his three-year stint into the head job at Ole Miss after leading the Bulldogs to the Division I-AA semifinals in 1982.

Tech's search for Brewer's successor led to what seemed like the school's own backyard with the hiring of A.L. Williams from nearby Northwestern State in Natchitoches. Williams, a Louisiana Tech graduate, amassed a 38-46-0 record in eight seasons as coach of the Demons.

In an unusual move, Hubert Boales was replaced as McNeese State head coach after going 4-6-1 in his only season at the helm of the Cowboys. John

McCann was named the new head man, with Boales taking McCann's position on the Cowboys' staff as defensive coordinator. Boales had been McNeese's defensive coordinator before replacing Ernie Duplechin in 1982.

Northeast Louisiana visited Texas-Arlington and was the first two Southland teams to open conference play in 1982. The Indians entered the game 1-1 on the season, falling 10-9 at Indiana State in their opener before losing 31-6 at home to Southwestern Louisiana. UT-Arlington entered the game 0-1 after a 21-14 loss to Western Michigan.

The Indians held a slim 13-10 halftime lead as Northeast Louisiana yielded 172 yards of total offense to the Mavericks. The NLU defense turned things around in the second half, holding the Mavs to only two first downs and 36 yards offense as the Indians went on to post a 16-10 victory.

The teams traded scores in the first half. Field goals by UTA's Scott Tennison and Northeast Louisiana's Jesse Garcia led to a 3-3 tie after one quarter. Texas-Arlington countered a 3-yard touchdown run by Bobby Craighead with a 42-yard gallop by Scotty Caldwell for a 10-10 tie in the second quarter. Northeast pulled ahead 13-10 on a 41-yard field goal by Garcia on the final play of the first half. The only score of the second half, a 27-yard field goal by NLU's Scott Martin, helped provide the Indians with their six-point triumph.

Craighead, who rushed for 136 yards, switched to tailback after playing tight end a year earlier as the Indians sought more of a ground attack in 1983. He rushed for 158 yards in the season opener against Indiana State.

Maybe it was playing before a national TV audience on WTBS, or perhaps it was playing on a Thursday night, but something seemed to bring out the best in Northeast Louisiana in its home game against Arkansas State.

Despite the short week of preparation, Northeast amassed a school-record 317 yards on the ground while holding Arkansas State, the nation's fifth-best rushing team, to 94 ground yards. Also, NLU continued its propensity for turning an opponent's mistakes into points in taking an eye-opening 45-7 win.

Late in the first quarter, Bubba Ash's recovery of an Arkansas State fumble gave Northeast the ball at the A-State 35. Four plays later, NLU had a 7-0 lead. Shortly after taking a 14-0 lead, safety Bruce Daigle returned an interception down to the 1-yard line to set up another quick score for Northeast Louisiana.

The SLC-opening loss dropped Arkansas State to 2-2 on the season.

Two days later, Williams made his Southland coaching debut as Louisiana Tech hosted Lamar. Williams was still seeking his first win as Bulldogs coach as Tech was off to a 0-2 start with losses to New Mexico State and Southern Mississippi. Lamar went into its first SLC game of the year 1-2.

Playing at home for the first time in 1983 did nothing to help the Bulldogs' early-season turnover problems against Lamar. For the second time in three games, Louisiana Tech turned the ball over a school-record 10 times. Including the five turnovers in the Southern Mississippi contest, the Bulldogs turned the ball over 25 times in their first three games.

Lamar only managed 85 yards total offense against Louisiana Tech but got more than enough help from the mistake-prone Bulldogs as Tech had six interceptions and four lost fumbles in an 18-12 Cardinals triumph. Cornerback Donald Rawls picked off three of the errant throws, and of the turnovers, six came in the first half as Lamar built an 18-0 lead.

Mitchell Bennett returned a punt 60 yards for a touchdown, Ricky Fernandez kicked a 23-yard field goal and a safety when Tech quarterback Jordan Stanley was tackled in the end zone provided the Cardinals with their first-quarter points. A 2-yard pass from Ray Campbell to Louis Landry in the second quarter made it 18-0 at the break.

Louisiana Tech's lone touchdown came on a 1-yard run by Nate Williams in the third quarter. Rodney Clay, Lamar's backup quarterback, took an intentional safety in the fourth quarter that narrowed the score to 18-9. Roberto Dager's 29-yard field goal pulled Tech to within 18-12 with 4:25 left in the game.

After a week in which all seven Southland teams either played non-conference games or had open dates, North Texas State finally made its SLC debut against Arkansas State.

Played Oct. 8, 1983, in Little Rock, the Eagles used a balanced offense and strong defense to blank Arkansas State 17-0. North Texas rushed for 123 yards and passed for 131 while the Eagles' defense came up with three fumbles, two sacks and two interceptions.

A 43-yard Todd Smith field goal early in the second quarter gave North Texas a 3-0 lead. Following a fumble by Arkansas State quarterback Tim Langford at the Indians' 32, a 27-yard strike from Eagles quarterback Greg Carter to Brady Davis helped set up a 6-yard touchdown toss to Tim Wasson for a 10-0 lead at the 7:35 mark of the second quarter. The game's only other score came in the middle of the fourth quarter on a 9-yard draw by fullback Carlen Charleston.

The victory in the Eagles' Southland Conference debut improved North Texas to 4-2. North Texas gave Corky Nelson a win in his debut with a 32-3 victory over West Texas. Following a 20-13 loss to Oklahoma State, the Eagles beat New Mexico State and New Mexico while losing to Texas leading up to the Arkansas State game.

Arkansas State's fourth-consecutive loss dropped the Indians to 0-2 in the Southland and 2-4 overall.

Making his Southland debut as a head coach the same day was McCann of McNeese State. The Cowboys went into their game at Louisiana Tech 3-1. McNeese opened with wins over Northwestern State, Southeastern Louisiana and West Texas before falling to Nicholls State. In the win over West Texas, McNeese running back Buford Jordan rushed for 172 yards to run his career total to 3,408 to become the Southland Conference's all-time rusher.

An open date gave the Cowboys an extra week to prepare for their game against Louisiana Tech, which was coming off a 17-14 triumph over Tennessee-Chattanooga.

McNeese got off to a slow start despite the rest, falling behind 17-0 at halftime. David Brewer tossed two first-quarter touchdowns, one from 13 yards out to Chris Tilley and the other a 6-yard strike to Karl Terrebonne. Dager added a 23-yard field goal in the second quarter to make it 17-0 at the break.

Feeling a sense of urgency, the Cowboys drove 74 yards on their opening possession of the second half to get on the scoreboard on a 1-yard run by Don Richards. Art Hamilton's interception of a Brewer pass at the Bulldogs' 36 set up a 21-yard Tony Whittington field goal as McNeese pulled to within a touchdown at 17-10 going into the final quarter.

Hamilton picked off another errant Brewer pass moments later, leading to a 5-yard Jordan touchdown run to tie the game four plays into the fourth quarter.

Louisiana Tech regained the lead on a 43-yard Dager field goal and Steve Fisher's interception of a Cowboys pass with 3:51 left in the game seemed to have the Bulldogs on the brink of victory.

The Bulldogs were forced to punt after the interception, giving the ball back to the Cowboys at the McNeese 22-yard line with 2:12 left in the game. A 42-yard pass from Richards to Keith Ortego, along with runs of 5 yards by Jordan and 11 by Richards moved the Cowboys to the 10-yard line. Jordan, who rushed for 152 yards in the game, waltzed along the sideline for the game-clinching touchdown with 17 seconds remaining to give McNeese a 24-20 triumph.

On the same day North Texas and McNeese were playing their first Southland games of the season, Northeast Louisiana had a chance to make its SLC mark 3-0 with a win at Lamar. An open date, coming off the heels of the Thursday game against Arkansas State, left NLU idle for 16 days going into the Lamar game while the Cardinals entered the contest coming off a 15-14 loss to Texas Southern.

The layoff had Northeast coach Pat Collins a bit concerned about his team's offensive timing. The rust was evident early as quarterback Rodney Horn connected on only 5 of 15 passes in the first half.

What the break also seemed to do was give fresh legs to the NLU defense. The Indians constantly harassed Lamar's quarterbacks, sacking them 11 times for more than 70 yards in losses. The defense also staved off an early threat by the Cardinals when David Outley intercepted a pass in the end zone on a drive that was set up by a Craighead fumble at the NLU 42.

After a scoreless first quarter, the Indians took a 2-0 lead when an attempted lateral by quarterback Rodney Clay deep in Lamar territory went through the end zone for a safety. A 47-yard Garcia field goal following the ensuing free kick made it 5-0. A 1-yard run by Craighead made it 11-0 at halftime. The only score of the second half came when backup quarterback Alvin Brown tossed a 28-yard touchdown pass to Tag Rome in the fourth quarter to give Northeast a 17-0 win.

With Northeast Louisiana playing a non-conference game against Nicholls State the following week, it gave the rest of the Southland Conference teams a chance to pick up a bit of ground on the Indians. Taking full advantage was North Texas as the Eagles pulled off a 17-10 victory at McNeese State to move their SLC record to 2-0.

The Cowboys lost more than a Southland Conference game as Jordan suffered a knee injury late in the first half. He rushed for 49 yards prior to the injury, leaving him 163 yards shy of becoming the all-time rusher in Louisiana collegiate history.

Four plays into the game, North Texas had a 7-0 lead on a 62-yard punt return by Tony Meriwether. Derrick Batiste's 49-yard punt return later in the opening quarter helped to set up a 7-yard pass from Richards to Richard Andrews to tie the game. The Mean Green took a 10-7 halftime lead on a 25-yard Thomas Bresnehan field goal with 3:13 remaining before intermission.

North Texas built its lead to 10 points at 17-7 when Carter scored on an 8-yard run to cap a 65-yard drive early in the fourth quarter.

The Cowboys failed to take advantage of favorable field position in the second half. McNeese began four possessions inside North Texas territory but capitalized only once on a 32-yard Whittington field goal with 4:38 left in the game for the 17-10 final.

Texas-Arlington and Arkansas State, meanwhile, each picked up their first Southland wins of the season. UTA blanked Lamar 21-0 while Arkansas State topped Louisiana Tech 21-7.

Randy Johnson rushed for 111 yards and two touchdowns in the Mavericks' win over Lamar. UTA, which evened its record at 1-1 in the Southland and 3-3 overall, recorded its first shutout since blanking Idaho State 48-0 in 1979. Lamar dropped to 1-2 in the conference and 2-5 overall.

Johnson set the tone early, racing 39 yards to set up his first touchdown run from a yard out to give Texas-Arlington a 7-0 lead on its initial possession of the game.

The 7-0 lead stood up until the fourth quarter when Caldwell scored from a yard out to make it 14-0. A fumble by Lamar's Ron Garner on the ensuing kickoff at the Cardinals' 37 eventually led to Johnson's 3-yard touchdown run for the 21-0 final.

Arkansas State scored on its first three possessions of the game on two short touchdown runs by Langford and a 19-yard scamper by Dwayne Pittman. Langford, whose second touchdown gave Arkansas State a 21-0 lead, actually fumbled the ball into the end zone, but was recovered by Pittman. Tech, 0-3 in the SLC, got its lone score on a 24-yard pass from Brewer to Tilley with 2:42 remaining in the game. Arkansas State improved to 2-1 in the league.

The Indians made it two-in-a-row with a 24-14 victory at McNeese State.

Keying Arkansas State's win was its wishbone offense as McNeese surrendered 325 yards on the ground in falling behind 24-0.

Arkansas State led 21-0 at halftime on first-quarter touchdowns runs of 28 and 48 yards by Pittman. Langford added a 2-yard run in the second quarter.

After the Indians extended the lead to 24-0 on a 28-yard Scott McDonald field goal in the third quarter, McNeese came up with its two scores in the fourth quarter on touchdown runs of 5 and 24 yards by Simon Jordan, the younger brother of Buford.

Non-conference victories over Nicholls State and Southeastern Louisiana extended 6-1 Northeast Louisiana's winning streak to six games going into its Southland Conference home game against McNeese State.

An inspired NLU defense limited the Cowboys to two first-half field goals by Whittington. The Northeast offense got a record-tying performance by Garcia. Garcia, who missed four field goals, including three from beyond 50 yards in a season-opening loss to Indiana State, booted three field goals in excess of 50 yards against McNeese. The only other time such a feat took place in NCAA history was when Wyoming's Jerry Depoyster kicked three field goals beyond 50 yards in a win over Utah State in 1966.

Garcia's effort alone would have been enough to give the Indians the win in a 37-6 triumph. More than enough insurance was provided by a pair of touchdown passes from Horn to Rome, a 12-yard run by Chris Lott and a 93-yard kickoff return by Craighead.

The victory was the seventh straight for the Indians since their 10-9 season-opening loss. The result of the McNeese game, coupled with Louisiana Tech's surprising 25-18 win at North Texas, gave NLU sole possession of first place in the Southland Conference.

Following a week off, the Eagles seemed on their way to a big Southland win at home over Louisiana Tech before Brewer, the Bulldogs' quarterback, got hot in the final five minutes of the game.

Brewer fired two touchdowns to rally Tech to a 19-18 lead, with the go-ahead score coming on an 8-yard touchdown pass to Tilley with 27 seconds left in the game. On the ensuing possession, Douglas "Tank" Landry deflected a pass by Carter. Tech safety Ray Wilmer came up with the ball and raced 38 yards for a touchdown with 11 seconds left in the game for the 25-18 final to improve the Bulldogs to 1-3 in the SLC as North Texas dropped to 2-1.

Arkansas State was unable to make it three straight, falling at home to a suddenly hot Texas-Arlington squad 28-19.

The Indians fell behind 21-0 before starting to rally. A 12-yard halfback pass by Erven Beasley late in the third quarter and a 49-yard scoring run by Langford early in the fourth quarter made it 21-19.

UT-Arlington countered by driving 76 yards. Facing third-and-13 near midfield, a 38-yard pass from reserve quarterback Kraig Hopkins to Andre Gray kept the drive alive. Two plays later, Caldwell, who rushed for 128 yards, scored to make the final 28-19.

The loss dropped Arkansas State to 2-3 in the Southland and 4-5 overall. UTA's fifth win in its last six outings improved the Mavericks to 2-1 in the SLC and 5-3 overall.

Teams streaking in opposite directions met a week later in Lake Charles when McNeese State played host to Texas-Arlington. UTA was riding a four-game winning streak while the Cowboys lost three-straight games heading into the Southland Conference affair.

A 47-yard Whittington field goal provided the only points of the first half. McNeese stretched its lead to 10-0 in the middle of the third quarter on a 6-yard run by Subester Brooks, who was making his first start at quarterback for the Cowboys.

The Mavericks finally got on the scoreboard early in the fourth quarter on a 1-yard run by Randy Johnson to cap an 80-yard drive early in the fourth quarter before tying the game on a 36-yard Scott Pennison field goal.

McNeese State regained the lead on a 36-yard Whittington field goal for a 13-10 Cowboys advantage. In the closing minute of the game, McNeese fullback Ronnie Landry scored on a 5-yard run after Batiste intercepted a deflected Danny Jackson pass and a facemask penalty set up the Cowboys at the UTA 13.

Texas-Arlington tacked on a touchdown on a 10-yard pass from Jackson to Gray with 33 seconds left in the game as McNeese held on for a 20-16 triumph.

The outcome left both teams 5-4 overall. McNeese moved to 2-3 in the SLC while Texas-Arlington dropped to 2-2.

No team, meanwhile, was on a streak like Northeast Louisiana. The Indians took a seven-game winning streak into their game at rival Louisiana Tech. The Bulldogs were on a modest two-game winning streak going into the NLU game, the first time all season Tech won back-to-back contests.

A stingy Northeast Louisiana defense and several Tech turnovers allowed the Indians to walk away with a 17-0 road win to remain unbeaten in the Southland with one conference game remaining. The only points in a hard-fought first half came on a 34-yard Garcia field goal with 4:04 remaining before halftime. Garcia's kick was set up by Mike Turner's interception of a David Brewer pass.

The Indians took advantage of several Tech mistakes to add to their led in the second half. The first miscue of the third quarter came when punt returner Doyle Adams fumbled at the Louisiana Tech 16. A 1-yard sneak by Horn made it 10-0 with 11:15 remaining in the period. Howard Terrebonne's interception of a pass from Tech backup quarterback Kyle Gandy on the Bulldogs' next possession set up the final NLU score. The Indians traveled 61 yards, with a 7-yard halfback pass from Craighead to Joey Evans making the final 17-0.

Northeast Louisiana clinched no worse than a share of the Southland title, the first conference crown in the 53-year history of the NLU football program.

It was up to North Texas to try and keep the pressure on the front-running Indians. A win at home against Lamar would move the Eagles to 3-1 in the Southland Conference, setting up a showdown the following week against NLU.

North Texas didn't generate much offense but didn't need to as Lamar was shut out for the third time in its last four games as the Eagles captured a 10-0 triumph.

Smith's 54-yard field goal in the first quarter were the game's only points until the third period when Scott Toman's 23-yard pass to Nathan Williams produced the game's lone touchdown.

The Cardinals, who scored a total of six points over a span of 17 quarters, dropped to 1-3 in the Southland and 2-7 overall. North Texas, 3-1 in the conference and 6-3 overall, won the game despite being limited to one first down and 20 yards of total offense in the opening half.

The scenario was set. A win by Northeast Louisiana at home against North Texas would give the Indians the undisputed Southland Conference title with a perfect 6-0 record. A North Texas victory would move the Eagles to 4-1 and put them in position to tie for the league crown a week later with a win over Texas-Arlington.

In one of the most important games in school history, Northeast Louisiana was without Horn, its starting quarterback. Horn missed the game with a right thumb injury sustained in a midweek dorm accident. That put control of the offense in the hands of Brown, who was making his first start before a regional television audience on ABC.

What the fans saw both in the stands in Monroe and out in TV land was a young quarterback making early mistakes, with an opportunistic North Texas squad taking advantage of its opportunities.

A 20-yard field goal by Bresnahan on the Mean Green's opening possession of the game gave North Texas a 3-0 lead. On the Indians' next two possessions, Brown had trouble exchanging the handoff with his running backs. The result was a pair of fumbles in NLU territory that led to quick North Texas touchdowns. Carter touchdown passes of 37 yards to tailback Charleston and 20 yards to fullback Richard Buckingham gave the Mean Green a 17-0 lead with time still remaining in the opening quarter.

NLU's lone score came on a 26-yard touchdown pass from Brown to Lott late in the second quarter to make it 17-7 at halftime. The Indians could not recover from the early deficit with North Texas as the Mean Green added fourth-quarter scores on a 7-yard touchdown reception by Merriweather and a 22-yard Bresnahan field goal for the 27-7 final.

On the same day North Texas was positioning itself for a possible automatic bid to the Division I-AA playoffs, Arkansas State and Louisiana Tech were closing out Southland Conference play.

Arkansas State managed to even its league mark at 3-3 with a 24-14 win at Lamar.

Lamar hung in with Arkansas State through the first half before in Indians pulled away. The teams were tied 7-7 at halftime. Beasley had touchdown runs of 1 and 8 yards for the Indians, while Langford passed for a touchdown and McDonald kicked a 24-yard field goal to lead Arkansas State.

Arkansas State tied Memphis 14-14 a week later to conclude the season 5-5-1.

Louisiana Tech closed out Southland play with a 24-17 win at Texas-Arlington. The Bulldogs finished 2-4 in the SLC and moved to 4-6 overall as Tech won for the third time in its last four outings.

Tech led 14-0 at halftime and 17-3 going into the fourth quarter. The Bulldogs' points came on Brewer touchdown passes of 9 yards to Bobby Fowler and 29 yards to Mike Dellocono, and a field goal. UTA tied the game on a 39-yard Caldwell run and a 16-yard pass from Jackson to Reggie Brooks.

The Bulldogs' game-winning touchdown was set up when blitzing safety Aldon Kelly caused Jackson to fumble, with linebacker John Paul Lacque recovering at the Maverick 22 with slightly more than five minutes remaining in the game. Five plays later, Brewer scored from 2 yards out for the 24-17 final. Tech lost 13-9 in its season finale a week later to end 4-7.

McNeese State and Lamar closed out their seasons the following week as the Cowboys won in Beaumont 17-7 to finish 3-3 in the Southland and 6-5 overall. Lamar ended the year at the bottom of the SLC at 1-5 along with posting a 2-9 overall mark.

In his second game back from an injury, Jordan rushed for 157 yards to become Louisiana's all-time collegiate rusher. The McNeese tailback finished his career with 4,156 yards, topping the mark of 4,035 yards by LSU's Charles Alexander.

His 157 yards also allowed Jordan to reach 1,007 on the season, becoming the first player in Southland Conference history to top 1,000 yards in three-consecutive seasons.

A 36-yard punt return by Batiste and a 15-yard pass from Lamar's Kenneth Vaughn to Danzell Lee led to a 7-7 tie at halftime.

Jordan also closed his career with a touchdown, scoring on a 26-yard run and Whittington added a 26-yard field goal. Whittington's field goal was No. 16 on the season for the kicker, allowing him to establish a new single-season school record.

The record by Jordan was a tremendous individual accomplishment but the Southland Conference's focus was in Denton for North Texas' game with Texas-Arlington. A win would allow the Eagles to share the SLC crown with Northeast Louisiana at 5-1. North Texas also would earn the league's automatic bid to the playoffs since the Eagles beat NLU in head-to-head competition. A Mean Green loss would give Northeast the conference title and a playoff bid. At 8-3 overall, the Indians were pinning their hopes on an at-large berth in the playoffs should North Texas win its game with UTA.

North Texas built a 10-0 lead before the Mavericks cut their deficit to three points on a 15-yard run by Caldwell in the second quarter. Leaving nothing to chance, North Texas exploded for three touchdowns to build a 31-7 halftime lead on its way to a 53-15 victory.

Carter accounted for three touchdowns. He scored on a 26-yard run while tossing touchdown strikes of 8 yards to Tim Kerschen and 18 yards to Sid More. Buckingham scored a couple of touchdowns on runs of 1 and 16 yards.

North Texas concluded the regular season 8-3 while UTA finished 2-4 in the Southland and 5-6 overall.

Playing in Reno, Nevada, to open the Division I-AA playoffs, North Texas found itself trailing 7-0 less than two minutes into the game when University of Nevada-Reno quarterback Eric Beavers connected with Scott Threde on a 17-yard scoring strike for a quick seven-point edge.

The Mean Green defense would not allow Nevada-Reno to score again in the first half, allowing North Texas to tie the score at halftime on a 13-yard pass from Carter to Wasson with 39 seconds remaining in the second quarter.

North Texas took its first lead a minute into the second half on a 33-yard Bresnahan field goal for a 10-7 edge for the Eagles. The three-point margin held up until the 14:07 mark of the fourth quarter when Carter hooked up with Williams on a 24-yard pass to put the Wolf Pack back on top 17-13. A 24-yard Marty Zendejas field goal less than three minutes later extended Nevada-Reno's lead to seven points at 20-13.

A 12-yard pass from Carter to Davis with 4:45 remaining in regulation forced overtime.

Nevada-Reno knocked the Mean Green out of the playoffs when Zendejas connected on a 32-yard field goal in overtime and ended North Texas State's season at 8-4.

LOUISIANA TECH COMES
UP A BIT SHORT

North Texas found out rather quickly that the 1984 season would not be a repeat of 1983. With only one non-conference game under their belt, the Eagles opened Southland play at Lamar and suffered a 10-6 defeat. The Mean Green went into the game against Lamar 1-0 after a season-opening win over Angelo State. Lamar entered the contest 0-1 after losing 13-7 to Texas Southern.

A 66-yard touchdown pass from Lamar quarterback Dennis Haskins to Dwayne Dodd less than two minutes into the game and a 50-yard second-quarter field goal by Ricky Fernandez proved to be enough for the Cardinals against North Texas.

Lamar's defense held the Eagles to 72 total yards as both teams moved to 1-1 overall in the SLC opener for both teams.

After a week in which all Southland teams were involved in non-conference action, North Texas, coming off a 24-6 loss to SMU, returned to league play at Louisiana Tech.

Like North Texas, Louisiana Tech's offense was having trouble scoring points early in the 1984 season, getting off to a 1-3 start.

A 52-yard pass from Louisiana Tech quarterback David Brewer to Lifford Jackson in the first quarter and a 3-yard touchdown run by Joe Rasco staked the Bulldogs to a 14-0 halftime lead. The Brewer-to-Jackson connection represented the first offensive touchdown for the Bulldogs in 13 quarters.

The only offensive points the Eagles could generate were a pair of Todd Smith field goals. The only touchdown for North Texas came when Johnny Schindler blocked and returned a Tech punt attempt 27 yards for a touchdown.

On the same day North Texas fell to 0-2 in the Southland, Lamar also was playing its second conference game of the season, hosting 2-1 Texas-Arlington. UTA went into its league opener 2-1, including a season-opening victory over West

Texas to give Chuck Curtis a win in his debut as a college head coach. Curtis, who took over at UTA after being head coach at Cleburne High School in Texas from 1981-1983 was a one-time SMU assistant who was quarterback Charley Conerly's backup with the NFL's New York Giants in 1957.

Lamar seemed on its way to a rare win over Texas-Arlington, jumping out to a 10-0 halftime lead. The Mavericks, however, rallied in the second half for a 13-10 victory to top Lamar for the 10th-straight time. Scott Tennison's 47-yard field goal proved to be the difference in UTA's three-point triumph.

McNeese State made its 1984 Southland debut a week later as the second-ranked team in Division I-AA when the Cowboys hosted Louisiana Tech. The Cowboys were off to a 4-0 start despite the fact Buford Jordan took his more than 4,000 career rushing yards to the United States Football League. Jordan would later play for the NFL's New Orleans Saints.

An opportunistic Louisiana Tech squad took advantage of several early breaks to take a 24-3 halftime lead against McNeese State. Richie Sims returned a blocked punt 11 yards for a touchdown to give the Bulldogs a 7-0 lead only 27 seconds into the game. David Green's 2-yard run capped a 64-yard drive that was aided by two, 15-yard penalties against the Cowboys to give Tech a 14-0 lead. A fumbled snap by McNeese quarterback Don Richards two plays into the ensuing drive set up a 22-yard George Benyola field goal as the Bulldogs went on to build its 24-3 halftime lead.

The McNeese defense tossed a shutout in the second half, allowing the Cowboys to rally. Runs of 18 and 3 yards by Tony Hunter made the score 24-17. McNeese had a chance to tie the game late in the fourth quarter, but a fourth-down pass from the Bulldogs' 12-yard line was dropped by Keith Ortego in the end zone.

Still seeking its first Southland win of the season, North Texas visited Arkansas State in the Indians' conference opener. Arkansas State went into the game 3-2. One of the losses was a 22-21 heart-breaker at Texas A&M leading up to the North Texas encounter.

Narrow losses continued to plague the Eagles. North Texas held a 9-7 lead in the fourth quarter against Arkansas State but could not hold on as the Eagles fell 14-9, dropped their fourth-straight game following a season-opening victory.

The crushing blow for the Eagles came when Arkansas State's Rickey Jemison broke loose on a 40-yard ramble with less than seven minutes remaining in the game. A recovery of a Sid Moore fumble at the North Texas 42 by Indians defensive end Marvin Neloms set up the winning score.

North Texas advanced inside the Indians' 30-yard line in the closing moments but Eagles quarterback Mike Rhone was thrown for three-straight losses to end the threat.

The Mean Green trailed 7-6 at halftime before gaining the lead on a 27-yard Smith field goal early in the third quarter following a fumble by Arkansas State quarterback Dwane Brown.

Also playing its initial Southland Conference game of the year that same day was Northeast Louisiana, which was off to a 3-1 start.

Northeast Louisiana's SLC debut got off to a bit of a shaky start when Cardinals linebacker Eugene Seale returned a Rodney Horn interception 29 yards for a touchdown on the Indians' first possession of the game. Even after the Indians built a 20-7 lead, things did not seem so secure when two passes totaling 69 yards from Lamar quarterback George Levias to Rodney Clay set up a 1-yard Burton Murchison touchdown run to close the gap to six points at 20-14.

That changed minutes later when the Indians answered with a 3-yard pass from Horn to Mike Suggs to rebuild the Northeast Louisiana lead to 27-14. Freshman running back Steve Avery, making his first start, was the workhorse on the march, rushing for 42 yards on the 80-yard drive. Jimmy Harris put the game away with a 4-yard run to make the final 34-14.

Like in its win over McNeese, Louisiana Tech struck quickly a week later at home against Arkansas State.

It took a little longer than 27 seconds, but the Bulldogs again got an early edge when Jordan Stanley hooked up with Cleve Bailey on a 65-yard touchdown connection on Louisiana Tech's first offensive snap to give Tech a 7-0 lead. This time, the early lead would not last long as the Indians responded with a 22-yard Jim Wiseman field goal and a 9-yard run by Keith Weaver to tie the game 10-10.

Stanley followed his first career touchdown pass with the second at the 3:35 mark of the second quarter – again hitting Bailey, this time for 38 yards – as Louisiana Tech took a 17-10 halftime lead. The only other score in the game was a 42-yard Benyola field goal midway in the third quarter to give the Bulldogs a 20-10 triumph as Tech moved to 3-0 in the Southland.

While Louisiana Tech was soaring at 3-0 in the Southland, at the other end of the spectrum, North Texas State's woes continued. The Eagles' 26-7 home loss to McNeese stretched the North Texas losing streak to five games as the Mean Green fell to 0-4 in the SLC. McNeese squared its conference mark at 1-1 with the triumph while improving to 5-1.

The Cowboys fell behind 7-0 when Lance White raced 90 yards with a mid-air fumble, but the McNeese State defense would not yield a single point in the victory. Not only did the McNeese defense not allow a point, it set up four of the Cowboys' five scores in the contest.

Richards scored on a 3-yard run following a Mean Green fumble to tie the game in the second quarter. Moments later, Vance Robichaux's fumble recovery set up a 45-yard Tony Whittington field goal. A Mike Catrera recovery of another Eagles fumble set up a 4-yard Tony Hunt run for a 17-7 halftime lead for McNeese.

Another North Texas fumble led to a 1-yard touchdown run by Richards in the fourth quarter and a Whittington field goal later in the period provided the 26-7 final.

With Louisiana Tech taking on Northwestern State in non-conference action, Texas-Arlington and Northeast Louisiana, both 1-1 in the SLC, looked to pick up ground on the Bulldogs when the teams met in Monroe in a game that featured a heavy rain that left about a half-inch of water on the Malone Stadium field and turned the playing surface into a muddy mess.

A short punt gave NLU the ball at the Texas-Arlington 43 early in the game. The Indians could pick up only a few yards, but instead of trying to punt on fourth down in an attempt to pin the Mavericks deep, Indians coach Pat Collins sent in Teddy Garcia to attempt a 50-yard field goal. Horn, the holder on the attempt, took the snap and tried to pass. The fake field goal pass fell incomplete, giving UTA good field position.

The only points of the first half came on a 34-yard field goal by Tennison to give Texas-Arlington a 3-0 lead at halftime. He hit on field goals of 32 and 38 yards in the third quarter to give the Mavericks a 9-0 advantage. NLU's only score came on a 7-yard pass from Horn to Joey Evans with 2:26 left in the game as the Indians, ranked No. 10 entering the game, fell to 5-2 on the season, including 1-1 in the Southland. UTA improved to 5-2 overall and 2-0 in the conference.

A rain storm also greeted McNeese State in its game at Arkansas State.

McNeese led 3-0 on a 38-yard Whittington field goal before Arkansas State pulled ahead 7-3 in the final minute of the first half. The Indians gained possession at the Cowboys' 8-yard line following a blocked Benny May punt. Brown, the Arkansas State quarterback, scored one play later to give the Indians a four-point halftime edge.

Arkansas State extended its lead to 13-3 early in the third quarter when Brown scored on a 1-yard run after an interception gave the Indians the ball at the McNeese 34.

McNeese responded early in the third quarter, putting together a 77-yard drive and pulling to within three points at 13-10 when Hunt capped the drive on a 1-yard dive with 8:27 remaining in the third quarter. Arkansas State answered with a 40-yard field goal by Frank Richards to up its lead to 16-10.

The Cowboys tied the game on a 19-yard touchdown pass from Don Richards to split end Richard Anderson with 28 seconds left in the game. McNeese missed out on a chance to win the game when Ortego, the Cowboys holder, was unable to handle the snap from center on the conversion attempt, leaving the game a 16-16 tie.

The result left both teams 1-1-1 in the SLC. McNeese moved to 5-1-1 overall and Arkansas State 4-3-1.

Louisiana Tech struggled to a non-conference victory over Northwestern State by the unusual score of 5-0 but the Bulldogs continued to show the ability to win close, low-scoring games as Tech looked to go 4-0 in the Southland with a triumph over Lamar.

Playing in Beaumont, the Bulldogs couldn't seem to shake the one-win Cardinals as Louisiana Tech held a narrow lead of 12-7 going into the fourth quarter.

The break the Bulldogs needed finally arrived when Lamar quarterback Brent Watson, who was sacked seven times in the game, fumbled when pounded by a pair of Tech rushers. Walter Johnson's fumble recovery at the Cardinal 35 set up a 14-yard touchdown pass from Kyle Gandy to Lester Mills for a 19-7 lead with 4:31 left in the game. It was Gandy's first action since suffering a broken wrist against Southwestern Louisiana in the second game of the season. Benyola's school-record-tying 52-yard field goal with 36 seconds remaining in the game made the final 22-7.

Besides Louisiana Tech, Texas-Arlington was the only other unbeaten team in the Southland Conference as the 2-0 Mavericks hosted 1-1-1 Arkansas State.

The Mavericks showed they were not in Louisiana Tech's class, falling 51-21 to Arkansas State as UT-Arlington yielded 444 yards total offense and allowed the Indians running back duo of Jemison and Preston Maddox to score a combined five rushing touchdowns.

"It was the first time we really turned our offense over to Dwane Brown," explained Arkansas State coach Larry Lacewell. "He was a young quarterback and we tried to do things the hard way. We called all the plays and didn't give Dwane much freedom.

"The wishbone is a check-off offense. You better be able to check out of a certain play and usually it's one option or the other option. We allowed him to do that in that game. Texas-Arlington just wasn't ready for it. We just went up and down the field."

Despite the big rushing numbers, it hardly looked like an Arkansas State rout through the first quarter. Trailing 7-0, UT-Arlington responded with a 19-play drive, culminated on a 17-yard pass from quarterback Phil Blue to Charles Walker to tie the game. A fumble on the ensuing kickoff led to a Mavericks touchdown three plays later for a 14-7 UTA advantage.

Arkansas State responded by scoring on its next four possessions to pull away. Jemison, who rushed for 104 yards, scored on runs of 3 and 1 yard before Richards kicked a career-tying 47-yard field goal on the final play of the first half to stretch the Indians' lead.

Jemison added a 44-yard jaunt at the start of the third quarter and split end Judious Lewis scored on a 26-yard end-around on the Indians' way to the 30-point victory.

At Lake Charles, Northeast Louisiana held a two-point lead at halftime with a baseball-like score of 5-3 against McNeese State. NLU's Garcia and McNeese's Whittington each had first-half field goals. The difference came when May, the Cowboys punter, was unable to control the center snap on a punt attempt from the McNeese end zone and had to fall on the ball for a safety.

A 52-yard touchdown run by Kirby Bonvillain in the third quarter gave NLU a 12-3 lead. Trailing by nine points early in the fourth quarter, McNeese elected to try for a fourth-down conversion from its own 30-yard line. Indians defensive tackle Mike Yost brought down Richards for a 2-yard loss. Northeast took advantage of the excellent field position as Avery scored four plays later to give the Indians a 19-3 win that improved NLU to 2-1 in the Southland and 6-2 overall. McNeese dropped to 1-2-1 in the SLC and 5-2-1 overall.

Northeast Louisiana's win over McNeese put the Indians in position to have a major say in the outcome of the Southland Conference race. Up next for the Indians was a home game against Louisiana Tech. A win by the Bulldogs would move Tech to 5-0 in the SLC and clinch no worse than a tie for the league title. A victory by the Indians had the potential to put NLU, Texas-Arlington and Arkansas State in contention.

NLU jumped out to a 9-0 lead on a 5-yard touchdown pass from quarterback Rodney Horn to Chris Lott and a 50-yard Garcia field goal. The touchdown was set up by linebacker Ronnie Washington's interception of a Gandy pass at the Northeast 44. Louisiana Tech made it 9-7 at halftime on a 16-yard touchdown reception by Mike Sherman to cap a 79-yard drive at the 9:24 mark of the second quarter. The touchdown was the first allowed by the NLU defense in 10 quarters.

Louisiana Tech took its first lead of the game at 10-9 on the Bulldogs' first possession of the second half on a 40-yard Benyola field goal. Trailing by a point, the Indians got the ball at their own 16 for one last opportunity in the closing moments. Passes of 22 and 20 yards from Horn to Lott helped to advance the ball into Bulldog territory. With 55 seconds left in the game, Garcia booted a 45-yard field goal to give NLU a 12-10 win to snap Tech's five-game winning streak.

Texas-Arlington took advantage of the Louisiana Tech loss, defeating McNeese State 24-20 at home to run its conference record to 3-1.

A week after having trouble scoring against Northeast Louisiana, the Cowboys exploded for 17 first-half points at Texas-Arlington.

McNeese scored on three of its first four possessions on a 5-yard scamper by Hunt, a 2-yard run by Stewart and a 42-yard Whittington field goal for its 17-point advantage. UTA made it 17-7 at halftime on a 79-yard touchdown strike on the colorful combination of Blue to Donald White.

Trailing 20-7, the Mavericks put themselves back in the game early in the fourth quarter when tailback Scotty Caldwell scored on a 2-yard run to make the score 20-14. The Cowboys fumbled on the ensuing kickoff, giving the ball right back to UTA. Tennison hit a 43-yard field goal four plays later as the Mavericks closed to within three points at 20-17.

Caldwell sprinted 33 yards on a 60-yard drive later in the fourth quarter to set up his own 2-yard touchdown run to give the Mavericks a 24-20 come-from-behind victory. The UTA tailback rushed for more than 100 yards in the second half. By contrast, the Cowboys, who were averaging 193 yards a game on the ground, were limited to 89 yards as a team.

Along with moving to 3-1 in the Southland, the Mavericks improved to 6-3 overall. McNeese fell to 1-3-1 in the Southland and 5-3-1 overall.

Playing an afternoon game the following week against North Texas State, Northeast Louisiana had a chance to share the Southland crown if the Indians could beat the Mean Green and their next opponent, Arkansas State, both on the road, while Texas-Arlington, which still had Louisiana Tech on the schedule, would have to lose once.

The stakes were set and the objective clear when the Indians faced North Texas, which was winless through four SLC games. Despite everything that was on the line, the Indians gave a lackluster performance.

Northeast Louisiana surrendered 10 points in the first quarter to the Mean Green. Opening the first quarter going against a 21-mile-per-hour wind, the Indians were unable to generate much offense and punter Kevin Duhe got off three kicks, none more than 26 yards. That gave North Texas great field position and the Eagles were determined to take advantage of it.

It was actually a fumble that set up the first score for North Texas. The Mean Green took their first possession at the NLU 32 following a Kenneth Johnson fumble. Smith's 43-yard field goal gave North Texas a 3-0 lead less than two minutes into the contest.

After the Mean Green botched two scoring opportunities on a fumble and missed field goal, North Texas took its next possession at its own 46 following a 20-yard Duhe punt. Freshman running back Monty Moon capped the drive five plays later on a 24-yard run for a 10-0 North Texas lead with 4:15 remaining in the opening quarter. Garcia kicked a 37-yard field goal with 9:10 remaining in the first half to make the score 10-3. For Garcia, who would go on to kick in the NFL, the field goal was his ninth straight, setting a new school and Southland Conference mark.

Neither team was able to mount much offense in the second half, allowing Northeast Louisiana to remain in the game. Midway in the fourth quarter, the Indians offense began to click. Two passes from Horn to Evans totaling 42 yards moved the ball to the North Texas 22. Runs by Horn and Bonvillain advanced the ball to the 10. Horn tried to force the ball to a well-covered Lott in the end zone. North Texas safety Jay Saad made a leaping grab of Horn's pass, ending the Indians' hopes.

Motivation would not be a problem for the Louisiana Tech Bulldogs in their final regular-season game at home against Texas-Arlington. Having learned of Northeast Louisiana's 10-3 upset by North Texas earlier in the day, all Tech had to do was defeat the Mavericks to capture the outright Southland Conference title.

The Bulldogs would not wait for some dramatic finish, jumping out to a 20-0 halftime lead on their way to a 34-0 whipping of UTA. Two Benyola field goals, a 3-yard run by Green and a 25-yard pass to Sherman gave Tech its halftime lead. Gandy also fired touchdown passes of 16 yards to Paddy Doyle and 59 to Todd Breske in the game.

Tech's win allowed the Bulldogs to capture their eighth conference title since joining the Southland in 1971. Finishing the regular season a week before all the other SLC teams gave Louisiana Tech, 5-1 in the conference and 7-4 overall, a week off to prepare for the Division I-AA playoffs.

The results of the Northeast Louisiana and Louisiana Tech games already known to Arkansas State, the Indians knew they had no shot at the Southland title in their home game against Lamar. Still, a win over the Cardinals would move Arkansas State to 3-1-1 in the SLC, but more importantly, a 6-3-1 record might keep the Indians in line for an at-large bid to the playoffs.

Arkansas State's powerful ground game was on display once again. The Indians amassed 500 of their 601 yards on the ground as Jemison rushed for 134 yards.

"We executed the offense about as well as we could," said Lacewell.

The outcome was still in doubt as a pair of 16-yard touchdown passes from Watson to Clay allowed the Cardinals to rally to within a single point at 14-13 in the third quarter until Arkansas State scored the final 23 points of the game for a 37-13 victory.

The knockout blows came on a quarterback sneak by Brown in the third quarter and 12-yard run by Jemison in the fourth. Brown's touchdown was set up by a 74-yard reverse by Lewis.

Arkansas State's home game at Northeast Louisiana was the one game of consequence in the Southland Conference during the final week of the 1984 season. A win over NLU would allow Arkansas State to finish 7-3-1 and be in line for an at-large berth to the playoffs.

About the last thing Arkansas State wanted to happen took place on its first offensive play when Mike Turner returned an interception 56 yards for a touchdown.

Arkansas State quickly settled down, scoring on three of its next four possessions to take a 24-7 halftime lead. The first two touchdowns were 1-yard runs by Jemison. Jemison was one of three running backs to rush for more than 100 yards as Arkansas State amassed 409 yards on the ground out of its wishbone offense.

Jemison rushed for two more touchdowns in the second half and Northeast Louisiana's other points came on a 36-yard pass from Horn to Lott one play after NLU recovered a muffed punt to make the final 38-14 as Arkansas State closed the regular season 7-3-1 and Northeast Louisiana 7-4.

"That was a satisfying victory for us because they had embarrassed us a year or two before on national television and they beat us pretty bad," said Lacewell, referring to Arkansas State's 45-7 loss a year earlier to NLU. "It was kind of a get-even game. Pat Collins was a good friend of mine and I had never done this in my life, but called a fake field goal at the end of the game just to send a message. I don't think we scored on it. I probably shouldn't have done it."

In the other two games to close out the season, Texas-Arlington blanked North Texas 22-0 to finish 4-2 in the Southland and 7-4 overall while McNeese defeated Lamar 34-14 to end the year 2-3-1 in the SLC and 7-4 overall. North Texas and Lamar finished with identical 2-9 records, including 1-5 in the conference.

In UTA's win, Caldwell rushed for 101 yards and scored a touchdown while McNeese intercepted six passes against Lamar. Cowboys' cornerback Todd McArthur tied a school record with three interceptions in the game. Linebacker Joey Granger picked off two passes while the other interception was recorded by Mark Hamilton.

Arkansas State's 7-3-1 record was not only good enough to get in the Division I-AA playoffs - the 10th-ranked Indians managed to host in the opening round against a familiar foe, the University of Tennessee at Chattanooga. Arkansas State blanked the Moccasins 16-0 on the road in Week 2 of the regular season.

The Indians took advantage of several UTC mistakes to build a 23-3 halftime lead. Four plays after the Moccasins fumbled the opening kickoff, Jemison scored on a 1-yard run less than two minutes into the contest. Arkansas State used a bit of trickery for its second score when Farrell Wilson ran 24 yards for a touchdown on a guard-around play. I.J. Chapman's 57-yard interception with two seconds left in the half gave the Indians their 20-point lead on the way to a 37-10 victory. UTC's only points in the first half came on a 25-yard Scott Geim field goal following a fumble by Brown.

Arkansas State rushed for 219 yards in the game. The Indians allowed Tennessee-Chattanooga 243 total yards, 80 of which came on a late drive when the game already had been decided.

"Frankly, we were kind of surprised to be in the playoffs," said Lacewell. "It took a great spurt out of us late in the season to make it and we were kind of like, 'What are we doing here?' But we won the game and it was exciting for us because we had some lean years prior to that."

Louisiana Tech's opening-round playoff game at home against Mississippi Valley was an offensive showcase. The Bulldogs rolled up 703 yards of total offense, including 408 rushing and 295 passing. Their Southwestern Athletic Conference foes had 618 total yards. Where the Delta Devils couldn't keep up with the Bulldogs was on the scoreboard as Tech proved unstoppable in a 66-19 triumph.

Tech held a 10-6 lead after one quarter before erupting for four scores in five second-quarter possessions to blow the game open 38-19 at halftime. The scores came on a pair of 1-yard runs by Green, an 8-yard touchdown reception by Gerry Jones and a 5-yard Jones run.

Another offensive explosion in the third quarter saw the Bulldogs' lead stretch to 40 points at 59-19.

All of Valley's points came in the first half on a 1-yard pass from quarterback Willie Totten to Curtis Debardlabon, a 1-yard run by Carl Byrum, and a 64-yard bomb to Jerry Rice. Totten attempted 75 passes in the game, completing 44 for

485 yards, but threw six interceptions. Rice, the future Hall of Fame receiver of San Francisco 49ers fame, finished with nine catches for 155 yards.

The Bulldogs had to hit the road to Jackson, Mississippi, for their quarterfinal playoff game against undefeated and top-ranked Alcorn State, another SWAC opponent.

Like the previous week against Mississippi Valley, Louisiana Tech came up with an offensive onslaught in the second quarter to put the Delta Devils away. Unlike the Valley game, this time the game was scoreless before the Bulldogs erupted.

Gandy tossed for 254 yards and three touchdowns in the first half. He threw touchdown strikes of 12 yards to Sherman, 8 yards to Mills and 5 yards to Breske. Tech opened the second-quarter scoring on a 5-yard run by Jones. Even the defense, which held Alcorn to minus-67 yards rushing, got in on the scoring when Walter Johnson sacked Braves quarterback Richard Miles in the end zone for a safety.

Tech built its lead to 44-0 before the Braves scored three late touchdowns to make the final 44-21.

Arkansas State had much farther to travel for its second-round playoff game, going all the way to Bozeman, Montana, to take on second-ranked Montana State.

Behind the wishbone attack, the Indians averaged 41 points per game over their last four outings going into the Montana State encounter but were held scoreless by the Bobcats. All 14 of Arkansas State's points in a 31-14 defeat came from Indians strong safety Billy Ray Bowers. Bowers returned a pair of interceptions for touchdowns to give the Indians a 14-0 lead early in the second quarter.

A mistake-prone Indians offense was held to 186 yards rushing, including only 63 in the second half. Causing most of the Arkansas State miscues was Clete Linbarger. The Bobcats defensive end recovered three fumbles, forced another and had an interception.

Meanwhile, Montana State quarterback Kelly Bradley, the Big Sky Conference Offensive Player of the Year, was just as dominating on offense, passing for 313 yards and three touchdowns. He had a scoring strike of 6 yards to Darin Dietrich to make it 14-7 at halftime. In the second half, he hooked up with Kelly Davis from 6 yards out and 12 yards to Dietrich. The sophomore quarterback also scored on a 1-yard run in the 31-14 victory that ended Arkansas State's best season since 1975 at 8-4-1.

"There was a snowstorm the night before," Lacewell recalled. "Our players had never seen anything like that. We weren't equipped uniform-wise or anything else like that. The field the next day, they had plowed it and raked it off and it was really slick.

"The wishbone is a lateral offense. The quarterback has to have the ability to go down the line of scrimmage and cut up and it was miserable for us."

Unlike its first two playoff games, there would be no big offensive explosion in Louisiana Tech's semifinal playoff game against Middle Tennessee State in Murfreesboro, Tennessee, but one long run made the difference in the Bulldogs' 21-13 win.

The Bulldogs held a one-point lead when Green broke loose on an 80-yard gallop with 7:59 left in the game to secure the win for Louisiana Tech. Green's long run came as an unexpected bonus. Prior to his run, Middle Tennessee had bottled up the Bulldogs' running game to the tune of 12 yards.

Sims' 37-yard return of a blocked Middle Tennessee punt provided the only touchdown of the first half. The Blue Raiders made it 7-3 at halftime on a 33-yard Kelly Potter field goal. Middle Tennessee took its only lead of the game midway in the third quarter on a 2-yard run by Gerald Anderson. An 11-yard pass from Gandy to Breske put Tech on top 14-10. Potter's field goal made it 14-13 before Green broke loose on the ensuing possession to help send the Bulldogs to the national championship game in Charleston, South Carolina.

Louisiana Tech's opponent in the title game was Montana State – the same Montana State that eliminated Arkansas State by shutting down the Indians' powerful ground game.

To this day, Gandy may not know what hit him on Dec. 15, 1984. Gandy was sacked 11 times for 101 yards in losses and four of the Bulldogs' seven turnovers were interceptions by the quarterback as Montana State hammered Louisiana Tech 19-6 in the Division I-AA championship game. History shows that Bobcats defensive end Mark Fellows pounded Gandy for five sacks, while his line mates, Pat Sikora and Linebarger joined in for an additional two sacks apiece.

Montana State scored all 19 of its points in the first half. All but one of the Bobcats' scores came off of Bulldog miscues.

Mark Carter's 33-yard field goal gave Montana State a 3-0 lead. That score was set up by one of Gandy's four interceptions in the game. A partially-blocked Tech punt set up the Bobcats' next score, a 17-yard touchdown pass from Bradley to tight end Joe Bignell to make it 9-0. Bradley's 33-yard strike to Bignell in the second quarter gave Montana State a 16-point advantage and Carter's 48-yard kick with six seconds left gave the Bobcats a 19-0 halftime lead.

Louisiana Tech, which ended its season at 10-5, earned its only score of the game on Gandy's 10-yard pass to Sherman with 48 seconds remaining in the contest.

Arkansas State went into its 1985 Southland Conference opener at McNeese State a misleading 2-2 on the season, with the Indians' two losses being by close margins to Southeastern Conference schools. Arkansas State's losses were 22-14 to Mississippi State and 18-16 to Ole Miss. McNeese went into its league opener 1-2.

The Indians led 6-3 at halftime but McNeese took advantage of a pair of outstanding defensive plays to gain the lead in the second half. An interception by Marcel Mills set up a 25-yard Lance Wiley field goal and linebacker Don Moseley's tackle of Indians quarterback Duane Brown in the end zone gave the Cowboys an additional two points.

Tony Johnson capped McNeese's only long possession of the game, scoring on a 4-yard run to conclude a 74-yard drive.

Arkansas State's only points in the second half came on a 49-yard pass from Brown to Gerald Patterson. The Indians attempted two late field goals but both were wide and short of the target as A-State fell 15-13.

Two Stuart Reid field goals were countered by a 34-yard Wiley boot as the Indians took a 6-3 halftime edge.

"I was as mad as I've ever been at my team," said Arkasas State coach Larry Lacewell. "It was a long bus ride home and I made up my mind that we were a good football team, to not over-coach them and leave them alone. From that moment on, we played well the rest of the season."

Louisiana Tech opened up defense of its Southland title a week later at North Texas State. The Bulldogs went into the contest riding a three-game winning streak after opening the season with a 28-0 loss at Southern Mississippi. North Texas sported a 2-2 record, with the Mean Green's two losses coming against Oklahoma State and Texas Tech.

The 3-1 start gave the Bulldogs confidence going into their game at North Texas State. No one was more confident that Jordan Stanley. The quarterback, making his second start of the season, hit on 18 of 23 passes for 200 yards – and that was just in the first half – as the Bulldogs built a 24-0 halftime lead. By the time he was done, Stanley hooked up with nine different receivers, passed for 250 yards and a touchdown as Tech took a 33-8 win.

Stanley connected on all five of his throws on Louisiana Tech's first scoring drive, capped by a 1-yard run by Joe Rasco. Following a George Benyola field goal, a halfback pass from Garlon Powell to Roderick Wright made it 17-0. A 41-yard reception by Mike Sherman set up a 1-yard touchdown pass to Lester Mills to end the first-half scoring. Benyola added three field goals in the second half.

North Texas avoided the shutout on a 45-yard pass from Mike Rhone to Marcus Camper in the fourth quarter.

Louisiana Tech topped 30 points for the third week in a row in taking a 35-3 home win over McNeese State that moved Tech to 2-0 in SLC play and 5-1 overall.

McNeese scored first on a 25-yard Wiley field goal that seemed to serve as a wake-up call for the Bulldogs. After a 49-yard Benyola field goal tied the game, Louisiana Tech went ahead to stay on a 21-yard touchdown run by Bobby Leitz early in the second quarter. Benyola would go on to kick two more field goals in the game, while Stanley and Wright would hook up on touchdown passes of 41 and 68 yards. Stanley threw a third touchdown in the game when he hit Rasco from 5 yards out.

As quickly as Louisiana Tech found itself 2-0 in the Southland, the Eagles of North Texas State were dropping to 0-2 as the Mean Green had no answer for Arkansas State's Preston Maddox in a 56-0 drubbing in Jonesboro. The Arkansas State running back scored three rushing touchdowns and had a touchdown reception as the Indians amassed 433 yards to build a 28-0 lead by halftime.

It was a complete team effort for Arkansas State, which evened its record at 1-1 in the Southland and 3-3 overall. The Indians' defense, top-ranked in the SLC, held the Mean Green to 111 yards of total offense, only 40 of which came on the ground. The Arkansas State defense also recovered three fumbles and intercepted four passes.

Making their Southland debuts that same day were Lamar and Northeast Louisiana. Both teams went into the encounter in Beaumont 3-1 on the season. The Indians' lone loss was a 31-17 defeat at the hands of the Texas A&M Aggies.

Northeast Louisiana was in control from the start against Lamar. The Indians scored less than 90 seconds into the game and kept on rolling in an easy 37-14 victory.

Mike Wooten, who rushed for 140 yards, scored the first of his two touchdowns on the opening drive of the game. After his 45-yard scamper, Teddy Garcia added a 32-yard field goal to make it 10-0. A 2-yard pass from Bubby Brister to Chad Peterson made it 17-0 at intermission. Another Brister touchdown, this one a 4-yard toss to Mike Manzullo on the opening possession of the second half, made it 24-0.

Brister, who entered the game as the top-rated passer in Division I-AA, passed for 212 yards and two touchdowns. Brister was in his second season at quarterback for the Indians following a short stint in professional baseball.

The NLU defense held Burton Murchison, Division I-AA's leading rusher to 109 yards. Not only did the Indians hold him below his average of 172, they also kept him out of the end zone. So he did the next best thing – he threw a 44-yard pass to flanker Derek Anderson to make it 24-8. The only other score the Cardinals would manage was an 11-yard pass from quarterback Dave Money to Rodney Clay with six seconds remaining in the game for the 37-14 final.

UT-Arlington was the last team to play its initial Southland game of the 1985 season when the 2-3 Mavericks hosted Lamar.

Mavericks quarterback David Bates passed for 260 yards and tossed touchdown passes of 70, 51 and 30 yards in a 37-17 victory for UTA. Bates' favorite target was Keith Arbon, who hauled in five catches for 180 yards and a touchdown.

The result left both teams 3-3 overall while Lamar dropped to 0-2 in the Southland.

Louisiana Tech found itself on the wrong end of a fourth-straight 30-plus point outing in a 31-13 loss at Arkansas State. The loss snapped a five-game winning streak for Louisiana Tech and left both teams at 2-1 in the Southland Conference.

Dwane Brown ran the Indians' wishbone offense to near perfection. He carried the ball 27 times for 152 yards and passed for 92 as Arkansas State held the ball almost twice as long as the Bulldogs. Doug Landry, the rugged Tech linebacker, who would go on to play three years in the Canadian Football League, was in on 23 tackles, but neither he nor his teammates could stop the option.

"When a quarterback can run the ball 27 times, you are going to occupy the clock," said Lacewell. "We kept the ball from Louisiana Tech and it was something they couldn't stand because they wanted to throw the ball."

Louisiana Tech, trailing by 11 points at halftime, came up with a Benyola field goal to make it 21-13 in the third quarter, but the Bulldogs would be held scoreless the remainder of the game. Arkansas State, meanwhile, added a 26-yard Reid field goal and a 2-yard touchdown run by Maddox in the second half.

Arkansas State built its first-half lead on a 12-yard run by Duane Brown, a 7-yard touchdown pass from the Indians' quarterback Cazzy Francis and a 3-yard reception by tight end Ray Brown. An interception and fumble set up the first two scores. Louisiana Tech's points came on a Benyola field goal and a 3-yard Rasco run.

"It was an extremely satisfying win for us. We had a hard time against them over the years. It was a fun time for us beating Louisiana Tech," Lacewell said.

With Louisiana Tech playing non-conference foe Northwestern State and Arkansas State having the week off, Texas-Arlington looked to take its spot atop the Southland Conference as the league's only 2-0 team with a home win against Northeast Louisiana.

Northeast Louisiana's defense had trouble containing the Mavericks' well-balance offense, while the Indians' offense suffered a severe blow in the first quarter after losing Chris Jones, the teams' star receiver, with a knee injury.

The Indians responded quickly to an early Scott Roper field goal when Brister hooked up with Benny Mitchell on a 63-yard touchdown strike to take a 7-3 lead. Bates, who threw for 160 yards, got the first of his two touchdowns in the game in the closing seconds of the first half on an 8-yard toss to wingback James White to give UTA a 10-7 halftime edge.

Picking up where they left off to close the first half, the Mavericks opened the third quarter by driving 82 yards. The march ended on a 33-yard touchdown pass to Arbon to make it 17-7. Tony Brown, who rushed for 167 yards in the game, upped the Texas-Arlington lead to 24-7 on a 7-yard run early in the fourth quarter. NLU's only score in the second half came on a 22-yard touchdown pass from Brister to Manzullo as the Indians fell 27-13.

After scoring 28 points in blanking Southwest Texas a week earlier in non-conference action, the Cowboys could have used a few of those points against Southland foe North Texas State.

For the first time in 141 games, McNeese failed to score but the Cowboys could take some solace in the fact they didn't allow any points either in a scoreless tie. It was the second time in three outings that North Texas failed to score.

With rain falling in Lake Charles starting two days before game day, the Cowboys Stadium field was not conducive to scoring and it showed as neither team amassed 200 yards of total offense.

Each team missed out on scoring opportunities. Flip Johnson's 58-yard punt return for a touchdown was called back by a holding penalty. Smith, the Mean Green kicker, missed field goal attempts of 50 and 43 yards. The 43 yarder came with 10 seconds left in the game.

The result left McNeese 1-1-1 in the SLC and 3-3-1 overall. North Texas moved to 0-2-1 in the conference and 2-5-1 overall.

A missed 30-yard field goal by Roper with six seconds left in the game dropped Texas-Arlington from the unbeaten ranks in the Southland with a 13-12 loss at Arkansas State in an afternoon encounter.

Roper field goals of 32, 38 and 50 yards staked the Mavs to a 9-0 halftime lead.

His late miss benefitted Arkansas State and the kicker would go on to help the Indians in later years.

"When UTA dropped football that year, we recruited him and he came here and he was a good kicker for us," said Lacewell. "Thank the Lord Roper missed the field goal that night. They probably deserved to beat us."

Trailing 12-7 after another Roper field goal, a 71-yard scamper by Brown less than a minute into the fourth quarter put the Indians on top by one point. A two-point conversion attempt failed but Arkansas State held on for the win.

UTA missed putting more points on the board. Of 18 offensive possessions, 10 ended up in Arkansas State territory but the Mavericks were unable to produce a single touchdown.

Texas-Arlington dropped to 2-1 in the SLC and 4-4 overall. Arkansas State moved to 3-1 in the conference and 5-3 overall.

Louisiana Tech joined Arkansas State at 3-1 in the Southland Conference later in the day in a contest decided by one point.

Tech held a 23-16 lead at Lamar when the Bulldogs elected to attempt a field goal on a rain-soaked field to stretch the lead to 10 points with 2:20 left in the game. Benyola's attempt was wide left, giving the ball back to the Cardinals at the 24-yard line.

Three passes by Brent Wilson moved the ball to the Tech 7. His fourth pass of the drive, a touchdown toss to Clay with seven seconds left in the game, pulled Lamar, which entered the game 0-2 in the SLC, to within one point at 23-22. Instead of a game-tying extra point, the Cardinals elected to go for the win with a two-point conversion attempt. The attempt failed but pass interference was called against the Bulldogs, giving Lamar another shot. Wilson then pitched to Murchison, the Cardinals' All-America tailback, who had rushed for 184 yards in the game. The quarterback's pitch bounced off of the prolific running back's shoulder pads and Tech's own All-America, defensive tackle Donald Washington, pounced on the loose ball to preserve the win.

Three Benyola field goals gave the Louisiana Tech kicker an SLC single-season record 20 and the Bulldogs the early lead. Tech trailed 10-9 at halftime and the game was tied 16-16 when the Bulldogs came up with what proved to be the game-winning touchdown in the fourth quarter. A series of turnovers by both teams ultimately gave the ball back to Tech at the Lamar 49. From the 1-yard line, Powell got the ball. As he tried to cross the goal line, he lost control of the football. Tech guard Joe Taylor fell on the ball in the end zone, allowing the Bulldogs to eke out the victory.

After the scoreless tie a week earlier, McNeese State could produce only 10 points at Northeast Louisiana. Luckily for the Cowboys, their defense recorded a school-record third-straight shutout to take a 10-0 Southland win over the Indians.

Again playing on a wet field, the Cowboys and Indians waded through a scoreless first half. Wiley broke the scoreless deadlock with a 45-yard field goal midway in the third quarter. Vance Robichaux's recovery of a Bubby Brister fumble at the NLU 22 set up a 14-yard touchdown run by Perry Myles to make it 10-0 midway in the fourth quarter.

The Indians reached the McNeese 8-yard line late in the game after an interception but the drive came to an end on Mark Hamilton's interception of a Brister pass in the end zone.

McNeese improved to 2-1-1 in the Southland Conference and 4-3-1 overall. Northeast Louisiana fell to 1-2 in the league and 4-4 overall.

An unusual season continued a week later for McNeese State. After three consecutive shutouts, the Cowboys recorded their second tie in three weeks against Texas-Arlington.

Brown scored on a 2-yard touchdown in the first quarter at McNeese to end the Cowboy defense's scoreless streak at 13 quarters. The Mavericks would manage only a field goal the remainder of the game but the Cowboys could do no better than 10 points themselves, resulting in a second deadlock in Southland Conference play for McNeese.

After Wiley kicked a 25-yard field goal in the second quarter, UTA's Roper countered with a 29-yard effort as the Mavs took a 10-3 halftime lead.

With both teams struggling offensively in the second half, the Cowboys brought in David Anderson off the bench. The senior quarterback provided the spark McNeese was looking for, tossing a 41-yard touchdown pass to Arthur Alexander with 56 seconds left in the third quarter to salvage a tie for the Cowboys.

Each team missed out on scoring opportunities in the fourth quarter. David Verrett recovered a Mavericks fumble in the McNeese end zone to prevent a score. Two Cowboys drives ended with a fumble and an interception.

The result left McNeese 2-1-2 in the Southland and 4-3-2 overall. Texas-Arlington moved to 2-1-1 in the conference and 4-4-1 overall.

Louisiana Tech dropped out of a first-place tie in the Southland with Arkansas State when the Bulldogs suffered a 13-9 home loss to Northeast Louisiana.

Tech scored on its opening possession versus Northeast Louisiana when Powell galloped 41 yards to set up Rasco's 1-yard run for a 6-0 lead. The game quickly turned to a defensive battle as the only other points produced in the first half were field goals as the Bulldogs took a 9-3 halftime lead. Tech was limited to 56 yards in the opening half and NLU 63.

A Teddy Garcia field goal early in the second half made the score 9-6. The Indians took a 13-9 lead on a 1-yard run by Mike Wooten on a 21-yard drive set up by a Stanley fumble when hit by a hard-charging Cyril Crutchfield. A fake punt attempt from midfield early in the fourth quarter failed for the Bulldogs, who were unable to mount a serious threat the remainder of the game in falling by four points.

At the bottom of the Southland standings, Lamar lost 20-0 at North Texas State to drop to 0-4 in the conference as the Cardinals' losing streak reached six games. The Eagles' first SLC win of the season moved North Texas to 1-2-1 in the league and 3-5-1 overall.

North Texas recorded its first shutout since 1983 with the win over Lamar. The last time the Eagles' defense came up with a shutout, the Cardinals were the victim, falling 10-0.

The Eagles got the best of the Cardinals in a battle of teams winless in SLC play. Gene Pool, a freshman, tossed a pair of touchdown passes and Todd Smith added two field goals to pace North Texas.

Murchison, who entered the game as the leading rusher in Division I-AA, set a new single-season Southland record for Lamar. His fourth carry of the game gave him the new mark at 1,268 yards. He went on to rush for 102 yards in the contest on 26 attempts.

Arkansas State maintained a leg up on Louisiana Tech the following week with a road win over hapless Lamar. Coming off a 41-12 non-conference win over Southern Illinois, the Indians defeated the Cardinals 21-0 as Lamar failed to score for the second week in a row.

Brown accounted for all the scoring in Arkansas State's triumph. The Indians quarterback scored on touchdown runs of 3 yards in the second quarter and 14 yards in the third. He also hooked up with Francis on a 56-yard touchdown strike in the second quarter as Arkansas State's fifth-consecutive win improved the Indians to 4-1 in the Southland and 7-3 overall. Lamar dropped to 0-5 in the conference and 3-7 overall.

Arkansas State's top-rated defense held Murchison to a season-low 44 yards. Murchison, who was averaging 151 yards per game, left the contest in the second quarter with a headache.

Louisiana Tech's loss to Northeast Louisiana ended any hopes of the Bulldogs gaining the Southland's automatic bid to the Division I-AA playoffs. Still, a win over Texas-Arlington in Tech's regular-season finale would allow the Bulldogs to finish the season 8-3 and perhaps be in line for an at-large berth to the playoffs. Louisiana Tech needed a Northeast Louisiana upset of Arkansas State the following week to force a conference co-championship. The league's automatic bid in that scenario would still go to Arkansas State since the Indians beat Tech in head-to-head competition.

Tech yielded a 33-yard touchdown pass from Bates to Keith Arbon on the opening possession of the game. Led by Doyle Adams, who intercepted two passes and recovered a fumble, the only other points Tech allowed the remainder of the game was a late touchdown on a fake field goal.

Tech got a 29-yard interception return for a touchdown by Adams, three Benyola field goals and two Stanley touchdown passes to give the Bulldogs a 29-14 win. That left the Bulldogs 8-3 overall and 4-2 in the SLC but there would ultimately be no postseason bid for Louisiana Tech.

In Monroe, it was bombs away for Northeast Louisiana against North Texas State as Brister threw for 227 yards and the Indians rediscovered the long ball.

The game was tied 10-10 until Billy Brewer scored on a 14-yard run to give North Texas a 17-10 lead with 11:13 left in the game. With about a minute remaining, Brister decided it was time for the long ball once again. Again, he launched one in the direction of Mitchell. The NLU receiver hauled in the pass and waltzed into the end zone some 60 yards later to make the score 17-16. A 2-point conversion pass from Brister to tight end Keith Rufus gave the Indians an 18-17 lead.

Time was running out as the Mean Green got into position to attempt a 46-yard field goal. Kevin Chatman, who had connected from 35 yards earlier in the game, was playing in place of Smith, North Texas' normal kicker who was injured in an intramural soccer game the previous week. Chatman's kick was wide to the right, allowing NLU to claim an improbable 18-17 win and clinch another winning season.

Unlike two weeks earlier against Louisiana Tech, Northeast Louisiana was unable to play the role of spoiler against Arkansas State. Arkansas State's 31-23 triumph in the regular-season finale in Monroe allowed it to capture the Southland Conference title with a 5-1 league mark and 7-4 overall record. NLU ended its season 6-5.

A 49-yard touchdown pass from Brister to Keith Rufus gave Northeast a 17-10 halftime lead. Arkansas State tied the game with 5:12 remaining in the third quarter when a partially-blocked Kevin Duhe punt set up a 30-yard end-around by Francis. Arkansas State took its first lead of the game when Francis got past the NLU secondary to haul in a Brown pass as the 70-yard score gave A-State a 24-17 lead with 6:57 left in the game on its way to a 31-23 win and the SLC title.

"It was thrilling for me because this group of kids had gone through so much as freshmen," said Lacewell. "We beat a good Northeast Louisiana team. They were all-out. They ran faked punts and faked field goals and an onside kick. They did everything."

Lamar, meanwhile, closed out its 1985 season with a 28-7 home loss to McNeese State. The Cardinals concluded the year on an eight-game losing streak and wound up winless in the Southland Conference and 3-8 overall.

McNeese jumped out to a 21-0 first-quarter lead and coasted to its win over Lamar.

Brian McZeal, who rushed for 78 yards to set the freshman rushing record for McNeese with 809 yards, scored on a pair of 1-yard runs for the Cowboys in the opening quarter. McZeal topped the previous mark of 766 yards set by Buford Jordan.

Sandwiched between McZeal's two runs were a 20-yard reverse by Nelson Joseph that helped McNeese to a three-touchdown lead after one quarter.

The score held up until the fourth quarter when Lamar came up with its only touchdown of the game on a 14-yard pass from Smith to Levias. Johnson scored on a 3-yard run for McNeese later in the quarter for the 28-7 final.

The lone bright spot for the Cardinals was the 140-yard effort by Murchison to secure the national Division I-AA rushing title.

McNeese finished tied second with Louisiana Tech in the Southland at 3-1-2 and ended the season 6-3-2 overall.

Lamar lost in Ken Stephens' final game as Cardinals coach. Stephens, who finished with a four-year mark of 11-33, announced his resignation days before the McNeese game.

Needing a win at North Texas State to avoid a losing season, the Texas-Arlington Mavericks were unable to even manage a tie against the Eagles.

Chapman kicked a 32-yard field goal with 1:43 left in the game to give North Texas a 13-10 lead. A 35-yard attempt by Roper with eight seconds left was wide right, handing the Mavs a cruel three-point loss in what proved to be the last game for the Texas-Arlington program.

UTA dropped the sport after the 1985 season so the defeat to North Texas meant the Mavericks closed out its final year of football at 4-6-1, including 2-3-1 in the Southland Conference. North Texas ended with an identical record to UT-Arlington both overall and in the Southland.

Sixth-ranked Arkansas State was able to host its opening-round Division I-AA playoff game and the visitors didn't have to travel very far for the contest. Arriving from north Louisiana was Grambling State and legendary coach Eddie

Robinson. Earlier in the season, Robinson passed Alabama's Paul "Bear" Bryant to become the winningest coach in the history of college football.

"It was an emotional game and I wasn't quite sure who my players were for. I remember getting off the bus and my entire team ran off and wanted his autograph," Lacewell said of Robinson.

Robinson and his Tigers found themselves in a defensive struggle against the Indians. Grambling State suffered from poor field position throughout the game as Arkansas State punter Stacy Gore pinned the Tigers inside their own 16-yard line six times in 11 Grambling possessions. While Arkansas State had better field position, the Indians were unable to cash in. On three occasions in which Arkansas State advanced inside the Grambling 22-yard line, the Indians failed to come away with a single point.

A trick play helped to produce the only points in the first half. Facing third-and-12 late in the second quarter, Arkansas State's Ray Brown rambled 25 yards on a guard-around play before being hauled down at the Grambling 1-yard line. It took three plays but Rickey Jemison finally scored from a yard out with 45 second left in the half for a 7-0 Indians lead.

The 7-0 score held up until early in the fourth quarter when Grambling marched 80 yards to tie the game. Chauncey Allen, playing in place of starter Terrell Landry at quarterback, completed four passes for 69 yards during the drive. The big toss was to John McFarland, who broke loose for 52 yards before being brought down from behind at the Arkansas State 6-yard line. Three plays later, Landry was inserted into the game and scored from a yard out to tie the contest with 11:21 left in the game. The touchdown drive was the only time in the contest that Grambling crossed midfield.

Taking possession at its own 45 with 2:07 left in the game, Arkansas State eventually faced a third-and-2 at the Grambling 30-yard line. Sophomore Homer Rhodes, playing in place of an injured Maddox, turned a shovel pass into a 12-yard gain down to the 18. Jemison raced 11 yards down to the Tigers' 7-yard line with nine seconds left.

Instead of sending in Reid, the Indians' regular kicker who has missed two earlier field goals in the game, Arkansas State coach Larry Lacewell opted for Frank Richards. Richards, who missed all three of his field goal attempts during the regular season, connected from 25 yards out to give Arkansas State a 10-7 victory that advanced the Indians to the next round of the playoffs.

"Our kicking game was terrible," said Lacewell. "It was just a flip of the coin. I remember ole Frank made it and all were shocked."

Regardless of what the outcome may have been, the game allowed Lacewell the opportunity to face the two winningest coaches in college football history at the time during his career.

"I had now played against the two winningest coaches in the history of (college) football; Coach Bryant at Alabama and Coach Robinson. Someone asked me how it felt. I said, 'It feels pretty dumb. I wish I was playing against the losingest coaches,'" Lacewell joked.

Trailing 24-10 on a snow-covered field and a frigid wind blowing in Reno, Nevada, the Arkansas State Indians finally got hot in the final six minutes of their second-round Division I-AA playoff game.

Lewis Brown's 12-yard touchdown run, a punt block by Brad Dent and Greg Zachry's recovery of a blocked punt rallied the Indians to within one point with 3:10 left in their game against Nevada-Reno. After the final score, Reid slipped while attempting to kick the extra point and Arkansas State continued to trail 24-23.

Arkansas State regained possession near midfield with 1:22 left in the game and proceeded to use a few familiar plays from the Indians' opening-round playoff game against Grambling State. A 17-yard guard-around by Ray Brown and a shovel pass for 12 yards – this time by Andre Tate – helped Arkansas State reach the Nevada 13 before calling timeout with 27 seconds remaining on third down. The Indians elected to kick the field goal on third down in case there was some sort of miscue on the play, Arkansas State might have another attempt on fourth down.

Richards, who provided the game-winning kick against Grambling a week earlier, was sent onto the field. The snap from center was high, with holder Butch Snider pulling in the ball and running before suffering a 10-yard loss.

Wolf Pack players celebrated what they thought was a victory. With the play coming on third down and with time still remaining on the clock, Nevada was assessed a delay-of-game penalty and 19 seconds was placed on the clock. Richards' next attempt was from 35 yards out. This time, the snap from center was too wide for Snider to control. Richards ran after the ball before being brought down by Nevada defenders, bringing Arkansas State's season to an end.

"I think I made a dumb mistake," said Lacewell. "I think I shouldn't have told my team that because my center about turned purple when I said something about a bad snap. Sure enough, he snapped it and it was a world record over (the holder's) head. The only reason we got another chance, even though we recovered it, was because they (the Wolf Pack players) ran out on the field, grabbed the ball and thought the game was over."

   Arkansas State took a 10-7 halftime lead on Dwane Brown's 25-yard touchdown run on the Indians' first possession of the game and a 37-yard Richards field goal with three seconds left in the first half.

   Nevada scored on three-consecutive possessions in the third quarter on a 49-yard pass from quarterback Eric Beavers, a 46-yard Marty Zendejas field goal and a 15-yard touchdown reception by Thai Ivery to build its 24-10 lead at the 3:41 mark of the third quarter on its way to the 24-23 victory that ended Arkansas State's season at 9-4.

ARKANSAS STATE'S LAST SLC HURRAH

Following the 1985 season, Texas-Arlington opted to drop its football program. The Mavericks' other sports programs continued to compete in the Southland but the loss of the school left the conference a six-team football league.

McNeese State and North Texas State were the first two teams to kick off Southland Conference action in 1986. The Cowboys entered the contest 1-2 on the season while the Eagles were 1-1, with the defeat being a 48-28 loss to Texas A&M.

The Cowboys led 10-7 in the second quarter at North Texas State before the Eagles used a big special teams play and a time-consuming offense to put away McNeese 21-13.

Marcus Camper returned a punt 60 yards for a touchdown in the second quarter to give the Eagles a 14-10 halftime edge. A 2-yard run by Billy Brewer in the third quarter extended the North Texas lead to 21-10. Lance Wiley's 36-yard field goal made it 21-13 in the fourth quarter.

North Texas, which rushed for 288 yards, used up four minutes on a drive down the stretch and later intercepted a McNeese pass with 1:40 left in the game to preserve the eight-point victory.

The Eagles were unable to make it two in a row in Southland play, dropping a narrow 17-10 decision a week later at 2-2 Louisiana Tech.

A series of North Texas mistakes allowed Louisiana Tech to begin its first three possessions inside the Mean Green's 40-yard line. The Bulldogs didn't take full advantage of the North Texas miscues, but did produce 10 points on a 26-yard Matt Stover field goal and a 1-yard Garlon Powell run.

That allowed the Mean Green to stay in the game as North Texas pulled to within seven points at 10-3 with a 43-yard Todd Smith field goal. Midway in the fourth quarter, North Texas put together it's only sustained drive when quarterback Bron Beal's 1-yard touchdown run capped a 73-yard drive to make it 17-10. Louisiana Tech faced a fourth-and-1 at the Mean Green 11 and instead of a field-goal attempt for a possible 10-point lead with 2:54 left in the game, the

Bulldogs failed on a conversion attempt when Powell was stopped short. That gave North Texas one last chance, but the Eagles fumbled at their own 46, allowing Tech to take the seven-point victory.

Off to an 0-4 start under new coach Ray Alborn, Lamar was looking to reverse its fortunes in the Cardinals' Southland Conference opener at Northeast Louisiana. Ironically, Alborn, who coached Rice from 1978-83, made his debut as Lamar coach against the Owls. A 28-14 defeat to the Owls was followed by losses to Sam Houston State, Stephen F. Austin State and Texas A&I going into the league opener versus NLU.

Northeast Louisiana went into the encounter with Lamar 1-4 on the season, with the Indians lone win a 17-14 decision against Southwest Texas State.

The Cardinals seemed to serve notice from the opening play of the game that they were out to turn their season around with the start of conference play. Kevin Simon returned the opening kickoff 52 yards to set up quarterback Shad Smith's 29-yard touchdown pass to flanker Dwayne Dodd for a quick 7-0 lead. An exchange of turnovers resulted in Norrtheast Louisiana starting a possession at its own 1-yard line. NLU's Tommy Minvielle entered the fumbling act, with linebacker Michael Jackson recovering for Lamar. It took four plays, but tailback Burton Murchison finally plowed through for a 14-0 Cardinals lead. A later 4-yard run by Murchison gave Lamar a 21-0 lead.

Two Teddy Garcia field goals made it 21-6. On Lamar's first play from scrimmage following Garcia's second field goal, Charles Durham returned a Smith interception to the Cardinals' 23. Two plays later, a scrambling Walter Phythian found Mike Manzullo for a 22-yard touchdown. A two-point conversion attempt failed, but the Indians overcame their poor start to trail only 21-12 at halftime.

Garcia's third field goal of the game inched the Indians closer at 21-15. NLU drove 80 yards in the fourth quarter with Jimmy Harris' 1-yard run tying the game. Garcia's extra point with 4:52 left in the game gave Northeast Louisiana a 22-21 lead.

Needing only a field goal go win, Lamar reached the NLU 6-yard line with approximately three seconds left in the game. With Lamar coaches frantically trying to call a timeout, the officials apparently never saw any player signal for a stoppage of play and time ran out on the winless Cardinals.

Louisiana Tech improved to 2-0 in SLC play with a 28-16 win over McNeese State in Lake Charles. Stover kicked a school record-tying four field goals in the game, including three in the first half. Along with the three field goals, the Bulldogs also added a safety and a 61-yard pass from Jordan Stanley to Paddy Doyle to lead 18-16 at halftime. Besides a fourth Stover field goal, Tech also added a 4-yard run by Powell in the second half. Powell, who rushed for 107 yards in the game, had his fourth 100-plus yard rushing effort of the season.

A field goal and a pair of 2-yard touchdown runs by McNeese quarterback Scott Dieterich allowed the Cowboys to cut an 18-3 deficit to 18-16 at halftime.

Louisiana Tech faced a tough task in trying to get to 3-0 in the Southland when the Bulldogs hosted fourth-ranked Arkansas State. The defending SLC champions were the final team to play their initial conference game in 1986.

Following up on their strong 1985 season, the Indians lost only once in their first six games going into the league opener. Arkansas State was 4-1-1 with the only blemishes on the Indians' record coming against Southeastern Conference schools. Arkansas State lost 24-9 at Mississippi State and tied Ole Miss 10-10 on the road.

A Stover field goal and two Powell touchdown runs gave the Bulldogs a 17-7 halftime lead. Powell's first score was set up on a fake punt by Tech, while the later score came from a yard out following a 49-yard pass from Stanley to Rod Wright.

Two field goals by Scott Roper, the former UTA kicker, made the score 17-13 in the second half. Taking over at the Louisiana Tech 44 with 2:31 left in the game, the Indians used three running plays and a 13-yard pass from quarterback Dwane Brown to Fred Barnett to reach the 9. Two plays later, Brown hit Barnett from 5 yards out with 55 seconds left in the game. The ball was knocked away from Barnett, the future Philadelphia Eagle and Miami Dolphin receiver, but he was ruled to have had control of the ball and the touchdown stood.

"After (Barnett) caught the ball and took a step and threw it straight up. It looked like it was knocked loose but he was celebrating and there was a discussion on the play but they ruled it in our favor," Arkansas State coach Larry Lacewell recalled.

Individual records were accumulating for McNeese State but so were the losses as the Cowboys dropped to 0-3 in the Southland Conference in a 37-17 home loss to Northeast Louisiana.

Tony Citizen rushed for 43 yards in the game, giving him 848 on the season through only seven games. That established a new freshman rushing record for McNeese, which had been set only a year before by Brian McZeal. Also, Flip Johnson had nine catches in the game to give him a school-record 84 career receptions.

The more effective numbers in the game, however, belonged to the Indians. Minvielle rushed for three touchdowns, quarterback Stan Humphries tossed for two scores and Garcia kicked a season-long 46-yard field goal in NLU's victory. Like

Bubby Brister before him, Humphries had a stint in minor league baseball before quarterbacking the Indians.

Two 1-yard runs by Minvielle and touchdown passes from Humphries to Tommy Jackson and Chris Jones gave the Indians a 38-3 halftime lead. The only points for McNeese came on a 37-yard Wiley field goal in the first quarter.

Garcia's field goal and a 3-yard run by Minvielle rounded out NLU's scoring in the second half. The Cowboys countered with a pair of touchdown passes from Dieterich to Johnson.

Along with falling to 0-3 in the Southland, McNeese dropped to 1-6 overall, guaranteeing only the second losing season for the Cowboys in 15 years. Northeast Louisiana moved to 2-0 in the SLC and 3-4 overall.

A week later at Arkansas State, McNeese State saw a 10-7 halftime deficit increase by an additional 10 points in the third quarter on a 21-yard touchdown pass from Brown to freshman halfback Dennis Forrest and a 23-yard Roper field goal.

Arkansas State faced a few anxious moments when the Cowboys drove 62 yards to set up Dieterich's touchdown run from a yard out to make it 20-14 with 6:35 left in the game. The Indians responded by moving 64 yards on the ensuing drive before Roper connected on his third field goal of the game, this one from 34 yards out with 1:39 left to secure a 24-14 Arkansas State triumph.

McNeese's sixth-consecutive loss dropped the Cowboys to 1-6 overall and 0-4 in the Southland. Arkansas State improved to 2-0 in the SLC and 6-1-1.

Lamar's 17-3 non-conference victory over Southwest Texas State a week earlier gave Alborn his first win as coach and ended the Cardinals' 13-game losing streak but they had no such luck when returning to league action against North Texas.

Even with Billy Brewer missing the game while nursing an injury, the Cardinals were no match for visiting North Texas State in a 33-13 loss. Following non-conference victories over Northwestern State and TCU, the triumph over Lamar gave the Mean Green a three-game winning streak for the first time since 1983 as North Texas improved to 5-2 overall and 2-1 in the Southland.

Spreading the carries around, 10 Eagle ball carriers amassed a total of 369 yards on the ground. A 2-yard touchdown run by Carl Brewer and an 83-yard sprint by Monte Moon staked the Mean Green to a 14-0 halftime advantage. Darren Collins added a 37-yard run for North Texas in the second half and Todd Smith kicked two field goals.

In the only Southland encounter a week later, Lamar seemed perhaps on the verge of earning an elusive first conference win at home against Louisiana Tech when Mike Andrie kicked a 43-yard field goal to tie the game 20-20. The Bulldogs, however, made sure that didn't happen by scoring the final 19 points of the contest for a 39-20 triumph.

A 46-yard field goal by Stover on the ensuing possession following Andrie's kick gave Tech the lead again at 23-20. The field goal was Stover's eleventh in a row, establishing a new Southland record. Andrie's punt attempt on the Cardinals' next possession was blocked. He recovered in the end zone for a safety, making the score 25-20.

Tech pulled away on two, fourth-quarter touchdowns. The first was a 10-yard run by Derrick Douglas while the final score of the game occurred when linebacker Neal Atkins recovered a fumble by Lamar quarterback John Evans in the end zone.

Louisiana Tech, which improved to 3-1 in conference and 5-3-1 overall, had its most productive offensive outing of the season. Bob Garrett, making his first start at quarterback since the opening game of the season, was 18 of 23 passing for 238 yards. The Bulldogs amassed 434 yards total offense, including 238 passing and 196 rushing.

Any thoughts the Bulldogs had of winning the Southland Conference came to an abrupt halt at the hands of rival Northeast Louisiana in Monroe. The Indians converted several early Louisiana Tech turnovers into a Garcia field goal and a 12-yard touchdown pass from Stan Humphries to David Christmas. Garcia and Stover exchanged field goals to make it 13-3 at halftime.

It was much the same in the second half. Tech punter Barry Bowman was brought down by a hard-charging Northeast Louisiana special teams squad as he tried to scoop up a low center snap. After taking over at the Louisiana Tech 17, Humphries scored on a 1-yard run four plays later to make it 20-3. All the Bulldogs could come up with in the second half was a 48-yard field goal as the 20-6 defeat dropped Tech to 3-2 in the SLC and 5-4-1 overall. NLU remained unbeaten in Southland play at 3-0 as the Indians improved to 5-4 overall.

Second-ranked Arkansas State joined Northeast Louisiana at 3-0 in the Southland with a 43-21 victory at North Texas State. The well-rested Indians went into the game coming off an open week while North Texas was coming off a heartbreaking 27-26 loss at Nevada-Las Vegas that snapped a three-game winning streak for the Mean Green.

The Eagles' defense had no answer for Arkansas State's offense, which rolled up 455 yards. Roper tied the single-game SLC record with five field goals.

Roper's first field goal came less than three minutes into the game. A 2-yard run by Brown and Roper's second field goal gave the Indians a 13-0 lead after one quarter. The Arkansas State kicker would go on to add three more field goals while

Brown helped to account for two more touchdowns on a 76-yard run and a 42-yard pass to Cazzy Francis.

Arkansas State had little trouble moving to 4-0 in the Southland Conference with a 56-7 home domination of Lamar. The Cardinals entered the game coming off a 47-23 victory over Central Oklahoma for their second win of the season but any confidence factor didn't carry over to league play as Lamar fell to 0-4 in the SLC.

Brown rushed for a career-high 181 yards rushing – 153 in the first half – as second-ranked Arkansas State rolled up 575 yards of total offense. The Arkansas State quarterback had scoring runs of 21 and 78 yards in the first half as the Indians built a 28-7 lead by intermission.

Mike Adams made sure there would be no rally attempt by the Cardinals when he returned the second half kickoff 99 yards for a touchdown for the 8-1-1 Indians.

For yet another year, Northeast Louisiana found itself unbeaten in Southland Conference play late in the season and facing a crucial league game. At 3-0, a win at North Texas State would make the Bulldogs undefeated going into the season finale against Arkansas State.

Northeast and North Texas were involved in a 7-7 tie as the two teams traded early touchdowns. The Eagles got on the scoreboard first on a 19-yard option keeper by Beal. NLU tied the game when Minvielle capped a 45-yard drive with a touchdown run from a yard out.

North Texas responded to Minvielle's touchdown by marching 78 yards for a score of its own. Collins ended the drive with a 5-yard run for a 14-7 lead. The turning point came three plays later when Mean Green defensive end Tom Middaugh sacked Humphries and caused a fumble. The ball was recovered by Mike Minter of North Texas at the NLU 30. On the first play from scrimmage, Beal ran down the line on the option and then dropped back to pass. He lofted the ball to tight end Todd Joseph for the touchdown to make it 21-7.

The Eagles, who rushed for 259 yards in the game, used 13 plays to travel 73 yards to open the second half. Billy Brewer's 13-yard touchdown run made it 28-7. NLU scored late to make the final appear closer at 28-20, but the loss snapped the Indians' four-game winning streak to even their record at 5-5. North Texas ended the year 3-2 in the Southland and 6-4 overall for its first winning season since 1983.

On the final week of the regular season, Louisiana Tech defeated Southwestern Louisiana 23-14 in non-conference play to conclude the 1986 season 6-4-1 overall and 3-2 in the SLC. A.L. Williams, the Louisiana Tech coach, announced 10 days before the USL contest that he would step down as coach after the game to accept a position as assistant athletic director at the school.

At the bottom of the standings, Lamar lost 38-7 at McNeese State to end the season 0-5 in the Southland and 2-9 overall. Lamar's conference losing streak was extended to 16 games over the span of three seasons. McNeese, picking up its first victory since the season opener, snapped a nine-game losing streak to also finish 2-9 overall and 1-4 in the conference.

The few noteworthy moments in the game belonged to McNeese. Citizen ran for 94 yards to finish with 1,088 yards in capturing the Southland Conference rushing title. Dieterich ended the season with 2,121 passing yards and 2,097 total yards to lead the SLC in both categories. Johnson finished as the top receiver in the conference with 164 catches.

With the preliminaries out of the way, it all came down to the Arkansas State-Northeast Louisiana game in Jonesboro. NLU's loss to North Texas allowed Arkansas State to clinch at least a share of the title and that made the stakes higher for Northeast. At 3-1 in the Southland, a victory would leave the teams tied for the league title but NLU would get the conference's automatic bid to the Division I-AA playoffs by virtue of its head-to-head victory. With a 5-5 record going into the game, there would be no at-large berth for Northeast Louisiana.

Arkansas State, by contrast, was all but assured a spot in the playoffs. A win would give Arkansas State the outright Southland title. Entering the game as the second-ranked team in Division I-AA, a loss to Northeast Louisiana was unlikely to keep Arkansas State out of the postseason.

A 40-yard Roper field goal in the first quarter was answered by a 9-yard touchdown pass from Humphries to Benny Mitchell less than two minutes into the second quarter to give Northeast Louisiana a 7-3 lead. Arkansas State responded by scoring the next 20 points of the game for a 23-7 lead early in the fourth quarter. A 52-yard scoring strike from Brown to Francis, two Roper field goals and a 4-yard run by James McCarley helped Arkansas State build its lead.

Phythian entered the game in relief of Humphries two series into the fourth quarter. Three plays into his first drive, he heaved a pass to Charles Andrews for an 87-yard touchdown. A two-point conversion made it 23-15.

After a 30-yard Roper field goal made it 26-15, Phythian was at it once again. Throwing the ball four times in an eight-play drive, the quarterback connected with Jones on a 13-yard toss to make it 26-21. Arkansas State recovered an onside kick attempt and ran off the final 1:54 of the game to secure a perfect 5-0 Southland Conference mark.

"We won two championships back-to-back and that's so difficult in the Southland Conference to do that. The teams are so equal. It's very seldom to win conference championships back-to-back. It was a big day for us to do it at home," said Lacewell.

Arkansas State, which extended its home non-beaten streak to 18 games, concluded the regular season 9-1-1. Northeast Louisiana ended its season 5-6 overall, including 3-2 in the SLC.

As Arkansas State was preparing for its game against Northeast Louisiana, word broke that the school was planning to join Louisiana Tech, and perhaps, Lamar, in the newly-formed American South Conference. That meant Arkansas State's third-consecutive Division I-AA playoff run would be its last as a member of the Southland Conference.

Second-seeded Arkansas State had little trouble in its opening playoff game as the host Indians dominated Sam Houston State 48-7.

Leading the way for the Indians was fullback Rickey Jemison, who had a career-high 157 yards rushing. Brown, the Arkansas State quarterback, produced 215 yards of total offense with 145 yards passing and 70 rushing as part of an Indians attack that produced 594 yards.

The game was tied 7-7 in the first quarter before Arkansas State built a 20-7 edge at halftime. The Indians scored touchdowns on four of their five possessions in the second half to blow away the Bearkats, the champions of the Gulf Star Conference.

Touchdown runs of 10 yards by Brown, 63 by Forrest and 36 yards by Jemison made it 41-7 after three quarters.

It wasn't only the Arkansas State offense that was dominant. The Indians' defense limited a Sam Houston State offense that went into the game averaging 411 yards to 97 rushing and 53 passing. Bearkats quarterbacks Reggie Lewis and Bryan Osterhaus were a combined 4 of 22 passing against the Indians. SHSU's only score came on a 1-yard run by Lewis late in the first quarter.

Arkansas State's quarterfinal playoff encounter at Delaware was the same as the Sam Houston State game – and then some.

Jemison set a career record for the second week in a row with 159 yards rushing and instead of waiting to score on four of five possessions in the second half as they did against Sam Houston State, the Indians scored on nine of 12 possessions – including touchdowns on their first three drives. Arkansas State produced 646 yards of offense in the 55-14 demolition of the Blue Hens.

Despite touchdown runs of 7 and 72 yards by Jemison, along with a 52-yard pass from Brown to Barnett, Delaware stayed in the game in the early going behind the play of Rich Gannon. The future quarterback of the Minnesota Vikings, Washington Redskins, Kansas City Chiefs and Oakland Raiders guided the Blue Hens to a 70-yard scoring drive culminated in a 28-yard run by Bob Norris and tossed a 10-yard pass to Gregg Penasuk to make the score 21-14 in the second quarter.

A 32-yard Roper field goal with 3:09 remaining in the first half gave Arkansas State a 31-14 halftime lead. While Arkansas State blanked the Blue Hens in the second half, the Indians added an additional 24 points on an 8-yard run by Forrest, a Roper field goal, and two touchdown runs by Andre Tate.

Delaware's Wing-T offense managed to produce 421 yards in the loss as Gannon passed for 228 yards and rushed for 67.

"We didn't stop him," Lacewell said of Gannon. "It was one of those games where we would get the ball and score they would get the ball and moved it. Thank the Lord they turned it over more than they should have."

Arkansas State went into its Division I-AA semifinal game at home against Eastern Kentucky without the services of Jemison, the Indians running back who set single-game personal highs for rushing in each of the previous two games.

With Jemison nursing a strained knee, freshman Richard Kimble got his first career start at fullback. On the opening play from scrimmage, Kimble fumbled on his own 9-yard line. The Arkansas State defense bailed out the Indians' offense by keeping the Colonels off the scoreboard. It was one of four occasions in the contest in which the Arkansas State defense stopped Eastern Kentucky inside the Indians' 10-yard line.

Kimble and the rest of the Arkansas State offense settled down with the freshman running back gaining 95 yards as the Indians managed 200 on the ground without Jemison. Luckily, Arkansas State still had a healthy Brown, who accounted for three touchdowns for the Indians.

A 21-yard run by Forrest down to the Eastern Kentucky 39 eventually set up a quarterback sneak by Brown from a yard out for a 7-0 Arkansas State lead with 2:14 remaining in the first quarter. Brown kept the ball on an option keeper and scored on a 19-yard run to make it 14-0 with 3:36 remaining in the opening half.

After an exchange of turnovers, Eastern Kentucky quarterback Mike Whitaker, who was sacked four times by a harassing Indians defense, tossed an 18-yard strike to Frank Davis with 1:10 left in the second quarter for a 14-7 halftime score.

Whitaker wasn't so fortunate to open the third quarter. An errant throw by the Colonels' quarterback was picked off by Vincent Barnett, who ran the ball back to the Eastern Kentucky 6-yard line. On third-and-goal from the 7-yard line,

Brown hit tight end James Waldrop for the touchdown that gave Arkansas State a 21-7 lead less than two minutes into the second half.

Eastern Kentucky countered with a 23-yard Dale Dawson field goal but Arkansas State mounted an 11-play, 68-yard drive that ran the clock down to 4:47 before Roper connected on a 36-yard field goal that secured a 24-10 victory that sent the Indians to the Division I-AA championship game.

Played six days before Christmas on a Friday at the Tacoma Dome in Tacoma, Washington, the Division I-AA championship game, also known as the Diamond Bowl, showed that Ham can be tough to swallow.

That was especially true for Arkansas State. The Indians simply were unable to stop the Hambone, the offense named for Georgia Southern quarterback Tracy Ham. Ham rushed for 180 yards, passed for 360 and accounted for four touchdowns to lead the defending champion Eagles to a dominating 48-21 win and the national championship.

For all of big numbers for Ham and the Georgia Southern offense, the Eagles could have won by a much larger margin. Georgia Southern scored on its first seven possessions but on four of the drives the Eagles had to settle for field goals.

Also, Ham's 540 yards of total offense to top his championship-game record set the previous year, came despite his not playing the final 10 minutes of the contest.

"Tracy Ham is the best wishbone quarterback I've ever seen," Lacewell declared. "We didn't see anybody offensively my whole 11 years at Arkansas State like him. He proved it by going to Canada and breaking all of their records.

"I've never seen one guy in college football that would just totally dominate a game. Football is a team game. You've got to have receivers, running backs, whatever. Frankly, he didn't need anybody but himself."

Georgia Southern, 13-2 under coach Erk Russell, the former Georgia Bulldogs defensive coordinator, was as dominant to its road to the championship game as in was in the title contest against Arkansas State. The Eagles defeated North Carolina A&T 52-21 in the opening round of the playoffs. In the quarterfinals, Georgia Southern won 55-31 over Nicholls State, which had finished second to Sam Houston State in the Gulf Star Conference. A 48-38 victory over Nevada-Reno, an old Southland Conference postseason nemesis, put the Eagles in the national championship game for the second-consecutive year.

Playing with a national TV audience via ESPN but with a disappointing crowd of only 4,419, the Eagles struck early and often. A 20-yard Tim Foley field goal less than five minutes into the game and a 1-yard run by fullback Gerald Harris gave Georgia Southern a 10-0 lead.

Arkansas State had 424 yards of total offense, 95 of which came on a late first-quarter drive. A 15-yard run by Boris Whitehead made it 10-7 with 3:08 remaining in the first quarter.

That was as close as Arkansas State would get. While the Indians rushed for 343 yards, 240 came in the second half long after the game was decided.

"We should have gone for it (on fourth down) every time because we could not stop them," said Lacewell.

The second quarter was all Georgia Southern. Foley kicked field goals of 30, 25 and 36 yards, while Ham scored on a 25-yard run to give the Eagles a 26-7 halftime lead. Ham scored on runs of 31 and 11 yards in the third quarter while all the Indians could counter with was a safety. After a 79-yard bomb from Ham to split end Ricky Harris with 10:52 left in the game, the Georgia Southern quarterback was done for the day – and so were the Indians.

"I think if we had played any other team in the country, I think we probably would have won the game. We were that great a team but we were not great against him," said Lacewell, again referring to Ham.

Arkansas State's final season in the Southland Conference ended with a 12-2-1 record. The 12 wins represented a school record for the most wins in a single season.

MAJOR MEMBERSHIP CHANGES AND A NATIONAL CHAMPIONSHIP

The 1987 season ushered in the biggest one-year change in the membership of the Southland Conference.

The departure of Louisiana Tech, Arkansas State and Lamar caused the league to go looking for new members. Added to the SLC in 1987 were Northwestern State, Sam Houston State, Southwest Texas State and Stephen F. Austin State. All had been members of the Gulf Star Conference. With so much turnover so quickly, it was impossible to get all of the teams to play one another on their schedules. That meant several non-league games had to be "designated" conference games. Northeast Louisiana, for example, had to play designated conference games against recent league foes Louisiana Tech and Arkansas State.

There was change at McNeese State as well. Following the 1986 season, John McCann was dismissed as coach and the new Cowboy in charge was Sonny Jackson. Jackson was hired away from Nicholls State, which he guided to the 1986 Division I-AA quarterfinals.

All of the changes made Northeast Louisiana's Pat Collins the dean of Southland Conference coaches. Collins was entering his seventh season at the helm of the NLU program.

Louisiana Tech, Arkansas State and Lamar left the Southland for new the new American South Conference, joining the likes of Southwestern Louisiana, the University of New Orleans and Texas-Pan American.

With UNO and Pan American having no football programs, the American South Conference was a basketball-centric league, causing the football programs to play as Division I-AA independents while making the transition to Division I-A.

Louisiana Tech competed as a Division I-AA independent through 1988 before becoming Division I-A. Arkansas State was a Division I-AA independent through 1991. Lamar competed as an independent on the Division I-AA level through 1989 before dropping its football program. Lamar brought back football on the Division I-AA level in 2010 and returned to the Southland Conference in 2011.

Southland Conference play began early in 1987 with a pair of games only two weeks into the season. Northwestern State and Southwest Texas both made their league debuts on September 12, 1987, as the Demons faced McNeese State and the Bobcats took on North Texas State.

McNeese went into the game 0-1 on the season coming off a 34-31 loss against Northern Iowa in Jackson's debut as Cowboys coach. Northwestern State was 1-0 and coming off a 23-20 upset victory over former Southland member Arkansas State, which was ranked No. 2 in Division I-AA.

Northwestern State was led by fifth-year coach Sam Goodwin. In his first four years at the helm, he led the Demons to a 19-24-1 record.

McNeese and Northwestern State met 36 times on the gridiron but 1987 was the first time the two school competed as Southland Conference rivals when they met in Natchitoches, Louisiana. The Cowboys led the all-time series 23-13.

The Demons jumped out to a 16-0 halftime lead on a 1-yard run by quarterback Rusty Stack, a 19-yard Keith Hodnett field goal and an 11-yard run by John Stephens.

McNeese scored off the second-half kickoff on a 30-yard Lance Wiley field goal but the Cowboys would produce no more points the rest of the game. Meanwhile, Northwestern countered with 23 points in the second half, including 20 in the third quarter. Slack added a 4-yard touchdown run in the second half and a 21-yard scoring strike to tight end Orlan Lockhart. In the middle of those two scores, Kevin Lewis returned a punt 69 yards for a touchdown. Hodnett added a field goal in the fourth quarter to make the final 39-3.

Southwest Texas went into its game at North Texas 0-1 following a season-opening loss at home in San Marcos, Texas, to Texas A&I. The Bobcats were blanked in the contest 2-0.

The Bobcats were led by fifth-year coach John O'Hara. O'Hara sported a 23-21 record, including a Lone Star Conference co-championship in 1983.

North Texas went into the game against Southwest Texas 0-1 after opening the season with a 69-14 loss at Oklahoma, the top-ranked team in Division I-A.

Limited to a pair of Keith Chapman field goals, North Texas held a 6-0 lead until David Haass of Southwest Texas connected on a 34-yard field goal to close the margin to three points. The Eagles put the game away with two touchdowns in the final 4:16 of the contest on a 3-yard run by backup quarterback Scott Davis and a 17-yard scamper by Tony Baker to give North Texas a 20-3 triumph.

On the same day Northwestern State and Southwest Texas were making their Southland debuts, Northeast Louisiana visited Louisiana Tech.

The Indians may or may not have been looking to send a message to their former, though "designated" conference rivals. The message that was delivered loud and clear was that Stan Humphries and NLU's new one-back offense meant business. Humphries threw for 377 yards and the Indians built a 31-7 halftime lead on their way to blasting Tech 44-7 before a Joe Aillet Stadium-record crowd of 24,925.

"It started out throwing the football out of it and a lot of fullback traps and things like that," Humphries said of the new offense. "Eventually as the year went along, we got better and better with two backs and a little bit of I-formation and play action and things like that toward the end of the year.

"I just think the system overall, as far as blocking scheme passing game-wise and route combinations and things like that was something that kind of fit our players' profiles and what we were capable of doing."

Collins, Humphries' head coach, said the one-back offense was a fairly novel idea in college football in the late 1980s.

"First of all, the idea was let's spread them out and get people one-on-one," Collins explained. "It was relatively new. Nobody was really doing it at the time. You had a chance to see a lot of different schemes defensively and we got better at it as time went on.

"We found out as we got into the season that we would have to add something to the offense, so we had a two-back offense and not just a one-back so we were able to get those crucial yards when we needed them."

Northeast Louisiana drove the length of the field on the opening possession of the game. Fullback Tommy Minvielle's touchdown run from a yard out gave NLU a 7-0 lead and the Indians never let up. Two short touchdown runs by T-back Andrew Hargroder were sandwiched around a 4-yard touchdown toss from Humphries to Jeff Steele for a 28-0 lead. Kicker Teddy Garcia's third extra point following Steele's touchdown reception gave him 155 career points and established a new school record. He later added a field goal to account for NLU's 31 points in the first half. Tech's only points in the opening half came on a 10-yard pass from quarterback Bob Garrett to Paddy Doyle.

"Being the first game of the year and beating your arch rival with a new offensive system, we came out and we played like we hadn't missed a beat and we were at midseason form. We played really, really well. We threw the ball and we ran the ball when we needed to. It was kind of a total domination that game. We had a ton of confidence after that game was over with," said Humphries.

McNeese State also helped Stephen F. Austin usher in its membership in the Southland Conference as the Cowboys hosted the Lumberjacks in SFA's first-ever league game on September 19, 1987.

The Nacogdoches, Texas, school entered its game with McNeese 1-0-1 on the season. SFA opened with a 7-3 win at West Texas and a 13-13 tie at home against Prairie View.

Guiding the Lumberjacks was sixth-year coach Jim Hess. Hess led SFA to a 35-19-1 mark in his first five years, including a Gulf Star Conference co-championship in 1985. The Lumberjacks were coming off a 5-6 season in 1986, the only losing season under Hess.

McNeese State's defense led the Cowboys to their first win of the season with a 20-8 victory over Stephen F. Austin. The Cowboys held the Lumberjacks to 136 total yards. SFA running back Michael Horace, who entered the game averaging 122 yards on the ground as the second-leading rusher in the Southland, managed only 28 against McNeese.

An 11-yard pass from Scott Dieterich to Carlos McGee and a pair of Wiley field goals in the second quarter gave McNeese a 13-0 halftime lead. SFA rallied in the second half on a 28-yard pass from Dustin Dewald to Chris Edwards and a safety to move to within five points at 13-8. The safety came when Dieterich was tackled in the end zone by Johnny Hendrix.

The Cowboys put the game away on a 1-yard run by Tony Citizen. A 34-yard pass from Dieterich to McGee set up Citizen's touchdown run.

Northeast Louisiana's game at Southwest Texas, meanwhile, was a carbon copy of the opener against Louisiana Tech. Northeast Louisiana won by an identical 44-7 score while jumping out to a 23-7 halftime lead. Garcia also continued his assault on the record books.

Garcia kicked an extra point following a 15-yard touchdown reception by Minvielle in the first half. That gave Garcia 35-straight extra points, tying a school record. Following a 65-yard touchdown reception by tight end Jackie Harris later in the second quarter, Garcia missed the extra point to snap his streak. He connected on a 42-yard field goal with 17 seconds remaining in the half. The kick gave him 13 field goals in a row, giving him a Southland Conference record.

The Bobcats were trailing 23-7 at the start of the second half when tailback Gerald Bickham fumbled at his own 10-yard line midway in the third quarter. T-back Cisco Richard scored from a yard out five plays later and the rout was on.

Fourth-ranked Northwestern State spotted North Texas State a 12-0 lead before catching fire in the fourth quarter at home against the Mean Green.

Failing to score through three quarters, the Demons used a trick play to get back in the game. Tracy Palmer threw a 10-yard halfback pass to Stack but a missed extra point left Northwestern trailing 12-6.

Northwestern State used a more conventional method to take a 13-12 lead on Slack's 47-yard touchdown toss to Lockhart. The Demons had a chance to pad their lead but Hodnett missed a 43-yard field goal attempt with 7:20 remaining in the game.

Late in the game, a fumble by Slack was recovered by Tom Middaugh at the Demons' 46. Facing fourth down, Davis' toss to receiver Marcus Camper kept the drive alive. With 30 seconds left in the game, Chapman booted a 22-yard field goal to give the Mean Green a 15-13 triumph.

North Texas took an unusual 5-0 lead at halftime on a safety and a 41-yard Chapman field goal. The first loss of the year dropped the Demons to 2-1 on the season, including 1-1 in the Southland. North Texas remained in a tie with Northeast Louisiana for the top spot in the SLC at 2-0.

In the only Southland Conference encounter a week later, seventh-ranked North Texas moved to 3-0 in league play with a 38-16 victory at McNeese State.

The Cowboys rallied from an early 14-0 deficit to trail 14-10 at halftime but could manage only a late touchdown in the second half in falling to the Eagles.

Down by two touchdowns, McNeese State pulled to within four points at halftime on a 26-yard Wiley field goal and a 5-yard run by Citizen. The second half, however, especially the fourth quarter, belonged to the Eagles.

The Mean Green stretched a 17-10 lead after three quarters on a 3-yard pass from Bron Beal to Tony Cook, a 22-yard interception return for a touchdown by Derrick Wiggins and a 53-yard pass from Davis to David McGinty to make it 38-10.

Baker scored on touchdown runs of 25 and 1 yard within a five-minute period in the first quarter to give the Eagles their 14-0 lead. The only other score in the game was a fourth-quarter touchdown reception of 4 yards by McGee from freshman quarterback Hud Jackson, the coach's son.

Sam Houston State made its Southland Conference debut in one of the Bearkats' two "designated" league games, taking on Texas Southern at home in Huntsville, Texas, on October 3, 1987.

The Bearkats were coached by Ron Randleman. In his sixth year at Sam Houston State, Randleman had a record of 33-23-1 going into the 1987 season, including a Gulf Star Conference co-championship in 1985 and the outright title in 1986. Randleman was coach at Pittsburg State for six years prior to moving on to Sam Houston State, leading the Gorillas to the NAIA national finals in 1981.

SHSU entered the Texas Southern game 3-2 on the season. The Bearkats defeated Angelo State, Texas A&I and Texas Southern while suffering losses to Montana State and Houston.

The Bearkats dominated Texas Southern 45-7 for their first-ever Southland Conference victory.

Northeast Louisiana, coming off a 26-14 non-conference win over Nicholls State, was looking to match North Texas State at 3-0 in the Southland in a battle of ranked teams as the second-ranked Indians visited eighth-ranked Northwestern State. Coming off the loss to North Texas, an open date gave the Demons an extra week to prepare for NLU.

The Demons were clinging to a 31-27 lead in the closing seconds when Northwestern State attempted to convert on fourth down from the NLU 17. Quarterback Scott Stoker, in for an injured Slack, was stopped short, giving the ball to the Indians with 16 seconds remaining.

Humphries, who would later quarterback the San Diego Chargers to the Super Bowl, hit Steele with a pass at the NLU 40. Steele bounced off several would-be tacklers and reached the Demons' 48. On the final play of the game, Humphries heaved the ball into the end zone in a jump ball situation, with Harris hauling in the pass for a 33-31 Indians triumph. Harris, a future Green Bay Packers tight end, caught the game-winner after it had been deflected in the end zone.

"I know a lot of people who are from Northwestern over the years that are good friends of mine," said Humphries. "The actual last two plays of the game, the Northwestern coaches were in the elevator because they thought they had won. Once they exited the elevator, they heard all the screaming and yelling going on and they ran to the tunnel to see what had happened and they saw the scoreboard that we had won.

"I've heard about it through the years. One of my good friends is a guy who was keeping the clock and they gave him a bunch of crud because there was only one second left in the game after we completed that pass to midfield. A good home-field clock operator would have let the clock run out. It's a lot of fun memories in that kind of a game."

The ending typified the kind of game the two ranked teams played. NLU produced 20 points in the second quarter of the high-scoring affair to take a 27-14 lead at halftime. The Indians' points in the quarter came on a 12-yard pass from Humphries to Mike Manzullo, an 11-yard run by Minvielle and a 55-yard Garcia field goal.

Northwestern State scored on the opening possession of the second half on a 40-yard touchdown pass from Stoker to Floyd Turner, the future New Orleans

Saints, Indianapolis Colts and Baltimore Ravens receiver. The Demons later added a 3-yard touchdown run by Stoker and a Hodnett field goal to lead 31-27.

NLU remained unbeaten at 4-0 while the Demons' second-straight loss dropped Northwestern State to 2-2.

Sam Houston State's first Southland encounter that was not a "designated" game came when the Bearkats visited North Texas.

The Eagles entered their home game against Sam Houston State ranked No. 3 in Division I-AA but had a struggle on their hands until late in the Southland Conference tilt.

Behind a 206-yard rushing effort by Luther Turner and two third-quarter touchdowns by quarterback Reggie Lewis, the Bearkats took a 24-21 lead into the fourth quarter.

The North Texas defense shut down the Bearkats the rest of the way and after a 25-yard touchdown run by Davis, the Eagles pulled away for a 41-24 victory to remain unbeaten in the SLC at 4-0. North Texas improved to 5-1 overall while SHSU dropped to 1-1 in the conference and 3-3 overall.

A late rally lifted the Demons to a 24-21 Southland win at Southwest Texas State to snap a three-game Northwestern State losing streak and kept the Bobcats winless on the season.

Trailing 21-17, the Demons started their game-winning drive at their own 20-yard line. Stoker, who entered the game in the third quarter in place of an ineffective Slack, completed passes of 15 yards to Lockhart and 35 to Al Edwards to advance Northwestern to the Bobcats' 30. Following a first-and-goal from the 4-yard line, an illegal motion penalty moved the Demons back to the 9. Stoker hit Lockhart for the go-ahead score with 35 seconds left in the game.

The Bobcats quickly moved into Demons territory in the closing seconds. SWT quarterback Ron Rittimann hooked up Eric Tennessee for 34 yards, with the receiver being brought down at the Northwestern 3-yard line as time expired.

Northwestern trailed 14-7 at halftime before tying the game early in the second half on a 6-yard pass from Stoker to Turner. The score was set up when a partially-blocked Bobcats punt was recovered by Randolph Hayes at the SWT 31.

The Bobcats got a break of their own moments later when free safety Andre Horton returned an errant Slack pass to the Northwestern 2. Reggie Rivers scored one play later to put SWT back on top at 21-14. A 27-yard Hodnett field goal with 4:35 showing in the third quarter made it 21-17 and set the stage for the late Demons rally.

Northwestern State evened its record at 2-2 in the Southland and 3-3 overall. SWT remained winless through six games, including 0-3 in conference play.

Following North Texas State's win over Sam Houston State, the Eagles suffered their second loss of the season, falling 19-10 at Division I-A TCU. An open date gave the Mean Green an extra week to get over the loss to the Horned Frogs before returning to Southland Conference play at Stephen F. Austin.

The Eagles' undefeated record in league play was in serious jeopardy when Larry Centers scored on a 1-yard run to give the Lumberjacks a 14-13 lead in the fourth quarter.

The Eagles drove downfield in the closing moments, reaching the SFA 21 to set up Chapman's 38-yard game-winning field goal to lift North Texas to a 16-13 triumph.

By avoiding the upset, North Texas, now ranked No. 5, stayed unbeaten in SLC play at 5-0 while improving to 6-2 overall. The Lumberjacks fell to 1-2 in conference play and 3-4-1 overall.

In the three weeks following Northeast Louisiana's last Southland game against Northwestern State, the Indians went through a 1-2 stretch, losing to Lamar and Southwestern Louisiana but defeating two-time defending national champion Georgia Southern 26-17. The NLU-Georgia Southern game was a contest of Top 10 teams as the Indians went into the game ranked No. 6 while Georgia Southern was No. 8.

A struggling Humphries was benched during the three-game stretch.

"I wasn't playing well and (Collins) just wanted to shake it up a little bit, shake me up a little bit and bring me back to reality or something like that, and it did," said Humphries.

"That was a mistake on my part," revealed Collins. "You can't alternate. You can't get anything going. You can't get the chemistry going that you need when you alternate quarterbacks."

Humphries and the Indians continued to roll once back in Southland play, topping visiting McNeese State 37-10 to move to 4-0 in the conference. A fifth-consecutive loss dropped the Cowboys to 1-7 on the season.

Making his first start in three weeks, Humphries threw for a career-high 382 yards and had three touchdowns to lead Northeast Louisiana past McNeese.

The game was tied 3-3 in the second quarter until the Indians scored the final 17 points of the opening half. Humphries threw touchdown passes to Manzullo and Kenneth "Bump" Johnson and Garcia added his second field goal of the half to give NLU a 20-3 lead. Two weeks earlier against Georgia Southern, Garcia kicked the 46th field goal of his career to set a new Southland record.

Garcia's field goal on the Indians' first possession of the second half gave the kicker 50 for his career. Moments later, Humphries' third touchdown pass of the game, this one to Jones, made it 30-3. A 2-yard touchdown run by Phythian rounded out the scoring for Northeast. The only touchdown for McNeese came when safety Berwick Davenport snatched the ball from NLU third-team quarterback Doug Pederson and raced 26 yards for a touchdown.

"We kind of got back on track and playing like we did earlier in the year and maybe gained some of the confidence we had lost for a two- or three-week span," said Humphries.

Following Northwestern State's win over Southwest Texas, the Demons lost 23-0 to Louisiana Tech in the final State Fair Classic between the two teams in Shreveport before the Demons jumped back into Southland competition at Sam Houston State.

Limited to 30 yards of offense in the opening half, including zero passing, the Demons fell behind 13-0 against Sam Houston State on the way to a 34-7 loss.

SHSU scored on its opening possession of the game on a 10-yard run by Turner to cap a 79-yard drive. The Bearkats added two field goals late in the first half. Billy Hayes booted a school-record 54-yard field goal to make it 10-0. Hayes connected from 23 yards out to make it 13-0 when Stephens fumbled at his own 16 while the Demons were attempting to run out the clock.

Down 20-0, the Demons' only points came in the third quarter on a 1-yard run by Mike O'Neal to cap an 80-yard drive.

Northwestern fell to 2-3 in conference play and 3-5 overall. SHSU improved to 2-1 in the league and 5-3 overall.

Sam Houston State's next game was a road contest at Stephen F. Austin. The teams boasted one of the longest rivalries in collegiate football history as both schools had been playing each other yearly since 1924, except for the World War II years of 1942-45. The 1987 contest was the first time the schools met for "The Battle of the Piney Woods" as members of the Southland Conference.

Lewis threw for 248 yards and a touchdown to pace the Bearkats past SFA 31-17. The Sam Houston State quarterback also rushed for 70 yards in the victory.

Senior tight end Ricky Eggleston scored on a 46-yard touchdown catch for SHSU's first score of the game and raced 41 yards on another reception to set up the Bearkats' second touchdown.

All of the scoring came in the first half. The Bearkats' defense limited SFA to 81 yards of total offense in the final two quarters.

The Bearkats improved to 3-1 in the Southland and 6-3 overall with the win while SFA dropped to 3-5-2.

A season-long trend continued for McNeese State in the Cowboys' Southland Conference home game against Southwest Texas State. McNeese allowed the Bobcats to jump out to an early lead, only to see the Cowboys rally to make a game of it at halftime before fading in the second half in a 26-10 loss.

A 33-yard touchdown pass from Rittimann to Mike Murphy and a 4-yard pass from Haass to Matt Barber staked the Bobcats to a 14-0 lead in the second quarter. A 46-yard pass from Dieterich to Jeff Delhomme made it 14-7 at halftime and a Wiley field goal in the middle of the third quarter rallied the Cowboys to within four points.

The Cowboys would not score again. Meanwhile, SWT added a 25-yard pass from Rittimann to Darrell Grant and a 19-yard Kyle Matlock field goal for a 24-10 lead. The final indignity for McNeese came when Jackson was sacked in the end zone for a safety late in the game.

McNeese fell to 1-4 in the Southland and 1-8 overall with its sixth-consecutive loss. The Cowboys would go on to split their final two non-conference games. Jackson lost to his former team, Nicholls State, before closing the year with a win over Lamar. The victory over the Cardinals allowed McNeese to avoid its first-ever 10-loss season. Southwest Texas, winners of three straight, improved to 1-3 in the conference and 3-6 overall.

Following Northeast Louisiana's win over McNeese, the Indians faced Division I-A foe Southern Mississippi in a game that featured two future NFL quarterbacks. Opposite Humphries was Brett Favre, a freshman who earned the role as the Golden Eagles' starting quarterback earlier in the season.

Humphries, a senior, and his Indians got the best of Favre the USM 34-24.

"That was probably the game of the year that turned our season around and got us believing that we were pretty good and what we were capable of doing," Humphries said. "We totally dominated that game at Southern Miss. That's what gave us the confidence going into the final two conference games and into the playoffs."

Northeast Louisiana's defensive scheme helped to styme Favre and the Golden Eagles' offense, according to Collins.

"Because of the scheme we were doing with the five defensive backs we were able to do numerous blitz packages and some of it was zone blitz and it gave us an opportunity to put speed on the field and I think that made a huge difference," said Collins of the then-unique 4-2-5 alignment.

In a battle of conference unbeatens, the 4-0 Indians seemed eager to put the game away in the first half against 5-0 North Texas State in Monroe. Northeast Louisiana totally dominated the opening half to take a 21-0 lead. Touchdown passes from Humphries to Steele and Manzullo, along with a two-point conversion and two Garcia field goals gave NLU its 21 points. Garcia's second field goal of the game gave him 238 points, a new Louisiana collegiate kick-scoring record.

North Texas came out in the second half seeking to copy the Indians' first-half performance. Davis, the Eagles' quarterback who was held to six yards rushing in the first half, scampered 63 yards on the Mean Green's first possession of the second half to put his team on the scoreboard. After Garcia and Chapman, his North Texas counterpart, traded field goals early in the fourth quarter, Tony Shaw's interception of a Humphries pass set up an 18-yard touchdown pass from Davis to halfback Billy Brewer to make the score 24-17.

Three plays into the ensuing drive, Humphries fumbled when blindsided on a sack, giving the ball right back to the Eagles at the NLU 7. A keeper by Davis from a yard out with 1:23 left in the game pulled North Texas to within one point at 24-23. Chapman's conversion attempt bounced off the right upright. The miss allowed Northeast Louisiana to clinch no worse than a tie for the SLC title.

"I was shocked (North Texas coach Corky Nelson) kicked the extra point. I thought he was going to go for two," Collins recalled.

Like Stephen F. Austin's series with Sam Houston State, the Lumberjacks' rivalry with Southwest Texas had a long, storied history. Just as with Sam Houston, SFA and Southwest Texas played every season since 1923, with the exception of the World War II years.

SWT entered the 1987 contest on a three-game winning streak after opening the season with six-consecutive losses. The Lumberjacks went into the contest having lost the first two of four SLC contests to open the season. The 16-14 loss to North Texas and the 31-17 defeat at the hands of Sam Houston State left SFA 3-5-1 through nine games.

A 24-yard field goal by Stephen F. Austin's Bert Jones in the first quarter held up until the final quarter when the Lumberjacks looked to pat their lead with another Jones kick. The attempt, from 37 yards out, was blocked by A.J. Johnson, who raced 59 yards for a touchdown for what proved to be the winning points in Southwest Texas State's 7-3 victory.

The Bobcats missed a 43-yard field goal on their opening possession of the game. A 46-yard interception return by SFA's Keith Ellison set up Jones' field goal for the game's only points until Johnson's return.

SFA's Larry Centers led all rushers with 131 yards but the story of the game was defense. SWT linebacker Brad Fulks had 12 tackles, two fumble recoveries and an interception while Arnold Baker, a Bobcats defensive end, recorded 14 tackles.

Southwest Texas improved to 2-3 in the Southland and 4-6 overall. SFA fell to 1-4 in the league and 3-6-1 overall.

Because of the quirk in scheduling, Sam Houston State's home game against Western Illinois was a "designated" Southland Conference game for the Bearkats.

The choice of Western Illinois as a conference opponent may not have been sitting too well with Bearkats partisans at the start of the fourth quarter with Sam Houston State clinging to a 21-18 advantage. That changed quickly as touchdown runs of 1 and 61 yards by Turner and a 59-yard interception return for a touchdown by Billy Anderson allowed SHSU to pull away for a 42-18 victory.

Having clinched no worse than a tie for the Southland title, Northeast Louisiana needed a win in the final week of the regular season to finish unbeaten in the league. Arkansas State was no longer a member of the Southland, but like the Louisiana Tech game to open the season, the contest against A-State in Monroe was a "designated" conference game for Northeast Louisiana.

Arkansas State may no longer have been a member of the SLC, but seemed fit for a spoiler's role, especially after it took advantage of numerous Northeast mistakes to build an early lead. One play after Steele fumbled at his own 3-yard line, Arkansas State fullback Richard Kimble ran in for a touchdown and a 7-0 lead. A 1-yard run by Kimble to cap an 86-yard drive following a Humphries interception made it 14-0. Another Humphries interception set up a 15-yard option keeper by Arkansas State quarterback Duane Brown and a 21-0 lead. Humphries salvaged the first half with a short option keeper for a touchdown and a two-point conversion run to make it 21-8 at halftime.

After Northeast Louisiana pulled to within 21-14 in the third quarter, a 15-yard run by Richard tied the game 21-21. A 16-yard Garcia field goal with slightly less than 10 minutes remaining gave NLU its first lead of the contest at 24-21. Northeast put the game away with 2:19 remaining in the fourth quarter on a 1-yard keeper by Humphries. The 31-21 victory gave NLU the Southland Conference championship and an automatic bid to the Division I-AA playoffs.

While NLU was wrapping up the conference title, a pair of rivals met for the first time as members of the Southland Conference.

The series between Sam Houston State and Southwest Texas predated the series each school had with Stephen F. Austin. Both of those rivalries began in 1923. The Bearkats and Bobcats first met on the football field in 1919.

Sam Houston State and SWT took a few short breaks along the way, so the series was not as continuous as the other two. The Bearkats and Bobcats did not meet in 1918 because of World War I. The teams failed to meet each other in 1928, 1930 and 1935. World War II caused stoppage of the series from 1943-45. From that point on, the teams met each year with the 1987 encounter marking the 66th meeting between the two schools. SWT went in the 1987 contest with a 48-36-4 series lead.

SWT and Sam Houston State both were on hot streaks closing out the season as both teams were on four-game winning streaks going into the season finale in San Marcos.

Turner, who rushed for 175 yards in the game, scored on a touchdown run with 46 seconds left in the game to push Sam Houston State's lead to 24-14. Southwest Texas quickly drove 80 yards in only five plays, with Rittimann's 5-yard touchdown pass to Murphy making the score 24-21 but with only with three seconds left in the game, time finally ran out on the Bobcats and their four-game winning streak.

The victory allowed Sam Houston State to finish 5-1 in the Southland and 8-3 overall. Southwest Texas ended 2-4 in the conference and 4-7 overall for its third-consecutive losing season.

Another long rivalry to make its way to the Southland Conference involved Stephen F. Austin and Northwestern State as the two teams met in the 1987 season finale in the Battle for Chief Caddo. The winner of the game received the Chief Caddo trophy. Made of solid wood, standing almost seven-and-a-half feet tall and weighing in excess of 330 pounds, it is the largest trophy in college football.

The trophy derived its name from an Indian chief whose tribe was responsible for settling the locations of what is now Natchitoches, Louisiana – the home of Northwestern State – and Nacogdoches, Texas – the home of Stephen F. Austin State University.

The first meeting between the two schools was in 1924 but the Chief Caddo trophy wasn't awarded until 1961. Northwestern State led the all-time series 28-13-2, although SFA took a four-game winning streak going into the 1987 encounter.

Northwestern State ended the 1987 season in style as Stephens, the future New England Patriots running back, scored two touchdowns and set a new school record in the Demons' 33-21 win at Stephen F. Austin.

Stephens rushed for 104 in the game. That gave him 3,057 yards for his career, 10 more than Joe Delaney to top the Northwestern State rushing chart.

SFA turned a Gilbert Galloway fumble into a 3-yard touchdown pass from Todd Hammel to Derrick Wright and a Galloway interception by David Whitmore into a 1-yard touchdown run by Centers for a 14-3 lead. The Demons closed to 14-13 on a 1-yard run by Pete Ellis and 34-yard Hodnett field goal. A 1-yard run by Centers, the future Arizona Cardinal runner, extended the Lumberjacks' halftime lead to 21-13.

The Northwestern State defense blanked SFA in the second half. The Demons offense, meanwhile, recovered an onside kick to open the third quarter which led to a 1-yard run by Stephens to make it 21-19. A 1-yard run by Ellis gave Northwestern the lead at 26-21 before Stephens closed out his prolific career with a 21-yard touchdown jaunt.

Not only did the victory allow Northwestern to finish with a winning record for the first time since 1984 at 6-5, the Demons also bounced back from a 1-2 Southland start to break even at 3-3 in their first year in the league. SFA finished its season 3-7-1 overall, 1-5 in conference play.

North Texas State and Sam Houston State both finished the regular season 5-1 in the Southland. Although the Bearkats finished 8-3 overall and the Mean Green 7-4, it was North Texas that earned an at-large bid to the Division I-AA playoffs. Not only did the Mean Green win the head-to-head encounter between the two teams 41-24, among their losses were games to the likes of Oklahoma and TCU. Additionally, North Texas spent much of the season highly ranked in Division I-AA.

The Mean Green's opponent in the opening round of the playoffs was none other than Southland Conference champion Northeast Louisiana. The Indians won the regular-season contest 24-23 at home but North Texas was given another shot at NLU, again in Monroe.

Like in the first game, Northeast Louisiana jumped out to a halftime lead. North Texas actually struck first on a 28-yard Chapman field goal. His miss from 42 yards out on the Mean Green's next possession must have given Eagles fans chills, recalling the closing moments of the previous encounter between the two teams.

Those fears weren't abated in the first half of the playoff game as the Indians went on to score 17 points to lead by 14 at halftime. Following Chapman's miss, NLU drove 75 yards with Minvielle's 1-yard run giving Northeast a 7-3 lead. After a Garcia field goal, the Indians gained their 17-3 halftime margin on a 5-yard touchdown pass from Humphries to Harris. The final score of the half was set up on linebacker Duke Marcus' interception of a Davis pass at the North Texas 40.

Unlike the first game, Northeast Louisiana continued to add to its lead in the second half. The Indians turned a fumble by Eagles running back Edsel Ford into a 30-yard Garcia field goal. After forcing the Mean Green to punt, NLU drove 64 yards to set up a 5-yard run by Richard on an option pitch. Another Garcia field goal, this one from 21 yards out, made the score 30-3. Ford added a 3-yard touchdown run to make the final 30-9.

"We didn't mind at all playing them a second time," Collins said. "A lot of people have a phobia about playing the same team twice but we felt like going into that game that we had something else in mind. The kids were looking down the road, taking it one game at a time but thinking of playing for a national championship."

"Being able to play a team you just played two or three weeks earlier, realizing how close that game was, it really made us focus real hard on that playoff game. We played well and came out and did what we had to do to win the game," said Humphries.

Playing at home for the second week in a row in the playoffs, Northeast Louisiana trailed Eastern Kentucky 7-0 at halftime before an offensive eruption occurred in the third quarter that featured scores on six-straight possessions.

The offensive explosion saw the Indians fall behind before tying the game 23-23 early in the fourth quarter, only to quickly fall behind once again. A snap through the legs of Humphries deep in NLU territory was chased down by the quarterback in the end zone for a safety. The Colonels scored off of the ensuing free kick with tailback Elroy Harris' 25-yard run giving Eastern Kentucky a nine-point advantage at 32-23.

With Humphries throwing the ball all over the field, the NLU quarterback finally found Johnson for an 8-yard touchdown strike to make it 32-30 with 4:27 left in the game. Northeast Louisiana caught a break when on a third-and-1 situation on the ensuing possession, Colonels offensive tackle Paul Lichtefeld was called for a procedure penalty. An incomplete pass then forced a punt, giving the ball back to the Indians at the Northeast 13 with less than three minutes remaining in the game.

Humphries, in the midst of a record-setting performance, drove the Indians down the field to set up a 48-yard Garcia field goal to give Northeast Louisiana a dramatic 33-32 victory to send the Indians to the Division I-AA semifinals. Humphries ended the game with 486 yards passing and a NCAA playoff-record 521 yards of total offense. That broke the mark previously held by Tracy Ham of Georgia Southern.

"You pass the 50 and you have the confidence in your kicker. You know Teddy knocks through the long field goal to win the game. He was a veteran kicker, a senior, someone who had done it all year for you," Humphries said of Garcia.

If Northeast Louisiana fans thought the first two playoff games at home were exciting, they turned out to be just opening acts for what was to take place in the Indians' Division I-AA semifinal game at home against Northern Iowa.

A pair of 1-yard touchdown runs by Minvielle and Richard, a 31-yard interception return for a touchdown by Cyril Crutchfield, along with Humphries touchdown passes to 7 yards to Manzullo and 43 yards to Kenneth Burton gave Northeast Louisiana 35 points in the first half. Northern Iowa quarterback Mike Smith fired touchdown passes of 15 yards to Sherrod Howard and 29 yards to Brian Baker to account for the Panthers' points in a furious first half that ended 35-14.

The second half was the opposite of the first as the only points Northeast scored was on an 8-yard pass from Humphries to Richard. Smith, meanwhile, rifled four more touchdowns in the second half. His total of six set a new NCAA playoff record. Two more touchdowns to Baker made the score 35-27. After Richard fumbled the kickoff following Baker's second touchdown of the third quarter, Smith struck again on a 12-yard screen pass to flanker Wes Anderson. A two-point conversion try failed, making the score 35-33. Humphries' touchdown pass to Richard increased the Indians advantage to eight points at 41-33.

A 5-yard pass from Smith to Howard with seven seconds left in regulation made the score 41-39. Howard's two-point conversion pass to fullback Woody Wright forced overtime.

NCAA overtime rules called for each team to have a possession starting at the opposition's 25-yard line. If the score was tied after the first possession, play continued until a winner was determined. Each team would continue to have one possession per overtime period.

Northern Iowa got the ball first but failed to score when Northeast Louisiana linebacker Terry Jones recovered an Errol Peebles fumble at the 1-yard line. The ball was again placed at the 25-yard line for NLU's possession. Instead of running any plays, Indians coach Pat Collins elected to send Garcia onto the field on first down. His kick was wide right, forcing a second overtime.

Northeast Louisiana got the ball first in the second overtime. The Indians were unable to move the ball but this time Garcia hit from 41 yards away to give NLU a 44-41 lead. Now, the Panthers needed either a touchdown to win or a tying field goal to send the game to a third overtime. Two plays gained a total of 4 yards for Northern Iowa. A pass on third down was broken up in the end zone by Northeast cornerback Stephone Avery. Danny Helmer was sent onto the field to attempt a 38-yard field goal. He hooked his kick to the left, giving NLU a 44-41 win and sending the Indians to the NCAA championship game.

"I had great confidence in Teddy Garcia," said Collins. "That's why when we held them that first time, I felt we had played long enough and had a long season, we would kick the ball. He missed it by a little bit. The second one could have been good from 60 yards."

The NCAA Division I-AA championship game against Marshall in Pocatello, Idaho, marked the first time Northeast Louisiana played away from home in the playoffs.

Northeast's 21-13 halftime lead didn't last long as the Thundering Herd exploded for 251 yards and 29 points in the third quarter. A short touchdown pass from Marshall quarterback Tony Petersen to Keith Barber, only one play after the two connected on a 55-yard hookup, pulled the Thundering Herd to within two points at 21-19. A fumble by Richard on the next possession set up another Petersen-Barber touchdown, with a two-point conversion giving Marshall a 27-21 lead.

The points were now flowing freely as a 9-yard touchdown from Humphries to Harris put Northeast Louisiana back on top. Marshall countered with a 17-yard touchdown pass from Petersen to Bruce Hammond. A two-point conversion gave the Thundering Herd a 35-28 lead. Minvielle's second fumble of the day led to a touchdown by Ron Darby to extend Marshall's lead to 14 points at 42-28.

Humphries, who threw for 436 yards in the game, began a late rally for NLU. He drove the Indians 74 yards with a 23-yard pass to Harris advancing the ball to the Marshall 10. On the next play, Humphries' screen pass to Johnson produced a touchdown. The quarterback hooked up with Harris for a two-point conversion to make the score 42-36.

An onside kick by Northeast was unsuccessful, but the Indians got the ball back on a defensive stop. Hitting on 5 of 6 passes in an 80-yard, seven-play drive, Humphries tied the score with a 2-yard run. Garcia's successful extra point gave Northeast Louisiana a 43-42 lead with 7:19 left in the game.

The game now belonged in the hands of the Indians defense. Until the stop that gave NLU the ball for the go-ahead score, the Indians had been unable to contain the Thundering Herd in the second half, surrendering 29 points and 251 yards in the third quarter alone.

On Marshall's possession following Northeast Louisiana's go-ahead score, the Thundering Herd reached the NLU 22 before a Darby fumble was recovered by Indians cornerback Richard Green at the 7. The Marshall defense forced a punt and got the ball back on the Northeast 39 with 1:22 left in the game. After Peterson was sacked by Troy Brown on first down, his desperation pass over the middle was intercepted by safety Perry Harper to seal the national championship for Northeast Louisiana.

"In the fourth quarter, I broke the national championship game record for passing in a game and the next series the quarterback from Marshall broke my record," Humphries recalled. "It was one of those games, up and down and we were able to make a play at the end of the game with the interception to seal the win."

Northeast Louisiana, Humphries said, gave its fans one of the most exciting postseason experiences on its way to a national championship.

"It was a wild ride," said Humphries. "Those games in the playoffs were all tight. There were a lot of points scored. It was like a shootout every week.

"People today still talk about those playoff games and the last-second things that happened. The excitement of both teams going up and down the field and putting points on the board and being able to come out on top, it was a wild ride."

"It's a wonderful thing. It's something you dream about. It was a weird thing. It was like a team of destiny," Collins said.

THREE TIMES THE FUN

It didn't take long for Northeast Louisiana to begin defense of its national championship and Southland Conference title in 1988. After opening up with a 22-6 non-conference win at Nicholls State, the Indians played at McNeese State to open conference play. The Cowboys went into the game 1-0 with a season-opening victory over Mississippi College.

Mistakes doomed the Indians against McNeese State. Second-ranked Northeast Louisiana turned the ball over six times and allowed the Cowboys to begin nine possessions inside Indians territory in a 23-0 NLU loss. The loss snapped a winning streak of nine games for the Indians that included a 4-0 run through the 1987 playoffs. It was the first time Northeast had been shut out in 30 games – the last time coming in a 10-0 loss to McNeese in 1985.

NLU quarterback Walter Phythian was unable to match his 254-yard, two-touchdown performance from the season opener. Against the Cowboys, he was 9 of 24 passing with four interceptions. One of Phythian's interceptions by McNeese linebacker Eric LeBlanc set up a 7-yard touchdown from quarterback Scott Dieterich to Jeff Delhomme with 30 seconds remaining in the first half to give the Cowboys a 10-0 lead. McNeese jumped out to a 3-0 lead on a 34-yard Lance Wiley field goal.

Wiley added two field goals in the second half, the first set up on another Phythian interception. The Cowboys drove for the game's final score in the fourth quarter, traveling 70 yards to set up Tony Citizen's 1-yard run for a 23-0 blanking of Northeast Louisiana.

Northeast Louisiana was back in conference action a week later against Southwest Texas State in the Indians' first home game of the season.

With less than two minutes remaining in the game, the Indians found themselves trailing 27-26. A loss by Northeast Louisiana would drop the Indians to 0-2 on the young Southland Conference season. No team had ever won a SLC crown with more than one loss.

A 4-yard run by Bill Jones with 1:53 left in the game had given the Bobcats their 27-26 lead. Northeast got the ball for one last chance at its own 34. After an incomplete pass, Phythian hit receiver Kenneth Burton with back-to-back passes to advance the Indians to the Southwest Texas 45. When a third-and-6 play came up 3 yards short, NLU sent kicker Derek White into the game. White's kick from 50 yards out with 17 seconds remaining lifted the Indians to a 29-27 triumph and kept Northeast Louisiana alive in the SLC race.

Northeast had to rally at the end after taking a 20-7 halftime lead against the Bobcats. Trailing 7-3, the Indians quickly moved ahead on a 15-yard run by Phythian and a 39-yard interception return by safety Hiram Porter. Porter's interception came only two plays after Phythian's touchdown run. A 23-yard White field goal gave NLU its 20-7 halftime lead.

SWT quarterback Ron Rittimann put the Bobcats back in the game early in the third quarter on a 13-yard touchdown pass to Mike Murphy. After a 26-yard touchdown reception by Cisco Richard brought the NLU lead to 26-14, Southwest Texas responded once again. Rittimann scored on a 1-yard run to get the Bobcats close before Jones' score put SWT ahead and set the stage for White's dramatic kick.

The Bobcats quickly fell to 0-2 with a 27-10 home loss to Stephen F. Austin. The victory was the first for the Lumberjacks in San Marcos since 1974. SFA went into the game 2-1 on the season with wins over Prairie View and Lamar following a season-opening loss at Southern Mississippi.

Rittimann had a tough outing against the Lumberjacks, hitting on only 9 of 30 passes for 97 yards.

SFA running back Larry Centers, who rushed for 111 of his 130 yards in the first half, scored on a 2-yard run to give the Lumberjacks a 7-0 lead. A.J. Johnson took in a short pass from Rittimann and sidestepped a pair of defenders on his way to a 23-yard touchdown to tie the game after one quarter. A 26-yard pass from SFA quarterback Todd Hammel to Dave Kelley and a Chuck Rawlinson field goal was answered only by a Jason Howes field goal, allowing the Lumberjacks to take a 17-10 halftime lead.

The only score in the second half came on a 28-yard run by SFA's Michael Horace. Southwest Texas failed on two occasions in the second half to convert on fourth down from inside the Lumberjacks' 36-yard line.

Stephen F. Austin made it two-in-a-row in the Southland with a 20-3 triumph at Northeast Louisiana. The Lumberjacks moved to 4-1 overall while NLU, coming off a non-conference loss to Arkansas State, dropped to 3-2 overall and 1-2 in the conference.

The Lumberjacks' top-rated defense held true to form in the win over Northeast Louisiana. SFA sacked Phythian 10 times and intercepted three passes. With nine dropped passes by Indians receivers, Phythian finished only 8 of 33 and NLU was limited to 240 total yards.

White gave Northeast Louisiana a 3-0 lead when he kicked a field goal on the Indians' opening drive of the game. NLU would not score again the remainder of the game. The Lumberjacks, meanwhile, took a 10-3 lead at halftime on a game-tying Rawlinson field goal and a touchdown toss from Hammel to Centers. Centers hauled in a short pass from Hammel along the sidelines and scooted 89 yards for a touchdown.

The Lumberjacks increased their lead in the second half on a 48-yard touchdown reception by Joe Bradford and a 36-yard Rawlinson field goal with two minutes left in the contest.

Northwestern State, meanwhile, went into its Southland opener at home against Southwest Texas 2-1 on the season.

Six different players scored for Northwestern State and the Demons used a dominating second half in a 49-21 victory over Southwest Texas State.

Following a 7-7 tie after one quarter, the teams combined for five touchdowns in a high-scoring second quarter. Northwestern's scoring came on a 10-yard run by Kenneth DeWitt and touchdown passes from Scott Stoker of 69 yards to Floyd Turner and 37 yards to Orlan Lockhart. SWT scored twice in the quarter on an 86-yard touchdown return by Johnson and a 3-yard run by Jones. Jones' touchdown came with 54 seconds left in the half to pull the Bobcats to 28-21 at the break.

Northwestern State put the game away in the second half by scoring three more touchdowns on runs by Gilbert Galloway, Paul Frazier and Brian Driskill while blanking SWT over the final 30 minutes.

North Texas State went into its Southland Conference opener at home against Northeast Louisiana as the top-ranked team in Division I-AA. The Eagles were 5-1 on the season. Included in the five wins was a season-opening upset of Texas Tech. The only loss for the Eagles came against Texas when the Longhorns needed a touchdown in the final minute for a 27-24 win to avoid another upset bid by the Mean Green.

The Eagles were seeking revenge against Northeast Louisiana. North Texas lost twice to NLU the previous season, including in the opening round of the playoffs, on the Indians' march to the national championship. The Indians were not the same team from a year earlier. NLU was reeling at 1-2 in Southland play but did have three conference encounters under its belt while North Texas was playing its initial league game of the season.

NLU didn't seem quite ready to give up.

Northeast Louisiana led by eight points at halftime but an Indians turnover gave North Texas the ball at the NLU 7-yard line only two plays into the third quarter. North Texas quarterback Scott Davis ran to his right on the next play for the touchdown. A two-point conversion attempt left the Mean Green trailing 21-19. A blocked punt in the end zone gave Northeast Louisiana an additional two points to make the score 23-19.

Moments later, Davis broke loose on a 38-yard scramble with slightly more than seven minutes remaining in the game to put the Eagles on top 26-23.

Doug Pederson, making his first collegiate start in place of the injured Phythian, positioned his Indians where they needed to be. Having tossed for almost 300 yards and two touchdowns, Pederson drove his team from the Northeast Louisiana 25-yard line to the North Texas 16 in the game's final minute. Pederson spotted Anthony Burns in the back of the end zone, but the quarterback's pass was out of reach. The three-point loss also put the Southland Conference race out of the Indians' grasp as NLU fell to 1-3 in the SLC and 3-3 overall.

The Indians had given a good accounting of themselves against Division I-AA's top-ranked team, especially in the first half. Northeast Louisiana led 21-13 at halftime but could produce only a safety in the game's final 30 minutes.

After a Keith Chapman field goal gave the Eagles a 3-0 lead following a Northeast fumble, Pederson tossed his first touchdown of the game when he connected with Jeff Steele on a 22-yard toss. Steele's 55-yard return of a North Texas punt helped to set up Richard's touchdown run on a sweep to make it 14-3. The Eagles cashed in on a fumbled punt by Steele later in the first half as Chapman's 29-yard field goal made it 14-6. After a 65-yard punt return for a touchdown by Marcus Camper made it 14-13, Pederson guided NLU on a 68-yard drive that was capped on his 6-yard toss to Anthony Burns to give the Indians their 21-13 halftime lead.

Elsewhere, Northwestern State built an early lead behind the running of Mike O'Neal at McNeese State and then held off a late Cowboys rally for a 25-20 triumph.

O'Neal scored on three 1-yard runs and Hodnett added a 21-yard field goal to produce the Demons' points.

"He wasn't that impressive in the course of a game, except for when we needed short yardage," Demons coach Sam Goodwin said of O'Neal. "He was our starting fullback, but when we needed a yard or two, he would get it."

Trailing 25-3, the Cowboys scored the final 17 points of the game on a 1-yard run by Brian McZeal, a 30-yard Wiley field goal and a 6-yard pass from Hud Jackson to Brian Champagne.

McNeese blocked two punts and intercepted a pass in the fourth quarter to get back in the game but missed out on a couple of scoring opportunities when Wiley missed a pair of field goals.

The final team to play its initial Southland Conference game was Sam Houston State. The Bearkats went into their game against rival Stephen F. Austin sporting a 3-2 record.

Neither team was able to produce as much as 200 yards of total offense in a contest that featured the two top-rated defenses in the nation.

Trailing 3-0, the Lumberjacks took a 7-3 lead at the start of the second quarter on a 3-yard touchdown run by Horace. The score was set up on a 43-yard punt return by Bruce Alexander. A defensive back, Alexander intercepted two passes as SFA went on to take a 17-10 decision that improved the Lumberjacks to 3-0 in the Southland.

Top-ranked North Texas, meanwhile, moved to 2-0 in the Southland with a 38-16 victory at McNeese State as the Eagles improved to 5-1 overall. McNeese lost for the fourth-consecutive time after a 3-0 start to drop to 3-4 overall and 1-2 in the SLC.

A pair of early interceptions set the tone in the encounter. The Eagles picked off Dieterich on the Cowboys' first possession of the game to set up a 58-yard touchdown pass from Davis to David McGinty. After another interception, Keith Chapman kicked a 40-yard field goal to give the Mean Green a 10-0 lead in the first quarter.

North Texas added 10 more points in the second quarter for a 20-0 Eagles lead at intermission. Camper scored a pair of touchdowns in the second half on a 69-yard punt return and a 9-yard pass from Davis as the Mean Green cruised to victory.

McNeese, which was held to 83 yards rushing, failed to cross midfield in the opening half of play.

North Texas State and Northwestern State each looked to match SFA at 3-0 in the Southland a week later with the top-ranked Eagles visiting Sam Houston State and the Demons facing Northeast Louisiana in Shreveport. The Lumberjacks, meanwhile, were involved in a non-conference affair against Eastern Washington.

The Eagles entered their game at Sam Houston State with the No. 1 ranking in the nation but faced a Bearkats team that led Division I-AA in defense.

SHSU forced two fumbles, an interception and foiled a fake-punt attempt by the Eagles to only trail 10-3 at halftime.

The Eagles' run-and-shoot offense was held to 288 yards in the game but came alive on their first two possessions of the second half.

A 5-yard touchdown run by McGinty to open the third quarter and a 5-yard scoring pass from Davis to Camper helped North Texas pull away for a 24-3 victory. North Texas improved to 6-1 overall as SHSU fell to 0-2 in the conference and 3-4 overall.

The Demons were determined to get revenge for a heart-breaking loss the previous season to Northeast Louisiana. Northwestern State saw the Indians travel 87 yards in two plays, scoring on a 48-yard jump-ball pass in the end zone on the final play in a 33-31 loss. NLU went on to win the Division I-AA championship while the Demons lost three of their next four games.

There was no need for such dramatics this time around as Northwestern State built a 27-3 lead on its way to a 27-15 victory in the resumption of the State Fair series in Shreveport.

The Demons led 10-3 at halftime before extending the advantage to 24-3 on a pair of third-quarter touchdowns. Ken DeWitt raced 55 yards with the second-half kickoff to eventually set up a 20-yard touchdown run by Frazier. Stoker hooked up with Mark Mayfield on a 33-yard touchdown toss later in the quarter to give Northwestern its 24-3 lead.

After the Demons upped the lead to 27-3 on a Hodnett field goal, the Indians gave Northwestern State a few anxious moments.

A pass from Pederson, the future Green Bay Packer and Miami Dolphin quarterback, to Richard from 33 yards out capped a 71-yard drive in the fourth quarter. Steele capped an 80-yard drive on a 3-yard run to make it 27-15.

Northeast Louisiana recovered a Demons fumble at the Indians' 21 with 2:15 remaining in the game. The Indians reached the Northwestern State 20 but Pederson stepped out of bounds while scrambling on fourth down to end NLU's comeback hopes.

The Demons matched North Texas at both 3-0 in Southland play and 6-1 overall. NLU fell to 1-4 in the conference and 3-5 overall.

While North Texas and Northwestern State were tied atop the Southland, Southwest Texas was still seeking its first conference win of the season at McNeese State. The Bobcats got off to a good start as a pair of touchdown runs by Jones staked SWT to a 14-7 halftime lead.

The lead would not last as the Cowboys scored 17-consecutive points to build a 24-14 advantage early in the fourth quarter. After a 29-yard touchdown pass from Dieterich to McZeal tied the game, the McNeese tailback added a 2-yard run and Wiley connected on a 30-yard field goal to put the Cowboys up by 10 points.

Jones scored his third touchdown of the game after Wiley's field goal to cut the Bobcats' deficit to three points. SWT crossed midfield in the closing seconds but Howes' 50-yard field goal attempt fell short, allowing the Cowboys to snap a four-game losing streak with the 24-21 victory.

Dieterich hit on 10 of 15 passes for 119 yards to become McNeese's all-time leader in career completions, attempts and yards.

McNeese evened its record at 2-2 in the Southland Conference and 4-4 overall. Southwest Texas fell to 0-4 in the league and 3-5 overall.

All 3-0 Southland teams were in conference action a week later with the headliner being the North Texas-Stephen F. Austin clash in Nacogdoches. North Texas entered the game top-ranked in the nation while SFA was No. 9. Like the Eagles, the Lumberjacks also were 6-1 overall.

Although the rankings and records were very similar between the two teams, the game represented a contrast in styles. North Texas managed its No. 1 ranking by featuring the third-best scoring offense in the country. SFA, meanwhile, boasted the second-best defense in Division I-AA.

A 3-3 tie after one quarter spoke to the closeness of the game everyone expected when Chapman and Rawlinson exchanged field goals in the opening period. The only score of the second quarter came on a 1-yard run by Centers to give the Lumberjacks a 10-3 halftime edge.

North Texas drove to the SFA 29 to open the second half but a Davis pass was deflected by the Lumberjacks' David Whitmore into the hands of Bobby Henry with the interception ending the threat.

The Lumberjacks marched 80 yards, culminated with a 10-yard touchdown pass from Hammel to Centers for a 17-3 SFA lead with five minutes remaining in the third quarter.

North Texas rallied to within a touchdown when Davis hooked up with Tony Cook from 35 yards out early in the fourth quarter.

The North Texas quarterback completed six-straight passes as the Eagles reached the Lumberjacks' 43 later in the quarter. Davis' next attempt was picked off by Keith Ellison, the SFA defender's second interception of the game, to preserve the 17-10 triumph for the Lumberjacks.

Davis passed for 308 yards in the game but he was constantly harassed by SFA defenders. The Lumberjacks sacked Davis seven times and forced six interceptions while holding North Texas to 24 points below its seasonal average.

In Natchitoches, Stoker passed for two touchdowns and DeWitt rushed for two more as the Demons kept pace with SFA with a 49-14 win over Sam Houston State.

One of Stoker's touchdown passes was a 69-yard bomb to DeWitt. Stoker's other touchdown toss was 44 yards to Frazier. DeWitt also scored on a pair of 4-yard runs.

Northwestern State's defense shut down the Bearkats, intercepting five passes while allowing only 73 yards through the air. One of the interceptions, by David Chitman, was returned 44 yards for a touchdown to stake the Demons to a 7-0 lead on Northwestern State's way to a 28-7 halftime lead.

"One place we did have a lot of talent was our secondary, which was as good as anybody's anywhere," said Goodwin. "I always felt like if you had a strong secondary, you would be in the game because you weren't going to give up easy scores and most times teams had trouble marching down the field if they don't get a big play. That (1988 Northwestern State) team gave up very few big plays."

The Demons improved to 7-1 overall. Sam Houston State, which fell to 0-3 in the SLC and 3-5 overall, got its only points on a 5-yard touchdown pass from Bart Bradley to Scott Ford in the second quarter and a 72-yard run by Curtis Thomas in the final quarter.

Northwestern State's next test came a week later at North Texas against an Eagles team still reeling from their loss to SFA. The Demons, ranked No. 11, entered the game 4-0 in the Southland Conference and 7-1 overall and North Texas, now the seventh-ranked team in the nation, could seemingly ill afford another loss if the Mean Green hoped to keep their title aspirations alive.

A 20-yard Chapman field goal gave North Texas a 3-0 lead and the Eagles appeared on their way to more points before Demons defensive back Randy Hilliard raced 80 yards with an errant throw by Mean Green reserve quarterback Bron Beal to give Northwestern State a 7-3 edge.

DeWitt scored on a 4-yard run to make the score 13-3 on a drive that was set up by a 1-yard punt by Beal into a strong wind, giving the Demons the ball at the North Texas 30. A 2-yard run by Pete Ellis gave Northwestern State a 19-3 halftime lead.

The Demons built their lead to as much as 25-3 in the second half before North Texas scored two late touchdowns on short runs by Davis and fullback Monty Moon to make the final 25-17.

North Texas, which had been ranked No. 1 in the nation until a loss to Stephen F. Austin, fell to 3-2 in the SLC with its second-straight loss and 6-3 overall.

In Lake Charles, the McNeese State Cowboys, well rested after an open date, jumped out to a 24-0 halftime lead on their way to a 37-0 rout of Sam Houston State.

SHSU, which boasted the top-ranked defense in Division I-AA only two weeks prior to the McNeese encounter, surrendered 476 yards of total offense to the Cowboys. McZeal led the way with 113 yards rushing while Dieterich and Jackson each tossed two touchdown passes in a 227-yard air attack.

Dieterich's first touchdown pass, a 40-yard strike to Champagne, staked the Cowboys to a 7-0 lead. A 9-yard run by Mark LeBlanc made it 14-0 after one quarter. Following a Wiley field goal, Jackson hit Citizen with a 21-yard touchdown pass for a 24-0 halftime lead.

The two McNeese quarterbacks each added another touchdown pass in the second half. Also, Wiley kicked four extra points to give him 77-straight conversions, breaking the McNeese, Louisiana collegiate and Southland Conference record for consecutive conversions. The old mark of 75 was set by former Cowboys kicker Don Stump in the 1970s.

McNeese improved to 3-2 in the SLC and 5-4 overall. The Bearkats fell to 0-4 in the conference and 3-6 overall.

It was now Stephen F. Austin's turn to try and match Northwestern State at 5-0 in the Southland when the Lumberjacks hosted McNeese State a week later while Northwestern State faced Jackson State in a non-conference affair.

An exchange of first-half kicks by Wiley and Rawlinson led to a 3-3 tie at the break, but the second half belonged to the Lumberjacks, now the nation's top-ranked team. Wiley's kick tied the game midway in the second quarter following a delay of more than 10 minutes because of threatening weather conditions.

The Lumberjacks drove down to the McNeese 10 with the second-half kickoff to break the tie on a 26-yard Rawlinson field goal.

Stephen F. Austin mounted another long drive, this time culminating the 80-yard march with a touchdown on a 5-yard run by Centers. The Lumberjacks iced the game with a 1-yard run by Centers following a Dieterich fumble at the McNeese 14 to give SFA a 20-3 victory.

Needing a win to keep whatever playoff hopes it had still alive, North Texas snapped a two-game losing streak with a 30-10 win at Southwest Texas State.

Chapman kicked three field goals and Eagles defensive lineman Rex Johnson returned an interception 70 yards for a touchdown to help spark North Texas.

North Texas concluded Southland play 4-2 overall while Southwest Texas dropped to 0-5 in the conference.

Sam Houston State joined Southwest Texas at 0-5 in the Southland with a 17-3 loss at Northeast Louisiana that allowed the Indians to conclude conference play at 2-4.

Phythian, starting in place of an injured Pederson, guided NLU to a 17-3 lead at halftime that would hold up for the remainder of the contest.

The Indians were sharp on their first two possessions of the game. Phythian hit Richard with a 14-yard touchdown pass to cap an opening 65-yard drive. On NLU's next possession, Phythian hit Harris at the Sam Houston 42. The tight end broke a tackle and then rambled the remaining yards to conclude a 56-yard touchdown reception to give the Indians a 14-0 advantage. Two weeks earlier in a 24-3 non-conference win over Lamar, Harris, seeing action for only the third time since early-season knee surgery, hauled in 16 passes to set a new Southland Conference single-game mark.

A 39-yard field goal by Chris Nowels right before halftime gave Northeast its first-half total of 17 points. The Bearkats, who were held to minus-5 yards passing and 176 on the ground, scored their only points on a 43-yard Billy Hayes field goal. The kick came after Sam Houston State could advance the ball no more than 13 yards following a short NLU punt.

In the final week of the regular season, North Texas defeated Rice 33-17 in non-conference play to keep its playoffs hopes alive at 7-4. In other non-league affairs, Northeast Louisiana was blanked 23-0 by Louisiana Tech to finish with a losing record at 5-6 a year after winning the national title and McNeese State defeated Lamar 22-17 to end the year 6-5 as the Cowboys secured their first winning season in three years.

In a Southland encounter among last-place teams, Southwest Texas defeated Sam Houston State 10-3 to avoid the conference cellar. The Bobcats finished the year 1-5 in the SLC and 4-7 overall. SHSU ended 0-6 in the league and 3-8 overall.

A 2-yard pass from David Haass to Matt Barber late in the first quarter proved to be enough points for the Bobcats. A fumble by Greg Pagel late in the first half set up a 47-yard field goal by Hayes to make it 7-3 at the half before SWT added the only points of the second half with a field goal.

All of the attention on the final week of the 1988 regular season was on Northwestern State's game at Stephen F. Austin.

Not only was the battle between two nationally-ranked teams, top-ranked SFA boasted a unit that was best in the nation in total defense and second in scoring defense going into the encounter against No. 10 Northwestern State.

Scoreless after one quarter, the Demons drove the length of the field in the second quarter to take the lead. Keys to the drive were a 28-yard pass from Stoker to Turner and Frazier's 38-yard run that moved the ball down to the 1-yard line. It took O'Neal three times but he finally scored to give Northwestern State a 7-0 lead early in the second quarter.

Frazier rushed for 84 yards in the game. The SFA defense, which went into the contest yielding only 65 yards per game on the ground, gave up 265 against the Demons.

A 27-yard Mayfield touchdown run on a reverse upped the Demons' lead to 14-0. The Lumberjacks made it 14-7 at the half following a 33-yard pass from Hammel to Bradford.

Following a halftime rain that turned an already wet field into a sloppy mess, the Demons mounted another long drive in the third quarter. A 17-yard pass from Stoker to Turner from the SFA 25 on third down kept the drive alive. Stoker later scored on a 2-yard keeper to cap an 85-yard drive to put Northwestern up 20-10.

A 1-yard run by Marvin Davis with 5:21 left in the game tightened the score at 20-17 but the Demons managed to mount yet another long, time-consuming drive to run out the clock to capture their first-ever Southland Conference title.

"That was a tremendous accomplishment for that group of kids," Goodwin said of winning the Southland title. "We weren't real big. Our quarterback was 5-7, 155 pounds. Our center was 5-11, 220 but he started four years.

"Our guys, every week, just came to play. It overachieved more than any team I ever coached."

Both teams moved to 9-2 overall with the outcome. The Demons finished a perfect 6-0 in Southland play while the Lumberjacks dropped to 5-1.

Thanks to a 7-4 finish, tough schedule and a stint as the top-ranked team in the country, North Texas made the Division I-AA playoffs with an at-large berth, giving the Southland Conference three teams in the playoffs for the first time ever.

The Eagles played at Marshall in the opening round while Stephen F. Austin, the second-place team from the Southland, hosted Jackson State. Northwestern State, despite being the SLC champion, opened the playoffs at Boise State.

North Texas, the No. 10 seed, was involved in a defensive struggle at sixth-seeded Marshall. The Thundering Herd, the Southern Conference champions, scored the game's only points on an 8-yard touchdown pass from John Gregory to Mike Barber after a muffed punt.

While trying to run out the clock, Gregory fumbled at his own 45 with 1:27 remaining in the game. The Eagles could not take advantage as a Davis pass was intercepted by Marshall's Rondell Wannamaker at the Thundering Herd's 35-yard line with 43 seconds left in the game as the 7-0 final ended North Texas' season at 8-4.

In Stephen F. Austin's game against Jackson State, a 73-yard strike from Hammel to Bradford late in the first quarter were the only points either team could manage in the first half as the Lumberjacks took a 7-0 lead to the locker room.

The Lumberjacks' much-heralded defense sparked Stephen F. Austin in the second half. SFA cornerback Johnnie Hendrix's 48-yard interception return for a touchdown early in the third quarter made it 14-0. The lead increased to 17 points two possessions later with a field goal before SFA rounded out the scoring on a 1-yard run by Horace early in the fourth quarter to give the Lumberjacks a 24-0 victory.

SFA's defense held the Tigers to 72 yards rushing and 87 passing. Lewis Tillman, who broke many of Walter Payton's Jackson State records, was limited to a season-low 48 yards on the ground.

Temperatures below 40 degrees and a strong wind greeted the eighth-ranked Demons in the Southland Conference champions' opening-round playoff game at Boise State.

Northwestern State linebacker Mark Newstrom came up big for the Demons. His interception of a Duane Halliday pass on a ball tipped by Broncos tight end Jeff Lindsley gave the ball to Northwestern at the Boise State 39 in the first quarter. On the first play from scrimmage, Stoker connected with Turner to give the Demons a 7-0 lead. Newstrom's pick was one of five interceptions thrown by Boise State quarterbacks in the game.

A 20-yard pass from reserve quarterback Rusty Slack to Lockhart set up a 1-yard O'Neal run to give the Demons a 13-0 halftime lead.

Boise State tied the game 13-13 with two quick third-quarter touchdowns on a pair of 2-yard runs by Chris Thomas.

Northwestern failed on an opportunity to break the tie when Steve Compton recovered a blocked Broncos punt deep in Boise State territory. The Demons failed to score on fourth-and-inches, but the result left the Broncos pinned up against their own goal line.

The Demons held, forcing another punt. Newstrom was the man on the spot once again, blocking Tom Schiller's punt for a safety to put Northwestern State on top 15-13.

Following the free kick, DeWitt went on to score on a 14-yard run to help the Demons advance with a 22-13 victory.

"We didn't play well, I didn't think. Our defense did, but offensively, we didn't do real well. There was snow everywhere the day before the game. On the day of the game, they got a tractor out there and they had that blue turf and had big piles of snow on the outside of the game field and it was cold," Goodwin remembered.

A week later in the Division I-AA quarterfinals in Statesboro, Georgia, Stephen F. Austin's defense could not duplicate its effort against Jackson State. Georgia Southern, winners of two national titles in the previous three years, rushed for 281 yards against the vaunted Lumberjacks defense in SFA's 27-6 loss. Eagles quarterback Raymond Gross rushed for 161 yards and passed for 136 against the Lumberjacks.

SFA's defense did the job in the first half as the Lumberjacks took a 6-3 lead at halftime. A pair of Rawlinson field goals was countered by a 24-yard kick by Georgia Southern's Mike Dowis for the only scoring in the opening 30 minutes.

Like SFA in its game against Jackson State, it was defense that turned the game around in the second half, only this time it was by the Lumberjacks' opponent. Taz Dixon's 44-yard interception return of an errant Hammel throw to the 1-yard line set up Ernest Thompson's touchdown run to put the Eagles on top 10-6 to kick-start 24 unanswered points by Georgia Southern.

A Dowis field goal and a 3-yard touchdown run by Frank Johnson made it 20-6. SFA appeared to get back in the game on a 21-yard scoring strike from Hammel to tight end Brad Barfield but the play was wiped out because of a penalty. A 52-yard pass from Gross to Tony Beiser accounted for the game's final score.

Horace rushed for 140 yards in a losing effort as SFA ended its most successful season ever at 10-3.

Northwestern State, meanwhile, faced another team from Idaho on the road in the second round of the playoffs, squaring off against the top-ranked Idaho Vandals.

The Demons struck first on a 20-yard Hodnett field goal before Idaho roared back with 28 points later in the opening quarter. Three Northwestern State turnovers led to the four Vandals touchdowns, including three touchdown passes by future NFL quarterback John Friez. Two of Friez's touchdowns went to John Jake.

"With as good a defense and secondary as we had, it looked like we had never played football before," Goodwin said. "They were throwing the ball all over us. I thought it was going to be 100-0 at one point."

Despite the terrible start, the Demons managed to make it 35-24 at halftime thanks to three second-quarter touchdowns.

Touchdown passes of 20 yards to DeWitt and 15 to Al Edwards from Stoker gave the Demons their first two scores. After another Friez touchdown pass, Northwestern pulled to within 11 points at halftime on a 5-yard run by DeWitt.

After all the scoring in the first half, the second half turned into a field-goal kicking contest. Thayne Doyle hit on a 23-yard attempt to make it 38-24 as Friez only played one series in the final 30 minutes. Two Hodnett field goals, including one from 53 yards, made it 38-30.

With all the offense in the game, it came down to the Idaho defense in the final two minutes. Needing a touchdown and two-point conversion to force overtime, the Demons marched inside the Vandals' 10-yard line in the closing moments. The Idaho defense held off the Demons on four tries from within the 7-yard line as a pair of carries by both Stoker and fullback Pete Ellis failed to gain the necessary yardage before Northwestern, which ended its season at 10-3, turned the ball over on downs.

"We didn't have any timeouts left," Goodwin recalled. "We were a run-first team and we're thinking four plays and four (actually seven) yards, we can get it running the ball."

The result left Goodwin still questioning himself many years later.

"We probably should have thrown once," said Goodwin. "At least that would have stopped the clock if it was incomplete and give us a little more time to set up. We ran four-straight plays and we didn't score.

"If we could have scored and gone for two to force overtime, we really had outplayed them the second half. The momentum was in our favor."

SFA REACHES NATIONAL CHAMPIONSHIP GAME

Northeast Louisiana began a new era in more ways than one with the start of the 1989 season. Gone was coach Pat Collins, the architect of the Indians' national championship team in 1987. NLU unveiled both a new coach and a new twist to the offense as Dave Roberts, who matriculated from Western Kentucky as the Indians' head coach, brought the no-huddle offense along with him.

After opening the season with a 29-13 victory over Nicholls State, the Indians jumped right into Southland Conference play against McNeese State and the tightly-contested league opener in Monroe led to both teams pulling out all the stops.

After a scoreless opening quarter, Reggie McKay's 2-yard run and a 28-yard Robert Tallent field goal gave Northeast a 10-0 lead that would last until the fourth quarter. Early in the fourth quarter, McNeese surprised the Indians by running a guard-around play. Guard Kenneth Pierce picked up a faux fumble and rambled 16 yards into the end zone. An inadvertent whistle by the officials called the play dead at the 5-yard line. Two plays later, Tony Citizen scored from 3 yards out to make it a 10-7 game. The Cowboys took the lead for the first time at 14-10 when Troy Jones raced 53 yards with a punt for a touchdown. It was the third-straight game in which Jones returned a punt for a touchdown, setting a new school and Southland Conference record.

Down by four points with less than three minutes remaining in the game, the Indians faced an all-important third-and-1 at the McNeese 37. Instead of a run play to pick up a first down, quarterback Doug Pederson threw to a wide-open Jackie Harris for the touchdown. The grab was one of the tight end's 11 catches in the game. NLU secured the win with Terrell Haynes' interception of a Cowboys pass with 1:41 left in the game as the Indians improved to 2-0 overall and 1-0 in SLC play, while McNeese fell to 2-1 overall and 0-1 in the conference.

The Cowboys went into the contest 2-0 with season-opening wins over Mississippi College and Samford.

Northeast Louisiana was back in Southland action a week later at Southwest Texas. It was the Indians' first road game of the season while the Bobcats were playing the third of four home games to open the year. SWT split its first two games, losing to Texas A&I before blanking Prairie View 41-0.

After a 20-yard field goal by Jason Howes in the first period, Southwest Texas scored 17 points in the second quarter to take a 20-0 halftime lead. The Bobcats' points came on a 1-yard run by Willie Bickham, a 13-yard run by Reggie Rivers and a 37-yard Howes field goal.

Freshman quarterback Kevin Smith, who rushed for 92 yards and passed for 94, scored on an 11-yard run midway in the fourth quarter for a 25-0 SWT lead. Northeast, which was limited to a total of 73 yards that included minus-9 net yards rushing, got its only points with 3:30 left in the game on a 16-yard pass from Pederson to Kenneth Burton.

McNeese State also was facing Southland competition for the second week in a row as the Cowboys visited Northwestern State. The defending conference champions had a tough start to the season, losing road games to Southwest Missouri State and Eastern Illinois before taking a 38-14 decision over East Texas in the Demons' home opener.

The Demons trailed 17-15 late in their game against McNeese. Two pass interference calls and three passes from quarterback Scott Stoker to Al Edwards totaling 46 yards helped to move Northwestern State to the 9-yard line. Following a Demons timeout, the Cowboys called time to try and ice Northwestern kicker Chris Hamler. Hamler booted a 25-yard field goal as time expired to give his team an 18-17 triumph.

McNeese led 10-7 at halftime before stretching its advantage on a 9-yard touchdown pass from Scott Dieterich to Carlos McGee for a 10-point Cowboys edge. Edwards scored on a double-reverse and Stoker added a two-point conversion run to make it 17-15 at the end of three quarters.

In the only Southland Conference matchup a week later, the Demons traveled to Southwest Texas.

Northwestern State found itself in a 14-14 tie in the fourth quarter and facing fourth down against the Bobcats. It seemed time to punt the ball and turn the game over to the Northwestern defense. Instead, Demons punter Mark Contreras passed 17 yards to Adrian Hardy to keep the drive alive at midfield.

Later in the possession, Stoker took off on what appeared clear sailing and a 28-yard touchdown run. An inadvertent whistle, however, blew the play dead.

After all the intrigue, the 20-play, 8:46 drive ended with a 22-yard Hamler field goal for a three-point Northwestern lead with 9:45 left in the game.

While the Demons labored to gain the lead, Northwestern put it out of reach in a matter of seconds. Three plays following Hamler's kick, defensive back Randy Hilliard raced 24 yards on an interception return for a touchdown and a 24-14 lead. Northwestern would add a late Stoker touchdown run to turn a close game into a 31-14 victory.

Northwestern led 14-7 at halftime on a 10-yard pass from Stoker to Jerry Roberson and a 5-yard run by Stoker. SWT's only score in the opening 30 minutes came on a 9-yard run by Bickham. The Bobcats tied the game in the third quarter on a 1-yard Bickham run.

The Demons' quest for three Southland wins in a row was a tall order when Northwestern State hosted fourth-ranked North Texas State. The Eagles went into their first conference game of the year 3-1 on the season, with their only loss being 20-17 to Kansas State.

The Demons' Steve Compton raced 94 yards for a touchdown on an interception return only five plays in to the game to set the tone for the contest. Compton's interception was not the only defensive highlight for Northwestern, which limited the Eagles to 148 total yards. The Demons completely shut down the Mean Green running game, holding North Texas to 18 yards on 21 attempts.

Following Compton's return, the Demons added a 2-yard scoring run by Pete Ellis and a 4-yard pass from Stoker to Brad Brown in the second quarter. A 14-yard touchdown run by Danny Ford with 14:16 left in the game gave Northwestern State a 27-0 lead.

The Eagles' only score came minutes later on a 2-yard run by Darrin Collins as the Demons went on to take a 30-7 victory.

Also playing its initial Southland Conference game of season that same day was Stephen F. Austin. Gone was Jim Hess, who parlayed the Lumberjacks' success the previous season into the head job at Division I-A New Mexico State. SFA defensive coordinator Lynn Graves was elevated to head coach.

The Lumberjacks went into the Southwest Texas game 3-1 on the season. SFA opened the season with a win over Jackson State, the same team the Lumberjacks defeated in the opening round of the 1988 playoffs. The lone loss for the Lumberjacks was to Boise State.

Southwest Texas grabbed a 10-0 lead on a 24-yard Howes field goal and Heath Johnson's 63-yard interception return for a touchdown. Before the first quarter was over, however, SFA gained a 12-10 advantage. On the first play following Johnson's interception return, Lumberjacks quarterback Todd Hammel connected with Patrick Jackson on a 77-yard scoring strike but the conversion attempt was blocked. Hammel, who passed for 377 yards and accounted for four touchdowns, hooked up with Eric Wright on a 28-yard touchdown pass. A pass on a two-point conversion attempt failed, leaving SFA with a two-point edge.

Howes put SWT back on top 13-12 with another field goal before Hammel added a 4-yard touchdown run and a 24-yard pass to Wright to give the Lumberjacks a 25-13 lead at the break.

The only scoring in the second half came on a 2-yard run by SFA's Larry Centers and a second interception return for a touchdown by the Bobcats. This time, it was Glenn Mangold who returned an errant pass 16 yards for a touchdown but it wasn't enough for SWT as Graves won his first conference game as Lumberjacks head coach with a 32-21 triumph.

SFA won the game despite 223 yards in penalties and seven turnovers.

Sam Houston State was the last team to make its Southland debut in 1989 when the Bearkats hosted Northeast Louisiana. SHSU went into the game 1-4, with the Bearkats' only win coming over Texas Southern. Northeast Louisiana's loss to Southwest Texas earlier in the season was the start of a three-game losing streak for the Indians heading into the SHSU encounter.

Sam Houston State took the lead less than two minutes into its game against NLU when a midair Terrance Quarles fumble fell into the waiting arms of Bearkats linebacker Doc Livingston, who raced 35 yards for a touchdown. SHSU's only other points came on a pair of second-half field goals by Mark Klein.

Cisco Richard sparked the Indians with a 2-yard run with 24 seconds remaining in the first half and an 83-yard punt return for a touchdown in the third quarter on NLU's way to a 21-13 victory. The game's only other score came on a 37-yard pass from Pederson to Harris in the second quarter that tied the game 7-7.

North Texas State had played three-straight games on the road but finally playing at home against Stephen F. Austin did little to change the Mean Green's fortunes.

The Lumberjacks built a 14-0 lead in the second quarter on a 62-yard punt return by Tim Fields and a 4-yard touchdown run on a reverse by Jackson. North Texas rallied to within four points on a 50-yard Keith Chapman field goal and a 1-yard touchdown run by Erric Pegram.

SFA put the game away in the third quarter. A 65-yard scoring strike from Hammel to Jackson sparked a 21-point fourth quarter to give the Lumberjacks a 35-16 victory.

The Eagles dropped to 0-2 in the Southland and 3-3 overall. SFA improved to 2-0 in the conference and 5-1 overall.

With three-consecutive Southland victories the Demons were hoping an open date would not slow their momentum going into their next conference game against Northeast Louisiana in Shreveport.

Trailing 14-7, a punt pinned Northwestern State back at its own 1-yard line with less than five minutes remaining in the game. Stoker went to the air right away. He spotted a streaking Robinson for a 99-yard touchdown play to pull the Demons to within one point of the Indians.

An over-enthusiastic Demons squad drew an unsportsmanlike penalty for excessive celebration, moving the conversion kick back 15 yards. Hamler missed the 35-yard extra point. The Indians were guilty of being offside on the play, giving Hamler another chance. This time, he connected to tie the game with 4:24 left in the game.

Late in the game, a fumble by Demon punt returner Pat Clark was recovered by Mack Dellafosse at the Northwestern State 39. Six plays later, Tallent's 41-yard field goal attempt with 29 seconds remaining came up short, resulting in a 14-14 tie.

By salvaging a tie, the Demons extended their unbeaten streak to 11 games. The Demons moved to 3-0-1 the SLC and 4-2-1 overall. NLU moved to 2-1-1 in the league and 3-3-1 overall.

Thanks to his 99-yard touchdown pass, Stoker threw for 294 yards against the Indians. That gave him a career total of 4,113 yards, making him the all-time passing leader at Northwestern State.

NLU broke a scoreless tie in the third quarter on a 4-yard pass from Pederson to Harris. After the Demons tied the game later in the quarter on a 65-yard pass from Stoker to Carlos Treadway, the Indians took a 14-7 lead in the fourth quarter on a 3-yard run by Pederson.

The outcome proved costly for Northwestern State. While the Demons were involved in a deadlock with Northeast Louisiana, Stephen F. Austin was pounding McNeese State 42-14 to remain unblemished in Southland play at 3-0.

McNeese simply was unable to stop Hammel. The SFA quarterback threw for 377 yards and four touchdowns as the No. 5 Lumberjacks cruised to 6-1 on the season.

Hammel was hot from the start. He tossed a pair of 15-yard touchdown passes to Joe Bradford and Centers scored on a 1-yard run as SFA jumped out to a 21-0 lead after one quarter.

Two more Hammel touchdown passes, one to Dave Kelly from 15 yards out, and another to Bradford from 10 yards away, gave the Lumberjacks a 35-0 lead in the third quarter.

McNeese, which fell to 0-3 in the SLC and 3-4 overall, scored its two touchdowns in the fourth quarter on a 30-yard pass from Hud Jackson to Citizen and a 10-yard strike from third-team quarterback Wes Watts to Brent Ferdinand.

Elsewhere, the woes continued for North Texas as the Eagles fell to 0-3 in the Southland with a 14-6 home loss to Sam Houston State.

North Texas built a 6-0 lead on a pair of Chapman field goals but was unable to cross the goal line against Sam Houston State. With the Eagles leading 3-0, North Texas linebacker Trent Touchstone intercepted a Bearkats pass that led to a 26-yard field goal and a 6-0 Mean Green lead early in the second quarter.

The Bearkats took the lead with less than four minutes remaining before halftime. Chris Kadlecek recovered a Wally McNeely fumble at the North Texas 22 to set up a 3-yard touchdown run by Elijah Nauls for a 7-6 SHSU lead.

Nauls added another 3-yard touchdown run, this time to cap a 16-play drive that ate up almost nine minutes of the third-quarter clock for the final score of the game.

The Bearkats' defense kept the Eagles out of the end zone with two defensive stops inside the Sam Houston State 10-yard line. SHSU's defense made its final stand with 8:12 left in the game by turning away North Texas on a fourth-and-1 conversion attempt at the Bearkats' 24-yard line.

With Stephen F. Austin playing Eastern Washington in non-conference action, Northwestern State looked to regain some ground a week later at Sam Houston State.

Reeling from the tie with Northeast Louisiana, the Demons struggled against Sam Houston State. Stoker tossed six interceptions in the game, three coming in Bearkats territory in the first half, in a 26-3 upset.

Thanks to Demons miscues, SHSU was able to eke out a 10-3 halftime lead despite only three first downs in the opening two quarters. Following a 28-yard Hamler field goal, the Bearkats scored the final 10 points of the first half on a 45-yard pass from Ashley Van Meter to Claude Stewart and a 35-yard Klein field goal.

The Bearkats pulled away in the second half on a pair of short Claude Thomas touchdown runs and a 53-yard Klein field goal. A fumble by Demons tailback Randy Wright set up Thomas' first touchdown run only four minutes into the second half. Klein's 53-yard kick was set up by the fifth of Stoker's six interceptions.

Northwestern fell to 3-1-1 in the Southland and 4-3-1 overall. SHSU improved to 2-1 in the conference and 3-5 overall.

In Lake Charles, Citizen rushed for 182 yards to move into second place behind only Buford Jordan on the McNeese career rushing list and scored a touchdown as the Cowboys snapped a three-game Southland Conference losing streak with a 21-7 victory over Southwest Texas.

The McNeese tailback, who raised his career total to 2,924 yards, scored on a 1-yard run to give the Cowboys a 7-0 lead. Citizen's touchdown came after a guard-around play by Pierce. Earlier in the season against Northeast Louisiana, Pierce scored on a similar play.

A 19-yard run by Eric LeBlanc made it 14-0 at halftime.

The Bobcats avoided the shutout on a 31-yard pass from Eric Turner to Delwin Manning with 19 seconds left in the contest.

McNeese improved to 1-3 in the SLC and 4-4 overall. Southwest Texas also moved to 1-3 in the conference and 3-5 overall.

Stephen F. Austin's 42-36 non-conference win at Eastern Washington moved the Lumberjacks to 7-1 and extended SFA's winning streak to six games heading back into Southland play at home against Sam Houston State.

SHSU was never in the game against the fourth-ranked Lumberjacks. Hammel tossed touchdown passes of 77 and 19 yards in the first half as Stephen F. Austin built a 35-0 halftime lead on its way to a 45-7 rout of the Bearkats.

Hammel was 25 of 40 passing in the game for 534 yards and set school records for passing in a season and career yardage. Through nine games, the SFA quarterback amassed 3,123 yards and brought his career total to 6,390.

While SFA was one win away from capturing the Southland title, a struggling North Texas team was still seeking its first conference win when it visited McNeese State. The Eagles were coming off a game in which it felt the wrath of a SMU team that had been embarrassed by Houston in a 74-point loss. The Mustangs took their frustrations out on North Texas, handing the Mean Green a 35-9 defeat that extended the Eagles' losing streak to five games.

The Cowboys simply dug themselves too deep a hole against North Texas, falling behind 24-0 at halftime on their way to a 31-19 loss to the Eagles.

McNeese rallied for two touchdowns in the third quarter on a 1-yard run by Dieterich and a 30-yard pass from the quarterback to Ferdinand to trail 24-13. The Eagles halted the Cowboys' momentum in dramatic fashion when quarterback Scott Davis hooked up with Victor McGolothin on a 62-yard bomb. Dieterich tossed 11 yards to Jeff Delhomme to make the final 31-19.

North Texas built its 24-0 lead on a 47-yard Chapman field goal, a 1-yard pass from Davis to Charles White, a 2-yard run by Wally McNeely and a 14-yard run by Davis.

Both teams moved to 4-5 overall. McNeese dropped to 1-4 in the Southland while North Texas improved to 1-3 in league play.

So many records were set in the Northeast Louisiana-Stephen F. Austin game, the most sophisticated super computer likely would have an easier time calculating pi than most football fans would have digesting all the new marks.

Among the more remarkable facets of the game were the new passing records. Hammel was 31 of 45 passing for 571 yards and a new school and Southland Conference-record eight touchdowns. Not to be outdone, Pederson passed for 619 yards, a NCAA Division I-AA record. The NLU quarterback's 46 completions tied the I-AA record and set new school and SLC marks. His 71 attempts set new school and conference marks as well.

When you start adding up all the new standards for combined yards by the two teams, the record totals seemed endless. In the end, the scoreboard read 66-45 in favor of the home-standing Lumberjacks. It seems almost an aside that SFA clinched the Southland Conference title.

The teams traded scores throughout most of the game with the second-quarter spread proving to be the difference. The teams were tied 10-10 after one quarter before SFA outscored the Indians 35-21 in the second quarter.

NLU and Stephen F. Austin traded touchdowns to open the second quarter when Richard's 83-yard punt return was answered by Hammel's 43-yard touchdown pass to Michael Bratsch. The Indians took their only lead of the game on Pederson's 75-yard bomb to Jeff Steele for a 24-17 edge.

It was at that point the Lumberjacks scored three-straight touchdowns to build a lead they would never relinquish. Centers started things off with a 6-yard touchdown run before Hammel tossed touchdown passes of 55 yards to Wright and 21 yards to Bradford to make the score 38-24. The teams then traded touchdowns as the Indians scored on a 9-yard pass from Pederson to Keith Bilbo and Hammel connected with Pat Jackson from 5 yards out to make it 45-31 at halftime.

Hammel threw three more touchdowns in the second half; 64 yards to Anthony Landry, 2 yards to Kelly, and 60 yards to Jackson. Kelly, who caught Hammel's first touchdown pass, along with Jackson, were the only two SFA pass catchers with more than one touchdown.

Northeast added two touchdowns in the second half on Pederson throws of 34 yards to Kendall Farrar and 12 yards to Steele.

The result meant SFA improved to 9-1 overall and remained unbeaten in the Southland Conference at 5-0. Northeast fell to 4-5-1 and 2-2-1 in the conference.

Although nothing could match the SFA-Northeast Louisiana fireworks, McNeese State's 31-14 win at Sam Houston State provided a noteworthy moment of its own as Citizen rushed for 79 yards to top 3,000 in his career.

Citizen rushed for two 1-yard touchdown runs in the first quarter as McNeese built a 21-0 lead after one period. The other score for the Cowboys in the opening quarter came on a 5-yard pass from Dieterich to Ferdinand.

Both of the Bearkats' touchdowns came on runs by Nauls.

The McNeese defense forced six turnovers, including four interceptions. Mike Pierce picked off two of the errant throws and had 15 tackles in the contest.

McNeese concluded Southland play 2-4 and the Cowboys needed a non-conference win over Lamar to finish with a winning season. Although Citizen rushed for 226 yards against the Cardinals, the Cowboys lost 22-17 to conclude the season at 5-6.

About the only noteworthy aspect of Southwest Texas' game at North Texas State was the fact both teams entered the encounter 1-3 in the Southland.

The Eagles seemed to be mere minutes away from winning their second conference game in a row. North Texas was trying to protect a lead of less than a touchdown in the closing minutes against the Bobcats. Southwest Texas had the ball at its own 28-yard line with less than a minute remaining in the game when Turner, the Bobcats quarterback, hit split end Mike Collins over the middle at the Eagles' 40. Collins side-stepped a North Texas defender and raced past the Mean Green's secondary on his way to a 72-yard touchdown with 45 seconds left in the game that gave SWT a 25-20 triumph.

Having already clinched the Southland title, the only intrigue left for Stephen F. Austin in its regular-season finale at Northwestern State was to see if the Lumberjacks could finish unbeaten in conference play.

The season finale featured a Demons unit that was top-rated in the Southland in total defense and scoring defense against the Lumberjacks' nation-leading offense.

The Demons' defense held SFA, which went into the game averaging 38 points and 504 yards per game, to 318 yards. That resulted in a 17-17 tie, but the Lumberjacks really didn't seem to mind. The tie gave 9-1-1 SFA its only blemish on its conference record but the Lumberjacks already had secured the Southland title and an automatic bid to the playoffs. Meanwhile, the outcome cost the Demons a shot at a .500 mark. Northwestern finished the year 4-5-2 and 3-1-2 in the Southland after opening conference play at 3-0.

Northwestern built a 10-7 halftime lead on a 22-yard interception return for a touchdown by David Chitman and a 32-yard Hamler field goal. SFA's score came on a 4-yard run by Centers.

After a 3-yard pass from Stoker to Treadway gave the Demons a 17-7 lead in the third quarter, the Lumberjacks tied the game in the fourth period on a 27-yard Chuck Rawlinson field goal and a 5-yard run by Hammel.

Each team missed a chance to pull out the win by missing on long field goal attempts in the final moments. Rawlinson missed from 54 yards out with 16 seconds remaining while Hamler was short on a 56-yard attempt as time expired.

Southwest Texas blanked Sam Houston State 24-0 in San Marcos, allowing the Bobcats to finish in third place in the Southland at 3-3. The win allowed SWT to end the season 5-6 but it didn't prove to be enough to save John O'Hara's job as coach. In his seven years leading the Bobcats, his teams sported a 36-41 record. O'Hara went 16-6 in his first two years after inheriting a two-time Division II national champion from Jim Wacker but his teams went 20-35 over the next five seasons. SHSU finished 3-8 overall, including 2-4 in the Southland.

A 56-yard pass from Turner to Mike Murphy down to the 5-yard line set up a 1-yard run by Bickham to break up a scoreless tie early in the third quarter and gave Southwest Texas a 7-0 lead. That opened the floodgates for the Bobcats in the second half as SWT added a 33-yard Howes field goal, a 25-yard interception return for a touchdown by safety Michael Sims and a 1-yard touchdown reception by Brian Parks. The short touchdown reception by the Bobcats' tight end was set up when Mangold, a senior defensive tackle for SWT, caused a fumble while sacking Bearkats quarterback Trevor Spradley.

In a tightly-contested finale, Northeast Louisiana was held to two Tallent field goals through three quarters to trail North Texas State 20-6 before starting to rally in the fourth quarter.

The Indians scored 19 points in the fourth quarter on a 5-yard run by McKay along with Pederson touchdown passes of 5 yards to Harris and 52 yards to Farrar to lead 25-20 with 2:01 left in the game. North Texas regained the lead at 28-25 with only 37 seconds left in the game on a 31-yard touchdown pass from Davis to Carl Brewer and a two-point conversion

Starting at their own 20-yard line, the Indians took advantage of a pass interference call and two Pederson passes totaling 37 yards to set up a 45-yard field goal attempt by Tallent with three seconds left in the game. Eagles defender Harry Casey broke through the line and blocked Tallent's kick, allowing North Texas to claim a three-point win.

North Texas ended the season 5-6 overall, including 2-4 in the Southland. The Indians finished with a losing record at 4-6-1. History shows Northeast Louisiana with a 5-5-1 record in 1989 after Louisiana Tech was forced to later forfeit its 24-6 win over NLU.

Stephen F. Austin's opening-round game in the Division I-AA playoffs was not for the faint of heart.

Played in Nacogdoches, the Lumberjacks were trailing by four points with less than three minutes left in the game and facing fourth-and-16 from the Grambling State 36. A pass by Hammel to Jackson appeared to be off the mark. Jackson, the SFA receiver somehow managed to make a diving, finger-tip grab to keep the drive alive after a 23-yard gain.

Facing fourth down again, this time from the 4-yard line and needing 2 yards for a first down, Hammel passed to Bratsch for a gain down to the 1-yard line. Hammel scored on a sneak on the next play to give the Lumberjacks a 59-56 victory.

The fact the Lumberjacks were able to complete passes down the stretch should not have been a surprise. The teams combined to put the ball in the air 100 times for 923 yards and 11 passing touchdowns. Despite those numbers, there were no interceptions and only two holding penalties in the game.

Jackson and Wright each had two touchdown catches for the Lumberjacks while Centers had eight receptions for 150 yards. Grambling receiver Steven Glover had six receptions for 211 yards and scored three touchdowns. His final touchdown catch from 45 yards out with 4:11 left in the contest had given the Tigers a 56-52 lead.

SFA led 7-6 after one quarter before Grambling built a 27-7 lead. The Lumberjacks rallied back to trail 27-21 at halftime.

The ball was not expected to be put in the air 100 times in the Division I-AA quarterfinals as the Lumberjacks took on a Southwest Missouri State team that boasted the top running game in the nation.

Playing at home for the second week in a row in the postseason, the plan for the Lumberjacks was to try and get Southwest Missouri to reluctantly put the ball in the air. Meanwhile, the Bears' strategy was to do whatever it took to keep the ball away from SFA's potent offense.

Both factors turned in favor of SFA. The Lumberjacks held a Southwest Missouri team that had averaged 309 yards per game on the ground to a season-low 93. Meanwhile, the Bears' strategy to keep the ball away from Stephen F. Austin backfired as Southwest Missouri failed on four of five attempts to convert on fourth down.

Hammel, who threw for 405 yards and four touchdowns, connected on scoring tosses of 63 yards to Jackson and 22 yards to Centers to give SFA a quick 13-0 lead. Hammel's strike to Jackson came only two plays into the game.

An 18-yard touchdown run by Tony Gilbert early in the second quarter rallied Southwest Missouri to within 16-10. By the 11:24 mark of the fourth quarter, the Lumberjacks pulled away for a 48-18 lead. During the stretch, Rawlinson kicked a 51-yard field goal and Roland Dumes, who rushed for 103 yards, scored on runs of 37 and 62 yards on the Lumberjacks' way to a 55-25 victory.

A heavy snowstorm greeted Stephen F. Austin as the Lumberjacks went on the road for the first time in the postseason as SFA faced Furman in Greenville, South Carolina, in the Division I-AA semifinals.

Stephen F. Austin built a 21-7 halftime lead on Hammel touchdown passes of 34 yards to Kelly and 5 yards to Bradford, along with a 14-yard run by Centers. Furman's only score in the opening 30 minutes came on a 23-yard pass from Patrick Baynes to Don Clardy early in the second quarter. Furman fullback Billy Stockdale scored on a 1-yard run with 13:22 left in the game but a missed conversion attempt left the Paladins trailing 21-13.

The Paladins, looking to reach the Division I-AA championship game for the third time in five years, marched 80 yards in the snow in 18 plays in the closing moments. A 1-yard run by Stockdale made it 21-19 with 19 seconds showing in the fourth quarter. Stockdale got the call on the two-point conversion attempt but his off-tackle run was stuffed by the Lumberjacks, sending SFA to the national championship game for the first time in school history.

Stephen F. Austin's quest for a national title would not be an easy one. SFA not only faced a Georgia Southern team seeking its third national title in five years and looking to become the only team in NCAA history to go 15-0 in a season, the Lumberjacks had to take on the Eagles on Georgia Southern's home field. On top of that, the Lumberjacks faced a championship game-record crowd of 25,725 – most of whom were partisan Georgia Southern fans.

If that wasn't enough motivation for the Lumberjacks, all they had to do was think back to a year earlier when Georgia Southern eliminated SFA from the playoffs with a 27-6 victory in the Division I-AA semifinals.

Georgia Southern led 20-17 at halftime thanks to a 34-yard run by quarterback Raymond Gross, a fumble recovery in the end zone by Terrance Sorrell and a pair of Mike Dowis field goals. SFA's points came on a 1-yard run by Hammel, a 12-yard touchdown reception by Centers and school record-tying 52-yard field goal by Rawlinson.

The Lumberjacks eventually built a 34-27 lead before Georgia Southern tied the game on a 1-yard run by Ernest Thompson with 5:58 left in the game. Facing a heavy rush on the ensuing possession, Hammel tossed his fourth interception of the game. On third-and-goal from the 3-yard line, SFA defenders David Temple and Roderick Stansell held Joe Ross for no gain. Dowis kicked a 20-yard field goal to give the Eagles a 37-34 lead with 1:41 left in the fourth quarter.

Stephen F. Austin failed to get into field goal range in the closing moments when Hammel threw his fifth interception of the game with 27 seconds left in the contest.

The loss, nor the interceptions, could take way Hammel's accomplishments. He closed out his career with a record 5,364 passing yards. Hammel also set a Division I-AA playoff record with 1,449 yards and 14 touchdown passes.

The Lumberjacks completed their best-ever season at 12-2-1.

When Southwest Texas began Southland Conference play at Northeast Louisiana to usher in the 1990 season, it was with a new man leading the way. The new top Bobcat was Dennis Franchione. Franchione, left his alma mater, Pittsburg State, to take the SWT job. In five seasons as coach, he led the Gorillas to a 53-6 record. Franchione became the second former Pittsburg State coach in the Southland, joining Sam Houston State's Ron Randleman.

Franchione won his debut as Southwest Texas coach with a 15-7 win over Texas A&I but brought a 1-2 record into the game against 1-1 Northeast Louisiana.

After trailing Northeast Louisiana 17-9 at halftime, Southwest Texas pulled ahead 27-23 in the fourth quarter on a 5-yard touchdown run by backup quarterback Greg Pagel with 7:32 left in the game.

NLU lined up in its new run-and-shoot with four receivers and bruising fullback Roosevelt Potts in the backfield, to attempt one final drive with 4:05 left in the game. A pass interference penalty against the Bobcats, a 7-yard pass to Cisco Richard for a third-down conversion, and an 11-yard Richard run helped advance the Indians to the SWT 13. Richard, who was lined up as a receiver in the formation, hauled in a dump pass from Doug Pederson and raced in for the needed 13 yards to cap a 77-yard drive and give Northeast a 30-27 lead with 1:36 remaining in the game.

Southwest Texas reached the NLU 16 in the closing seconds but two incomplete passes and a sack of Pagel by safety Michael Young caused time to expire before the Bobcats could run off another play.

NLU built its 17-9 halftime lead on a 41-yard Rob Tallent field goal, an 8-yard fumble return by Chris Houston and a 1-yard run by Erich Cox. With Pagel guiding the way, Southwest Texas rallied to eventually take a 27-23 lead. Pagel, who entered the game in place of injured starter Gilbert Price, threw a 24-yard touchdown pass in the second quarter and ran for a pair of touchdowns in the second half before the Indians came back to pull out the win.

Northwestern State and North Texas State vied in the only Southland Conference encounter a week later in Denton. After opening the season with losses to Eastern Illinois and Nicholls State, the Demons edged East Texas 24-17 to snap a seven-game non-winning streak stretching back to the 1989 season. North Texas was 2-1, its lone early-season loss again coming against Texas A&M.

The Eagles' defense was unable to stop Northwestern State's John Tappin. The junior flanker scored three touchdowns, including two on catches of 76 and 66 yards. Meanwhile, the Demons' defense limited the Mean Green to 1-of-12 third-down conversions and 207 yards of total offense in Northwestern's 28-18 victory.

Tappin's 76-yard touchdown reception and his 18-yard run on a reverse staked the Demons to a 14-3 halftime lead. His 66-yard touchdown catch from Brad Brown gave Northwestern State a 28-3 lead in the third quarter.

North Texas fought back, scoring twice in the third quarter. Erric Pegram, who went on to play for four NFL teams, scored on a 1-yard run to cap a 69-yard drive. Brown fumbled on the first play of the Demons' ensuing possession, setting up a 5-yard keeper by quarterback Scott Davis but the Eagles could get no closer than 10 points.

At Lake Charles a week later, the Northeast Louisiana Indians faced a McNeese State team now coached by former NLU assistant Bobby Keasler. Keasler replaced Sonny Jackson, who produced a 13-20 record in three years at McNeese.

The Cowboys were struggling at 1-3 entering their first Southland Conference game of the season, allowing almost 500 yards of total offense and 33.5 points per game. McNeese reduced those numbers significantly, holding the Indians to 88 yards rushing, 222 passing and 14 points.

McNeese did all the scoring in the first half on a 25-yard Eric Roberts field goal and a 1-yard run by Wes Watts to lead 10-0. Northeast put itself back in the game midway in the third quarter when Richard caught a pass for 25 yards and then rushed for another 25 to set up a 1-yard touchdown run by Potts to make it 10-7. NLU seemed to have positioned itself for a shot at taking the lead shortly after Potts' touchdown when Dickey Caston returned a Cowboys punt to the McNeese 24. An illegal block penalty nullified the run and forced the Indians to take possession at their own 10.

Instead of possibly tying the game or taking the lead, the Indians fell further behind two series later when McNeese running back Erwin Brown scooted 52 yards for a touchdown and a 16-7 lead. The Cowboys made it 10-7 on another Roberts field goal to lead 19-7 before Northeast added a 3-yard run by Richard in the middle of the fourth quarter to make the final score 19-14.

On the same day Keasler picked up his first Southland victory, Franchione had a second chance to get his initial conference win when Southwest Texas hosted Stephen F. Austin. The Lumberjacks, the defending SLC champions, were looking to league play to help turn their season around after a 1-3 start. SWT was coming off a 33-30 win over the Colonels heading into the game with the Lumberjacks.

The Bobcats took an early lead and took advantage of five SFA turnovers to blank the Lumberjacks 24-0. Southwest Texas scored off its opening drive when Reggie Rivers, who rushed for 176 yards in the game, capped the 80-yard drive with a 4-yard run.

Southwest Texas' second touchdown was set up by an interception. Bobcats defensive lineman Mike Slater tipped a pass by Lumberjacks quarterback Scott Barrick that was picked off by Chad Coleman. The SWT linebacker raced back to the Stephen F. Austin 37 to eventually set up a 9-yard touchdown run by Gilbert for a 14-0 halftime lead.

The only scoring in the second half came on a 38-yard Robbie Robertson field goal and a 4-yard run by Price.

Stephen F. Austin dropped to 1-4 for the Lumberjacks' worst start since 1981. The defeat also marked the first time SFA had been shut out since a 3-0 loss to Eastern Washington in 1987, a span of 39 games.

A week later, Sam Houston State became the final team to open Southland play in 1990 at Northeast Louisiana. The Bearkats went into the game 1-4 on the season. SHSU's lone win came against Angelo State.

The Bearkats faced a NLU team that played its most complete game through six weeks of the season in Sam Houston State's 27-10 loss. Getting good performances from the offense, defense and special teams, the Indians evened their record at 3-3 overall and moved to 2-1 in the Southland.

The Indians, who rolled up 446 yards while allowing only 150, came up with a pair of Richard touchdown runs in the first quarter to lead 14-0. NLU drove 57 yards for its first touchdown while the second was set up by the special teams when Keith Bilbo recovered a Bearkats fumble at the Sam Houston State 17. Following an 11-yard touchdown pass from Bearkats quarterback Danny Thomas to Randy Ray in the second quarter, the Indians countered with a 24-yard Tallent field goal to lead 17-7 at halftime.

Following Ray's touchdown reception, the Northeast defense did not allow a first down for nine-straight possessions. In that span, the Bearkats amassed a total of 30 yards. On offense, Potts rushed for 109 yards while Pederson completed 16 of 18 passes for 160 yards.

Special teams contributed directly to the next score when Richard returned a third-quarter punt 71 yards for a touchdown. Each team added field goals the remainder of the game to make the final 27-10.

McNeese State, meanwhile, used two big plays on offense and a record-setting big play on defense to take sole possession of first place in the Southland Conference at 2-0 with a 38-21 home win over Northwestern State.

Watts connected on scoring bombs of 73 yards to Jeff Delhomme and 76 yards to Adam Henry in the first half. The McNeese quarterback also passed 28 yards to Brown as the Cowboys built a 21-7 halftime lead.

With the score 21-14 in the third quarter, McNeese cornerback David Easterling returned an interception a school-record 96 yards for a touchdown to put the Cowboys back on top by two touchdowns. McNeese scored the final 10 points of the game on a 38-yard Roberts field goal and a 7-yard run by Robbie Vizier.

Northwestern State's points came on two touchdown runs by quarterback Brad Brown and a 2-yard run by Brian Driskill.

Meanwhile, Stephen F. Austin's slide continued with a 31-24 home loss to North Texas.

Barrick passed for 255 yards, including a stretch of eight-consecutive completions on a 14-play, 73-yard drive in the third quarter that was culminated on a 7-yard touchdown run by Kirby McNeil to give SFA a 24-21 lead.

From that point on, the North Texas defense put the clamps on Barrick. The Eagles intercepted the SFA quarterback on three-straight possessions in the fourth quarter while holding the Lumberjacks to 20 yards of total offense in the final period.

Coming off a career-high 203 yards rushing against SMU, Davis scored on a touchdown run in the fourth period against SFA to put North Texas on top 28-24. Brad Allen later added a 39-yard field goal to seal a 31-24 win for the Eagles.

While Davis scored the go-ahead touchdown on the ground, his passing proved effective. He was 21 of 43, both season highs, for 245 yards. Greg Mathews, a true freshman, stepped up in place of the injured Tony Cook with six catches for 99 yards.

McNeese State was looking to start 3-0 in the Southland Conference for the first time since 1980 a week later, but things didn't look too promising for the Cowboys after falling behind 14-0 in the second quarter at North Texas.

After a 1-yard touchdown run by Robert Blowers and a 5-yard pass from Davis to Blowers, McNeese managed a 38-yard Roberts field goal to trail 14-3 at halftime.

North Texas seemed poised to put the game out of reach early in the third quarter when a 29-yard punt return by Mathews gave the Eagles the ball at the McNeese 22. Unable to advance the ball, the Eagles lined up for a 40-yard field-goal attempt by Brad Allen. Cowboys' cornerback Ronald Soloman blocked the kick and Eric LeBlanc scooped up the ball for McNeese at the Cowboys' 45-yard line. As LeBlanc was being tackled, he pitched to Soloman, who raced 70 yards for a touchdown to make the score 14-10.

McNeese's special teams came up big once again late in the third quarter. Lamar Thomas blocked a Bart Helsley kick to set up a 22-yard Roberts field goal to make the score 14-13 less than 30 seconds into the fourth quarter.

On McNeese's next possession, Roberts booted a 39-yard field goal with less than five minutes remaining to give the Cowboys a 16-14 triumph.

Along with special teams, McNeese's defense played a key role down the stretch. Of North Texas' 154 yards rushing in the game, only 31 came in the second half.

The result left both teams 4-3 overall. UNT dropped to 1-2 in the Southland.

At Natchitoches, teams going in opposite directions met when Southwest Texas visited Northwestern State.

Rivers, ranked second in Division I-AA in rushing, ran for 129 yards and scored two touchdowns in a 22-12 win over the Demons. The fourth-straight win for the Bobcats improved SWT to 5-3 overall and 2-1 in the Southland. The Demons, losers of three in a row, fell to 2-5 overall and 1-2 in the SLC in dropping their third home game in four outings.

Northwestern scored on its opening possession and held a 9-7 lead at halftime. James McKellum's 4-yard run capped an opening 80-yard drive and Chris Hamler booted a 42-yard field goal with two minutes remaining in the half to give the Demons their points. SWT's only score came on an 11-yard run by Rivers.

After the Demons extended their lead to 12-7 on a Hamler field goal, the Bobcats gained the lead by one point on a 1-yard run by Todd Scott late in the third quarter.

Failing to convert on fourth down early in the fourth quarter, the Demons gave the ball to Southwest Texas at the Northwestern 33. Rivers' 9-yard touchdown run six plays later and a two-point conversion gave the Bobcats a 10-point lead they would not relinquish.

Elsewhere, Sam Houston State used a strong running game and an opportunistic defense to earn its first Southland Conference win of the season with a 23-3 home victory over Stephen. F. Austin.

Bearkats running back Curtis Thomas rushed for 218 yards, including a 9-yard touchdown, to pace Sam Houston State. Thomas' effort was the second-most ever by a SHSU runner behind only McNeil Moore. Moore rushed for 286 yards against Lamar in 1951.

Along with Thomas, Bearkats quarterback Ashley Van Meter scored on a touchdown run and Mark Klein kicked three field goals to pace SHSU.

The Bearkats' defense, which recovered four fumbles and had an interception, held SFA to 83 yards of total offense, including minus-49 rushing.

Riding a three-game conference winning streak, Southwest Texas was looking to claim a share of the Southland title a week later with a victory at home over unbeaten McNeese State

Kip Texada's interception of a Bobcats pass shortly after McNeese State had taken a 17-16 lead in the fourth quarter seemed to put the Cowboys in a position to retain sole possession of first place.

Eric Foster's 9-yard run to cap a 57-yard drive put the Cowboys on top by a point and Texada's interception gave the ball back to McNeese at the SWT 12. Two plays into the drive, however, the Cowboys fumbled, giving the ball back to the Bobcats.

Southwest Texas quickly moved into field goal position. Robertson's 42-yard attempt as time expired was wide. A roughing-the-kicker penalty moved the ball closer and gave Robertson another shot. This time, he connected from 30 yards out to give the Bobcats a 19-17 triumph.

The result left both teams 3-1 in the Southland while Southwest Texas improved to 6-3 as McNeese dropped to 4-4.

Robertson field goals of 20 and 50 yards gave SWT a 6-0 lead after one quarter before McNeese rallied on a 5-yard run by LeBlanc in the second quarter for a 7-6 Cowboys edge at the break.

Roberts, who connected on at least one field goal in all eight McNeese games, hit from 27 yards in the third quarter to give the Cowboys a 10-6 advantage that would last until the fourth quarter.

An 11-yard halfback pass from Rivers to Scott Smith for a touchdown and a 27-yard Robertson field goal early in the fourth quarter put SWT on top 16-10. Foster, who rushed for 161 yards in the game, scored on his 9-yard run to set the stage for Robertson's game-winning kick.

In Monroe, Northeast Louisiana turned up the defensive pressure, especially in the second half, to take a 14-3 win over Northwestern State to match Southwest Texas and McNeese at 3-1 atop the Southland. For the first time in years, the long series between NLU and Northwestern State was played on a campus site instead of Shreveport where the game had become known as the State Fair Classic.

A 7-3 halftime lead stood up for the remainder of the game until NLU added a touchdown in the fourth quarter. The Indians forced six of the Demons' seven turnovers in the second half and held Northwestern State to 40 yards of total offense over the final two quarters. Northwestern had amassed 203 yards in the first half despite trailing by four points when the Demons only were able to answer a 2-yard touchdown run by Richard in the opening quarter with a 47-yard Hamler field goal in the second quarter. Richard caught five passes in the game for a career total of 156. That broke the all-time Southland Conference record of 155 set by Pat Holder of Abilene Christian from 1968-70.

With neither team able to score throughout most of the second half, the Demons remained in the game. That changed with Pederson's 11-yard touchdown pass to Kenneth Burton early in the fourth quarter. Houston's interception of a Brown pass set up Northeast Louisiana at the Northwestern State 22. It looked as though the Demons might escape unscathed when Tallent missed a 35-yard field-goal attempt. Northwestern defensive lineman Greg Necaise was flagged for being offside on the play, setting up fourth-and-inches. Bryant Broady's 1-yard run gave the Indians a first down that eventually set up Burton's touchdown reception.

The Demons dropped their fourth-straight game to fall to 2-6 overall and 1-3 in conference play.

At Huntsville, Pegram rushed for a career-long 76-yard run to give North Texas an early 7-0 lead but the Eagles' offense was unable to produce much else in a 26-14 loss.

Pegram accounted for 126 of the Eagles' 201 yards on the ground. After Pegram's early touchdown, the Bearkats scored 20-consecutive points on two Klein field goals and a pair of touchdown runs by Thomas. Thomas finished with 150 yards rushing.

The SHSU defense continually harassed Davis, holding the North Texas quarterback to minus-8 yards rushing and 98 passing while recording four sacks.

North Texas' defense, meanwhile, allowed 441 yards as Van Meter rushed for a season-high 163 yards.

The Mean Green dropped to 1-3 in the SLC and 4-4 overall. Sam Houston State improved to 2-1 in the conference and 3-5 overall.

With Southwest Texas having a bye week and Northeast Louisiana playing a non-conference game against Louisiana Tech, McNeese State had a chance to take a half-game lead in the standings the following week with a win at struggling Stephen F. Austin.

Things couldn't seem to get much worse for Stephen F. Austin. The Lumberjacks found going into the McNeese game that their one win on the season over Nicholls State became a forfeit when SFA was ruled to have used an ineligible player. That officially dropped the Lumberjacks' record to 0-8.

Despite that, the Lumberjacks found themselves with a narrow 3-2 halftime lead against the Cowboys. Neither team could generate much offense in the first half. SFA's three points came on a 53-yard Chuck Rawlinson field goal after the Lumberjacks gained possession at the McNeese 42 on an interception. The Cowboys' only points came when Joey Bernard and Martin Bonura brought down Barrick in the end zone for a safety at the 8:20 mark of the second quarter.

Rawlinson made it 5-2 on a 37-yard field goal in the third quarter before McNeese gained its only lead on a 49-yard run by Vizier to put the Cowboys on top 9-5.

The rest of the game belonged to the Lumberjacks. Barrick hit Eric Wright with a 37-yard touchdown strike to give the lead back to Stephen F. Austin at 12-9 going into the fourth quarter. SFA scored three more times in the final quarter on a Rawlinson field goal, another Barrick to Wright pass and Anthony Cuney's 72-yard interception return to make the final 30-9.

McNeese fell to 3-2 in the SLC and 4-5 overall. The Lumberjacks recorded their first official win of the season to move to 1-3 in the conference and 1-8 overall.

Meanwhile, two teams seemingly going in opposite directions met when Sam Houston State visited Northwestern State. SHSU went into the encounter with a two-game Southland winning streak to reach 2-1 in the conference while the Demons dropped two-in-a-row after a league-opening victory to head into the contest 1-2 in the SLC.

The Demons trailed 10-0 at halftime before scoring all of their points in the second half – 20 in the fourth quarter. A 33-yard touchdown pass from Brown to Tappin provided the game's only points of the third quarter. Tappin's 74-yard scamper in the fourth quarter gave the Demons their first lead at 13-10. Northwestern's final two scores came on a 21-yard pass from Andrew Roach to David Gordy and a 3-yard run by Brown as the Demons' 27-10 triumph left both teams 3-6 on the season.

SHSU scored on its first two possessions of the game on a 29-yard run by Thomas and a 21-yard Klein field goal. Thomas finished with 169 yards rushing on 24 carries.

Stephen F. Austin's win over McNeese State a week earlier proved to be a one-time thing. The Lumberjacks gave another solid effort but fell at Northeast Louisiana 10-3 to drop to 1-9 overall, including 1-4 in the Southland. NLU's victory moved the Indians to 4-1 in the conference.

No two games could be such polar opposites as the 1989 and 1990 Northeast Louisiana-Stephen F. Austin encounters. In 1989, the Lumberjacks scored 35 points in the second quarter in a 66-45 victory in Nacogdoches. The 1990 matchup in Monroe saw a combined total of 13 points.

NLU's defense came through once again, holding the Lumberjacks to 139 total yards while sacking SFA quarterbacks six times. The offense, meanwhile, led by Potts' 136 yards rushing, produced when it had to.

Potts carried the ball five times for 51 yards in a 76-yard drive opening drive to set up a 27-yard Tallent field goal. Potts toted the pigskin seven times in an 80-yard drive right before halftime to set up a 9-yard touchdown pass from Pederson to Burton to give the Indians a 10-0 halftime lead. The only points in the second half came on a 38-yard field goal by Rawlinson in the fourth quarter as NLU prevailed 10-3.

With an extra week to prepare coming off an open date, Southwest Texas had a chance to match Northeast Louisiana at 4-1 in the Southland Conference with a home win over North Texas.

The Bobcats boasted the No. 2 rushing offense in the nation, averaging 303.7 yards per game. Rivers, the Southland's leading rusher with an average of 115.8, got his yards, rushing for 129 against the Eagles.

Still, North Texas managed to contain the Bobcats' ground game. The Eagles' offense held onto the ball for 20 minutes in the opening half to lead 13-9 at intermission. Meanwhile, the North Texas defense held the Bobcats to 115 rushing as a team.

The Eagles' defense came up with a big play on the first snap from scrimmage when linebacker Byron Gross brought down Price in the end zone for a safety. A Tom Patrick field goal helped to give North Texas a 5-0 lead.

A 55-yard run by Rivers set up a 20-yard touchdown pass from Price to Scott Moore for a 6-5 SWT edge after one quarter. A 7-yard run by Davis and the quarterback's two-point run made it 13-6 before a 42-yard Roberson field goal made it 13-9 at the break.

Patrick's 25-yard field goal in the fourth quarter made it 16-9 and set up a dramatic finish.

A 5-yard pass from Price to Moore with slightly more than two minutes remaining in the game pulled the Bobcats to within a single point.

Going for two points and the win, Price once again targeted Moore. Moore caught the ball in the back of the end zone but the SWT receiver was flagged for pushing off on North Texas defender Walter Casey, allowing the Eagles to hold on for the 16-15 triumph.

The loss dropped SWT to 3-2 in the Southland and 6-3 overall. North Texas improved to 6-4 overall and 2-3 in the conference.

Needing a win in its home game against Sam Houston State to have any chance to remain in the Southland race, McNeese State edged the Bearkats 13-6 to move to 4-2 in the conference and end a two-game slide. The loss dropped SHSU to 2-3 in the league.

An exchange of field goals provided the only points in the first half. Ron Alexander quickly changed that, racing a school-record 93 yards with the second-half kickoff to put McNeese on top 10-3. Roberts added an 18-yard field goal in the fourth quarter to make it 13-3. The kicker's first-quarter field goal gave him 18 on the season to establish a new single-season mark for McNeese.

Klein provided all of SHSU's scoring, adding a 26-yard field goal in the fourth quarter as the Cowboys held on for a 13-6 victory.

McNeese closed out the season with a 27-7 non-conference loss at home to Weber State to end the year with a losing record at 5-6.

You had to give Northeast Louisiana and North Texas credit – they sure knew how to give some excitement to the final week of the 1990 regular season with the Southland Conference title on the line.

Things didn't quite look that way from the start with the game's first points not coming until the second quarter on a 43-yard Tallent field goal. From that point on until the fourth quarter, the Eagles seemed to be the team playing with greater urgency. After Tallent's field goal, Davis put his team on top 6-3 on a 31-yard touchdown pass to Velton Morgan. A fumble by Potts at the NLU 15 right before halftime set up a 27-yard Patrick field goal to make the score 9-3. North Texas increased the lead to 15-3 when James Walton returned a blocked punt 8 yards for a touchdown in the third quarter.

Trailing by 12 points, the Indians took possession of the ball at their own 20 with 8:59 left in the game. After advancing the ball to the NLU 44, Pederson spotted Richard at the North Texas 35. Richard scooted past a couple of Eagle defenders and sailed into the end zone for a 56-yard touchdown play that pulled Northeast to within five points at 15-10 at the 8:04 mark of the fourth quarter.

Clinging to a five-point lead, the Eagles used up slightly less than six minutes to advance to the NLU 36. Pegram was brought down for a 2-yard loss by Rod Moon, forcing a punt. The punt gave the ball to the Indians at their own 1-yard line with 1:40 left in the game.

Two passes to Burton brought the ball to the Northeast 34. Pederson hit Richard in stride at the North Texas 40. Eagles cornerback Sean Mayes made an unsuccessful attempt to push Richard out of bounds, but the shifty runner raced the remaining yards to complete a 66-yard touchdown and give the Indians a 16-15 lead.

Not taking a chance on the possibility of a long kickoff return, NLU elected for a squib kick. North Texas recovered at midfield with 50 seconds left in the game. That was enough time for the Mean Green to reach the Northeast 19 and set up Patrick for a 37-yard field goal attempt with five seconds left in the game. Moon penetrated the line and blocked Patrick's kick to secure the conference championship for Northeast Louisiana.

The win gave the Indians a 5-1 conference record and 7-4 overall mark. North Texas concluded the season 6-5 overall, including 2-4 in the SLC.

With Northeast Louisiana wrapping up the Southland title and McNeese already having secured second place, the remaining conference games on the final week of the season were a matter of jockeying for third place.

In Huntsville, Southwest Texas seemed well on its way to closing out the season with a victory over Sam Houston State as the Bobcats led 25-11 early in the fourth quarter before Van Meter, the Bearkats' quarterback, got hot.

A 54-yard bomb from Van Meter to Greg Lockhart set up a 7-yard touchdown toss to Brian Gloden. Van Meter scrambled in for the two-point conversion to make the score 25-19 with 11:58 remaining in the game.

The recovery of a bad snap on a punt attempt put the Bearkats back in business at the SWT 8-yard line. Van Meter and Gloden hooked up again, this time from 2 yards out with 1:18 left in the contest. Klein kicked the extra point to give SHSU a 26-25 triumph.

Southwest Texas built a 14-3 halftime lead on a 2-yard touchdown run by Price and the quarterback's 63-yard pass to Danny Faust in the first quarter. A 39-yard run by Charles Oliver and a 2-point conversion in the third quarter made it a three-point game before the Bobcats answered on a Robertson field goal and a 5-yard run by Price for SWT's 25-11 lead to set up the Bearkats' late rally.

The result left both teams in a tie for third place in the Southland at 3-3. Southwest Texas ended the season 6-5 overall and Sam Houston State 4-7.

Northwestern State's defense put the clamps on Stephen F. Austin in a 20-3 home win that allowed the Demons to join Sam Houston State and Southwest Texas at 3-3 in the conference and bring a long season to an end for the Lumberjacks.

Northwestern held SFA to 119 yards and yielded a school-record-low four first downs. The Lumberjacks did not pick up their initial first down of the game until there was less than two minutes remaining in the opening half. Leading the defensive charge was Necaise, the Demons' defensive end, with four quarterback sacks. Necaise finished the 1990 season with 16 sacks.

Brown's 24-yard scramble for a touchdown and a 21-yard Hamler field goal gave the Demons a 10-0 halftime lead. Northwestern extended the lead to 17-3 on a 22-yard run by McKellum. SFA didn't score until the 4:47 mark of the third quarter on a 22-yard Rawlinson field goal.

By winning their final three games, the Demons ended the season with a 5-6 record. SFA, which reached the Division I-AA finals a year earlier, finished 1-10 overall and 1-5 in the conference.

Two players and one quarter were too much for Northeast Louisiana in the opening round of the Division I-AA playoffs at Nevada-Reno. Treamelle Taylor and Ray Whalen factored in two of the Wolf Pack's three touchdowns in a 21-point second quarter that proved to be the difference in the Indians' 27-17 loss.

Trailing 7-0, Taylor's 53-yard punt return in the second quarter set up Whalen's 16-yard touchdown run to tie the game. Taylor then caught an 8-yard touchdown pass from Fred Gatlin to give Nevada-Reno the lead. The score was set up when Pederson fumbled after being hit by defensive end Mark Drahos, with Matt Clafton recovering at the NLU 21. Whalen added a 24-yard run to give the Wolf Pack a 21-7 lead and more than enough points for the win.

NLU, which had taken a 7-0 lead on a 1-yard run by Richard in the first quarter, added a 1-yard run by Potts on its first drive in the second half to make it 21-14. That was as close as the Indians would get as Nevada-Reno added two Kevin McKelvie field goals in the fourth quarter for the 27-14 win to eliminate the Indians.

NICHOLLS DEBUTS WITH
BIG SLC UPSET

Nicholls State University in Thibodaux, Louisiana, joined the Southland in 1991, giving the conference eight football-playing schools. Although the Colonels were newcomers to the league, Nicholls was no stranger to most of the SLC schools. Nicholls has been members of the Gulf Star Conference with Northwestern State, Sam Houston State, Southwest Texas and Stephen F. Austin. In addition, Nicholls and McNeese State played each other on an almost yearly basis since the early 1970s. Although a non-conference opponent in 1990, the Colonels faced all of the SLC except for North Texas State.

The Colonels were coached by Phil Greco. In his fifth year at Nicholls, Greco, a former assistant coach at Northeast Louisiana, Southern Mississippi and Tulane, guided the Colonels to a 22-21-1 record as a Division I-AA independent.

Nicholls State's invitation to join the Southland was a long time in coming as far as the school was concerned, but once in, it didn't take long for the Colonels to make their conference debut. Played September 7, 1991, Nicholls began life as a member of the SLC at Northeast Louisiana. Each team went into the game with a game under its belt. Nicholls lost its season opener 7-3 against Texas A&I, a nationally-ranked Division II foe, while NLU defeated Division I-A Southwestern Louisiana 21-10.

The Colonels knew the task before them would be difficult, especially when taking several factors into account: Nicholls trailed 14-2 in the series between the two teams; the Colonels hadn't beaten Northeast Louisiana since 1986 and hadn't won at Malone Stadium since 1979; NLU had never lost a home opener at Malone Stadium since the stadium opened in 1978; the Indians were picked first in the preseason Southland Conference poll, while the Colonels were picked last.

None of that seemed to matter to the school located along the banks of Bayou Lafourche in south Louisiana. Powered by a running attack that amassed

282 yards and produced two 100-yard rushers, the Colonels upset Northeast Louisiana 15-10.

David Craig Robinson, who rushed for 122 yards, scored on a 55-yard burst to give the Colonels a 7-0 lead. Northeast tied the game later in the first quarter on a 3-yard Greg Robinson run. A 20-yard Rob Tallent field goal was countered by a 19-yard Skip Shelton field goal on the final play of the first half for a 10-10 tie at intermission.

The Colonels managed only five points in the second half but that proved to be enough as the Nicholls defense took over. Roosevelt Potts, who rushed for 78 yards in the first half, was held to minus-2 in the final two quarters. Also, the Indians committed four of their five turnovers in the second half.

A 24-yard Shelton field goal put Nicholls on top 13-10 in the third quarter. The final two points for the Colonels came when a lateral by NLU quarterback Ches Liles went out of the end zone for a safety in the fourth quarter.

Liles, who suffered an injury to the little finger of his left hand in the game, was replaced by Robert Cobb in the second half. Cobb completed his first three passes to lead the Indians to the Nicholls 14. His fourth pass was intercepted by Darryl Pounds at the goal line with 13:30 left in the game. Northeast continually turned the ball over down the stretch and never seriously threatened the Colonels' 5-point lead.

Along with David Craig Robinson, the Colonels' other 100-yard rusher in the game was Jarvis Lillie with 101.

Following an open date and a 25-17 non-conference win over Troy State, the Colonels had a chance to move to 2-0 in the Southland before the majority of the league's teams had even played a single conference game.

Nicholls saw Southwest Texas take advantage of a pair of second-half turnovers to spoil the Colonels' first-ever Southland Conference home game at Guidry Stadium with a 19-10 win for the Bobcats. Holding a mere 3-0 lead at halftime, SWT extended its advantage to 10 points. A 40-yard pass from quarterback Gilbert Price to Danny Faust set up a 1-yard touchdown run by Todd Scott. When Price wasn't throwing the ball, he was hurting the Colonels with his running ability. Price rushed for 145 yards in the game as the Bobcats' flexbone option attack amassed 275 yards on the ground.

Nicholls put itself back in the game on a 39-yard Shelton field goal with 3:23 remaining in the third quarter before turnovers doomed the Colonels. Rob Woodard's interception of a Joey Primus pass gave SWT the ball at the Nicholls 47. That eventually set up a 21-yard Robbie Robertson field goal for a 13-3 Bobcats lead with 9:41 left in the game. Clyde Washington fumbled the ensuing kickoff, with Heath Johnson recovering for the Bobcats at the Nicholls 23. Scott scored his second touchdown from a yard out as SWT put the game out of reach at 19-3 with 6:55 remaining in the game.

The result left both teams 2-1 overall.

Southwest Texas became the second team to try and jump out to 2-0 in the Southland Conference when the Bobcats hosted Northeast Louisiana.

Northeast Louisiana, coming off a 21-13 upset of top-ranked Georgia Southern and a 17-7 victory over Mississippi College, put Robinson to good use against Southwest Texas. Robinson broke loose on a 77-yard gallop late in the first quarter to give the Indians a 10-8 lead. The running back, who rushed for 159 yards in the game, added an 18-yard touchdown run on Northeast's next possession to stretch the lead to 17-8. That would be more than enough to give NLU its first Southland Conference win of the season as neither team could score in the second half.

Southwest Texas took a 8-0 lead on its opening possession of the game when Price's 15-yard pass to Scott Moore capped a 74-yard drive and the Bobcats added a two-point conversion on a Greg Pagel run. A 37-yard Tallent field goal made it 8-3 before the Indians took the lead with their touchdown late in the first quarter.

McNeese State played its league opener a week later at Nicholls. The Cowboys went into the encounter 1-2 on the season. After starting with losses to seventh-ranked Northern Iowa and Southwest Missouri State, McNeese picked up its initial win of the season with a 31-3 victory over Montana.

After Nicholls took a 3-0 lead after one quarter on a 25-yard Shelton field goal, Eric Foster scored touchdowns in each of the next three quarters.

All of Foster's scores were set up by either the Cowboys' special teams or defense. A 37-yard punt return by Ron Alexander set up a 46-yard ramble by Foster to give McNeese a 7-3 lead one play into the second quarter. Foster, who rushed for 139 yards in the game, gained all 39 yards on a third-quarter drive and scored on an 8-yard run on a drive set up by a Lance Guidry interception.

Foster made the final 21-3 when he scored on a 2-yard run in the fourth quarter to culminate a 5-yard drive set up by Guidry's block of a Shelton punt.

When North Texas faced Northwestern State in Natchitoches in the Southland opener for both teams, the Mean Green had a new man roaming the sidelines.

Dennis Parker took over the program from Corky Nelson following Nelson's nine-year run and 48-52-1 record. A veteran high school coach, Parker became the coach at North Texas after his Marshall High team won the 1990

Texas state championship. Parker led Marshall to a 56-27-1 record in seven years at Marshall.

North Texas was off to a 1-2-1 start. After a season-opening 24-0 victory over Abilene Christian, the Eagles scored a combined two points in losses of 40-2 against Oklahoma and 72-0 against Nevada. North Texas tied Southwest Missouri State 21-21 and had an extra week to prepare for Northwestern State because of an open date.

Northwestern State, meanwhile, was 2-2 heading into its conference opener.

The first conference game under a new coach is always a moment of joy, but on the sideline opposite North Texas, the Demons were dealing with heavy hearts. Northwestern State was playing its first game after offensive lineman Bill Britt was paralyzed from the waist down during a hunting accident a week earlier.

Perhaps emotions got the best of Northwestern State early in the game as the Demons turned the ball over three times in the opening quarter. Despite the turnovers, the Demons still managed a 14-10 lead after one quarter when the Eagles were unable to take complete advantage of the miscues.

After a Deon Ridgell 20-yard touchdown run staked the Demons to a 7-0 lead, the Northwestern State running back fumbled on back-to-back possessions. The first was recovered by the Eagles at the 1-yard line, leading to a Joey Missildine touchdown run one play later. A Ridgell fumble at the Northwestern State 18 led to a 19-yard Kevin McDaniel field goal. John Tappan fumbled on a kickoff return but the Demons eventually forced a punt. When Brad Brown scored on a 4-yard run, the Demons managed a 14-10 halftime lead.

Leading 17-10 and facing a first-and-25 situation in the fourth quarter, the Demons put the game away when James McKellum turned a screen pass from Chris Gilliam into a 50-yard touchdown and a 24-10 triumph.

Also playing their initial Southland games of the season were eighth-ranked Sam Houston State and Stephen F. Austin. The Bearkats hosted Nicholls State while SFA was at home against Southwest Texas.

Sam Houston State entered its game against Nicholls 3-0-1 on the season, its only blemish being a 21-21 tie at Western Illinois.

After a 24-yard Shelton field goal extended the Colonels' halftime edge of three points to 13-7, the Bearkats responded with a 44-yard run by Broderick Davis to set up Davis' 7-yard touchdown scamper one play later to give Sam Houston a 14-13 edge with 8:07 remaining in the third quarter. On the ensuing kickoff, old third-quarter woes came back to haunt the Colonels when Kelvin Dandridge fumbled, with Bearkats kicker Chris Batten recovering at the Nicholls 38. A 3-yard pass from Danny Thomas to Kregg Lunsford capped a 10-play drive to give SHSU a 21-13 lead.

Sam Houston State, 4-0-1 overall and 1-0 in the Southland, came up with an insurance touchdown on a 39-yard touchdown run by Davis with 10:23 left in the game. The 28-19 final dropped the Colonels to 2-4 overall and 1-3 in conference play.

Stephen F. Austin went into its first SLC game of the season on a three-game losing streak. After opening with a 50-9 whipping of Arkansas-Monticello, the Lumberjacks lost to Jackson State, Boise State and Youngstown State to drop to 1-3.

Special teams played a big role in Stephen F. Austin's 31-15 loss to Southwest Texas. Moments after a 1-yard run by Scott capped a 12-play drive to give the Bobcats a 7-0 lead in the first quarter, Woodard blocked a Lumberjacks punt that was recovered by Craig Hemphill in the end zone for another touchdown. Hemphill tackled SFA punter Leo Araguz at the 5-yard line late in the second quarter to set up a touchdown pass from Price to Anthony Wood for a 21-0 Bobcats lead. A 48-yard Chuck Rawlinson field goal as time expired in the second quarter gave SFA its only points of the first half.

The closest the Lumberjacks got in the second half was 24-9 following a 77-yard touchdown pass from Clint Bounds to Marcus Henderson in the fourth quarter.

In Monroe, No. 10 Northeast Louisiana broke McNeese State's streak of not allowing a touchdown at 12 quarters on a 3-yard run by Robinson in the second quarter for a 10-0 halftime lead for the Indians. NLU scored the game's first three points on a Tallent field goal in the first quarter. The Indians were without Lyles, their starting quarterback, who was injured a week earlier in a game against Southwest Texas. Cobb guided the NLU attack against the Cowboys.

Leading by 10 points to open the third quarter, the Indians fumbled the second-half kickoff, giving the ball to McNeese at the Northeast 34. Eight plays later, Foster scored on a 5-yard run to make it 10-7.

The score held up until the Cowboys got the ball for one last possession at their own 20-yard line with 1:22 left in the game and no timeouts remaining. Passes from Eric Acheson to Adam Henry and Marcus Bowie advanced the ball 46 yards. After reaching the 9-yard line, Eric Roberts kicked a 26-yard field goal with six seconds left in the game for a 10-10 tie.

"That was a big turnaround for us," said McNeese coach Bobby Keasler. "We weren't expected to win that ball game and we hung around and had a chance to tie it up."

McNeese moved to 1-0-1 in the SLC and 2-2-1 overall with the outcome. Northeast Louisiana moved to 1-1-1 in the conference and 4-1-1- overall.

The Cowboys' defense was ranked sixth in Division I-AA heading into their Southland Conference clash at Northwestern State a week later, but it was the Demons' "Purple Swarm" that did a number on McNeese State.

Northwestern State's defense limited McNeese to 217 yards of total offense and set up two touchdowns for the Demons' offense.

The Northwestern State defense handed the ball to the offense at the McNeese 44 late in the first quarter on a fumble recovery by Randy Bullock. Gilliam scored from 10 yards out on a keeper for a 7-0 Northwestern lead. Roberts kicked a 25-yard field goal with 14 seconds remaining in the second quarter to pull the Cowboys to within four points at halftime.

Northwestern extended its advantage to 10 points at 13-3 on a 6-yard run by Brown with slightly more than nine minutes remaining in the third quarter. Adrian Hardy's interception return to the McNeese 20 set up a 9-yard touchdown run by Gilliam with 3:20 left in the game to hand the Cowboys a 20-3 defeat.

"When we played Northwestern it was always a dog fight," said Keasler.

Sam Houston State matched Northwestern State at 2-0 in the Southland with a 27-15 home triumph over Northeast Louisiana.

Sixth-ranked Sam Houston State built a 14-0 halftime lead, but the Bearkats really made their statement on a drive to open up the second half in their home game against Northeast Louisiana.

The Bearkats mounted a 74-yard drive that took 18 plays and used up nine minutes on the clock before Davis scored on a 4-yard run to give Sam Houston State a 20-0 lead. After the Indians scored on a 31-yard Tallent field goal and a 17-yard run by Potts to make it 20-9, fortune smiled on Sam Houston State. Receiver Ray Malone fumbled after a pass reception at the NLU 5 but the loose ball eluded several Indian defenders as it rolled to the end zone. Claude Stewart, Malone's fellow receiver, fell on the ball for a touchdown to give the Bearkats 27-9 lead with 11:16 left in the game.

Northeast Louisiana managed to score on a 29-yard pass from Wendal Lowrey to Vincent Brisby to make it 27-15 with 4:55 remaining, but with the time used up by the Bearkats at the start of the quarter, there just was not enough time for the Indians to rally. Sam Houston State improved to 5-0-1 overall and 2-0 in the SLC while the 12-point loss dropped NLU to 4-2-1 overall and 1-2-1 in the league.

While Northwestern State and Sam Houston State were moving to 2-0 in the Southland, the North Texas Eagles were earning Parker's first conference win as Mean Green coach.

A McDaniel field goal, a safety, and a 10-yard touchdown pass from freshman quarterback Mitch Maher to Richard Clark gave North Texas an 11-7 lead heading into the fourth quarter.

The Eagles were still clinging to their four-point advantage when Maher fumbled the ball while setting up to pass at his own 44 in the fourth quarter. SFA took advantage when Bounds eventually scored on a 1-yard run to put the Lumberjacks on top 14-11.

Down by three points, the Eagles punted the ball away with 1:59 left in the game and turned the game over to their defense. The North Texas defense came through when linebacker Brad Koch knocked the ball loose from SFA running back Reno Moore. Moore's mid-air fumble was recovered by Eagles defensive back Wayne Walker.

Like Bounds, another backup quarterback would get his chance to shine. After three Maher fumbles, the freshman was replaced by senior Wendell Mosley. Mosley fired an 8-yard touchdown pass to J.R. Selexman with 33 seconds left in the fourth quarter to give the Eagles an 18-14 lead.

Donald Ericks' interception of a Lumberjacks pass at the Eagles' 4-yard line on the final play of the game allowed North Texas to earn its first Southland Conference victory of the season.

North Texas improved to 1-1 in the SLC and 2-3-1 overall. The Lumberjacks dropped to 0-2 in the conference and 1-5 overall.

Sam Houston State was looking to move to 3-0 in the Southland a week later when the fifth-ranked Bearkats visited North Texas State.

SHSU's ranking didn't seem to faze the Eagles – at least not in the first half. The North Texas defense held the Bearkats to 26 total yards in the first two quarters while the Mean Green offense dominated time of possession. For all their success controlling the tempo, the Eagles' offense managed to penetrate the SHSU red zone only twice in the first half. The only points North Texas could muster was 7-yard touchdown pass from Mosley to Luis Silva in the second quarter to give the Eagles a 6-0 halftime lead.

The second half was a different story. Starting its second drive of the third quarter at the North Texas 33, quarterback Ashley Van Meter, playing in place of struggling Thomas, tossed a 27-yard pass to Malone. That set up Van Meter's 4-yard touchdown run to give the Bearkats a 7-6 edge.

With the Eagles selling out on defense to stop the run, the Bearkats went to the passing game behind Van Meter. He completed passes of 25 yards to Greg Lockhart and 16 yards to Curtis Thomas to set up Thomas' 9-yard touchdown in the fourth quarter for a hard-fought 14-6 triumph for Sam Houston State.

"It was a night game and we were very ragged," Bearkats coach Ron Randleman recalled. "Sometimes those night games on the road are tough."

After coming off the bench a week earlier to rally North Texas over Stephen F. Austin, Mosley was intercepted four times by the Bearkats, including three times in the second half.

Along with moving to 3-0 in the Southland, the unbeaten Bearkats improved to 6-0-1 overall. North Texas dropped to 1-2 in the league and 2-4-1 overall.

Northwestern State was unable to match Sam Houston State at 3-0 as the Demons lost 24-9 at home to Northeast Louisiana.

The loss proved costly to the Demons in more ways than one. Not only did the loss snap a three-game winning streak, Northwestern State lost Gilliam to a broken elbow on the first drive of the contest.

Without Gilliam, the Demons only managed 164 yards of total offense as backup quarterbacks for Northwestern threw four interceptions.

Still, Northwestern managed a 3-0 halftime lead because of the Indians' own struggles. NLU committed a total of seven turnovers, including five in the opening 30 minutes of play. As a result, the only points in the opening half came on a 44-yard Jeff Powell field goal on the Demons' opening drive.

Other than the opening drive, the Demons would not pick up a first down until the third quarter. NLU, meanwhile, used a 26-yard Tallent field goal on the first drive of the second half and a 2-yard run by Potts to take a 10-3 lead going into the fourth quarter.

The Demons pulled to within 10-9 in the fourth quarter on a 2-yard run by Ridgell on a drive set up by an Indians fumble at the Northeast Louisiana 15.

NLU mounted two 80-yard drives in the fourth quarter to pull out the win. Lowrey, thrust into action because of injuries to the Indians' top two signal callers, scored on a 1-yard run to cap the first long drive. Chris Williams culminated the next drive on a 3-yard run with 3:51 left in the game to give the Indians the 24-9 victory.

The Demons fell to 4-3 overall and 2-1 in the Southland. NLU improved to 2-2-1 in the league and 5-2-1 overall.

At Lake Charles, the home field didn't seem particularly friendly to the Cowboys early in their game against Southwest Texas when McNeese State fell behind 15-0 in the first quarter.

Foster fumbled on the first play from scrimmage, giving the Bobcats the ball at the McNeese 26 to open the game. Scott made the Cowboys pay for the miscue when he scored on a 1-yard run. Minutes later, Scott scored on a 5-yard run and a two-point conversion pass from Pagel to Moore gave SWT a 15-0 advantage.

A pair of Roberts field goals were sandwiched around Robertson's three-pointer as the Bobcats took an 18-6 lead at intermission.

The McNeese defense turned the tide in the second half, forcing two Southwest Texas turnovers that the Cowboys' offense converted into touchdowns in the fourth quarter. McNeese got the ball at the SWT 4-yard line after defensive end Ken Naquin forced a Scott fumble that was recovered by Ronald Scott. It took four plays, but Foster finally scored from a yard out to make the score 18-13.

McNeese got the ball back at its own 38 with 4:45 remaining in the game after linebacker Sean Judge's recovery of a Price fumble. A 25-yard toss from Acheson to Collins provided the biggest chunk of yardage as the Cowboys marched toward the SWT end zone. Foster raced the final 12 yards with 3:30 left in the game to put McNeese on top 19-18.

A two-point conversion attempt failed, but the Cowboys' defense sacked the Bobcats' quarterback twice and was able to run out the clock for the one-point triumph.

McNeese improved to 2-1-1 in the Southland and 3-3-1 overall. Southwest Texas fell to 2-2 in the conference and 4-3 overall.

An open date a week earlier seemed to refresh Nicholls as the Colonels recorded their first shutout victory since 1988 in a 24-0 blanking of Stephen F. Austin.

Unlike the trend that led to three-straight losses entering the SFA game, the Colonels built upon a narrow 7-0 halftime lead by taking advantage of an opponent's mistakes instead of committing them.

A 32-yard Shelton field goal less than three minutes into the second half gave Nicholls a 10-0 lead. The score was set up on Tyrone Dominique's recovery of a Mike Goddard fumble at the SFA 20. Lillie's tackle-breaking 42-yard run on the Colonels' next possession helped to set up a 1-yard touchdown run by Robinson to make it 17-0. Lillie, who rushed for 134 yards, scored the game's final touchdown on a 5-yard run with 5:43 left in the third quarter. That score was set up on a fumble recovery by Kevin George at the Lumberjack 27.

Nicholls moved to 3-4 overall and 2-3 in the Southland, while SFA fell to 1-5 overall and 0-3 in league action.

The struggling Lumberjacks used a bit of early trickery in their home game against Sam Houston State to upset the fifth-ranked Bearkats 13-3 and drop SHSU from the ranks of the unbeaten.

SFA was forced to punt on its opening possession of the game but instead of kicking the ball away, Araguz tossed a 43-yard pass from punt formation to Tim Fields down to the Bearkats' 12-yard line. That led to a 22-yard Rawlinson field goal for a 3-0 lead that stood up until the third quarter.

After the Bearkats tied the game on a field goal, Rawlinson kicked a school-record 58 yarder to put Stephen F. Austin back on top at 6-3. SFA put the game away in the fourth quarter on a 40-yard touchdown pass from Goddard to Fields.

SFA, which held the Bearkats to 162 total yards, improved to 1-3 in the Southland and 2-6 overall. Sam Houston State dropped to 3-1 in the conference and 6-1-1 overall.

"That was an afternoon game up there and Michael Bankston was hurt," Randleman said. "When Stephen F. Austin saw he was not going to play, it really fired them up.

"He (Bankston) was instrumental in a lot of ball games, but not in that one."

The Sam Houston State loss opened the door for McNeese State to gain ground on the Bearkats when the Cowboys hosted North Texas State.

After spotting North Texas a 3-0 lead on a 21-yard McDaniel field goal, the Cowboys defense clamped down on the Eagles and forced eight turnovers in McNeese State's 41-3 rout of the Mean Green in Southland Conference play.

Brian Brumfield and Lance Guidry each had two of the Cowboys' five interceptions and the McNeese defense also forced three fumbles.

"I thought we played good defense the whole time we were there (at McNeese). That was the one thing I told the staff, 'I said we were going to be good on defense and good in the kicking game,'" said Keasler.

Foster scored on a pair of short touchdown runs to give McNeese a 14-3 lead after one quarter. Defensive end Dana Scott recovered a fumble by Moseley in the end zone and Roberts kicked a 49-yard field goal to give McNeese a 24-3 halftime lead.

McNeese added 17 points in the second half, including a 16-yard pass from Pat Neck to tight end Bobby Smith on a fake field goal attempt.

The Cowboys improved to 3-1-1 in the SLC and a half-game behind Sam Houston State in the conference race. McNeese moved to 4-3-1 overall. North Texas fell to 1-3 in the league.

Without Gilliam, Northwestern State turned to Brad Laird at quarterback in the Demons' Southland Conference road game at Southwest Texas State. The Bobcats showed the true freshman quarterback no mercy, turning three-straight

Laird interceptions into scores as part of a 21-point second quarter in SWT's 24-0 victory.

Southwest Texas broke a scoreless tie after one quarter on a 45-yard touchdown pass from Price to Reggie Leday. Woodard picked off Laird's first interception of the game, setting up the Bobcats at the Demons' 18. Scott scored on a 6-yard run three plays later for a 12-0 lead.

Woodward was at it again moments later, returning an errant Laird throw 31 yards down to the Northwestern State 14. Price hooked up with Moore on a 3-yard toss four plays later to make it 18-0.

Laird's third interception was picked off by Johnson and returned to the Demons' 39. That set up a 26-yard Ray Whitehead field goal with 2:30 remaining before halftime.

The loss was the first time a Sam Goodwin-coached Demons team was shut out in a Southland Conference game.

SWT improved to 3-2 in the league and 5-3 overall. Northwestern State evened its conference record at 2-2 and 4-4 overall.

The Demons continued to struggle offensively in a 13-3 loss a week later at Sam Houston State, now ranked tenth in the nation.

Powell's 22-yard field goal in the first quarter represented the only points produced by the Demons in two games. The Bearkats, ranked seventh in the nation in defense, limited Northwestern State to 199 yards of total offense, including only 65 rushing on 40 attempts.

The Bearkats produced all of their points in the second quarter on a pair of short touchdown runs by Charles Oliver. Oliver's first touchdown was set up by Charles Harris' fumble recovery at the Demons' 7-yard line.

SHSU remained in first place in the Southland Conference with the win, improving to 4-1 in the league and 7-1-1 overall. Northwestern fell to 2-3 in the SLC and 4-5 overall.

McNeese State, meanwhile, managed only 168 yards of total offense and a 7-7 tie in its Southland Conference home game against Stephen F. Austin but it was enough to keep the Cowboys in the league race. The Cowboys moved to 3-1-2 in the Southland to set up a showdown at Sam Houston State.

McNeese managed a tie with SFA by holding the Lumberjacks to 163 yards. It was an emotional game for the Lumberjacks, who were playing their first game under interim coach Phil Bounds after Lynn Graves was fired earlier in the week. SFA fell to 2-6-1 with the loss.

The Cowboys took a 7-0 lead at halftime on a 9-yard pass from Wes Watts to Tom Perry in the second quarter. Chris Fontenette, who rushed for 93 yards in the game, scampered 70 yards in the drive to set up the touchdown toss.

Stephen F. Austin tied the game in the third quarter on a 15-yard run by Henderson.

McNeese had a shot to win the game when Roberts set up for a 37-yard field goal with 2:57 left in the game. Roberts' kick was wide right, leaving the game in a tie.

Coming off an eight-turnover performance in its loss to McNeese, the Eagles next faced Southland newcomer Nicholls State, which was ranked sixth in the nation in turnover margin.

The Mean Green turned the tables on Nicholls, failing to turn the ball over for the first time all season while forcing the Colonels into six miscues.

North Texas took advantage of a fumbled pitch and fumbled punt return to score two of its three first-half touchdowns to take an 18-6 halftime lead. The Eagles' scores came on a 2-yard pass from Maher to David Brown, a 3-yard run by Charles White and a 4-yard pass from Maher to White. Maher played in place of Mosley, who missed the game after complaining of painful headaches during the week and failed to accompany the Eagles to the game.

McDaniel kicked two second-half field goals to increase the score to 24-6. Following McDaniel's second kick, Robinson returned the ensuing kickoff 90 yards for a touchdown to make the score 24-13 in the fourth quarter. A 1-yard run by Lillie with 2:06 in the game rallied the Colonels to within 24-19.

The Eagles recovered an onside kick but Nicholls eventually got the ball back. Keith Wilkerson's recovery of a Colonels fumble with 50 seconds left in the contest enabled North Texas to secure its first road win of the season.

North Texas moved to 2-3 in the Southland and 3-5-1 overall. Nicholls fell to 2-4 in the conference and 4-5 overall.

The Cowboys trailed 7-6 at halftime in their final Southland Conference game of the season the following week at Sam Houston State. McNeese led 6-0 after one quarter on a pair of Roberts field goals. The first, from 25 yards out, was set up by Terry Irving's recovery of a Bearkats fumble. A fumble by Matt Daigle at the McNeese 47 eventually led to an 11-yard touchdown pass from Van Meter to Brian Gloden to give the Bearkats a 7-6 halftime edge.

McNeese built a 16-7 lead in the third quarter on a 33-yard Roberts field goal and a 3-yard Fontenette run. The Bearkats countered with 10 points of their own on an 8-yard run by Harris before a 35-yard Mark Klein field goal put SHSU ahead 17-16 with 9:44 left in the game.

After Roberts missed a 37-yard field goal with 2:32 left in the game, the Cowboys forced a Sam Houston State punt to get the ball back at its own 47. Following an incomplete pass and a 4-yard scramble by Acheson, the quarterback found Skeet Owens along the sideline for a 38-yard completion. Roberts connected on a 28-yard field goal with two seconds left in the game to give McNeese a 19-17 win to send the Cowboys to the Division I-AA playoffs.

The result meant jubilation for the Cowboys.

"It was the first conference championship. It was a great day. I can still see the faces on those kids in the dressing room. It was unbelievable how they felt. We had players that probably overachieved," said Kealer.

It meant something else to the Bearkats.

"Bankston got hurt on the field goal and couldn't get off the field. They had to stop the clock and it gave them a chance to kick the field goal. I wanted to go out and drag him off the field, but he's a big guy," Randleman jokingly said.

The win lifted McNeese to 4-1-2 and earned the Cowboys no worse than a share of the SLC title for the first time since 1980. At 5-3-2 overall, McNeese only had a non-conference game with Tennessee-Martin left on the schedule.

Although Sam Houston State fell to 4-2 in the league, it still could share the conference title by beating Southwest Texas in the Bearkats' SLC finale, but SHSU's loss put a lot of teams back in the running.

Despite Stephen F. Austin's tough season, the Lumberjacks entered their home game against Northeast Louisiana allowing an average of 86 yards per game to rank third in the nation in pass defense. The Lumberjacks yielded 96 to Brisby – on one play. By the time the Indians receiver was done, he had amassed 206 receiving yards. NLU went on to total 349 yards through the air and 225 on the ground to fly past SFA 48-20.

Brisby's school-record 96-yard bomb in the second quarter broke open a 13-10 game. After a Lumberjacks field goal, a 28-yard run by Potts gave the Indians a 27-13 halftime lead. Tallent kicked three of four extra points in the half. The lone miss, on his second attempt, snapped a NLU-record of 54-straight points after touchdown.

SFA narrowed the margin to seven points at 27-20 early in the third quarter on a 55-yard touchdown reception by Fields, but the Lumberjacks would not score the remainder of the game. Meanwhile, a pair of touchdown runs by Williams allowed NLU to pull away and improve to 6-3-1 overall and 3-2 in the Southland. Stephen. F. Austin fell to 2-7-1 overall and last in the conference at 1-4-1.

At Denton, Brown fumbled the opening kickoff for North Texas and Southwest Texas scored four plays later on a 5-yard run by Price as the Eagles returned to their old, bad habits in a 36-8 loss to the Bobcats.

The fumble was the first of five turnovers for North Texas and Southwest Texas took full advantage, scoring all but six of its points off of Mean Green miscues.

Following Price's touchdown run, he tossed a 34-yard touchdown pass to Moore later in the first quarter. Scott added a pair of short touchdown runs in the second quarter as SWT put the game away by halftime with a 26-0 lead.

Trailing 36-0, North Texas avoided the shutout when Maher tossed a 26-yard touchdown pass to Clayton George in the fourth quarter.

The win allowed Southwest Texas improve to 4-2 to stay in the hunt for a possible Southland Conference co-championship as the Bobcats moved to 7-3 overall. North Texas dropped to 2-4 in the league and 3-6-1 overall.

Two 4-5 teams met in Northwestern State's final road game of the 1991 season at Nicholls State.

Trailing 3-0 after a 36-yard Shelton field goal, Hedrick's 1-yard touchdown run to cap a drive that began at midfield, gave Northwestern State a 7-3 lead. The touchdown was the first for the Demons in three games. Northwestern later sacked Primus, the Nicholls quarterback, in the end zone for a safety to lead 9-3 at halftime.

Nicholls attempted to rally after a 12-yard touchdown run by Lawann Latson increased the Colonels' deficit to 13 points at 16-3 in the fourth quarter.

Playing in place of an injured Primus, Carl Disher directed the Colonels on a 64-yard drive, which was culminated on Disher's 6-yard touchdown pass to John Brown.

Down 16-10 with slightly more than two minutes remaining in the game, the Colonels elected to try an onside kick. Rob Floyd recovered for Northwestern and the Demons were able to run out the clock for the six-point triumph. Northwestern improved to 3-4 in the SLC while Nicholls fell to 2-4. The Colonels closed out the regular season with a 40-6 loss to Georgia Southern to conclude 4-7 – the fourth non-winning season in five years for Nicholls.

Needing a win in the week's final season to claim a share of the Southland Conference title and a possible at-large bid to the Division I-AA playoffs, Sam Houston State turned to its defense in the Bearkats' all-important game at Southwest Texas.

The Bearkats forced a pair of Southwest Texas turnovers that the Sam Houston State offense turned into its only touchdowns of the game. The first miscue led to a 3-yard run by Harris to give SHSU a 7-0 lead less than two minutes into the game. Early in the fourth quarter, another SWT turnover set up an 11-yard Van Meter run that extended the Bearkats' lead to 20-3.

Southwest Texas began a furious rally following Van Meter's run. A snap over the head of the SHSU punter through the end zone for a safety got things started and made the score 20-5.

A 4-yard run by Price inched the Bobcats a bit closer at 20-11. SWT recovered an onside kick, setting up a 32-yard field goal to make it a six-point game at 20-14 with 4:52 left in the contest.

SWT had two final possessions to try and gain the lead in the closing minutes but the Bearkats' defense stepped up once again. On the first occasion, four-consecutive incomplete passes by Price ended the drive at the Bobcats' 44. SHSU's Harris fumbled two plays later, giving the ball back to Southwest Texas at its own 40. The drive ended at the 29 when Price came up short on a fourth-down conversion attempt, allowing Sam Houston State to hold on for a 20-14 victory.

Along with Sam Houston State's other defensive accomplishments in the game, the Bearkats held the nation's second-best rushing attack to a season-low 119 yards.

"We had a great defense that year, not just Bankston," said Randleman. "Our front four was about as good as I ever had – Johnny Black, Eric January and Willie Lacy. Those guys were all athletic. We didn't do a lot of things defensively. We were able to play pretty basic and play pretty well. Consequently, offensively that year we were not too exotic because we didn't want to put our defense in a bad situation."

The Bearkats' 5-2 Southland record matched McNeese State's winning percentage of .714 as the Cowboys sported a 4-1-2 conference mark. SHSU finished the regular season with an 8-3-1 overall mark while Southwest Texas ended the year 7-4.

Northeast Louisiana's offense ended the 1991 season on a high note in the Indians' 44-21 Southland Conference home win over North Texas.

Lowrey had a career night, passing for 305 yards and four touchdowns. His favorite target, Brisby, tied a school record with three touchdowns catches and 179 yards receiving. The running game was not left out as Potts rushed for 140 yards to become the third runner in NLU history to top 1,000 yards in a season.

North Texas quarterbacks failed to enjoy the success of Lowrey. Eagle quarterbacks were constantly harassed as the Indians recorded five sacks, including one in the end zone for a safety.

A 42-yard interception return for a touchdown by North Texas defensive back Tomur Barnes narrowed the gap to 21-13 at one point but the Indians went on to score the next 23 points to cruise to the victory.

NLU concluded the regular season 4-2-1 in the Southland and 7-3-1 overall. North Texas finished 2-5 in the conference and 3-7-1 overall.

At Natchitoches, the Demons wasted little time in securing a winning season in front of the home folks against Stephen F. Austin. Northwestern State scored 17 points in the first quarter and 14 in the second on its way to a 52-0 trouncing of the Lumberjacks.

Northwestern finished 6-5 overall and 4-3 in the Southland Conference by winning its final two games of the season. The Lumberjacks, who suffered their worst margin of defeat in 15 years, ended the season 2-8-1 overall and 1-5-1 in the SLC.

Demons senior linebacker Andre Carron had 12 tackles in the game to finish his career with 519 tackles. Carron shattered the all-time school mark, topping former record-holder Gary Reasons of New York Giants fame by 125 tackles.

Carron even got in on the scoring for the Demons. Lining up at fullback, Carron scored Northwestern's final touchdown on a 1-yard run in the fourth quarter.

Brown and McKellum, another pair of seniors, each scored two touchdowns. Brown scored the game's first touchdown on a 22-yard run in the first quarter. He added a 1-yard run in a 14-point third quarter. McKellum scored on runs of 5 and 80 yards as the Demons rushed for a season-high 294 yards.

Even the Demons' defense, which set a new school record by holding the Lumberjacks to 70 total yards, managed to score. Darius Adams returned an interception 44 yards for a touchdown in Northwestern State's largest margin of victory in 33 years.

Sam Houston State did receive an at-large bid to the playoffs as the Bearkats traveled to Murfreesboro, Tennessee, to take on Middle Tennessee State.

Thomas, who rushed for 135 yards, scored on a 5-yard run late in the first quarter of a game played in a constant rain. Klein missed the extra point, which would come back to haunt the Bearkats.

A 42-yard field goal by Blue Raiders kicker Garth Petrilli in the second quarter was answered by Thomas' second touchdown of the day to give Sam Houston State a 13-3 halftime lead. The touchdown was set up by Orlando Williams' third blocked punt of the season. Petrilli provided the only points of the third quarter on a 33-yard field goal.

The Blue Raiders trailed by seven points in the fourth quarter but the margin could have been closer if not for two missed field goals by Petrilli. Middle Tennessee was forced to punt with 10 minutes left in the game but a roughing-the-kicker call against SHSU kept the drive alive.

Middle Tennessee's Joe Campbell, who rushed for 202 yards, scored on a 2-yard run 13 plays later. Klein's earlier miss meant the Blue Raiders only needed to kick the extra point to tie the game 13-13 and force overtime.

With the ball placed at the opponents' 25-yard line, the Bearkats got the ball first in overtime. Thomas' third touchdown run of the night, this one from a yard out, put Sam Houston State on top. Klein's extra-point attempt hit the right upright, leaving the Bearkats with a 19-13 edge.

Campbell scored from 10 yards out on Middle Tennessee's overtime possession. Petrilli's kick was good, giving the Blue Raiders a 20-19 triumph to end Sam Houston State's season at 8-3-1.

McNeese State's Southland Conference title earned the Cowboys the right to open the playoffs at top-ranked Nevada.

Things looked bleak for the Cowboys when they trailed 15-3 at halftime and 22-3 going into the fourth quarter.

McNeese mounted two long drives in the fourth quarter. Acheson capped a 97-yard drive with an 18-yard touchdown strike to Henry. The Cowboys quarterback later hooked up with Fontenette on a 10-yard touchdown toss. A two-point conversion pass failed, leaving the score at 22-16 with 5:53 left in the game.

The Cowboys' defense forced the Wolf Pack to punt twice in the closing minutes. On the first occasion, McNeese, in turn, was forced to punt. Another exchange gave the ball back to the Cowboys at their own 20-yard line. McNeese reached the Nevada 47 before Nevada took over on downs and ran out the clock.

Nevada used big plays to build its lead. After a 2-yard run by Keith Washington, Wolf Pack quarterback Fred Gatlin hit Bryan Reeves on a 48-yard touchdown strike for a 10-0 Nevada advantage. A safety gave the Wolf Pack two more points before Gatlin tossed 48 yards to Chris Singleton to give Nevada a 22-3 lead going into the fourth quarter.

"We were right there. We felt like we had to a chance to win at one point," said Kealser. "They were an excellent football team. Playing on the road, they were tough in their stadium but we were just excited about getting in the playoffs that first time."

McNeese ended the 1991 season 6-4-2.

VIC THE DEMON VERSUS
CHIEF BRAVE SPIRIT

Maybe the Southland schedule makers knew the Northeast Louisiana Indians were chomping at the bit going into the 1992 season. It had been a long year for the Indians in terms of looking for revenge after losing to conference newcomer Nicholls State in the Colonels' first-ever SLC game that handed the Indians their first-ever home-opening loss at Malone Stadium.

A year earlier, each team had a non-conference game under their belts going into the SLC opener but for the first time since 1972, a Southland encounter took place in Week 1 of a season.

The tone was set for the 1992 season only 12 seconds into Nicholls State's opener against Northeast Louisiana in Thibodaux. On the Colonels' first play from scrimmage, a pass by quarterback Joey Primus was tipped by Tommy Fagan, with Bennie Bazley picking off the ball and scampering 24 yards for a touchdown. Bazley's score was the first of three touchdowns as the Indians built a 21-3 halftime lead.

Northeast Louisiana, looking to avenge its 15-10 loss a year earlier, left little doubt of the game's outcome early in the second half. The Indians opened the half with a 43-yard touchdown toss from Wendal Lowrey to Stepfret Williams. A blocked Nicholls punt on the Colonels' opening possession of the half led to a 4-yard Duke Doctor touchdown to make it 35-3 less than five minutes into the third quarter. NLU would add a 23-yard Rob Tallent field goal before the Colonels would come up with their only touchdown of the game on a 36-yard pass from Henri Ransefore to David Johnson to make the final 38-10.

The next set of Southland openers would not take place for another three weeks. One of the teams making its 1992 conference debut was Southwest Texas State.

The Bobcats featured a new coach after Dennis Franchione left SWT for the University of New Mexico. He would go on to coach Texas Christian, Alabama and Texas A&M before returning to San Marcos in 2011 at the school now called Texas State University.

Jim Bob Helduser, an assistant coach at Southwest Texas first hired by John O'Hara in 1986, was promoted to head coach in 1992.

Helduser and his Bobcats made their Southland debut at Northeast Louisiana. SWT went into the game 2-1 on the season, opening with wins over Texas A&I and Texas Southern before losing to nationally-ranked Youngstown State. After the season-opening victory over Nicholls, NLU lost to Southwestern Louisiana and Eastern Kentucky heading into the Southwest Texas encounter.

With Northeast Louisiana and Southwest Texas featuring the top two offenses in the Southland, a shootout was expected. It came as quite a shock to the fans of both teams when the only three points scored through three quarters was a 32-yard field goal by the Bobcats' Ray Whitehead in the first quarter.

A 42-yard field goal by Whitehead early in the fourth quarter gave SWT a 6-0 lead. Northeast Louisiana took the lead for the first time with 11:11 left in the game on a 12-yard run by Roosevelt Potts to cap a 58-yard drive. Holding a one-point lead, the Indians got the ball back at their own 43 with 2:56 left. Greg Robinson popped through a gaping hole in the line and then blazed a total of 57 yards to give NLU a 13-6 win.

The loss marked the second-straight game Southwest Texas had lost to a ranked team after leading for three quarters.

Also playing its first conference game of the season that day was McNeese State. Traveling to take on Nicholls State, the Cowboys went into the game 1-2 on the season. A 50-12 drubbing by Division II Texas A&I dropped the Colonels to 0-2 going into the McNeese affair.

The Cowboys fell behind 17-7 before scoring 14 points in the final quarter for a 21-17 victory over Nicholls.

After a 31-yard Skip Shelton field goal less than a minute into the fourth period put the Colonels up by 10 points, the Cowboys began to rally.

Nicholls was looking to add to its 10-point advantage when a Shelton field-goal attempt was blocked by Eric Kidd. Ron Alexander picked up the loose ball and raced to the Colonels' 25. Four plays later, backup quarterback Kerry Joseph tossed a 10-yard touchdown pass to Adam Henry to cut the McNeese deficit to three points at 17-14 with 8:27 remaining in the game.

McNeese won the game 21-17 when Joseph scored on a 10-yard run with 1:45 left in the game to cap a 66-yard, 11-play drive.

Nicholls built a 14-7 halftime lead on a pair of Jarvis Lillie touchdown runs in the second quarter. His 1-yard run to give the Colonels a 7-0 advantage came after an interception by linebacker Brett Adams of an Eric Acheson pass at the McNeese 19. Lillie's other score came on a 42-yard scamper. The Cowboys' only touchdown in the first half came on a 1-yard run by Joseph in the second quarter.

The Colonels reverted to their earlier ways as a lack of offense and turnovers led to an early deficit in a 38-13 loss at Southwest Texas State in the only Southland encounter a week later.

A pair of Scott Smith touchdowns runs gave the Bobcats a 13-0 lead. Craig Hemphill returned an errant Ransefore pass 25 yards for a touchdown and a field goal gave SWT its 24-0 halftime lead.

Nicholls yielded 439 yards total offense against the Bobcats' spread-option attack. The Colonels lost seven players to injuries in the game including the team's two starting safeties, Darryl Pounds and Troy Griffin.

The Colonels fell to 0-4 overall and 0-3 in the Southland as their losing streak stretched to a school-record seven games over the course of two seasons. Southwest Texas evened its record at 2-2 overall and 1-1 in the SLC.

Heads had to be turning in almost whiplash-like conditions a week later to keep up with all the scoring in the second and third quarters of the Northeast Louisiana-McNeese State game in Lake Charles. In those two periods alone, the teams combined for 59 points in the Indians' 52-35 triumph.

Lowrey tossed for 352 yards and a NLU-record tying five touchdown passes to solidify his spot as the team's top quarterback and the Indians' hold atop first place in the Southland Conference at 3-0 in league play. McNeese fell to 2-3 overall and 1-1 in conference play.

Despite the final score the first quarter ended with a 7-3 lead for ninth-ranked Northeast on Lowrey's first touchdown of the game, a 48-yard strike to Brisby. Brisby would finish the game with five catches for 170 yards and two touchdowns.

Lowery tossed four of his five touchdown passes in the first half. Brisby hauled in a bomb for a 77-yard touchdown, while Robinson had a 66-yard touchdown reception and tight end James Boyette caught one from 4 yards out. McNeese, meanwhile, had touchdown runs of 4 yards by Eric Foster and 3 yards by Matt Daigle to trail 28-14 at intermission.

After Tallent added a third-quarter field goal to make it 31-14, the Cowboys struck for two touchdowns in the third quarter to pull to within three points at 31-28. Starting with Daigle's touchdown in the second quarter, McNeese scored on three of four possessions to get back in the game. The two third-quarter scores came on runs of 14 yards by Joseph and 22 by Henry Fields.

Lowrey responded by throwing his fifth touchdown pass of the game, a 36-yard connection with Doctor to stretch the Northeast Louisiana lead to 10 points at 38-28. The Indians followed with touchdown runs of 4 yards by Potts and 15 yards to Robinson to pull away for the eventual 52-35 victory.

"Northeast was loaded. They had players from all over the world," said Keasler. "I thought we played them pretty tough but they just outmanned us right there at the end."

The Southland's two new coaches met for the first time when John Pearce and his Lumberjacks traveled to take on Helduser and Southwest Texas in Stephen F. Austin's conference opener. Pearce, a veteran high school coach in Texas, took over as SFA coach after serving three years as an assistant at Texas A&M.

SFA went into its first conference game 2-2 on the season, alternating wins and losses through four games.

A pair of Chris Fontana field goals gave SFA a 6-0 lead before Southwest Texas gained the halftime lead on a 19-yard touchdown pass from quarterback John Hygh to Scott Moore with three seconds remaining in the second quarter.

Southwest Texas built a lead of 11 points at 17-6 on a 8-yard run by Donald Miller with less than six minutes left in the game but SFA quickly countered on a 59-yard strike from Mike Goddard to Tim Fields and a two-point conversion to rally to within 17-14.

The Lumberjacks got the ball back twice in the closing moments. The first drive ended when SWT linebacker John Douglas forced a Goddard fumble. On SFA's final possession with only seconds remaining, Goddard was sacked and then threw a 14-yard pass to Shawn York as time expired.

Northwestern State and North Texas gave their fans everything they might have wanted, and then some, as both teams played their first Southland games of the season when the two teams met in Denton. The Demons were 3-1 on the season with Northwestern State's lone loss to Troy State. North Texas was 1-3, opening with a victory over Abilene Christian before losing to SMU, Southwest Missouri State and Texas.

The Mean Green jumped out to a 21-7 halftime lead a 37-yard pass from Mitch Maher to Clayton George and a pair of Terrance Brown touchdown runs.

A 44-yard field goal by Richard DeFelice in the third quarter gave North Texas a 24-13 lead but the Demons quickly cut the deficit when Darius Adams returned the ensuing kick 96 yards for a touchdown – only the second kickoff return for a touchdown by Northwestern State in 19 years.

An 18-yard touchdown run by Northwestern State quarterback Brad Brown gave the Demons a 34-31 lead in the fourth quarter. The Eagles reached the Demons' 5-yard line and spiked the ball with 45 seconds remaining on third down. On fourth down, DeFelice kicked a 22-yard field goal to tie the game but the stoppage of the clock left Northwestern State with more than 30 seconds and two timeouts remaining.

The Demons recovered an onside kick at the North Texas 38 with 29 seconds left in the game. After a 19-yard run by Deon Ridgell, Brown ran for no gain but positioned the ball in the middle of the field. Jeff Powell booted a 36-yard field goal with four seconds remaining to give Northwestern State a 37-34 triumph.

Also opening up Southland play that same day was Sam Houston State. The Bearkats went into their game at Nicholls State 3-1 on the season, with the Bearkats' only loss being a 45-14 defeat at Rice.

For the third time in five games, Nicholls turned the ball over on its first possession which led to an opponent's touchdown. This time, Kevin Riley's interception return of a Ransefore pass led to a 3-yard touchdown run by Dana Sherman. After a 20-yard scramble for a touchdown by Bearkats' quarterback Ashley Van Meter made it 13-0, the Colonels rallied to take a 16-13 halftime lead. A 39-yard keeper by Ransefore on the final play of the opening quarter made it 13-7. Early in the second quarter, Lillie fumbled while going into the end zone, with Clyde Washington recovering for Nicholls to tie the game. A 36-yard Shelton field goal with 7:39 remaining in the second quarter gave the Colonels their three-point halftime edge.

A 30-yard Shelton field goal early in the fourth quarter stretched the Nicholls advantage to six points at 19-13. Charles Oliver's 5-yard run with 4:26 left in the game tied the score. The Bearkats missed out on their chance to win the game when Michael Morris blocked the extra-point attempt, with the teams having to settle for a tie. The blocked extra point was one of two in the game. Along with the missed extra points, the teams combined to miss five field goals, lose four fumbles and toss two interceptions.

The tie left Nicholls at 0-4-1 overall and ended the Colonels' losing streak at seven games but extended their non-winning streak to eight games. Nicholls moved to 0-3-1 in the Southland Conference. SHSU fell to 3-1-1 in its conference opener.

Northeast Louisiana switched from a high-powered passing attack to a strong running game to down Sam Houston State 38-10 in Monroe. Robinson and Potts became the first NLU running back tandem since 1973 to each rush for more than 100 yards in the same game. Robinson rushed for 139 yards and three touchdowns while Potts amassed 108 yards and figured in two touchdowns as the Indians gained a total of 258 yards on the ground.

Potts gave eighth-ranked Northeast a 7-0 lead on a 33-yard touchdown pass from Lowrey. His other score came on an 18-yard touchdown run in the third quarter. Robinson scored on runs of 4, 34 and 6 yards. The Indians led 17-3 at halftime and added the first two touchdowns of the second half for a 31-10 lead on their way to the win.

NLU improved to 4-0 in the Southland and 5-2 overall with its fourth-straight win. Sam Houston fell to 3-2-1 overall and 0-1-1 in the conference.

Coming off the loss to Northeast Louisiana, the Cowboys took out their frustrations with a 29-0 home blanking of Northwestern State.

Despite the final score, the Cowboys only led 8-0 at halftime. A 22-yard Jose Larios field goal and a safety when Brown, the Demons' quarterback, threw the ball away to avoid a sack in the end zone, gave McNeese a 5-0 lead after one quarter. Larios added three more points on a 46-yard field goal in the second quarter.

The Demons reached the McNeese 26 late in the first half but came away with no points when Powell's field goal attempt was off target.

McNeese freshman running back Bryan Foster scored on second-half touchdown runs of 3 and 16 yards while Joseph threw a 22-yard touchdown pass to Reggie Collins as the Cowboys pulled away for the 29-0 victory.

The Cowboys improved to 2-1 in the Southland Conference and 3-3 overall. Northwestern State fell to 1-1 in the league and 4-2 overall.

Elsewhere, a pair of touchdown passes by Maher helped North Texas build a 14-3 lead heading into the fourth quarter of the Eagles' Southland encounter at Stephen F. Austin. The Lumberjacks rallied to within three points at 14-11 less than a minute in the final period on a 1-yard run by Leonard Harris and a two-point conversion pass from James Ritchey to Fields.

Unlike a week earlier against Northwestern State, the Mean Green didn't let the lead completely slip away. Maher, who passed for 241 yards, tossed his third touchdown pass of the game when he hooked up with George from 10 yards out to secure a 21-11 win to snap North Texas' four-game losing streak.

The North Texas defense forced five turnovers, including two interceptions by cornerback Tomur Barnes.

The result left both teams 2-4 overall while the Eagles evened their Southland record at 1-1 and SFA dropped to 0-2.

Northeast Louisiana's rivalry with Northwestern State always had been a battle but not in the form the 1992 encounter will be remembered.

NLU never trailed in its game at Northwestern State but the Indians just couldn't seem to deliver the knockout punch until the fourth quarter. Touchdown runs by Robinson and Sammie Fudge were countered by a 9-yard Ridgell scamper as Northeast built a 14-7 halftime lead.

Northwestern made it a one-point game at 14-13 when the Demons drove on their opening possession of the second half to set up a 22-yard Powell field goal. After stopping the Indians on two-straight drives, the Demons got the ball back at the Northeast 44. Northwestern was unable to take advantage of the favorable field position when Fagan intercepted a Brown pass.

Fifth-ranked NLU scored less than a minute later on a 15-yard run by Potts to take a 21-10 lead. The Demons made it a 21-18 game with 6:50 remaining in the contest on a 2-yard Brown run and a two-point conversion. Like they had done throughout most of the game, the Indians responded after the Demons closed the gap. This time, a 12-yard run by Robinson with less than three minutes left gave NLU a 10-point cushion for the 28-18 final.

Northeast improved to a perfect 5-0 in SLC play with its fifth win in a row and 6-2 overall, while Northwestern fell to 1-2 in the conference and 4-3 overall.

While Northeast Louisiana couldn't seem to come out with the knockout blow until late, such was not the case for the battle between the two mascots from each team. Vic the Demon, the Northwestern State mascot, and his NLU counterpart, Chief Brave Spirit, seemed to be involved in a mock scuffle sometime during the first quarter. Things got out of hand when Chief Brave Spirit ripped off Vic's head. The headless Demon then slammed the Chief onto the concrete surface of Turpin Stadium. Like good mascots should, they gained notoriety for their schools by being featured on CNN's Play of the Day.

Doug Ireland, Northwestern State's longtime Sports Information Director, had a birds-eye view of the event from the pressbox.

"There was a break in the action. I think it was a quarter shift," Ireland recalled. "Both teams had their punt teams on the field. The mascots were doing their typical byplay and nobody in the pressbox gave it any notice. Then you began to hear audible crowd reaction, especially from the student side, which was packed since it was NSU-NLU.

"People tried to figure out what was going on and someone said, 'Look,' and noticed there was a fracas going on between the mascots. It couldn't have been more than 10-15 seconds long but it was amusing to watch because at that point in time, nobody sitting in the pressbox had an appreciation for what was going to unfold and how this would very much be the most memorable event of that game or any game, arguably, in some respects."

At first, many in the stadium thought the action was just playacting by the mascots.

"It looked like the typical interaction that mascots have," Ireland said. "At some point, it became too aggressive. The playacting turned into wrestling and the NLU mascot ripped our guy's head off and that's when things when crazy and he (the Demons mascot) just waylaid the guy."

From that point, the event took on a life of its own.

"It still pops up on specialty programs and anytime there is a mascot incident at any level, ESPN's got it and it will show up on 'Sportscenter,' again," said Ireland. "I'll get texts from all over the country, 'Hey, I'm in the airport in Austin and I just saw the mascot fight.' It's a sliver of offbeat history. About 36 hours after it happened, it was CNN's 'Play of the Day' and it just took over from there."

Both 2-1 in Southland play, McNeese State and Southwest Texas needed to continue to win in order to have any hope of catching Northeast Louisiana as the two teams met in San Marcos.

McNeese experienced a reversal of fortune in the first half against Southwest Texas. A week after blanking Northwestern State 29-0, McNeese was shut out in the opening half against the Bobcats.

Two Whitehead field goals staked SWT a 6-0 lead after one quarter before a 3-yard run by Harold Adams in the second quarter gave the Bobcats a 13-0 lead at the break.

The Cowboys turned things around in the second half, limiting Southwest Texas to 60 total yards while tossing a shutout over the final two quarters.

McNeese began to rally when Larios kicked a 39-yard field goal in the third quarter. In the fourth quarter, Cowboys linebacker Vincent Landrum forced a Bobcats fumble that was recovered by Martin Bonura at the SWT 10. The turnover proved costly for the Bobcats when Joseph hit Erwin Brown with a 13-yard touchdown pass three plays later to make the score 13-10.

Taking over at their own 34 following a short punt, the Cowboys marched into Southwest Texas territory. Joseph tossed a long one that Henry hauled in for a 47-yard touchdown with 2:12 left in the game for a 17-13 McNeese victory.

McNeese, which won its third game of the season in the closing minutes, improved to 3-1 in the Southland and 4-3 overall. SWT, also 4-3 overall, dropped to 2-2 in conference play.

"These guys never quit and I think that won over a lot of people," Keasler said of his Cowboys.

Running back Charles Harris and the Sam Houston State running game hardly needed any help in its Southland Conference home game against North Texas but the Bearkats got it anyway.

Harris almost doubled his single-game average by rushing for 133 yards and scored a school-record four touchdowns on the ground. Meanwhile, the Bearkats used a blocked punt and an interception to set up two touchdowns. In total, SHSU blocked two punts on its way to a 34-14 victory over the Eagles.

The victory margin could have been larger but Sam Houston State missed two field goals and the Eagles came up with a goal-line stand inside the North Texas 1-yard line.

For all of the Bearkats' success on the ground, Sam Houston State needed two touchdowns inside the final three minutes of the first half to take a 14-7 halftime lead. Following a 3-yard touchdown run by Harris, a fumble by Brown of North Texas set up another short touchdown run by Harris to give SHSU a seven-point halftime lead.

The Bearkats improved to 1-1-1 in the Southland and 3-3-1 overall. North Texas slipped to 1-2 in the conference and 2-5 overall.

Nicholls State managed to stay away from its usual early-game woes, and as a result, the Colonels found themselves trailing only 7-6 at halftime at Stephen F. Austin in a game pitting two teams still seeking their first conference win of the season. The Colonels waited until the second half to revert to form as miscues allowed the Lumberjacks to score 14 points in a span of 2:12 to keep Nicholls winless on the season with a 21-6 victory.

A pair of Shelton field goals countered a 17-yard touchdown pass from Mike Goddard to Michael Pearce as Nicholls trailed by only one point at halftime. After holding the SFA offense in check throughout the first half, the Colonels' fortunes began to change late in the third quarter. Wade Booker turned a screen pass into a 30-yard gain down to the Nicholls 8. On the next play, Booker ran wide left for the touchdown and a 14-6 SFA lead.

On the ensuing possession, Charmyst Amie returned a Primus interception down to the Nicholls 24. Three plays later, York made an over-the-shoulder grab of a Goddard pass for an 11-yard touchdown. The 21-6 score with 13:54 left in the game was sufficient to give the Lumberjacks a win that improved SFA to 3-4 overall and 1-2 in the Southland. Nicholls fell to 0-6-1 overall and 0-4-1 in the league as the Colonels saw their non-win streak reach 10-straight games.

With Northeast Louisiana enjoying an open week, McNeese State looked to inch closer to the Indians in the standings in the Cowboys' game at North Texas State.

Dramatic endings had become almost spooky for McNeese in 1992 and it was only appropriate that the Cowboys' Southland Conference game at North Texas on Halloween Night ended with another heart-pounding finish.

After a 1-yard run by Maher gave the Eagles a 25-19 lead with four minutes left in the game, Chris Fontenette returned the ensuing kickoff 54 yards to give the Cowboys excellent field position.

A 20-yard pass from Joseph to Henry for a fourth-down conversion and an 11-yard reception for a third-down conversion moved the Cowboys deep into North Texas territory. Joseph connected with Eric Foster on a 3-yard touchdown strike with 1:24 left in the game to lift McNeese to a 26-25 win over the Mean Green.

The win kept McNeese in serious Southland Conference contention with a 4-1 league record as the Cowboys improved to 5-3 overall.

McNeese raced off to a 12-3 halftime lead on short touchdown runs by Bobby Guercio and Bryan Foster. North Texas gained its first lead at 16-12 in the third quarter on an 84-yard bomb from Maher to Michael High and a 2-yard run by Terrance Brown.

As befitting the night, the Cowboys regained the lead in a bizarre fashion. Eric Foster fumbled after hauling in a Joseph catch, with teammate Damien Joseph picking up the ball and racing 64 yards for a touchdown for a 19-16 McNeese advantage. The Eagles rebuilt their lead to 25-19 before the Cowboys rallied for another come-from-behind victory.

A dramatic fourth-quarter rally allowed Sam Houston State to take a 34-23 victory over visiting Stephen F. Austin.

The Lumberjacks led 23-20 before Van Meter connected with Claude Stewart on a 59-yard scoring strike with 5:02 left in the game to give Sam Houston State a 27-23 edge. With less than two minutes remaining in the contest, SHSU linebacker Anthony Miller returned an interception 39 yards for a touchdown to seal a 34-23 victory for the Bearkats.

A 64-yard touchdown pass from Van Meter to Stewart and a Marcus Hajdik field goal gave the Bearkats a 10-3 halftime lead. SFA had taken a 3-0 lead on a 38-yard Fontana field goal.

Fontana's third field goal of the game broke a 13-13 tie going into the fourth quarter. A 21-yard Oliver run put Sam Houston State on top 20-16 before SFA regained the advantage at 23-20 on a 3-yard run by Harris. Harris became the first freshman in Lumberjacks history to top 200 yards in a game, finishing with 202 yards against the Bearkats.

The Bearkats improved to 2-1-1 in the SLC and 5-2-1 overall. Stephen F. Austin fell to 1-3 in the conference and 3-5 overall.

Meanwhile, it was a Brown-out in Northwestern State's 20-17 Southland Conference home win over Southwest Texas.

Demons quarterback Brad Brown hit Steve Brown with a 5-yard touchdown pass with 30 seconds remaining in the game to lift Northwestern to the three-point victory. A pass of 43 yards intended for Danny Faust in the end zone was broken up by Demons defender Fred Thompson to secure the triumph.

A wild fourth quarter saw the Bobcats tie the game at 10-10 on a 5-yard run by Hygh. Powell's 32-yard field goal put the Demons back on top at 13-10.

On the ensuing kickoff, Faust hauled in a lateral by Maurice Williams from across the field and scampered 80 yards to the Northwestern State 6 to set up a 1-yard run by Smith to put the Bobcats on top 17-13 with 6:28 remaining in the game.

Northwestern State converted on fourth down three times in the drive to set up the Brown-to-Brown connection for the victory.

The Demons moved to 2-2 in the SLC and 5-3 overall in snapping a two-game losing streak. Southwest Texas fell to 2-3 in the league and 4-4 overall.

With 5-0 Northeast Louisiana playing a non-conference game against Eastern Washington, McNeese State had yet another chance to inch closer to the Indians in the Southland in the Cowboys' game at Stephen F. Austin.

The McNeese State defense made sure the Cowboys would need no late-game heroics against Stephen F. Austin, holding the Lumberjacks to 54 yards rushing and 84 passing while safety Lance Guidry scored two touchdowns in a 28-3 victory.

Guidry closed the first-half scoring on a 42-yard fumble return for a touchdown to give McNeese a 21-3 halftime lead. He provided the only score in the second half on a 23-yard interception return for a touchdown.

Prior to Guidry's fumble return; the Cowboys had scored the first 14 points of the game on a 1-yard run by Fontenette and a 13-yard run by Guercio. SFA's only points came on a 48-yard Fontana field goal in the second quarter.

McNeese improved to 5-1 in the Southland and 6-3 overall. SFA fell to 3-6 with the loss.

Northwestern State, meanwhile, dropped its second Southland Conference game in three-straight home outings in a 42-19 loss to Sam Houston State.

Special teams blunders doomed the Demons as the Bearkats blocked three punts, returning two for touchdowns in the rout. The two returns for touchdowns came on back-to-back possessions.

SHSU was leading 21-7 in the third quarter when Orlando Williams raced 20 yards with his recovery for a touchdown. On the Demons' next possession, Sean Thomas scored after a 39-yard return to give the Bearkats an insurmountable 35-7 lead.

The Demons fell to 2-3 in the SLC and 5-4 overall. Sam Houston State improved to 3-1-1 in the conference and 6-2-1 overall.

Nicholls State went into its Southland game at North Texas coming off its only win of the season with a 27-24 non-conference triumph over Southern University for the Colonels' first victory since a 21-7 win over the Jaguars 363 days earlier.

Unfortunately for Nicholls, the Colonels reverted back to form in their 31-2 loss to North Texas. The Colonels scored on their opening possession on a 39-yard Shelton field goal and after the kicker missed a field goal late in the half, Nicholls trailed only 7-3. After less than six minutes had elapsed off the game clock, the Colonels were down 17-3 on their way to the 28-point defeat.

Following Shelton's 47-yard miss against a stiff wind, Maher completed a pair of 30-yard passes as part of a four-play, 70-yard drive. Maher's second 30-yard strike to David Brown gave the Eagles a 14-3 lead with 3:56 remaining before halftime. A 36-yard DeFelice field goal made it 17-3 at intermission before North Texas scored on its first two possessions of the second half and the rout was on.

North Texas moved to 3-6 overall and 2-3 in the Southland, while Nicholls fell to 1-7-1 and 0-5-1 in conference play.

Top-ranked Northeast Louisiana returned to Southland play after a two-week break that included an open date and a 41-31 non-conference victory over Eastern Washington.

Potts rushed for 130 yards to become Northeast Louisiana's all-time rusher as the Indians defeated Stephen F. Austin 41-22 to move closer to another Southland Conference title. The big fullback's effort gave him 2,904 yards, topping Joe Profit's career mark of 2,818 set in 1970.

The win, the seventh straight for Northeast, moved the Indians to 6-0 in conference play and 8-2 overall. Stephen F. Austin, playing two reserve quarterbacks because of injuries, lost its sixth game in seven outings to fall to 3-7 overall and 1-5 in the SLC.

NLU put the game away early, scoring on its first four possessions to build a 24-0 halftime lead. Two touchdown runs by Robinson, a Tallent field goal and a 40-yard touchdown reception by Brisby gave the Indians a big cushion at intermission.

The Lumberjacks scored the first two touchdowns of the second half on a 6-yard run by Harris and a 9-yard touchdown pass from Blake Armstrong to Pearce to make it 24-14 but SFA would not score again until late in the game after the contest had been decided.

Potts' record overshadowed two records set by Brisby. His 14-yard touchdown catch in the fourth quarter gave him a total of 17, a new school career record. Brisby's yardage reached 996 in the game for a new single-season mark at NLU.

The Cowboys made it two games in row in which McNeese State needed no last-minute heroics with a 37-14 home victory over Sam Houston State to close out Southland Confernce play.

McNeese finished 6-1 in SLC play and secured no worse than a second-place finish in the league. The Cowboys, 7-3 overall, kept their hopes alive for a share of the conference crown. A loss by Northeast Louisiana against North Texas in the final week of the regular season would allow McNeese the share the title. McNeese's only remaining game was a non-conference affair at Weber State.

Sam Houston State dropped to 3-2-1 in league play and 6-3-1 overall.

Short touchdown runs by McNeese's Fields and Guercio were countered by a pair of Chris Batten field goals as the Cowboys took a 14-6 lead at intermission.

The Cowboys pulled away in the second half on three Larios field goals, a touchdown run by Fields and a 2-yard pass from Acheson to Warren. The Bearkats' only points in the second half came on a 60-yard pass from Van Meter to Harris and a two-point conversion in the third quarter.

Elsewhere, North Texas won back-to-back games for the first time since 1990 with a dramatic 13-10 triumph at Southwest Texas State.

A 70-yard punt return by Faust down to the North Texas 15-yard line set up a 1-yard touchdown run by Williams to give Southwest Texas a quick 7-0 lead. A 26-yard DeFelice field goal made it 7-3 at halftime.

The Eagles trailed 10-3 and faced a crucial fourth-and-3 at the SWT 28 in the fourth quarter when a scrambling Maher hooked up with George on a 20-yard completion. Terrance Brown eventually scored on a 1-yard run to tie the game 10-10 with 5:19 left in the contest.

DeFelice kicked a 20-yard field goal with 1:01 left in the game and the Bobcats fumbled on the ensuing kickoff, enabling North Texas to capture the three-point victory.

Southwest Texas entered the game with the Southland Conference's top rushing offense averaging 269.9 yards per game, but was limited to 158 on the ground by the Mean Green defense.

North Texas evened its SLC mark at 3-3 while moving to 4-6 overall. Southwest Texas dropped to 2-4 in the conference and 5-5 overall.

Only days before the Colonels' game at Northwestern State, Nicholls announced Phil Greco would be dismissed as football coach following the season. With only two games remaining in the 1992 gridiron campaign, there would be no win-one-for-the-outgoing-coach scenario. Nicholls managed a total of six points over its final two games in falling to the Demons 44-6 before closing the season with a 21-0 non-conference home defeat to Troy State to finish 1-9-1 overall, including 0-6-1 in the SLC.

Nicholls found itself down 23-0 at halftime against the Demons. Trailing 44-0, the Colonels avoided the shutout on an 11-yard run by Mark Thomas with 5:30 remaining in the game.

Northwestern State, which improved to 6-4 overall and 3-3 in the SLC, scored on its first possession of the game when David Howard turned a screen pass from Brown into a 36-yard touchdown. A 12-yard run by Ridgell, a 9-yard keeper by Brown, and a 32-yard field goal by Powell made it 23-0 at halftime. The Demons poured it on midway in the third quarter when a 51-yard pass from Brown to Guy Hendrick on a fake reverse set up a 3-yard scoring run by Howard.

Not even Mother Nature could rain on Northeast Louisiana's parade in the final week of the 1992 regular season. NLU scored more than 40 points for the third-straight week on a cold, rainy day in Denton, Texas, as the Indians defeated the Eagles 47-25 to capture the school's fourth Southland Conference championship.

Northeast Louisiana's eighth-straight win of the season gave the Indians a perfect 7-0 conference mark to end the regular season at 9-2 overall. North Texas ended its season 4-7 overall and 3-4 in the league.

The Indians, tied with The Citadel for the top spot in Division I-AA, established several milestones on their way to the victory. The running back tandem of Robinson and Potts each topped the 1,000-yard mark on the season. Robinson concluded the regular season with 1,011 yards and Potts 1,004. Brisby became the first NLU receiver in history to top 1,000 receiving yards in a season with 1,050. Lowrey finished the year by hitting on 147 completions in 227 attempts for a completion percentage of 64.7. That set a new Southland Conference single-season mark, topping the old record of 63.5 set by Steve Haynes of Louisiana Tech in 1975.

There were a few anxious moments for the Indians in the game. After NLU took the early lead, North Texas pulled to within two points at 16-14. Potts scored two of his three rushing touchdowns in the final five minutes of the second quarter to give the Indians a 30-14 lead at the break.

A 1-yard run by Terrance Brown in the fourth quarter closed the Eagles to within eight points at 33-25. Potts, however, put the game out of reach with his third rushing touchdown of the game – this one from 21 yards out – to make it 40-25. Wallace Toomer then returned an interception 38 yards for a touchdown for the 47-25 final.

In the Battle of Chief Caddo, the Demons used a strong defense to close out the 1992 season with a 24-10 victory at Stephen F. Austin. Northwestern State's defense limited the Lumberjacks to 111 yards of total offense and shut out SFA in the second half.

Clinging to a six-point lead of 16-10 at halftime, the Demons scored early in the third quarter to put the game away. A 15-yard interception return by Adrian Hardy down to the Lumberjacks' 6 set up the game's final score. Brown scored on fourth-and-goal from the 1-yard line and added a two-point conversion run for a 24-10 lead Northwestern would never relinquish.

After the Demons' initial score of the game, Marcus Henderson's 98-yard kickoff return set up Harris' 1-yard dive. Northwestern countered on a 2-yard run by Hendrick to put the Demons on top for good late in the first quarter.

Northwestern State finished its season 4-3 in the Southland Conference and 7-4 overall. SFA ended 1-6 in the conference and 3-8 overall.

Van Meter of Sam Houston State and Southwest Texas State's Faust each scored three touchdowns as the teams met in Huntsville to close out the 1992 season in a game played in a heavy thunderstorm.

Two touchdown runs by Faust and a two-point conversion gave SWT an early 15-0 lead. Van Meter countered with touchdown tosses of 33 yards to Stewart and 29 yards to Red Jones to make the score 15-13 at halftime.

Faust and Van Meter each accounted for another touchdown to leave Southwest Texas with a 22-20 edge in the third quarter. SWT was forced to punt from its own 32-yard line late in the third quarter. Jeff Brandes' kick was blocked by SHSU's Jeff Jordy and the ball scooted out of the end zone for a safety that provided the game's final points in a 22-22 tie.

The deadlock ended Sam Houston State's season at 6-3-2 overall and 3-2-2 in the Southland. SWT finished 5-5-1 overall, including a 2-4-1 mark in the conference.

McNeese State's second-place finish in the Southland Conference and 8-3 overall record earned the Cowboys a trip to Moscow, Idaho, to take on No. 5 Idaho in the opening round of the Division I-AA playoffs.

Fields rushed for 223 yards but he saved his best effort for last. With McNeese trailing 20-17, the Cowboys got the ball at their own 29 with 1:29 left in the game. A 34-yard burst by Fields allowed McNeese to advance into Idaho territory. After a 28-yard pass from Joseph to Skeet Owens to the 1-yard line, Fields scored from a yard out two plays later to put the Cowboys on top 23-20 with 28 seconds left in the game.

The Vandals reached the McNeese 35 on the ensuing possession but a 52-yard field goal attempt by Mike Hollis was wide left as the Cowboys won in the closing minutes for the sixth time in 1992.

Hollis hit on field goals of 36 and 37 yards in the third quarter to give Idaho its 20-17 lead.

McNeese, which moved to 9-3 on the season, trailed 14-10 at halftime. The Cowboys scored the game's first 10 points on a Larios field goal and a 68-yard gallop by Fields. Idaho took the lead with two touchdowns in the second quarter on Doug Nussmeier touchdown passes of 17 yards to Walter Saunders and 19 yards to Yo Murphy.

In its playoff opener, top-ranked Northeast Louisiana showed its balanced attack was superior to a one-man show. Robinson rushed for a NCAA-playoff and NLU-record 250 yards. Potts, his backfield mate, rushed for 122 yards as the Indians amassed a school-record 502 yards on the ground. NLU's passing game also clicked as Chez Liles came off the bench to throw for 140 yards and three touchdowns. Two of the touchdowns went to Williams for 118 yards. Meanwhile, Alcorn State quarterback Steve "Air" McNair attempted 73 passes. When it was all added up, the Indians came up with a 78-27 domination of the Braves in the opening round of the I-AA playoffs in Monroe.

Everything seemed to work in unison for Northeast Louisiana, which established new playoff records for points scored with 78 and total yards with 742. By contrast, McNair had little help. The highly-touted sophomore quarterback completed 32 of his throws for 386 yards and two touchdowns, but threw five interceptions and was sacked five times. To go along with his passing, McNair, a future NFL star, accounted for 456 yards of total offense, mostly by scrambling for 68 of his team's 103 yards on the ground.

Alcorn State equaled Northeast Louisiana's 20 points in the second quarter. Unfortunately for the Braves, that was the only quarter they could match the Indians. Thanks to 17 points in the first quarter, NLU built a 37-20 halftime lead.

Northeast scored the first 17 points of the game on a 17-yard run by Potts, a 32-yard Tallent field goal and a 16-yard run by Robinson. A 1-yard run by Brown and an 11-yard touchdown pass from McNair to Price were sandwiched around a 1-yard touchdown run by Potts to make it 30-14. By halftime, Robinson had rushed for 175 yards.

The Indians completely blew out Alcorn in the second half, including a 27-0 pasting in the third quarter. NLU's scores in the third quarter included touchdown passes of 86 and 32 yards to Williams.

Back in the second week of the regular season, the Cowboys made the decision to take three points off the board in a home game against Northern Iowa. Instead of a possible game-tying field goal, McNeese opted to try for a touchdown after a penalty on the field-goal attempt gave the Cowboys a first down deep in Panthers territory. The gamble failed as Northern Iowa stopped McNeese on three downs and Larios missed his second field-goal attempt as the Cowboys lost 21-18.

In a quarterfinal rematch at Northern Iowa, the Cowboys would be faced with no such decision. The Panthers' defense held McNeese to 186 yards and forced seven turnovers as No. 3 Northern Iowa eliminated the Cowboys with ease with a 29-7 triumph.

Northern Iowa scored on the opening possession of the game, marching 60 yards for a touchdown. William Freeney, a defensive standout at linebacker who also saw a bit of action on offense, capped the drive with a 1-yard run to give the Panthers a quick lead.

A Joseph fumble at the McNeese 31 set up a touchdown pass from quarterback Jay Johnson to Tim Mosley early in the second quarter. A blocked punt for a safety gave Northern Iowa two more points before Kenny Shedd hauled in an 11-yard pass from Johnson to give the Panthers a 22-0 halftime lead.

McNeese's only points in the game came when Fontenette returned the second-half kickoff 100 yards for a touchdown. The return set a new school and Division I-AA playoff record. The previous mark of 99 yards was set by Mike Cadore of Eastern Illinois in 1987.

"That dome is tough for us to play in. Our players weren't old enough. We didn't have many seniors. They made some big plays. They had a wideout that we just couldn't cover," said Keasler.

The Cowboys ended the season at 9-4.

Northeast Louisiana picked an inopportune time to be on the wrong end of a 40-point score. The Indians, coming off a 78-27 win in the opening round of the playoffs and having scored at least 40 points in each of their final four games, couldn't reach half that amount in a 41-18 loss to Delaware in the Division I-AA quarterfinals.

Despite playing at home, top-ranked NLU had no answers for the Blue Hens' Wing-T offense as eighth-ranked Delaware pulled off the upset by rushing for 376 yards. It didn't help matters any that the Indians lost their top two quarterbacks in the game and committed a season-high seven turnovers.

Lowery left the game with a scratched cornea and Liles suffered a sprained shoulder. Robert Cobb, the third-team quarterback, played the entire second half.

Delaware built a 21-10 halftime lead on a cold day in Monroe on touchdown runs of 3-yards by Lanue Johnson, 4 yards by quarterback Bill Vergantino and a 37-yard interception return by Brian Quigg. The Blue Hens spread the carries around as four different players rushed for at least 50 yards in the game.

A recovery of a Northeast Louisiana fumble on the opening kickoff of the second half set up a 2-yard run by Vergantino to build the Delaware lead to 18 points at 28-10. Cobb's 4-yard touchdown pass to Brisby and a two-point conversion attempt made it 28-18 with 12:29 left in the game. NLU, which concluded its season at 10-3, would get no closer as the Blue Hens scored the final two touchdowns on a 42-yard run by Johnson and a 3-yard run by Daryl Brown for the 41-18 final.

MCNEESE WINS FIRST-EVER HOME PLAYOFF GAME

Northeast Louisiana began defense of its conference title in 1993 in what would be the Indians' final year in the Southland when NLU elected to start the transition toward Division I-A status in 1994.

The Indians seemed eager to show it was a notch above other Division I-AA opponents with its 51-30 thrashing of Nicholls State in the Southland Conference opener for both teams in Thibodaux. All three of NLU's wins on the season came against I-AA foes, with the Indians outscoring those opponents 125-48. Northeast opened the season with wins of 34-13 over Eastern Washington, 40-14 over Eastern Kentucky as well as its trouncing of Nicholls. NLU's lone loss was to Division I-A Southern Mississippi 44-37. Against the Colonels, NLU scored on seven of its first eight possessions as the Indians rolled up 542 yards of total offense.

NLU had a 31-point second quarter to turn a 13-7 edge after one period into a 44-16 blowout by halftime. Robert Cobb was 13 of 18 passing for 269 yards and two touchdowns before giving way to backup Raymond Philyaw early in the second period.

The second-quarter onslaught included touchdown runs of 23 yards by Alabama Crimson Tide transfer Irving Spikes and 2 yards by Kendall Bussey, plus touchdown passes of 40 yards from Cobb to Duke Doctor and 62 yards from Philyaw to Dennis Bamburg. The NLU defense added a score of its own when Tito Wooten returned an interception 34 yards for a touchdown.

Nicholls, playing its first conference game under new coach Rick Rhoades, scored two fourth-quarter touchdowns against NLU reserves to account for the final margin.

Rhoades spent the previous three years as offensive coordinator at the University of Kentucky under Bill Curry. Rhoades was the offensive line coach at Alabama for one year before following Curry to Kentucky. As head coach of Troy

State from 1985-87, Rhoades led the Trojans to the Division II championship in 1987.

The loss to Northeast Louisiana dropped Nicholls to 0-3. Nicholls lost its season opener to Livingston State 51-42 in a game in which the Colonels debuted their new Stack-I offense. The offense, which featured an I-formation backfield with three backs lined up behind the quarterback, produced the most points a Nicholls team had scored in five years. In the Colonels' second game of the season, Rhoades lost to his former Troy State team 24-17.

Playing a conference game for the second week in a row, Northeast Louisiana had another big opening half at home against Northwestern State, jumping out to a 26-3 halftime lead. Touchdown passes from Cobb to Doctor and Kevin Washington, along with a 27-yard Miller field goal and a 20-yard run by Spikes gave the Indians their points in the first half. The only points for the Demons came on a 37-yard Trea Ward field goal.

The Demons were not exactly ready to concede any superiority to Northeast. After allowing 255 yards of total offense in the first half, Northwestern held NLU to 90 yards over the final two quarters to blank the Indians the remainder of the game to mount a furious rally.

Northwestern scored the only points of the third quarter on a 15-yard run by fullback Danny Alexander. A 5-yard run by Shannon Harris only moments into the fourth quarter made it 26-17.

Brad Laird's 4-yard touchdown pass to Jared Johnston made it a two-point game at 26-24 with six seconds left in the game. Jason Fernandez recovered the onside kick at the Northeast Louisiana 49 with two seconds remaining. The game appeared to end when Laird was sacked by James Folston. A face mask penalty, however, gave the Demons the ball at the NLU 34 for one final play. Ward's 51-yard field goal attempt was short and wide to the right as the Indians held on for the two-point triumph.

By escaping with the win, Northeast improved to 4-1 overall and 2-0 in the Southland. Northwestern State fell to 1-3 in its conference opener. The Demons had opened the season with losses to Southern University and Troy State before topping East Texas 30-19.

For the third time during the season, fourth-ranked Northeast Louisiana faced a Southland opponent playing its first conference game of the season when the Indians hosted 2-2 McNeese State.

Northeast Louisiana had the statistical edge in most categories in the first half but trailed 21-19. That was due to the Indians settling for four Miller field goals in five trips inside the red zone. Two of the Cowboys' scores in the first half came on a pair of 51-yard touchdown passes from Kerry Joseph to Adam Henry.

A 1-yard run by Henry Fields and a 37-yard Jose Larios field goal put the Cowboys on top 31-19 in the fourth quarter. Spikes, who was held to 76 yards rushing, scored on a 3-yard run to make it 31-26. Larios added another 37-yard field goal to give McNeese State the 34-26 victory.

After being blanked in the second half against Northwestern State, the Indians managed only one touchdown in the final two quarters against McNeese. Along with holding Spikes to 50 yards below his rushing average, the Cowboys limited Cobb to 99 yards passing in the second half and without a touchdown for the first time in the 1993 season. The Cowboys, who improved to 3-2 overall, also forced three NLU turnovers.

"I thought we did a good job of getting things cranked up at halftime. We played better defense the second half. Our kids hung in there and found a way to win," said Keasler.

Two other games that same day marked the 1993 Southland Conference debuts for four teams as Sam Houston State hosted Stephen F. Austin while Southwest Texas visited North Texas State.

Sam Houston State went into the SFA encounter 2-2 on the season. The Lumberjacks were 3-1 on the year. After opening with a loss to Idaho, SFA defeated Youngstown State, Livingston State and Boise State.

Playing without its top two running backs, halfback Leonard Harris and fullback David Loeb, Stephen F. Austin still managed a 24-7 lead in the fourth quarter before having to hold off Sam Houston State.

Making up for the loss of the two running backs was James Ritchey. The sophomore quarterback, who rushed for 104 yards, had touchdown runs of 17 yards in the second quarter and 6 yards in the fourth period as SFA built its lead before Richey was forced from the game with an injured left shoulder.

The Bearkats rallied in the fourth quarter on a pair of 13-yard touchdown passes from quarterback Dwight Gross to Red Jones, the second making the score 24-20 with 1:43 left in the contest. Sam Houston State forced a punt on SFA's ensuing drive but got the ball back with only 35 seconds remaining and was able to run only two plays before time expired in the Lumberjacks' four-point loss.

In Denton, North Texas State went into its league opener against Southwest Texas 2-2 on the season. The Mean Green were dominated 76-14 by powerful Oklahoma to start the season and North Texas followed that with a loss to Northern Arizona before picking up victories over Southwest Missouri State and Abilene Christian. SWT was 1-3 on the season as the Bobcats opened with a win over

Texas A&M-Kingsville before taking a three-game losing streak into the North Texas encounter.

Against Southwest Texas, North Texas quarterback Mitch Maher accounted for five touchdowns and the Eagles needed every one of them in a 35-28 victory over the Bobcats.

One of Maher's few mistakes in the game, a third-quarter interception returned to the North Texas 28 by Brian McCray, set up a 37-yard Ray Whitehead field goal to pull the Bobcats to within 21-20.

Maher responded with his third and final rushing touchdown early in the fourth quarter to extend the North Texas lead. Luis Silva turned a pass from Maher into a 27-yard touchdown to put the Eagles on top 35-21. SWT added a 10-yard touchdown run by Michael Ivory with 49 seconds left in the contest to account for the final margin.

The victory represented the first time the Eagles won a Southland opener and achieved a three-game winning streak under Dennis Parker. It marked the first time North Texas won three-in-a-row since the 1989 season.

Northeast Louisiana rebounded from its loss to McNeese State as Cobb produced the best game of his career a week later in the Indians' 40-21 win at Southwest Texas. The NLU quarterback threw for a career-high 343 yards and three touchdowns to ignite the Indians. Northeast improved to 5-2 overall and 3-1 in the Southland.

All three of the touchdowns came in a 256-yard first half passing performance for Cobb as Northeast built a whopping 37-14 halftime lead. Spikes got NLU's offense started with a 26-yard touchdown run that was part of a 24-point opening quarter for the Indians. Cobb fired touchdown passes of 27 yards to Stepfret Williams, 8 yards to Charles Randolph and 15 yards to Washington. Miller also added a field goal and the Northeast defense even produced points in the first half on a 71-yard fumble return by cornerback Larry Whigham.

For SWT, 1-5 overall and 0-2 in the SLC, most of its offense came from quarterback John Hygh and running back Donald Wilkerson. Hygh rushed for 156 and a touchdown. Wilkerson ran for 95 yards and a pair of touchdowns as the Bobcats amassed 380 rushing yards out of their option offense.

In Lake Charles, an 80-yard pass from Maher to Troy Redwine late in the first quarter set up a 2-yard run by Terrance Brown for a 7-0 Eagles lead against McNeese State to signal what might be a high-scoring Southland Conference affair.

Things settled down at that point as the only other scoring in the first half came on a pair of Larios field goals, allowing the Cowboys to trail only 7-6 at halftime.

North Texas stretched the lead to 11 points going into the fourth quarter on a 25-yard Richard DeFelice field goal and a 34-yard pass from Maher to Redwine.

McNeese began to rally in the fourth quarter on a 47-yard Larios field goal. The Cowboys' only touchdown of the game, a 30-yard run by Chris Fontenette, pulled McNeese to within 17-15.

Down by two points, the Cowboys marched into Mean Green territory to set up another Larios field goal attempt. Larios' fourth field goal, from 29 yards out with one minute left in the game, lifted McNeese to an 18-17 triumph.

North Texas had one last opportunity but on fourth down, Zack Bronson intercepted his sixth pass of the season to secure the Cowboys' victory.

McNeese improved to 2-0 in the Southland and 4-2 overall. North Texas fell to 3-3.

Meanwhile, Stephen F. Austin dominated the statistical battle in the first half of its home game against Nicholls, but Lumberjack mistakes allowed the Colonels to trail only 21-14 at halftime. A Nicholls miscue to open the third quarter sank any hopes of a Colonels rally. A fumble by Pounds of the second-half kickoff set up a quick score for SFA. Four plays after Pounds' turnover, Lumberjacks quarterback Mike Goddard hit Kevin Goodwin with a 9-yard touchdown strike in the left corner of the end zone for a two-touchdown lead on Stephen F. Austin's way to a 35-21 victory.

The Lumberjacks, 5-1 overall and 2-0 in the Southland Conference, amassed 308 yards total offense in the first half compared to 109 for the Colonels. Still, a 44-yard interception return for a touchdown by Tedrick Henry of a Goddard pass, a missed field goal and a Lumberjack fumble at the Nicholls 2-yard line kept the Colonels in the game. Still winless after six games, Nicholls fell to 0-3 in the SLC.

Elsewhere, Northwestern State fought back from a 17-0 first-quarter deficit a week later at Sam Houston State.

The Demons took the lead for the first time late in the third quarter at 24-20 on a 1-yard run by Deron Reed to cap a drive that started at the SHSU 35 following Steve Readeaux's interception of a Gross pass. Readeaux's interception was one of three in the game by the Northwestern State defense.

Sam Houston State regained the lead at 27-24 on a 14-yard run by Charles Harris. Northwestern pulled to within a point at 27-26 when an attempted punt by the Bearkats went through the end zone.

The Demons marched 53 yards in the closing moments. Arthur Hunter's 2-yard run and a two-point conversion with 1:01 left in the game gave Northwestern State a dramatic 34-27 victory.

Northwestern improved to 2-1 in the Southland and 3-3 overall. SHSU fell to 0-2 in the conference and 2-4 overall.

McNeese State scored the first 37 points of the game a week later in their Southland home game against Sam Houston State to cruise past the Bearkats 37-14 and into sole possession of first place in the SLC.

The Cowboys' win, which improved McNeese to 3-0 in the league and 5-2 overall, coupled with Northeast Louisiana's 26-10 triumph over Stephen F. Austin, put McNeese all alone in first place.

Despite the large margin of victory, the Cowboys only led 13-0 at halftime on two first-quarter Larios field goals and a 27-yard pass from Joseph to Thomas Simon in the second quarter. Larios, the nation's leading kicker, added another field goal later in the game. His three boots gave him 10 successful kicks in a row while hitting on 16 of 19 for the season.

The Cowboys made no doubt about the outcome with a 24-point third quarter. After a 28-yard Larios field goal, McNeese added three touchdowns in the quarter on a 17-yard touchdown reception by Henry, a 1-yard run by Bryan Foster and a 22-yard scamper by Fontenette for a 37-0 lead. Henry's reception gave him a school-record 12 career touchdown catches.

McNeese picked off four passes in the game, including two by Bronson to give the national leader eight on the season.

SHSU reserve quarterback Stacey Arrambide factored in both of the Bearkats' fourth-quarter touchdowns on a 6-yard pass to Montoya Boyce and a 5-yard scoring run.

In Northeast Louisiana's 26-10 home win over No. 10 Stephen F. Austin, Cobb followed up his performance against Southwest Texas with an even better game against the Lumberjacks. The NLU quarterback threw for 346 yards and four touchdowns to pace the Indians. The win put NLU in sole possession of second place in the Southland Conference at 4-1 and 6-2 overall.

NLU led 12-10 in the first half as Cobb threw touchdown passes of 22 yards to Williams and 14 yards to Randolph. SFA, 5-2 overall and 2-1 in the Southland, countered with a 4-yard run by Harris and a 29-yard Brian Minton field goal.

Unlike a few previous games during the season when Northeast Louisiana jumped out to a big lead and then had to hold off an opponent's late charge, this time it was the Indians tossing a shutout in the second half. The Northeast defense limited SFA to 97 total yards in the second half and sacked Richey six times in the game. NLU also held SFA to 24 points below their season average. Meanwhile, the only scores of the second half came on a pair of touchdown passes from Cobb to Bamburg.

Like its game against Sam Houston State, Northwestern State had to rally once again at North Texas State.

Trailing 31-24, the Demons tied the game on a 4-yard keeper by Laird with 4:06 left in the game. Josh King's recovery of an Eagles fumble on the ensuing kickoff gave the ball back to Northwestern. Mike Allen's 16-yard touchdown on a reverse put the Demons on top 38-31 with 2:17 remaining in the game.

North Texas responded with a 62-yard march. Throwing the ball on all eight plays of the drive, Maher hit Clayton George on a 12-yard scoring strike to make it 38-37 with 55 seconds left in the game. Going for two points and the win, Maher's rushed throw was a bit off-target for intended receiver David Brown. The Demons recovered the onside kick to hold on for the one-point victory.

The win left Northwestern State a half-game back in the Southland Conference race with the Demons' final three league games all at home. Northwestern improved to 3-1 in the SLC and 4-3 overall. North Texas, a one-point loser for the second-straight week, fell to 1-2 in the Southland and 3-4 overall.

North Texas led 21-10 at halftime behind a touchdown reception by Brown and 2-yard Brown run. Maher added a 1-yard run.

The Demons pulled ahead 24-21 on a couple of 5-yard runs, one by Alexander and the other by Chip Wood.

Perhaps it was a case of bottled-up frustration, but when Nicholls State found someone it could beat up on, the Colonels never let up. Nicholls scored on its first four possessions and built a lead of 35-10 at halftime on its way to a 63-37 home win over Southwest Texas State.

The first win of the season moved the Colonels to 1-6 overall and 1-3 in Southland play and ended a school-record 10-game losing streak dating back to the 1992 season. The initial win of the Rhoades era dropped SWT to 1-6 overall and 0-3 in the conference.

Nicholls stayed away from the mistakes that haunted it throughout the season and executed its option offense to the tune of 556 yards, including a school-record 436 rushing. Unlike past games, the Colonels stayed away from long-yardage situations, averaging 8.9 yards per play, also a school record. The Colonels also played opportunistic football in the first half, converting two Bobcat fumbles into touchdowns and scoring another following a shanked Southwest Texas punt.

One reason for the Colonels' offensive output was the success of their wingbacks. Three wingbacks scored touchdowns, including Reggie Rogers, who rushed for 96 yards. Along with the wingbacks, Corey Thomas, the Nicholls quarterback, rushed for 164 yards.

McNeese State's hold on first place in the Southland Conference seemed in jeopardy a week later when the Cowboys trailed 14-0 at halftime at Stephen F. Austin.

After a scoreless first quarter, the Lumberjacks produced the only points in the opening half on a 4-yard run by Curtis Luper and a 7-yard pass from Ritchey to Perry Freeman.

McNeese put itself back in the game with two touchdowns in the third quarter to tie the game on an 18-yard run by Joseph and a 7-yard touchdown reception by Henry.

SFA regained the lead in the fourth quarter on a 7-yard run by Luper but a missed conversion attempt by Minton left the Lumberjacks with a six-point edge.

The Lumberjacks forced McNeese to punt on the ensuing possession but gave the ball back to the Cowboys on a Harris fumble at the SFA 37. Joseph drilled Skeet Owens with a 12-yard touchdown strike with 1:09 left in the game and Larios kicked the extra point to give McNeese a 21-20 triumph.

McNeese remained unbeaten at 4-0 in the Southland while improving to 6-2 overall. The Lumberjacks fell to 2-2 in the conference and 5-3 overall.

Meanwhile, Northwestern State seemed perfectly positioned. The Demons were a half-game out of first place in the Southland and were at home to take on a Southwest Texas team that had lost six games in a row. That didn't seem to bother Wilkerson and his Bobcat teammates very much.

The Demons were unable to stop the SWT running back. Wilkerson rushed for 195 yards and scored two touchdowns as the Bobcats upset Northwestern State 22-15.

Down 22-7, a 3-yard run by Deon Ridgell and a two-point conversion less than a minute into the fourth quarter pulled the Demons to 22-15. Northwestern drove down to the Bobcats' 7 on its next drive. Laird went back to pass before scrambling down to the 1-yard line. The Demons quarterback was hit by SWT linebacker Scott Swinnea and the ball popped loose. The ball rolled back to the 7, where it was recovered by Bobcats safety Todd Seibert to end the threat.

The Bobcats were able to burn off the final 6:07 by holding onto the ball for 12 plays to run out the clock.

Wilkerson touchdown runs of 43 and 7 yards, along with a 38-yard Whitehead field goal allowed SWT to take a 15-7 halftime lead. The Bobcats extended the lead to 22-7 on a 1-yard run by Hygh. The score was set up by Damion Branch's block of a Demons punt.

The loss dropped Northwestern to 3-2 in the conference and 4-4 overall. Southwest Texas won its first league game to improve to 1-3 in the SLC and 2-6 overall.

Along with Southwest Texas, Sam Houston State also picked up its first Southland win with a 29-27 victory at North Texas State.

Sam Houston's Harris showed once again he loved playing against North Texas. After scoring four touchdowns a year earlier, the running back rushed for a career-high 215 yards and two touchdowns in the Bearkats' 24-14 victory.

Harris broke a 14-14 tie on a 61-yard gallop in the third quarter and Chris Batten chipped in a 39-yard field goal with less than a minute remaining to account for the final 10-point margin.

A 1-yard touchdown run by Maher and his 7-yard touchdown pass to George allowed the Eagles to tie the game at halftime. North Texas failed to score in the second half as the Bearkats blocked two DeFelice field-goal attempts in the third quarter.

The result left both teams 1-3 in the Southland and 3-5 overall.

McNeese State made sure Southwest Texas State would not make it two wins in a row as the Cowboys jumped out to a 20-0 lead in their Southland Conference road game at Southwest Texas and cruised to a 27-7 victory for McNeese's fifth-consecutive win.

A 68-yard pass from Joseph to Henry in the first quarter staked the Cowboys to an early lead. McNeese put the game away by halftime with a 13-point second quarter. A pair of Larios field goals and a 1-yard touchdown run by Fields put the Cowboys up by 20 points at halftime.

The Bobcats cut the deficit in half with a 10-point third quarter on a 39-yard Whitehead field goal and a 30-yard run by Donald Miller.

McNeese made sure SWT would get no closer as Fields scored on a 9-yard run in the fourth period for the 27-7 victory.

The Cowboys remained perfect in SLC play at 5-0 while improving to 7-2 overall.

Like in a pair of games earlier in the season, relying on a much-needed two-point conversion in the closing seconds of the game proved costly once again for the Eagles in their home game against Stephen F. Austin.

After a 23-yard Minton field goal gave the Lumberjacks an eight-point cushion at 29-21, the Eagles drove 63 yards in less than three minutes to rally to within 29-27 with 24 seconds left in the game on a 4-yard touchdown reception by David Brown.

When SFA defensive lineman Chris Roberson's hit on Maher caused an errant throw by the North Texas quarterback, the Eagles lost their third game of the year on a failed two-point conversion in the closing moments.

Luper rushed for 179 yards and two touchdowns for SFA. The Eagles hurt their own cause as two fumbles and a muffed punt led to 15 SFA points.

A fourth-consecutive loss dropped North Texas to 3-6 overall and 1-4 in the Southland. The Lumberjacks moved to 3-2 in the SLC and 6-3 overall.

Wins over Southwest Texas and Southern University had Nicholls State gunning for its third-straight victory after an 0-6 start when the Colonels visited Sam Houston State.

The Colonels seemed to take a liking to winning, coming up with yet another way to pull out a victory at home against Sam Houston State. Nicholls linebacker Ivan Williams blocked Batten's field-goal attempt with 1:04 left in the game to preserve a 20-19 triumph.

Trailing by one point, the Bearkats took possession of the football at their own 43-yard line with five minutes remaining in the game. SHSU drove down to the Nicholls 3 before setting up for the field goal. The Colonels called their final timeout of the game before Batten's field-goal attempt. Williams' block helped Nicholls improve to 3-6 overall and 2-3 in the Southland. The Bearkats fell to 3-6 overall and 1-4 in league play.

Nicholls held a 14-6 halftime lead and got what proved to be the game-winning points on a short drive set up by a SHSU penalty. The Bearkats lined up to punt from their own 33, but punter Josh Farrell threw the ball to Brian Benford, who raced down to the Colonels' 47-yard line. SHSU was called for having an ineligible man downfield, and with the loss of down on the penalty, Nicholls gained possession at the Bearkats' 28.

Four plays later, Roscoe Griffin scored on a 6-yard run and Adam Diel's conversion gave Nicholls a 20-6 lead with 6:55 remaining in the third quarter.

A week later, McNeese State was taking no chances in its Southland Conference encounter at Northwestern State. The Cowboys scored the game's first 10 points and cruised to a 34-7 victory over the Demons to clinch no worse than a share of the conference title and capture the league's automatic bid to the Division I-AA playoffs.

A 9-yard pass from Joseph to Henry and a Larios field goal gave McNeese its 10-0 lead. The Demons cut the deficit to three points at 10-7 on a 1-yard run by Laird but touchdown passes of 10 and 11 yards to Owens, one in the second quarter and the other in the third, allowed the Cowboys to build their lead to 24-7.

McNeese added the final 10 points of the game in the fourth quarter for the 34-7 victory.

McNeese moved to 6-0 in the Southland and 8-2 overall. The Demons evened their record at 3-3 in the SLC and 5-5 overall.

Northeast Louisiana played its most complete game of the season in a 48-10 win at Sam Houston State as the Indians looked to keep pace with McNeese State. Cobb tossed four touchdown passes and Spikes rushed for 137 yards to top the 100-yard mark for the sixth time during the season, NLU's defense, meanwhile, held Harris to 65 yards. With 40 yards in losses, the Indians held Sam Houston to 52 yards rushing as a team and only 178 passing.

NLU, 8-2 overall and 5-1 in the Southland Conference, scored 24 points in each half. The first-half scores came on a 22-yard Miller field goal, short touchdown runs by Baron Bradley and Foster, along with a 35-yard pass from Cobb to Bamburg. Second-half scoring for the Indians consisted of a Miller field goal and a touchdown pass to Doctor and two to Wyatt.

The Bearkats fell to 3-7 overall and 1-5 in the conference.

Stephen F. Austin, meanwhile, was looking to make a statement for an at-large playoff bid with its 29-7 home victory over Southwest Texas State. While a Southland title was not likely, the Lumberjacks' 7-3 record and strength of schedule seemed to work in Stephen F. Austin's favor. All three of SFA's losses were to teams ranked in Division I-AA's top 10 and the Lumberjacks handed top-ranked Youngstown State it's only loss of the season.

A pass from Jones to Ronnie Smith and a touchdown toss from Ritchey to Pearce were countered by a 1-yard Wilkinson run as SFA took a 13-7 halftime lead. Ritchey's 65-yard strike to Chris Jefferson in the third quarter made it 19-7. The Lumberjacks added a touchdown run by Luper and a Christian Fontana field goal in the fourth quarter while SFA blanked the Bobcats in the second half for the 29-7 triumph.

A lopsided, mistake-free effort gave Nicholls its first win of the season and set the Colonels on the path to a three-game winning streak. A lopsided, mistake-filled game brought the winning streak to an abrupt halt at North Texas State.

The mistakes included: Three lost fumbles, one of which was returned for a touchdown; a muffed kickoff, which led to a touchdown; a blocked punt that led to a score; and yielding a touchdown on a kickoff return. All took place in the opening 30 minutes that saw the Colonels fall behind 49-7 at halftime on their way to a 63-21 defeat. It was the first time in school history that an opponent scored more than 60 points against Nicholls and was the team's worst defeat since a 59-9 loss to McNeese State in 1981.

Two plays into the game, Thomas fumbled at the Nicholls 17-yard line to eventually set up a 5-yard touchdown pass from Maher to Redwine and set the tone for the game. Chris Brown would go on to rush for three touchdowns and the Eagles closed the first half on a school-record 96-yard touchdown pass from Maher to Redwine.

North Texas improved to 4-6 overall and 2-4 in the SLC. Nicholls fell to 3-7 overall and 2-4 in the conference.

McNeese State captured its first outright Southland Conference title since 1980 with a 27-0 home win over Nicholls State in the 1993 regular-season finale.

Following a scoreless first quarter, No. 5 McNeese got more than enough points to win with a 17-point second quarter. Short touchdown runs by Fontenette and Dorian Dunmiles along with a 45-yard Larios field goal gave the Cowboys the lead at halftime. McNeese added a Larios field goal in the third quarter and an 8-yard pass from Joseph to Lupe Nunez in the fourth quarter for the 27-0 victory.

McNeese limited Nicholls to 116 total yards. As the Cowboys were building a 17-0 lead, the McNeese defense held the Colonels to zero yards in the second quarter while forcing two fumbles and an interception.

The Cowboys concluded the regular season a perfect 7-0 in the Southland and 9-2 overall. Nicholls finished 3-8 overall, including 2-5 in the conference.

Fourth-ranked Northeast Louisiana, meanwhile, closed out its tenure in the Southland Conference in record-setting fashion. Not only did the Indians defeat North Texas 61-31 in Monroe to secure a bid to the Division I-AA playoffs, they also put up some staggering offensive numbers.

NLU, which closed the regular season 9-2 overall and 6-1 in the Southland, amassed a season-high 614 yards of total offense. The attack was well-balanced as the Indians rushed for 267 yards and passed for 347.

A slew of offensive records were established by the Indians. Spikes provided two of the new marks. Spikes rushed for 254 yards to set the new single-game rushing mark at NLU, while breaking the single-season mark of 1,328 yards set by Jimmy Edwards in 1972.

Cobb threw for 347 yards and four touchdowns. He became the first quarterback in Northeast Louisiana history to throw for 3,000 yards in a single season, topping the old school record of 2,964 yards by John Holman.

Big plays were the order of the day for the NLU offense. Of Cobb's four touchdown passes, three went for at least 57 yards. One of Spikes' touchdown runs was a 57-yard scamper.

North Texas, which concluded its season 4-7 overall and 2-5 in the SLC, was happy to be part of the offensive fireworks, at least for the first half. The Eagles rolled up 524 yards of total offense and matched NLU's scoring for most of the opening two quarters, trailing 33-24 at the break.

Maher's 10-yard touchdown pass to David Brown early in the third quarter made it a two-point game at 33-31. Maher ended the game with 323 yards passing and three touchdowns, but threw four interceptions. Terrance Brown rushed for 190 yards.

Despite the early touchdown throw, Maher was limited to 96 yards passing in the second half as the Indians pulled away by scoring the final 28 points of the game. Three of the final four touchdowns were on passes by Cobb.

Stephen F. Austin staked its own claim to a postseason berth as the Lumberjacks jumped out to a 38-10 lead at Northwestern State on SFA's way to a 51-20 trouncing of the Demons.

SFA led 14-3 after one quarter on a pair of touchdown passes from Ritchey to Goodwin before erupting for 24 points in the second quarter. Luper and Harris had short touchdown runs in the quarter, Fontana kicked a 41-yard field goal, and Goodwin hauled in another touchdown reception, this one from Goddard.

The Lumberjacks, who rushed for 307 yards and passed for 239, finished 5-2 in the SLC and 8-3 overall. Northwestern finished below .500 both in the league and overall. The Demons closed the 1993 season 3-4 in the conference and 5-6 overall.

In San Marcos, Southwest Texas lost 35-10 to Sam Houston State as the Bobcats finished off their worst season since 1960. SWT finished in last place in the Southland Conference at 1-6 while going 2-9 overall. The Bobcats were 2-8 in 1960. The Bearkats closed the year 4-7 overall, including 2-5 in the SLC.

A 34-yard Whitehead field goal in the first quarter gave Southwest Texas a 3-0 lead and the Bobcats appeared headed for more until SHSU's Mitchell Moore intercepted a Hygh pass at the Bearkats' 11-yard line.

The Bearkats marched following the turnover, scoring on an 18-yard pass from Gross to Jones and the rest of the game belonged to Sam Houston State. The Bearkats added a 1-yard run by Harris with 22 seconds left in the second quarter for a 14-3 lead at the break.

Harris, who rushed for 151 yards in the contest, made it 21-3 in the third quarter. The only other points the Bobcats could muster the remainder of the game came on a 4-yard run by Scott Smith in the third quarter.

Stephen F. Austin received the postseason bid to the playoffs it had hoped for and the Lumberjacks were sent to Troy State against a Trojans team that made the postseason in their first year of eligibility in Division I-AA.

A 4-yard pass from Troy State's Kelvin Simmons to Eric Polite was countered by a 7-yard strike from Ritchey to Pearce, leaving the Trojans with a 7-6 edge. After that, Orlando Parker made his presence felt for Troy State.

Only 22 seconds after SFA scored, Parker hauled in a 51-yard touchdown pass to up Troy's lead to 14-6 after one quarter. The Trojans were leading 21-12 at halftime when Parker raced 88 yards with the second-half kickoff for a 28-12 lead on Troy State's way to a 42-20 victory.

SFA finished the season 8-4.

Fourth-ranked Northeast Louisiana was at home for the first round of the Division I-AA playoffs, taking on Idaho, featuring left-handed gunslinger Doug Nussmeier.

The future New Orleans Saints and Indianapolis Colts quarterback helped produce touchdowns on two of Idaho's first three possessions. He hit Sherriden May with a 17-yard touchdown for the first score and ran in from 5 yards out to account for the other. NLU, meanwhile, countered with a 7-yard pass from Cobb to Williams and a 22-yard Miller field goal to trail 14-10 at halftime.

Trailing 27-16, the Indians pulled to within three points with 9:34 left in the game on a 26-yard touchdown reception by Bamburg and a two-point conversion. Idaho drove the field, eventually facing third-and-goal. Nussmeier rolled to his left and was pursued by a host of NLU defenders. The quarterback, who finished with 322 yards through the air, tossed an underhanded pass that was caught by Andy Gilroy in the end zone.

On the first play of the ensuing drive, Cobb and Williams hooked up on a 73-yard bomb to again pull Northeast Louisiana to within three points, this time at 34-31.

That would be the last score of the game. Nussmeier came up with runs of 7 yards for a third-down conversion and 7 yards on a fourth-and-5 situation to run out the clock on the Indians.

The loss ended the Indians' season at 9-3 and closed out Northeast Louisiana's stint in the Southland Conference – a stint that included the 1987 national championship and four conference titles.

Southland Conference champion McNeese State trailed by eight points at halftime of its opening-round playoff game against William & Mary.

The Cowboys struck quickly in the second half, scoring on their opening drive of the third quarter on a 6-yard run by Fields. Joseph added a two-point conversion run to tie the game at 28-28. McNeese forced the Tribe to punt on their next possessions, getting the ball back at the Cowboys' 39. McNeese marched to the William & Mary 8-yard line to set up a 25-yard Larios field goal for a 31-28

Cowboys edge. Larios added a 46-yard field goal with 1:46 left in the game for a six-point advantage.

William & Mary, which entered the game ranked No. 10 in Division I-AA, reached the Cowboys' 20-yard line with 30 seconds left in the game but the drive ended with an incomplete pass on fourth down.

No. 5 McNeese, which moved to 10-2 and won its first-ever home playoff game, fell behind early when it fumbled on its third play of the game. The Tribe took advantage when quarterback Shawn Knight scored on a 5-yard scramble. McNeese quickly responded when Joseph connected with Henry on a 58-yard strike to tie the game.

The Tribe fumbled the ensuing kickoff, giving the ball right back to McNeese at the William & Mary 8-yard line. Joseph tossed into the end zone three plays later. Tribe defensive tackle Tim Kagle tipped the ball, which fell into the arms of Michael Warren for a 4-yard touchdown to give the Cowboys a 14-7 lead.

William & Mary mounted a 95-yard, 17-play drive to tie the game. Troy Keen's 1-yard run capped the drive with 13 minutes remaining in the first half. Keen added a touchdown run with 14 seconds remaining in the second quarter to give the Tribe their eight-point lead and set the stage for the Cowboys' second-half rally.

"That's the first time our fans had ever heard of or seen people like William & Mary. Later we played teams like Delaware and Youngstown State. They were not familiar with those people but I think they found out William & Mary had a good football team. It was a battle. They were very physical," Keasler said.

The win over the Tribe advanced McNeese State to the quarterfinals against top-ranked Troy State, which defeated Stephen F. Austin in the opening round of the playoffs. Playing at home for the second week in the postseason, the Cowboys seemed unable to stop the passing barrage of Simmons in the first half.

Simmons completed his first 10 passes of the game and threw for 327 yards in the opening two quarters as the Trojans jumped out to a 21-0 lead.

A 32-yard pass from Simmons to Parker gave Troy State a 7-0 lead. After hitting on all five passes on his opening drive, Simmons repeated the feat on his second possession. This time, the drive was culminated not in a pass but a 16-yard Simmons run to give the Trojans a 14-0 lead after one quarter.

Simmons hooked up again with Parker in the second quarter. Parker hauled in Simmons' pass near midfield and fought off several would-be McNeese tacklers before speeding the rest of the way for an 87-yard touchdown and a 21-0 Troy State lead.

McNeese finally got a score of its own when Erwin Brown raced 18 yards for a touchdown on a reverse. Simmons and company came right back when the quarterback hooked up with Daniel Brady on a 31-yard touchdown pass.

The Cowboys scored the final two touchdowns of the first half on a 7-yard run by Fields and a 2-yard pass from Joseph to Nunez with 10 seconds remaining to cut the deficit to only seven points at 28-21.

McNeese fought back from the Trojans' early offensive onslaught but each team could manage only one touchdown the rest of the way. Troy rebuilt its lead to 14 points on a 7-yard run by Simmons with 29 seconds remaining in the quarter to cap a 98-yard drive. Along with throwing for 372 yards and three touchdowns, Simmons also scored two rushing touchdowns to lead a Trojan attack that amassed 570 yards of total offense.

The Cowboys made the final 35-28 on a 19-yard touchdown run by Joseph with 10:08 left in the game.

McNeese finished the 1993 season 10-3 as the Cowboys lost for the first time in nine games and snapped an eight-game home winning streak.

The departure of Northeast Louisiana to pursue Division I-A status caused the Southland Conference to revert to a seven-team football league in 1994.

Northwestern State and Nicholls State opened up Southland play in 1994, each with two games under its belt. The Demons went into the game 1-1 while the Colonels were unbeaten through two games, including a 16-7 victory over Connecticut to spoil Skip Holtz's debut as Huskies coach.

Playing with Brad Laird at quarterback for the first time in the 1994 season, the Demons came up with their biggest offensive output of the year in a 35-3 win over Nicholls. Laird, who was held out of the first two games because of sprained throwing shoulder, had very modest numbers against the Colonels. The junior quarterback only was 5 of 11 passing for 47 yards but guided an overpowering rushing attack that gained 311 yards. Leading the ground game for the Demons was Clarence Matthews, who had a career-high 129 yards.

The Demons spread the carries around. Along with a 75-yard scamper by Matthews for a touchdown, other first-half scores came on a 15-yard run by Danny Alexander and a 2-yard run by Terry Williamson as Northwestern built a 21-3 halftime lead. Adam Diel provided the only Nicholls points with a 48-yard field goal as time expired in the opening half.

Northwestern State's defense provided the only points of the second half. Grant Crowder returned an interception 15 yards for a touchdown while Steve Readeaux rambled 50 yards on a fumble return.

All of the remaining Southland teams, with the exception of McNeese State, made their conference debuts three weeks later. Stephen F. Austin hosted Sam Houston State and North Texas State visited Southwest Texas State.

Sam Houston State entered the Stephen F. Austin game unbeaten through five games while the Lumberjacks were 1-2-1

Lumberjacks quarterback James Ritchey accounted for five of Stephen F. Austin's six touchdowns in SFA's 42-6 domination of Sam Houston State. SFA's defense held Bearkats running back Charles Harris to 17 yards and the only points SHSU could muster were two Marcus Hajdik field goals.

Ritchey fired touchdown passes of 28 yards to Chris Jefferson and 4 yards to Walter Terry while the Bearkats countered with Hajdik's two field goals for a 14-6 halftime lead for SFA.

The Lumberjacks quarterback had touchdown runs of 12 and 4 yards in the third quarter and a 65-yard scoring strike to Jefferson in the fourth quarter on SFA's way to the 42-6 victory.

North Texas' game at Southwest Texas marked the Southland debut of Matt Simon as Mean Green coach. Simon took over the North Texas program after two years as an assistant at New Mexico under former SWT coach Dennis Franchione. Prior to his stint at New Mexico, Simon had been an assistant at the University of Washington for 10 years.

The Eagles went into their game against Southwest Texas 2-2 on the season. North Texas' two losses were by margins of 21-17 to Montana and 36-34 to Oklahoma State.

Southwest Texas, meanwhile, was 3-2 with victories over Northern Iowa, Cal State-Northridge and Sonoma State.

Using an option attack, the Mean Green rushed for 166 yards, led by Eteka Huckaby's 131-yard effort, in North Texas' 27-14 win. The teams were tied 14-14 at halftime before the Eagles outscored the Bobcats 13-0 in the second half on a 1-yard run by Cedric Cromer and a 9-yard pass from quarterback Mitch Maher to David Brown. Brown finished with 152 reception yards.

McNeese State entered its initial Southland Conference game of the 1994 season at North Texas State with a 4-1 record and ranked No. 5 in Division I-AA. The Cowboys had been second-ranked while winning their first four games before falling to then-fifth ranked Youngstown State 28-8.

Coming off an open date, the Cowboys trailed North Texas 23-17 entering the fourth quarter before the Eagles came up with a pair of breaks in the final period. An attempted pass by McNeese quarterback Kerry Joseph was ruled a fumble and recovered by North Texas at the McNeese 38. Maher hit Luis Silva with a 33-yard touchdown pass to extend the North Texas lead to 13 points at 30-17. Brett Renfro later returned a Joseph fumble 87 yards for a touchdown and a two-point conversion gave the Eagles a 37-17 victory.

North Texas and McNeese exchanged field goals in the first quarter. The Cowboys built a 10-6 lead before Maher hit Brown with a 10-yard touchdown toss just before halftime for a 13-10 advantage for the Eagles.

McNeese suffered its first Southland Conference defeat in 13 games. North Texas and McNeese both moved to 4-2 overall, while the Eagles improved to 2-0 in SLC play.

"It was one of those games where we just didn't play well and we ended up paying for it," said McNeese coach Bobby Keasler.

Stephen F. Austin and Northwestern State joined North Texas at 2-0. The Lumberjacks defeated Nicholls State 24-10 on the road while the home-standing Demons overwhelmed Sam Houston State 54-0.

After losing to Northwestern State, Nicholls defeated Samford 24-6 to move to 3-1 as the Colonels equaled their win total of the entire 1993 season. Nicholls went into its game coming off a 35-14 loss to seventh-ranked Troy State.

Stephen F. Austin played to its strengths while denying the same to the Colonels, all of which led to a 24-10 road win for the Lumberjacks. SFA, ranked first in the Southland Conference and eighth nationally in rushing defense, held Nicholls to 105 yards on the ground. The Colonels, who entered the game with the second-best rushing offense in the nation, were held to 203 yards below their average.

Trailing 10-9 at halftime, the Lumberjacks pulled ahead for the first time when Harris scored on a 5-yard run. A two-point conversion attempt failed as SFA led 15-10 midway in the third quarter. Ritchey's 15-yard touchdown pass to Jefferson late in the third quarter and Brian Minton's 19-yard field goal with less than four minutes remaining in the game accounted for the 24-10 final.

Northwestern State went into its game with Sam Houston State coming off an open date a week after the Demons upset then-No. 4 Troy State 24-10, handing the Trojans their first regular-season loss in 18 games.

The Demons produced their biggest offensive day of the season against SHSU. Alexander rushed for a career-high 132 yards as Northwestern rolled up a season-high 414 yards on the ground. Going into the game, the Bearkats only had been allowing 114 yards rushing.

The Demons built a lead of 27-0 at halftime and 40-0 after three quarters. Alexander also scored on a 23-yard reception while Laird fired two touchdown passes. Brian Jacquet had a pair of touchdown runs in the second half.

Northwestern improved to 2-0 in the Southland and 4-2 overall. SHSU, which started the year 5-0, dropped its second game in a row to fall to 0-2 in the conference and 5-2 overall. The 54-point total was the highest for the Demons since a 59-26 win over Angelo State in 1981. The defeat was SHSU's worst in 53 years, equaling a 54-0 loss to Texas A&M.

The Demons' win over Sam Houston State set up an early-season Southland showdown the following week between two 2-0 conference teams when Northwestern State hosted North Texas.

Thanks in part to Maher's three scoring runs and a touchdown pass, the Mean Green built a 28-18 lead in the fourth quarter. After recovering a fumble, the Demons drove 69 yards, culminating the drive on a 2-yard run by Matthews with three minutes left in the game to inch within three points.

Northwestern State's defense held, giving the ball back to the Demons. North Texas defensive tackle Stan Thomas intercepted a Laird pass with 1:26 remaining in the game, allowing the Eagles to hold on for a 28-25 victory.

The win allowed North Texas to get off to a 3-0 SLC start for only the third time in 12 years. On the other two occasions, the Eagles went on to make the playoffs. Northwestern State dropped to 2-1 in the conference and 4-3 overall.

Playing its fourth-consecutive game on the road, McNeese State, now ranked No. 10, bounced back from the North Texas loss with a 30-6 win at Sam Houston State.

The Cowboys led 7-3 at halftime before erupting for 23 points in the second half. Vincent Landrum's block of a Hajdik punt for a safety provided the first points of the second half. After Hajdik kicked a 32-yard field goal, Jose Larios countered with a 20-yard boot to give McNeese a 12-6 lead going into the fourth quarter.

McNeese put the game away in the fourth quarter on touchdown runs of 1 and 20 yards by Chris Fontenette and a 37-yard Larios field goal for the 30-6 victory.

The two field goals gave Larios 43 for his career, a new all-time McNeese record. Joseph, who amassed 130 yards of total offense in the game, raised his career total to 5,078, also a new all-time record for the Cowboys.

McNeese's defense had a big hand in the win as well, holding the Bearkats to 96 total yards.

The Cowboys evened their conference record at 1-1 while improving to 5-2 on the season. Sam Houston State fell to 0-3 in the league and 5-3 overall.

In San Marcos, Nicholls State and Southwest Texas squared off, each looking for its first Southland Conference win of the season.

Nicholls State couldn't stop Donald Wilkerson when it counted most in the Colonels' encounter versus Southwest Texas State. The Bobcats running back rushed for 126 yards in the first half to stake his team to a 21-13 halftime lead. The Nicholls defense then shut down Wilkerson and the rest of the SWT offense until the game's final drive.

Trailing 26-21 with 3:50 left in the game and needing to drive 71 yards for the game-winning touchdown, the Bobcats handed the ball over to Wilkerson. Southwest Texas fed the ball to Wilkerson five times in seven plays, with the running back amassing 64 yards. With Nicholls keying on Wilkerson, SWT quarterback David Williams hit Cyril Adkins with a 4-yard touchdown pass with less than a minute remaining in the game to give the Bobcats a 27-26 victory.

Down by eight points at halftime, Nicholls dominated the line of scrimmage on both sides of the ball for most of the second half. A 9-yard option keeper for a touchdown by quarterback Corey Thomas and a failed two-point conversion left the Colonels down by two points at 21-19 at the 3:35 mark of the third quarter. Nicholls took its only lead of the game when Thomas went back to pass from his own 19-yard line and hit Derrick Maxwell at midfield. Maxwell broke away from the Bobcat secondary and raced the remaining yards to give the Colonels a 26-21 advantage before SWT's late rally.

The loss dropped the Colonels to below .500 for the first time during the season, falling to 3-4 overall and 0-3 in the Southland.

North Texas, playing its final home game of the season, faced a Sam Houston State team a week later that was going in the opposite direction of the Eagles. While the Mean Green sported a three-game winning streak to remain undefeated in Southland play, the Bearkats were in the midst of a three-game losing skid that left SHSU winless in the conference.

Looking for a chance to play classic spoiler, the Bearkats scored on an 8-yard pass from freshman quarterback Chad Schramek to Bennie Wiley in the fourth quarter that rallied Sam Houston State to within four points at 21-16.

SHSU got the ball back with slightly more than four minutes left in the game. Because of numerous injuries, the Bearkats were without their starting running back, quarterback, wide receiver, tight end and two offensive linemen, yet drove 69 yards before North Texas linebacker Benny Cherry picked off a Schramek pass in the end zone with 41 seconds remaining to preserve five-point victory for the Eagles.

North Texas had built its lead by scoring touchdowns in each of the first three quarters on two Maher touchdown passes and a 9-yard run by Wayne Coleman. Maher's first touchdown pass came on the Eagles' initial snap of the game and was an 84-yard bomb to Brown. The touchdown toss was No. 62 of Maher's career, allowing him to top the all-time conference mark, previously held by Abilene Christian's Jim Lindsay.

The Eagles improved to 4-0 in the Southland and 6-2 overall while SHSU dropped to 0-4 in the league and 5-4 overall.

Looking to stay on the heels of North Texas State, Northwestern State bounced back from its loss to the Eagles with a 41-17 road win over Southwest Texas.

Northwestern led 17-3 at halftime before SWT pulled to within 20-17 on third-quarter touchdown runs of 53 yards by Claude Mathis and 11 yards by Wilkerson.

Laird responded with a 53-yard bomb to James Brock to set up the quarterback's 1-yard touchdown run. A 50-yard scoring run by Matthews and a 2-yard run by Laird allowed the Demons to pull away.

Northwestern improved to 3-1 in the Southland and 5-3 overall.

In Lake Charles, McNeese State's defense rose to the occasion in the Cowboys' 13-9 win over Stephen F. Austin. The Cowboys limited SFA's conference-leading rushing attack to 42 yards and held the Lumberjacks to 269 total yards. McNeese's defense also scored a touchdown and intercepted three passes.

Larios kicked two field goals and Chad Reeves recovered a fumble in the end zone to give McNeese a 13-3 halftime lead. McNeese's lead was a slim three-point margin late in the first half until Lamont Glenn stripped the ball from Ritchey and Reeves recovered in the end zone. The Lumberjacks' only points came on a 36-yard Minton field goal.

SFA didn't have to travel far for its lone touchdown of the game in the fourth quarter. A Joseph fumble at the McNeese 4 set up a 1-yard run by Ritchey to make the final 13-9.

The result left both teams 2-1 in conference play. McNeese improved to 6-2 overall while the Lumberjacks dropped to 4-3-1.

A week later, North Texas seemed on cruise control on its way to clinching the Southland Conference title, building a big halftime lead in its game at Stephen F. Austin. A Jeff Graham field goal and three Maher touchdown passes gave the Eagles a 24-0 lead going into the final two quarters of the contest.

Taking advantage of a pair of Eagle fumbles, SFA tightened things up a bit on touchdown runs by Harris and Kerry Bennett but a 37-yard pass from Maher to Troy Redwine left North Texas with a seemingly comfortable 30-14 lead going into the fourth quarter.

A 25-yard Dameian Vallery touchdown run and a 5-yard touchdown reception by Champ Traylor, along with a pair of two-point conversions, tied the game in the fourth quarter. Following a 28-yard Minton field goal, the Lumberjacks had their first lead of the game at 33-30.

The odds of any sort of North Texas rally seemed mighty long when the Eagles faced fourth-and-26. Maher, who passed for a career-high 486 yards, connected with tight end Silva on a 38-yard toss to keep the drive alive.

Facing third-and-10 from the Lumberjack 15 with six seconds showing, Maher tossed into the end zone for Brown. The pass fell incomplete, with Eagle partisans calling for a pass interference call on SFA safety Ryan Thomas. UNT didn't get the call and had to settle on a 32-yard Graham field goal with two seconds left in the game to salvage a 33-33 tie.

Although the tie kept the Eagles from clinching the conference crown, it did allow North Texas to run its unbeaten streak to five games as UNT moved to 4-0-1 in the Southland and 6-2-1 overall. The Lumberjacks moved to 2-1-1 in the league and 4-3-2 overall.

Elsewhere, McNeese State's run defense again was up to the task in the Cowboys' 34-10 Southland Conference home win over Southwest Texas.

Wilkerson, the second-leading rusher in the nation with an average of 160 yards per game, was held to 73 yards on 25 attempts by the Cowboys' defense. McNeese also held the Bobcats to 50 total yards in the second half.

The Bobcats scored first on a 7-yard pass from Williams to Adkins but would add only three more points the rest of the way on a 38-yard field goal by Ray Whitehead in the third quarter.

Following a 37-yard Larios field goal in the first quarter, the Cowboys took a lead they would never relinquish when Landrum returned a blocked punt for a touchdown in the second quarter. That gave McNeese a 10-7 lead before the Cowboys made it 13-7 at halftime on another Larios field goal.

Other than Whitehead's field goal, the rest of the second half was all McNeese as the Cowboys scored 21 points on two touchdown runs by Joseph and a 35-yard gallop by Fields. Fields led all rushers with 135 yards.

McNeese improved to 3-1 in the Southland and 7-2 overall. Southwest Texas fell to 1-3 in the league and 4-5 overall.

Nicholls State, meanwhile, had been making strides during the 1994 season. A non-conference victory a week earlier over Southern University gave the Colonels their fourth win of the year. It marked the first time Nicholls had won as many games in a season since a 4-7 mark in 1991.

One thing the Colonels hadn't done in 1994 was win a game in the Southland Conference. Nicholls had its best chance going into its road game at Sam Houston State. After a 5-0 start, the Bearkats lost four-consecutive SLC games going into the Nicholls tilt.

Nicholls held the Bearkats to 125 total yards and the Colonels offense played opportunistic football in taking a 24-0 win over SHSU. The Nicholls offense managed only 248 yards but took advantage of opportunities provided by its defense to move to 1-3 in SLC play and 5-4 overall. Sam Houston State dropped its fifth-straight game to fall to 0-5 in league play and 5-5 overall.

The Colonels eked out a 3-0 lead at halftime before taking advantage of one of the Bearkats' mistakes early in the second half. An interception of a Schramek pass by Tyrone Houston on a ball tipped by Todd Harris gave the Colonels the ball at the SHSU 41. Three plays later, a tackle-breaking run of 40 yards by Thomas gave Nicholls a 10-0 lead with 13:34 still remaining in the third quarter. The Nicholls quarterback had been held to minus-18 yards rushing prior to his touchdown run. Other Colonel scores included a 14-yard touchdown run by Thomas later in the third quarter and a 50-yard interception return by Clarence Wiggins early in the fourth period.

With another chance to capture the Southland Conference championship a week later, North Texas quickly fell behind 7-0 at Nicholls State on a 13-yard run by Thomas.

Special teams provided the first points of the game for the Eagles when Kelon Wilson blocked a punt that rolled out of the end zone to make the score 7-2 in the first quarter. Seldom-used freshman running back Hut Allen, forced into action because of injuries, made the most of his opportunity, scoring on a 5-yard run. Allen finished the game with 112 yards rushing and 75 receiving. Following Allen's touchdown, a two-point conversion run by Maher gave North Texas a 10-7 edge.

North Texas was leading 17-7 before another special teams play allowed the Eagles to secure the game by halftime. Terry Watson returned a second blocked punt 34 yards for a touchdown and a 24-7 Mean Green lead at halftime.

Nicholls never seriously threatened the Eagles' lead from that point, allowing North Texas to capture the SLC title with a 31-17 victory.

North Texas stretched its unbeaten streak to six games as the Eagles concluded Southland play at 5-0-1 and moved to 7-2-1. It was the Mean Green's first Southland title since 1983. The Eagles' unbeaten streak was snapped, however, with a 38-20 loss to former SLC foe Northeast Louisiana. Nicholls dropped to 1-4 in the SLC and 5-5 overall.

In Natchitoches, a clash of two teams sporting 3-1 Southland Conference records met when the Demons played host to McNeese State.

The Demons took a 7-0 first-quarter lead on a 1-yard keeper by Laird to cap an 83-yard drive. Northwestern missed out on several other scoring opportunities in the first half. Jason Fernandez missed a 30-yard field goal. The Demons were turned away on two other occasions when they were stopped on downs at the McNeese 33 and after Laird was intercepted at the 2-yard line by Zack Bronson.

That allowed the Cowboys to stay in the game, eventually tying things up 7-7 at halftime on a 30-yard pass from Joseph to Terence Davis in the second quarter.

McNeese's fifth-ranked defense limited the Demons to 85 yards in the second half. Meanwhile, the Cowboys scored three times in the final 30 minutes to pull away. The go-ahead score came on a 1-yard run by Fields on a drive set up by a Northwestern fumble at the Demons' 31. Joseph put the game away with two four-quarter touchdowns, one of 15 yards to Joseph Warren and the other a 3-yard strike to Marrico Wilson.

For a team accustomed to playing on grass, the Cowboys found playing on Northwestern State's artificial turf to be a tough transition, according to Keasler.

"We used to hate to play on that carpet," the McNeese coach said. "Our kids didn't like playing on it. We played very timid."

McNeese improved to 4-1 in the SLC and 8-2 overall. Northwestern fell to 3-2 in the conference and 5-5 on the season.

In San Marcos, Stephen F. Austin led 24-0 with 12 minutes left in the game but had to hold on to defeat Southwest Texas 24-19.

A pair of 1-yard runs by Ritchey and Terry gave SFA a 14-0 halftime lead. A 24-yard Minton field goal in the third quarter and Cesar Cespedes' return of a blocked punt for a touchdown gave the Lumberjacks their 24-0 lead early in the fourth quarter.

Southwest Texas began to rally back when Wilkerson, held to a season-low 58 yards rushing, scored on a 1-yard run for the Bobcats' initial score of the contest. Williams, SWT's freshman quarterback who was sacked five times in the game, got hot in the final minutes of the game. He tossed a pair of 10-yard touchdown passes to Mathis to finish with 339 yards in the game as the Bobcats closed to within five points.

The Bobcats were driving once again until Lumberjacks safety Thomas Sitton picked off Williams at the Stephen F. Austin 17-yard line with 10 seconds left in the game to preserve the win for SFA.

SFA improved to 3-1-1 in the Southland and 5-3-2 overall. Southwest Texas dropped to 1-4 in the conference and 4-6 overall.

The Cowboys, back up to No. 8 in the nation, secured a second-place finish in the Southland Conference and a Division I-AA playoff berth with a 41-24 home win over Nicholls State to close out the 1994 regular season.

McNeese ended the regular season at 9-2 overall, including 5-1 in the Southland. Nicholls finished 5-6 overall and 1-5 in the conference.

Joseph also secured his spot in the McNeese record books. By hitting on 9 of 18 passes for 215 yards and three touchdowns, he became the Cowboys' all-time passer. Joseph finished the regular season with career totals of 367 completions for 4,931 yards and 36 touchdowns.

The McNeese quarterback factored in the Cowboys' first two touchdowns of the game. He scored on a 1-yard run and tossed an 11-yard pass to Damien Morris to give McNeese a 14-0 lead after one quarter. The Cowboys scored twice more in the second quarter on a 1-yard run by Bryan Foster and a 26-yard Larios field goal. Nicholls managed one score in the first half, a 1-yard run by Roscoe Griffin to trail 24-7 at the break.

Joseph tossed two more touchdowns in the second half. He connected with Morris on a 58-yard strike and hooked up with Davis from 43 yards out as the Cowboys pulled away for the 41-24 victory.

Northwestern State, 5-2 at one point, dropped its season finale at Stephen F. Austin 34-14 to finish the year with a losing record.

Northwestern was tied 13-13 with SFA going into the fourth quarter before Lumberjacks scored the final 21 points of the game, fueled by Demons mistakes.

SFA's recovery of an attempted punt return by Brock on the final play of the third quarter gave the Lumberjacks the ball at the Northwestern 43. That set up Harris' 1-yard touchdown run 10 plays later to break the tie. Harris helped increase the Lumberjack advantage to 14 points at 27-13 on a 14-yard touchdown run one play after Cody Mahon's interception of an errant Laird pass.

Aaron DeLaTorre sealed the win for SFA when he returned a Demons' fumble 23 yards for a touchdown with 4:25 left in the contest.

Northwestern, which finished 5-6 overall and 3-3 in the Southland, got a 189-yard performance from Matthews, becoming only the fourth running back in Demons history to top 1,000 yards for a season.

The Lumberjacks finished 6-3-2 overall and 4-1-1 in the SLC but it was not good enough to earn SFA at at-large berth in the Division I-AA playoffs.

Sam Houston State went into its season finale at home against Southwest Texas looking to close out the year with at least one Southland win. After starting the season 5-0 against non-conference competition, the Bearkats lost five league games in a row going into the game with SWT. The outcome of the contest would determine if SHSU would finish the season with a winning or losing record.

As befitting two struggling teams, the score was tied 10-10 at halftime. A 27-yard run by Stacy Arrambide and a 31-yard Hajdik field goal gave the Bearkats a 10-0 edge before SWT tied the game at the break on a 4-yard run by Wilkinson and a career-best 48-yard field goal by Whitehead. Whitehead's kick came with four seconds left in the first half.

The Bobcats would not score again. Sam Houston State, meanwhile, added a 37-yard touchdown pass to Red Jones and a 2-yard Arrambide run to lead 24-10 going into the fourth quarter. Hajdik's second field goal of the game and a 10-yard run by Harris accounted for the final scoring in the game.

SWT's Wilkerson ran for 153 yards on 33 carries to establish a new Southland single-season rushing record with 302 carries for 1,569 yards.

The result left Sam Houston State, Southwest Texas and Nicholls State at the bottom of the Southland standings at 1-5. SHSU finished 6-5 on the year while Southwest Texas concluded the season at 4-7.

Making its first Division I-AA playoff appearance since 1988, North Texas had to take a long journey to Idaho. In facing Boise State, North Texas was taking on a Broncos team that had lost only once all season and was ranked No. 3 in the nation.

The Eagles had to deal with other elements as well, including a 29-degree temperature and a blue artificial field. Despite that, it was the Broncos who were feeling blue after a big second quarter by the Mean Green.

The teams traded scores in the first quarter, leading to a 10-10 tie. North Texas countered a 40-yard pass from Boise State's Troy Hilde to Ryan Ikabe and a 29-yard Greg Erickson field goal with an 8-yard run by Maher and a 31-yard Graham field goal.

North Texas controlled the second quarter with a 19-yard touchdown pass from Maher to Vertis McKinney and another Graham field goal to lead 20-10 at the break.

Despite the North Texas lead, there were some chinks in the Mean Green's armor. The Eagles built their lead relying on the arm of Maher. The senior quarterback and holder of most all-time passing records at North Texas, was 21 of 32 passing for 226 yards in the first half. Meanwhile, the Eagles' running game was limited to an average of less than three yards per carry.

Boise State continued to shut down the North Texas ground attack in the second half. The lack of a ground game limited the Eagles' ability to run the clock and also altered the effectiveness of Maher. North Texas' seven second-half drives concluded with five punts and two interceptions. After a strong first half, Maher was 8 of 19 for only 37 yards passing in the final two quarters.

Still, the Eagles seemed on the verge of a knockout punch in the third quarter. North Texas was on the march for another potential score still leading 20-10 when Maher was picked off at the Boise State 21-yard line.

In a flash, the Eagles' lead disappeared. The Broncos had their own trouble moving the ball but an opportunistic defense allowed Boise State to rally. A 35-yard pass completion down to the 1-yard line set up a 1-yard run by K.C. Adams to make the score 20-17 with less than eight minutes remaining in the game.

Moments later, another Maher interception set up a 6-yard touchdown reception by Willie Bowens for a 24-20 Broncos lead with 5:38 remaining in the contest and all Boise State would need to eliminate the Mean Green from the playoffs.

The loss ended the Eagles' season at 7-4-1 and ended North Texas' tenure in the Southland Conference. North Texas announced earlier in the year it was leaving the league and moving up to Division I-A. The Eagles would be moving to the Big West Conference. In an ironic twist, Boise State also had plans to join the Big West.

In another opening-round game, McNeese State used big plays to blow past No. 6 Idaho as the fifth-ranked Cowboys defeated the Vandals 38-21.

The game got off to a slow start with neither team scoring in the first quarter. Larios broke the ice with a 22-yard field goal and Idaho gained a 7-3 edge on a 6-yard pass from Brian Brennan to Dwight McKenzie.

It was at that point that the big plays began. On the first play from scrimmage after Idaho's touchdown, Joseph broke loose on an 83-yard sprint to give McNeese a 10-7 halftime advantage. The McNeese quarterback ended up running for a career-high 177 yards in the game.

Picking up where he left off in the first half, Joseph hooked up with Davis on an 83-yard bomb less than three minutes in the second half to give the Cowboys a 10-point cushion at 17-7. Not wanting to be left out, Fields scampered for a school-record 90-yard touchdown run on McNeese's next possession to give the Cowboys all the points they would need with a 24-7 lead.

The teams traded scores the remainder of the game as the Cowboys advanced to the quarterfinals with the 17-point victory.

Things looked bleak for McNeese State in the Cowboys' Division I-AA quarterfinal playoff game at home against Montana.

The Cowboys trailed 27-7 going into the fourth quarter and McNeese's option attack was affected by a soft, muddy field. If the Cowboys were to have any chance to rally, McNeese likely would have to go to the air.

So, Joseph passed 15 yards to Davis early in the fourth period but the touchdown toss still left the Cowboys trailing by 13 points. A Grizzlies gambit, however, failed when a fake punt went awry when a pass was broken up by Cowboys cornerback Damon Gladney, giving the ball back to McNeese at the Montana 33. Fields, who managed to rush for only 27 yards in the game, eventually scored on a 1-yard run to pull the Cowboys to within six points at 27-21 with 6:42 remaining in the game.

Wasting little time, Joseph tossed to Morris. The receiver caught the ball at the 7-yard line and fell into the end zone with 4:13 left in the game. Larios' extra point gave McNeese the lead for the first time at 28-27.

The McNeese defense held and gave the ball back to the Cowboys' offense. Montana's defense, in turn, forced McNeese to give up the ball on downs. The Grizzlies drove into Cowboys' territory and Andy Larson kicked a 37-yard field goal with eight seconds left in the game to give Montana a dramatic 30-28 victory.

"We didn't play well early," said Keasler. "We had our chances and let it slip past. That was a heartbreaker."

Montana led 14-7 at halftime. The Grizzlies scored first on a 7-yard pass from Dave Dickerson to Mike Erhardt. McNeese tied the game later in the first quarter on a 28-yard pass from Joseph to Morris. Dickerson was forced to leave the game with an injury, but Bert Wilberger, the backup quarterback, guided Montana to a 14-7 halftime lead with a 19-yard touchdown pass to Scott Gurnsey in the second quarter.

The Grizzlies increased the advantage by scoring the only points of the third quarter on Wilberger touchdown passes of 6 yards to Gurnsey and 43 yards to Shalon Baker for a 27-7 Montana lead. Dickerson and Wilberger combined to complete 43 of 75 passes for 537 yards and four touchdowns in the game.

McNeese, which ended its season 10-3, only managed 63 yards rushing. Along with Fields, Joseph also was held to 27 yards on the ground. The McNeese quarterback brought the Cowboys back by hitting a career-high 21 of 47 attempts for 283 yards but it wasn't quite enough as McNeese bowed out in the quarterfinals.

MISSING OUT ON ALL-SOUTHLAND
I-AA TITLE GAME

The departure of North Texas reduced the Southland to a six-member football league. With the SLC now down to five conference games, most teams had at least four games under their belts before beginning league play in 1995.

Nicholls State went into its conference opener at Northwestern State 0-5 under first-year coach Darrin Barbier. Rick Rhoades resigned early in 1995 and was replaced by Barbier, a highly-successful coach at Hahnville High School in Louisiana. Barbier led the Tigers to two state championships in six years, one of which came during a 15-0 campaign in 1994.

One of the few highlights from the first five games of the season for Nicholls was Nakia Lumar's performance against Samford. The running back rushed for 182 yards, including a record 91-yard touchdown scamper. His touchdown run was the longest in both Nicholls and Southland Conference history. He broke the school record of 80 yards set by Lionel Vital in 1984. The SLC mark of 90 yards was shared by Steve Eaton of Southwest Texas and Charles Harris of Sam Houston State.

Northwestern State, by contrast, took a three-game winning streak into its conference opener. The Demons lost to Southern and Troy State before bouncing back with victories over Delta State, East Texas State and Boise State.

Clarence Matthews rushed for more than 170 yards for the second week in a row, saving his best attempts for when they counted most in the Demons' 34-14 win over the Colonels.

A 6-yard touchdown by Matthews, who finished with 171 yards rushing, gave Northwestern a 20-14 lead with 10:29 remaining in the game. The score came moments after winless Nicholls had taken a 14-13 advantage on cornerback Reggie Davis' 62-yard return for a touchdown of a fumble by Demons quarterback Brad Laird.

Matthews went on to a 15-yard touchdown run and Anthony Williams scored from 10 yards out to make the final 34-14.

The teams were tied 7-7 after one quarter when Lumar and Northwestern's William Williber traded touchdowns. A 30-yard Greg Mueller field goal gave the Demons a 10-7 halftime edge.

On the same day Barbier was making his Southland debut as Nicholls coach, Stephen F. Austin and Sam Houston State were renewing their long rivalry. SFA was off to a 4-0 start and ranked No. 4 in the nation. Along with eye-opening wins over Northern Iowa and Youngstown State, the Lumberjacks defeated Angelo State and Henderson State for its perfect start. Sam Houston State was off to a 3-2 start.

SFA running back Kerry Bennett rushed for three of his school-record tying four rushing touchdowns in the first half as the Lumberjacks built a 24-7 halftime lead on their way to a 38-22 victory at Sam Houston State.

Bennett finished with only 42 yards rushing but Dameian Vallery, playing in place of an injured Leonard Harris, rushed for 93 yards. The Lumberjacks' production wasn't limited to the running game as three Stephen F. Austin receivers had at least 72 reception yards as SFA amassed 410 total yards to help give SFA its best start ever through five games.

Trailing 31-15 in the fourth quarter, Kevin Pesak hauled in a 42-yard touchdown catch for SHSU. The Bearkats' tight end had a career-best nine catches for 116 yards.

At 0-6 and with a losing season already assured, things were not working well and it was time for a change at Nicholls. So, the Colonels junked the Stack-I offense first brought in by Rick Rhoades in favor of an I-formation option attack and played true freshman Brad Zeller at quarterback.

While the play of both the I-formation and Zeller provided a few bright spots, Colonels mistakes led to the same old results as Nicholls fell 56-3 at Stephen F. Austin.

The fourth-ranked Lumberjacks took advantage of several Nicholls mistakes and a strong wind to score on five first-half drives and improved to 6-0 on the season and 2-0 in Southland play. SFA, ranked third in the nation in scoring defense at 7.6 points per game, yielded only one field goal in dropping the Colonels to 0-7 overall and 0-2 in the conference.

Off to its worst start in school history, Nicholls tried to shake things up by using former starting quarterback Corey Thomas as a punt returner. Thomas muffed his first attempt at fielding a punt, setting up the Lumberjacks at the Nicholls 21. Vallery's second touchdown run of the game gave SFA a 14-0 lead.

The Lumberjacks took advantage of excellent field position due to a short punt into a strong wind to set up a 5-yard touchdown pass from quarterback James Ritchey to Bennett to make it 21-0. On the Colonels' next possession, punter Quinn Guidry dropped the ball before getting off a punt of only two yards. One play later, Ritchey hooked up with Chris Jefferson on a 51-yard touchdown strike on the final play of the first quarter to make it 28-0.

Nicholls trailed 35-0 before finally getting on the scoreboard. Zeller showed his running ability, going 46 yards on a draw to eventually set up a 36-yard Adam Diel field goal with 7:47 remaining in the opening half.

Northwestern State joined Stephen F. Austin at 2-0 in the Southland Conference with a record-setting defensive performance in the Demons' 24-2 triumph at Sam Houston State.

The Demons held SHSU to a school-record minus-10 yards rushing. The Bearkats finished with only 157 total yards as Northwestern State took advantage of four Sam Houston State turnovers. Northwestern, meanwhile, amassed 406 yards of total offense.

Northwestern State took a 2-0 lead in the first quarter when SHSU quarterback Chad Schramek was penalized for intentional grounding while attempting to pass from his own end zone.

Matthews scored on a pair of runs, while Brian Jacquet caught a 25-yard pass from Laird and Mueller kicked a 25-yard field goal.

SHSU's only points of the game came after Matthews' second touchdown, a 17-yard run in the fourth quarter. Following the touchdown, Dedrick Mango returned a blocked extra-point attempt back for two points.

Sam Houston State's next opponent was McNeese State. The Cowboys went into their Southland Conference opener at home as the top-ranked team in Division I-AA. It was a distinction the Cowboys earned while facing a brutal early-season schedule. Among McNeese's victories were wins over then No. 6 James Madison 30-24, then No. 12 Central Florida 49-7, which was led by future NFL quarterback Dante Culpepper, and defending two-time Division I-AA national champion Youngstown State 31-3 as part of the Cowboys' 6-0 start.

Bobby Keasler, McNeese State's coach, said he knew from the start that he had a very good team entering the 1995 season.

"We still had Kerry Joseph at quarterback and Henry Fields at running back and we were very good on defense. I thought we had the two best linebackers in the conference with Chad Reeves and Vince Landrum. Vince was an All-American for us. I thought we were pretty well fixed up as a football team. The kicking game was excellent," the McNeese coach said.

The Bearkats already had two conference games under their belt but it hardly showed in a 20-0 loss. Offensively, the Cowboys got a game-leading 137 yards rushing by Henry Fields, while Kerry Joseph rushed for 113 yards. Jose Larios provided the only points of the first half on a pair of field goals in the second quarter. McNeese put the game out of reach in the fourth quarter on a 22-yard run by Joseph and the quarterback's 36-yard scoring toss to Warren.

McNeese's defense, which recorded its first shutout of the season, limited the Bearkats to 42 yards rushing and 119 passing.

Also playing its initial Southland Conference game that same day was Southwest Texas State. The Bobcats were 2-4 going into their game at Nicholls State.

The ball seemingly bounced the right way for winless Nicholls, or so it appeared, against Southwest Texas.

Clinging to a 28-25 lead, the Bobcats were driving for a game-clinching score when running back Aaron Allen apparently fumbled going into the end zone with the Colonels recovering. On the play, however, an inadvertently blown whistle by one of the officials ended the play at the 1-yard line and SWT retaining possession. Two plays later, David Williams scored on a quarterback sneak to give the Bobcats a 35-25 triumph.

Nicholls rallied from a 28-7 halftime deficit to make it a close game in the second half. The Colonels marched 80 yards with the second-half kickoff, with Tawaskie Anderson's 11-yard touchdown run making it 28-14. A 33-yard Diel field goal, along with a 4-yard touchdown run by Anderson and a two-point conversion by Zeller made it 28-25 with 8:17 remaining in the game.

From that point, the Bobcats just gave the ball to Claude Mathis, the Southland Conference's leading rusher. Mathis, who finished with 152 yards on 31 carries, rushed seven times for 43 yards in what proved to be the game-winning drive.

In perhaps the biggest regular-season game in Southland history, top-ranked McNeese State visited No. 3 Stephen F. Austin in a clash of unbeaten teams.

As might have been expected of two such closely-matched teams, the game was scoreless until the late stages of the first half. That changed quickly when Joseph connected with Warren on a 13-yard touchdown strike to give McNeese a 7-0 lead with 4:01 remaining in the second quarter. Cowboy strong safety Marcus LeBlanc then intercepted a Ritchey pass, giving the ball back to McNeese. Joseph connected with Terence Davis on a 33-yard toss with 3:05 showing that gave McNeese a 14-0 halftime lead.

McNeese's quick lead in the second quarter almost disappeared just as fast in the third period. A fumbled snap by Joseph gave the ball to the Lumberjacks at the Cowboys' 33. Harris raced in on the very next play to make it 14-7. A 47-yard field goal by Larios was blocked by Damiyon Bell and returned back to the McNeese 18 by Jason Speights. That led to a 36-yard Brian Minton field goal to make it 14-10.

The rest of the game, especially the third quarter, belonged to Joseph and McNeese. The Cowboys quarterback hit on 9 of 10 pass attempts in the third quarter. He scored on a 2-yard run before tossing touchdown passes of 16 yards to tight end Marrico Wilson and 44 yards to Davis on a flea flicker for a 34-10 McNeese lead.

SFA linebacker Jeremiah Trotter, who went on to play 12 years in the NFL, mostly with the Philadelphia Eagles, returned an errant Joseph pass 12 yards in the fourth quarter to account for the 34-16 final.

Photo courtesy Stephen F. Austin sports information

Jeremy Moses, who played quarterback at Stephen F. Austin from 2007-2010, is the only player in Southland Conference history to win the Walter Payton Award.

Photo courtesy Stephen F. Austin sports information

Stephen F. Austin linebacker Jeremiah Trotter was a 1996 All-American who went on to play in the NFL for 11 seasons, mostly with the Philadelphia Eagles.

Photo courtesy McNeese State sports information

McNeese State running back Buford Jordan, who played for the Cowboys from 1980-1983, was the first player in Southland Conference history to rush for 4,000 career yards.

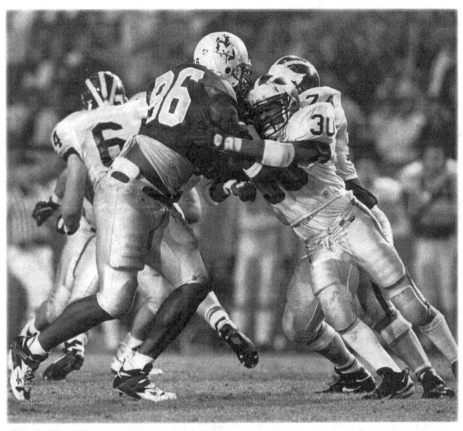

Photo courtesy McNeese State sports information

Kavika Pittman (86) of McNeese State was a 1995 All-American who went on to play nine years in the NFL.

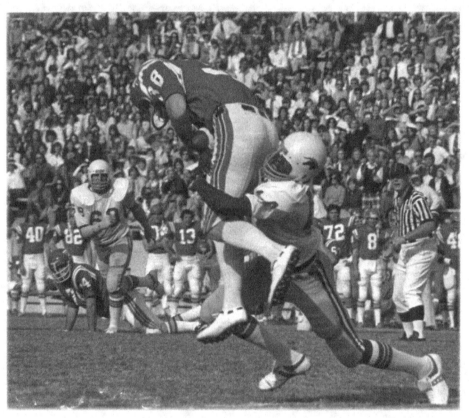

Photo courtesy Louisiana Tech sports information

Louisiana Tech receiver Roger Carr was a two-time All-American who became a first-round pick in the NFL and enjoyed a 10-year NFL career.

Photo courtesy Louisiana Tech sports information

Louisiana Tech defensive lineman Fred Dean was a four-time All-Southland selection and is a member of the Pro and College Football Hall of Fame.

Chet Douthit was a receiver on an Arkansas State squad that won the College Division national championship in 1970.

Photo courtesy Arkansas State sports information

Arkansas State linebacker Bill Bergey was one of the first star
defenders in the Southland Conference and went on to play in
the NFL for 12 years.

Photo courtesy Sam Houston State sports information

A two-time All-American at Sam Houston State, Timothy Flanders finished his career as the all-time career rushing leader in the Southland Conference.

Photo courtesy Sam Houston State sports information

Sam Houston State defensive lineman Michael Bankston was a three-time All-Southland pick who went on to play nine years in the NFL.

Photo courtesy Northwestern State sports information

Northwestern State offensive lineman Marcus Spears (76) was a 1993 Outland Trophy semifinalist who went on to play 12 years in the NFL.

Photo courtesy Don Sepulvado/Northwestern State sports information

A 1991 All-American, Northwestern State linebacker Andre Carron (94) is the all-time career sacks leader in the Southland Conference.

Photo courtesy Central Arkansas sports information

Central Arkansas quarterback Nathan Brown was the
Southland Conference's Offensive Player of the Year in 2007
and the 2008 Player of the Year.

Central Arkansas' Larry Hart was the Southland Conference's Defensive Player of the Year in 2008 and 2009.

Photo courtesy Randy Bergeron/Southeastern Louisiana sports information

Simmie Yarborough, who played at Southeastern Louisiana from 2008-2011, had 2,780 reception yards and 30 touchdowns for the Lions in his career.

Photo courtesy Randy Bergeron/Southeastern Louisiana sports information

A first-team All-Southland selection in 2012, Robert Alford went on to play for the Atlanta Falcons in the NFL.

Photo courtesy Nicholls State sports information

Quarterback Yale Vannoy helped to lead the Nicholls State Colonels to the Football Championship Subdivision playoffs in 2005.

Photo courtesy Nicholls State sports information

A two-time All-American, defensive back Lardarius Webb of Nicholls State went on to play for the Baltimore Ravens of the NFL.

Photo courtesy Texas State sports information

A 1996 and 1997 All-American, Texas State's Claude Mathis is second among the all-time rushing leaders in the Southland Conference.

Photo courtesy Texas State sports information

Named the second-team punter on the Southland Conference's all-time football team, Texas State's Cory Elolf was a 2004 All-American.

Photo courtesy Louisiana-Lafayette sports information

Rafael Septien, who played for Southwestern Louisiana from 1974-1976, went on to play 10 years in the NFL and was a 1981 Pro Bowl selection.

Photo courtesy Louisiana-Lafayette sports information

A player at Southwestern Louisiana from 1976-1978, defensive back Ron Irving is second on the Ragin' Cajuns' all-time interception list with 19.

Defensive lineman Al Lucas, who played for Troy from 1996-1999, was awarded the 1999 Buck Buchanan Award as the outstanding defensive player on the FCS level.

Photo courtesy Louisiana-Monroe sports information

A 1989 All-American, Northeast Louisiana tight end Jackie Harris went on to play for four teams during a 12-year NFL career.

Photo courtesy Louisiana-Monroe sports information

A defensive end at Northeast Louisiana from 1987-1990, Anthony Williams went on to play in the Canadian Football League.

Photo courtesy Jacksonville State sports information

A receiver at Jacksonville State from 1996-1999, Joey Hamilton is the Gamecocks' all-time leading receiver with 2,903 yards.

Photo courtesy Abilene Christian sports information
Abilene Christian quarterback Jim Lindsey,
a 1970 All-American, was the NCAA record
passing leader by the time he concluded his
career with the Wildcats.

Photo courtesy Abilene Christian sports information

A 1969 All-American, Abilene Christian linebacker Chip Bennett also was the 1969 College Division Player of the Year.

Photo courtesy Lamar University sports information

Quarterback Phillip Primm helped Lamar to either outright or shared Southland Conference titles during the first three years of the league's existence from 1964-1966.

Photo courtesy Lamar University sports information

Eugene Seale (53) a linebacker at Lamar from 1983-1985, made the Southland's all-time second-team defense and spent six years in the NFL.

Quarterback Mitch Maher threw for more than 8,500 yards in his career at North Texas from 1991-1994.

Photo courtesy North Texas sports information

North Texas linebacker Byron Gross was a 1990 All-American who
started every game of his career, a span of 46 consecutive games.

Photo courtesy Trinity University sports information

Earl Costley, who played at Trinity from 1970-1973, is second on the Tigers' all-time rushing list with a total of 3,980 yards.

Photo courtesy Trinity University sports information

Trinity's Marvin Upshaw (right), the brother of Pro Football Hall of Famer Eugene Upshaw, enjoyed a nine-year NFL career of his own.

"We played an excellent offensive game," said Keasler. "We came up with big plays with Kerry Joseph running the ball and throwing the ball to Terence Davis. We just took over. I think that set us up a little bit when you beat Stephen F. at Stephen F."

Fresh off a 42-39 non-conference victory over Division I-A Northeast Louisiana, Northwestern State took a six-game winning streak into its Southland Conference home game against Southwest Texas.

Northwestern and SWT were locked in a 14-14 tie before the passing duo of Williams and Paul Pine got hot in the fourth quarter for the Bobcats. A 14-yard pass from Williams to Pine with 10:13 remaining broke the tie. Williams, who threw for 232 yards, put the game away when he connected with Pine on a 15-yard scoring pass with 2:46 showing to knock off the Demons 28-14.

Northwestern State managed a 14-14 tie at halftime on a 24-yard run by Matthews in the first quarter and a 40-yard touchdown reception by Pat Palmer.

The Demons slipped to 2-1 in the Southland and 6-3 overall. SWT improved to 2-0 in the conference while evening its overall record at 4-4.

Southwest Texas put its 2-0 Southland mark on the line a week later when the Bobcats hosted top-ranked McNeese State.

McNeese State's rushing defense rose to the occasion yet again, shutting down Mathis, the prolific Southwest Texas runner, in the Cowboys' 28-7 win over the Bobcats.

Mathis entered the game leading the nation in all-purpose yards and was ranked eighth in rushing as he managed to rush for more than 100 yards in seven of SWT's eight games. His numbers took a hit against the Cowboys as McNeese's defense held him to 62 yards rushing. The Cowboys limited the Bobcats to 64 yards rushing as a team and 284 total yards.

Despite the impressive defensive numbers, the Cowboys only managed a 7-0 lead at halftime. The lone score of the first half came on a 9-yard run by Joseph in the second quarter.

A 32-yard pass from Joseph to Chris Fontenot in the third quarter gave McNeese a 14-0 lead. Fields, who rushed for 141 yards in the game, scored on a 1-yard run in the fourth quarter to put the Cowboys up by three touchdowns. McNeese rounded out its scoring on a 3-yard touchdown reception by Warren.

The McNeese defense missed out on its second shutout in three weeks when the Bobcats scored on a 14-yard pass from Williams to Allen in the fourth quarter.

McNeese moved to 3-0 in the SLC and 9-0 overall. Southwest Texas dropped to 2-1 in the conference and 4-5 overall.

A pair of teams still seeking their first Southland Conference win of the season met when Sam Houston State visited Nicholls State.

The Colonels limited their usual first-half mistakes, leading to a 17-17 tie after two quarters but Nicholls was unable to score the entire second half and made a costly mistake late in the game that enabled the Bearkats to take a 24-17 victory.

A punt return by Eric Anderson down to the Nicholls 11 was called back because of a running-into-the-kicker penalty against SHSU. The Bearkats ended up taking possession at their own 36, but a personal foul by the Colonels moved the ball to the Nicholls 49. A 14-yard third-down conversion pass from Schramek to Pesak moved the ball down to the Nicholls 18 and eventually set up a 3-yard touchdown run by Wayne Coleman to make it 24-17 with 7:04 left in the game.

Playing their best first half of the season, the Colonels produced 17 points in the opening two quarters. A Diel field goal and a pair of two short runs by Rondell Honor provided the scoring for Nicholls. Honor's second touchdown, a 1-yard run just before halftime, tied the score. The touchdown was set up by a 60-yard gallop down to the 3 by Monte Dugas.

The Bearkats' first two scores came on a Marcus Hajdik field goal and a 2-yard run by Coleman. SHSU took a 17-10 lead on the only turnover of the first half when Bearkats defensive lineman Ulric Robertson pulled down a Zeller pass at the line of scrimmage and rambled 35 yards for a touchdown.

SHSU improved to 4-5 overall and picked up its first conference win in four tries. The 0-10 mark represented to most losses for Nicholls in a single season. Nicholls fell to 0-4 in league play.

The Cowboys certainly proved to be more good than lucky in getting off to a 9-0 start, but a little luck didn't hurt in McNeese State's Southland Conference home game against Northwestern State.

An exchange of field goals provided the only scoring in the first half until the Cowboys came up with a touchdown right before halftime. A 37-yard punt return by Zack Bronson gave McNeese the ball at the Demons' 20. The Cowboys continually handed the ball to Fields, who finally scored on a 5-yard run with 57 seconds remaining in the second quarter.

Donnie Ashley returned the second-half kickoff down to the Northwestern 17. Fields got the ball for three-straight carries down to the 1-yard line. Joseph decided to do the honors himself, but fumbled into the end zone. An alert Warren fell on the ball right before it scooted through the back of the end line to give McNeese a 17-7 lead.

Larios added a field goal in the third quarter and Laird, the Northwestern State quarterback, scored on a 1-yard run in the fourth period to give McNeese a 20-10 victory.

Matthews became the first opposing runner to top 100 yards against McNeese's top-ranked defense. The Demons running back finished with 122 yards. Matthews also set new Northwestern State records for rushing yards in a season and career all-purpose yards, topping Joe Delaney in both categories.

"Matthews was an excellent running back. We knew he would get his yards but we had to force them to do something else," said Keasler.

McNeese stayed unbeaten in the conference at 4-0 and overall through 10 games.

An open date gave Stephen F. Austin and extra week to mull over its loss to McNeese State and when the Lumberjacks returned to the field, they took out their frustrations on Southwest Texas in SFA's 50-21 trouncing of Southwest Texas in Nacogdoches.

Ritchey tossed first-half touchdown passes of 2 yards to Mikhael Ricks, 44 yards to Jefferson and 57 yards to Kevin Goodwin as SFA built a 44-0 halftime lead. Ritchey's backup, Mike Quinn, also threw two touchdown passes to Brandon Walker and another to Oyedokum.

The Lumberjacks' defense held Mathis, the Southland's rushing leader, to 32 yards on the ground. Meanwhile, Vallery rushed for 144 yards for SFA.

Williams threw for 316 yards for SWT, which fell to 2-2 in the Southland and 4-6 overall. SFA improved to 3-1 in the conference and 8-1 overall.

Playing on a Thursday night to close out the 1995 season, fifth-ranked Stephen F. Austin amassed 373 yards rushing in a 25-20 win at Northwestern State.

Harris rushed for 181 yards and Vallery 169 to pace a potent Lumberjacks ground attack. Harris scored on a 3-yard run in the second quarter to help SFA take a 12-7 halftime lead.

A 79-yard touchdown pass from Ritchey to Goodwin in the third quarter stretched the SFA lead to 18-7 before Northwestern countered with a 5-yard run by Williber to make it 18-13. Vallery's 66-yard touchdown run later in the third quarter effectively put the game away but the Demons did manage the game's final score on a 15-yard touchdown reception by Palmer in the fourth quarter.

Matthews scored the game's first touchdown in the opening quarter to give him a school-record 13 for one season. His 172 yards allowed him to top 100 yards in a game for the 12th time, a new school career record.

SFA finished 9-1 overall and 4-1 in the Southland. Northwestern State ended the season 6-5 overall and 2-3 in the conference.

If ever a game was an example of two teams going in opposite directions, it was McNeese State's regular-season finale at Southland Conference foe Nicholls State. The Cowboys were seeking to end the regular season unbeaten while the Colonels were looking for a year-ending victory to avoid a winless campaign.

The Cowboys left no doubt which scenario would prevail. McNeese jumped out to a 24-0 lead and allowed the Colonels only one score in a 31-6 win for the Cowboys. The outcome marked only the third time in school history the Cowboys posted a perfect season. McNeese went 8-0 in 1963 and 11-0 in 1979.

Joseph tossed a 41-yard pass to Damien Morris and Larios kicked a 25-yard field goal to give McNeese a 10-0 lead after one quarter. The quarterback re-injured his right shoulder in the second quarter and would not return. Joseph originally suffered the injury a week earlier in the Cowboys' 20-10 win over Northwestern State.

Tim Leger, the backup quarterback, tossed touchdown passes of 5 and 11 yards to Davis in the second quarter to give McNeese a 24-10 halftime lead.

Each team scored once in the second half. The only points for Nicholls came on a 44-yard run by Zeller as the Colonels finished winless under Barbier, their first-year coach.

Fields rushed for 121 yards in the game to reach 4,160 career yards to break the career record of Buford Jordan.

McNeese finished a perfect 11-0 on the season, including 5-0 in the Southland Conference. Nicholls ended 0-11 overall and 0-5 in league play.

Closing the 1995 season in San Marcos, Sam Houston State spotted Southwest Texas a 7-0 lead before scoring the next 19 points on its way to a 26-20 triumph over the Bobcats.

Mathis, who rushed for 117 yards, accounted for all 80 yards on SWT's opening possession, including a 68-yard touchdown run, to give the Bobcats a 7-0 lead. SHSU responded with a 4-yard run by Bennie Wylie and a 20-yard Hajdik field goal in the second half to give the Bearkats a 9-7 halftime edge.

Coleman, who rushed for a career-high 163 yards, scored on a 56-yard run in the third quarter and Hajdik added another field goal as the Bearkats extended their lead to 19-7 before going on to take the 26-20 victory.

The result left both teams 2-3 in the Southland. Sam Houston State finished 5-5 overall and SWT 4-7.

Stephen F. Austin and visiting Eastern Illinois combined for almost 1,000 yards of offense in the opening round of the Division I-AA playoffs, but it was a late defensive play that helped to seal a 34-29 victory for the Lumberjacks.

While the total yardage was quite close, the teams accumulated the yards in opposite fashion. SFA amassed 491 yards, 390 of which came through the air. Eastern Illinois ground up 484 yards, 318 of which came from its running game.

The Lumberjacks jumped out to 14-0 lead on runs of 21 yards by Harris and 7 yards by Ritchey. SFA would go on to add a 24-yard Minton field goal but Eastern Illinois countered with touchdown runs of 2 and 1 yard by running back Willie High and a two-point conversion to trail 17-15 at halftime.

The two-point halftime margin was as close as the Panthers would get the remainder of the game as Eastern Illinois blew a scoring opportunity early in the third quarter. High broke loose on a scamper from his 31 before stripped of the ball by Speights, the Stephen F. Austin cornerback. Ron Powell recovered the loose ball for the Lumberjacks at the SFA 15.

Ritchey, who threw for a career-high 390 yards, fired touchdown passes of 56 and 23 yards to Ricks in the second half. After SFA took its biggest lead of the game at 45-15, Eastern Illinois quarterback Pete Mauch countered with scoring strikes of 10 yards to Charlie Roche and 25 yards to Tom Hess in a span of less than a minute. The touchdown pass to Hess closed the margin to 34-29 with 5:14 left in the game.

The Panthers managed to get the ball back and it wasn't until Pat House's interception at the Eastern Illinois 48-yard line with 1:30 left in the game that the Lumberjacks had secured the victory.

As the top seed in the Division I-AA playoffs, McNeese State received an opening-round home game against old postseason foe Idaho.

The tone was set from the start. Davis returned the opening kickoff 30 yards. A 41-yard pass from Joseph to Fontenot set up a the first of four Larios field goals as the Cowboys would go on to build a 30-0 lead midway in the second quarter on their way to a 33-3 victory.

McNeese, which moved to 12-0, scored on its first five possessions as Joseph accounted for 217 yards of total offense in the opening two quarters of the game. By contrast, the Cowboys' defense limited Idaho to 29 yards in the Vandals' first five possessions of the contest.

Joseph had a hand in setting up most of the Cowboys' scores. A 53-yard toss to Morris set up a Larios field goal and a 32-yard pass to Davis led to a 6-yard touchdown run by Dorian Dunmiles. His 47-yard strike to Davis gave McNeese a 30-0 lead.

"We felt our speed was better than theirs and it was proved that night," Keasler said. "We came up with big plays and they just couldn't get anything going. We dominated that game."

Idaho, which lost to McNeese three times in four tries in the opening round of the playoffs, only managed a third-quarter field goal in the game.

"When you come into Cowboy Stadium, especially at that time of year, those big-ole hogs from up north, they can't breathe that south Louisiana air and that makes it tough for them and we were used to it," said Keasler.

The running game played a key role in Stephen F. Austin's quarterfinal playoff game at Appalachian State. The Lumberjacks' defense limited Appalachian State's normally prolific running attack to 72 yards on 34 attempts. Meanwhile, SFA got a 180-yard effort from Harris as the Lumberjacks defeated the previously unbeaten Mountaineers 27-17.

Appalachian State took a 7-0 lead on a 2-yard pass from quarterback Scott Satterfield to Frank Leatherwood. SFA ran off the next 13 points on a pair of Minton field goals and a 17-yard run by Vallery before a field goal by the Mountaineers' Jay Sutton made the score 13-10 in favor of the Lumberjacks at halftime.

The teams exchanged turnovers early in the third quarter, ultimately leading to a 6-yard touchdown pass from Satterfield to Aldwin Lance to put the Mountaineers on top 17-13 but Appalachian State would not score again.

Ritchey, who threw for only 144 yards in the game, connected with Jefferson on a 49-yard pass to set up a 2-yard touchdown run by Harris that gave SFA a 20-17 lead in the fourth quarter. Harris added a 6-yard touchdown run to seal the Lumberjacks' 27-17 victory.

In Lake Charles, McNeese State quick-strike plays were put to good use in a 52-18 drubbing of Delaware in the Division I-AA quarterfinals.

Joseph tossed for a career-high five touchdown passes, with Terence Davis and Wilson hauling in two apiece, and the Cowboys returned two kickoffs for scores.

The game started quietly enough on a 41-yard field goal by Sean Leach. Unfortunately for Delaware, the Blue Hens had to kick off. Ashley returned the kick 92 yards for a touchdown and Delaware would never lead again.

Joseph's first touchdown pass, a 44-yard strike to Davis, gave McNeese a 14-0 lead after one quarter. A short touchdown pass to Wilson and another to Terence Davis helped the Cowboys build a 31-6 halftime lead.

Freshman William Davis returned the second-half kickoff 96 yards to make it 38-6. Touchdown passes to Wilson and Ashley gave McNeese a lead of as much as 52-12 before Delaware scored the game's final touchdown.

Fields rushed for 115 yards as the Cowboys rolled up 421 yards of total offense. The McNeese defense, meanwhile, forced six turnovers. The Cowboys intercepted three passes, two by Bronson.

Although McNeese won by a large margin, the Cowboys entered the game leery of Delaware's vaunted Wing-T offense.

"We had to come up with a game plan. Gosh, almighty, they pull both tackles and they had a lot of misdirection. We had to be really solid on defense and hone in on doing the things you are coached to do. We had to play a little slower up front," said Keasler.

With Stephen F. Austin and McNeese State advancing to the Division I-AA semifinals, each was one win away from creating an All-Southland Conference national champion game. The University of Montana, the Lumberjacks' host in one of the semifinal contests, made sure that wasn't going to happen by spanking SFA 70-14.

The first winter storm of the season to hit the area and game-time temperatures that never topped 10 degrees put the Lumberjacks' offense in deep freeze. SFA was limited to 52 yards rushing on 35 attempts while the Grizzlies kept warm with 473 yards passing and 196 rushing.

While the final score was indicative of the type of beating the Lumberjacks took in the game, SFA trailed only 21-14 at one point in the second quarter.

Following a 33-yard touchdown pass from Montana's All-America quarterback Dave Dickenson to Joe Douglass, a failed onside kick by the Grizzlies gave SFA the ball at the Montana 42-yard line. Harris, who was held to 43 yards rushing, scored on a 2-yard run to make it 21-14 with less than four minutes remaining in the opening half.

The Lumberjacks would never be that close again. Dickenson, a future Canadian Football League fixture, tossed a 20-yard touchdown pass to Raul Pacheco. Montana got the ball back with less than a minute remaining in the second quarter but it was more than enough time for Dickenson to eventually find Nathan Dolan on a 23-yard scoring toss to give the Grizzlies a 35-14 halftime lead.

Montana added another 35 points in the second half as Dickenson ended up tossing for 370 yards in the game and five touchdowns. He also had a 6-yard rushing touchdown in the first half.

The loss for SFA was the program's worst defeat since a 64-0 loss to West Texas State in 1930. The Lumberjacks, who concluded the season at 11-2, were outgained 669-264 in the semifinal loss.

Reaching the Division I-AA semifinals for the first time in school history, top-ranked McNeese State played at home once again against Marshall, led by future Georgia Bulldogs coach Jim Donnan.

A wind in excess of 20 miles per hour greeted the two teams. The Cowboys had the wind at their backs to open the game and forced Marshall to punt on its opening possession. McNeese drove 66 yards, with Fields scoring on a 1-yard run to give the Cowboys and early 7-0 advantage.

Facing the wind, the Cowboys went three-and-out on three-consecutive possessions in the second quarter. Taking over at its own 47, the Thundering Herd tied the game on a 24-yard pass from freshman quarterback Chad Pennington, a future NFL first-round pick, to Ricky Carter.

The teams traded punts later in the second half, with a kick by Marshall's Chris Hanson being downed at the McNeese 1-yard line. On first down, Rusty Struppeck was tackled in the end zone for a safety to give the Thundering Herd a 9-7 edge at halftime.

Going against the wind in the third quarter, Fields took a direct snap from center out of shotgun formation and raced to his left for a 51-yard touchdown. A two-point conversion attempt failed, leaving the Cowboys with a 13-9 lead.

The Thundering Herd answered with a 75-yard drive. Pennington capped the drive on a 2-yard touchdown pass to LaVon Colclough. The extra-point attempt was blocked as Marshall took a 15-13 lead with 2:24 remaining in the third quarter. Marshall was unable to take full advantage of a first-and-goal at the McNeese 4, but a 23-yard Tim Openlander field goal extended the Thundering Herd's lead to five points.

Needing a touchdown to win, the Cowboys reached the Marshall 29 but a penalty and a pair of sacks forced McNeese to punt the ball away. With 2:47 left in the game, Marshall's Chris Parker, the all-time rusher in Southern Conference history, raced 18 yards for a touchdown to give the Thundering Herd a 25-13 win to advance to the championship game on its own home field, while the Cowboys season ended with a 13-1 record.

The success the Cowboys had in 1995, Keasler said, was built around team unity.

"We tried to build a team that believed in each other and they really did. I've never seen a team so close. They still keep in touch with each other to this day," the McNeese coach said.

THE SOUTHLAND FOOTBALL LEAGUE

Losing schools each of the previous two years that were seeking to move up to Division I-A status left the Southland with only six football-playing members. To rectify that, the conference added Troy State in 1996 as a football-only member. So, for football only, the Southland Conference became known as the Southland Football League.

It didn't take newcomer Troy State long to play its initial SFL game or to show that it meant to be a force in the newly-named league.

The Trojans had two games worth of experience before taking on Nicholls State. Troy State was 2-0 going into its encounter with the Colonels, opening the season with victories over Alcorn State and Eastern Kentucky.

Troy State was coached by Larry Blakeney. In his sixth season at Troy, Blakeney successfully guided the Trojans from Division II to Division I-AA. His teams went 5-6 and 10-1 the final two years in Division II. Blakney's teams went a combined 21-6-1 from 1993-95 as a Division I-AA independent, including reaching the Division I-AA semifinals in the school's first year of eligibility for the playoffs.

Nicholls State went into its game with Troy State 1-1. After opening with a 44-10 loss to Northeast Louisiana, the Colonels defeated Mississippi Valley State. The victory over the Delta Devils gave Darren Barbier his initial win as Nicholls coach after the Colonels went 0-11 during his first year at the helm. The win snapped a 14-game losing streak dating back to the 1994 season.

"Getting a win was a big monkey off of our backs," Barbier said. "We knew it would happen. We knew the program was going in the right direction. Obviously, it was a big win. We had been 0-13 (under Barbier). We needed a win."

Played September 21, 1996, in Troy, the fourth-ranked Trojans were just too much for the Colonels. Nicholls committed four turnovers and a special teams blunder that the Trojans turned into 31 points on their way to a 37-7 triumph.

Troy took advantage of early Nicholls mistakes to score on five of its first six possessions to lead 27-7 at halftime. Meanwhile, the Trojan defense limited the

Colonel offense to 73 first-half yards, 58 of which came on Nicholls' final possession of the first half.

The Trojans' first possession was the only one in which Troy State had to travel a long distance to score. Matt Huerkamp's 42-yard field goal capped a 60-yard drive to give the Trojans a 3-0 lead.

Maurice Stringer's 53-yard punt return down to the Nicholls 19 set up the next Trojans score. Six plays later, Troy took a 10-0 lead on a 4-yard run by Arrid Gregory.

A fumble by Nicholls running back Nakia Lumar two plays into the ensuing possession gave the ball right back to Troy at the Colonels' 39-yard line. Five plays later, Troy Donelson's 11-yard run made it 17-0 with 3:25 still remaining in the opening quarter.

On the first play of the ensuing possession, a Brad Zeller pass was tipped by Dale Watson and intercepted by Demetric Shipman. That set up a 32-yard Huerkamp field goal for a 20-0 Trojans lead with seven seconds left in the first quarter.

Nicholls finally forced a Trojans punt, but when Dominic Brown tried to field an end-over-end kick, he fumbled, giving the ball right back to Troy at midfield. That set up a 1-yard run by Daniel Griffin to make it 27-0.

The Colonels drove 82 yards in 10 plays and used up the first 5:20 of the third quarter to earn their only score of the game. Zeller's 1-yard sneak capped the drive to make it 27-7 at the 9:36 mark of the third quarter.

"We were overmatched in that game. With the four turnovers, that just made it worse," Barbier said. "That wasn't a game that we penciled in that we had a chance to win. They were one of the premiere programs in the country at the time. We just tried to get better. Our whole mission that year was to just get better every week and not worry about the scoreboard."

For the second time in four games, Troy State faced an opponent ranked in the Top 10. Like the previous encounter against then No. 10 Eastern Kentucky, the third-ranked Trojans were on the road against No. 7 Stephen F. Austin.

Facing ranked opponents was nothing new to the Lumberjacks as well. Stephen F. Austin went into its Southland Conference opener at home with a 2-1 mark after wins over Eastern New Mexico and Delta State before suffering a 38-12 loss at Northern Iowa. SFA went into the game against Northern Iowa ranked third in the nation while the Panthers were No. 5.

SFA grabbed a 3-0 lead on a 32-yard Ryan Smith field goal before the Trojans countered on a 9-yard touchdown pass from Stan Davis to Ryan Pearson.

After the teams traded field goals in the third quarter, Troy State maintained a four-point edge at 10-6.

A 7-yard touchdown reception by Mike Oyedokun gave SFA what proved to be a 13-10 victory. The winning scored was set up by 55-yard pass from Peyton Jones to Chris Jefferson.

Open dates gave both Stephen F. Austin and Sam Houston State an extra week to prepare for their rivalry in Nacogdoches.

The 1-4 Bearkats went into their Southland opener on a three-game losing streak.

Pat House, who rushed for 152 yards for SFA, had a touchdown run and the Lumberjacks added a field goal for a 10-7 lead going into the final minutes of the game.

The Lumberjacks held a three-point advantage despite converting only once in 13 tries on third down. With SFA forced to punt with 4:04 left in the game, Yohance Bree, the Sam Houston State return man, scampered 71 yards for a touchdown to put SHSU on top 14-10.

Starting at its own 20-yard line with 1:10 left in the game, SFA reached the Bearkats' 25 but hard-charging linebacker Matthew Chapman of SHSU hit Mike Quinn while the Lumberjacks' quarterback was attempting to pass. Quinn's pass fell incomplete in the end zone, allowing Sam Houston State to hold on for the four-point win.

After the loss to Stephen F. Austin, Troy State bounced back with a 37-6 win over Alabama State before heading back into Southland action at home against McNeese State.

The Cowboys learned early in 1996 that there would be no repeat of the 1995 season, going into the Troy State encounter 2-3.

Rob Baldwin kicked field goals of 30 and 35 yards to give the Cowboys a 6-0 lead midway in the second quarter.

Troy took the lead later in the quarter on a 2-yard touchdown run by Donelson but the Cowboys claimed the halftime advantage at 12-7 on a 78-yard pass from Tim Leger to Chris Fontenot.

McNeese's five-point lead held up until late in the fourth quarter. With three minutes left in the game, Donelson tossed a halfback pass to Jeff Hammond. The extra point was blocked, leaving the Trojans with a scant 13-12 lead. A turnover gave the ball back to Troy State at the Cowboys' 17 with 2:46 left in the game. Huerkamp's 28-yard field goal secured the win for the Trojans.

Like McNeese State and Sam Houston State, Northwestern State also was making its Southland debut that day when the Demons hosted Nicholls State.

The Demons went into the game 3-1 on the season, their only loss being to rival Northeast Louisiana.

After their loss to Troy State, the Colonels had an open date before earning a 10-3 non-conference victory over Samford heading into the Northwestern game.

The Demons fell behind by scores of 3-0 and 10-7 before building a 17-10 halftime lead against Nicholls.

A 69-yard pass from Warren Patterson to Pat Palmer and a 2-yard run by Anthony Williams put Northwestern State on top 14-10. Eric Collins' 32-yard field goal on the final play of the first half gave the Demons a seven-point edge at halftime.

Field goals of 42 and 28 yards by Adam Diel in the third quarter rallied the Colonels to within one point at 17-16.

Holding Northwestern to no points in the second half, the Colonels got their big break in the fourth quarter when defensive back Jack Nicoll blocked the punt of Shane Barbaro, the nephew of former Colonels great and NFL safety, Gary Barbaro, with Nicholls taking possession at the 23-yard line and 1:43 left in the game. After two short running plays, Zeller spiked the ball to stop the clock. Diel, who had kicked three field goals in the game, but missed from 52 yards out in his previous attempt, booted a 37 yarder to give Nicholls a 19-17 victory.

The outcome, the first-ever Southland win for the Colonels under Darren Barbier, evened Nicholls' league record and 1-1 and moved the team above .500 at 3-2 overall. The victory also represented the first time the Colonels had won back-to-back games in Barbier's two seasons as coach. It also marked the Colonels' first Southland win since 1994. Northwestern State fell to 3-2 overall and 0-1 in the SFL.

"It was a character check," Barbier said. "Can we win a close game? Teams go through phases in building a program and that was our second phase. The first was for us to learn to compete, and I think we did that. Then we had to learn how to win and I think (the win over Northwestern State) took us to the next phase."

Southwest Texas State was six games into its 1996 season when the Bobcats played their first Southland Football League contest at Troy State. SWT went into the game 3-2 with wins over Grand Valley State, Hofstra and Idaho and losses to Eastern Washington and Southern Utah.

A pair of Trojan running backs accounted for almost 200 of the team's 291 yards rushing in sixth-ranked Troy State's 24-13 victory over the Bobcats.

Gregory rushed for 103 yards and Joe Jackson 93 to pace Troy State. Meanwhile, the Troy State defense contained Claude Mathis. The Southwest Texas runner entered the game as the leading rusher in the SFL but was held to a total of 65 yards, only 17 in the second half.

Troy trailed 13-10 until Jackson scored on a 6-yard run to cap a 78-yard drive to give the Trojans a 17-13 edge at the 6:03 mark of the third quarter.

Down by four points, the Bobcats were on the move early in the fourth quarter when David Williams tossed to Russell Peevy. The ball deflected off the hands of the Southwest Texas tight end and was intercepted by Shane Black. Black raced 62 yards down to the SWT 33. Davis scooted 20 yards two plays later to put the Trojans on top 24-13.

At Thibodaux, Stephen F. Austin's offense was struggling to put points on the board so the Lumberjacks turned to their defense to post a 27-11 win over Nicholls State.

Stephen F. Austin, 4-2 overall, 2-1 in the Southland, led 7-3 midway in the third quarter until defensive back Todd Holmes returned a Zeller interception 31 yards for a touchdown to give the Lumberjacks a 14-3 edge. On the Colonels' next possession, SFA linebacker Larry Echols stepped in front of another Zeller pass attempt, returning the errant throw 54 yards for a touchdown and a 20-3 lead at the 6:54 mark of the third quarter.

Nicholls, which fell to 1-2 in the SFL and 3-3 overall, got its only points of the first half on a 43-yard Diel field goal with 44 seconds remaining in the second quarter. The Colonels' second-half points came on a safety and a 1-yard run by Richie Delatte with 3:46 remaining in the game.

"I thought we had a chance to win that one," Barbier said of the SFA game. "We were in the game awhile and then we turned it over. We learned some lessons. We learned that if we were going to compete in conference, we can't turn the ball over."

Elsewhere, the Demons snapped a two-game losing streak behind two long touchdowns apiece from Williams and Palmer as Northwestern State rolled up 599 yards of total offense in a 38-21 home triumph over Sam Houston State.

Williams had touchdown runs of 69 and 24 yards and finished with 119 yards rushing. Palmer amassed 165 yards and caught touchdowns receptions of 71 and 70 yards. Meanwhile, Brian Jacquet rushed for a career-high 110 yards.

The Demons broke away from a scant 14-6 halftime lead with a 17-point third quarter.

Both teams moved to 1-1 in SFL play while Northwestern improved to 4-2 on the season and the Bearkats fell to 2-5.

Sam Houston State scored early at home a week later against McNeese State and bounced back from the loss to Northwestern State with a 30-25 triumph over the Cowboys.

Dedrick Manigo's 27-yard interception return for a touchdown on the first play from scrimmage and a 35-yard Marcus Hajdik field goal gave the Bearkats a 10-0 lead in the first quarter. The Cowboys responded with a field goal, safety and a 1-yard touchdown run by Earnest McGowan in the second quarter to take the lead before a 2-yard Elmore Armstrong run gave SHSU a 17-13 halftime edge.

Trailing 24-13, a 65-yard touchdown pass from Leger to Donnie Ashley late in the third quarter rallied the Cowboys to within five points. Jerod Jones recovered Joey Mouton's fumble on the ensuing kickoff and skipped 5 yards into the end zone to give McNeese a 25-24 lead.

McNeese State returned the favor with five minutes left in the game when Chris Hall's recovery of a Cowboys fumble gave Sam Houston State the ball at the Cowboys' 36. Two unsportsmanlike penalties against the Cowboys advanced the ball to set up a 3-yard run by Armstrong to pull out a 30-25 triumph for the Bearkats.

SHSU moved to 2-1 in the Southland Football League and 3-5 overall while McNeese dropped to 0-2 in the conference and 2-5 overall.

When Nicholls State traveled to take on Southwest Texas, both teams knew Daylight Standard Time was on the horizon. What they didn't know was that the outcome of the game wouldn't be decided until five overtimes.

Nicholls was only a few minutes away from winning the game in regulation, clinging to a 20-14 lead. However, a tired Colonels defense that spent most of the second half on the field, allowed SWT to travel 74 yards before Mathis tied the game on a 1-yard run with 2:11 remaining in regulation. The Bobcats could have avoided overtime, but Matt Wieland's conversion kick was blocked by Murphy Edwards, sending the game to overtime.

Some fans thought the moment got the best of Barbier by his reaction on the sidelines.

"Back in the 1990s, I had a terrible habit of chewing tobacco. I had a big ole wad of tobacco in my mouth and Murphy Edwards is running off the field after blocking the extra point. I go and jump on him and my chin hits his shoulder pads and I swallow my tobacco. I started throwing up right there on the sidelines. It appears that the excitement is getting to me that I can't take the pressure of the situation. I was really throwing up a wad of tobacco," Barbier recalled with a chuckle.

In past years, the game would have ended in a tie. The NCAA's newly-instituted overtime called for each team to have at least one possession, starting at the opponents' 25-yard line. If the game was tied after each team had a possession, the game continued until a winner emerged.

Nicholls got the ball first in the initial overtime and had to settle on a 29-yard Diel field goal. Mathis suffered an injury to his neck area in Southwest Texas' first overtime and the game was delayed for 20 minutes. The Bobcats ultimately had to settle on a 38-yard game-tying field goal by Wieland.

The teams continued to match scores during the next three possessions. Aaron Allen had a 12-yard run for Southwest Texas and Nicholls countered with a touchdown run by Terrence Spears from a yard out to make the score 30-30 and send the game to a third overtime. Diel and Wieland traded field goals in each of the third and fourth overtimes to force the fifth extra period.

Nicholls got the ball first in the fifth overtime and faced a second-and-goal at the 1-yard line. Two running plays failed to produce a touchdown. The Colonels lined up to kick a field goal but then called timeout. After the timeout, Nicholls elected to go for the touchdown. Spears got the call and was hit immediately but managed to lunge forward to break the plane of the goal line. Diel's conversion gave the Colonels a 43-36 lead.

"It was a tough call," Barbier said of opting against a field goal. "We felt we hadn't stopped them. They scored three-straight touchdowns in the second half and they matched us score-for score in overtime. I thought our defense was just about spent and I didn't think a field goal would hold up. I thought it gave us the best chance to win the game."

After the Bobcats gained 1 yard, Quincy Sorrell got a hand on a pass by Williams. The Nicholls linebacker bobbled the ball before securing it and racing 94 yards for a touchdown to give the Colonels a dramatic 49-36 victory.

Like the tobacco incident, there were other shenanigans going on along the Nicholls sideline in the long overtime game.

"We had a booster on our sideline. In those days, you used to have cords (on the coaching headsets) and you used to have a helper with the cords. One of our boosters asked if he could do that because he thought it would be fun. He wasn't in the greatest shape but I let him do it. Sure enough, he picks the worst game to do it. We played and extra hour-and-a-half. At the end of the game, he was on the bench getting oxygen and said, 'I'm never doing this again,'" said Barbier, laughing while recalling the incident.

Nicholls moved to 2-2 in the Southland and 4-3 overall with the win. Southwest Texas fell to 0-2 in the SFL and 3-4 overall.

Still seek its first Southland Football League win of the season, McNeese State used a 24-point third quarter to build a 37-24 lead at home against Stephen F. Austin but it would not last.

Quinn hit Mikhael Ricks with an 11-yard touchdown in the fourth quarter as the Lumberjacks pulled to within six points at 37-31 before Quinn hooked up with Ricks from 15 yards out with 15 seconds left to tie the game. Smith kicked the extra point to give SFA a 38-37 triumph.

The loss in the closing seconds overshadowed a school-record-tying five touchdown passes by Leger. He tossed two touchdowns to Damien Morris along with one each to Fontenot, Pat Matthews and Andre Perkins.

McNeese trailed from the opening kickoff when SFA's Freeman Perry raced 94 yards with the opening kickoff. Leger's first touchdown pass to Morris tied the game before the Lumberjacks added a Smith field goal and a 3-yard run by KaRon Coleman. Leger's second touchdown strike to Morris allowed the Cowboys to trail only 17-13 at halftime.

The Cowboys fell to 0-3 in the SFL and 2-6 overall. SFA improved to 3-1 in the league and 6-2 overall.

Like McNeese State, Southwest Texas was still seeking its initial Southland win of the year when the Bobcats hosted Northwestern State. Just like the Cowboys, SWT would have to wait at least another week to achieve the goal.

The Bobcats allowed two early touchdowns in excess of 50 yards and it was all downhill from there for Southwest Texas in a 49-0 blowout against Northwestern State.

Demon fullback Robert Robertson had a tackle-breaking 51-yard pass reception for a touchdown and Williams scored on a 56-yard reverse on Northwestern State's way to a 21-0 halftime lead.

With Mathis hampered with a lingering neck injury from the Nicholls State game, the Bobcats were impotent on offense, limited to 113 yards. Mathis entered the Northwestern State game in the second quarter and finished with zero yards on five carries. Allen, normally a receiver, started in Mathis' place and rushed for 67 yards.

The loss was the first shutout for Southwest Texas in nine years. SWT dropped to 0-3 in the Southland Football League and 3-5 overall. Northwestern State improved to 2-1 in the conference and 5-3 overall.

Next up for Northwestern State was a home game at Troy State. Following their win over Southwest Texas, the Trojans defeated rival Jacksonville State 31-21 to improve to 7-1 on the season. Not that they needed it, an open week gave the Trojans an extra week to prepare for the Demons.

Jackson and Gregory were back at it again for Troy State at Northwestern State. The fifth-ranked Trojans ground out 267 yards rushing behind two early touchdowns by Jackson and a 109-yard effort by Gregory in Troy's 26-13 victory.

Northwestern State, which entered the game with Division I-AA's sixth-best rushing offense at 272 yards per game, was held to 160 by the Trojans' defense. Also hurting the Demons' cause were 13 penalties and a blocked punt.

The blocked punt came only moments after a 15-yard run by Jackson gave Troy State a 7-0 advantage on the Trojans' first possession of the game. The blocked punt set up a 1-yard Jackson scoring run to quickly put Troy on top 14-0.

Northwestern State managed to make it a 14-7 game on a 31-yard pass from reserve quarterback Brandon Emanuel to Palmer before Huerkamp kicked a 29-yard field goal to give the Trojans a 17-7 lead at the break.

Troy State improved to a league-leading 4-1 and 8-1 overall with the win. Northwestern evened its SFL record at 2-2 in falling to 5-4 overall.

With Nicholls State and Sam Houston State both 2-2 in the Southland, someone was going to move above .500 in league play when the two teams met in Thibodaux.

That distinction went to Nicholls with a 20-10 triumph but the win meant more than just moving above .500 for the Colonels as they guaranteed themselves their first winning season since 1988.

The turnaround from 0-11 in 1995 to a winning season marked only the second time in either Division I-A or Division I-AA football history that such a feat occurred. The only other time it happened was when Idaho State went from 0-11 in 1979 to 6-5 the following season.

Nicholls only trailed 7-3 at halftime despite being held to 77 yards total offense in the opening half. Lumar immediately sparked the Colonels when he returned the second-half kickoff 95 yards down to the Bearkats' 5-yard line. Lumar got the call two plays later and scored from 2 yards out, and suddenly, Nicholls was on top 10-7.

The Bearkats tied the game at 10-10 on a 38-yard Hajdik field goal moments later, but Colonels quickly countered. Nicholls drove 68 yards to set up a 26-yard Diel field goal as the Colonels regained the lead at 13-10 with 3:54 remaining in the third quarter.

Two plays into the ensuing possession, Nicholls linebacker Robert Martin forced a fumble by Bennie Wyle, with Anthony Saul recovering for the Colonels at the SHSU 11-yard line. The Colonels put the game away two plays later on a 10-yard touchdown strike from Zeller to Kip Rohner.

Along with topping .500 in the Southland, the Colonels improved to 6-3 overall. SHSU fell to 3-6 overall and 2-2 in the conference.

While the winner of the Nicholls-Sam Houston State game moved above .500 in the Southland, the victor of the Southwest Texas-McNeese State game on the same day would pick up its first win in the Southland Football League.

Mathis and his Southwest Texas Bobcats became the latest team to exact revenge on McNeese State in 1996. Mathis entered the 1995 encounter between the teams as the nation's leader in all-purpose yards and No. 8 in rushing but was held to 62 yards in a 28-7 loss. He rushed for 174 yards and scored two touchdowns in the Bobcats' 16-13 win at McNeese to keep the Cowboys winless in SFL play.

After an exchange of field goals between Wieland and McNeese State's Shonz LaFrenz, Mathis, who had been hobbled by injuries, scored on a 1-yard run to give the Bobcats a 9-3 lead at halftime. A 34-yard field goal by LaFenez in the third quarter pulled the Cowboys to within three points.

Mathis gave SWT just enough of a cushion when he broke loose on a 34-yard run in the fourth quarter to extend the Bobcats' lead to 16-6 before McNeese scored the final touchdown of the game on a 1-yard McGowan run.

The Cowboys dropped to 0-4 in the SFL and 2-7 overall. Southwest Texas improved to 1-3 in the league and 4-6 overall.

It indeed took at least another week for McNeese State to win its initial Southland game of the year as the Cowboys avoided a potential winless league season with a 20-3 triumph at Northwestern State.

The Cowboys took advantage of a Demons team that was down to their third-team quarterback. Mark Gibson got the start in place of Patterson, the injured starter. Patterson suffered a groin pull a week earlier in a loss to Troy State. Emanuel, the second-team quarterback, was lost for the season in the game against Troy with an ankle sprain.

McNeese took a 7-0 lead on a 1-yard run by McGowan late in the first quarter. Collins' 23-yard field goal with 13 seconds remaining in the second quarter made it 7-3 at halftime.

The Cowboys drove 80 yards with the second-half kickoff to increase their lead to 10 points at 13-3 when Leger capped the drive with a 1-yard run. Derrick Beavers, who rushed for 111 yards, put the game away with a 36-yard touchdown run with 6:16 left in the game.

Northwestern, which was averaging 432 yards a game, was limited to 263. The loss marked the first time the Demons were held without a touchdown in 31 games.

McNeese improved to 1-4 in the SFL and 3-7 overall. Northwestern State fell to 2-3 in the conference and 5-5 overall.

On the same day McNeese State was earning its first Southland win, a 23-yard touchdown run by Davis to cap an 80-yard drive on Troy State's opening possession set the tone in a 35-14 win at Sam Houston State that secured the SFL title for the Trojans.

The Bearkats were unable to stop a Trojans running game that amassed 436 yards on the ground. Gregory and Jackson combined for three touchdowns and 358 yards rushing as Troy won the Southland crown in its first year in the league.

After Davis' touchdown, a 12-yard sprint by Jackson and a 74-yard gallop by Gregory gave Troy State a 21-0 halftime lead.

The Bearkats' offense came to life in the third quarter as a 49-yard touchdown pass from freshman quarterback Albert Bradley to Louis Hutchison and a 12-yard run by Bradley made the score 21-14.

After an exchange of fumbles, a 29-yard scoring pass by Davis to Andy Swafford and a touchdown run by Jackson allowed Troy to wrap up the SFL championship.

Troy State improved to 5-1 in the conference and 9-1 overall while earning its fourth-consecutive playoff bid. The Trojans would go on to defeat Samford 50-10 in non-conference play in the final week of the 1996 regular season to improve to 10-1 heading into the playoffs.

SHSU dropped to 2-3 in the league and 3-7 overall.

Whatever chance Stephen F. Austin had for a potential Southland Football League co-championship came to an end with Troy State's win over Sam Houston State and the Lumberjacks' surprising 31-19 loss at Southwest Texas.

Mathis rushed for a Southland-record 310 yards against No. 7 SFA. His effort broke the old mark of 304 set by McNeese State's Tony Citizen against Prairie View in 1986.

Southwest Texas scored on its first possession on a 28-yard touchdown pass from Williams to Travis Bush. After the Lumberjacks cut into the lead on a pair of field goals, the Bobcats countered with a 50-yard run by Mathis and a 5-yard pass from Williams to Peevy for a 21-6 SWT advantage.

SFA rallied to within two points at 21-19 before Williams tossed his third touchdown pass of the game, this one to Terrance Hatton, and SWT added a field goal as the Bobcats went on to take the 31-19 victory.

The Lumberjacks slipped to 3-2 in the SFL and 7-3 overall. Southwest Texas improved to 2-3 in the conference and 5-5 overall.

Stephen F. Austin's late-season slide continued. The Lumberjacks didn't allow the Demons a lot of big plays, but the big plays they did get proved to be the difference as SFA closed the 1996 season with a 17-10 loss at Northwestern State.

All three of the Demons' scores came from long distance. Eric Collins kicked a 45-yard field goal, Jeff Spikes scampered 75 yards for a touchdown run and Williams blazed 75 yards for Northwestern State's three scores in the game. Williams' touchdown with 13:18 left in the contest proved to be the game winner.

The Demons' defense also came up big with a school-record 11 sacks and held SFA to minus-25 yards rushing. Northwestern State's defense also stopped the Lumberjacks from within the 2-yard line on four downs with eight minutes left in the game to preserve the victory.

A 3-yard run by House gave Stephen F. Austin a 7-3 lead at halftime.

SFA finished the season 7-4 overall and 3-3 in the Southland. Northwestern State concluded its season at 6-5.

Nicholls State went into the 1996 season just hoping to win a game. After escaping with a narrow 29-19 victory over Division II Harding College, the Colonels went into their season finale 7-3 and thinking of postseason possibilities.

Trailing 16-10 at McNeese State with only 2:38 left in the game and needing a touchdown to keep any playoff hopes alive, Nicholls quickly moved 83 yards to set up Zeller's game-tying touchdown with 11 seconds left in the game. Diel added the conversion, giving the Colonels a dramatic 17-16 triumph.

With little more than character to play for in a 3-8 season, McNeese broke a 10-10 tie with 2:44 left in the game when Charles Ayro intercepted a Zeller pass and returned it 25 yards for a touchdown to give the Cowboys the lead. LaFrenz's extra-point attempt was blocked by Ivan Williams, leaving McNeese with a six-point edge with 2:44 remaining in the game.

The Colonels drove downfield quickly, with Zeller connecting on 8 of 12 passes on the drive. His final attempt was a 12-yard connection to Thomas down to the McNeese 4-yard line with 18 seconds left in the game. On the next play, Zeller was hit behind the line of scrimmage on a draw play but managed to break a tackle on his way into the end zone for the touchdown. Diel, who had a field goal blocked earlier in the game, booted the extra point to give Nicholls the win.

"We called a quarterback draw. We caught them in a man-under type coverage where they kind of ran off the linebackers and Zeller scored pretty easily," Barbier said.

Lumar rushed for 109 yards in the game to finish with 1,072 yards, becoming the first Nicholls player to top 1,000 yards rushing in a season.

The win, which improved the Colonels to 4-2 in the Southland Football League and 8-3 overall, coupled with Stephen F. Austin's 17-10 loss to Northwestern State earlier in the day, gave Nicholls sole possession of second place in the SFL behind league champion Troy State.

In Huntsville, Sam Houston State closed the season on a winning note with a 29-17 come-from-behind win over Southwest Texas.

A pair of Hajdik field goals allowed the Bearkats to trail only 10-6 at halftime. A 3-yard touchdown run by Bradley in the third quarter gave SHSU the lead before a 10-yard touchdown run by Williams put SWT on top 17-13.

Hajdik's third field goal of the game, this one from 33 yards out, followed by touchdown runs of 11 yards by Armstong and 4 yards by Bradley rallied the Bearkats.

Mathis rushed for 157 yards to finish the season with 1,593 to set a new Southland single-season rushing mark. He ended the season with 16 rushing touchdowns, a new school record.

The Bearkats ended the season 3-3 in the SLC and 4-7 overall. Southwest Texas finished the year 2-4 in the league and 5-6 overall.

The good news for the Colonels was that their 8-3 record earned Nicholls State a berth to the Division I-AA playoffs. The bad news was that Nicholls ended up seeded last in the 16-team field and had to travel to take on the top-ranked and defending national champion University of Montana in Missoula, Montana.

Montana scored on its first possession and the Colonels were unable to execute their ball-control game plan and gave the Grizzlies a short field to work with, resulting in a 48-3 loss in the opening round of the Division I-AA playoffs.

Meanwhile, the Montana defense held Nicholls to only 129 total yards, including 64 rushing and 65 passing. By contrast, the Grizzlies passed for 447 yards and rolled up 545 yards of total offense.

With the game-time temperature at 27 degrees and a biting wind, Montana quarterback Brian Ah Yat, a native of Hawaii, connected on all four of his attempts in an opening six-play drive, including a 27-yard touchdown pass to Raul Pacheco. Ah Yat finished 30 of 48 passing for 363 yards.

"We were not used to playing on a frozen field," said Barbier. "It was like we were taking baby step and they were running like gazelles on an iced-over field. I guess it would have been different if they had come down here and we played in the swamp and they tried running through the swamp."

Although trailing 10-0 and outgained in first-quarter yardage 164-64, the Colonels were still in the hunt when Ricky Wilson returned an errant Ah Yat pass to the Montana 9-yard line. Nicholls lost yardage against a stout Montana defense and had to settle on a 42-yard Diel field goal. It would prove to be the only points for the Colonels.

"When we intercepted a pass early in the game and got down to the 5-yard line and we ended up kicking a field goal, I knew we were in a lot of trouble," said Barbier. "We were just overmatched. We had gotten our program to where we could compete in our conference but we were not ready to compete on a national scale at that time."

Greg Fitzgerald's block of a Quinn Guidry punt gave Montana the ball deep in Nicholls territory and set up a 12-yard touchdown run by Josh Branen. Another Ah Yat to Pacheco touchdown, this one from 11 yards out at the 3:05 mark of the second quarter made it 24-3 at the break. At halftime, the Colonels trailed in total yards 317-32.

Branen added a touchdown run in the second half and Justin Olsen hauled in a pair of scoring passes, one from Ah Yat and another by Darren Rowell. A Jack Dennehy interception of a Corey Lambert pass set up a Larson field goal with 1:57 left in the game to make the final 48-3 as Nicholls' turnaround season ended at 8-4.

"At the time, the reward was making the playoffs," Barbier said. "I don't think we ever had visions of winning a national championship. It would have been nice to go up there and upset them but to do that would have literally been another 'Miracle on Ice.'"

The biggest one-year turnaround in college football history earned Barbier the Eddie Robinson Award as the top coach in Division I-AA in 1996.

"The first year was such a learning experience. We made a few changes offensively and defensively. I kind of gave up by defensive coordinator's duties. I made a mistake my first year; I never should have done that. We made some administrative moves that made our team better, which allowed our kids to compete. Once we allowed our kids to compete and understand what we did better, we had some success. We had great character kids. That's why I was able to win the Eddie Robinson Award, because of the kids and the coaches."

While Troy State won the Southland title in its first year in the league, it was hardly the first-ever playoff appearance for the Trojans.

A former Division II national champion, Troy State advanced to the Division I-AA playoffs in each of the Trojans' previous three seasons as an independent prior to joining the SFL. Troy reached the I-AA semifinals in 1993 before being knocked out in the first round of the playoffs in 1994 and 1995.

Opening the playoffs at home, Troy and Florida A&M traded the lead six times in the contest.

Gregory, who rushed for 166 yards and two touchdowns, put the Trojans up for good at 29-25 with 6:57 remaining in the game on a tackle-breaking 15-yard run.

Trailing by four points, a 21-yard touchdown run by Gregory with 56 seconds left in the second quarter to cap a 90-yard drive, gave Troy a 13-10 halftime edge.

The Rattlers regained the lead on their first possession of the second half on a 20-yard pass from Florida A&M quarterback Oteman Sampson to Juan Torro. After Troy took a 19-17 lead on a 6-yard run by Jackson, the Rattlers countered once again. A 14-yard touchdown pass to Robert Wilson on a drive set up by a Gregory fumble and a two-point conversion gave Florida A&M a 25-19 advantage with 3:21 remaining in the third quarter. A 45-yard Huerkamp field goal less than a minute into the fourth quarter rallied the Trojans to within three points and set the stage for Gregory's game-winning score.

The teams moved the ball in opposite fashion. Gregory's yardage was part of a 273-yard effort by Troy State. Meanwhile, the Rattlers passed for 261 yards. Sampson was 20 of 38 passing in the contest.

Troy State's defense constantly harassed Murray State quarterback Mike Cherry in the Trojans' 31-3 home win over the Racers in the Division I-AA quarterfinals.

The Trojans' defense showed it meant business from the start, sacking Cherry on the first play from scrimmage. The befuddled Murray State quarterback ended up connecting on only 18 of 40 passing attempts for 180 yards and four interceptions. Troy's defense was just as stout against the run, holding the Racers to 27 yards on 12 carries.

With that sort of defensive effort, the Trojans put the game away by halftime. Jackson scored on a 1-yard run following Murray State's initial possession and Davis added a 6-yard touchdown run in the second quarter to give Troy a 14-0 halftime lead.

Murray State's only points came on a third-quarter field goal before the Trojans put an exclamation point on their victory with a 17-point final quarter. Huerkamp kicked a 27-yard field goal while Jackson and Terrell Smith each added 1-yard scoring runs for the 31-3 final.

The win over Murray State set up a trip to frigid Montana for the Trojans against the Grizzlies in the Division I-AA semifinals.

Maybe it was the frozen field that had been covered all week or perhaps it was just the quality of play by the Grizzles, but the Trojans were completely overwhelmed in a 70-7 rout.

If the game had lasted only two series, it would have been a different outcome for the Trojans. Pratt Lyons returned an errant Ah Yat pass 16 yards for a touchdown on Montana's second series of the game to give Troy State an early 7-0 lead.

With the Troy State offense unable to score in the game, Montana overcame the deficit later in the first quarter. Ah Yat rebounded from his early interception by tossing 6 yards to Mike Erhardt and 21 yards to Branen to give the Grizzles a 14-7 lead on their way to scoring 70 unanswered points.

Ah Yat fired two more touchdown passes in the second quarter, hooking up with Pacheco on a 31-yard strike and Joe Douglass from 5 yards out. Branen scored on a 2-yard run and Andy Larsen kicked a 25-yard field goal to give Montana a 38-7 halftime lead.

Montana passed for 454 yards in the game. Ah Yat finished 22 of 40 for 295 yards before giving way to Rowell, who threw for an additional 159 yards.

Troy State, which ended the 1996 season at 12-2, was limited to 34 yards rushing and 84 passing. The Trojans' top rusher was Smith with 22 yards on two carries, while Davis was 14 of 39 passing for 79 yards with two interceptions.

MCNEESE REACHES
DIVISION I-AA FINALS

For the second year in a row, the Southland added another football-playing member. The addition of Jacksonville State in Jacksonville, Alabama, in 1997 was the conference's second foray into the state of Alabama in as many years. The addition of the Gamecocks made the Southland Football League an eight-team conference.

Like rival Troy State, Jacksonville State was in its early stages of the transition from Division II to Division I-AA. Also like Troy, the Gamecocks enjoyed past success, winning the Division II national championship as recently as 1992.

Jacksonville State received a quick introduction into the SFL, facing Sam Houston State with only one game under its belt – a 47-42 loss to Southwest Missouri State. SHSU went into the game 0-2 with losses to Angelo State and Texas A&M.

The Gamecocks were seeking their first win under new coach Mike Williams.

Based on Jacksonville State's first-ever Southland Football League game, the Gamecocks may have figured life in the new league would be exciting.

Playing at Sam Houston State, the Gamecocks trailed the Bearkats 21-14 heading into the fourth quarter. Jacksonville State tied the game early in the fourth quarter on a 9-yard touchdown pass from quarterback Montressa Kirby to Ronald Bonner.

The game was still tied when Jacksonville State forced a Bearkats punt and got the ball back at the Gamecocks' 40-yard line with 2:58 left in the contest. Two runs by Kirby picked up 14 yards. Two pass completions to Bonner and another to Cedric Allen gave the Gamecocks a first down at the 13-yard line with less than a minute remaining in the game. Kirby went back to Bonner once again, connecting with the Jacksonville State receiver with 49 seconds left in the game to lift the Gamecocks to a 21-14 triumph in their first-ever SFL game and Williams garnering his initial victory.

Kirby finished with 354 yards passing and 74 rushing. Bonner and Joey Hamilton each topped 100 yards in receiving. Bonner hauled in 12 catches for 139 yards while Hamilton had 124 yards on eight receptions.

A 16-yard pass from Kirby to Hamilton produced the game's first score. After a 1-yard touchdown run by SHSU's Elmore Armstrong, Jacksonville State countered with a 3-yard scoring run by Michael Daies to give the Gamecocks a 14-7 lead after one quarter.

Armstrong broke a 14-14 tie at halftime with his second 1-yard touchdown run for the only points of the third quarter.

A week later, a pair of playoff teams from 1996 met to open SFL play when Troy State visited Nicholls State. The Trojans were off to a 3-0 start while Nicholls was 1-1.

Coming off an open date, well-rested Nicholls kicker Kyle Leisher, a freshman, booted a 29-yard field goal with 4:25 remaining in the game to lift the Colonels to a 22-20 victory over the defending SFL champions.

Nicholls built a 19-7 lead before the second-ranked Trojans rallied. Clifford Ivory's 76-yard return for a touchdown of an errant throw by Colonels quarterback Brad Zeller made the score 19-14 at the 4:43 mark of the third quarter. Troy took its only lead of the game with 9:03 remaining in the contest on a 4-yard run by Steven Kelley.

The Colonels went on a clock-eating five-minute drive to set up Leisher's game-winning kick. Nicholls defensive back Dedric Clark helped to preserve the victory by intercepting Adam Russell with 1:13 remaining in the contest.

Following a 34-16 non-conference loss to Alabama-Birmingham, the Gamecocks found out things might not be so easy in the SFL following a 27-6 home loss to McNeese State.

Jacksonville State faced a Cowboys team determined to prove the 3-8 season of 1996 was an aberration.

"They were embarrassed," McNeese coach Bobby Keasler said of his Cowboys. "When you go 3-8, people will talk about you. Just like when you are 13-1, people will talk about you. But they would rather be 13-1 than 3-8. It really worked on them. When they came in for two-a-days, I've never seen a group of kids grab it by the back end and go to work. They kept saying to each other that this will not happen again and that's just what they believed in."

Kirby found out the Cowboys meant business. The Gamecocks quarterback, who entered the game averaging 366 yards of total offense, was held to 63 yards passing and 5 rushing. The McNeese defense also intercepted six passes, including three from Kirby.

A 10-yard touchdown run by William Davis and a 23-yard Shonz LaFrenz field goal gave McNeese a 10-0 halftime lead. The Gamecocks' only score came on a 4-yard Kirby run in the third quarter but McNeese added a 66-yard touchdown pass from Blake Prejean to Chris Fontenot, a 47-yard return by Donnie Ashley and a LaFrenz field goal for the Cowboys' 21-point victory.

McNeese, which opened the season with wins over Southeastern Oklahoma, Southwest Missouri and Northern Iowa, moved to 4-0 overall while Jacksonville State dropped to 1-1 in the SFL and 1-3 overall.

In Natchitoches, Northwestern State was opening up SFL play against Nicholls State. The Demons were 1-1 on the season after starting with a loss to Southern, followed by a victory over Henderson State.

As with Nicholls State a week earlier, the Demons had a week off going into their SFL opener. Fresh legs allowed Northwestern State defenders to continually harass Zeller, the Nicholls State quarterback. Zeller was sacked five times and threw three interceptions in Northwestern State's 19-0 triumph.

The Demons drove 80 yards on the opening possession of the game, culminating the drive on a 26-yard pass from Brandon Emanuel to Chris Pritchett for a 7-0 lead. Northwestern made it 13-0 at halftime on a 19-yard pass from Warren Patterson to Pat Palmer.

Leading 7-0 late in the first quarter, the Demon defense ended a Nicholls threat when Kenny Wright intercepted a Zeller pass in the end zone.

Northwestern made the final 19-0 when Tony Maranto returned an interception 35 yards for a touchdown with less than five minutes remaining in the game. It was the safety's second interception return for a score of the 1997 season.

The only SFL matchup a week later saw seventh-ranked Troy State visiting a Southwest Texas team making its league debut under first-year coach Bob DeBesse. DeBesse, a former Bobcat player from 1978-80, took over as coach after serving the previous five years as offensive coordinator at the University of Minnesota. The Bobcats were off to a 2-1 start under their new coach. Southwest Texas won DeBesse's debut with a victory over Cal State-Sacramento. After being edged by Hofstra 28-24, SWT nipped Montana State 28-26.

It may or may not have had anything to do with a short week of preparation because of a Thursday night game, but the SWT-Troy State game was a showcase of turnovers.

The turnover woes even affected normally sure-handed Southwest Texas runner Claude Mathis, who lost two fumbles in the game. SWT managed a 17-14 halftime lead despite four turnovers. Troy State's turnovers proved more costly, with two of the miscues leading directly to Bobcat touchdowns.

David Williams scored on a 1-yard run to cap Southwest Texas' opening drive of the game but the Bobcats' turnovers began on the following two possessions when the SWT quarterback threw an interception and Mathis lost his first fumble of the contest.

Troy State failed to take advantage of the two mistakes and fell behind 14-0 when Russell, while under heavy pressure, had a pass deflected and intercepted by Brady Schley. Schley raced 56 yards to put the Bobcats on top by two touchdowns. SWT's defense came up with seven sacks in the game after the Trojans failed to allow a sack through their first four contests.

The Trojans put themselves back in the game by taking advantage of Southwest Texas' next two turnovers. Mathis' second fumble led to a 7-yard touchdown run by Kelley. After a field goal by SWT's Ross Doctoroff, an interception by Williams led to a 12-yard touchdown pass from Russell to Letrell Brown to make the score 17-14 at halftime.

Neither team scored again until late in the third quarter when Kent Laster's interception of a Russell pass led to a 25-yard touchdown run by Mathis. Mathis rushed for 159 yards in the game after a slow start.

Southwest Texas put the game away less than a minute into the fourth quarter when Russell, again under pressure, had his pass picked off by William Welch. Welch scooted 17 yards for a touchdown to give the Bobcats a 31-17 victory.

A full slate of Southland Football League games a week later saw Stephen F. Austin make its league debut at home against Jacksonville State. The Lumberjacks were off to a 3-1 start, with their only defeat being a 24-10 loss at Montana.

The Lumberjacks were in control from the start in their game against Jacksonville State. A 54-yard touchdown pass from Peyton Jones to Mikhael Ricks and a pair of Ryan Smith field goals gave Stephen F. Austin a 13-0 lead early in the second quarter. KaRon Coleman returned a punt 54 yards to set up his own 2-yard touchdown run two plays later for a 19-0 SFA advantage.

Jacksonville State's first score came when Marvelle Granville rambled 68 yards for a touchdown after Jones was stripped of the ball. The defensive end's touchdown made it 19-7 with less than a minute remaining in the third quarter.

Isiah Stoker scored on a 20-yard run early in the fourth quarter as SFA went on to take a 41-15 victory.

In Lake Charles, McNeese State showed it was worthy of its new No. 4 ranking with a 50-7 thrashing of Northwestern State.

McNeese only led 13-7 at halftime before exploding for 37 points in the second half. LaFrenz kicked five field goals while Prejean tossed two touchdown passes to Damien Morris and another to Davis.

The McNeese defense contributed to the scoring spree when Bruce Bolden returned an interception 47 yards for a touchdown and Ronnie McZeal raced 46 yards with a fumble return.

McNeese improved to 2-0 in the SLC and 6-0 overall, with Northwestern State falling to 2-3 overall and 1-1 in conference play.

"It was just unbelievable how we just totally fell apart," Northwestern State coach Sam Goodwin said. "I talked to the team that night. I was concerned about my job. We had a talented team and were 2-3 and it just looked bad."

Leisher, Nicholls State's freshman kicker, booted a game-winning field goal in the closing seconds for the second time in 1997 to lift the Colonels past Southwest Texas 29-28.

A high-scoring first half in Thibodaux saw the Bobcats take a 21-17 lead at intermission. Nicholls scored 17 points in the opening quarter on short touchdown runs by Terrence Spears and Nakia Lumar, along with a Leisher field goal. SWT countered with 21 points in the second quarter on a 2-yard keeper by Williams, a 30-yard pass from Williams to Cyril Adkins and a 5-yard run by Mathis.

Nicholls trailed 28-17 before scoring the final 12 points of the game. The rally began in the third quarter on Leisher's second field goal of the game, this one from 27 yards away. Tawaskie Anderson's 8-yard run early in the fourth quarter pulled the Colonels to within two points at 28-26.

The Colonels marched 71 yards for the winning score following a failed 27-yard Doctoroff field goal with 3:44 left in the game that was partially blocked by Ed Dillon. A 33-yard pass from Zeller to Kajuan Billings set up Leisher's game-winning field goal.

Nicholls moved to 4-2 overall and 2-1 in the Southland while SWT fell to 3-2 overall and 1-1 in the league.

Meanwhile, Troy State hosted a Sam Houston State team coming off an open date and both offenses seemed to take the first two quarters off as the squads battled through a scoreless opening half.

Joe Jackson scampered 59 yards with the first big play of the game with slightly less than five minutes remaining in the third period. Four plays later, Jackson scored from 14 yards out to give Troy State a 7-0 edge.

The Bearkats answered early in the fourth quarter on a 3-yard pass from senior Chad Schramek to Kevin Pesak to tie the game.

SHSU had a chance to win the game in regulation but James Dummer missed on a 42-yard field goal with one second remaining.

Dummer made amends moments later when another 42-yard attempt was successful to give the Bearkats a 10-7 lead at the start of overtime.

The Trojans turned to Jackson on their overtime possession. He got the call for seven carries, advancing the ball to the 1-yard line. On third-and-goal, Mareno Philyaw ran around left end on a quarterback keeper to give Troy a 13-10 triumph.

Troy State improved to 1-2 in the Southland Football League and 4-2 overall by snapping its two-game losing streak. Sam Houston State dropped to 0-2 in the SFL and 2-4 overall.

A week later, Stephen F. Austin looked to join idle McNeese State at 2-0 in the Southland Football League when the Lumberjacks visited Troy State.

Stephen F. Austin took a quick 7-0 lead in its game at Troy State in record fashion. Jones hit Ricks down the sideline for a 97-yard touchdown, the longest pass play in school history.

Most of the remainder of the game consisted of relatively short scoring possessions. One such drive came moments after Ricks' big catch when Troy State's Kelly scored on a 2-yard run to cap a 40-yard drive. The teams traded field goals for a 10-10 tie at the break.

The Lumberjacks took advantage of two third-quarter drives that began near midfield to put Stephen F. Austin on top. SFA began its opening possession of the second half at the Trojans' 49 and cashed in on a 30-yard Smith field goal. A 50-yard drive was culminated on a 20-yard pass from Jones to Freddy Lyons to give the Lumberjacks a 20-10 lead.

Lawrence Tynes provided the only points of the second half for the Trojans with a 31-yard field goal with 2:57 left in the game to account for the 20-13 final.

SFA moved to 2-0 in the Southland and 5-1 overall. Troy State, the defending conference champions, dropped to 1-3 in the league and 4-3 overall.

In Natchitoches, the Bobcats were the unfortunate opponent the day Northwestern State decided to retire the jersey of former Demons great and New Orleans Saints and Atlanta Falcons quarterback Bobby Hebert.

Perhaps drawing inspiration from the ceremonies, Patterson, the present-day Demons quarterback, fired three touchdown passes to Pritchett as Northwestern State built a 23-0 lead by the third quarter on the way to a 31-3 rout of Southwest Texas. Pritchett had scoring receptions of 76, 21 and 22 yards. The three receiving touchdowns tied the single-game school record last achieved by Hebert's former top target and future Miami Dolphin receiver Mark Duper.

The Demons' defense had as much to do with the rout as Patterson and Pritchett. Northwestern State held Mathis to 20 yards on 11 carries while sacking Williams seven times. The Demons limited the Bobcats to 67 yards, a Northwestern State record for fewest yards allowed to an opponent in a single game.

SWT's only points came on a field goal set up by a blocked punt.

The outcome left both teams 3-3 overall. Southwest Texas dropped to 1-2 in the Southland Football League while Northwestern State improved to 2-1.

Instead of last-second field goals in favor of Nicholls, it was a fourth-quarter turnover that proved costly to the Colonels in a 24-17 loss at Sam Houston State.

The game was tied 17-17 when the Bearkats' Carlton Fortson returned a Zeller interception 18 yards down to the Nicholls 31. Schramek, who came off the bench in the second half in relief of starter Albert Bradley, tossed an 18-yard touchdown pass to Armstrong to give SHSU a 24-17 lead with 12:04 left in the game.

Nicholls had taken a 17-14 halftime lead on a 13-yard run by Anderson, an 8-yard pass from Zeller to Rocky Curl and a 27-yard Leisher field goal. The Bearkats tied the game midway in the third quarter on a 28-yard Dummer field goal and the SHSU defense went on to blank the Colonels in the second half.

The Colonels fell to 4-3 overall and 2-2 in the Southland while Sam Houston improved to 3-4 overall and 1-2 in league play.

Stephen F. Austin's win over Troy State set up a battle of ranked teams that were both off to 2-0 Southland Football League starts when the Lumberjacks hosted McNeese State.

The Lumberjacks entered the game ranked No. 10 in the nation, while the Cowboys were No. 2. Also, both teams boasted stout defenses. SFA entered the game with the fourth-ranked defense in the nation while McNeese had allowed only three rushing touchdowns all season.

SFA managed to amass 345 yards of total offense but had trouble scoring against the Cowboys' defense. The only points produced in the first half came on a 15-yard touchdown run by Derrick Blaylock, only the fourth rushing touchdown allowed by McNeese.

The Lumberjacks' defense, meanwhile, held McNeese to minus-22 yards rushing and constantly harassed Prejean. The Cowboys' quarterback was sacked five times and SFA linebacker Jeremiah Trotter had four tackles for losses.

Smith connected on field goals of 32 and 47 yards in the second half to give Stephen F. Austin a 13-0 lead. McNeese got back in the game on a 6-yard run by Davis to cap one of the few sustained drives of the contest. Davis' touchdown capped a 71-yard, 13-play drive to make the score 13-7 with 6:56 remaining.

The Cowboys forced SFA to punt on the ensuing possession. Ashley raced 68 yards for an apparent touchdown. A holding penalty wiped out the score and three plays later, reserve quarterback Tim Leger threw an interception.

Stoker became the workhorse down the stretch, getting the ball 10 times in the next 11 plays as the Lumberjacks ran out the clock for a 13-7 triumph that left Stephen F. Austin as the only unbeaten team in SFL action.

The result left both teams 6-1 overall. SFA improved to 3-0 in the league as McNeese fell one game behind the Lumberjacks in the conference race.

In the only other SFL encounter that day, Nicholls State won at Jacksonville State to move to 3-2 in the league while extending the Gamecocks' losing streak to four games.

Nicholls managed to overcome four fumbles, pouring rain and a 17-minute delay because of lightning to gain its first road win of the season with a 16-14 victory over Jacksonville State.

The Colonels led 10-0 at halftime on a 24-yard Leisher field goal and a 3-yard run by Kendall Joseph. Jacksonville State gained the lead with a 14-point third quarter. The go-ahead touchdown came when the Gamecocks' Warren Blair jarred the football loose from Zeller, with Eric Mims scooping up the ball and sprinting 8 yards for the touchdown.

Nicholls, which was held to minus-4 yards in the third quarter, came up with the game-winning drive early in the fourth quarter. A 10-yard run by Joseph along with a personal-foul call against JSU got the Colonels rolling. Joseph later capped the 52-yard drive with a 4-yard touchdown run with 10:13 left in the game for a 16-14 edge. The victory marked the fourth time in the season Nicholls rallied for a win in either the fourth quarter or overtime.

The Colonels had lost all three of their previous road games before the victory at Jacksonville State. The win improved Nicholls to 5-3. Jacksonville State fell to 1-6 overall and 1-3 in the SFL.

Looking to remain unbeaten in Southland Football League play as well as extend its winning streak to five games, Stephen F. Austin fell behind 21-16 heading to the fourth quarter of the Lumberjacks' home game against Southwest Texas.

A 4-yard run by Stoker and a 37-yard Smith field goal gave SFA a 26-21 lead before Mathis put the Bobcats back on top at 28-25 on a 31-yard touchdown run with six minutes left in the game.

Stoker came through one more time, scoring on a 2-yard run to give the Lumberjacks a 31-28 triumph.

SWT built a 14-10 halftime lead with touchdowns in each of the first two quarters, including a 67-yard pass from Williams to D'Angelo Torres. The Lumberjacks' first-half points came on a 40-yard Smith field goal and a 41-yard run by Coleman.

Stephen F. Austin moved to 4-0 in the Southland and 7-1 overall. SWT fell to 1-3 in the league and 4-4 overall.

As SFA was moving to 4-0, McNeese State and Northwestern State both were looking to stay within a game of the league-leading Lumberjacks. McNeese's task involved a home game against Sam Houston State while Northwestern State was at Troy State.

McNeese saw the Bearkats take the lead less than three minutes into the game. Sam Houston State's Fabian Johnson blocked Brian Stewart's punt and Jeff Jones returned the loose ball 14 yards for a touchdown.

SHSU's early touchdown seemed to be a wake-up call for the Cowboys as McNeese responded with four unanswered scores to take a 24-7 lead by the third quarter. A 40-yard run by Davis and a 35-yard pass from Prejean to Fontenot gave the Cowboys a 14-7 lead after one quarter. A 1-yard run by Earnest McGowan gave McNeese a 21-7 lead at halftime that LaFrenz extended by three points on a 43-yard field goal in the third quarter. Earlier in the game, LaFrenz missed a field goal to snap his string of consecutive kicks at 13.

The Bearkats ended McNeese's scoring spree on a 1-yard run by Schramek to make the score 24-14 after three quarters. The Cowboys outscored SHSU 14-7 in the final quarter for the 38-21 final.

No. 8 McNeese improved to 3-1 in the SFL and 7-1 overall. The Bearkats dropped to 1-3 in the conference and 3-5 overall.

Meanwhile, on a field better suited for mud wrestling than football, Northwestern State eked out a 14-13 victory at Troy State to put the Demons back in the SFL race. The Demons improved to 3-1 in the conference and 5-3 overall with Northwestern's third-straight win. Troy State fell to 1-4 in the Southland and 4-5 overall.

Northwestern State scored on its opening drive when fullback Rob Robertson hauled in pass from Patterson on fourth-and-goal from the Trojans' 2-yard line. The conversion attempt failed when the ball went through the hands of Maranto, the Demons' holder, leaving Northwestern with a 6-0 lead.

Troy countered moments later when Andy Swafford returned the ensuing kickoff 88 yards to give the Trojans a 7-6 edge.

Wright, the Demons' sophomore safety, deflected an option pitch by the Trojans and recovered the loose ball at the Troy 28 to set up Northwestern's next score later in the first quarter.

Ronnie Powell eventually scored on a 3-yard run and Patterson hit Palmer with a two-point conversion pass with 1:09 remaining in the opening period to give the Demons a 14-7 lead.

Troy State came up with its only drive of the game in the second quarter, advancing 74 yards to set up a 2-yard keeper by Philyaw. This time, it was the Trojans' turn to botch the extra point on the muddy field as the ball slipped through the hands of Troy holder Wes Garner.

The one-point margin held up as Troy State never seriously threatened again, failing to advance any deeper than the Northwestern State 39 in a game that was delayed 25 minutes during halftime because of the foul weather.

Stephen F. Austin ran into a sharp Schramek in the Lumberjacks' Southland Football League road game the following week at Sam Houston State. The senior Bearkats quarterback passed for 350 yards and Bennie Wylie came up with late heroics to hand the seventh-ranked Lumberjacks their first conference loss while ending SFA's five-game winning streak. Facing fourth-and-1 with 1:22 remaining in the game, Wylie broke loose on a 48-yard touchdown scamper to give Sam Houston State a 33-27 victory.

The loss dropped the Lumberjacks to 4-1 in the SFL and allowed other league teams to get back into the thick of the conference race.

Wylie's score was his second of the game on fourth down. Earlier in the contest, he scored on fourth down from a yard out. Erik Polk added touchdown runs of 9 and 11 yards for the Bearkats.

SFA's first Southland loss dropped the Lumberjacks to 7-2 overall. Sam Houston State improved to 2-3 in the league and 4-5 overall.

McNeese State and Northwestern State both took advantage of SFA's loss. The Cowboys defeated Southwest Texas 31-21 while the Demons pounded Jacksonville State 42-21.

In San Marcos, Southwest Texas was looking to add to a 21-17 lead with a field-goal attempt late in the third quarter. The kick was blocked and McNeese's Delphfrine Lee scooped up the ball and raced 86 yards for a touchdown to put the Cowboys on top 24-21 on the final play of the third quarter. McNeese went on to add a 5-yard touchdown run by McGowan in the fourth quarter to give the Cowboys the 31-21 victory.

SWT led 7-3 after one quarter when Mathis, who rushed for 168 yards in the game, scored on a 32-yard run. McNeese countered with a 1-yard McGowan run and Prejean passed 21 yards to Morris. Williams tossed a 5-yard pass to Terrance Hatton and a two-point pass left the Cowboys with a 17-14 edge at halftime.

The Bobcats gained their only lead of the game when Williams scored on a 16-yard run prior to Lee's return of the blocked field goal.

McNeese improved to 8-1 overall. Southwest Texas fell to 1-4 in the conference and 4-5 overall.

In Natchitoches, Powell topped 200 yards rushing for the second time in the season, including a Northwestern State-record 93-yard touchdown run, to pace the Demons past Jacksonville State.

Along with forcing a three-way tie for the SFL lead, the Demons moved to 6-3 overall. The Gamecocks fell to 1-4 in the conference and 1-8 overall after dropping a school-record seventh-straight loss.

Robertson added three touchdowns on a pair of short runs and a 30-yard touchdown reception.

Kirby, the Jacksonville State quarterback, threw for 380 yards and two touchdowns but the Gamecocks were held to 16 yards rushing.

Stephen F. Austin, McNeese State and Northwestern State all won their games the following week to reach 5-1 in the Southland, meaning the league title would not be decided until the final week of the regular season.

If Stephen F. Austin had any doldrums remaining from the Sam Houston State loss, Ricks put the Lumberjacks at ease quickly when he scored on a 79-yard reception on SFA's second possession of the game against Nicholls State on SFA's way to a 39-7 home victory.

Perry Eliano's interception of a Zeller pass gave the ball to the Lumberjacks at the Colonels' 25. After a penalty backed up Stephen F. Austin, a 34-yard pass from Jones to Ricks set up 2-yard touchdown run by Coleman for a 13-0 SFA lead.

A 6-yard touchdown reception by Ricks made it 19-0 before Nicholls came up with its only score of the game on 2-yard run by Spears with 12:22 remaining in the second quarter. Big plays in the drive included a 59-yard pass to Julius Alcee and a 22-yard run by Zeller.

The only score of the second half was a 77-yard run by Stoker.

Stephen F. Austin improved to 5-1 in the SFL and 8-2 overall. Nicholls dropped to 3-3 in the conference and 5-5 overall.

Along with keeping pace in the SFL, the Cowboys made Bobby Keasler the winningest coach in McNeese State history with a 10-7 home win over Troy State.

Keasler picked up win No. 65 in his eighth season, edging past Jack Doland.

"It makes you feel like you are doing the right thing. There had been some good coaches to come through that university. It's quite an accomplishment by a lot of folks, players, staff, all your support group," Keasler said of the milestone win.

A 4-yard run by Prejean in the first quarter gave McNeese the lead in the low-scoring affair. The Trojans tied the game on a 27-yard run by Philyaw in the second quarter.

The Trojans looked to take the lead in the fourth quarter on a Clyde Williams field goal attempt. The kick was blocked and the Cowboys gained possession at their own 8-yard line. McNeese marched 60 yards to set up a 37-yard game-winning field goal by LaFrenz.

McNeese missed out on a couple of scoring opportunities earlier in the game. LaFrenz had one field goal blocked and missed another from 52 yards out when the ball hit the crossbar.

The Cowboys moved to 5-1 in the Southland and 9-1 overall. Troy State fell to 1-6 in the league and 4-6 overall.

Northwestern State, the only of the three contenders playing on the road, exploded for 21 third-quarter points to make sure it stayed a three-way race while running its winning streak to five games with a 35-19 victory over the Bearkats.

Leading 7-0 on a 1-yard run by Emanuel in the first quarter, the quarterback got the second-quarter scoring frenzy started with an 80-yard touchdown strike to Palmer.

Two interceptions led to the Demons' next two scores. The first came when a pass attempt by Schramek was batted by B.J. Williams, with the Northwestern defender snatching the football and sprinting 55 yards for a touchdown.

Maranto returned another Schramek interception 47 yards down to the 1-yard line. After a Demons penalty, Emanuel scored on an option keeper to put Northwestern on top 28-0. The pick was the sixth of the season for Maranto, who returned two interceptions for touchdowns earlier in the season.

A 5-yard touchdown run by Wylie in the third quarter and a 23-yard touchdown pass from Bradley to Larry Nixon early in the fourth quarter made the score 28-13 but the Bearkats could get no closer.

Powell missed out on his third 200-yard rushing game, finishing with 181, as Northwestern improved to 5-1 in the SFL and 7-3 overall. SHSU, which lost for the fourth time in its last six games, fell to 2-4 in the Southland and 4-6 overall.

In the only game that day with no SFL title implications, Southwest Texas won at Jacksonville State 35-27 in a game that focused on Mathis.

Needing only 38 yards to become the all-time career rusher in the Southland Football League, the senior runner got his 38 yards – and a whole lot more. When he was done, the Bobcats' All-American ran for 308 yards to give him a total of 4,606 yards with one game remaining in his career.

Playing on a Thursday night, the Demons earned a share of the Southland title with a 38-24 home win over Stephen F. Austin.

Involved in a three-way tie for the Southland Football League lead going into the game, the teams showed they were moving in different directions in the regular-season finale as the Demons won for the sixth-straight time while the Lumberjacks dropped two of their final three games.

The result left both teams 8-3 overall, but more importantly, the Demons moved to 6-1 in the SFL while the Lumberjacks finished 5-2.

Following a 3-3 tie after one quarter, Northwestern State scored three-straight times in the second quarter. A blocked punt and an interception helped to set up the first two scores of the quarter, a pair of 2-yard runs by Powell. The Demons running back finished with 126 yards and three touchdowns in the contest.

Northwestern's third touchdown of the quarter came on a 38-yard pass from Emanuel to Palmer. Emanuel passed for 288 yards in the game while Palmer finished with 216 yards, the most ever for a Demons player in a game. Palmer also ended the game with 99 receptions and 2,233 yards, both career records.

SFA managed to make it 24-10 at halftime on a 32-yard touchdown pass from Jones to Zach Woods with 18 seconds left in the second quarter.

Ricks caught a pair of touchdown passes for SFA and finished with 136 yards as the teams traded touchdowns in each of the final two quarters.

When Troy State played host to Jacksonville State in the 1997 season finale, also on a Thursday night, it marked the 59th time the teams met in The Ol' School Bell rivalry, although it was the first time as members of the Southland Football League.

Both teams already had secured losing seasons but the Trojans proved to be too much for the Gamecocks in a 49-0 rout.

Troy State managed to dominate despite being without Jackson or Kelley. Phillip Jones proved to be more than an adequate replacement as the tailback rushed for 145 yards and tied a school record with four touchdowns.

Of Phillip Jones' four touchdown runs, only one was a long as 9 yards out. Philyaw and Moreo Jones each added rushing touchdowns for the Trojans while Swafford returned a punt 69 yards for another score.

Phillip Jones' first two touchdowns were set up by turnovers. The first came following Antonio Thompson's interception of a Kirby pass and the other occurred after a T.J. Heatherly fumble recovery.

Aware of the results of the Northwestern State-Stephen F. Austin encounter from two days earlier, the Cowboys knew a win in the 1997 season finale at Nicholls State would give McNeese State a Southland Football League co-championship. It also would give McNeese the league's automatic bid to the Division I-AA playoffs by virtue of the Cowboys' 50-7 win over the Demons earlier in the season.

A 79-yard bomb from Prejean to Ashley on the second play from scrimmage signaled the type of big game that would unfold. Before the game was out, Prejean tossed two more touchdown passes of 65 and 34 yards, and linebacker Wayne Cordova returned an interception 24 yards for a touchdown in the Cowboys' 31-13 victory. Prejean finished the year with 2,062 yards passing, becoming the first quarterback in McNeese history to top 2,000 yards in a single season.

Nicholls added a big play of its own on a 64-yard pass from quarterback Brad Smith to Alcee in the fourth quarter, but by then it was much too late as the Colonels still trailed 24-13 on their way to the 31-13 loss.

No. 7 McNeese led 10-3 going into the fourth quarter before the two teams exploded for a combined 31 points in the final period.

The Cowboys finished the regular season 10-1 for the biggest single-season turnaround in school history after McNeese went 3-8 in 1996.

Nicholls concluded the season 5-6 overall, including 3-4 in the Southland.

The remaining game the final week of the regular season featured teams near the bottom of the SFL standings.

In San Marcos, Sam Houston State won a high-scoring 35-30 finale over Southwest Texas. The result left both teams 2-5 in the SFL and 5-6 overall. It was the sixth-consecutive losing season for Southwest Texas.

Sam Houston State built a 35-10 halftime lead as the Bearkats produced 321 yards in the opening two quarters. Leading the way was Schramek. In his final game, he passed for 263 yards and three touchdowns in the opening half.

A touchdown run by Williams with less than 12 minutes remaining in the game rallied the Bobcats to within 35-30 but SWT was unable produce points on its final three possessions in suffering the five-point loss to close the season.

Mathis was held to 63 yards rushing in the game, well below his season average of 154. He concluded his career as the Southland's all-time rusher with 4,691 yards. He also set a single-season conference mark with 1,595 yards.

While McNeese entered the playoffs as the top team from the Southland, Northwestern State earned an at-large playoff berth following its victory over SFA, sending the Demons to Spokane, Washington, to take on 10-1 Eastern Washington, the Big Sky Conference champion.

The Demons were no match for the Eagles, who scored on all five of their first-half possessions in building a 27-3 halftime lead en route to a 40-10 opening-round playoff victory.

Rex Prescott scored on a 41-yard run, Harry Leons tossed a 70-yard touchdown strike to Steve Correa and Josh Atwood kicked the first of his two field goals to give the Eagles a 17-0 lead after one quarter.

"We were never in the game," Goodwin said. "They had a couple of tight ends that were about 6-7 and probably 280. We had never seen anybody like that in our league.

"Defensively, we didn't have an answer for them."

The only points the Demons could muster in the first half came on a 37-yard Collins field goal. Atwood followed with a 22-yard kick and Prescott scored from a yard out to make it 27-3 at the break.

Prescott finished with 102 yards rushing. His backup, Mike McKenzie, rushed for 129 yards and a pair of touchdowns in the second half as the Eagles rolled up 241 yards on the ground.

Despite the lopsided loss, the Demons outgained Eastern Washington on the ground. Northwestern amassed 267 yards, 206 by Powell. It was Powell's third game of the season in which he rushed for more than 200 yards. Pritchett scored on a 10-yard run early in the fourth quarter for the only touchdown for Northwestern State, which ended its season 8-4.

McNeese State, meanwhile, held a 10-0 lead in the first half of its opening playoff game at home against Montana but the lead could have been more for the Cowboys.

Trailing by 10 points, the Grizzlies were forced to punt from deep in their own territory. Jake Dennehy's kick was blocked by Marcus LeBlanc and recovered by Jake Morrison at the 4-yard line. Dennehy made amends when he intercepted Prejean on the very next play. Montana responded with a 99-yard drive, with Brian Ah Yat's 17-yard pass to Jeremy Watkins pulling the Grizzlies to within three points at halftime.

Ah Yat was picked off by Lee at the Montana 34 midway in the third quarter. Davis raced 34 yards for an apparent touchdown but an illegal block against McNeese pushed the Cowboys to midfield. The Cowboys ended up settling on a 29-yard LaFrenz field goal for a 13-7 lead.

It took only 40 seconds for the Grizzlies to come up with a go-ahead touchdown in the closing minutes. With Montana held to minus-18 yards rushing, the Grizzlies' ability to move the ball was limited to the passing game. Ah Yat responded, completing two short passes to Travis Walker and a 24-yard gainer to

Raul Pacheco. The Montana quarterback drilled a 33-yard strike to Justin Olsen with 1:30 left in the game to put the Grizzlies on top 14-13.

McNeese started its final possession at the 20-yard line. A short pass from Prejean to Davis, along with a personal-foul penalty against the Grizzlies, moved the ball to the Cowboys' 47. A third-down conversion advanced McNeese to the Montana 32. Prejean tossed to Ashley at the 22, who fought off a would-be tackler and raced the remaining yards for the touchdown to give the Cowboys a 19-14 victory.

"We kept saying we owed those folks and we had them at home. When you come into Cowboys Stadium…and it was hot that night. Those big guys they had just melted, but we didn't. We hung in there with them and made some plays," said Keasler.

It was defense to the rescue and then some for McNeese State in its quarterfinal playoff game at Western Illinois.

A pass into the flat by Western Illinois quarterback Jeff Hecklinski was picked off by Jerod Jones. With an open field in front of him, Jones sprinted 69 yards for a touchdown to give the Cowboys a quick 7-0 lead.

That would prove to be the only touchdown of the first half. The Leathernecks rallied for two Keith Jones field goals to trail 7-6 at halftime but Western Illinois easily could have had the lead if not for the effort of the McNeese defense.

A fumble in the second quarter gave the Leathernecks the ball at the McNeese 5-yard line but when Western Illinois was unable to move the ball, it had to settle on a 24-yard Jones field goal. The Leathernecks drove inside the Cowboys' 10-yard line on their next possession but once again had to settle on a Jones field goal, this time from 32 yards away.

Just like Western Illinois, the Cowboys were unable to move the ball on offense, finishing with 151 total yards. Clinging to a one-point lead, McNeese increased its cushion when Ashley returned a punt 39 yards for a touchdown to put the Cowboys on top 14-6 with 3:34 left in the fourth quarter.

Western Illinois' Aaron Stecker, a future NFL running back, scored on a 3-yard run with 8:24 left in the game but when a two-point conversion pass attempt failed, McNeese was able to hold on for a 14-12 triumph. Stecker's touchdown extended his scoring streak to 13-straight games, although the Cowboys held him to under 100 yards rushing for only the third time all season.

McNeese, which moved to 12-1 in advancing to the semifinals, won the game despite not scoring on offense in a game played in frigid temperatures.

"That is the coldest I've ever been in my life," Keasler declared. "They had to put something on the field because the field was solid ice. They had played on it and it had gotten kind of muddy, and all of a sudden, it was strictly ice. We go in after warm-ups and had to change socks because we had ice in our socks. We got back out and it's 19 degrees and we pulled that out. We like to froze to death but the kids played well."

Following a scoreless first quarter, the Cowboys fell behind 7-0 in their semifinal game at the University of Delaware after a 7-yard run by Craig Cummings. McNeese responded with two touchdowns later in the quarter on a 13-yard run by Davis and a 70-yard bomb from Prejean to Morris to give the Cowboys a 14-7 lead at halftime.

A 21-yard LaFrenz field goal made it 17-7 but Delaware closed to 17-14 by the end of the third quarter on a 33-yard pass from Matt Nagy to Cummings. Nagy's 20-yard pass to Greg McGraw early in the fourth quarter put the Blue Hens on top 21-17.

LaFrenz booted a 31-yard field goal with 6:09 left in the game to pull the Cowboys to within one point at 21-20.

Trailing by a point, McNeese faced fourth-and-1 at its own 48. Prejean tossed in the direction of Fontenot. The ball almost was intercepted by Dominick Banks but Fontenot fought off the Delaware defender for a 4-yard gain to keep the drive alive.

"We had been running that stretch play and I suggested why don't we run a bootleg off that and hit the tight end in the flat and get a first down. We needed about three yards," Keasler recalled.

The Cowboys drove 57 yards to set up LaFrenz for a potential game-winning field goal from 31 yards – the same distance he hit from moments earlier to make it a one-point contest. The Blue Hens called timeout with five seconds left in the game in an attempt to ice the kicker. LaFrenz's kick was true once again for a 23-21 win to send McNeese to the national championship game for the first time in school history.

"We were very lucky to have good kickers," Keasler said. "We were going to be good on defense and be good in the kicking game. We had people in the kicking game that could hurt you, even our punter. We just felt we did a good job with the kicking game."

McNeese State's semifinal win sent the Cowboys to the national championship game in Chattanooga, Tennessee, against a Youngstown State team that already had won three national titles in the 1990s.

For a team making its first appearance in the national finals and feeling understandable jitters, the Cowboys couldn't have asked for much better field position to open the game. McNeese began each of its first three offensive possessions beyond its own 40-yard line.

Despite the favorable field position, however, the Cowboys had little to show for it in terms of points. The opening possession stalled when an offensive face-mask penalty erased a first-down play.

On McNeese's second possession, Fontenot dropped what seemed like a sure touchdown catch, causing the Cowboys to settle on a 22-yard LaFrenz field goal.

"People said, 'if he had caught that we would have won.' I said, 'yeah, if he hadn't of caught the one at Delaware we wouldn't be here,'" said Keasler.

McNeese came away with no points on its third possession when Youngstown's Mike Stanec blocked LaFrenz's 41-yard field goal attempt.

The Penguins, meanwhile, came up with a 21-yard Mark Griffin field goal with 2:19 remaining in the second quarter for a 3-3 tie at halftime.

LaFrenz kicked third-quarter field goals of 37 and 46 yards to give McNeese a 9-3 lead going into the fourth quarter.

The Cowboys were in possession of the ball and clinging to their six-point advantage when Penguins linebacker Jeff Fackrell intercepted a Prejean pass. The only turnover of the game gave Youngstown the ball at its own 34-yard line midway in the fourth quarter.

"We are driving down again, all we had to do was kick another field goal and then we threw an interception. You can't throw interceptions; you can't fumble the ball, not when it's that close of a game. You can't make mistakes and we made a mistake and lost the ball game," said Keasler.

Penguins quarterback Demond Tidwell opened the drive with a 22-yard pass to tight end Tim Tyrell. Following an 8-yard completion to Willis Marshall, Tidwell hooked up with Mark Cox for a 14-yard gain down to the McNeese 7-yard line.

Tidwell was sacked on third down by Charles Ayro but the Cowboys' linebacker was flagged for grabbing Tidwell's facemask. Ayro had poked Tidwell in the eye during the incident and the quarterback had to leave the game for a play. Backup quarterback Jared Zwick entered the game and fumbled the snap. A false start had been committed by the offense, so the fumble was nullified.

Back in the game, Tidwell sent Cox into motion. As Cox passed receiver Renauld Ray, the ball was snapped. In man-to-man coverage, two defenders were opposite Cox and Ray. Both defenders followed Cox and Ray was left open in the left corner of the zone. Tidwell spotted Ray and the 9-yard touchdown toss with 8:08 remaining handed the Cowboys a heart-breaking 10-9 loss.

McNeese ended the season 13-2, falling in the lowest-scoring championship game in the history of the Division I-AA playoffs.

It was an especially bitter loss, considering how far the Cowboys had come in a year's time.

"The kids had busted their cans coming off a 3-8 season and play in THE game and fall short by one point, it's like cutting your heart out," said Keasler.

DEMONS REACH I-AA SEMIFINALS
FOR FIRST TIME

For the first time in three years, the Southland did not add a new member to its ranks. There also were no head coaching changes, so the league featured a sense of stability, if not headline-grabbing moments, going into the 1998 season.

Most teams had three games of experience going into the opening weekend of conference play.

In one of the openers, Jacksonville State visited Nicholls State. The Gamecocks went into the encounter 2-1. A 19-13 triumph over Alabama A&M in the season opener snapped a nine-game losing streak for Jacksonville State. The Gamecocks' lone loss was a high-scoring 51-32 defeat at powerhouse Georgia Southern.

The Colonels went into the game 1-1.

Jacksonville State opened at a Nicholls State team that was playing on its home field for the first time in 1998. Colonel fans were naturally excited to see their team play, but the Nicholls band proved to be a bit too exuberant.

After Nicholls scored on a 2-yard run by Kendrick Barnes to give the Colonels a 20-15 lead with 1:38 left in the game, the Gamecocks got the ball back one last time.

Jacksonville State quickly drove downfield, aided by an unsportsmanlike penalty against the Nicholls band. Earlier in the game, the band had been warned for playing while the Gamecocks had the ball. Jacksonville State quarterback Montressa Kirby fired a 13-yard touchdown strike to Ronald Bonner with three seconds left in the game to give the Gamecocks a 21-20 triumph.

Nicholls had built a 14-9 halftime lead thanks to two big plays by Colonel defender Robert Martin. From deep in Jacksonville State territory, Martin stripped Daniel Kirkland of the ball, with Murphy Edwards recovering in the end zone for a 7-0 lead late in the first quarter. The Colonels' other score in the first half came in the second quarter when Martin hit Kirby's arm as the quarterback attempted to pass, with Terry Irby recovering at the Nicholls 33. Eight plays later, Sullivan Turner scored on a 2-yard run to make it 12-3. After the Gamecocks scored on a 14-yard touchdown pass by Kirby, a blocked conversion attempt was returned by Kevin Johnson for two points to give the Colonels their five-point halftime lead.

Also opening up SFL play that day were Northwestern State and Southwest Texas State. The Demons were off to a 3-0 start while the Southwest Texas was 2-1.

The "big play" sunk Southwest Texas against No. 8 Northwestern State. Three of the Demons' touchdowns came from at least 38 yards and another long-distance play set up an additional score in SWT's 34-10 loss.

A 74-yard bomb from Warren Patterson to Eric Granger set up the Demon quarterback's 6-yard touchdown toss to T.J. Sutherland to give Northwestern State the early lead. Patterson connected with Granger on a 46-yard strike on the Demons' next possession to make it 14-0.

Jermaine Jones returned a Bobcats' fumble 74 yards for a touchdown for a 21-0 Northwestern State lead after one quarter.

Patterson hooked up with Ronnie Powell on a 38-yard touchdown pass right before halftime as the Demons took a 28-3 lead to the locker room.

The only touchdown for Southwest Texas came on a 6-yard run by ReShawn Brown in the fourth quarter. Brown was held to 38 rushing yards and the Bobcats were limited to 147 total yards. Brown's score was the first touchdown in 10 quarters for the Bobcats.

The Demons' Purple Swarm defense recorded 10 sacks and held the Bobcats to 147 total yards as Northwestern improved to 4-0 for the first time since 1980.

It was career victory No. 100 for Sam Goodwin as a college coach, including a mark of 91-78-3 as Demons coach.

An inspired Jacksonville State team was back in Southland Football League action five days later when the Gamecocks hosted Stephen F. Austin. With a conference win already under their belt and playing before a televised audience, the Gamecocks were looking to go 2-0 for the first time ever in league play on the Division I-AA level. Plus, a fourth win of the season would double Jacksonville State's victory total of the previous two years combined.

Stephen F. Austin, meanwhile, went into the game 1-3 on the season.

With that as the backdrop, the Gamecocks jumped out to a 16-7 first-quarter lead.

Excellent field position due to a pair of Eurosius Parker punt returns set up Jacksonville State's first two scores. After starting the first possession at the SFA 38 the Gamecocks had to settle on a 37-yard Brad Hopkins field goal. Kirby capped a short drive on a 14-yard draw for a 10-0 lead.

The Lumberjacks made it 10-7 when KaRon Coleman took a handoff from Peyton Jones and then passed to the SFA quarterback for a 9-yard touchdown pass. Kirby hooked up with Joey Hamilton on a 66-yard scoring strike with two seconds left in the opening quarter for Jacksonville State's 16-7 lead.

Stephen F. Austin made it 16-13 with a 42-yard Mike McCary field goal in the third quarter but the Lumberjacks would get no closer in falling 22-16.

Two days later, 3-1 Troy State and 2-2 Sam Houston State played their first Southland Football League game of the 1998 season when the Trojans visited the Bearkats.

The Trojans allowed the Bearkats to rally to within three points midway in the fourth quarter of their encounter but would let SHSU get no closer in Troy State's 17-14 victory.

Trailing 17-7, Matt Buss hit Matt Dominguez with a 15-yard touchdown pass to pull Sam Houston State to within a field goal. Buss got SHSU on the scoreboard in the second quarter on a 38-yard touchdown toss.

Lawrence Tynes, a kicker on two Super Bowl-winning New York Giant teams, kicked three field goals in the game for the Trojans. Troy State's only touchdown came on Thad Buttone's 11-yard halfback pass to quarterback Brock Nutter.

"Lawrence Tynes has certainly proved his mettle over the years," said Troy State coach Larry Blakeney.

The close result, said, Blakeney, was typical of the Trojans' tenure in the Southland.

"None of them (wins in the Southland) were easy. There were some great coaches and really great players and teams in that league," said Blakeney.

Playing on a Thursday a week later in Thibodaux, Nicholls State and Sam Houston State were the next Southland Football League teams to play coming off a short week of preparation.

Being at home seemed to work in the Colonels' favor early in the game as Nicholls built a 30-14 halftime lead on a 4-yard run by Tawaskie Anderson, a 94-yard interception return by Aaron Smith, a 60-yard pass from Brad Zeller to Curtis Johnson, a 28-yard run by Zeller, and a 41-yard Kyle Leisher field goal.

The Bearkats wiped away a 19-point deficit in the second half. A 33-yard pass from Buss to Jonathan Cooper and a 3-yard run by Elmore Armstrong inched SHSU closer before James Dummer connected on a 28-yard field goal to tie the game 33-33 with 5:49 remaining.

Nicholls then used a pass interference call, a 17-yard pass from Zeller to Julius Alcee and a 17-yard run by Johnson to set up a 38-yard game-winning Leisher field goal with 1:46 left in the game.

SHSU fell to 0-2 in conference play and 2-4 overall. Nicholls evened its league mark at 1-1 while improving to 2-3 overall.

Two days later, McNeese State played its opening SFL game when the Cowboys hosted Jacksonville State. McNeese entered the game 4-0 and as the top-ranked team in Division I-AA.

The Cowboys' Jessie Burton had taken the SFL by storm. In the season opener against Southeastern Oklahoma, he broke loose on a 47-yard touchdown run on his first carry as a collegiate player on his way to a 142-yard performance. In McNeese's win over Southern Utah, Burton had seven rushing touchdowns and 42 points to set new McNeese marks while also tying the Southland Conference and Division I-AA records.

Against Jacksonville State, McNeese trailed at halftime for only the second time all season, falling behind 14-7. Kirby scored on a 1-yard run with 12 seconds remaining in the first quarter for a 6-0 Gamecocks lead. A 37-yard halfback pass from Tywone Dyson to Hamilton and a two-point conversion made the score 14-0 with 6:08 remaining in the opening half.

The Cowboys pulled to within a touchdown at halftime on a 1-yard run by Burton with 1:21 remaining in the opening half.

McNeese's late first-half score was the start of 30 unanswered points for the Cowboys. In a 23-point second half, Blake Prejean tossed a pair of touchdown passes, Ronnie McZeal returned an interception 37 yards for a touchdown and Shonz LaFrenz added a field goal.

The Cowboys improved to 5-0 by winning its SFL opener. Jacksonville State fell to 2-1 in the league and 4-2 overall.

With one loss between the two teams and both off to 1-0 starts in the Southland Football League, McNeese State's game at Northwestern State the following week classified as a showdown.

The defending league co-champions also were among the best in the nation. McNeese was top-ranked in Division I-AA while Northwestern State was No. 8.

Northwestern marched 75 yards with the opening possession of the game. Powell's 2-yard run gave the Demons a 7-0 lead less than five minutes into the contest.

The early touchdown was no harbinger for a high-scoring game. After Northwestern State's quick touchdown, the Demons would not score again until the fourth quarter.

Things were just as tough for the McNeese offense. The Cowboys' first seven possessions produced four turnovers, two punts and one lone field goal.

Trailing 7-0 late in the first half, McNeese faced first-and-10 from the Demons' 12-yard line. William Davis, who had switched from wide receiver to running back in 1997 and was now back at receiver, appeared to haul in a touchdown pass from Prejean but Northwestern State defender Mike Green stripped the ball from the receiver.

McNeese State coach Bobby Keasler viewed the play differently than the officials.

"We threw a touchdown pass in the end zone. As soon as we caught it, (Davis) made two steps and the Northwestern State guy ripped it out and they called it incomplete," Keasler said.

The Cowboys ended up having to settle on a 20-yard LaFrenz field goal with seven seconds remaining in the second quarter to trail by four points at the break.

Still down by four points, the Cowboys traveled 97 yards in the closing seconds of the third quarter. Burton, the SFL's leading rusher was held to 61 yards in the game but came up with his most important carry of the day, a 15-yard scamper for a touchdown to give McNeese a 10-7 lead with 51 seconds remaining in the quarter.

With the Demons' offense shut down following their opening score, the Northwestern State defense provided a helping hand early in the fourth quarter. Prejean, who had not thrown an interception all year, was picked off by Northwestern's Jones at the McNeese 44.

It took seven plays, including a key third-and-11 conversion, to give the Demons the lead at 14-10 on a 2-yard run by Patterson with 9:51 left in the game.

McNeese threatened later in the game, reaching the Northwestern 20-yard line but a 6-yard gain on a pass from Prejean to Eric Chew on fourth down came up a yard short. Jones intercepted a Prejean pass on the final play of the game to preserve the win for the Demons.

The result left both teams 5-1 overall. Northwestern State moved into a two-way tie for first place in the SLC with a 2-0 mark, while McNeese dropped to 1-1 in the league.

A Thursday playing date for Stephen F. Austin's SFL opener against Jacksonville State was followed by an open date, meaning the Lumberjacks had a gap of 16 days between their game against the Gamecocks and SFA's home contest versus Troy State.

If the Lumberjacks didn't work on stripping the ball with their extra preparation time, it sure would have been a surprise to Troy State. The Trojans turned the ball over on their first play from scrimmage and four times over the opening nine minutes of the contest.

SFA took a bit of advantage from the turnovers yet led only 13-7 at halftime. McCary kicked an early 28-yard field goal and Isiah Stoker scored on a 3-yard run. McCary added a 40-yard field goal as the second quarter expired for the Lumberjacks' 13-7 edge.

Troy State's lone score of the first half came on an 11-yard run by Wayne Thomas to make the score 10-7 moments prior to McCary's second field goal.

Stoker broke loose on a 72-yard ramble early in the fourth quarter for a 20-7 SFA lead before the Trojans countered on a 13-yard pass from Nutter to Callarious Williams to make the score 21-14 with 12:41 remaining in the game.

The Trojans moved from their own 39-yard line to the Stephen F. Austin 32 late in the game before Brian Sullivan hit the arm of a scrambling Nutter. The Troy State quarterback fumbled, with Sullivan recovering with 1:25 left in the game to secure the victory for SFA. It was Sullivan's second fumble recovery of the game and the last of the Trojans' six turnovers.

The outcome left both teams 1-1 in the SFL. The Lumberjacks improved to 2-4 in snapping a three-game losing streak while the Trojans slipped to 4-2.

One game not played the same day as the Northwestern State-McNeese State and SFA-Troy State games was Nicholls State's contest at Southwest Texas. The game had to be postponed because of heavy flooding in the San Marcos area. The result of the postponed game, coupled with an open date for Southwest Texas following its non-conference game against Southern Illinois, gave the Bobcats a 19-day break before playing their next game at Troy State.

The Bobcats seemed to be chomping at the bit to get some game action. SWT opened the game by going on a 77-yard drive in 14 plays and used up 7:18 to set up a Doctoroff field goal. Southwest Texas, which would be held to 10 yards rushing in the game on 33 attempts, would not score again until the fourth quarter.

Troy State grabbed the lead late in the first quarter on a 4-yard run by Al Lucas. The defensive lineman lined up in the backfield and scored two plays after a fumble by SWT quarterback Spergon Wynn.

Neither team would score again until the Trojans marched 90 yards to open the second half. An 18-yard pass from Nutter to Williams put Troy on top

14-3. A career-best 42-yard field goal by Tynes gave the Trojans their biggest lead of the game at 17-3 only four seconds into the fourth quarter.

With Southwest Texas unable to generate any offense following its opening drive, the Bobcats' defense helped to put SWT back in the game. A fumble by Troy State's Tony Donelson at the Trojans' 28 set up a 17-yard run by Wynn two plays later. A fumble by Thomas on Troy's next possession at the 33 set up a touchdown strike to James Stewart one play later. Two touchdowns in a span of 28 seconds allowed the Bobcats to tie the game 17-17 with 4:31 remaining in the fourth quarter.

The Trojans would have the last say when Nutter hooked up with Daniel Brown for a 42-yard gain to set up an 18-yard Tynes field goal with 1:50 left on the clock to give Troy State a 20-17 triumph.

SWT dropped to 0-2 in the Southland Football League and 2-4 overall. Troy State improved to 2-1 in the conference and 5-2 overall.

Perhaps experiencing a letdown after an upset of then top-ranked McNeese, Northwestern State, now No. 4 in the nation, managed only a 7-3 halftime lead at Nicholls State. A 4-yard run by Brian Jacquet was countered by a 27-yard Leisher field goal to account for the halftime score.

The offenses for both teams finally got on track, combining to score on four-straight possessions early in the second half.

Jacquet's second short touchdown run, this one from a yard out, extended Northwestern's lead to 14-6. Nicholls answered with a 3-yard dive by Anderson but a two-point conversion pass from Zeller to Jarrad Poirrier was stopped short, allowing the Demons to cling to a 14-12 edge.

Three plays later, Patterson hooked up with Chris Pritchett on a 77-yard touchdown toss to extend the Northwestern State lead to 21-12. The Colonels responded once again, this time Sullivan Beard out-leaped a Demons defender to bring down a 39-yard pass to set up a 1-yard Anderson run and the Colonels again trailed by two points, this time at 21-19 with 40 seconds remaining in the third quarter.

Each team missed field goals in the second half before Patterson teamed up with Granger on a 26-yard touchdown pass to give the Demons what appeared to be a comfortable 28-19 lead with 3:36 left in the contest.

The stubborn Colonels gave it one more rally attempt. A 57-yard pass from Zeller to Kajuan Billings set up a 2-yard run by the Nicholls quarterback to make it 28-26 with 1:43 left in the game.

An onside kick attempt was recovered by Northwestern's David Jones and returned to the Nicholls 23. The Demons were able to run out the final 1:38 to escape with a two-point victory that moved Northwestern to 3-0 in the Southland and 6-1 overall. Nicholls fell to 1-2 in the conference and 2-4 overall.

For the second week in a row, the Cowboys fell behind when an opponent marched for a touchdown on the opening possession of the game. This time, it was a 3-yard pass from Jones to KaRon Coleman to give Stephen F. Austin a 7-0 lead at Lake Charles.

McNeese, now ranked No. 5 in the nation, answered with two second-quarter touchdowns to take a 14-7 lead at intermission. The Cowboys tied the game on a 14-yard run by Sherif Lott, who was subbing for an injured Burton. McNeese gained the lead when linebacker Wayne Cordova returned an interception 20 yards for a touchdown.

The Cowboys increased their lead to 10 points at 17-7 on a third-quarter field goal by LaFrenz. A 9-yard touchdown pass from SFA's Travis Fallon to Nasser Avyad later in the third quarter and a 27-yard McCary field goal midway in the fourth period tied the game 17-17.

McNeese won the game when LaFrenz kicked a 26-yard field goal with 1:33 remaining in the game.

The Cowboys improved to 2-1 in the Southland and 6-1 overall. SFA fell to 1-2 in the conference and 2-5 overall.

Meanwhile, teams going in the opposite directions met when Jacksonville State hosted Sam Houston State.

Kirby, who passed for 174 yards and three touchdowns, hit Jake Carlton with a 20-yard scoring toss to break a tie and give the Gamecocks a 17-10 halftime lead. Kirby hooked up with Hamilton on a 39-yard pass less than a minute into the fourth quarter for a 24-10 advantage on Jacksonville State's way to a 31-19 victory.

Jacksonville State moved to 2-1 in the Southland and 6-2 overall, clinching the Gamecocks' first winning season since 1995. SHSU's fifth-straight defeat dropped the Bearkats to 0-3 in the conference and 2-5 overall.

Both Southwest Texas and Stephen F. Austin had their share of first-half struggles in another Thursday night SFL affair, this time in San Marcos.

A dropped pass in the end zone by Drew Svoboda on what appeared to be a sure touchdown and two missed field goals by McCary led to a scoreless first half for Stephen F. Austin. Luckily for the Lumberjacks, the game was a defensive battle as the Southwest Texas offense had its own struggles.

A 30-yard interception return by Southwest Texas cornerback Kendall Jones to the Bobcats' 48 set up the only score of the first half. Wynn hooked up with tight end Justin Young on a 14-yard scoring strike to give the Bobcats a 7-0 lead in the first quarter.

The lone score would hold up until the Lumberjacks came up with a big break late in the third quarter. A bad snap over the head of SWT's Rick Barrow deep in Bobcats territory forced the Southwest Texas punter to run down the ball at his own 6-yard line. SWT's defense held, but on a 21-yard field goal attempt, holder Chad Stanley tossed to Svoboda. This time Svoboda held onto the ball for a 4-yard touchdown to tie the game 7-7.

Three pass completions by Wynn on a fourth-quarter drive, two to D'Angelo Torres and one to Stewart, advanced the ball to the SFA 12-yard line. Torres' first catch was good for 38 yards to kick-start the drive. Wynn faked a handoff before racing to his right for the 12-yard touchdown to put the Bobcats on top 14-7.

Southwest Texas stopped two late SFA drives. One ended on a Marcus Pierce interception. In the final two minutes, Sterling Rogers deflected a pass on fourth down to preserve the seven-point triumph for the Bobcats.

The Bobcats improved to 1-2 in the SFL and 3-4 overall. Stephen F. Austin fell to 1-3 in the league and 2-6 overall.

Two days later, a 41-yard run by Tony Taylor on Northwestern State's opening possession against Troy State gave the Demons an early lead in a key Southland Football League game in Natchitoches. Playing in place of injured Powell, the red-shirt freshman rushed for a game-high 161 yards.

Phillip Jones' 3-yard option run tied the game 7-7. The Demons regained the lead 10-7 on a 41-yard Thomas LaToof field goal. The field goal was set up by a Trojan fumble at the Troy 20 late in the first quarter.

Troy State moved ahead on the following possession on a 6-yard touchdown run by Thomas for a 14-10 Trojans lead early in the second quarter. Thomas finished with 101 yards rushing and Jones had 118 yards as both backs topped 100 yards in the contest.

Northwestern missed out on a chance to take the lead in the third quarter following a blocked punt. The Demons reached the Troy State 3-yard line before a pass intended for Joel Comeaux was tipped and intercepted by Antonio Thompson in the end zone with less than five minutes remaining in the quarter.

The only points either team could muster in the second half came on a 24-yard LaToof field goal as the Demons moved to within one point at 14-13. Northwestern had a third-and-1 at the 5-yard line but Jacquet was tossed for a 2-yard loss, forcing the Demons to settle on LaToof's field goal.

Troy used up the final 5:21 of the clock with a 12-play, 68-yard drive to hold on for the win that left both teams 6-2 overall. The loss snapped a nine-game home winning streak for the Demons. It also ended a six-game win streak for Northwestern State in conference play.

The result left both Troy State and Northwestern State 3-1 in the SFL. Idle Jacksonville State also sat at 3-1 and McNeese State could join the crowd with a win at Sam Houston State.

Lott again proved to be a more than an adequate replacement for Burton, rushing for three touchdowns in McNeese State's 35-13 win to force a four-way tie atop the SFL.

No. 5 McNeese led 21-6 at halftime on a 10-yard run by Lott, a 4-yard pass from Prejean to tight end Pat Matthews and a 74-yard fumble return by safety Joe Judge. The Bearkats' only points came on a pair of field goals by Dummer.

Lott scored on a pair of 1-yard runs in the second half. SHSU was able to respond with only a 2-yard Buss run in the Cowboys' victory.

Along with the tie for first place in the Southland, McNeese improved to 7-1 overall. Sam Houston State dropped to 0-4 in the conference and 2-6 overall.

All four teams atop the Southland Football League were in conference action a week later as the schools looked for some separation going into the stretch drive of the season.

Two of the teams with 3-1 SFL records met when Northwestern State visited Jacksonville State.

Taylor showed his performance in the Troy State game was no fluke, rushing for 230 yards and three touchdowns in Northwestern State's 53-36 win at Jacksonville State.

Jacksonville State scored on four of its first five possessions, including three touchdowns in the second quarter to build a 28-17 first half lead. The Gamecocks' scores came on a 1-yard run by Kirby and a pair of Kirby touchdown passes.

Northwestern State, now ranked No. 9, came up with the first three touchdowns of the second half to build a 39-28 lead. Taylor started things off with a 1-yard touchdown run, his second rushing touchdown of the game. Fullback Dick Drago added a 5-yard touchdown run and Jones returned a punt 47 yards for a touchdown to account for the other two scores. The Demons scored on six-straight possessions behind backup quarterback Brad Spangler, who replaced an injured Patterson in the second quarter.

After Jacksonville State rallied to 39-36 on a 47-yard pass from Kirby to Hamilton, Jacquet countered with a 1-yard touchdown run with 1:10 left in the third quarter to extend the Demon advantage to 46-36. Taylor's third touchdown run of the game from 12 yards out midway in the fourth quarter accounted for the final margin

"I thought the Jacksonville State game was the turning point of the season," Demons coach Sam Goodwin said. "We didn't play too well against Nicholls. Jacksonville State was not a powerhouse, but at half, we're behind and Patterson got hurt. The only guy we had was Brad Sprangler. Sprangler was about 5-9, 170 pounds. He's not real strong or real fast. I really thought our season was probably over. If we don't win that one, we're done."

The win allowed the Demons to, at worst, remain tied for the SFL lead at 4-1 as Northwestern improved to 7-2 overall. Jacksonville State, suffering its first loss of the season at home, fell to 3-2 in the Southland and 6-3 overall.

McNeese State joined Northwestern State at 4-1 with a 27-0 blanking of Southwest Texas in Lake Charles as a healthy Burton rushed for 122 yards and two touchdowns.

Now ranked No. 3, the Cowboys built a 20-0 halftime lead with a 17-point second quarter. Leading 3-0 following a 33-yard LaFrenz field goal in the first quarter, McNeese put the game away before halftime on a 3-yard run by Burton, a 62-yard punt return by Davis and a 24-yard LaFrenz field goal.

The only points of the second half came on Burton's 3-yard touchdown run.

McNeese's defense held the Bobcats to 16 yards rushing and sacked SWT quarterbacks 12 times. Defensive end Blair Bradley had four of the sacks for the Cowboys.

The Cowboys improved to 4-1 in the SFL and 8-1 overall. Southwest Texas fell to 1-3 in the conference and 3-5 overall.

Troy State showed it meant to remain a Southland contender as well as the Trojans amassed season-best totals of 470 yards total offense and 301 rushing in a 31-10 home win over Nicholls State. The victory improved the Trojans to 4-1 in the SFL and 7-2 overall. The loss, the third straight for Nicholls, dropped the Colonels to 1-3 in the league and 2-6 overall.

The Trojans took a 7-0 lead on their first play of the game on an 80-yard bomb from Nutter to Philyaw. Despite that, the Trojans only managed a 10-3 halftime lead as the only other scores in the opening half came as the teams traded field goals.

Troy pulled away in the second half. Lucas, a defensive lineman who also played fullback, scored on a pair of 1-yard runs in the third quarter. Lucas' first score capped a drive that lasted more than five minutes while his second touchdown came only four plays following a turnover on the Colonels' ensuing possession. Meanwhile, the Trojan defense held Nicholls to one touchdown in the second half on a 6-yard run by Anderson in the third quarter that made the score 24-10.

Along with Nicholls State and Southwest Texas, the only two other teams not in Southland contention met when Sam Houston State hosted Stephen F. Austin. Both teams went into the game 2-6 overall.

While the records going into the game may have been the same, the play on the field was quite different. The Bearkats were unable to contain SFA's running game as the Lumberjacks picked up 284 of their 328 yards on the ground in a 38-7 victory.

Coleman rushed for 145 yards and two touchdowns while Stoker added 75 yards along with scoring two touchdowns of his own.

The Bearkats tied the game 7-7 at the 12:42 mark of the second quarter on a 2-yard run by Adrian Thomas but Sam Houston State would not score again.

Jay Stegall put SFA on top for good with a 7-yard touchdown run midway in the second quarter. A 47-yard McCarty field goal gave the Lumberjacks a 17-7 halftime lead.

Coleman scored both of his touchdowns in the second half and Stoker added a 2-yard scoring run as SFA pulled away.

SHSU remaining winless in the Southland at 0-5 while the Lumberjacks improved to 2-3 in the league.

At least one of the 4-1 teams atop the SFL would fall behind in the league race a week later as ninth-ranked Troy State hosted third-ranked McNeese State.

With that as the backdrop, it was quite understandable the game would be a tightly-contested four-point affair going into the fourth quarter.

A 6-yard touchdown run by Prejean gave the Cowboys a 7-0 lead in the first quarter. Troy State made it 7-3 at halftime on Tynes' 21-yard field goal with 21 seconds remaining in the second quarter.

The score remained the same until McNeese pushed its advantage to 10-3 early in the fourth quarter.

McNeese put the game away midway in the final period. An 11-yard touchdown pass from Prejean to Andre Perkins put the Cowboys up by two touchdowns. A bad snap on a punt attempt gave the ball back to McNeese, setting up a 73-yard Prejean strike to Keffian Smith to put the game out of reach with a 23-3 Cowboys victory.

Along with the all-important Southland Football League victory, the Cowboys also improved to 9-1 overall. Troy dropped to 4-2 in the SFL and 7-3 overall.

Getting his first start since the season opener, Spangler and the Northwestern State offense was even more productive than it was a week earlier against Jacksonville

State as the Demons routed Sam Houston State 59-3 in Natchitoches to remain tied with McNeese atop the Southland standings.

Spangler passed for 326 yards and three touchdowns and the Demons scored on eight-straight possessions as Northwestern improved to 5-1 in the SFL and 8-2 overall. The Bearkats remained winless in the conference through six games in dropping to 2-8 overall.

The Northwestern quarterback tossed a 35-yard touchdown to Pritchett for the only score of the first quarter. A 3-yard run by Taylor, a 66-yard punt return by Jones and Spangler's 36-yard touchdown strike to Granger gave the Demons a 28-3 halftime lead. SHSU's only points in the game came on a 26-yard Dummer field goal less than a minute into the second quarter.

A 56-yard pass from Spangler to Nathan Black opened a third-quarter scoring barrage in which the Demons added 24 more points to build a 52-7 lead going into the fourth quarter.

Although a Southland Football League title seemed unlikely, Jacksonville State still had a lot to play for in the closing weeks of the 1998 season. Sporting a 6-3 record with two games remaining, the Gamecocks had an opportunity for an 8-3 season after winning only one game the previous year.

With that in mind, every time Southwest Texas rallied against Jacksonville State in their encounter in San Marcos, the Gamecocks seemed to answer back.

Trailing 13-0 at halftime, the Bobcats rallied to within five points early in the second half with a safety and a 2-yard touchdown run by Brown that was set up a partially-blocked punt. The Gamecocks countered with a 5-yard touchdown pass from quarterback Kirby to Jeremy Harper and a two-point conversion to stretch Jacksonville State's lead to 13 points at 21-8.

Down 24-15, the Bobcats cut the deficit momentarily to three points on a 44-yard touchdown pass from Wynn to Tyson Olivo. The extra-point attempt was blocked, with Jacksonville State's Parker going the distance for two points in the opposite direction. Instead of being down by two points, SWT trailed 26-21.

Southwest Texas was in possession of the ball with Jacksonville State clinging to its five-point lead when a Bobcats fumble was returned 32 yards for a touchdown by Carnell Buford for a 33-21 Gamecocks lead with 1:33 left in the game.

Wynn tossed a 44-yard touchdown pass to Torres with 48 seconds left in the game to make the final 33-27.

Jacksonville State improved to 4-2 in the Southland and 7-3 overall. SWT fell to 1-4 in the league and 3-6 overall.

In Thibodaux, poor field conditions because of a day-long rain and a stingy Nicholls defense allowed the Colonels to hold Stephen F. Austin, the top-rushing team in the Southland, to 87 yards on the ground, leading to a 14-7 victory over the Lumberjacks.

Leading 6-0 going into the fourth quarter, the Colonels mounted an 80-yard, 17-play drive that used up 9:16 on the clock to put the game away. Running 10 times and passing seven, the Colonels came up with four third-down conversions before Barnes scored on a 3-yard run. A two-point conversion pass from Zeller to Poirrier gave Nicholls a 14-0 lead with 7:34 remaining in the game.

SFA closed to 14-7 with 2:35 left in the game on 3-yard touchdown run by Coleman that was set up by a 42-yard pass from Fallon to John Acker. An attempted onside kick was recovered by the Colonels, who were able to run out the clock.

Nicholls, 2-3 in the SFL, 3-6 overall, scored the only points of the first half on a pair of Leisher field goals. A 23-yard field goal by Leisher with three seconds remaining in the second quarter following a 21-yard Beard punt return, gave the Colonels their six-point edge.

SFA fell to 2-4 in the Southland and 3-7 overall.

Northwestern State and McNeese State each went into the final week of the 1998 regular season with 5-1 marks, so the Southland Football League title was definitely on the line. Neither team seemed to have a matchup advantage as each faced a club sporting only three wins on the season. Northwestern State played at 3-7 Stephen F. Austin while McNeese was at home against Nicholls State.

Ranked third in the nation, McNeese was assured a spot in the Division I-AA playoffs, even if the Cowboys didn't capture the Southland Football League title but a win over Nicholls possibly could have lifted them to a higher playoff seeding.

The Cowboys gained a slight edge, leading 14-10 at halftime. McNeese took a 7-0 lead in the first quarter on a 4-yard run by Burton. Nicholls countered with a 29-yard Leisher field goal and a 5-yard pass from Zeller to Terrell Lewis in the second quarter before Burton hauled in a 9-yard touchdown pass from Prejean to give the Cowboys a four-point edge at halftime.

A Sean Johnson interception return for a 28-yard touchdown put Nicholls on top 17-14 before the Cowboys came up with the next three scores. McNeese regained the lead midway in the third quarter on a 3-yard run by Prejean. A 27-yard LaFrenz field goal and a 4-yard run by Burton gave the Cowboys what seemed like a comfortable lead of 30-17 with 4:37 remaining in the game.

Zeller hooked up with Beard on a 20-yard touchdown pass with 3:19 left in the game to close the Colonels' deficit to six points. The duo hooked up again, this time from 45 yards out with eight seconds remaining to tie the game. Leisher kicked the extra point to give Nicholls a 31-30 upset victory.

"That's the worst we played and we put 30 points on the board. We just didn't play well on defense. We haven't stopped them yet. It was a track meet – and we don't like track meets. We like to win on defense and use that kicking game to keep you bottled up," said Keasler.

The highlights for the Cowboys in an otherwise disappointing loss were Burton's three rushing touchdowns to give him a school single-season record of 19 touchdowns. Linebacker Charles Ayro had three tackles in the game, raising his total to a McNeese record-best 463.

McNeese concluded the regular season 9-2 overall, including 5-2 in the Southland Football League. Nicholls improved to 4-6 overall, 3-3 in conference play.

Meanwhile, things looked quite comfortable for Northwestern State as the Demons built a 28-0 lead late in the first half at Stephen F. Austin with a second-straight Southland Football League title on the line.

A desperation pass from 39 yards out from Fallon to Lawrence Pullen on the final play of the first half made it 28-7. Coleman scored on a 1-yard run on the Lumberjacks' first possession of the second half to narrow the gap at 28-14.

The Demons maintained a two-touchdown lead through three quarters but when Stoker scored on a 14-yard run less than a minute into the fourth period, Northwestern State's lead dwindled to 28-21.

Things went from comfortable to harrowing as the Demons saw the Lumberjacks drive down to the Northwestern 24 with less than five minutes remaining. Looking for Ayyad in the corner of the end zone, Peyton Jones threw in the direction of the SFA receiver. As he had done throughout the season, Northwestern State's Jermaine Jones came up with the big play. He picked off the potential game-tying pass attempt with 3:40 left in the game.

"Jermaine Jones was about 5-8 and they had a receiver about 6-4, 6-5, and they throw the ball up in the air and Jermaine goes up with that big ole kid and is able to knock the ball out of his hands," Goodwin recalled.

A 46-yard halfback pass from Jacquet to Black set up a Spangler sneak from a yard out with 1:34 left in the game for a 35-21 Northwestern State win that secured the Demons the SFL's automatic bid to the playoffs.

Northwestern State, which finished the regular season 6-1 in the Southland and 9-2 overall, built its 28-0 lead by scoring twice in each of the first two quarters. Short touchdown runs by Drago and Jacquet gave the Demons a 14-0 lead after one quarter. Northwestern made it 28-0 on scoring runs of 2 yards by Jacquet and 4 yards by Spangler.

SFA, which finished the season 2-5 in the conference and 3-8 overall, suffered a pair of interceptions inside the Northwestern 20-yard line in the first quarter – two of four interceptions the Lumberjacks suffered in the contest.

A possible postseason berth was on the line for the winner of the Jacksonville State-Troy State game in Jacksonville as both teams went into the clash 7-3 on the season.

Thanks to a dominating defense that held Jacksonville State to 192 total yards, including only eight rushing, Troy State got all the points it would needed in the second quarter on its way to a 31-7 victory over the Gamecocks.

Phillip Jones scored on a 6-yard run and Mareno Philyaw on a 30-yard reverse for a 14-0 lead. Battone, who rushed for 113 yards, scooted 58 yards for a touchdown late in the period to give Troy a 21-0 halftime lead.

Troy State held a 28-0 lead before Jacksonville State came up with its only score of the game on a 4-yard pass from Kirby to Carlton with less than a minute remaining in the third quarter.

The Trojans closed the regular season 8-3 while Jacksonville State concluded the year 7-4.

In another rivalry game, Sam Houston State won its season finale at home with a 31-24 victory over Southwest Texas to snap an eight-game losing streak for the Bearkats.

The Bearkats were staring at a potential nine-game losing streak to close the 1998 season when Sam Houston State trailed in the fourth quarter against Southwest Texas State. For a team that saw a 17-10 halftime lead turn into a 24-17 deficit against SWT and had scored a total of 10 points combined in its previous two games, needing two scores down the stretch to pull off the win seemed, well, like a stretch.

A 9-yard touchdown pass from Buss to Dominquez tied the game but there was still 8:37 left in the contest. Sam Houston State got the ball back at its own 28-yard line. Doing what they had not done most of the season, the Bearkats mounted a long, time-consuming drive. Taking 12 plays, SHSU used up 5:06 on the clock before Joe Rauls scored on a 1-yard run with 1:20 remaining in the game for a 31-24 lead.

When Jartis Watts intercepted a Bobcats pass with 1:09 left in the game, the Bearkats saw their frustrating eight-game losing streak come to an end as Sam Houston State ended the season on a positive note.

Southwest Texas had tied the game 10-10 on a 7-yard run by Brown and a 26-yard Doctoroff field goal in the second quarter. The Bobcats pulled ahead in the third quarter at 24-17 on a 2-yard run by Brown and Myron Coleman's recovery of a blocked Bearkats punt in the end zone for a touchdown.

Sam Houston State ended the year 1-6 in the SFL and 3-8 overall. Southwest Texas dropped to 1-5 in the conference and 3-7 overall with one game remaining in the season.

On the same day the best teams in Division I-AA were playing in the opening round of the playoffs, two squads, each with losing records, squared off in a game that had no significance on a national level. The 3-7 Southwest Texas Bobcats were playing host to the 4-6 Nicholls State Colonels in San Marcos.

The fact the game was even being played was a symbol of fortitude for those involved from both schools. The game was originally scheduled to be played a month earlier but had to be postponed when 16 inches of floodwater inundated south central Texas.

If anyone could empathize with the people of south central Texas, it was the folks of south Louisiana, who had endured their share of natural disasters through the years from hurricanes and resulting floodwaters.

As the rescheduled game approached, supporters of Nicholls State decided to come up with some sort of symbol that would bring a bit more focus to what was a meaningless end-of-the-season game to the rest of the country. It was determined a wooden boat paddle, something the people of both regions were well acquainted with, would be that symbol. After all, a paddle could be used in both good and bad times – good times such as for recreational boating and even as a huge spoon for gigantic dishes of jambalaya, and bad times in flooding search-and-rescue missions.

The paddle would be painted in the colors representing each school and would be awarded to the winning team on an annual basis. Thus, the "Battle for the Paddle" was born.

Like with most good rivalries, stories are told or closely guarded. Most are exaggerated.

One such story involved the paddle following a Nicholls State win over Southwest Texas in a game played in Thibodaux. The paddle made the rounds of Thibodaux bars to celebrate the Colonels' victory. At one stop, a Colonels player used the paddle on the ample backside of a Nicholls coed, resulting in a broken paddle. A new paddle was made for the Battle of the Paddle, as close to a carbon copy of the original as possible. The original paddle was pieced together and now resides in one of the town's sports bars.

In the first "Battle for the Paddle," the Colonels scored twice in the third quarter to turn a 13-10 deficit into an 11-point advantage going into the fourth period.

Playing in his final game as a Colonel, Zeller tossed a 16-yard touchdown pass to Alcee to ignite the Nicholls comeback. A 1-yard dive by Barnes put the Colonels on top 24-13 with one quarter remaining.

Wynn and Torres, who staked the Bobcats to a quick 7-0 lead on an 18-yard touchdown pass less than three minutes into the game, rallied Southwest Texas in the fourth quarter. A 38-yard strike from Wynn to Torres only seconds into the final quarter made it 24-21. Moments later, an interception of a Zeller pass set up a 29-yard Wynn-Torres hookup to give SWT a 28-24 lead. A 46-yard Leisher field goal was all the Colonels could muster the rest of the way as the Bobcats nabbed the "Paddle" with a 28-27 triumph.

In the opening round of the playoffs, Phillip Jones raced 80 yards for a touchdown on Troy State's first play from scrimmage in the Trojans' Division I-AA playoff opener at Florida A&M. The play was called back because of a holding penalty and the Trojans never could get in sync in the first half of their eventual 27-17 loss to the Rattlers.

The penalty was one of numerous mistakes for Troy, both physical and otherwise, as the Trojans were doomed by two crucial lost fumbles.

A 1-yard touchdown run by Florida A&M quarterback Pat Bonner, a 10-yard touchdown pass to Tariq Qaiyim and a pair of Juan Toro field goals gave the Rattlers a 20-3 halftime lead. Bonner's touchdown run was set up by the Trojans' first lost fumble.

The Trojans, who produced only 74 yards in the first half, put themselves back in the game in the third quarter. Troy State marched to a 15-yard touchdown run by Jones with the second-half kickoff to trail 20-10. Julius Terrell returned an errant Bonner throw 40 yards for a touchdown on the Rattlers' ensuing possession, leaving the Trojans behind by only three points.

Troy State seemed poised to grab the lead after taking over at its own 20-yard line following a Florida A&M punt. Thomas broke loose on a 43-yard gallop to get the drive going. Jones advanced the ball 10 yards but fumbled after being hit.

The Rattlers made Troy pay dearly for the second fumble as Bonner tossed a 30-yard pass to Qaiyim to put the game away at 27-17.

"They were nobody to sneeze at. They were a good, well-oiled football program," Blakeney said of the Rattlers.

Troy State concluded the 1998 season at 8-4.

McNeese State's loss to Nicholls in the regular-season finale dropped the Cowboys to a No. 6 seed but they still managed a home playoff game against the University of Massachusetts, the No. 11 seed.

McNeese trailed 21-3 at halftime and was down 21-9 early in the fourth quarter. UMass was down 3-0 before the Minutemen scored three touchdowns in the second quarter. UMass' scores came on a 2-yard run by Kevin Quinlan, and touchdown passes of 31 yards from quarterback Todd Bankhead to receiver Adrian Zullo and 7 yards to tight end Kerry Taylor.

All of McNeese's points through three quarters came on LaFrenz field goals. Trailing 21-6, Cowboys defensive end Brian Gill intercepted a Bankhead pass at the Minutemen's 12-yard line. After Matthews dropped what appeared to be a sure touchdown in the end zone on second down, McNeese had to settle on a 25-yard LaFrenz field goal to make it 21-9 with 13:40 remaining in the game.

McNeese got its only touchdown of the game on a 10-yard pass from Prejean to Davis with 9:33 left in the game to make the score 21-16. LaFrenz added a 29-yard field goal to cut the Cowboys' deficit to two points with 4:52 remaining in the game.

The Cowboys reached the UMass 35-yard line in the closing minutes. LaFrenz, who connected on four field goals to keep McNeese in the game, was brought to attempt a game-winning 52 yarder with 1:42 left in the contest. His kick was long enough but wide to the right, ending McNeese's season with a 21-19 defeat.

McNeese concluded its season 9-3.

Northwestern State showed why it earned the No. 2 overall seed in the Division I-AA playoffs with a resounding 48-28 opening-round win at home over Illinois State.

The Demons rolled up a school-record 650 yards of total offense, including 306 rushing. Although no Northwestern back rushed for more than 100 yards in the game, the Demons spread the production around as Jacquet ran for 97 yards, Taylor 90 and Powell 73.

Spangler tied a single-game school record with four touchdowns passes. Pritchett was on the receiving end of three of the scoring strikes, hauling in touchdown grabs of 35, 60 and 53 yards.

A 29-yard touchdown run by Taylor and two touchdown passes from Spangler to Prichett gave the Demons a 21-0 lead after one quarter. The only other score of the opening half was a 1-yard pass from Illinois State quarterback Kevin Glenn to Scott Preusker with 3:39 remaining in the first half as the Redbirds cut the deficit to two touchdowns at the break.

Jacquet scored two rushing touchdowns and Spangler hit Sutherland with a 59-yard touchdown strike as the Demons built a 42-21 lead going into the fourth quarter.

"They ran a lot of crossing routes," Goodwin said of the Redbirds. "They weren't real deep but we hadn't seen much of that and we had a hard time stopping it. We were the better team but it took us awhile to pull away."

The Demons saw quarterfinal opponent Appalachian State run 86 plays and control the clock for 36:49 but Northwestern State made effective use of big plays for the second week in a row to take a 31-20 home victory to advance to the Division I-AA semifinals for the first time in school history.

A Chris Barden field goal in the first quarter and a 27-yard touchdown pass from David Reaves to Daryl Skinner with 5:52 remaining in the second quarter staked the Mountaineers to a 10-0 lead.

It was at that point the Demons started to make use of their big plays. A 58-yard pass from Spangler to Granger with less than five minutes remaining in the second quarter finally got Northwestern on the scoreboard. Another Spangler-to-Granger connection, this one from 77 yards with 1:25 remaining before halftime, gave the Demons a 14-10 lead at intermission.

A 1-yard touchdown run by Appalachian State's Terrence McCall was countered by a 2-yard run by Spangler before Barden connected on a 38-yard field goal on the final play of the third quarter to leave the Demons with a scant 21-20 lead going into the final period.

Another pair of big plays, this time a 47-yard pass from Spangler to tight end Gant Gremillion and a 35-yard run by Powell set up a 2-yard touchdown run by the Northwestern State quarterback to stretch the Demons' lead to 28-21.

Skinner returned the ensuing kickoff 77 yards down to the Demons' 17. The Northwestern State defense, which held the Mountaineers to 82 yards rushing on 47 carries – 118 below Appalachian's season average – stiffened and forced a Barden field goal attempt. The 34-yard kick was wide left, allowing the Demons to maintain their eight-point edge.

LaToof added a 32-yard field goal with 3:12 left in the game as the Demons recorded an 11-win season for the first time since 1939 in advancing to the semifinals against a Massachusetts team that had knocked Northwestern State's SFL brethren McNeese State out in the opening round of the playoffs.

Three touchdowns in the second quarter gave Northwestern State a 21-14 halftime lead over Massachusetts and left the Demons only 30 minutes away from playing for the Division I-AA national championship.

Playing at home for the third-straight time in the postseason, the Demons used a 20-yard run by Powell, a 31-yard pass from Spangler to Granger and a 1-yard run by Jacquet for their 21-14 lead. Jacquet's touchdown broke a 14-14 tie only 1:04 before halftime.

A 20-yard run by Quinlan was countered by a 29-yard LaToof field goal, leaving the Demons with a 24-21 lead going into the final quarter.

Northwestern, which committed four turnovers in the game, came up with its most costly miscue early in the fourth quarter. With the Demons still clinging to a three-point lead, Spangler bobbled a snap from center and then tried to split two defenders. His pass was intercepted by UMass linebacker Khari Samuel.

Using a fake reverse, Bankhead hit a wide-open Matt Jordan for a 49-yard touchdown to give UMass a 27-24 lead with 10:34 remaining in the game.

"Up until that point, I thought we were going to win the game. They had a hard time stopping us running the football," recalled Goodwin.

Coming off a week in which the Northwestern State defense held Appalachian State to 118 yards below its season-rushing average, the Purple Swarm defense was unable to stop Marcel Shipp of UMass.

The future Arizona Cardinals and Houston Texans runner rushed for 24 of his game-high 190 yards on a scoring gallop with 2:39 left in the game to extend the UMass lead to 34-24.

"We knew he was a pretty good running back but we had no idea how really good he was," Goodwin said of Shipp. "He dominated us.

"We felt like we could keep him under control. We knew he would get some yards but no way did we think he could do that to our defense. In the fourth quarter, once they got the lead, we just couldn't stop them."

Each team added a touchdown in the closing minute to make the final 41-31 as Northwestern State ended its season at 11-3.

After several years of stability, there were three coaching changes in the Southland Football League at the start of 1999 and more intrigue to follow as the season progressed.

McNeese State's Bobby Keasler, a former assistant at Northeast Louisiana, returned to Monroe to take over the now Division I-A program. Keasler was replaced by Cowboys assistant Kirby Bruchhaus, McNeese's defensive coordinator.

At Stephen F. Austin, John Pearce was replaced by Mike Santiago. Santiago spent nine seasons as an assistant at McNeese State prior to being named the head coach of the Lumberjacks. Before going to McNeese, Santiago had assistant coaching stints at North Carolina State, Northern Arizona, Western Michigan and Southwest Texas. He also was a scout for the NFL's Cleveland Browns in 1984.

Darren Barbier departed Nicholls State after the 1998 season and was replaced by Daryl Daye. A Louisiana native, Daye was defensive line coach and defensive coordinator at Liberty University from 1991-98.

The first of the new coaches to make his Southland Football League debut was Santiago when his Lumberjacks hosted Southwest Texas. Stephen F. Austin went into the game 1-1. Santiago won his debut when the Lumberjacks opened with a 51-34 victory over Abilene Christian. SFA lost to Utah State leading up to the Southwest Texas game.

Southwest Texas was 1-1 as well with a win over Midwestern State and a loss to South Florida.

The difference between Stephen F. Austin quarterback Wes Pate and his Southwest Texas counterpart, Spergon Wynn, in the Lumberjacks' Southland Football League opener against the Bobcats was that Pate lasted all four quarters.

Each quarterback had a hand in all the touchdowns scored in the game. Wynn scored on a pair of short runs for a 14-14 tie before leaving the game in the third quarter. He returned to the game but was not as effective   after suffering a leg injury.

Pate countered with a 30-yard touchdown run and scoring passes to Freddy Lyons and Zach Woods to give the Lumberjacks a 21-14 lead in the second quarter. His 47-yard touchdown run on an option keeper on the first play of the second half put SFA on top by 14 points.

The only other points of the second half came on a 33-yard field goal by SWT's Justin Martinez to make the final 28-17.

A week later, Daye made his SFL debut when the Colonels visited Jacksonville State. The Colonels were 0-2 on the season. After making a winner of Keasler in his first game as Northeast Louisiana coach in a 27-10 Colonels loss, Nicholls had an open date before falling to Western Illinois 14-13 in a game played in New Orleans' Tad Gormley Stadium.

Jacksonville State went into the Nicholls game 1-1 with a loss to Alabama A&M and a victory over Union College in Kentucky.

The Colonels went into their 1999 SFL opener averaging only 11.5 points per game. By the time the first quarter was over against the Gamecocks, Nicholls found itself in a 21-21 tie.

The surprisingly strong offensive output did not end there. A 43-yard Kyle Leisher field goal with 12:24 remaining in the game gave Nicholls a whopping 45-21 lead. Could the Nicholls defense hold off the Jacksonville State offense became the question down the stretch.

A 3-yard touchdown run by Jacksonville State's backup quarterback, Reggie Stancil, made the score 45-28 and began a furious Gamecocks comeback.

Following a 15-yard touchdown pass from Stancil to Joey Hamilton with 4:39 remaining in the game, a successful onside kick gave the ball back to Jacksonville. The Gamecocks took advantage when Stancil and Lorenzo Banks hooked up on a 6-yard touchdown strike to make it 45-42 with 3:12 remaining in the contest but that was as close as Jacksonville State would get as the Colonels picked up their first win under Daye.

Nicholls earned the win behind a career day by quarterback Brad Smith. He ran for 97 yards and two touchdowns while throwing for a career-high 337 yards and three touchdowns. Smith connected with Sullivan Beard on touchdown passes of 97 and 80 yards as the Colonels amassed 478 total yards, a Nicholls single-game record.

Playing away from home for the fourth-straight game a week later to open the season, the Colonels could not duplicate the Jacksonville State effort, falling 42-17 at 3-1 Northwestern State.

Against the Colonels, Tony Taylor, who rushed for a game-high 194 yards, and Troy Sumrall, each rushed for two touchdowns as the Demons built a 28-3 halftime lead. The only points for Nicholls in the opening half came on a 33-yard Leisher field goal with 2:03 remaining before halftime.

The Demons put the game away early in the third quarter when Terrence McGee returned an interception 34 yards for a touchdown on the first play of the second half.

It was Bruchhaus' turn to make his Southland Football League debut when his McNeese State Cowboys visited Stephen F. Austin. Bruchhaus and his Cowboys were off to a 1-3 start. After opening with a loss to Northern Iowa, the Cowboys defeated Texas A&M-Kingsville 24-10 to give Bruchhaus his first win as McNeese coach.

Unlike SFA's Santiago, Bruchhaus would not get a win in his initial Southland outing as five turnovers doomed McNeese State in a 40-14 loss to the Lumberjacks.

An 83-yard bomb from Blake Prejean to Eric Chew gave McNeese a 7-0 lead before the Lumberjacks began to take advantage of Cowboy mistakes. One such occasion occurred with McNeese trailing 14-7. The Cowboys had the ball deep in their own territory when SFA's Kyle Dews returned an errant McNeese pass 20 yards for a score and a 20-7 lead for the Lumberjacks. Ted Woodard, who had his extra-point attempt blocked following Dews' touchdown, kicked a 26-yard field goal for a 23-7 Stephen F. Austin lead at halftime.

Trailing 26-7, a 5-yard pass from Prejean to Jimmy Redmond made it 26-14 in the third quarter but that was as close as the Cowboys would get in the 40-14 victory for the Lumberjacks.

A rare midseason coaching change in the Southland took place in Jacksonville State. After a 34-18 non-conference loss to Samford, Mike Williams abruptly resigned as Gamecocks coach. Jeff Richards, the Gamecocks' assistant head coach and offensive coordinator, was named Jacksonville State's interim head coach. Richards came to Jacksonville State in 1998 after stints as an assistant at Southeast Missouri State, Arkansas State and Southern Mississippi.

It really didn't seem to matter to Chris Chaloupka who the coach was at Jacksonville State. The Sam Houston State quarterback, an Oklahoma State transfer, tied a single-game school record with five touchdown passes as the Bearkats opened Southland Football League play with a 51-17 domination of the Gamecocks.

The Bearkats pulled away from a slim 17-10 halftime lead on third-quarter touchdown passes of 9 yards to Matt Dominguez and 45 yards to Larry Nixon. Chaloupka added an 18-yard scoring strike to Nixon in the fourth quarter while Adrian Thomas rushed for two touchdowns.

Jacksonville's only score in the second half came on a 3-yard run by Stancil in the fourth quarter.

The win in Sam Houston State's SFL opener improved the Bearkats to 3-2 overall. The three wins through five games equaled SHSU's entire win total of the previous season.

Jacksonville State dropped to 0-2 in the league and 1-4 overall.

Four non-conference wins to open the season helped to give Troy State the No. 2 ranking in the nation going into the Trojans' Southland Football League opener at home against Northwestern State. Included in Troy's 4-0 start was a season-opening upset of Cincinnati.

Already having a conference game under their belts, the Demons gave Troy everything it could handle as Northwestern wiped out an early 10-0 deficit to lead 21-17 at halftime.

Wayne Thomas' 2-yard run and a 22-yard field goal by Lawrence Tynes gave the Trojans the early lead.

With Brad Spangler back in action after missing several weeks with a strained medial collateral ligament in his knee, the Demons got on the scoreboard on a 34-yard pass from the quarterback to Travis Fleming.

After Troy countered with a 66-yard strike from Nutter to Philyaw, the Trojans still held what seemed like a comfortable 17-6 lead. A 20-yard run by Tony Taylor and a two-point conversion, however, followed by Mike Green's recovery in the end zone of a blocked punt with 4:43 remaining before halftime suddenly gave the Demons a 21-17 edge.

The Demons maintained their four-point lead until early in the fourth quarter when Phillip Jones' dive from a yard out allowed the Trojans to escape with a 24-21 victory.

Troy's conference-opening win moved the Trojans to 5-0 on the season while Northwestern fell to 1-1 in the SFL and 2-4 overall.

In Thibodaux, the second annual "Battle for the Paddle" had the Colonels looking like a boat without an oar after losing Smith with a concussion in the second quarter in the SFL clash.

On a day in which yards were hard to come by because of sloppy conditions caused by days of rain, Nicholls struggled both on the ground and through the air. The Colonels were held to 78 yards rushing and 114 passing. Of the 78 rushing yards, 51 came on one drive late in the third quarter and 34 of the passing yards came on the opening possession of the game.

Southwest Texas, 1-1 in the SFL and 2-3 overall, alternated running backs Bronson Sanders and Lee Davis with good results. Sanders finished with 73 yards on 18 carries and a touchdown while Davis had 71 yards on 16 attempts. Wynn was 13 of 25 passing for 109 yards in the miserable conditions.

Despite winning the statistical battle, the Bobcats needed a bit of trickery and the aid of a turnover to take a 16-0 victory.

Facing fourth down at the Nicholls 9-yard line with 21 seconds remaining in the opening half, SWT lined up for a field-goal attempt. Bobcats' holder Travis Rush took the snap from center and rolled to his right before hitting a wide-open Eric Diogu in the end zone for a 7-0 halftime lead.

Southwest Texas extended the lead to 13-0 early in the fourth quarter on a 4-yard run by Sanders that came four plays following a fumble by Colonels backup quarterback Cooper Collins. Ross Doctoroff added a 39-yard field goal to account for the final margin.

Looking to move to 3-0 in the SFL, members of the Lumberjacks' offense had to be shaking their heads at what transpired in the first quarter of Stephen F. Austin's encounter at Sam Houston State.

Interception returns of 35 yards by Chris Foster and 58 yards by James Burnett for touchdowns staked the Bearkats to a 14-0 lead in what appeared would be a defensive battle.

From that point on, both defenses seemed to take the rest of the game off as the two teams combined for an eye-popping 1,324 yards of total offense.

For all the big numbers, the biggest ended up in favor of the Lumberjacks. Stephen F. Austin amassed a Southland Football League-record 717 yards of total offense as Pate passed for 345 yards and running back KaRon Coleman accumulated 297 all-purpose yards as SFA took a wild 45-31 victory.

Coleman rushed for 216 yards. Included in his scores were touchdown runs of 65 and 63 yards along with a 54-yard scoring reception.

The SFA defense, meanwhile, didn't exactly shut down the Bearkats. SHSU amassed 607 total yards as Chaloupka passed for a school-record 479 yards.

After falling behind 14-0, the Lumberjacks scored the next 23 points. The Bearkats never led after blowing the early two-touchdown advantage and twice got to within two points – the first time at 23-21 on a 21-yard pass from Chaloupka to Jonathan Cooper and at 30-28 on a 49-yard strike to future Canadian Football League pass catcher Matt Dominguez from fellow receiver Jermaine Henderson. Dominguez ended the game with 186 reception yards.

The loss evened the Bearkats' record at 1-1 in the SFL and 3-3 overall. Stephen F. Austin remained unbeaten in league play at 3-0 and 4-2 overall.

In San Marcos, the Bobcats were less than five minutes away from taking second-ranked Troy State to overtime. With the score tied 17-17 in the fourth quarter, a stout SWT defense forced the Trojans into a fourth-and-34 punting situation.

D'Angelo Torres, the Bobcats' return man, fumbled after signaling for a fair catch, with Brent McAlliley recovering at the Southwest Texas 20. It took seven plays, but Nutter, the Troy quarterback, eventually scored on a 1-yard keeper with 4:35 left in the fourth quarter to give Troy State a 24-17 thriller.

An 8-yard fumble return by Rayshun Reed and a 48-yard Tynes field goal staked the Trojans to an early lead. SWT scored with four seconds left in the first half on a 16-yard pass from Wynn to Torres.

Troy extended its lead to 17-7 when Philyaw turned a screen pass from Nutter into a 59-yard touchdown on the first play from scrimmage in the second half. A 2-yard touchdown pass from Wynn to Diogu following a partially-blocked Trojans punt and 31-yard Martinez field goal that hit the goal post tied the game at the 11:17 mark of the fourth quarter.

Troy State stayed unbeaten at 2-0 in the SFL and 6-0 overall. Southwest Texas fell to 1-2 in the conference and 2-4 overall.

Meanwhile, McNeese State seemed headed to a second-straight SFL loss at Jacksonville State when Stancil fired a 15-yard touchdown pass to Cedric Allen with 50 seconds left in the game to give the Gamecocks a 26-23 lead.

A 38-yard pass from Prejean to Pat Matthews gave the Cowboys a bit of hope. Shonz LaFrenz, who had kicked three field goals earlier in the game, was called upon to try a 39-yard attempt to force overtime. His 39-yard kick as time expired gave McNeese new life.

In the first overtime, Aaron Pierce, who rushed for 161 yards, scored on a 2-yard run to give McNeese a 33-26 lead. Jacksonville State forced a second overtime when the Gamecocks tied the game on a 15-yard run by Roger Bell.

Jacksonville State was held to a 40-yard Brad Hopkins field goal and a 36-33 edge. Needing a touchdown for a win or a field goal to force a third overtime, McNeese quarterback Slade Nagle drilled Redmond with a 12-yard scoring strike to give the Cowboys a 39-36 triumph.

The Gamecocks led 19-6 at halftime but were held scoreless in the third quarter as McNeese rallied to within 19-13 going into the fourth quarter. After a 1-yard touchdown reception by Matthews and a LaFrenz field goal gave the Cowboys a 23-19 lead, Jacksonville State regained the advantage at 26-19 on Allen's touchdown catch to set the stage for LaFrenz's kick to force overtime.

McNeese improved to 1-1 in the Southland and 2-4 overall. Jacksonville State fell to 0-3 in the conference and 1-5 overall.

At home against Sam Houston State a week later, the Trojans marched 84 yards in eight plays with the opening drive of the contest to take a 7-0 lead less than three minutes into the game.

The ease in which Troy State drove for its first drive, which was culminated on a 2-yard run by fullback Thad Buttone, quickly demonstrated why the Trojans were now ranked the No. 1 team in Division I-AA.

By the time the game was over, Buttone had a school record-tying four touchdowns in Troy's 41-16 victory to remain unbeaten on the season. Along with his early run, Buttone also caught a 26-yard scoring pass from Nutter and added a pair of 1-yard touchdown runs.

Troy State's Chris Archie and his defensive mates were just as formidable as Buttone. The Trojans safety intercepted a school record-tying three passes in the game. Troy's defense limited the Bearkats' offense to 254 yards – almost 200 below SHSU's seasonal average while knocking Chaloupka out of the game with a concussion.

Even the Trojans' special teams was in top-ranked form as David Philyaw blocked a punt and recovered a fumble after a bad SHSU snap on another punt attempt.

Sam Houston State dropped to 1-2 in the SFL and 3-4 overall.

While Troy State may have been considered the No. 1 team in the nation, Stephen F. Austin still had a say as to who was the top team in the Southland Football League as the Lumberjacks put their 3-0 league record on the line against Nicholls State.

Stephen F. Austin didn't duplicate its offensive numbers of the previous week against Sam Houston State, but the Lumberjacks didn't have to in their home game against the Colonels.

By late in the first quarter, SFA already led 14-0 after scoring on its opening two possessions but lost Coleman and Blaylock to injuries. So, the Lumberjacks had to turn to Isiah Stoker and their defense.

Stoker rushed for 150 yards as the Lumberjacks amassed 427 yards of total offense. Meanwhile, the SFA defense recorded eight sacks and limited the Colonels to 170 yards of total offense.

A 15-yard pass from Pate to Woods and a 1-yard run by Blaylock prior to his groin injury gave Stephen F. Austin a 14-0 lead. Woodard added a pair of second-quarter field goals for a 20-0 Lumberjacks lead at the break.

After going scoreless in 10 quarters, the Colonels finally put some points on the board in the third quarter on a 14-yard run by Sullivan Turner. The drought-breaking touchdown came on only a 20-yard drive following an interception by Lee Rogers. The Colonels would not score again the remainder of the contest while SFA added an 18-point fourth quarter for a 38-7 victory.

The Lumberjacks remained unbeaten in SFL play at 4-0 while improving to 5-2 overall. Nicholls sank to 1-3 in the conference and 1-6 overall with the defeat.

Elsewhere, with two struggling teams meeting in Jacksonville State's SFL home game against Southwest Texas, the Gamecocks sensed their best chance to pick up a win with Richards as coach as Jacksonville built a 14-0 halftime lead.

Stancil passes of 9 yards to Allen and 17 yards to Hamilton left Southwest Texas behind by 14 points going into the second half.

Southwest Texas put itself back in the contest late in the third quarter. After a 21-yard Martinez field goal, the Bobcats recovered an onside kick at the Jacksonville State 32. Wynn connected with Tyson Olivo on an 8-yard touchdown toss as SWT rallied to within 14-10 with 2:49 remaining in the third quarter.

A 32-yard field goal by Hopkins with 7:53 left in the fourth quarter increased the spread to seven points. SWT reached the Jacksonville State 34-yard line late in the game but on fourth-and-10, Taylor Mitchell sacked Wynn with 50 seconds left to give the Gamecocks a 17-10 triumph to end a four-game losing streak for Jacksonville State.

The outcome left both teams 1-3 in the Southland and 2-5 overall.

In Lake Charles, the Cowboys held off a late charge from Northwestern State for a 20-17 win to give McNeese State back-to-back wins for the first time during the 1999 season.

A 10-10 tie after one quarter held up until the third quarter. McNeese doubled up on the Demons in the third quarter on a 44-yard pass from Nagle to Chew and a 29-yard LaFrenz field goal to lead 20-10 going into the fourth quarter.

Northwestern State cut the deficit to three points with 8:56 left in the game on an 11-yard pass from Spangler to Terry Brannagan.

Driving for a potential score late in the game, the Demons were turned away when Jarod Jones intercepted a Spangler pass in the end zone. A final Demons gasp came up short when Chris Pritchett was knocked out of bounds at the McNeese 5-yard line with no time remaining after hauling in a pass from Spangler.

McNeese improved to 2-1 in the Southland and 3-4 overall. Northwestern State fell to 1-2 in the conference and 2-5 overall.

Stephen F. Austin's quest to remain unbeaten in the Southland seemed cloudy like the afternoon sky going into the final two minutes of the first half in the Lumberjacks' home game a week later against Jacksonville State.

The game looked like it might be a scoreless battle after two quarters when the Gamecocks went into punt formation with less than two minutes remaining in the half. However, SFA's Richard Daniels got a hand on John Howard's attempt, with Woods recovering for SFA at the Jacksonville State 11-yard line. The Lumberjacks had to settle on a 23-yard Woodard field goal but it did give Stephen F. Austin a 3-0 lead with 1:52 to go in the second quarter.

DeKendrick Vidito's interception of a Stancil pass on the ensuing possession gave the ball right back to the Lumberjacks near midfield. SFA took full advantage of the latter break when Pate tossed 1 yard to Jay Stegall for a 10-0 halftime advantage for Stephen F. Austin.

The second half belonged to Stoker. Playing in place of the still-injured Coleman and Blaylock, Stoker rushed for a school-record 289 yards and two touchdowns in the second half. One of Stoker's touchdowns came on a 57-yard run. He also had a 76-yard jaunt to set up another score as SFA went on to take a 33-16 victory.

Jacksonville State's scores came in the fourth quarter with the Gamecocks trailing 30-0. A 10-yard touchdown run by Michael Daies, a safety, and a 2-yard run by Rondy Rogers accounted for Jacksonville State's points.

SFA stayed perfect in the Southland at 5-0, along with moving to 6-2 overall. Jacksonville State fell to 1-4 in the conference and 2-6 overall.

Troy State was far from a welcome visitor for a Nicholls State team suffering through offensive woes. The Colonels were unable to score in a 20-0 loss to the top-ranked team in the country.

The Trojans remained atop the nation at 8-0 overall while moving to 4-0 in the Southland. Nicholls fell to 1-7 overall and 1-4 in conference play.

As Nicholls had done earlier in the season, the Colonels stayed with an opponent for a half despite being unable to score. The Colonels only trailed 7-0 at halftime on a 16-yard run by Jones with 2:51 remaining before intermission.

Troy's second-half touchdowns came on a 10-yard run by Nutter and a 28-yard pass from the Trojans' signal caller to Mareno Philyaw.

Smith, the Nicholls State quarterback, was sacked nine times by the Trojans.

McNeese State could not make it three conference wins in a row, only managing three points in a 20-3 home loss to Sam Houston State. The victory marked the first time the Bearkats defeated McNeese in Lake Charles since 1970.

All of the first-half scoring came in the second quarter. The Bearkats produced 10 points in the period when Chaloupka, who threw for 314 yards in the game, connected with Cooper on a 7-yard scoring toss and Daniel Chappell kicked a 30-yard field goal. LaFrenz provided all of the Cowboys' points in the game when he booted a 29-yard field goal as McNeese trailed 10-3 at halftime.

The only other scoring in the game came on a 25-yard Chappell field goal and a 5-yard run by Thomas. Thomas finished the game with 125 yards rushing.

The result left both teams 2-2 in the SFL as Sam Houston State improved to 4-4 overall and McNeese slid to 3-5.

Northwestern State made Sam Goodwin the winningest coach in school history in the Demons' home game against Southwest Texas but had to rally to do so.

The Bobcats jumped out to a 21-12 lead after one quarter on a 52-yard punt return by Darrick Vaughn, a 44-yard interception return by Kendall Jones and a 20-yard pass from Wynn to Tyrone Darden.

The nine-point margin held up until the third quarter when the Demons defense set up a pair of touchdowns to give Northwestern State the lead.

An 8-yard touchdown pass from Spangler to Pritchett on a drive that was set up by a fumble recovery at the SWT 9 made it 21-19 less than four minutes into the second half. Slightly more than one minute later, Mike Green returned a Wynn interception 37 yards for a touchdown to put Northwestern on top 26-21.

The Demons later added a 29-yard Clint Sanford field goal in the third quarter and a 1-yard run by Taylor in the fourth quarter for a 36-21 Northwestern State victory.

Taylor rushed for 218 yards and three touchdowns in the game. The Demons amassed 314 yards on the ground against a SWT defense that had been allowing opponents no more than 85.4 yard rushing per contest – the fifth-best rushing defense in the nation.

The win, which improved Northwestern's record to 2-2 in the Southland and 3-5 overall, gave Goodwin a record of 101-85-3, passing the previous mark of 100-92-11 by Harry "Rags" Turpin.

Southwest Texas dropped to 1-4 in the conference and 2-6 overall.

The showdown that had been anticipated for weeks finally arrived when top-ranked Troy State, 4-0 in the Southland Football League, hosted 5-0 Stephen F. Austin.

Along with being top-ranked in the polls, Troy State entered the game No. 1 in the SFL in scoring defense while the Lumberjacks topped the league in scoring, averaging 35 points a game.

The Trojan defense had the better outing, holding the Stephen F. Austin offense to 143 yards. The Lumberjack defense, on the other hand, could not stop Troy State's running attack. All of those factors added up in a 27-7 victory for the Trojans.

Troy State rushed for 390 yards and controlled the clock for more than 45 minutes. The 390 yards came on a school-record 73 rushes. The 45:33 time of possession also established a new team record.

Jones and LeBarron Black each topped 100 yards in the game. Jones rushed for 183 yards and Black 122.

"That was a premiere performance by our defense and to be able to count out the clock. Every team has its patented way of winning games. When you are good at rushing as we were that year, it makes your defense better, normally," said Troy State coach Larry Blakney.

Black scored on a 4-yard run on Troy State's opening drive to set the tempo for the Trojans. Jones had a 1-yard scoring run and Tynes kicked a 24-yard field goal to give the Trojans a 17-0 halftime advantage.

SFA scored on its first drive of the second half as Stoker's 15-yard run made it 17-7 but the Lumberjacks would not score again. Black came up with a 3-yard run in the second half and Tynes a 31-yard field goal for the 27-7 final.

Troy State remained unbeaten at 9-0 overall, including 6-0 in the SFL. The Lumberjacks fell to 5-1 in the league and 6-3 overall as Stephen F. Austin's four-game winning streak came to a halt.

In San Marcos, McNeese State bounced back from the Sam Houston State loss with a narrow 10-7 win at Southwest Texas State.

McNeese took a 3-0 lead in the first quarter on a 40-yard LaFrenz field goal but trailed 7-3 at halftime after a 4-yard run by Wynn in the second quarter.

The Cowboys held SWT to 95 yards in the second half and pulled out the win when Prejean tossed an 18-yard touchdown to Jessie Burton with 1:29 remaining in the game.

Burton was most of McNeese's offense. The Cowboys finished with 219 total yards, with Burton rushing for 106 yards to go along with his 18-yard touchdown reception. McNeese's defense held the Bobcats to 154 yards passing and 76 rushing, while sacking Wynn four times.

McNeese improved to 3-2 in the SFL and 4-5 overall. Southwest Texas fell to 1-5 in the league and 2-7 overall.

Meanwhile, Taylor rushed for 170 yards and three touchdowns to pace Northwestern State to a 35-7 Southland home win over Jacksonville State.

Taylor's three touchdowns gave him 15 on the season, surpassing the Northwestern single-season record of 13 set by Clarence Matthews in 1995.

Northwestern built a 21-0 halftime lead on Taylor's touchdown runs of 4 and 20 yards, plus a 1-yard score by Sumrall. Taylor added his final touchdown on a 3-yard run with 3:32 remaining in the game.

Jacksonville State's only score came in the third quarter on a 36-yard pass from Tim Gallahan to Hamilton.

Northwestern improved to 3-2 in the SFL and 4-5 overall. The Gamecocks fell to 1-5 in the conference and 2-7 overall.

In Huntsville, Chaloupka and Dominguez were unstoppable in Sam Houston State's 69-17 thrashing of Nicholls State. The Bearkats quarterback and receiver hooked up on three touchdown strikes. Chaloupka finished with five scoring passes, also connecting with Thomas and Cooper on touchdown tosses. Dominguez had a 15-yard reception from backup quarterback Albert Bradley for his fourth touchdown of the game.

Nicholls led 3-0 on a Leisher field goal and rallied to within 14-10 on a 68-yard pass from Jarrad Poirrier to Curtis Johnson. Smith, the Nicholls quarterback, began the play with a lateral to Poirrier, who hooked up with a wide-open Johnson.

Chaloupka's three touchdown passes to Dominguez followed as the Bearkats pulled away for a 35-17 halftime lead.

The win pulled the Bearkats above .500 at 3-2 in the SFL and 5-4 overall. Nicholls dropped to 1-5 in the conference and 1-8 overall.

McNeese State faced a tough task a week later, hosting an unbeaten and top-ranked Troy State team looking to clinch the Southland Football League title to secure an automatic bid to the Division I-AA playoffs.

The Cowboys broke a 7-7 tie at halftime on a 2-yard pass from Nagle to Matthews early in the third quarter. After LaFrenz kicked a 32-yard field goal, Burton scored on a 2-yard run with 5:22 remaining in the period to give the Cowboys a surprising 24-7 lead.

McNeese State's defense made sure there would be no last-minute rally by Troy State, holding the Trojans to 26 yards of total offense in the fourth quarter. Troy's offense was never able to get on track the entire game as the Cowboys held the Trojans to 148 yards passing and 58 rushing while recovering four fumbles and intercepting two passes.

Burton, who rushed for 103 yards, gave McNeese a 7-0 lead on a 24-yard touchdown run in the first quarter. Troy State's only points of the game came on a 3-yard run by Black in the second quarter to tie the game at the break.

McNeese improved to 4-2 in the Southland and 5-5 overall. Troy State fell to 5-1 in the SFL and 9-1 overall.

With four of the SFL teams involved in non-conference games, the only other contest featuring league teams the same week as the Troy State upset was the Northwestern State-Sam Houston tilt. Both teams went into the affair 3-2 in Southland play.

Sam Houston State jumped out to a 7-0 lead early in the second quarter of its home finale against Northwestern State on a 1-yard run by Chaloupka. The score proved costly as the Bearkats' quarterback suffered a torn right patellar tendon on the play as was lost for the season.

With the loss of Chaloupka, the Bearkats' defense picked up the slack. Sam Houston State's defense forced a school-record eight Demons turnover in a 21-0 shutout of Northwestern State.

The turnovers proved to be especially opportune. Northwestern State reached the red zone eight times and failed to score on every occasion. SHSU forced six interceptions, three coming in the end zone to end Demon scoring threats.

Trent Taylor picked off two of the passes. Foster, Keith Davis, Todd Moebes and Jartis Watts all had interceptions as well. Watts and William Roberts also had fumble recoveries.

Replacing Chaloupka, Bradley tossed a 17-yard touchdown pass to Nixon to give the Bearkats a 14-0 halftime lead. The only score of the second half was on a 4-yard run by Joe Rauls.

The shutout marked the first time in 67 games that the Demons failed to score.

Sam Houston State moved to 4-2 in the Southland Football League, and at 6-4 overall, clinched its first winning season since 1994. Northwestern State dropped to 3-3 in the SFL and 4-6 overall.

Troy State's loss a week earlier to McNeese State dropped the Trojans from No. 1 in the nation to No. 6 and they were in no mood to play around with rival Jacksonville State in their quest to clinch the Southland Football League title and an automatic bid to the Division I-AA playoffs in the regular-season finale.

Playing at home, the Trojans sent an early message when Philyaw took a handoff from Jones on Troy State's opening play from scrimmage and scampered 62 yards for a touchdown for a quick 7-0 lead on Troy's way to a 35-16 victory.

"That's a big rivalry game and everybody sort of gets up to play and our guys did a good job against Jax State," said Blakeney.

Al Lucas barreled in from 2 yards out later in the first quarter and Jones scored from 2 yards as well in the second quarter and the Trojans were on their way to capturing the SFL title.

Troy State scored more than enough points by halftime to win the game; especially after all the Gamecocks could show for three trips deep into Trojans territory was a 20-yard Hopkins field goal.

The Gamecocks managed two touchdowns in the second half on scoring tosses of 80 and 9 yards from Stancil to Banks. The freshman receiver finished with 192 reception yards.

Troy State closed the regular season 10-1 overall, including 6-1 in the Southland. Jacksonville State ended the year 2-9 overall, 1-6 in the conference.

In Natchitoches, Coleman was back in form for the final game of the season, rushing for 164 yards in Stephen F. Austin's 29-14 win at Northwestern State. The victory allowed the Lumberjacks to claim a share of the Southland Football League title.

Northwestern State led 14-9 at halftime. Taylor scored on a 91-yard touchdown run in the first half and finished with 152 yards. He captured the SFL rushing title with 1,441 yards.

Coleman's 10-yard touchdown run early in the second half put SFA on top. He added two more scoring runs in the final five minutes of the game for the 29-14 final.

SFA finished 6-1 in the Southland and 8-3 overall but failed to capture an at-large berth in the Division I-AA playoffs. Northwestern State saw its two-year reign as conference champions come to an end. The Demons closed the 1999 season at 3-4 in the league and 4-7 overall.

After a 1-4 start, McNeese State closed out the season by winning five of its last six, including a 38-0 SFL road win at Nicholls State, to end the 1999 season with a winning record.

Along with finishing the year 6-5 overall, the Cowboys ended up 5-2 in league play.

McNeese dominated on both sides of the ball in the season finale, rolling up 417 total yards while limiting Nicholls to 169, including only 59 on the ground.

Despite the big statistical edge, the Cowboys only managed a 7-0 halftime lead due to a mistake-filled first half. A missed LaFrenz field goal and two fumbles by Burton cost McNeese potential points. Burton, who rushed for 103 yards, made amends with a 1-yard touchdown run in the second quarter to give the Cowboys their 7-0 edge at intermission.

While the game was played at Nicholls State, is seemed like Senior Night in the second half for the Cowboys. After a 2-yard run by Josh Chaumont made it 14-0 only 10 seconds into the third quarter, senior fullback Abe Abdmoulaie scored his first career touchdown on a 1-yard run. Abdmoulaie seemed to like scoring so much; he added his second touchdown moments later on a 15-yard pass from Nagle to give McNeese a 28-0 lead with 4:09 remaining in the third quarter.

Tarius Davis, another senior, scored his first career touchdown on a 66-yard punt return with 8:01 left in the game. LaFrenz, yet another senior, hit a 41-yard field goal with 49 seconds left in the game to make the 38-0 final. LaFrenz's kick was field goal No. 66 in his career, tying the career school record originally set by Jose Larios.

While McNeese managed to close out the year with a winning record, Nicholls State ended its season at 1-10 overall and 1-6 in the SFL under Daye, the Colonels' first-year coach. It marked only the second time in school history that the Colonels finished with double-figure losses in a season.

Like McNeese, Sam Houston State went into its final game of the season at Southwest Texas on a high note with a three-game winning streak. Such was not the case for the Bobcats, who entered the tilt on a five-game losing skid.

Looking to close the season with four-consecutive wins, Sam Houston State found itself trailing 20-14 with less than two minutes remaining in the game.

A missed field goal attempt by SWT that would have put the game away, gave the Bearkats one last chance, taking over at their 20-yard line with 1:34 left in the game. SHSU advanced to the Bobcats' 34-yard line but a failed fourth-down conversion attempt with 27 seconds left in the game allowed Southwest Texas to hold on for the win – its only victory over Sam Houston State in the 1990s.

The Bearkats fumbled on their opening possession of the game at their own 40-yard line and Southwest Texas was able to take advantage when Sanders scored on a 9-yard run less than four minutes into the game. A 6-yard touchdown pass from Wynn to Marvin Giddings gave the Bobcats a 13-0 lead after one quarter.

A Bobcats fumble led to a 5-yard touchdown run by Bradley early in the second quarter to make the score 13-7. Vaughn's interception of a Bradley pass gave the ball to Southwest Texas at its own 37 with 1:46 left in the half. SWT scored with slightly more than 30 seconds remaining in the half for a 20-7 lead on its way to the 20-14 triumph.

SHSU ended the season 4-3 in the Southland and 6-5 overall. Southwest Texas concluded the year 2-5 in the conference and 3-8 overall.

Opening the Division I-AA playoffs at home, Troy State jumped out to a 10-0 halftime lead on its way to a 27-7 victory over James Madison.

A 1-yard touchdown run by Lucas in the second quarter and a Tynes field goal gave Troy State its 10-0 halftime edge. The Trojans took advantage of the absence of Dukes quarterback Chris Paquette, who suffered a separated shoulder in the second quarter. With Paquette out of the game, Troy concentrated on shutting down Curtis Keaton. The James Madison running back, who entered the game averaging 158 yards per game on the ground, was held to 40 yards by the Trojans' defense.

Leading 10-0, the Trojans scored on their first drive of the second half. Troy State marched 75 yards before Buttone fumbled into the end zone but Jones recovered for a Trojans touchdown. Eric Sloan returned an interception to the 1-yard line, setting up a touchdown run by Lucas one play later to seal the victory for Troy.

"In the playoffs, you will face some very good teams. Whoever gets prepared the best and handles the situations that occur in a football game best will wind up winning. It happened to be our day," said Blakeney.

Playing at home against a Florida A&M team that knocked Troy State out of the playoffs the previous year, the Trojans struck quickly against the Rattlers.

Troy State used 10 plays to drive 73 yards on its opening possession of the game to grab a 7-0 lead on a 2-yard run by Lucas.

The Trojans had little time to enjoy the advantage, however, as the Rattlers tied the game less than a minute later. A 77-yard bomb from Florida A&M

quarterback JaJuan Seider to Demetrius Bendross three plays into the Rattlers' ensuing possession knotted up the contest.

Neither team could score the remainder of the first half, leading to a second-half showdown.

A fumble by Nutter at the Troy State 24 in the middle of the third quarter provided Florida A&M with a huge break. The Rattlers could not take full advantage but still gained the lead when Jeremy Edward kicked a 34-yard field goal.

Florida A&M's defense forced the Trojans to a three-and-out on Troy State's next possession, giving the ball back to the Rattlers' offense and their own 43. A 57-yard strike from reserve quarterback Quinn Gary to Bendross gave FAMU a 17-7 lead. Bendross ended the game with five catches for 164 yards.

Naazir Yamini blocked a Rattlers punt at the Florida A&M 24 but all the Trojans could get out of the turnover was a 29-yard Tynes field goal early in the fourth quarter. Tynes' kick was as close as the Trojans would get as the Rattlers again knocked Troy State out of the playoffs with a 17-10 victory.

"The Florida A&M guys had plenty of talent and a great coaching staff. They obviously could throw it and run it. They were tough to beat," Blakeney said.

Troy State ended the 1999 season 11-2.

The 2000 season saw the addition of three new coaches in the Southland Football League, some coming due to unusual circumstances.

Only two days following the 1999 season, Jacksonville State had its new man in veteran coach Jack Crowe. The former University of Arkansas head coach returned to the coaching ranks after spending five years in private business. A former head coach at Livingston, Crowe had stints as offensive coordinator at Wyoming, Auburn, Clemson, Arkansas and Baylor. After serving as head coach at Arkansas from 1990-92, he was the offensive coordinator at Baylor for three seasons.

In May 2000, Steve Roberts was named the head coach at Northwestern State, replacing Sam Goodwin. Goodwin left the Demons to return to Henderson State, his alma mater, as athletic director. Roberts was hired away from Southern Arkansas, where he guided the Muleriders to a 35-24-1 record in six years.

A month later, Kirby Bruchhaus abruptly resigned as head coach at McNeese State amid allegations of gambling on college and professional football games, a violation of NCAA rules. Tommy Tate, an assistant at McNeese since 1979, was promoted to head coach of the Cowboys.

The first of the new head coaches to make his Southland Football League debut was Crowe when his Jacksonville State Gamecocks visited Nicholls State. Both teams had played one game prior to the SFL opener with Jacksonville State losing 40-0 to South Florida while Nicholls defeated Central Arkansas 52-44. The win for Nicholls snapped an eight-game losing streak.

Poor field conditions due to three days of rain led to a defensive struggle but Jacksonville State was able to take advantage of six Nicholls turnovers while holding the Colonels to only 222 yards of total offense in a 10-3 victory for the Gamecocks.

Down 10-0 early in the second half, Nehemiah Lucas blocked a Jacksonville State punt, with Nicholls taking over at the Gamecocks' 30. The Colonels eventually settled on a 32-yard Kyle Leisher field goal for their only points of the game.

Late in the game, Nicholls began a drive from its own 1-yard line for the second time in the contest. Facing third-and-eight from at the Jacksonville 29, Scott Smith sacked Nicholls quarterback Brad Smith for a 7-yard loss. On fourth down with slightly more than two minutes remaining, Maxwell Thurmond intercepted a Brad Smith pass to end the Colonels' comeback attempt.

Jacksonville took advantage of a Nicholls turnover on the Colonels' first possession of the game when Delvin Hugley returned an errant Brad Smith pass 30 yards for a touchdown. The only other score of the game came on a 35-yard Brad Hopkins field goal early in the second quarter.

Tate and his McNeese State squad made their Southland debut several weeks later when the Cowboys hosted Stephen F. Austin. McNeese went into the game 3-1 on the season. Tate drew a tough opening assignment, facing the Miami Hurricanes, the fifth-ranked team in Division I-A. Following a 61-14 loss to coach Butch Davis' Hurricanes, the Cowboys won three-straight games going into the SFA encounter.

"We went in (the Miami game) with a 'nothing-to-lose' attitude and really played our hearts out. The effort was outstanding," said Tate. "It was a very talented team we went up against and our players came out of that game with a lot of confidence and ready to move on with the season.

SFA was off to a 3-1 start as well, with the Lumberjacks' only defeat being a loss to Northern Iowa.

McNeese State's defense limited a Lumberjacks team that had been averaging 37.5 points per game to 156 yards of total offense and one score – a 1-yard touchdown run by Gary Allen in the second quarter – in the Cowboys' 37-6 victory. Allen's touchdown came with 29 seconds left in the half to make the score 17-6.

The Cowboys' first-half points came on a 40-yard Charlie Hebert field goal in the first quarter along with second-quarter touchdown runs of 7 yards by Marcus Trahan and 9 yards by Aaron Pierce.

Trahan added a 1-yard run in the second half while Slade Nagle tossed touchdown passes of 52 yards to Jermaine Martin and 15 to Jeff Hamilton. Jessie

Burton rushed for 128 yards but his streak of seven-consecutive games with a touchdown came to an end.

The win avenged a 40-14 loss a year earlier for McNeese in which the Lumberjacks used a fake punt with five minutes left in the game to set up a final touchdown although SFA already was ahead by a comfortable margin.

Making his SFL debut that same day was Roberts of Northwestern State. The Demons went into their home game against Troy State 3-1 on the season. A win over Southern University gave Roberts his first win as Demons coach. Northwestern State's lone loss was to Central Florida.

Troy State was off to a 3-1 start as well, with the Trojans losing only to South Florida.

The Demons came up with a 24-point third quarter to take a 24-10 lead against fifth-ranked Troy State.

Northwestern State trailed 3-0 at halftime before coming up with a 15-yard Tony Taylor run, a 31-yard Clint Sanford field goal, a 36-yard pass from Ben Beach to T.J. Sutherland and an 86-yard punt return by Terrence McGee to build it's lead. Troy's only third-quarter score came on a 44-yard run by LeBarron Black.

After a 1-yard run by Wayne Thomas with 9:47 left in the game made the score 24-17, the Demons turned the game over to their defense.

The Trojans made one final march, reaching the Northwestern 1-yard line for first-and-goal with 3:44 remaining. Thad Buttone, the Troy State fullback, was stopped for no gain. A dive by Black moved the ball to within inches of the goal line. On third down, Black was dropped at the 2-yard line.

On fourth down, Trojans quarterback Brock Nutter went left on an option keeper. He fumbled the ball into the end zone and Troy State recovered. Being that Nutter was not the player to recover his own fumble on fourth down, by rule, the score was nullified and the Demons went on to take possession to preserve the 24-17 upset victory.

"It was a nightmare," said Troy State coach Larry Blakeney. "Any time you are in a close game like that and you can't convert, it's a nightmare."

In San Marcos, Southwest Texas was playing its first Southland Football League game of the year against a 1-4 Nicholls State team that was on the road for the fourth-straight week. Southwest Texas went into the game 2-2.

SWT returned a pair of Nicholls fumbles 16 and 58 yards for touchdowns in a 25-0 win over the Colonels on a rain-drenched field. Nicholls lost a total of six fumbles and threw an interception in the shutout loss.

Clenton Ballard's 16-yard fumble return for a touchdown in the first quarter staked the Bobcats to a 10-0 lead. Myron Coleman's 58-yard fumble return in the fourth quarter rounded out the scoring for the Bobcats. Nicholls was limited to 68 yards total offense as quarterbacks Smith and freshman Josh Son were a combined 1 of 7 passing for minus-1 yard.

Meanwhile, a season-long trend for Sam Houston State saved the day for the Bearkats in their Southland Football League opener at Jacksonville State.

Jacksonville State had the early momentum, leading 10-0 when the Gamecocks went into punt formation. The Bearkats blocked John Howard's punt and Keith Davis picked up the loose ball and scooted 12 yards for a touchdown to turn the game into a three-point affair. The block by Sam Houston State was the fifth blocked kick by the Bearkats in as many games.

With the score tied 17-17 early in the fourth quarter the Gamecocks elected to try and convert on fourth down rather than risking another punt near midfield. One play after an incomplete pass gave the ball to SHSU, Jerome Dabney turned a screen pass from Albert Bradley into a 50-yard gain to the 1-yard line. Bradley scored on the next play but Alex St. Peter missed the extra point, leaving the Bearkats with a six-point lead.

Jacksonville State rallied on a 2-yard run by quarterback Reggie Stancil but the Bearkats blocked the potential go-ahead score, leaving the game tied 23-23 with 6:03 remaining in the contest.

A 50-yard pass from Bradley to Jermaine Henderson helped to set up a 27-yard St. Peter field goal with 40 seconds left in the game to give the Bearkats a hard-fought 26-23 triumph.

Sam Houston State improved to 4-1 with the victory, losing only to Western Illinois 31-0 through five games.

Playing on a Thursday night, Troy State took advantage of early Southwest Texas turnovers and shut down the Bobcats' running game as the Trojans snapped their two-game losing streak with a 31-7 SFL home win.

A Nick Colbert interception of a Reagan George pass led to a 5-yard touchdown run by Wayne Thomas. James Griffin's luck was no better at quarterback for Southwest Texas as he threw a second-quarter interception Rayshun Reed returned 10 yards for a touchdown. SWT fumbled the ball away two plays into its next possession. The Trojans took advantage with a 21-yard Lawrence Tynes field goal for a 17-0 Troy lead.

The Trojans built their lead to 31-0 before SWT avoided the shutout with five minutes left in the game on a 9-yard touchdown pass from Griffin to Kenneth Samuels. The Bobcats were limited to 51 yards rushing.

Both teams moved to 1-1 in the Southland Football League while Troy State improved to 4-2 overall with Southwest Texas slipping to 3-3.

Two days later, McNeese State moved to 2-0 in the SFL with a 28-0 blanking of Jacksonville State in Lake Charles.

Limited to two Hebert field goals over the first two quarters, the Cowboys scored three touchdowns in the second half. A 9-yard run by Burton and a 31-yard pass from Nagle to Martin in the third quarter made it 21-0. Hampered by injuries sustained a week earlier, Burton saw limited action against the Gamecocks, finishing with 57 yards on nine carries.

McNeese's final score came on a 33-yard pass from Nagle to Marcus Trahan in the fourth quarter.

The Cowboys' defense, meanwhile, held the Gamecocks to 83 yards rushing and 132 passing as McNeese moved to 5-1 on the season. Jacksonville dropped to 2-3 overall, including 1-2 in the Southland.

Unveiling its new triple-option offense, Nicholls baffled 10th-ranked Northwestern State for three quarters as the Colonels played at home for the first time in five weeks.

Switching from the spread offense Nicholls had run since the 1999 season, the Colonels built a 19-6 lead. Nicholls managed to rush for 232 yards and hold the ball for 30:56 through three quarters before the Demons made a switch of their own.

At that point, Roberts benched Beach, the Northwestern State starting quarterback, in favor of Aubrey Jones. On Jones' first possession, he led the Demons on a 13-play, 73-yard drive, culminating in a 14-yard touchdown pass to Sutherland. With Jones at the helm, Northwestern State ran 12-straight plays before the touchdown toss to Sutherland to make the score 19-13 with 12:35 remaining in the game.

Nicholls held Taylor to 81 yards rushing through three quarters before he broke loose in the final period. Taylor rambled 66 yards to set up his own 1-yard touchdown run to put Northwestern State on top 20-19 with 8:53 remaining in the game.

Taylor finished with 198 yards in the game as he became Northwestern State's all-time leading rusher. His 3,135 career yards pushed him ahead of John Stephens on the school's all-time rushing list.

A 38-yard touchdown run by Jeremy London with 2:28 remaining secured the victory for Northwestern. The Demons took an intentional safety on the final play of the game as Northwestern rallied for the 27-21 triumph.

Son led the Colonels' new option attack with 107 yards. He was 1 of 3 passing for two yards.

Opening in a double-wing and I-formation offense, Son marched the Colonels to an opening Leisher field goal. A 1-yard touchdown run by Samuel Brooks and two more Leisher field goals gave Nicholls a 16-6 halftime lead but the Colonels could not avoid dropping their sixth-straight game to fall to 0-3 in the SFL and 1-6 overall.

Tenth-ranked Northwestern State improved to 2-0 in the conference and 5-1 overall.

For the second year in a row, the defenses seemed to take the game off in Sam Houston State's encounter at Stephen F. Austin.

While the offensive numbers were not quite as big as the previous year, the scoring was higher as the teams combined for 93 points – the largest single-game point total ever in the 75 meetings of the two institutions – as the Bearkats eventually posted a 52-41 victory.

Sam Houston State grabbed an early 10-0 lead and the Bearkats were up by as much as 24-7 before eventually trailing 27-24 at halftime. The Bearkats regained the lead when Chris Foster returned the second-half kickoff 91 yards for a touchdown.

The back-and-forth battle saw the Lumberjacks leading 41-38 and looking for a potential knockout punch early in the fourth quarter. On first down from the SHSU 34, Lumberjacks quarterback Wes Pate, who passed for 283 yards, was hit by DeJuan Davis while attempting to throw. Keith Davis, DeJuan's older brother, intercepted Pate's errant throw and raced to the SFA 30. Two plays later, Willie Thomas scored on an 18-yard run for a 45-41 Bearkats lead.

It was SHSU that ended up delivering the knockout blow when Eric Brown scored on a 3-yard run with 6:37 left in the game.

Along with moving to 2-0 in the Southland, the Bearkats improved to 5-1 overall. SFA dropped to 0-2 in the league and 3-3 overall.

A week later, Northwestern State defeated visiting McNeese State 37-34 to remain the only unbeaten team in Southland Football League play.

McNeese State's game at Northwestern State marked the 50th meeting between the two teams and both squads seemed ready to put on a show with first place on the line in the Southland Football League.

Northwestern had the hot hand early, scoring the game's first 20 points. A Sanford field goal and a 41-yard pass from Beach to Sutherland gave the Demons a 10-0 lead after one quarter. An 8-yard touchdown pass to Daniel Morgan and a second Sanford field goal in the second quarter gave Northwestern it's 20-point cushion.

McNeese, meanwhile, avoided a first-half shutout when Nagle hit Jimmy Redmond with an 18-yard touchdown strike with 35 seconds remaining before halftime.

McGee got the points back in a flash when he returned an errant Slade throw 72 yards for a touchdown in the third quarter to put the Demons back on top by 20 points at 27-7.

Now, it was time for the Cowboys' hand to turn branding-iron hot.

A 1-yard run by Nagle and a 25-yard scamper by Burton rallied McNeese to within 27-20 by the end of the third quarter.

The Cowboys tied the game on a 1-yard run by Luke Lawton with 9:19 left in the game. Another Lawton score from a yard out with 2:01 remaining in the contest gave McNeese its first lead at 34-27.

After watching the Cowboys score 27-straight points, nothing less than a perfectly-executed two-minute drill could save the Demons.

Four plays into the ensuing drive, Beach hit Devon Lockett for 26 yards down to the McNeese 9-yard line. On third-and-goal, Sean Weber hauled in a 4-yard strike to tie the game 34-34 with 50 seconds remaining.

With overtime looming, the Demons kicked off. Trahan, the Cowboys return man, fumbled, with Treymayne Madison recovering for Northwestern at the McNeese 37 with 43 seconds left in the game.

A pass to Bernard Green and two running plays advanced the ball to the 20-yard line. With four seconds left in the game, Sanford booted a 37-yard field goal to lift the Demons to a 37-34 triumph.

"We just fell behind early, came back and got the lead and had a chance to win it," said Tate. "We just made some errors at the end that gave them an opportunity and they took advantage of them.

"I remember our players coming out of that game with a lot of confidence with the performance they gave and knowing that we just made so many mistakes that cost us the football game."

Special teams play, a huge asset for Sam Houston State all season long, let the team down in the Bearkats' home game against No. 10 Troy State.

Three Tynes field goals helped Troy State to a 9-7 halftime lead. Special teams woes struck for the Bearkats on the opening play of the third quarter when Jonathan Carter sprinted 95 yards with the second-half kickoff for a 16-7 Trojans advantage.

Foster returned the ensuing kickoff to near midfield but SHSU was unable to take advantage of the field position when St. Peter was off the mark on a 47-yard field goal attempt – his third miss of the game.

It wasn't all bad for the Bearkats' special teams unit as the Davis brothers did it once again. Keith Davis blocked a Trojans punt and his younger brother, DeJuan, recovered and raced 6 yards for a touchdown to put Sam Houston State back in the game at 16-14 late in the third quarter.

The Bearkats' momentum was short-lived as they allowed Jabar Dunbar to scamper 58 yards with the ensuing kickoff to the SHSU 31. Nutter eventually hit LeQuateus Justice with a 4-yard touchdown toss for a 23-14 lead.

Sam Houston State marched 92 yards for a touchdown, capping the drive on a 2-yard run by Bradley with 50 seconds left to make the score 23-21. The Trojans recovered an onside kick attempt and held on for the two-point victory.

Both teams moved to 2-1 in the SFL and left Northwestern State as the only unbeaten team in conference play.

Meanwhile, Lee Davis and Bronson Sanders each topped 100 yards in the same game for the first time since the season opener as Southwest Texas defeated visiting Jacksonville State 28-24. The duo combined for 257 yards but the biggest carry of the game was a 2-yard run by Davis with 6:42 left in the contest to lift the Bobcats to the four-point triumph.

Southwest Texas improved to 4-3 overall, the first time the Bobcats had that many wins through seven games since a 4-3 start in 1992. SWT also moved to 2-1 in Southland play. Jacksonville State, meanwhile, dropped to 2-4 overall and 1-3 in the league.

Jacksonville State runner James Carlow also topped 100 yards in the game. His 46-yard touchdown run tied the game 14-14. The first of Davis' two touchdown runs put the Bobcats up by seven points in the third quarter.

A Gamecocks field goal and 10-yard run by Rondy Rogers gave Jacksonville State a 24-21 edge in the fourth quarter, setting the stage for Davis' game-deciding run.

In Thibodaux, teams each in the midst of losing streaks met when Stephen F. Austin played Nicholls State. The Lumberjacks entered the game with a three-game losing streak while the Colonels had lost six in a row.

Something had to give and it seemed only appropriate that the game was tied in the late stages. A 38-yard Leisher field goal allowed Nicholls to tie the game 20-20. SFA responded by driving 87 yards. A 51-yard pass from Pate to Lawrence Hamilton advanced the ball to the Colonels' 1-yard line. Pate scored on a keeper to give the Lumberjacks a 27-20 triumph.

Son, the Colonels' freshman quarterback, accounted for both of Nicholls State's touchdowns in the first half. He connected with Curtis Johnson on a 51-yard touchdown strike in the first quarter and scored on a 1-yard run in the second quarter.

Pate tossed 10 yards to Will Bowers for one score and hit Hamilton from 36 yards out for another.

SFA moved to 1-2 in the Southland Football League and moved back above .500 at 4-3 overall. Nicholls remained winless in the conference at 0-4 and 1-7 overall.

With Stephen F. Austin's penchant to blow 17-0 leads, the Lumberjacks tried to keep that from happening in their SFL game at Jacksonville State on a Thursday night by jumping out to a 27-0 advantage. It proved to be a good move for SFA.

A 2-yard touchdown run by Pate late in the first quarter started the scoring for the Lumberjacks. SFA made it 14-0 moments into the second quarter when Kevon Morton returned a blocked punt 3 yards for a touchdown. Two touchdowns to open the second half gave Stephen F. Austin its 27-0 margin.

The Gamecocks broke their scoring drought when quarterback Stancil tossed 33 yards to Herman Bell midway in the third quarter. Jacksonville State added touchdowns on back-to-back drives to trail only 27-21.

SFA was looking to put the game away with a field goal with 1:20 left in the game but an 18-yard attempt was partially blocked.

Facing fourth down in the closing seconds, a Stancil pass was tipped and Bell was unable to come up with the catch, allowing SFA to cling to a 27-21 triumph.

The Lumberjacks evened their SFL mark at 2-2 while improving to 5-3 overall. Jacksonville State dropped to 1-4 in the conference and 2-5 overall.

Two days later, Southwest Texas took advantage of two long fumble returns to set up scores in the Bobcats' 21-10 Southland home win over No. 5 Northwestern State.

The first fumble return by C.J. Carroll led to an 18-yard touchdown pass from Griffin to tight end Garrett Hagendorf. Sterling Rogers returned the second fumble 52 yards for a touchdown and a 14-0 SWT lead.

A 13-yard pass from George to Brian Foreshee made it 21-0 midway in the third quarter before the Demons got their only points on a 35-yard Sanford field goal and a 3-yard touchdown reception by Green.

The win marked the first time since 1992 that the Bobcats beat a team ranked in the Top 5 in Division I-AA. Northwestern State fell to 3-1 in the SFL and allowed numerous teams to join the hunt for first place.

In Huntsville, with McNeese State and Sam Houston State both 2-1 in the SFL, the winner of the clash would join Northwestern State and Southwest Texas atop the conference.

McNeese bounced back from its loss to Northwestern State in a big way, using a pair of big defensive plays to build an early lead the Cowboys would never relinquish in a 31-17 win over the Bearkats.

Cowboy defensive end Jimmy Abram rambled 58 yards on a fumble return less than two minutes into the game to give McNeese a 7-0 lead. Later in the quarter, defensive tackle Jerry Evans returned an interception 37 yards to set up a 2-yard touchdown reception by Lawton for a 14-0 lead.

After the Bearkats closed the gap to 14-3 on a 46-yard St. Peter field goal early in the second quarter, Pierce raced 56 yards for a touchdown and Trahan scored on a 1-yard run to give McNeese a 28-8 lead on the Cowboys' way to the 31-17 victory. Pierce, subbing for Burton, rushed for 133 yards.

In Troy, meanwhile, Troy State made it a four-way tie atop the SFL with a 41-12 thumping of visiting Nicholls State.

The Trojans jumped out to a 17-0 lead in the first quarter on a 46-yard field goal by Tynes, a 14-yard pass from Nutter to Carter and an 8-yard run by Black as Troy cruised to the victory.

Nicholls, winless in the SFL at 0-5 and 1-8 overall, got its only points on a 51-yard fumble return for a touchdown by Doug King and two Leisher field goals. Along with moving to 3-1 in the Southland, Troy improved to 6-2 overall.

At least one team was going to fall out of first place in the SFL a week later as McNeese State and Southwest Texas, both 3-1, squared off in Lake Charles.

Playing on a wet field in the rain, the Cowboys only could manage 247 yards of total offense but their defense limited Southwest Texas to 212 yards and only a field goal in McNeese State's 18-3 victory over the Bobcats.

McNeese scored all of its first-half points in the second quarter to take a 10-0 lead. A 23-yard Hebert field goal and a 2-yard run by Pierce gave the Cowboys the advantage at the break. Pierce was the workhorse for McNeese, carrying the ball 40 times for 106 yards.

"Aaron Pierce, he had 40 carries and the guy probably weighed about 170 pounds. He was just a real tough, strong kid," Tate recalled.

Southwest Texas got its only points in the third quarter on a 40-yard Justin Martinez field goal, but the Cowboys put the game out of reach in the fourth quarter on a 3-yard touchdown by Lawton and a two-point conversion run by David Latta.

Troy State kept pace with McNeese, taking a 6-0 win at Stephen F. Austin. Tynes provided the only points of the game on a 33-yard field goal in the second quarter and a 46-yard kick in the fourth quarter.

"There was pretty good defense played on both sides but it was rainy and cold and it was not perfect football weather. Our kids hung in and fought hard and Lawrence took care of us by getting us enough points to win," said Blakeney.

Along with improving to 4-1 in the Southland, Troy State improved to 7-2 overall. SFA dropped to 2-3 in the conference and 5-4 overall.

Northwestern State was not able to keep pace as the Demons did something at Jacksonville State they had not done in seven seasons - allow an opposing running back to gain more than 200 yards - leading to a devastating 28-24 loss.

Rogers rushed for 224 yards and the Gamecocks gained 332 yards as a team on the ground to hand No. 10 Northwestern State its second SFL loss in a row. Rogers rushed for two of his team's three touchdowns in the first half. Troy Sumarall countered with a pair of 2-yard touchdown runs and Sanford kicked a 27-yard field goal with 1:07 remaining in the first half for a 21-17 Jacksonville State lead.

Northwestern had a second-and-goal at the Jacksonville State 3-yard line but an unsportsmanlike penalty pushed back the Demons, forcing them to settle on Sanford's field goal.

The Demons took their only lead of the game at 24-21 when Kurt Rodriguez returned an interception for a touchdown in the closing seconds of the third quarter.

Northwestern fell to 3-2 in the Southland and dropped to 6-3 overall. Jacksonville State snapped a four-game losing streak in moving to 2-4 in the conference and 3-5 overall.

In the one game that day not involving a first-place team, Thomas racked up 197 all-purpose yards and accounted for three touchdowns as the Bearkats snapped a two-game losing streak with a 27-21 win at Nicholls State.

Following an early Leisher field goal for the Colonels, Thomas scored on runs of 1 and 12 yards to give Sam Houston State a 14-3 edge.

With SHSU leading 17-14, Brian Null hooked with Thomas on an 18-yard touchdown toss for a 10-point advantage on the Bearkats' way to the 27-21 victory.

The win moved Sam Houston State to 3-2 in SFL play and secured a second-straight winning season for the Bearkats as they improved to 6-3 overall. Nicholls remained winless in the conference through six games while dropping to 1-9 overall.

Troy State and McNeese State both entered their encounter with 4-1 records in the Southland Football League and the Trojans were looking for a title in their final year in the conference. Troy announced earlier that it was leaving the Southland to pursue Division I-A status.

Following a scoreless first quarter, McNeese took a 10-0 lead to the locker room on a 19-yard Hebert field goal and a 1-yard run by John Taylor in the second quarter.

Troy State gained the lead with a 17-point third quarter on a pair of touchdown runs by Carter and a 37-yard Tynes field goal. The Trojans made it 20-10 on a 23-yard Tynes field goal early in the fourth quarter.

McNeese fought back, scoring on a 3-yard Luke Lawton run with 6:09 left in the game but the Cowboys could get no closer in falling 20-16.

The win moved Troy State to 5-1 and secured no worse than a tie for the SFL title with one game remaining against Jacksonville State. McNeese dropped to 4-2. Troy moved to 8-2 overall with the win while McNeese fell to 7-3.

In a meeting of teams both sporting 3-2 SFL marks, Sam Houston State jumped out to a 17-0 lead at Northwestern State by scoring on three-consecutive possessions.

The Demons, meanwhile, were not so efficient on offense. Four of Northwestern State's trips inside the Bearkats' 30-yard line failed to produce points as SHSU came away with a 27-13 victory.

Northwestern State's only points in the first half came on a 48-yard run by Taylor.

After a 38-yard St. Peter field goal gave the Bearkats a 20-6 lead, Dink Watson's interception of a pass by Jones, the Demons' backup quarterback, gave Sam Houston State the ball at the Northwestern State 48. SHSU took advantage several plays later on a 15-yard screen pass for a touchdown from Null to Dabney to put the game away at 27-6 early in the fourth quarter.

The Demons were hampered by the loss of Beach, their starting quarterback, who suffered a separated shoulder in the first half.

Sam Houston State improved to 4-2 in the SFL and 7-3 overall. Northwestern State, at one point 6-1 on the season and ranked as high as No. 5 in Division I-AA, dropped to 3-3 in the conference and 6-4 overall.

Playing its final home game of 2000, a victory for Southwest Texas against Stephen F. Austin would allow Bobcat fans to witness a rare winning season.

Stephen F. Austin took a 7-0 lead by marching 80 yards with the opening kickoff, culminating the drive on a 20-yard pass from Pate to Bowers. At that point, the 17-point bug-a-boo hit SFA once again as the Lumberjacks were outscored by 17 points to fall behind 17-7.

The Bobcats answered with a drive of their own two possessions later. Facing fourth-and-2 from the SFA 30, Davis broke loose to tie the game. Southwest Texas converted Coleman's 25-yard interception return into a 20-yard Martinez field goal to give the Bobcats a 10-7 lead. SWT stretched the lead to 10 points moments later. After pulling off an onside kick, Griffin spotted Stephen Ross on a 48-yard touchdown strike less than a minute into the second quarter.

Hamilton turned a screen pass from Pate into a 64-yard score before SWT regained its 10-point margin to lead 24-14 on a 15-yard toss from Griffin to Tyrone Darden.

Stephen F. Austin made it 24-21 at halftime with a touchdown in the closing moments of the second quarter. The Bobcats made sure the Lumberjacks would make no further inroads, traveling 65 yards with the second-half kickoff. Davis capped the drive with a 6-yard run. An interception on SFA's ensuing drive set up an 11-yard strike to James Stewart for a 38-21 lead that would hold up for the remainder of the contest.

Southwest Texas moved into a three-way tie for second place with McNeese State and Sam Houston State at 4-2 in the Southland, one game behind Troy State. SWT's sixth win of the year secured a winning season for the Bobcats for the first time since 1991. SFA dropped to 2-4 in the league and 5-5 overall.

Third-ranked Troy State closed out its final Southland Football League game in style with a 28-0 win at rival Jacksonville State on a cold, rainy day.

The Trojans scored two early touchdowns and blanked the Gamecocks to claim their third and final SFL crown before departing the conference to pursue Division I-A status.

A 65-yard touchdown pass from Nutter to Carter on Troy State's opening play would be all the Trojans would need to top their rival. On Troy's next possession, Buttone tossed 33 yards to Carter for another touchdown and a 14-0 lead.

The Trojans forced Jacksonville State to punt on the opening possession of the third quarter and Heyward Skipper raced 55 yards for a touchdown to make it 21-0. Early in the fourth quarter, Buttone scored on a 1-yard run to cap an 81-yard drive to close out the scoring.

Jacksonville State's only serious threat came in the second quarter. Trailing by two touchdowns, the Gamecocks faced fourth-and-5 from the Troy 15. A screen pass from Stancil to Carlton lost 6 yards to end the drive.

"Our kids were really excited about playing. It was sort of a messy environment but one in which we took full advantage of and played awfully well," Blakeney said.

Troy State closed out the regular season 9-2 overall, 6-1 in the SFL. The Gamecocks, who were hoping to end the season with a win for a break-even record, finished 4-6 overall, including 2-5 in the conference.

Although there would be no SFL title for McNeese State in 2000, a win in the season finale over Nicholls State would allow the Cowboys to finish with an 8-3 mark and perhaps earn an at-large bid to the Division I-AA playoffs.

Rainy conditions led to a low-scoring affair. McNeese got all the points it would need in the first quarter on a 31-yard touchdown pass from Nagle to George Thompson and a 23-yard Hebert field goal.

The 10-0 lead held up through halftime before the Cowboys added two more points a safety in the third quarter. Arthur Goodly tackled Nicholls runner Sullivan Beard in the end zone to make the score 12-0.

Nicholls State's only score came on a 3-yard run by Chad Carter late in the third period. The score was set up when Bruce Bolden was hit by a punt and the Colonels recovered at the McNeese 15 as the Cowboys went on to take a 12-7 a victory.

"The field was real muddy and it was hard to sustain drives," Tate recalled. "You had to take advantage of field position and we did that with our defense and special teams and got enough points on the board to come away with the win."

McNeese ended the regular season 8-3 overall, including 5-2 in the Southland.

Nicholls concluded its year winless in the SFL and 1-10 overall with a 10-game losing streak. Officially, the Colonels mark became 2-9 overall and 1-6 in the Southland when Northwestern State was later forced to forfeit wins over Nicholls and Troy State for using an ineligible player. The forfeit also technically halted the Colonels' losing streak at five games.

Southwest Texas finished in a tie for second place with McNeese in the SFL at 5-2 with a season-ending 24-17 triumph at Sam Houston State.

Temperatures in the 40s, along with wind and rain, greeted the Bobcats in their 2000 season finale against Sam Houston State. The ball was hard to hold onto as each team fumbled three times. Yards came grudgingly as well as SWT finished with 258 yards to only 112 for Sam Houston State.

Davis picked up 67 of the Bobcats' yards on a touchdown run to give Southwest Texas a 7-0 lead. After a 5-yard scoring run by SHSU's Dabney, Griffin countered with a 9-yard touchdown run for a 14-7 Bobcats lead after one quarter.

Perhaps the biggest turnover of the game came when SWT defender Jason Washington returned a third-quarter interception 40 yards for a touchdown. Washington's score was part of a 10-point Bobcats scoring spree in a 30-second span that gave Southwest Texas a 24-10 lead on its way to the 24-17 victory.

The Bobcats' defense continually harassed Null and Bradley, the SHSU quarterbacks. Bradley was dropped behind the line numerous times for 46 yards in lost yardage.

Both teams concluded the season 7-4 overall. Southwest Texas, by winning four of its last five games, finished 5-2 in the SFL; it's best record since joining the league in 1987. Sam Houston State ended 4-3 in league play.

After a 6-1 start and a ranking of as high as No. 5 in the nation, Northwestern State's season ended with a wimper in a 17-3 loss at Stephen F. Austin.

The loss was the fourth-straight for the Demons to end the season. Northwestern finished the year 3-4 in the Southland Football League and 6-5 overall.

A 17-yard Sanford field goal in the first quarter was the only points the Demons could muster. The field goal gave him 14 on the season, a school single-season record.

SFA broke a 3-3 tie in the third quarter on a 19-yard pass from Peyton Jones to Hamilton in the third quarter and closed out the scoring on a 1-yard run by Allen with less than five minutes remaining in the game.

The lone solace for the Demons after the 6-1 start was the fact Northwestern State finished with a winning record for the fifth time in six seasons.

Even that was not meant to be. After Northwestern State was ruled to have used an ineligible player, the Demons were was forced to forfeit wins over Troy State and Nicholls State, leaving Northwestern with a SFL record of 1-6 and an overall mark of 4-7.

McNeese State's 8-3 record was good enough to earn a berth in the Division I-AA playoffs with the Cowboys opening the postseason at powerhouse Georgia Southern.

Georgia Southern struck quickly when quarterback J.R. Revere broke loose on a 63-yard scamper to give the Eagles a 7-0 lead. The Cowboys regrouped with a 34-yard Hebert field goal and a 37-yard pass from Nagle to Redmond to give McNeese a 10-7 lead after one quarter.

A 48-yard touchdown pass by Revere in the second quarter gave Georgia Southern a 14-10 lead but a 1-yard run by Pierce capped a 74-yard drive to give the Cowboys a 17-14 halftime edge.

Georgia Southern took control in the second half. While the Eagles' defense was shutting out McNeese the rest of the way, the Georgia Southern offense added a pair of touchdown runs by wingback Andre Weathers, a 10-yard run by Edmond Coley and an 11-yard run by Adrian Peterson for a 41-17 victory.

"They ran the triple option or spread option and that's what they were known for. They had an outstanding team and an outstanding tradition," Tate said of Georgia Southern.

Peterson's touchdown with 3:59 remaining in the game put an exclamation point on his season-high 203-yard effort. It was the running back's first action after missing the previous two weeks with a hyperextended elbow.

McNeese ended the 2000 season at 8-4.

Troy State opened the Division I-AA playoffs at home against Appalachian State. In the second week of the season, the Trojans defeated the Mountaineers 34-28 on the road.

A lot more was at stake as the Trojans now enjoyed the home-field advantage. Skipper electrified the home folks early, returning a punt 81 yards the first time the Trojans got their hands on the ball for a 7-0 lead.

The lead disappeared quickly as Troy returned the special teams favor on its next possession. Punter Matt Allen fumbled a snap from center, giving the ball to the Mountaineers at the Trojans' 3-yard line. Appalachian State went backward for a moment but ended up tying the game three plays into its drive on a 6-yard touchdown pass from quarterback Joe Burchett to Troy Albea.

After a 2-yard pass from Burchette to Jimmy Watkins culminated an 85-yard scoring drive, Skipper and the special teams factored in another score. This time, Skipper fumbled a punt return, setting up an 11-yard option keeper by Burchett for a touchdown. A two-point conversion pass attempt was intercepted by Chris Archie and returned for two points to make the score 19-9 at halftime.

After another fumble led to a 12-yard touchdown run by Watkins and a 26-9 Mountaineers lead, the Trojans attempted a late-game rally.

A 2-yard toss from Nutter to Buttone narrowed the margin to three points at 26-23 with less than six minutes remaining in the game. Appalachian State took 2:36 off the clock to eventually set up a 34-yard touchdown pass to Jose White to make the score 33-23.

The Trojans scored with less than two minutes left in the game on a 38-yard pass from Nutter to Carter to make the final score 33-30 as the Trojans were eliminated from the playoffs.

"When you get to the playoffs, you've got to play your best ball. You can't turn it over and can't give up big plays in the kicking game or big touchdown passes and that sort of thing. It will come back to haunt you," said Blakeney.

Troy State posted a 9-3 overall mark and 6-1 record in the Southland Football League in 2000. Factoring in the Northwestern State forfeit, the Trojans officially ended 2000 at 10-2, including going undefeated in seven conference games to close out their tenure in the SFL.

DEALING WITH SEPTEMBER 11

Troy State's departure left the Southland Football League with seven members for the 2001 season but the early part of the Southland season, like the rest of American society, would be remembered for something much more tragic.

The September 11, 2001, terrorists' attacks against the United States led to cancellation or postponement of most events across the country for several days. College football was no exception. The Southland, like the rest of college football, called off games scheduled for September 15, which was the third week of the regular season.

Prior to the terrorists' attacks, Nicholls State and Jacksonville State were the only two teams to have played a SFL game when the two teams met in Jacksonville.

Nicholls went into the game 0-1 on the season after being shut out 20-0 by Louisiana-Lafayette in the Colonels' 2001 opener. Jacksonville State was 1-0 with a win over Cumberland. While it might not have been to the extent of Georgia Tech's famed 220-0 win over the Bulldogs in 1916, the Gamecocks pounded Cumberland 72-10.

The final score was not the most noteworthy moment of the contest. Following Jacksonville State's second touchdown, Ashley Martin kicked an extra point, becoming the first female to play and score in a Division I football game. She finished with three extra points in the contest.

Quarterback Reggie Stancil staked Jacksonville State to all the points it would need in the first half of the Gamecocks' SFL opener against Nicholls State.

The junior quarterback tossed touchdown passes of 24 yards to Will Wagnon, 79 yards to Ralph Jenkins and 23 yards to Jason Poe for a 20-9 halftime lead on the Gamecocks' way to a 34-15 victory.

After being shut out in their season opener at Louisiana-Lafayette, the Colonels' first points of the season came in the first quarter at Jacksonville State when Colt Colletti scored on a 4-yard run for a 6-0 lead but only could add nine more points the remainder of the game.

Nicholls had taken a 9-7 lead midway in the second quarter when Chris Thompson blocked an attempted Gamecocks field goal to set up a 20-yard boot by freshman James Wilcox.

Four SFL teams played their initial conference games four weeks later when McNeese State hosted Stephen F. Austin and Northwestern State visited Sam Houston State.

McNeese went into the Stephen F. Austin game 3-1, its only defeat coming in a competitive 38-24 season-opening loss to Texas A&M. SFA went into the game 2-2 on the year.

Unlike McNeese State's first three wins, there would be no 50-point output for the fifth-ranked Cowboys in their game against Stephen F. Austin as the Lumberjacks returned three interceptions for touchdowns to sink McNeese State 26-14.

McNeese led 14-3 at halftime on a pair of short touchdown runs by Luke Lawton. The momentum swung in favor of the Lumberjacks when Jared Williams returned an interception 25 yards for a touchdown less than a minute into the second half to make the score 14-10. Following a 43-yard Ryan Rossner field goal, Maada Smith returned another interception 27 yards for a touchdown to give SFA a 20-14 lead. James Prince's 18-yard interception return for a touchdown with 2:54 left in the game gave the Lumberjacks the 26-14 victory.

"You never anticipate that. The three pick-6s are unusual. That gave them 21 points we couldn't defend," said Tate. "When you give up three touchdowns without your defense on the field, that's pretty hard to overcome."

Northwestern State and Sam Houston State both went into their encounter 3-1 on the season. The Demons upset Texas Christian for one of their wins, while the only loss was 24-0 to Oklahoma State.

Two touchdown runs by Joe Rauls and a touchdown pass from SMU transfer Josh McCown to Jonathan Cooper gave Sam Houston State a 17-0 third-quarter lead on its way to a 30-14 win over Northwestern State.

The arrival of McCown gave the Bearkats a problem most coaches would love to have – too many quarterbacks. In order to get some of that talent on the field, several of the quarterbacks moved to other positions.

Brian Null and Matt Buss saw action at receiver, Keith Heinrich moved to tight end and P.J. Traylor played safety.

"With all those quarterbacks on the field, it was an interesting season," said Sam Houston State coach Ron Randleman.

A 45-yard touchdown pass from Craig Naul, a LSU transfer, to Devon Lockett late in the third quarter got the Demons on the scoreboard but Northwestern

State was unable to compensate for a poor running game that produced only 57 yards.

Following Lockett's touchdown reception, SHSU put the game away on a 31-yard fumble return by Keith Davis for a 30-7 lead with 9:30 remaining in the game.

The Demons missed out on points in the first half when tight end Mark Peters fumbled into the end zone while attempting to score after a catch.

Southwest Texas finally made its SFL debut a week later when the Bobcats hosted McNeese State. SWT was off to a 4-1 start. The Bobcats went into the McNeese game riding a three-game winning streak following their 40-6 defeat at Missouri for SWT's only loss through five games.

McNeese State's Scott Pendarvis had an easier outing than his Bobcats counterpart, Cody McCauley, as the red-shirt freshmen both made their first career starts in the Southland Football League encounter.

Pendarvis hit on 12 of 18 passes for 169 yards and two touchdowns. A constantly-harassed McCauley, meanwhile, was 5 of 26 passing for 66 yards and was sacked six times.

The Cowboys trailed 3-0 after an 18-yard Justin Martinez field goal on the opening possession of the game before Pendarvis threw his first touchdown, a 38-yard strike to B.J. Sams in the second quarter, to give McNeese a 7-3 halftime edge.

Pendarvis added a 22-yard pass to Britt Brodhead early in the third quarter and fullback Andrew Robin rounded out the scoring on a 6-yard run with 4:32 left in the game.

McNeese held SWT to 67 yards rushing and 66 passing.

While Southwest Texas was playing its first SFL game of the season, Sam Houston State and Stephen F. Austin were moving to 2-0 in conference action as the Bearkats edged Nicholls State 35-31 and the Lumberjacks downed Jacksonville State 44-37.

McCown and Nicholls State's Josh Son showed completely different styles of quarterback play could prove productive, even in poor field conditions, when the Bearkats visited the Colonels.

Despite a driving rain, McCown hooked up with Heinrich on a 57-yard pass to set up a 10-yard toss to Cooper for a touchdown on the Bearkats' second possession of the game. McCown and Cooper hooked up on a 42-yard touchdown on SHSU's next drive for a 14-0 lead.

Son got the Colonels back in the game on a 40-yard touchdown run.

Both teams demonstrated early quick-strike ability but it was lightning strikes shortly after Son's touchdown run that forced both teams from the field. The game wouldn't resume action for two-and-a-half hours.

After play resumed, a Son fumble at the 5-yard line led to a McCown touchdown but the Nicholls quarterback made amends late in the first half by guiding the Colonels into position to add a 42-yard John Manly field goal to make the score 21-10 right before halftime.

A 30-yard touchdown run by Son at the 9:43 mark of the fourth quarter gave the Colonels their only lead of the game at 32-28.

SHSU responded by driving 55 yards. McCown and Cooper hooked up for their third touchdown toss of the game, this one from 15 yards out to give the Bearkats a 35-32 marathon victory.

By the time the game was done, McCown had thrown for 271 yards and four touchdowns, while rushing for another. Son, meanwhile, rushed for 189 yards and two touchdowns while passing for 93 yards and a touchdown.

"Thibodaux is not easy to get to," said Randleman. "We had done something different that year. I believe we ate in Lafayette. We ate our pregame meal earlier than usual. We were in that locker room and our guys are starved (because of the long weather delay). We sent our help out to the concession stands to buy hot dogs and candy bars."

The long delay was hard on the visiting Bearkats in another regard.

"You never know when you will get back out there. That was the tough thing. When you are home, you have more clothes and guys get to change and that sort of stuff and you can be a bit more relaxed. It was a tough situation," Randleman said.

Sam Houston State improved to 2-0 in the SFL and 5-1 overall. Nicholls fell to 0-2 in the league and 1-4 overall.

Things looked bleak for the Lumberjacks on a wet, slippery home field against Jacksonville State. Behind 251 yards of total offense by Rondy Rogers, including three rushing touchdowns and two scoring receptions, the Gamecocks led 30-17 going into the fourth quarter.

With Jacksonville State leading by 13 points, Stancil fumbled at his own 1-yard line. Williams, who was named the Division I-AA National Player of the Week for his performance against McNeese, recovered for the Lumberjacks. After SFA lost yardage on first down, Wes Pate connected with Eric Chapman on an 8-yard strike with less than nine minutes remaining in the game.

The Lumberjacks were backed up to their 5-yard line late in the game following a Jacksonville State punt. Stephen F. Austin worked its way into

Gamecocks territory. Pate tossed a short pass to Will Bowers. Bowers broke several tackles to power his way for a 26-yard touchdown to tie the game at 30-30 with 2:07 remaining. Pate finished the game with five touchdown passes, all to different receivers.

Jacksonville State reached the Stephen F. Austin 15-yard line in the closing seconds to set up a potential game-winning field goal by Steven Lee. After the Lumberjacks called two timeouts, the snap from center went through the hands of holder Josh Shaw to force SFA's second overtime game of the season.

The Gamecocks got the ball first in overtime and both teams scored touchdowns to force a second overtime period. SFA got the ball to start the second overtime and scored on an 8-yard pass from Pate to Courtney Garcia for a 44-37 lead.

With Jacksonville State needing a touchdown to stay alive, Stancil was sacked by an aggressive SFA defense and then tossed three-consecutive incomplete passes to end the game.

SFA moved to 2-0 in the Southland and 4-2 overall. The previously unbeaten Gamecocks fell to 1-1 in the conference and 4-1 overall.

Stephen F. Austin and host Sam Houston State were both looking to move to 3-0 in Southland Football League play when the teams met in a key conference showdown.

Facing a short week because of the encounter being played on a Thursday night, the Lumberjacks broke a scoreless tie in the second quarter on a 15-yard touchdown pass from Pate to Anthony Dingle. Sam Houston State tied the game on a 12-yard pass from McCown to Cooper.

Late in the first half, Pate was forced from the pocket while feeling pressure. His throw was off the mark, with P.J. Traylor making a leaping interception and racing 14 yards for a touchdown to give SHSU a 14-7 edge at halftime.

The Bearkats easily could have been trailing at the break but Rossner missed three field goals.

Stephen F. Austin tied the game on its opening possession of the second half on a 1-yard run by Pate. The Bearkats answered with a 32-yard touchdown pass from McCown to Cooper to give SHSU a lead it would not relinquish.

That didn't mean things wouldn't get dicey for the Bearkats down the stretch. With Sam Houston State leading 24-14, SFA's David Crocker returned a fumble to the SHSU 28. A penalty pushed the ball back to the 43 but the Lumberjacks eventually scored on a 10-yard pass from Pate to Dingle to make the score 24-21 with 1:53 remaining in the contest.

The Bearkats recovered the onside kick but were unable to run out the clock. Sam Houston State punted the ball down to the 8-yard line with only eight seconds remaining. The Lumberjacks managed to reach their own 44 when the game ended.

SHSU moved to 3-0 in the Southland and into sole possession of first place. The Bearkats improved to 6-1 overall. SFA dropped to 2-1 in the conference and 4-3 overall.

Two days later, Jacksonville State bounced back from its first loss of the season with a 38-17 win at home over Southwest Texas.

Rogers, who rushed for 179 yards, had a 9-yard touchdown run and Stancil tossed a scoring pass to Jake Carlton on the Gamecocks' way to a 24-0 halftime lead.

McCauley connected with Beau Robertson on a 24-yard touchdown pass early in the third quarter but the only other points the Bobcats could manage the remainder of the game was a 3-yard run by Bronson Sanders and a two-point conversion late in the third quarter. Sanders finished with 214 yards rushing in a losing cause.

Jacksonville State improved to 2-1 in the Southland Football League and 5-1 overall. SWT dropped to 0-2 in the conference and 4-3 overall.

In Natchitoches, Northwestern State fell behind Nicholls State 14-0 in the second quarter before the Demons scored on five of seven possessions on their way to a resounding 47-14 victory over the Colonels. The win evened Northwestern State's Southland mark a 1-1 and moved the Demons to 5-2 overall. Nicholls fell to 0-3 in the league and 1-5 overall.

A pair of short touchdown runs by Son had given Nicholls its two-touchdown advantage but the Demons defense held the Colonels to 91 yards over the final three quarters to pull away.

Northwestern State running back Jeremy Lofton rushed for 136 yards and three touchdowns, with 121 of the yards coming in the second half.

Lofton's 28-yard touchdown run early in the third quarter put the Demons on top for the first time at 19-14. Lofton appeared to be stopped at the Nicholls 25 but was never tackled. No whistle was blown and the Demons running back alertly continued on his way to the end zone.

A 38-yard touchdown run by Lofton made the score 26-14 before the Demons put the game away for all practical purposes moments later when Kendrick Llorens returned an errant Son pass 41 yards for a touchdown for a 33-14 Northwestern State lead.

Nicholls picked up its first on-field SFL victory in 17 games a week later and captured the symbolic oar in the "Battle for the Paddle," with a 33-14 home win over Southwest Texas in a confrontation featuring two winless teams in conference play.

SWT had won the three previous games since the yearly event became known as the "Battle for the Paddle."

Not counting a forfeit win over Northwestern State during the 2000 season, the Colonels had lost 16-straight Southland games before gaining the victory over the Bobcats. Nicholls improved to 1-4 in the SLC and 2-5 overall. SWT fell to 0-3 in the league and 4-4 overall.

Nicholls trailed 7-6 at halftime but dominated both sides of the ball early in the second half to score on its first three possessions of the half. The Colonels gained the lead on a 27-yard pass from Son to Isiah Mitchell.

Son scored on a 5-yard option keeper on the Colonels' next possession to extend their lead. Son ran in a two-point conversion attempt as Nicholls upped its lead to 20-7 with 4:06 remaining in the third quarter. Nicholls made it 27-7 by the end of the third quarter on a 16-yard run by Son.

Sanders, who rushed for 206 yards a week earlier against Jacksonville State, was held to 39 yards on 14 carries by the Colonels.

On the same day Nicholls was picking up its initial Southland win, Sam Houston State suffered its first conference loss with a 35-23 defeat at McNeese State.

Winners of four straight, an open date seemed to dampen the Bearkats' momentum entering their game against McNeese State.

The slow-starting Bearkats found themselves staring at a 28-0 deficit in the second quarter. McNeese quarterback Slade Nagle tossed a pair of touchdowns to tight end Jeff Hamilton during the early scoring spree. Hamilton added another scoring reception later in the game to tie a school record with three touchdown catches.

Trailing 28-14 at halftime, Sam Houston State cut into the deficit by another three points on the Bearkats' opening possession of the second half when Joey Price connected on a 23-yard field goal.

The Cowboys responded with Nagle's 3-yard touchdown strike to Hamilton.

McCown ended up tossing a Cowboys Stadium-record 61 passes in an attempt to rally the Bearkats.

"That was not our game plan," Randleman laughed.

McCown's 18-yard touchdown pass to Cooper made the score 35-23. SHSU reached the Cowboys' 43 late in the game but turned the ball over on downs to bring an end to the Bearkats' rally attempt.

Along with falling from the unbeaten ranks in conference play, the Bearkats slipped to 6-2 overall. McNeese improved to 2-1 in the SFL and 5-3 overall.

In Natchitoches, Nall returned from an injury in fine form, tossing for 338 yards and three touchdowns in Northwestern State's 42-17 rout of Jacksonville State.

The quarterback's lone touchdown pass of the first half, a 51-yard strike to Bernard Green, gave the Demons a 7-0 lead. A 3-yard run by Lofton and a 9-yard scamper by Troy Sumrall gave Northwestern a 21-3 halftime lead. Jacksonville State's only points in the first half came on a 38-yard field goal by Steven Lee.

The Demons added three more touchdowns in the second half, including touchdown passes by Nall of 2 yards to Nathan Black and 65 yards to Fredd Harrison.

Northwestern improved to 2-1 in the Southland Football League and 6-2 overall while Jacksonville State fell to 2-2 in the conference and 5-2 overall.

With Sam Houston State playing a non-conference game against Western Illinois, Northwestern State and Stephen F. Austin each had a chance to match the Bearkats at 3-1 with wins. The Demons visited Southwest Texas while the Lumberjacks were at home against Nicholls State.

A pair of 6-yard touchdown runs by Lofton helped the Demons take a 17-14 halftime lead against Southwest Texas on Northwestern State's way to a 20-17 triumph.

Still maintaining a three-point lead, a 50-yard pass from Nall to Black set up a 28-yard Clint Sanford field goal midway in the third quarter for what proved to be a huge six-point advantage as Justin Martinez's 36-yard kick with 1:23 remaining in the third quarter made it 20-17.

SWT threatened late in the game. Facing first-and-goal from the 2-yard line, a potential go-ahead touchdown was nullified because of a penalty. That eventually led to a Martinez 28-yard field goal attempt. His kick was blocked by Llorens, allowing the Demons to hold on for the three-point victory.

Northwestern improved to 3-1 in the Southland and 7-2 overall. The Bobcats fell to 0-4 in the conference and 4-5 overall.

The Lumberjacks, meanwhile, found themselves having to rally from a 14-7 deficit for a second week in a row. Unlike the Sam Houston State game, when Stephen F. Austin tied the game against Nicholls State, the Colonels could not immediately answer.

A 1-yard run by Chapman tied the game and an 11-yard toss from Pate to Dingle gave SFA a 21-14 lead in the third quarter. Stephen F. Austin tacked on two points in the fourth quarter on a safety before Nicholls scored on a 38-yard pass from Son to John Price with 3:03 left in the game to make the final 23-21.

Son factored in all three touchdowns for the Colonels. He scored on touchdown runs of 24 and 11 yards in the first half.

SFA improved to 3-1 in the Southland and 5-3 overall. Nicholls dropped to 1-4 in the league and 2-6 overall.

Following a 49-24 non-conference win over Western Illinois, Sam Houston State hosted Jacksonville State, looking for a win to maintain at least a share of the lead in the SFL.

The Bearkats looked like they might drop a second-straight league game when a 59-yard punt return for a touchdown by Neika Willis and a 44-yard touchdown pass from Stancil to Jenkins had Sam Houston State in a 14-3 hole.

SHSU wiped out the deficit by scoring 38-consecutive points. Included in the spree were two McCown touchdown passes to Cooper and another scoring toss to Rauls. The SHSU quarterback also scored on a 2-yard run as the Bearkats went on to take a 55-30 victory.

Jacksonville's final touchdown came on a 21-yard pass from reserve quarterback Anthony Mayo to Quincy Bowie. Martin kicked the extra point. Against Cumberland earlier in the season, Martin became the first female to score in a NCAA contest.

The win, No. 200 in the career of Bearkats coach Ron Randleman, lifted SHSU to 4-1 in the Southland and 7-2 overall. Jacksonville State dropped to 2-3 in the league and 5-4 overall.

"I never paid too much attention to that," Randleman said of the milestone victory. "You coach and you are just trying to win the next game."

Stephen F. Austin managed to match Sam Houston State at 4-1 in the Southland with a 30-21 victory at Southwest Texas.

Pate tossed for 417 yards and four touchdowns as Stephen F. Austin won its final home game of the 2001 season with a 35-13 victory over Southwest Texas.

Two field goals by SWT's Martinez and a 39 yarder by Rossner gave the Bobcats a 6-3 edge in the second quarter. After SFA built a 16-6 lead, McCauley's 46-yard touchdown pass to Lee Davis rallied SWT to within three points with 1:26 remaining before halftime but the Bobcats would not score again.

Pate fired two touchdown passes in each half. SFA added a 28-yard Rossner field goal and a safety in the second half. Dingle had 142 reception yards while Lawrence Hamilton finished with 116.

Along with staying in the Southland Football League hunt, SFA clinched a third-consecutive winning season with its sixth victory. Southwest Texas remained winless in conference play at 0-5 and dropped to 4-6 overall.

Northwestern State was unable to make it a three-way tie atop the Southland when the Demons suffered a 17-10 loss at McNeese State.

A 42-yard pass from Nagle to Jermaine Martin gave the Cowboys a 7-0 lead midway in the first quarter. The Demons countered with a Sanford field goal in the first quarter and a Harrison touchdown reception in the second to take a 10-7 halftime lead.

The McNeese defense would not allow Northwestern any more points, holding the Demons to a net zero rushing yards in the game.

McNeese pulled ahead 14-10 on a 1-yard run by Nagle in the third quarter and John Marino added a 37-yard field goal with 8:51 remaining in the fourth quarter as the Cowboys nipped the Demons 17-10.

The Cowboys moved to 3-1 in Southland play and 6-3 overall. Northwestern fell to 3-2 in the conference and 7-3 overall.

Sam Houston State clinched a share of the Southland Football League title a week later with a 31-13 victory at Southwest Texas.

The Bearkats did so in typical fashion. McCown passed for 379 yards, including a pair of scoring tosses to Heinrich. Heinrich finished with 149 reception yards in the game and Cooper 176. At one point in the game, 356 of SHSU's 373 total yards came through the air.

"When people would blitz, we would use him a lot on crossing routes," Randleman said of Heinrich. "He was a big, tall tight end, but he had great hands and pretty good speed. He was a tough matchup against certain defenses."

McCown, a future NFL quarterback, concluded the regular season with 210 completions, 2,884 yards passing and 29 touchdowns, all single-season school records. Cooper failed to catch a touchdown against the Bobcats but set a single-season school mark with 17 scoring receptions.

SHSU built a 24-7 lead in the third quarter. Southwest Texas came up with its two scores on a 9-yard touchdown pass from McCauley to Tyson Olivo in the third quarter and 7-yard run by Jerome Brooks with 8:34 remaining in the game.

The Bearkats, who earned a share of the Southland title for the first time since 1991, finished the regular season 5-1 in the conference and 9-2 overall. SWT failed to win a game in the league and concluded the season 4-7 overall.

Needing to win in its final Southland Football League game of the season to keep pace with Sam Houston State, the Lumberjacks came up with a touchdown to cut into Northwestern State's early 14-0 lead.

After Lofton scored on runs of 66 and 15 yards to give the Demons their two-touchdown lead, Pate hooked up with Hamilton on a 24-yard touchdown pass to make the score 14-7. The seven-point margin would not last long.

A 1-yard touchdown run by Lofton, who finished with a career-high 169 yards rushing, and a 22-yard Sanford field goal, extended the Demons' lead to 24-7. SFA added a field goal but Nall tossed a 5-yard touchdown pass to Green to give the Demons a 31-10 lead with less than three minutes remaining in the first half.

SFA added a touchdown for the only scoring by either team in the second half, sinking the Lumberjacks' playoff hopes with a 31-17 loss.

Nall passed for 213 yards in the game to give him 2,022 on the season to set a new Northwestern State single-season record. Green finished the season with 47 catches, also a new Demons mark.

The Lumberjacks finished Southland play at 4-2 and dropped to 6-4 overall. SFA closed the season a week later with a 55-3 loss to Kliff Kingsbury and the Texas Tech Red Raiders to conclude the season 6-5.

Northwestern State ended its season also 4-2 in the conference and 8-3 overall.

Meanwhile, McNeese State maintained control of its own destiny with a 34-27 Southland Football League road win at Nicholls State.

McNeese's win over Nicholls, coupled with Stephen F. Austin's 31-17 loss to Northwestern State and Sam Houston State's 31-13 win over Southwest Texas, meant all the Cowboys had to do was beat Jacksonville State in the season finale to earn the SFL's automatic bid to the Division I-AA playoffs.

The Cowboys moved to 4-1 in the SFL, a half-game behind league-leading SHSU. The Bearkats finished conference play 5-1 but their only conference loss was 35-23 to the Cowboys, meaning a win over Jacksonville would give McNeese the automatic bid because of the head-to-head tiebreaker.

McNeese did what it had to do against the Colonels, but it wasn't easy. Nicholls trailed 24-14 at the start of the second half before making a run at the Cowboys.

A total of 25 yards in penalties against the Cowboys, coupled with a 35-yard pass from Son to Phillip Brock, set up a 9-yard Brock touchdown run to pull Nicholls to within four points at 24-20 early in the third quarter.

The Cowboys countered on their next drive with a Marino field goal to make the score 27-20. Nicholls came up with a big break when a short Colonels punt rolled and hit Bradley Archie in the legs, with Travis Douglas recovering for Nicholls at the McNeese 37. Two plays later, Son hit Price with a 30-yard touchdown toss to tie the game 27-27 with 3:06 left in the third quarter.

McNeese answered once again, this time with a 12-yard pass from Nagle to Broadhead to put the Cowboys on top 34-27 on the first play of the fourth quarter.

Nicholls threatened twice down the stretch. The first time, the Colonels reached the McNeese 27 before turning the ball over on downs following an incomplete pass on fourth down. The Colonels advanced to the Cowboys' 23 later in the quarter but two incomplete passes following a Son sack turned the ball over to McNeese, which was able to run out the final 1:19 remaining on the clock.

While McNeese moved to 4-1 in the SFL and 7-3 overall with its big game remaining with Jacksonville State, Nicholls finished 1-5 in the Southland. The Colonels won at Division I-A Arkansas State 28-22 a week later in a game rescheduled because of the earlier terrorists attacks, to close the season 3-8.

McNeese held a 10-point lead in its all-important game at Jacksonville State and was less than 15 minutes away from clinching a share of its first Southland title since 1997 when the Cowboys gave their fans a few anxious moments.

Jacksonville State defender Reggie Spenser returned an interception 97 yards for a touchdown to cut the Gamecocks' deficit to three points at 24-21 with 11:27 left in the game. The Cowboys, however, gave their fans a lot to cheer about when Vick King, who rushed for 211 yards in the game, scored on a 1-yard run to cap a 57-yard drive with 5:19 remaining for a 31-21 victory.

"Vick King was an outstanding tailback and he really came into his own in that game," said Tate.

The win earned the Cowboys the SFL's automatic bid to the playoffs and McNeese's ninth trip to the Division I-AA playoffs since 1991.

A 19-point second quarter gave McNeese a 10-point halftime lead. Rogers, who rushed for 108 yards in the game, scored on a 6-yard run in the first quarter and a 26-yard Lee field goal early in the second quarter gave Jacksonville State a 9-0 lead.

McNeese moved ahead at the half on 6-yard runs by Lawton and King, along with a 16-yard gainer by Sams. The teams traded touchdowns in the third quarter before Spenser came up with his interception early in the fourth period.

The Cowboys finished SFL play at 5-1 along with posting an 8-3 overall mark. Jacksonville State finished 5-6 overall, including 2-3 in the conference.

McNeese State opened the playoffs at home against Maine in a contest that featured all of its scoring in the third quarter.

The Cowboys broke a scoreless tie in the third period on a 42-yard Hebert field goal. Maine countered less than two minutes later on a 27-yard touchdown pass from quarterback Jake Eaton to tight end Chad Hayes.

King, who rushed for 195 yards in the game, broke loose on a 58-yard gallop later in the third quarter to give the lead back to McNeese at 10-7. Maine's Royston English, who gained 144 yards on the ground, scored on a 4-yard run for what proved to be the winning score in the Black Bears' 14-10 triumph to eliminate the Cowboys from the playoffs.

"It was a disappointing loss but it was a good season and had a lot to build on," Tate reflected.

McNeese ended its season 8-4.

Sam Houston State, meanwhile, faced a two-week break before hosting Northern Arizona, the first time in school history the Bearkats played at home in the Division I-AA playoffs.

The Bearkats built a 24-14 halftime lead on a 2-yard run by Rauls, a 42-yard Price field goal, a 1-yard run by McCown on a drive set up by a Mark Hughes interception and a 31-yard run by Willie Thomas. Northern Arizona's first-half points came on Preston Parsons touchdown passes of 75 yards to Johnny Marshall and 12 yards to Tom Winn.

Down 31-24, Parsons tossed his fourth touchdown of the game, this one a 4-yard strike to Clarence Moore with 32 seconds left in the game to tie the score.

McCown hit receiver Matt Buss, a former quarterback, with a 58-yard strike to set up Alex St. Peter's 20-yard field goal as time expired for a 34-31 Sam Houston State triumph that advanced the Bearkats to the quarterfinals.

The victory, No.10 on the year for the Bearkats, tied a school record for most wins in a season.

A mistake-prone Bearkats squad was no match for No. 1 Montana, a playoff fixture that won a national title in 1995 and reached the championship game in 1996 and 2000. Playing on the road, Sam Houston State committed six turnovers, including five interceptions, in a 49-24 loss that eliminated SHSU from the playoffs.

The Grizzlies scored on all five of their possessions in the first half to build an insurmountable 35-10 halftime lead. John Edwards and Yohance Humphrey each rushed for a pair of touchdowns while Etu Molden had two scoring receptions for Montana.

Montana's defense picked off all five of its interceptions in the second half to eliminate any serious comeback attempt by the Bearkats.

McCown closed out his career by passing for 344 yards and two touchdowns but was intercepted four times. Cooper had nine receptions for 117 yards in a losing cause.

The Bearkats ended their most successful season ever at 10-3.

Yet another Southland team to fall to Montana in the playoffs, Randleman, like other SLC coaches over the years, couldn't help but appreciate the atmosphere at a Grizzlies home game.

"The fans are right on top of you, but they are good fans," Randleman said. "They really know when to yell and you really get a lot of penalties because they are all quiet and you get up to the line of scrimmage and they just exploded and it's extremely hard to hear. If you haven't been out there before to play them, it's difficult. To beat them anywhere would not be easy but to beat them at home, until you get the atmosphere figured out, it's a real challenge."

COWBOYS RETURN TO CHATTANOOGA

Jacksonville State and Nicholls State opened up Southland Football League play for the third year in a row when the teams met in Thibodaux for what would be the Gamecocks' final year in the conference in 2002. Jacksonville announced it was planning to join the Ohio Valley Conference in 2003.

The Gamecocks went into the game 1-1 on the young season while Nicholls was off to a 2-1 start.

Nicholls entered its SFL opener boasting the fourth-best rushing offense in Division I-AA. That seemed little solace as the Colonels entered the game without Josh Son at quarterback because of a groin injury and lost Phillip Brock, the team's best running back, in the second quarter with an ankle injury.

The lack of experienced offensive personnel limited Nicholls to only 139 yards rushing but the Colonels defense ended up saving the day in a 14-6 win that improved the team to 3-1.

Clinging to a 7-6 lead late in the third quarter, Nicholls defensive back Chris Thompson, a future NFL and Canadian Football League performer, intercepted a pass that bounced off the hands of Gamecocks receiver Ralph Jenkins and returned it 30 yards to give the Colonels a 14-6 lead with 2:20 remaining in the quarter.

Nicholls came up with a defensive stand late in the game. The Gamecocks faced fourth-and-7 at the Colonels' 15. A swing pass from Anthony Mayo to Rondy Rogers netted only 4 yards, allowing the Colonels to take over on downs to preserve the victory.

The Colonels took a 7-0 lead in the first quarter on a 4-yard run by James Morales and continued to lead by that margin until a 17-yard Reggie Stancil touchdown pass early in the third quarter made it 7-6 when JSU missed the extra-point attempt.

Almost three weeks later, Southwest Texas visited Northwestern State under new head coach Scott Stoker in the SFL opener for both teams. Stoker, a former Demons quarterback, was making his conference debut at Northwestern

State, returning to Natchitcohes after serving the previous eight seasons as an assistant at McNeese State

Northwestern State was off to a 4-1 start and ranked No. 7 under Stoker. Stoker's only loss through five games was a 45-7 defeat to the Georgia Bulldogs. Southwest Texas was 3-2 on the season, with losses of 42-0 to Minnesota of the Big Ten and to Portland State.

Playing on a Thursday night, Southwest Texas trailed by 16 points at halftime when the Bobcats attempted to rally in the second half. A 1-yard run by quarterback Cody McCauley on a drive set up by a punt return down to the Northwestern 11-yard line by Jarvis Smith began the comeback effort. A muffed punt by Toby Ziegler at his own 3-yard line set up a touchdown run by Lee Davis to move SWT to within two points at 23-21.

The Demons responded with a 10-play, 79-yard drive, with Derrick Johnese scoring on an 11-yard run to rebuild Northwestern's led to 30-21 as the Demons began to pull away on their way to a 40-27 victory.

The SFL opener improved Northwestern to 5-1 overall while Southwest Texas fell to 3-3.

Two days later, Sam Houston State and Stephen F. Austin made their 2002 SFL debuts when the Bearkats visited Jacksonville State and the Lumberjacks visited Nicholls State

Going into the Jacksonville State game 2-3, the Bearkats already equaled its loss total of the previous year and Sam Houston State appeared as though it would right the wrongs of a sub-.500 start by jumping out to a 13-0 lead against the Gamecocks.

A 4-yard pass from Vance Smith to Vincent Cartwright and a 5-yard run by Godfrey gave the Bearkats the lead. Meanwhile, the Gamecocks lost Mayo, their starting quarterback, late in the second quarter with an injury to his right knee. Mayo struggled prior to the injury, hitting on only 6 of 14 passes for 61 yards.

Stancil, who lost his starting job earlier in the season to Mayo, took over at quarterback for Jacksonville State. He promptly threw a 22-yard touchdown pass to Jenkins to get the Gamecocks back in the game. Following a safety to make the score 13-8, Stancil hit Jenkins on a 49-yard scoring strike on the final play of the first half to give Jacksonville State a 14-13 halftime edge.

Markee Coleman's 53-yard interception return for a touchdown less than three minutes into the second half increased the Gamecocks' advantage to 21-13.

After SHSU closed to within 21-19 on a 1-yard run by Godfrey only three seconds into the fourth quarter, the Gamecocks decided to hand the ball over to Kory Chapman. Chapman, playing in place of Rogers after the team's leading rusher suffered a sprained ankle, got the call eight times in an 80-yard drive. His final carry from 4 yards out gave Jacksonville State a 28-19 lead.

Joey Price connected on a 41-yard field goal slightly more than a minute later to make the score 28-22 but that would be as close as the Bearkats would get as SHSU lost its league opener to drop to 2-4 on the season.

SFA, off to a 3-2 start, entered its game at Nicholls State with the top-rated defense in the Southland and the Lumberjacks showed why they held the ranking by coming up with a big defensive play late in the game to set up a game-winning field goal in a 17-14 triumph.

Nicholls was driving for a potential game-winning score when the Lumberjacks' defense came up big. Facing fourth-and-3 at the SFA 28, the Colonels elected to go for the first down instead of trying a field goal on a field which had been totally chewed up after two weeks of tropical storms, hurricanes and almost daily downpours.

Son, the Nicholls quarterback, heaved the ball into the back of the end zone, with SFA defensive back Braxton O'Banion intercepting the ball and returning it 57 yards to give the Lumberjacks excellent field position at the Nicholls 43 with nine minutes left in the game.

The Lumberjacks, who improved to 1-0 the SFL and 4-2 overall, marched down to the Colonels' 1-yard line, but after being stopped two-straight plays for no gain, settled for Stephen Coker's 19-yard field goal, which proved to be the game-winner.

Coker's game-winning kick came only minutes after he had missed from 39 yards out when his plant foot slipped on the slop-like field and caused a low kick.

Nicholls, dropping its first conference game of the season and falling to 5-2 overall, was limited to 172 yards rushing by the SFA defense, only 79 in the first half.

The Colonels marched 71 yards on their opening possession of the second half. Rudy August's 5-yard run capped the drive to break a 7-7 tie. Tony Tompkins' 14-yard run later in the quarter tied the game at 14-14.

McNeese State went into its Southland Football League opener as the second-ranked team in Division I-AA. The Cowboys did so by getting off to a 4-1 start, with McNeese's only loss being 38-14 to Nebraska.

Like with previous losses to major programs, the defeat at Nebraska only served to boost the confidence of the Cowboys, according to McNeese coach Tommy Tate.

"We had a lot of returning players. A lot of players from the 2000 season were now seniors. It was a great roster with a lot of talented football players during that run from 2000 through 2003," said Tate.

Vick King rushed for 208 yards as McNeese State rebounded from the Nebraska loss with a 28-20 home victory over Jacksonville State.

McNeese led 21-10 at halftime but had to hold off the Gamecocks in the second half. A 32-yard pass from Stancil to Jenkins in the third quarter and a 36-yard Steven Lee field goal at the 8:31 mark of the fourth quarter rallied Jacksonville State to within one point at 21-20.

King scampered 78 yards to set up a 6-yard Luke Lawton touchdown run with 7:14 left in the game to provide the Cowboys with the eight-point victory.

The Cowboys improved to 5-1 by winning their conference opener while Jacksonville State fell to 1-2 in the SFL and 4-3 overall.

In San Marcos, Nicholls won its first road conference game since 1998 and guaranteed its first winning season since 1996 with a 24-21 win against Southwest Texas.

The Colonels built a lead of 24-7 after three quarters on touchdown runs by Son, David Plaisance and Rogers Williams and a 42-yard James Wilcox field goal before having to hold off the Bobcats. SWT made it close with a pair of touchdowns in the fourth quarter on a 43-yard pass from McCauley's to Sedrick Brown and a 1-yard run by Davis with 2:36 remaining in the game.

Nicholls picked up its first Southland road win since a 31-30 win at McNeese in 1998 and the six wins provided the Colonels with their first winning season since 1996 when they posted an 8-4 mark and reached the Division I-AA playoffs.

SWT fell to 0-2 in the conference and 3-4 overall.

Meanwhile, in a defensive struggle at Stephen F. Austin, neither the Lumberjacks nor the Sam Houston State Bearkats could score until SFA mounted a sustained drive in the third quarter.

Starting on their own 14-yard line, the Lumberjacks took 14 plays to travel 86 yards and used up 6:25 to take a 7-0 lead on a 3-yard touchdown pass from quarterback Michael Williams to Kevin Landry.

Sam Houston State, which failed to produce points on three drives that advanced inside the SFA 13-yard line, came up with its first score on a 42-yard Price field goal with 11:28 remaining in the game.

Leading by four points, Stephen F. Austin faced third-and-2 from the Lumberjacks' 47, when a pass attempt by Williams was intercepted by Michael Thompson, who returned the errant throw to the SFA 37.

Facing fourth-and-2 from the 29, Travis Tobaben hit Marcus Carter for 7 yards and a first down. A 2-yard dive by Maurice Harris with 6:36 remaining provided the game-winner in the Bearkats' 10-7 triumph.

The outcome left both teams 1-1 in the Southland. SFA fell to 4-3 overall while Sam Houston State improved to 3-4.

Playing on a Thursday night for the second time in the season, the Demons, now the third-ranked team in the nation, turned to the running back duo of Johnese and Shelton Sampson when trailing 14-7 at Nicholls State.

Johnese rushed six times for 38 yards and Sampson four times for 17 on an 80-yard drive to set up Kevin Magee's 1-yard sneak to tie the contest with 12:49 remaining in the game.

Another 1-yard quarterback sneak, this one on fourth-and-1 near midfield allowed the Demons to keep a drive alive late in the fourth quarter. A 15-yard pass from Magee to Mark Morris advanced the ball to the 5-yard line. Sampson ran for a first down at the 1-yard line before bouncing outside one play later to give Northwestern a 21-14 lead with 1:58 remaining.

The Colonels reached the Northwestern 37 when Son threw a pass into the end zone that was just off the fingertips of Vince Butler.

An offside call against the Demons on fourth-and-1 gave Nicholls another chance. On the next play, Son was sacked by Ahmad Willis and fumbled, with Northwestern's Chris Jones recovering with 26 seconds remaining for the seven-point win to hold off an upset bid by the Colonels.

Despite being held to 41 rushing yards at halftime, Nicholls found itself in a 7-7 tie at intermission. The Colonels' lone score of the half came on an 80-yard return by Plaisance when Nicholls forced the Demons to punt on their opening possession. Northwestern tied the game on a 20-yard pass from Magee to Zeigler with 1:57 remaining before halftime.

Northwestern improved to 2-0 in the Southland and 7-1 overall while Nicholls fell to 2-2 in the conference and 6-3 overall.

Second-ranked McNeese State led 14-10 at halftime against Sam Houston State before pulling away with a 23-point third quarter for a convincing 47-10 victory over the Bearkats two days later to keep pace with Northwestern State in the SFL.

Jermaine Martin returned the second-half kickoff 47 yards to set up a 1-yard run by quarterback Scott Pendarvis to give the Cowboys an 11-point advantage at 21-10. The Cowboys scored three more times in the third quarter on a pair of short runs by Lawton and Jacob Prim, plus a safety.

Lawton's touchdown capped a drive that began at the SHSU 12 after a Bearkats fumble. A bad snap out of the end zone earned the Cowboys a safety. McNeese added 10 points in the fourth quarter on a John Marino field goal and a 32-yard fumble return for a touchdown by Chris White.

The Bearkats' points came on a 46-yard run by Steve Smith in the first quarter and a Price field goal in the second quarter.

McNeese improved to 2-0 in the SFL and 6-1 overall. The Bearkats dropped to 1-2 in the league and 3-5 overall.

Meanwhile, Stephen F. Austin's 23-7 lead at Jacksonville State looked pretty comfortable in the second quarter of the Lumberjacks' game against the Gamecocks.

It took some doing, but the Gamecocks rallied to within three points by the 6:43 mark of the third quarter. Nick Pope kicked his first collegiate field goal, Coleman returned a blocked punt 65 yards for a touchdown and Lee added a 32-yard field goal to leave Jacksonville behind by only a 23-20 margin.

After SFA stretched its lead to 36-20, Jacksonville State countered with a 1-yard touchdown run by Marcus Mitchell with slightly more than seven minutes left to play in the game to make the score 36-28. With running backs Kory Chapman and Rondy Rogers suffering from nagging injuries, the Gamecocks' ground game was limited to 105 yards. Mitchell was Jacksonville State's leading rusher against SFA with 55 yards.

Maurice Daughtry gave the Gamecocks some hope late in the game when he returned a punt 35 yards to the SFA 20. On second-and-goal, Ralph Jenkins was dropped for a 6-yard loss on a reverse. Quarterback Anthony Mayo's third-down pass was incomplete, leaving Jacksonville State with fourth-and-goal from the 20. Freshman Maurice Mullins, who guided the Gamecocks to their first touchdown, replaced Mayo at quarterback. A quarterback draw by Mullins netted only 10 yards, turning the ball over to the Lumberjacks.

Jacksonville State got the ball for one last try. With the Gamecocks near midfield, Mayo failed to connect with a receiver on four-straight passes, allowing SFA to hold on for the 36-28 victory.

Stephen F. Austin improved to 2-1 in the SFL and 5-3 overall. Jacksonville State fell to 1-3 in the conference as its overall record moved to 4-4.

Seeming to like midweek games, Northwestern State found itself playing on a Thursday for a third time in 2002 in a Southland home game against Sam Houston State.

Johnese and Sampson were back at it again, each topping 100 yards to pace No. 3 Northwestern to a 38-10 win over the Bearkats.

Scoring on their first drive for the fourth time in the last five games, the Demons set the early tone on a 6-yard sweep by Johnese, who rushed for 101 yards in the game. Sampson, who amassed 118 yards on the ground, scored on a 3-yard run to cap an 83-yard drive. A 9-yard run by Johnese made it 21-0 with 9:30 remaining in the first half.

The Bearkats finally got on the scoreboard with 1:57 remaining in the first half on a 27-yard Price field goal.

Northwestern's defense was stingy once again, holding the Bearkats to a net 53 yards rushing and 121 passing as the Demons recorded six sacks for a league-leading 38 on the season.

The Demons remained unbeaten in the Southland at 3-0 and moved to 8-1 overall in winning their fifth-straight game and for the ninth-consecutive time at home.

SHSU fell to 1-3 in the conference and 3-6 overall.

Playing two days later, McNeese State knew it needed a win in its game at Stephen F. Austin to keep pace with Northwestern State.

The Cowboys did one better than Northwestern State against Sam Houston State, using a trio of backs instead of a duo to spread the ball around in a 42-13 SFL victory against Stephen F. Austin.

Marcus Trahan, King and Prim combined to rush for 264 yards and each scored a touchdown in the triumph over the Lumberjacks. Trahan rushed for 95 yards, King 94 and Prim 75 to pace the Cowboys' ground attack.

"We had three good tailbacks that kind of complemented each other. Prim was a big guy, King could do it all and Marcus Trahan was an outstanding tailback," said Tate.

After a scoreless first quarter, McNeese built an 18-0 halftime lead on three Marino field goals, a safety, and a touchdown run by Prim. King's touchdown came in the third quarter and Trahan scored in the final quarter.

SFA's points came on a pair of touchdown passes from Zeke Dixon to Anthony Dingle in the second half.

McNeese improved to 3-0 in the Southland and 7-1 overall. The Lumberjacks fell to 2-2 in the conference and 5-4 overall.

In Jacksonville, the odds of Southwest Texas tying up its game against the Gamecocks one more time going into the fourth quarter seemed to stretch the odds, especially considering the fact Bobcats had lost their previous eight SFL games dating back to 2000.

The Bobcats trailed twice early in the game and came back to tie the score before falling behind once more. Southwest Texas came through once again when

McCauley hooked up with Kenneth Samuels for a 65-yard touchdown pass to knot up the game 20-20.

Unlike earlier in the game, the Bobcats took things one step further. With the score still tied, Jarvis Smith returned a punt 68 yards for a touchdown with less than three minutes remaining to give Southwest Texas a 27-20 victory.

The Bobcats managed to snap their eight-game conference losing streak despite playing without their top two running backs. Davis suffered a concussion in the game and Brown had a sprained ankle. Terrell Harris more than picked up the slack, rushing for 166 yards on 25 carries to keep SWT's ground game intact.

Southwest Texas improved to 1-2 in the Southland and 4-4 overall. Jacksonville State fell to 1-4 in the conference and 4-5 overall.

For only the second time in five weeks, third-ranked Northwestern State found itself playing on a traditional Saturday instead of a Thursday night

Northwestern State led 10-6 at halftime on a fumble recovery by Zeigler in the end zone in the first quarter and a 25-yard Tommy Hebert field goal in the second period. Jacksonville State's only points in the half came on a 1-yard run by Mitchell in the second quarter.

From that point on, the Jacksonville State defense clamped down on the Demons' offense, holding Northwestern to 65 yards total offense, including only 23 rushing. The Demons finished the game with 60 yards rushing after averaging 282 yards during their five-game winning streak.

The Gamecocks gained the lead at 12-6 with 4:59 remaining in the third quarter on a 3-yard run by Mitchell to cap a 57-yard drive.

Jacksonville State came up with a trick play early in the fourth quarter to put the game away. Rogers hooked up with Jenkins in the back of the end zone on a 7-yard halfback pass to give the Gamecocks a 19-10 triumph.

The loss dropped Northwestern to 3-1 in the conference and 8-2 overall. Jacksonville State ended league play at 2-4 in moving to 5-5 overall. The Gamecocks would go on to lose to Georgia Southern 41-3 to conclude their final season in the Southland Football League with a losing record at 5-6.

Meanwhile, second-ranked McNeese State scored more than 40 points on a Southland Football League opponent for the third week in a row in the Cowboys' 47-7 home spanking of Southwest Texas. McNeese's win, coupled with Northwestern State's loss to Jacksonville State, moved the Cowboys into sole possession of first place in the SFL.

King, Trahan and Prim had another big game as the trio rushed for a combined 231 yards and four touchdowns. King ran for 97 yards and two touchdowns, Trahan had 73 yards and a touchdown while Prim added 61 and also scored.

Touchdown runs by King, Prim and Sams gave McNeese a 20-7 halftime lead. The Bobcats' only score came on a 1-yard run by Terrell Harris that tied the game 7-7 in the first quarter.

"When you can rush the ball for over 300 yards, it really opens up a lot of things in the passing game with play-action. It gives you an opportunity to throw to the tight ends and fullbacks and get some good throws down the field," Tate explained.

McNeese's defense, meanwhile, held the Bobcats to 131 total yards, including 29 passing. Of SWT's 102 rushing yards, 70 came in the first quarter.

Along with touchdown runs by King and Trahan in the second half, Pendarvis scored on a 1-yard run and he tossed a 1-yard pass to Lawton.

McNeese improved to 4-0 in the Southland and 8-1 overall. Southwest Texas dropped to 1-3 in the league and 4-5 overall.

Elsewhere, an open date proved beneficial for the Colonels who won their second conference road game of the season with a 34-16 triumph over Sam Houston State.

Nicholls, which moved to 3-2 in the Southland and 7-3 overall, rushed for 349 yards as four different running backs scored for the Colonels. Son attempted only three passes in the game, but he connected on two of the tosses for 74 yards.

SHSU, which dropped to 1-4 in conference and 3-7 overall, took a 7-0 lead in the first quarter on a 1-yard run by Godfrey.

After Nicholls tied the game on a 14-yard run by Brock, the Colonels took control by outscoring the Bearkats 14-3 in the second quarter. A 21-yard touchdown run by Brian Thomas and a 4-yard run by Travis Felder gave Nicholls a 21-10 halftime lead.

Coming off a loss, Northwestern State could take solace in that its showdown with No. 2 McNeese State was at Turpin Stadium, where the Demons were riding a nine-game winning streak stretching over two seasons.

That seemed to matter little to the Cowboys. McNeese built a 9-3 halftime lead that could have been more had the Cowboys not fumbled the ball away three times in the first quarter.

Like the previous week, a lack of offense doomed Northwestern State. The Cowboys held the Demons to 34 yards rushing and 164 total yards.

The Demons, now ranked No. 7, turned one of McNeese's first-quarter fumbles into a 22-yard field goal to give Northwestern a 3-2 lead after surrendering a safety less than four minutes into the game.

McNeese came up with the only other score of the first half on a 1-yard run by Prim early in the second quarter to give the Cowboys a 9-3 halftime edge. Martin turned a short pass from Pendarvis into a 42-yard gain down to the 1-yard line to set up Prim's touchdown.

The Demons appeared to regain the lead when Zeigler returned the ensuing kickoff 89 yards for a touchdown but the score was nullified by a holding penalty.

Trahan returned the second-half kickoff 63 yards to set up a 15-yard touchdown strike from Pendarvis to Sams to quickly extend the McNeese lead to 17-3 following a two-point conversion. A 32-yard Marino field goal made it 20-3 after three quarters.

Unlike recent games of spread-the-carries-around football, King carried the day for Cowboys with 121 yards rushing, including a 43-yard gallop with 6:44 left in the game to make the final 27-3.

McNeese moved to 9-1 overall and 5-0 in the Southland Football League to capture its second-straight conference title. A second-consecutive loss dropped Northwestern to 8-3 overall and 3-2 in the SFL.

In San Marcos, the Lumberjacks seemingly could not get their hands on the ball in the first half of Stephen F. Austin's final road game of the 2002 season against Southwest Texas.

Southwest Texas dominated time of possession, including using up nine minutes on one scoring drive to lead 14-7 at halftime. Davis scored on runs of 18 and 1 yard for the Bobcats' points. SFA's only score came on an 8-yard run by Tompkins.

Stephen F. Austin went to a quick-strike strategy in the second half. Gary Allen's 1-yard touchdown run on the Lumberjacks' opening drive of the third quarter capped a 57-yard drive that consumed slightly more than two minutes to tie the game. SFA needed only 57 seconds to score on its next possession when Dixon connected with Michael David on a touchdown toss to culminate a three-play drive to give the Lumberjacks a 21-14 edge.

Southwest Texas tied the game on a 3-yard run for Davis' third touchdown of the contest.

Stephen F. Austin countered with a 3-yard touchdown run by Dixon to put the Lumberjacks on top 28-21 early in the fourth quarter and Clay Gilbert added a 22-yard field goal to give SFA a 30-21 victory.

Defensively, senior Greg Pitts had 15 tackles to become the Bobcats' all-time leading tackler.

Stephen F. Austin moved to 3-2 in the SFL and 6-4 overall to earn its fourth-consecutive winning season. The Bobcats dropped to 1-4 in the conference and 4-6 overall.

Nicholls State seemed to face an almost impossible task going into the 2002 season finale at McNeese State. Not only were the Colonels facing the top-ranked team in the nation, the Cowboys were looking for a victory to become the first SFL team since 2000 to go undefeated in conference play. Additionally, a 10-1 finish likely would give McNeese home-field advantage throughout the Division I-AA playoffs.

The Cowboys made sure that happened when defensive back Rod Gulley intercepted a Yale Vannoy pass and returned it 40 yards for a touchdown with 1:11 remaining to secure a 33-21 victory over the Colonels.

Nicholls' option attack gave McNeese problems early in the contest as the Colonels built a 14-3 lead at one point on touchdown runs by Colt Colletti and Morales.

McNeese gained the lead by halftime when Lawton scored on a 4-yard run with 2:27 remaining before the break to put the Cowboys on top 23-21.

The Cowboys were clinging to a 26-21 lead before putting the game away on Gulley's interception return – the defensive back's eighth interception of the season.

Nicholls ended the season at 7-4 overall and finished 3-3 in the conference. The .500 Southland record was the Colonels' best league finish since a 4-2 mark in 1996.

Likely needing a win in the regular-season finale at Stephen F. Austin for an at-large playoff berth, Northwestern State trailed 28-21 heading into the fourth quarter after not having scored in the second half for three-consecutive games.

A fumble recovery by Darryl Lacy at the Lumberjacks' 18-yard line eventually set up a 1-yard Jeremy Lofton run to tie the game 28-28 at the 4:49 mark of the fourth quarter.

SFA needed only five plays to travel 65 yards to regain the lead. Dixon's 4-yard pass to Landry put the Lumberjacks back on top at 35-28 with only 2:10 left in the game.

The Demons answered with a 65-yard drive of their own. Needing seven plays to score, a 25-yard pass from Magee to Fredd Harrison tied the game again, this time at 35-35 with 1:28 to go in the contest.

Bryan McMillan, a red-shirt freshman, raced 25 yards after picking off an errant Dixon throw for a touchdown only 18 seconds later to give Northwestern an improbable 43-35 triumph.

The Demons had built a 21-0 lead by early in the second quarter. SFA stormed back, scoring the next 28 points. The Lumberjacks scored twice in the second quarter to trail 21-14 at halftime. A pair of 6-yard touchdown runs by Allen in the third quarter gave SFA its 28-21 lead entering the fourth period.

Northwestern moved to 9-3 overall and 4-2 in the Southland while the Lumberjacks fell to 6-5.

Playing for pride in a rivalry game, Sam Houston State ended the 2002 season on a positive note by snapping a three-game losing streak with a 21-14 home win over Southwest Texas.

Southwest Texas led 14-0 at halftime on a 71-yard run by Harris and a 30-yard pass from McCauley to Davis.

Sam Houston State tied the game with two touchdowns in the third quarter on scoring tosses by Smith of 33 yards to Jason Mathenia and 37 yards to Harris. Harris provided the game-winning score on a 25-yard run in the middle of the fourth quarter.

The outcome left both teams 4-7 on the season. Sam Houston State finished 2-4 in the Southland Football League and SWT 1-5.

Northwestern State faced a good news, bad news, scenerio. The good news for Northwestern was that the Demons advanced to the playoffs for the fourth time in six years. The bad news was the Demons again had to travel to Montana to take on the defending national champions.

The journey to Missoula, Montana, should have served as an omen for the Demons. First, the Demons' charter flight scheduled to depart on Thursday for the Saturday game, was pushed back to Friday because of a mechanical problem.

Fog kept the charter flight from flying into Missoula, causing the plane to land in Helena. The team then had to bus two hours on Friday, arriving in Missoula a mere 18 hours before the noon kickoff on Saturday.

It all seemed to take a toll as the Demons fell behind 35-0 by the midway point of the third quarter.

Montana scored less than three minutes into the game on a 26-yard run by David Gober and never trailed. A 23-yard pass from backup quarterback Brandon Neill to Tate Hancock in the first quarter and a 16-yard interception return for a touchdown by Herb Fernandez at the 7:06 mark of the second quarter gave the Grizzlies a 21-0 halftime lead. The Montana defensive end tipped a short pass from Magee into the air and hauled in the ball before rumbling in for the touchdown.

Trailing 35-0, the Demons finally got on the scoreboard on an 8-yard run by Johnese with 1:24 left in the third quarter. The only other score for Northwestern, which was held to 65 total yards in the opening half, was a 40-yard touchdown pass from Ben Beach to Harrison in the fourth quarter.

The loss ended the Demons' season at 9-4.

While Northwestern State was being dominated by Montana, top-seeded McNeese State more than had its hands full in the Cowboys' opening-round playoff game at home against Montana State.

King gave McNeese a 7-0 lead in the first quarter on a 9-yard touchdown pass from Pendarvis against a hungry Montana State squad that was making its first postseason appearance since 1984.

That would be the only score for the Cowboys in the first half, who lost King in the second quarter with a slight shoulder separation.

"Vick King was never the same after that shoulder injury," said Tate.

The Bobcats tied the game 7-7 at halftime on a 36-yard pass from freshman quarterback Travis Lulay to Aaron Hill midway in the second quarter.

An 8-yard pass from Pendarvis to Trahan early in the third quarter gave McNeese a 14-7 lead before Montana State tied the game again less than a minute into the final quarter on an 8-yard pass from Lulay, a future Canadian Football League quarterback, to Junior Adams.

Trahan picked up the slack in the absence of King, especially on a drive early in the fourth quarter. He carried the ball four times for 27 yards, including a 15-yard run down to the 1-yard line to set up a Pendarvis sneak for a 21-14 McNeese lead with 9:40 remaining in the game.

The Cowboys' defense came up big late in the fourth quarter. A third-down sack by blitzing McNeese safety Achille Fairchild on third down forced a Bobcats punt with less than three minutes left in the game.

Montana State forced a Cowboys punt with 1:22 left in the game. A fumble on the return was recovered by McNeese's Matt Gore. The Cowboys were able to run out the clock on a 21-14 victory that advanced 11-1 McNeese to the Division I-AA quarterfinals.

The Cowboys went from hosting one Montana team making a rare playoff appearance to taking on another that was a perennial postseason fixture. McNeese State was able to host for a second week in a row, facing the defending national champion Montana Grizzlies.

Montana showed why it was the defending champs, building and early 10-0 lead that stretched to 17-0 early in the third quarter.

A 42-yard Chris Snyder field goal in the first quarter and a 3-yard pass from John Edwards to Tate Hancock early in the second quarter gave Montana a

10-0 halftime lead. The Grizzlies stretched their advantage to 17 points on a 39-yard run by J.R. Waller early in the second half.

Ryan Corcoran came off the bench to replace an ineffective Pandarvis. The McNeese starter missed on his first 10 pass attempts as the Cowboys fell behind. Corcoran's 35-yard touchdown pass to Sams with 1:39 left in the third quarter finally got McNeese on the scoreboard.

A 19-yard run by Lawton early in the fourth quarter rallied McNeese to 17-14 but the Grizzlies answered with a 25-yard Snyder field goal to stretch the Montana lead to six points at 20-14 with 9:33 left in the game.

Corcoran and Sams hooked up once again. Facing third-and-goal from the Montana 17, the quarterback tossed a 17-yard strike to put McNeese on top 21-20 with 3:34 remaining. A 42-yard field goal with 58 seconds left increased the Cowboys' lead to 24-20.

"Ryan Corcoran – what a great reliever. He really stepped up in a big way," said Tate. "I know his teammates had a lot of confidence in him. He was outstanding coming off the bench."

Needing a touchdown to win, Edwards tossed a desperation pass 52 yards into the end zone as time expired. His pass was nowhere near a Montana receiver.

The hard-fought 24-20 victory advanced the 12-1 Cowboys to the Division I-AA semifinals.

McNeese State needed one more win to reach the national championship game for the second time in school history. Villanova had no plans to make it easy for the Cowboys, who were playing at home for the third time in the playoffs.

The Cowboys' offense was unable to produce points in the first half, scoring only on a 45-yard interception return by Fairchild to trail 21-7 at intermission.

McNeese marched early in the second half, facing a third down in Villanova territory. Pendarvis ran a sneak to pick up a first down but fumbled on the play. Jamison Young raced 87 yards in the opposite direction for a touchdown that would have given the Wildcats a three-touchdown lead. Instead, the officials ruled Pendarvis was down before the fumble, giving McNeese the ball back and a first down. Sams eventually scored on an end-around from 5 yards out to make the score 21-14. A 3-yard run by Andrew Robin left the Cowboys trailing 21-20 with 2:38 remaining in the third quarter.

Pendarvis threw to Sams a minute into the fourth quarter and the receiver used some shifty moves on his way to a 69-yard pass-and-run touchdown to give the Cowboys their first lead of the game at 26-21.

A 36-yard end-around by Martin less than four minutes later extended McNeese's advantage to 33-21. Villanova responded with its only score of the second half on a 6-yard run by Phil DiGiacomo to rally to within five points at 33-28 with 7:43 remaining in the game.

Prim scored with 14 seconds left to make the final 39-21 to send the 13-1 Cowboys to the national championship game.

"It was really electrifying at Cowboys Stadium that night. Villanova was a really good football team loaded with talent. Our players were not going to be denied that night," Tate recalled.

Villanova had taken a 21-7 halftime lead on two touchdown passes by Brett Gordon, who managed to throw for 354 yards despite having a broken thumb on his throwing hand, and a 1-yard run by Terry Butler.

A familiar venue and foe awaited the Cowboys in the 2002 Division I-AA national championship game.

In McNeese State's only previous appearance in the finals, the Cowboys played in Chattanooga, Tennessee, falling 10-9 to Youngstown State in 1997. The Cowboys' opponent in the 2002 title game was Western Kentucky, a team McNeese defeated 38-13 in the fourth week of the season.

The championship rematch was the opposite of the regular-season encounter in many ways. Sams set a new school record with 316 all-purpose yards in the Cowboys' regular-season victory. Against the Hilltoppers in the rematch, he was held to 69 yards receiving and 32 rushing.

"We weren't the same football team that we were earlier in the football season because of injuries and they were the same. They were probably a little bit better because they got a few guys back that were injured that didn't play against us earlier in the year," said Tate.

One of those players was Jon Frazier. The Western Kentucky running back proved to be the big game-changer in the championship game, amassed 249 yards of total offense, including 159 rushing, and scoring two touchdowns.

McNeese allowed 34 points in the championship, double the average the Cowboys allowed opponents during the regular season. On the flipside, the Hilltoppers held a McNeese squad that averaged 33 points per game to two field goals and a touchdown.

It all added up to a 34-14 national championship victory for Western Kentucky when McNeese left Chattanooga empty handed for the second time school history.

Played on a Friday, Western Kentucky's Karl Mazlowski picked off Pendarvis on the Cowboys' first offensive play of the national championship game. Pendarvis' errant throw set up the game's first touchdown, a 16-yard screen pass from Jason Michael to fullback Jeremi Johnson for what turned out to be the only score of the first quarter.

Frazier broke loose on a 55-yard run to give the Hilltoppers a 14-0 lead nine seconds into the second quarter. Peter Martinez kicked a 40-yard field goal in the second quarter while Marino hit from 30 and 24 yards out as Western Kentucky took a 17-6 halftime lead.

Three times in the game, the Cowboys advanced inside the Western Kentucky 15-yard line but only came away with two field goals.

A 49-yard reception by Johnson set up a 14-yard touchdown run by Frazier to increase the Hilltoppers' lead to 18 points at 24-6 less than four minutes into the second half. McNeese countered with its only offensive touchdown of the game on a 15-yard pass from Pendarvis to Lawton. A two-point conversion pass from the quarterback to Jeff Hamilton made it 24-14 with 3:49 remaining in the third quarter.

If the Cowboys had thoughts of another second-half championship-game rally, it was dashed when Frazier turned a screen pass into a 54-yard gain to set up a Michael touchdown. Michael's 2-yard run early in the fourth quarter made it 31-14. Martinez kicked a 23-yard field goal with 2:51 left in the game to give Western Kentucky a 20-point victory and a national championship.

"We gave up a couple of big swing passes on pressure situations. Offensively, they made some big plays and their fullback had a really big night. It was just a tough loss for us," said Tate.

McNeese ended the 2002 season 13-2. The Cowboys' only losses were to Division I-A Nebraska and in the Division I-AA championship game.

NAME CHANGES

The 2003 season was a year of name changes. With the departure of football-only member Jacksonville State, the Southland Football League reverted back to the name Southland Conference. Also, Southwest Texas State was now known as Texas State University at San Marcos.

With the Southland down to six teams, conference play began much later in the season for most teams than in past years. Most teams had at least five non-conference games worth of experience before starting league play.

Stephen F. Austin and Sam Houston State opened up Southland play on a Thursday night when the Lumberjacks visited the Bearkats. SFA went into the game 3-3 on the season while Sam Houston State was 1-4. SHSU opened with a win over Midwestern State before losing four-straight games.

The Bearkats were no strangers to playing on a Thursday night. The Southland opener against Stephen F. Austin was the third Thursday game for the Bearkats. The two previous Thurday encounters were losses but the Bearkats seemed eager to turn around their 1-4 start by jumping out to a 14-10 lead against SFA.

The Lumberjacks helped SHSU to build its lead with key breakdowns. On SFA's opening play from scrimmage, Tony Tompkins fumbled while attempting an option pass, with Sam Houston State recovering at the SFA 20. The Bearkats took advantage when Steve Smith scored on a 1-yard run nine plays later. The Lumberjacks were forced to punt on their next possession, with Stephen F. Austin allowing a 37-yard return by Bernard Campbell to the SFA 39. Another nine-play drive ended with a 6-yard touchdown pass from Wade Pate to Vin Cartwright.

Trailing 21-3, Stephen F. Austin rallied to tie the game 24-24 in the third quarter. Cliff Edwards scored on a 23-yard run and Braylon Lester returned an interception 26 yards for a touchdown to make the score 21-16 at halftime. After Sam Houston State opened the third quarter with a 48-yard Joey Price field goal,

Michael Williams connected with Chance Dennis on a 16-yard touchdown pass to tie the game at the 9:23 mark of the third quarter.

SHSU capped an 80-yard drive on a 2-yard run by Jason Godfrey on the final play of the third quarter to give the Bearkats the lead again at 31-24.

Still trailing by a touchdown, the Lumberjacks forced Sam Houston State to punt with less than three minutes remaining in the game. Ryan Smith blocked Curtis Parks' punt and SFA took over at the Bearkats' 11. Edwards scored on the next play to tie the game once again.

SFA had once last change, getting the ball back with 1:21 remaining. The Lumberjacks worked the ball into Bearkats territory and with time winding down, Ryan Rossner booted a 54-yard field goal with one second remaining in the contest to give Stephen F. Austin a 34-31 thriller.

Along with a new school moniker, there was another name change at Texas State. Manny Matsakis was the new coach of the Bobcats, replacing Bob DeBesse. A former head coach at Emporia State from 1995-98, Matsakis took over at the San Marcos school after serving as special teams coach at Texas Tech from 2000-02.

The Bobcats went into their Southland opener at home against Northwestern State sporting a 3-4 record. Matsakis lost in his debut by a whopping 72-8 margin at New Mexico before earning his first win against Angelo State. Another win came against a Southeastern Louisiana squad fielding a football team for the first time since 1995.

Northwestern State was off to a 5-2 start. One of the wins was against Division I-A rival Louisiana-Monroe (formerly known as Northeast Louisiana), while the two losses were to Tulane and Division I-AA power Northern Iowa.

Opening Southland Conference play against Northwestern State, the Bobcats faced one of the top defensive units in all of college football. The Demons were coming off a game in which Northwestern State set a new school record by holding Southeastern Louisiana to minus-13 yards rushing.

Northwestern State's defense again was a the top of its game, holding the Bobcats to 56 yards rushing and sacking Texas State quarterback Barrick Nealy nine times in a 49-19 victory.

Davon Vinson, the Demons' quarterback, was particularly efficient. He completed nine-straight passes to tie a school mark held by future New Orleans Saints and Atlanta Falcons quarterback Bobby Hebert for consecutive completions in a game. Vinson finished 10 of 11 passing for 145 yards.

While the Demons quarterback failed to throw a touchdown pass, Vinson scored three times running the football. A pair of short scoring runs by Vinson in the second quarter gave Northwestern a 14-13 halftime lead.

Vinson and Derrick Johnese added rushing touchdowns in the third quarter as the Demons pulled away. Texas State trailed 42-3 before scoring a pair of touchdowns late in the game against Northwestern State reserves.

McNeese State, the top-ranked team in Division I-AA, played its initial Southland Conference game a week later when the Cowboys hosted Sam Houston State. McNeese went into the game 5-1 and riding a four-game winning streak. The Cowboys' only loss was to Division I-A Kansas State.

Scott Pendarvis fired a school record-tying five touchdown passes as the Cowboys won a 55-37 shootout against Sam Houston State.

Along with Pendarvis' effort, Vick King rushed for 149 yards and two touchdowns to pace McNeese. Pendarvis tossed touchdown passes of 46 yards to B.J. Sams and 1 yard to Luke Lawton in the first quarter. He hooked up with Sams again on a 17-yard strike in the second quarter before tossing a 72-yard bomb to Britt Brodhead in the second quarter. John Marino added a 25-yard field goal in the second quarter to give the Cowboys a 29-17 halftime lead.

The Bearkats' first-half scores came on a 9-yard pass from Pate to Campbell in the first quarter, along with a 1-yard run by Godfrey and a 47-yard Price field goal on the final play of the second quarter.

Pendarvis' fifth touchdown pass was a 10-yard strike to Sams in the third quarter. King scored the game's final two touchdowns on runs of 12 and 2 yards.

McNeese moved to 6-1 while winning its league opener while the Bearkats dropped to 0-2 in the conference and 1-7 overall.

Also making its Southland debut that day was Nicholls State. On the road to face Northwestern State, the Colonels went into the clash 2-4. After opening with a 70-0 win over NAIA Bethel College, Nicholls went on a three-week cross-country journey. The Colonels flew to South Florida, followed by a trek to Portland State. The next week, a travel-weary squad bussed to Texas A&M-Kingsville. After losing all three road games, Nicholls beat up on Texas Southern 64-5 at home before falling 32-23 to Florida Atlantic in Fort Lauderdale, Florida.

After all the travel, Nicholls had a second open date in three weeks leading up to the Colonels' game at Northwestern State.

Nicholls and Northwestern State put on an interesting show. The Colonels scored on five of their first six possessions and amassed 415 yards of total offense against the nation's third-best defense in a 40-30 victory over the Demons.

The Colonels were especially effective in the first half, gaining 323 total yards in the opening two quarters while keeping the ball away from the Northwestern State offense with a time-consuming triple option attack.

Nicholls quarterback Josh Son showed no ill effects from a minor concussion suffered two weeks earlier, producing his best passing game of the season. The quarterback was 5 of 8 passing for 183 yards, including an 85-yard bomb to Vince Butler.

A high-scoring first half saw Nicholls take a 33-24 lead at intermission. The second half turned into a defensive battle. After a scoreless third quarter, each team produced a touchdown in the final quarter to account for the final score.

The conference-opening win, only the second victory in 14 tries for the Colonels at Turpin Stadium, moved Nicholls to 3-4 overall.

Meanwhile, Stephen F. Austin became the first time to reach 2-0 in Southland play with a 44-17 win at Texas State.

Stephen F. Austin fell behind 19-13 at halftime versus Texas State before exploding for 17-consecutive points on the way to the Lumberjacks' victory.

The 17-point run turned a six-point deficit into a 30-19 advantage. Highlighting the scoring spree was a 7-yard scoring run by Williams and a 7-yard interception return for a touchdown by SFA defensive lineman Kenneth Winters.

Texas State cut the deficit to three points on a 10-yard touchdown run by Morris Brothers early in the fourth quarter. The Lumberjacks countered with a 37-yard touchdown reception by Dennis before icing the game with 1:38 remaining on a 4-yard Eric Chapman touchdown run.

SFA improved to 2-0 in the Southland and 5-3 overall while Texas State dropped to 0-2 in the conference and 3-6 overall.

Texas State had a short week to prepare for top-ranked McNeese State, hosting the Cowboys on a Thursday night.

A pair of defensive scores for each team started off the McNeese-Texas State affair before both offenses settled down in a 38-28 victory for the Cowboys.

McNeese took a 7-0 lead seven seconds into the game when Jarrell Zeno returned an interception 12 yards for a touchdown. The Bobcats tied the score five minutes later on a 52-yard fumble return by Larry Hayden.

Pendarvis' 1-yard touchdown run with 41 seconds left in the first quarter gave McNeese a 14-7 edge. Brothers, who rushed for 149 yards in the game, scored on a 44-yard touchdown run in the second quarter and Marino countered with a 35-yard field goal as Texas State edged to within three points at 17-14 going into halftime.

McNeese stretched its lead when Pendarvis and Brodhead hooked up on a 73-yard touchdown pass early in the second half as the Cowboys went on to take a 10-point victory.

Cory Elolf set a new Texas State record with an 86-yard punt, topping the mark of 76 set by Bill Soyers in 1968.

The Cowboys moved to 2-0 in the SLC and 7-1 overall. Texas State fell to 0-3 in the conference and 3-7 overall.

Two days later, Nicholls State moved to 2-0 in the Southland for the first time in school history and joined McNeese and idle SFA atop the conference with a 37-12 win at home over struggling Sam Houston State.

Again, Son led the way for Nicholls. Guiding the nation's top rushing team, the quarterback ran for 68 yards to become the school's all-time leading rusher. Son ended the game with 2,483 yards, topping the school record by one yard, set by Oscar Smith. Smith played for Nicholls from 1981-82 and 1984-85.

Nicholls built upon a 24-6 halftime lead when Travis Douglas forced a Campbell fumble which was recovered by Kyle Freeman at the Bearkats 23. Three plays later, Travis Felder scored his second touchdown of the game as he turned the corner on a 7-yard run.

A 33-yard scoring strike from backup quarterback Travis Tobaben to Corey Zeno pulled the Bearkats to within 30-12 with 34 seconds remaining in the third quarter.

James Morales played most of the fourth quarter at quarterback for the Colonels, scoring on a 7-yard keeper with 12:43 remaining for the final score of the game as Nicholls evened its record at 4-4 after a 1-3 start to open the season.

SHSU dropped to 0-2 in the conference and 1-7 overall with the loss.

Texas State played a Thursday night game for the second week in a row when the Bobcats visited Nicholls State.

Nicholls was clinging to 17-13 lead midway in the fourth quarter when consecutive personal-foul calls against the Bobcats kept a Colonels drive alive.

Son was sacked on third-and-7 at the Texas State 47, which would have forced a punting situation. A personal-foul penalty against the Bobcats, however, moved the ball down to the 34 and kept the drive alive.

On the next play, the Bobcats committed another personal foul, moving the ball to the 19. Five plays later, Phillip Brock ran wide right for a 1-yard touchdown for a 24-13 Nicholls lead with 5:55 left in the game.

Nicholls added a 13-yard Son touchdown run with 14 seconds remaining to account for the final margin as the Colonels became the first team in the Southland to reach 3-0 in the conference in 2003.

The Colonels seemingly had no answers to Texas State's surprising game plan in the first half. Averaging 277 yards per game through the air, the Bobcats instead turned to their ground game. Texas State amassed 331 yards rushing and outgained Nicholls 485-243 in total yards.

After allowing 256 yards on the ground in the first half, the Nicholls defense adjusted, including coming up with three goal-line stands and forcing two fumbles.

Trailing 7-3 at halftime, Nicholls, which moved over .500 for the first time since a 1-0 start, regained the lead on its opening possession of the second half.

Big plays in the 65-yard drive included Son's only completion of the game – a 9-yard connection to Marcus Richardson – and a 28-yard Colt Colletti run. That eventually set up a 1-yard option keeper by Son for a 10-7 Nicholls lead with 8:28 remaining in the third quarter.

Nicholls fumbled deep in its own territory on its next two possessions but Texas State took advantage on only one of the opportunities - a 14-yard Brothers run to give the Bobcats a 13-10 edge.

Chris Crawford returned the ensuing kickoff a school-record 100 yards as Nicholls regained the lead at 17-13.

Texas State remained winless in four conference games and dropped to 3-8 overall with the loss.

Two days later, McNeese State headed into its Southland Conference home clash against a Stephen F. Austin team also sporting a 2-0 conference mark.

An expected tight outcome lived up to its billing as neither team managed more than a 10-point edge. SFA was the one to go up by 10 points on a 10-yard touchdown pass from Williams to Dennis and a 33-yard Rossner field goal in the second quarter to give the Lumberjacks a 17-7 advantage at halftime. SFA led 7-0 following Vernon Holman's recovery of a blocked punt in the end zone before McNeese tied the game on a 1-yard Lawton run.

McNeese inched closer in the second half on a pair of Marino field goals, one late in the third quarter and the other with 4:01 left in the game, to trail 17-13.

Trailing by four points, the Cowboys got the ball back at their own 34-yard line with 1:54 left in the game. A 24-yard pass to Sams and a pass interference call against the Lumberjacks on a fourth-and-5 play helped to move McNeese deep into SFA territory. Chris Thomas scored from a yard out with 1:54 left in the game to lift the Cowboys to a 20-17 victory.

McNeese remained perfect in the Southland at 3-0 while moving to 8-1 overall. SFA slipped to 2-1 in the conference and 5-4 overall.

In Huntsville, the Bearkats, seeking to end a seven-game losing streak, saw Northwestern State score a pair of touchdowns in less than a two-minute span to take a 17-10 halftime lead.

Sam Houston State turned the ball over on its opening drive of the second half but after Northwestern State failed to capitalize, the Bearkats scored on their next four possessions to take command of the game.

With the score tied 17-17, a mid-air fumble by Northwestern State's Issa Banna was hauled in by Greg Brown, who raced 46 yards to give the Bearkats a 23-17 lead with 13:24 left in the game.

Toby Zeigler fumbled the ensuing kickoff when belted by SHSU's Caleb Tubbleville, with Derrick Harris recovering for the Bearkats at the Northwestern State 22. That led to a 42-yard Price field goal and a 26-17 lead on Sam Houston State's way to a 29-24 triumph.

The win gave the Bearkats their first Southland win in four tries as SHSU moved to 2-7 overall. Northwestern State dropped to 1-2 in the SLC and 6-4 overall.

Nicholls State, Southland Conference co-leaders with McNeese State at 3-0, put its perfect league mark on the line at Stephen F. Austin. The Lumberjacks were key contenders for the conference title as well, sporting a 2-1 record going into the contest.

With the score tied 7-7, the Colonels lost Son when he reinjured ribs he hurt earlier in the season against Florida Atlantic. When Morales, the backup quarterback, left the game with a hamstring injury, the quarterbacking duties were left to Yale Vannoy.

The Lumberjacks took a 14-7 lead at the break when Tompkins turned a screen pass from Michael Williams into a 49-yard touchdown late in the second quarter.

Nicholls pulled to within four points at 14-10 on a 28-yard Jay Jones field goal at the start of the second half, but SFA put the game way with a pair of fourth-quarter touchdown passes from Williams to Michael Davis on its way to the 28-16 victory.

McNeese's clash with Northwestern State, meanwhile, was an even tighter affair than the Cowboys' earlier Stephen F. Austin encounter. The Cowboys led 6-3 at halftime as Marino kicked two first-half field goals and Northwestern State's Tommy Hebert booted a 19 yarder. The Demons had two first-and-goal chances in the first half but were limited to the one Hebert field goal.

A shanked punt gave Northwestern the ball at the McNeese 35 late in the third quarter. Following a false-start penalty, Vinson handed the ball to Johnese, who pitched it back to Vinson. The Demons quarterback hurled a strike to Derrick Doyle for a touchdown. Hebert's missed conversion attempt left Northwestern with a 9-6 edge.

Henry Smith returned the ensuing kickoff to midfield. King's 2-yard run on fourth-and-1 from the Demons' 40 kept the drive alive. On third-and-goal from the 3-yard line, Ryan Corcoran tossed to Sams for a touchdown and a 13-9 lead with 13:33 remaining in the game.

The Demons threatened late in the game, reaching the McNeese 5-yard line with 4:34 remaining. Following an incomplete pass on first down, a pitch to Johnese lost 3 yards. Vinson tossed to Johnese in the end zone but the Northwestern State running back was unable to come down with his feet in bounds. Vinson attempted to pass to what appeared to be an open Ben Bailey. The play was squashed, however, when Cowboys defensive end Mike Swanson deflected the ball with 3:29 remaining in the game.

King broke loose on a 41-yard run late in the game, allowing the Cowboys to run out the clock on a 13-9 triumph.

McNeese moved to 4-0 in the Southland and 9-1 overall. Northwestern State fell to 1-3 in the league and 6-5 overall.

Nicholls State was the only team left that could play spoiler in McNeese State's quest for another undefeated year in Southland play. The Colonels had entered the regular-season finale hoping for a long-shot scenario to the postseason. At 3-1 in the league, a win over McNeese could have created a three-way tie for first place. The Colonels found out before the game that the needed outcome that would give the automatic bid to Nicholls did not materialize when Stephen F. Austin defeated Northwestern State earlier in the day.

The Cowboys made all of that irrelevant, scoring the game's first 28 points as McNeese State cruised to a 63-28 victory.

Three plays into the game, Zeno recovered a Sedgwyn Thigpen fumble at the Nicholls 4-yard line. Pendarvis hit Matt Gore on the very next play go give McNeese a 7-0 lead.

King raced 41 yards to set up a 37-yard pass from Pendarvis to Sams for a 14-0 lead. Sams set a new school record for all-purpose yards on the play. He finished with 1,849 career yards, topping the previous record of 1,737 set by Flip Johnson in 1986.

A 9-yard touchdown run by King and a 67-yard pass from Pendarvis to Marcus Turner gave McNeese its 28-0 lead. Nicholls finally scored on a touchdown pass by Son to make it 28-7 at halftime.

Known for his running ability, Son passed for career-high 236 yards in the game. Son tossed a 61-yard touchdown pass to Butler in the second half. Pendarvis, meanwhile, threw his fourth score on the game on a 50-yard pass to Turner in the fourth quarter on the Cowboys' way to the 63-28 victory.

McNeese amassed 542 yards of total offense. The Cowboys' defense held the nation's third-best rushing attack to 188 yards, well below its average of 325 per contest.

In finishing 5-0 in Southland Conference play, McNeese stretched its conference winning streak to 16 games. The Cowboys concluded the regular season 10-1, their lone loss coming to Kansas State in Week 2. Nicholls ended its season 5-6 overall and 3-2 in the SLC.

"It was a good run for us. We were right in the Top 5 for three-straight years. It was a great run for our football program, our players and fans. It was a very exciting time for football at McNeese," said Tate.

Earlier, Stephen F. Austin fell behind 7-0 at Northwestern State but scored the next 34 points in a 44-14 domination of the Demons. Entering the game, the Lumberjacks still had hopes of a Southland Conference co-championship, needing a win over the Demons, coupled with a McNeese State loss to Nicholls. The Lumberjacks did their part, but later in the evening, the Colonels fell to the Cowboys 63-28, allowing McNeese to finish all alone in first place with a 5-0 league mark.

Down by seven points, Williams helped to account for Stephen F. Austin's next three touchdowns, more than enough points that the Lumberjacks would need to pull out the victory. The SFA quarterback hooked up on scoring tosses of 7 yards to Matt Bodley and 16 yards to Kevin Landry while adding a 1-yard touchdown run to make it 21-7.

Edwards contributed two touchdown runs and Rossner three field goals for SFA. The Demons' scores came on a 1-yard keeper by Vinson early in the game and a 2-yard run by Banna in the third period.

The Lumberjacks finished the season 4-1 in the Southland and 7-4 overall after going 6-5 in each of the previous three years. Northwestern State ended 1-4 in the conference and 6-6 overall.

In the other Southland Conference affair on the final day of the 2003 regular season, Texas State rushed for 405 yards, 246 by Terrell Harris, as the Bobcats snapped a 14-game winless streak against current Southland opponents with a 49-28 thumping of the Bearkats. The last league foe Texas State beat (other than departed member Jacksonville State 27-20 in 2002) was Sam Houston State in 2000.

The two sub-.500 teams battled to a 14-14 tie at halftime before Texas State took control in the second half. The Bobcats may have been inspired by a halftime ceremony in which the field was renamed "Jim Wacker Field at Bobcat Stadium," in honor of the late coach who led the school to two national championships.

Texas State seemed to put the game away in the blink of an eye. Harris broke loose on a 49-yard run to set up a 4-yard touchdown run by Nealy. Godfrey fumbled on the ensuing possession for SHSU with Harold Watson scooping up the ball and sprinting 18 yards for a touchdown. The two scores, which came in a span of seven seconds, turned a tied game into a 28-14 Texas State lead that the Bobcats would build into their eventual 49-28 victory.

Both teams ended the season 1-4 in the Southland Conference. Sam Houston State finished the year at 2-9 while Texas State ended up 4-8.

McNeese State seemed perfectly positioned to not only reach the Division I-AA championship once again, but to go one step beyond and claim a national title.

The Cowboys won the Southland Conference for the third-consecutive year and by entering the playoff as the No. 1 seed would enjoy home-field advantage until the finals for a second year in a row.

McNeese boasted an experienced, high-scoring offense. It hardly seemed like a fair fight. The Cowboys had not lost a first-round playoff game since 2001. No. 16 seed Northern Arizona had never won a Division I-AA playoff game before.

Falling behind early seemed no big deal for the Cowboys. A 9-yard pass from Lumberjacks freshman quarterback Jason Murrietta to Chris Nash late in the first quarter and an 11-yard toss to Ramen Green early in the second quarter for a 14-0 Northern Arizona lead wasn't anything McNeese couldn't overcome.

McNeese got three of the points back on a 27-yard Marino field goal midway in the second quarter. The Lumberjacks managed to increase their advantage to 18 points at halftime following a 7-yard touchdown pass to Clarence Moore for a 21-3 Northern Arizona lead.

The Cowboys were limited to three points in the first half, mostly due to poor starting field position. McNeese started five offensive possessions inside its own 22-yard line. Three of the drives began at the Cowboys' 2-, 3-, and 4-yard lines.

McNeese was accustomed to late-game heroics but there would be no rally this time around. Murrietta tossed two more touchdown passes in the second half and the Cowboys' offense never got on track in a shocking 35-3 blowout.

The Cowboys, who entered the game averaging 446 yards per game, were held to 190 by the Lumberjacks' defense. McNeese's defense surrendered 398 yards as the Cowboys suffered their worst defeat in playoff history.

Injuries, Tate said, played a role in the upset loss.

"We had a lot of starters that were in street clothes that night," said Tate. "I don't want to make any excuses with injuries. That's part of football. The next guy has got to step up and be ready to play."

"I do also want to give credit to the opponent," Tate added. "They had five senior offensive linemen that were really dominant that night and really instrumental in getting the win. They had a freshman quarterback but a lot of senior linemen and skilled people around him that really made them a good football team that night."

McNeese closed the 2003 season at 10-2.

COACHING UPHEAVAL II

Nicholls State was 3-0 in the Southland Conference for the first time ever with two games remaining in the 2003 season. The Colonels went into the final game of the regular season against top-ranked McNeese State needing a win to grab a share of the league title.

Officially, all of that was about as real as a dream sequence on the nighttime television soap opera, "Dallas."

A brewing academic fraud investigation led to a coaching change at Nicholls. Although he was not personally implicated, head coach Darryl Daye was dismissed for what school officials termed his failure to "maintain proper controls." Also, the Colonels were forced to forfeit all of their wins, leaving Nicholls winless for the 2003 season.

Daye's dismissal came only weeks before the start of the 2004 season, with defensive coordinator Jay Thomas being elevated to the top job. Thomas served two stints as an assistant at Nicholls from 1990-92 and again starting in 1999 before being named head coach.

The ordeal was not the only coaching change under unusual circumstances leading into the 2004 season. In January 2004, Texas State fired Manny Matsakis after a university investigation uncovered NCAA rules violations concerning extra hours of practice and voluntary summer workouts. School officials cited management issues as also leading to Matsakis' dismissal.

David Bailiff, a former player at what was then called Southwest Texas, was hired to replace Matsakis. Bailiff spent two stints as as assistant at his alma mater, including serving as defensive coordinator from 1997-2000. He was defensive coordinator at Texas Christian from 2001-03 before being named head coach at Texas State.

Despite the turmoil, Nicholls managed to win its 2004 season opener with a 37-14 home victory over Eastern Washington. The Colonels alternated wins and losses, going into their Southland Conference opener 3-2.

The Colonels opened Southland play at Sam Houston State against a Bearkats team that was off to a 4-1 start. Among SHSU's wins was a 41-29 thriller at home over Montana.

"They didn't handle our Texas hospitality any better than we handled their hospitality up there," said Randleman, referring to the hot and humid weather conditions in Huntsville, a stark contast to the frigid temperatures the Bearkats faced in their 2001 playoff loss at Missoula, Montana. "It was a warm night and they were dying."

Playing the previous Thursday gave the Bearkats a couple of extra days to prepare for their game against Nicholls State.

Looking to duplicate the success of the 2001 season when Sam Houston State brought in SMU transfer Josh McCown to play quarterback, the Bearkats turned the offense over to Dustin Long, a Texas A&M transfer, for the 2003 campaign.

Long was off his game against Nicholls in the 2004 encounter, throwing two touchdowns but suffering three interceptions. The Colonels could not take advantage, however, by losing three fumbles in a 38-10 loss to the Bearkats.

Stevie Smith took a swing pass from Long on SHSU's second play from scrimmage and turned it into a 75-yard touchdown to give the Bearkats the early lead.

A 1-yard touchdown run by Smith on a drive set up by a Yale Vannoy fumble gave the Bearkats a 14-0 lead after one quarter. Long culminated a 91-yard drive with a 27-yard pass to Brian Washington to give SHSU a 21-7 halftime lead.

The Colonels' only score in the first half came on 36-yard touchdown run by Colt Colletti early in the second quarter.

Also opening Southand Conference play that same day was McNeese State and Northwestern State. The Cowboys were not the same team that spent much of the previous season ranked No. 1 in the nation. McNeese was 2-3 on the season, the first time the Cowboys had been below .500 in eight years.

Northwestern State was off to a 4-1 start. The only blemish through five games was a narrow loss to Louisiana-Lafayette (formerly called Southwestern Louisiana).

As far as league foes were concerned, it was more than payback time for three-time defending Southland Conference champion McNeese State. Playing at home, Northwestern State was the first SLC team to try and dethrone the champs.

Featuring the top-ranked defense overall along with being No. 1 against the run, the Demons were stingy against McNeese, holding the Cowboys to 146 total yards, including minus-5 rushing. Northwestern's defense came up with six sacks and 16 tackles for loss.

The Demons took advantage of opportune field position to build a 24-3 halftime lead. One play after a shanked punt, Shelton Sampson scooted 31 yards for a touchdown less than two minutes into the game to give Northwestern a 7-0 advantage. A 32-yard pass from quarterback Connor Morel to Ben Bailey made it 14-0 before McNeese got its only points of the first half on a 23-yard John Marino field goal.

A 2-yard run by Derrick Johnese and a 43-yard Josh Storrs field goal gave the Demons their three-touchdown lead at halftime.

Davon Vinson added a touchdown run and touchdown pass in the second half as Northwestern continued to build its lead, ultimately winning by a 47-17 margin.

It marked the third time in the season that the Cowboys were beaten by at least 30 points.

Coming off an emotional win over McNeese, the Demons were a victim of poor timing as Northwestern State's next SLC encounter was at Nicholls State on a Thursday night. Thursday night games had been especially good to the Colonels, who had five wins in their last six Thursday games going into the contest against the Demons.

Much like the previous year, the Colonels used a surprisingly-productive passing game against No. 9 Northwestern State and the Demons' top-ranked rush defense.

Nicholls pulled away from a 17-14 halftime lead in a bizarre third quarter for Northwestern.

The Colonels were awarded two points when Morel, the Demons' quarterback, was penalized for intentional grounding in the end zone for a safety.

Two plays following the free kick, Vannoy threw into double coverage. Two Demon defenders ran into one another and the ball was tipped into the air and pulled down by Colonels tight end Jared Landrum who raced 54 yards for a touchdown to give Nicholls a 26-14 lead. The play gave Vannoy a season-high 230 yards passing. He also led the team in rushing with 72 yards.

Vannoy had been contained for most of the game by the Demons' defense. He only had four yards rushing until a 37-yard sprint helped to set up a Colletti touchdown in the third quarter.

Two examples demonstrated just what type of night it was for the Demons. The first came when three-straight penalties following a bad snap from shotgun formation led to a third-and-61 from the Northwestern 2-yard line.

The other came on a blocked field goal by Nicholls kicker Jay Jones. Although the kick was blocked, the ball bounced to holder James Wilcox, who completed a pass to Michael Young for a first down. On the next play, Cal Jones scored on a 16-yard run one play into the fourth quarter to give the Colonels a 40-14 lead that would hold up to the end of the game.

Both teams moved to 1-1 in Southland play with the outcome. Northwestern fell to 5-2 overall while Nicholls improved to 4-3.

Two days later, Texas State and Stephen F. Austin met in San Marcos in the Southland opener for both teams.

The Bobcats were off to a 2-4 start under Bailiff. Texas State won in Bailiff's debut against Angelo State but was on a three-game skid going into the SFA contest.

Stephen F. Austin was 5-1, with the Lumberjacks' only loss being a 31-24 defeat against Florida International

After Texas State's John Tyson capped an 80-yard drive on a 29-yard pass from quarterback Barrick Nealy to give the Bobcats a 7-0 lead, Stephen F. Austin countered with two touchdowns. With the score tied, Keldric Holman returned a fumble 12 yards for a touchdown to put the Lumberjacks on top 14-7.

The offenses for both teams were hampered by injuries to key players. Nealy entered the game with a nagging injury and Texas State also was without K.R. Carpenter and Terrell Harris.

Nealy reinjured his shoulder in the third quarter and was replaced by Chase Wasson. With the Bobcats trailing 14-10, Wasson raced 41 yards for a score for what proved to be the winning touchdown in Texas State's 17-14 victory.

For SFA, Derek Farmer entered the game with a hip pointer and departed the contest in the second quarter with a leg injury. Without the running back, the Lumberjacks were limited to 24 yards on the ground.

Texas State moved to 2-0 in the Southland a week later, using a strong second half for a 54-27 road beatdown of McNeese State.

Texas State allowed McNeese State to rally from a 17-point deficit to tie the game at halftime but the visiting Bobcats scored 23-consecutive points in the second half on their way to the 54-27 victory. The 54 points were the most scored by a Bobcats team since a 65-15 victory over Southern Utah in 1995.

The Bobcats scored in a variety of ways. Morris Brothers rushed for two touchdowns, Wasson tossed a 10-yard touchdown pass to Markee White, Nealy hit Tyson on a 10-yard pass, Domino Giametta and Walter Musgrove scored on fumble recoveries and Stan Jones kicked a 34-yard field goal. Texas State even came up with a safety in the victory.

Down 17-0, McNeese tied the game at halftime on a 15-yard pass from Chris Jones to Chris Thomas, a 1-yard run by Thomas and a 41-yard Marino field goal.

Texas State improved to 2-0 in the Southland Conference and 4-4 overall. McNeese fell to 0-2 in the league and 3-5 overall.

Sam Houston State joined Texas State at 2-0 in the Southland with a 31-28 road triumph over Stephen F. Austin.

A 24-yard Lance Garner field goal and Long touchdown passes of 51 yards to Jason Mathenia and 5 yards to Robert Garmon gave Sam Houston State a 17-7 halftime edge as the Bearkats went on to capture their sixth win of the season.

An old reliable aspect of the Bearkats' game paid dividends at the end of Sam Houston State's encounter at Stephen F. Austin.

Long and his Lumberjacks counterpart, Michael Williams, filled the air with footballs. Long passed for 361 yards and Williams 309. The Bearkats' quarterback tossed four touchdowns and had two interceptions. Williams threw three touchdowns and was picked off three times while playing with a groin injury. Each quarterback tossed a pair of touchdowns in the first half as SHSU edged the Lumberjacks 17-14 at the break.

SFA gained its first lead of the game at the 5:20 mark of the third quarter on a Joe Kutac's recovery of teammate Ron Middleton's fumble in the end zone for a 21-17 Lumberjacks advantage.

Long countered with his third touchdown pass of the game, a 35-yard strike to Mathenia to put Sam Houston State on top once again at 24-21.

The teams continued to trade leads. After a 14-yard touchdown pass from Williams to tight end Matt Bodley gave SFA the lead, the Bearkats reclaimed it at 31-28 on a 19-yard pass from Long to Bernard Campbell.

Trailing by three points, the Lumberjacks drove down for a potential game-tying field goal in the closing seconds of the game. Ryan Rossner's 40-yard attempt with 17 seconds was blocked by Steven Hagler, allowing the Bearkats to take a nail-biting 31-28 victory.

Sam Houston State improved to 2-0 the Southland Conference and 7-1 overall. SFA fell to 0-2 in the league and slipped to 5-3 overall.

The offensive numbers were staggering in Sam Houston State's Southland Conference home game a week later against McNeese State.

Touchdown runs of 83 and 5 yards by McNeese State's Chris Thomas gave the Cowboys a 35-24 lead – at halftime.

Thomas ended up rushing for 161 yards in the game but the really big numbers were rolled up by the passing game of both squads.

Long passed for a single-game school record 577 yards and tossed five touchdown passes as the Bearkats, ranked No. 4 in Division I-AA, amassed a team-record 655 yards of total offense. Three different SHSU receivers had more than 100 reception yards. Jarrod Fuller led the way with 137 yards and a touchdown while Mathenia hauled in nine catches for 165 yards and two scores while Vin Cartwright had 124 receiving yards.

The numbers were also as big for the Cowboys. Jones accounted for 265 of his team's school-record 644 yards of total offense. Along with Thomas' rushing effort, Andy Bertrand had 146 reception yards and two touchdowns.

A 2-yard run by Long in the third quarter allowed SHSU to make the score 35-31 before the Cowboys built their lead to 10 points on a touchdown pass from Jones to Bertrand.

The Bearkats responded with 21-straight points. A Mark Hughes interception of a Scott Pendarvis pass led to a 4-yard run by Smith. A 22-yard touchdown strike from Long to Mathenia put Sam Houston State on top 45-41 with 10:39 left in the game. Roberts' 26-yard touchdown catch increased the SHSU advantage to 52-41.

McNeese made it 52-47 with 1:55 remaining in the contest on a 3-yard touchdown pass from Jones to Guidry. The Cowboys recovered the onside kick and reached the Sam Houston State 17 before Hughes intercepted a Jones pass at the 3-yard line with 38 seconds left to preserve the seven-point victory for the Bearkats. The interception was the third of the game for Hughes.

SHSU moved to 3-0 in the Southland to take sole possession of first place in the conference while improving to 8-1 overall. McNeese dropped to 0-3 in the SLC and 3-6 overall.

In Natchitoches, Southwest Texas and Northwestern State both were looking for a win to stay in Southland Conference contention.

Northwestern State made a bold statement concerning its intentions, with the Demons scoring the first six times they had the ball in a resounding 44-7 win over Texas State.

Vinson and Derrick Doyle hooked up for two touchdowns, including an 8-yard connection, to give the Demons a 7-0 lead. Johnese, who rushed for 152 yards, scored on a 3-yard run and Tommy Hebert added a 25-yard field goal for a 17-0 Northwestern lead after one quarter.

Texas State's only score came less than a minute into the second quarter on a 15-yard pass from Wasson to Tyson. The Bobcats, limited to 169 yards of total offense, got almost half of the yards on the 80-yard scoring drive.

The Demons scored the next 21 points of the second quarter on a 6-yard Vinson run, an 8-yard Sampson run and a second Vinson-to-Doyle touchdown to put the game away at 38-7.

Both teams moved to 2-1 in Southland play. Texas State dropped to 4-5 overall while Northwestern State improved to 6-3.

Coming off an open date, Nicholls State put itself into the thick of the Southland Conference race for the third year in a row with a 41-23 win over Stephen F. Austin in the Colonels' 2004 home finale.

It was quite a fall for SFA. At one point in the season, the Lumberjacks were ranked as high as No. 5 in the nation. The loss to Nicholls was the third-straight conference defeat for SFA, which dropped to 0-3 in the SLC and 5-4 overall.

Colletti and Plaisance, a pair of senior running backs, each ran for more than 100 yards as the Colonels rushed for 401 yards versus the Lumberjacks.

Leading 20-10 at halftime, the Colonels mounted a 90-yard scoring drive to open the second half, culminating in a 17-yard touchdown run by Plaisance.

After Middleton turned a short pass from Williams into a 51-yard touchdown to pull SFA to within 27-17, a key ruling helped to seal the Lumberjacks' fate.

Early in the fourth quarter, a pass intended for Holman fell incomplete when it was batted away by Colonel defensive lineman Bryan Paille. After a discussion on the field, the officials ruled the play a lateral, and therefore a fumble, giving the ball to Nicholls.

Three plays later, Vannoy scored on a 3-yard run to effectively put the game away, making it 34-17 as Nicholls improved to 2-1 in the Southland and 5-3 overall.

It looked like something was going to have to give a week later in Sam Houston State's Southland Conference showdown at Northwestern State.

Now ranked No. 3 in the nation, the Bearkats boasted the second-ranked passer in the nation in Long. Northwestern State, meanwhile, featured the top-ranked defense in the country.

It was Sam Houston State's offense that gave as Long was held to a season-low 220 yards passing and failed to throw a touchdown for the first time all season. Additionally, the Demons held the Bearkats to almost 200 yards below their seasonal average.

"They played a lot of man," Randleman said of the Demons' defense. "The thing they could do that nobody else could seem to do is they had enough talent at their safeties that they could match up with your inside receivers. A lot of people have good enough corners but you can hurt them with your inside game."

Northwestern State, by contrast, rushed for 446 yards in the game, the most for a Demons team in their 27-year tenure as a Division I-AA program. Johnese rushed for a career-high 252 yards and two touchdowns to become the school's all-time scoring leader with a season of eligibility still remaining. His running mate, Sampson, rushed for 104 yards.

Demon turnovers allowed SHSU to stay in the game in the first half. A 41-yard fumble return for a touchdown by Hughes put the Bearkats on top 14-7. After Northwestern State tied the game again, a 43-yard Garner field goal gave Sam Houston State a 17-14 edge.

Northwestern State responded with a 14-play, 95-yard drive that was capped on a 7-yard run by Sampson that gave the Demons a lead they would never again relinquish at 21-17.

The Bearkats did manage to cut the deficit down to one point at 21-20 on a 38-yard Garner field goal with less than a minute remaining in the half but Johnese gave the Demons a 28-20 halftime edge with a 73-yard touchdown gallop.

After a 9-yard run by Fuller rallied SHSU to 38-27 with 6:26 left in the game, the Bearkats attempted an onside kick. The ball rolled out of bounds, giving possession to the Demons. Like it did most of the game, Northwestern Sate controlled to clock, adding a 9-yard run by Johnese with 38 seconds remaining to make the final 45-27.

The outcome left both teams 3-1 in the Southland. Sam Houston State fell to 8-2 overall while Northwestern State improved to 7-3.

With Texas State and Nicholls State both looking to join Northwestern State and Sam Houston State at 3-1 in the Southland Conference, the Bobcats' Nealy had one of the better outings of his career in the 2004 home finale for Texas State, throwing four touchdown passes in a 35-12 victory over the Colonels.

The Colonels were never in the game, falling behind 28-0 at halftime. Nicholls didn't put points on the scoreboard until a pair of short touchdown runs by Joseph Robbins in the fourth quarter.

Nealy tossed three of his four touchdown passes in the first half. Spreading the ball around, the quarterback hooked up with Carpenter, Randal Moshier and Douglas Sherman on the scoring strikes. Nealy added the other touchdown of the first half on a 39-yard run in the second quarter.

Texas State improved to 3-1 in the SLC and 5-5 overall. Nicholls dropped to 2-2 in the league and 5-4 overall.

Meanwhile, a pair of teams sporting 0-3 records in the Southland Conference met when Stephen F. Austin hosted McNeese State.

Perhaps a sign of how the season had gone for McNeese, the Cowboys' only score in a 55-7 loss to the Lumberjacks came from the defense. McNeese's only touchdown came when safety John Vigers returned a Williams fumble 65 yards late in the second quarter. By then, the Cowboys already were down 24-0.

The loss was the worst defeat for McNeese against a Division I-AA foe. McNeese turned the ball over seven times and yielded two touchdowns off of blocked punts as the Cowboys ensured a last-place finish in the SLC.

Following a 23-yard Rossner field goal in the first quarter, a Thomas fumble set up a 16-yard touchdown run by Middleton. A block of a Marino punt led to a 6-yard touchdown run by Louie Runnels and a 3-yard run by Michael Mott gave SFA its 24-0 lead.

Middleton ran for 114 yards to pace a season-best 223 rushing yards for the Lumberjacks. By contrast, the Cowboys were limited to 225 yards of total offense.

SFA picked up its first Southland win of the season while snapping a three-game losing streak. The Lumberjacks secured their sixth-consecutive winning season with the victory. McNeese dropped to 0-4 in the conference and 3-7 overall.

Things didn't look good in the 2004 regular-season finale for Northwestern State early against Stephen F. Austin, which entered the game with only one conference victory.

That didn't stop the Lumberjacks from taking a 13-0 halftime lead on an 82-yard pass from Williams to Tony Tompkins and a pair of Rossner field goals. When Rossner added a 28-yard field goal early in the third quarter, the Demons found themselves down by 16 points and a potential postseason bid slipping away.

The Demons didn't get on the scoreboard until a 9-yard run by Johnese at the 6:02 mark of the third quarter. A 2-point conversion pass by Vinson cut the Northwestern deficit to eight points.

Vinson's 1-yard dive with 59 seconds in the third quarter made the score 16-14. The quarterback's two-point conversion run tied the game going into the fourth quarter.

Another 1-yard Vinson run, this one at the 9:39 mark of the fourth quarter, gave the Demons their first lead of the game at 23-16.

Vinson hit Toby Zeigler with a 2-yard touchdown pass with 3:07 left in the game to give Northwestern a commanding 30-16 lead.

As a fitting tribute to the Demons' defensive effort in the second half, David Pittman returned an interception 57 yards for a touchdown with 1:49 remaining in the game to make the final 37-16

SFA ended its season 6-5 overall and 1-4 in the Southland.

The Demons moved to 8-3 overall and 4-1 in the SLC to capture a co-championship and the league's automatic bid to the playoffs.

After the disappointing loss to Northwestern State, Sam Houston State was not going to let a little rain stop it from securing as share of the Southland Conference title in the Bearkats' regular-season finale at home against Texas State.

The Bearkats did so without their usual big numbers. Long passed for a modest 255 yards by his standard and one touchdown. His lone scoring strike, an 8-yard toss to Roberts, came in the first quarter.

Fuller had 111 reception yards, including an 18-yard catch to set up a 2-yard touchdown run by Long late in the first half as the Bearkats went on to take a 27-9 victory.

Sam Houston State finished the regular season 4-1 in the SLC and 9-2 overall. Texas State concluded the year 5-6 overall, including 3-2 in the conference.

In Lake Charles, McNeese State avoided a rare winless Southland Conference record with a 30-9 win against Nicholls State.

The Cowboys broke a 3-3 tie on a 1-yard run by Thomas at the 6:31 mark of the second quarter to give McNeese a 10-3 halftime advantage. Thomas' touchdown was set up by a Colonels fumble at the Nicholls 25.

Thomas, who rushed for 121 yards, scored on runs of 4 and 6 yards in the third quarter before the Colonels' Vannoy countered with a 2-yard run as McNeese led 23-9 going into the final quarter. Kris Bush rounded out the scoring on a 1-yard run in the fourth quarter for the 30-9 final.

Avoiding the turnovers and penalties that hampered McNeese all season, the Cowboys amassed 418 yards of total offense. The McNeese defense, which allowed 47 or more points six times during the season, limited Nicholls' option attack to 231 total yards.

McNeese ended the season 4-7 overall, including 1-4 in the SLC. Nicholls moved to 5-5 overall and 2-3 in the conference.

Postseason appearances had become a fairly consistent occurrence in recent years for Northwestern State. So too was the Demons' first-round playoff opponent. For the third time, the Demons had to travel to take on perennial Division I-AA power Montana, ranked No. 7 going into the playoffs.

Northwestern State entered the game with the nation's top overall defense, allowing 250 yards per game. The Demons were also tops in rushing defense, holding opponents to a meager 78 yards per contest.

Touchdown runs of 24 and 61 yards in the first half by Montana's Lex Hilliard exceeded the rushing mark before halftime. Quarterback Craig Ochs' touchdown passes of 11 and 9 yards to Levander Segars gave the Grizzlies a 28-0 halftime lead.

Segars, who rushed for 111 yards in the first half, added touchdown runs of 30 and 2 yards in the third quarter on his way to a 171-yard rushing effort. Ochs finished with 234 yards passing and Montana piled up 543 yards in a 56-7 trouncing of the Demons.

Along with the gaudy offensive numbers, the Montana defense took a page out of the Demons' defensive playbook. The Grizzlies held Northwestern to two first downs and 29 yards of total offense in the first half while not allowing the Demons to cross midfield.

The only score for Northwestern came with the Demons trailing 42-0 in the third quarter on 10-yard pass from Vinson to Clayton Broyles.

Northwestern finished the season 8-4.

In another opening-round Division I-AA playoff game, the first quarter of the Bearkats' home contest against Western Kentucky proved to be an eye-opener for the Hilltoppers.

With the Bearkats leading 14-7, Robert Herron blocked Brian Claybourn's punt to set up a 3-yard touchdown run by Garmon and a 21-7 Sam Houston lead. Moments later, Corey Zeno blocked another punt for a safety that gave SHSU a 23-7 advantage.

The Bearkats blocked two punts in the first quarter against a Western Kentucky team that had not allowed a blocked punt all season. The safety gave Sam Houston State 23 first-quarter points. In their previous 11 games, the Hilltoppers had allowed 21 opening-quarter points all year.

The start of the second quarter was no joy for the Hilltoppers, either. Following the safety, Smith returned the ensuing free kick 30 yards that eventually set up a 4-yard touchdown run by Garmon for a 30-7 lead on the initial play of the second quarter.

Sam Houston State went on to take a 37-10 halftime lead on the Bearkats' way to a surprisingly-easy 54-24 victory.

"That might have been as good a game as we ever played while I was coaching. We played so good offensively, defensively and with our special teams, every facet of our game. I don't think they expected what we had," said Randleman.

Playing at Eastern Washington in the Division I-AA quarterfinals, the ninth-ranked Bearkats were uncomfortable competing at near-freezing temperatures and poor footing while playing on a natural surface for the first time all year. They also were in serious trouble, trailing 13-0 at halftime after failing to cross midfield in the opening two quarters.

A 9-yard run by Darius Washington six seconds into the fourth quarter gave the Eagles a 34-14 lead before Long warmed up his arm.

Forced to throw a school-record tying 61 times, Long began to rally the Bearkats. His 34-yard toss to Roberts early in the fourth quarter and an 8-yard touchdown run by Garmon made the score 34-28 with 3:34 left in the game.

Eastern Washington attempted to put the game out of reach on a 37-yard field goal attempt with 43 seconds left in the game. Cartwright blocked the kick, giving the ball back to the Bearkats' offense for one last try.

"We put in Cartwright, a receiver. He was a tall guy who could jump and he blocks the thing. When (the Eastern Washington players) lined up to kick the field goal, they were congratulating our guys for playing a good ball game," Randleman recalled.

Needing a touchdown and a conversion to win the game with less than a minute remaining, Long's first pass was incomplete. His next three attempts were complete as SHSU moved downfield. Long's following three passes all went to Mathenia as the Bearkats reached the Eagles' 7-yard line with time for one more play.

Long spotted Mathenia once again, this time for the touchdown with no time left on the clock to tie the game. Garner booted the extra point, giving Sam Houston State it's only lead of the game when it counted most with a 35-34 triumph that sent the Bearkats to the semifinals against Montana.

After struggling in the opening two quarters, Long was 30 of 44 passing for 377 yards in the second half. His favorite target, Mathenia, finished the game with career highs of 13 catches and 226 receiving yards as SHSU posted 11 victories for the first time in school history.

Playing at Montana against a team that was looking to reach the Division I-AA championship game for the fifth time in 10 years, the Bearkats knew they could not have a first half like the one they played a week earlier against Eastern Washington and survive.

With that in mind, Sam Houston State advanced to the Montana 9-yard line where it faced first-and-goal early in the game. Tuff Harris stepped in front of a Long pass attempt at the goal line and sprinted 75 yards down to the Bearkats' 25. On the first play following the turnover, Ochs, the Grizzlies quarterback, spotted tight end Willie Walden for the touchdown and a 7-0 Montana lead.

The Bearkats hung tough for most of the first half as Garner field goals of 37 and 40 yards enabled SHSU to trail only 7-6.

Harris came up big once again late in the first half. He returned another interception down to the Sam Houston State 4-yard line. It took the Grizzlies two plays to score following Harris' interception. Ochs tossed to Segars, but the ball bounced off of the intended receiver. Tate Hancock made a diving catch in the end zone, enabling Montana to take a 14-6 lead with 1:25 showing in the second quarter.

Montana scored less than five minutes into the second half on a 14-yard pass from Ochs to Jon Talmage and on a 7-yard run by Hilliard to stretch the Grizzlies' advantage to 28-7.

Sam Houston State's only score of the second half came on a 1-yard run by Smith with less than a minute remaining in the third quarter to make the score 28-13.

Dan Carpenter kicked a pair of field goals in the fourth quarter to make the final score 34-13.

Long passed for 375 yards in his final game as Sam Houston State closed its most successful season ever with an 11-3 record.

"You cannot get behind to those people up there. If you get ahead of them, you take them out of what they want to do and you can keep the crowd a bit more in check and that's how you've got to beat them," said Randleman.

It was the final game for Randleman, who retired as Bearkats coach following the 2004 season.

"I had pretty much decided going into the season that this would be it," said Randleman. "I loved coaching and felt we would have had a pretty good club the next year but you have to get off the merry-go-round sometime.

"The longer you coach, the wins are not quite as exciting and the losses were even more devastating than when you started out. I don't know why."

MOTHER NATURE AND THE SLC

Nicholls State and McNeese State went through a season of turmoil in 2004. For the Colonels, it was a coaching change only weeks before the start of the season in the wake of an academic fraud scandal. For the Cowboys, it was dealing with a year of paybacks by rivals leading to a 4-7 record after McNeese's recent success.

None of that could match the wrath of Mother Nature. Hurricanes Katrina and Rita struck south Louisiana in 2005 and while the Thibodaux area in general and the Nicholls community in particular came through mostly unscathed; the storms' impact left a lasting impression on the Colonels' football team.

Hurricane Katrina caused Nicholls' season opener at Utah State to be canceled. The Colonels' next game, at the University of Indiana, was in doubt only a few days before the contest was actually played.

Following a dispersal of players during Katrina's approach, the Colonels did not return to campus until the weekend prior to the Hoosiers game. As late as midweek, the game was in jeopardy until Indiana arranged for a charter flight from Baton Rouge.

McNeese, meanwhile, was hit with a double blow of hurricanes Katrina and Rita, leaving the lives of McNeese State student-athletes in an upheaval the entire season.

McNeese State's scheduled opener at home against Southern University was canceled because of Hurricane Katrina, making the Cowboys' 2005 debut a road game at fifth-ranked Georgia Southern.

The hurricanes caused other events in the Southland Conference to be overshadowed.

Two years after reviving its football program, Southeastern Louisiana began to compete for conference honors in 2005, increasing the number of football-playing schools in the league to seven.

The 2005 season also began another new era in football for the Hammond, Louisiana, school. Hal Mumme, the former University of Kentucky coach who resurrected the Lions program in 2003, took his pass-happy "Air Raid" offense with him to New Mexico State.

Taking over as the new coach at Southeastern was Dennis Roland. Roland spent two seasons as head coach at Belhaven College in Jackson, Mississippi, before being named to replace Mumme.

Mumme's offense produced video game-type numbers. The Lions' ability to move the ball and put points on the board quickly under Mumme put great pressure on the SLU defense. With that in mind, Roland installed a more balanced offensive attack and put renewed emphasis on defense.

A pair of other Southland schools, Sam Houston State and Stephen F. Austin, went through a coaching change in 2005 as well.

Ron Randleman retired as Sam Houston State's coach following the 2004 season and was replaced by Todd Whitten. Whitten was quite familiar with the Bearkats' program and the Southland Conference, being a former quarterback at Stephen F. Austin. He served as Sam Houston State's offensive coordinator in 1999 as was Tarleton State's head coach from 2000-04 before returning to Huntsville as head coach of the Bearkats.

Following Mike Santiago's fourth 6-5 mark in six years as Stephen F. Austin mentor, he was replaced as Lumberjacks coach by Robert McFarland for the 2005 gridiron campaign. A former SFA assistant, McFarland was the offensive line coach at East Carolina in 2004 before being named to replace Santiago.

Newcomer Southeastern Louisiana made its Southland debut on October 8, 2005, at home against Texas State. The Lions went into the game 1-2 on the season. After SLU won its opener against Alcorn State, the Lions lost to Northern Colorado and to Tulane in Baton Rouge. With Hurricane Katrina dumping its wrath on New Orleans, including the Louisiana Superdome, Tulane was a wandering nomad in the Division I-A college world.

Texas State entered the game 3-1 with, with the only loss being 44-31 at Texas A&M in a game that was moved up two days with the approach of Hurricane Rita.

The Lions only trailed 13-0 at halftime against Texas State despite being held to no first downs and only six yards of total offense with five minutes remaining in the second quarter.

Texas State scored its first-half points on a pair of touchdown runs by Douglas Sherman. SLU's offense showed a bit of life at the end of the first half, driving from its own 23 to the Texas State 10 when the Lions failed to convert on fourth down with 14 seconds remaining before halftime.

SLU drove 75 yards on the opening possession of the second half. The big play of the drive was Trey Willie's 54-yard toss to Hutch Gonzales down to the Texas State 2. Three plays later, Gonzales hauled in a pass that bounced off of Jamaal Jackson's hands to make the score 13-6. The Bobcats quickly countered when quarterback Barrick Nealy hit Demerious Johnson in the end zone to make Texas State's lead 20-6 at the 8:24 mark of the third quarter.

A 22-yard Jim Hall field goal was countered by a 15-yard run by Texas State's Daniel Jolly to give the Bobcats a 27-9 lead after three quarters. Tight end Jeff Guidugli's 1-yard touchdown reception pulled the Lions to within 12 points at 27-15 early in the fourth quarter. Texas State kicker Stan Jones hit a career-best 42-yard field goal to make the final 30-15.

Sam Houston State was another school affected by Hurricane Rita. The storm caused the cancelation of the Bearkats' game with Missouri State (formerly called Southwest Missouri State). SHSU had a scheduled open date the following week, meaning the Bearkats went three weeks before playing their Southland opener at home against Northwestern State.

The Bearkats went into the game 2-1 on the season. Sam Houston State won Whitten's debut 77-7 over an overmatched Bacone College team. SHSU lost to Houston 31-10 and Texas Tech 80-21 before the arrival of Hurricane Rita.

Like Sam Houston State, a cancelation and open date gave Northwestern State a break of 21 days before the teams met to open Southland play. The Demons went into the game 2-1 on the season. Northwestern State's season-opening win over Louisiana-Monroe gave the Demons the distinction of being the first Division I-AA team to garner 10 wins against Division I-A competition.

The long layoff was evident as both teams struggled to produce much offense, resulting in an exchange of field goals for a 3-3 tie at halftime.

Davon Vinson's 6-yard run in the third quarter provided the game's only touchdown as Northwestern took a 10-3 lead. SHSU made it 10-6 on a 52-yard Lance Garner field goal later in the third period.

The Bearkats reached the Northwestern 35-yard line late in the game but Carlo Stephens stopped Jason Godfrey on fourth-and-1 with 3:59 remaining, allowing the Demons to hold on for the four-point triumph.

Like Whitten at Sam Houston State, McFarland was making his Southland Conference debut when Stephen F. Austin hosted Nicholls State. The Lumberjacks went into the encounter 3-1. SFA won McFarland's initial game as coach with a

49-38 victory over Henderson State. After a loss to Montana State, the Lumberjacks bounced back with wins over Western Illinois and Southern Utah.

Nicholls was 1-2 on the season. The Colonels hung tough before losing at Indiana 35-31 in a game that almost wasn't played.

"We had to find our players (after being evacuated because of Katrina)," recalled Nicholls coach Jay Thomas. "We had players in Dallas, Houston, everywhere. By the Tuesday of that week, we probably had 98 percent of our players back and managed to get a game plan in. We had one player (who evacuated to Houston) in the Astrodome and we had to send someone to go and find him. That was like a needle in a haystack to get him to practice for the Wednesday."

The Colonels had ordered new uniforms for the season but had not yet arrived from their manufacturer's wearhouse on the Mississippi Gulf Coast.

"We had to fly out of Baton Rouge because the airport in New Orleans was shut down," Thomas recalled. "Indiana said we could wear their away jerseys. We were able to get our uniforms the day of the game. It was not the uniform we ordered, but it sufficed.

"To have three days to get ready to prepare for a Big Ten team, it was scary. We had an opportunity to win late but we lost it at the end."

After a 54-0 home win over Cheyney, Nicholls lost 26-13 at North Dakota State. A scheduled home game with Western Carolina the week after the Cheyney game was canceled because of Hurricane Rita.

"We had Katrina and Rita came on right after that. We didn't get the direct impact of Rita but it backed our water system up and that type of stuff. We had to get water shipped in from the Baton Rouge area," said Thomas.

Coming off a bye week, SFA produced the only points of the first half against Nicholls on a 25-yard touchdown pass from Zeke Dixon to Louie Runnels.

Nicholls exploded for 21 points in three-straight possessions to take the lead. Broderick Cole scored on a 45-yard run to cap a 98-yard drive to tie the game. After Cole scored on a 2-yard run on the Colonels' next possession to take the lead, Nicholls got the ball back seconds later after a Tyrel Williams fumble was recovered by Joseph Ogletree and returned to the Lumberjacks' 10-yard line. Cole scored his third quick touchdown – this one a 3-yard run on fourth down to put Nicholls on top 21-7.

The Lumberjacks forced overtime when Williams hauled in an 18-yard touchdown strike from Dixon with 32 seconds left in regulation to tie the game 21-21.

Nicholls got the ball first in overtime but came away with no points when Alex Romero missed on a 35-yard field-goal attempt. Jermone Brooks broke loose on SFA's first play of overtime, racing down to the 2-yard line. Two plays later, Brooks scored for a 27-21 victory.

Thomas and the Colonels were emotionally down after the heartbreaking defeat.

"I got advice from my dad after the game. With all we had been through, he said, 'you don't need to be out here moping about it. You need to figure out a way to get these guys ready to play for the rest of the season.' It got me motivated to be positive and our players remained positive," said Thomas, referring to his father, Larry, who was a high school football coach in Louisiana for 33 years.

Stephen F. Austin was the opponent for McNeese State's 2005 Southland Conference debut. The Cowboys were 2-1 on the season with wins over Georgia Southern and Texas Southern and a loss to Southern Mississippi.

The "home" game against Texas Southern was played at Northwestern State's Turpin Stadium in Natchitoches. McNeese was the Division I-AA version of Tulane's wandering nomads because of Hurricane Rita. McNeese students were displaced, with the Cowboys practicing at Southeastern Louisiana University in Hammond for three weeks following the storm. Hurricane Rita caused scheduled McNeese home games against Northwest Oklahoma State and Southern Utah to be canceled.

"It was challenging," said Matt Viator, an assistant coach on the 2005 McNeese State staff. "We owe Southeastern (Louisiana University) a lot for allowing us to relocate there. It was challenging to get all the players there and try to practice and do all that.

"It was also challenging because we were rebuilding at home. We had families here and it was challenging. Players had to get out of their apartments or dormitories and in terms of coaches, I had my house and my mother's house and you are trying to redo all of that and deal with insurance, and yet, you are in Hammond."

With McNeese State still not ready to host a football game, the Cowboys' Southland Conference "home" opener against Stephen F. Austin was slated to be played at the Gelena Park High School field in Houston, by edict of Southland commissioner Tom Burnett.

Instead of Houston, the game ended up being played closer to "home" at Cajun Field on the University of Louisiana-Lafayette campus.

The Cowboys jumped out to a 17-0 lead on their way to a 33-23 victory. A 34-yard pass from Chris Jones to Darrick Brown provided the game's first score. Blake Bercegeay added a 25-yard field goal to make it 10-0 after a Lumberjacks fumble at the SFA 9-yard line. Three plays into the second quarter, Jones hooked up with Quinten Lawrence on a 49-yard strike to give McNeese a 17-0 lead.

McNeese led 20-0 at halftime and was on top 26-10 going into the fourth quarter. The Lumberjacks cut into the deficit on a 63-yard pass from Danny Southall to Dominique Edison to make the score 26-16.

Each team added a touchdown in the closing moments. Chris Thomas scored on a 20-yard run for McNeese before the Lumberjacks ended the scoring on an 11-yard pass from Dixon to Edison for the 33-23 final.

In Natchitoches, Northwestern State used two late touchdowns in the second quarter to pull away from Southeastern Louisiana in a 31-10 victory over the Lions to move to 2-0 in the Southland Conference.

A 1-yard pass from Vinson to Brent Smith and a two-point conversion capped an 80-yard scoring drive with 2:38 remaining before halftime. On the Lions' next possession, punter Jim Hall couldn't handle the snap from center and was tackled by Keadrin Seastrunk and Keith Robinson at the SLU 5-yard line. Vinson's 1-yard toss to Seastrunk gave the Demons a 24-10 lead at the break.

SLU's points all came in the first half on a 42-yard Hall field goal and a 12-yard pass from Trey Willie to Merrick Lanaux.

Northwestern, which improved to 3-2 overall, got nine first-quarter points on a 23-yard Robert Weeks field goal and a 66-yard interception for a touchdown by Russ Washington.

SLU fell to 0-2 in the conference and 1-4 overall.

Meanwhile, after suffering last-minute losses to Indiana and Stephen F. Austin, the Colonels were determined not to let that happen in a home encounter with Sam Houston State.

Following a dominating first quarter in which Nicholls built a 17-0 lead, the Colonels saw the lead dwindle to 17-14 by halftime. Instead of letting the lead completely slip away as on previous occasions, the Colonels changed course when Joel Fontenot-Amedee raced 34 yards for a touchdown to re-establish Nicholls' lead at 24-14 midway in the third quarter.

After the Bearkats countered with a 40-yard Garner field goal, the Colonels offense responded again, this time on a 1-yard touchdown run by Joseph Tobias, putting Nicholls ahead 31-17 with 13:44 left in the game.

Nicholls added a short Zach Morgan touchdown run in the final two minutes in a 37-17 victory as the Colonels evened their Southland record at 1-1 while moving to 2-3 overall. The Bearkats fell to 0-2 in league play and 1-4 overall.

Leading the conference in passing offense at 289 yards per game, the Bearkats only gained 172 of their 264 total yards through the air.

"It was good we were able to get out early and get the lead and be able to control the clock a bit more and limit their possessions. That was a big shot in the arm. We needed a big win. It was a huge win for us and gave our guys the belief we could compete and make a run the rest of the season," said Thomas.

The Bearkats gave Whitten a win in his first game against his alma mater five days later as Sam Houston State scored on four of its first five possessions to build a 24-0 lead on SHSU's way to a dominating 52-24 Southland Conference home win over Stephen F. Austin on a Thursday night.

Sam Houston State rolled up 512 yards of total offense and the 52 points the Bearkats scored equaled the most points scored by either team in the series that dated back to 1923.

Phil Daugherty passed for 257 yards while Godfrey rushed for 164 and two touchdowns. Stevie Smith, who also scored twice, missed the century mark by a yard as the Bearkats won for the first time in 2005 since their season opener.

The outcome left both teams 1-2 in the Southland. Sam Houston State improved to 2-4 overall while SFA slipped to 4-2.

The loss overshadowed a 14-catch, 194-yard receiving performance by SFA's Chance Dennis.

Two days later, Nealy accounted for four touchdowns in Texas State's 31-16 home win over Northwestern State to give the Bobcats sole possession of first place in the Southland Conference.

Texas State took advantage of three-of-six first-half possessions starting inside Northwestern territory to build a 21-point lead. A 3-yard pass from Nealy to Tyrone Scott in the first quarter, along with a touchdown pass of 22 yards to Dameon Williams and an 11-yard Nealy run gave the Bobcats their 21 points.

The Demons rallied to within 21-10 by the close of the half on a 32-yard field goal by Weeks and a 3-yard Shelton Sampson run. Sampson's touchdown was set up by a blocked punt by Seastrunk. That would be as close as Northwestern could get as Nealy scored on a 5-yard run midway in the third quarter to stretch the lead to 28-10.

Texas State remained unbeaten in the Southland at 2-0 while moving to 6-1 overall and securing a winning season for only the third time since 1991. Northwestern State fell to 2-1 in the conference and 3-3 overall.

Southeastern Louisiana and McNeese State found themselves in an unusual position when they met for a Southland Conference encounter in Hammond. Only three weeks earlier, the Lions played in Baton Rouge against a displaced Tulane team because of Hurricane Katrina. Shortly after Katrina did her damage to southeastern Louisiana, Hurricane Rita left her share of destruction in southwestern

Louisiana. With damage done to Lake Charles and the McNeese campus, the Cowboys football program found refuge at SLU.

It wasn't exactly a college intramural contest, but there was a sense of familiarity beyond what goes on in games against state rivals. The Lions served as hosts, but that did not mean they intended to be hospitable on game day.

In fact, the Lions protected their home turf like they rarely had before. Southeastern Louisiana's defense held McNeese to a net 17 yards rushing and forced four turnovers. SLU allowed only two Cowboy scores in the game, a 1-yard sneak by McNeese quarterback Mark Fontenot and a 28-yard pass from Fontenot to Kris Bush with 5:58 left in the game. Meanwhile, Willie threw for a career-high 300 yards and two touchdowns for a 37-13 victory that gave the Lions their first win as members of the Southland Conference.

Willie's first touchdown pass to Gonzales gave the Lions a 7-0 lead on their way to a 16-7 halftime edge. The quarterback's other touchdown pass, a 25-yard connection with tight end Josh Taylor gave SLU a 30-7 advantage with 10:29 left in the game.

McNeese, which fell to 3-2 overall and 1-1 in the SLC, came up with the Fontenot-to-Bush connection to close the score to 30-14 before Jerald Watson countered with a 39-yard run with 5:03 remaining in the game to account for the 37-13 final.

The following week, sixth-ranked Texas State played at a Nicholls State team that had an extra week to prepare for their Southland Conference showdown because of a bye week.

A 76-yard touchdown run by Broderick Cole less than four minutes into the game, a 1-yard sneak by quarterback Yale Vannoy late in the first half, a 4-yard run by Anthony Harris early in the third quarter and a 3-yard option keeper by Vannoy gave Nicholls a 26-7 lead going into the fourth quarter.

The Bobcats stormed back in dramatic fashion in the fourth quarter, aided by a questionable decision by Jay Thomas, the Nicholls State coach.

With Nicholls clinging to a 26-21 lead with slightly more than three minutes remaining in regulation, Thomas elected to go for a first down instead of punting from the Colonels' 32 with Nicholls facing a fourth-and-2 situation.

Looking to pick up the first down and run out the clock, Harris was held for no gain, turning the ball over on downs. Three plays later, Jolly broke loose on a 23-yard scamper for a touchdown and Nealy added a two-point conversion pass to Scott as Texas State took its first lead of the game at 29-26 with 2:18 remaining.

Nicholls forced overtime when Romero connected on a 23-yard field goal on the final play of regulation.

Three plays into overtime, a pass interference call against Nicholls' Toney Edison gave the Bobcats a first down at the 10. On the next play, Edison redeemed himself by recovering a Jolly fumble, with the Colonels then needing only a field goal to win.

Nicholls managed to reach the 9-yard line before the drive stalled. Romero booted a 27-yard field goal for a 32-29 triumph that allowed the Colonels to move to 2-1 in the SLC and even their record at 3-3. Texas State slipped to 2-1 in the conference and 6-2 overall.

"We really felt like we had control of the entire game and then all of a sudden, they came back. They were really, really good," Thomas said of the Bobcats.

Meanwhile, the Cowboys finally ended their road warrior status, returning to Lake Charles to take on Sam Houston State. Because of damage to the stadium lights caused by Hurricane Rita, McNeese played SHSU in the first regular season day game at home since 1991.

McNeese held a 21-14 halftime lead before the Bearkats rallied to within one point on a 2-yard run by Godfrey at the 4:04 mark of the third quarter. Fontenot connected with Jeremy Haynes on a 21-yard touchdown pass early in the fourth quarter for a 28-20 advantage. Bercegeay stretched the lead by three more points on a 45-yard field goal, which proved to be enough of a margin when Bearkats quarterback Wade Pate tossed 5 yards to Brandon Perry for a 31-26 final.

Bercegeay kicked three field goals to give McNeese a 9-2 lead after one quarter. Corey Roberts had back-to-back touchdown catches in the second quarter to put SHSU on top 14-7. The Cowboys scored twice in the final 31 seconds of the first half on a 24-yard interception return for a touchdown by Chris Allen and a 9-yard touchdown pass by Fontenot to give McNeese its 21-14 lead at intermission.

McNeese improved to 2-1 in the Southland and 4-2 overall. The Bearkats dropped to 1-3 in the conference and 2-5 overall.

After Southeastern Louisiana showed it could win a Southland Conference game at home, the next test was trying to pick up a victory on the road. The Lions' first chance came a week after the McNeese contest with a game at Stephen F. Austin.

The Lions clicked in all areas on offense as Southeastern rolled up a season-high 526 yards in a 45-23 victory. Willie passed for a career-high 308 yards while Gonzales and Felton Huggins each topped 100 yards receiving. Mario Gilbert contributed three touchdowns as SLU evened its conference record at 2-2 and improved to 3-4 overall.

SFA, 4-4 overall and 1-3 in the SLC, scored on a 35-yard Cory Long field goal on the game's opening possession before the Lions responded with three-straight scoring drives of their own. Gilbert capped an 80-yard drive with a 3-yard run to give SLU a 7-3 lead after one quarter. Gilbert added a 13-yard run in the second quarter and Willie hooked up with Huggins on a 26-yard strike to make it 21-3. The Lumberjacks made the score 21-10 at halftime on a 7-yard pass from Southall to Dennis.

Southeastern Louisiana was pinned at its own 2-yard line following a punt in the third quarter. The Lions marched 98 yards, using up almost seven minutes on the clock and picking up three, third-down conversions along the way. Watson's 11-yard run with 3:17 remaining in the third period put SLU on top 28-10. Gilbert added his third rushing touchdown late in the third quarter to give Southeastern a 35-16 lead going into the fourth period.

Northwestern State, the defending Southland Conference champions, found itself in a crucial home game against Nicholls State. Both teams entered the game 2-1 the conference. The Demons' lone loss came to Texas State, while the Bobcats lost to the Colonels.

A win would keep the Demons in the race, while a victory by the Colonels would place Nicholls into a potential tie for first-place tie with Texas State.

With the score tied 24-24, a punt by Nicholls' Sean Comeaux pinned the Demons at the Northwestern State 1-yard line with 7:22 remaining in the game. Nicholls forced a punt, getting the ball back at the Demons' 43.

Cole scored on a 2-yard run with 1:38 left in the game to give the Colonels a 31-24 lead.

A 25-yard Zeigler kickoff return allowed the Demons to take possession near midfield. On third-and-long, Naton Stewart intercepted a Vinson pass to end the threat and secure the win for Nicholls.

"Now I know why I don't have any hair left," said Thomas.

Northwestern led 14-10 at halftime on a 33-yard Toby Zeigler run and an 8-yard run by Sampson. The Colonels' 10 points came on a 69-yard pass from Vannoy to Morgan and a 19-yard Romero field goal.

Nicholls led 24-17 in the second half before the Demons tied the game on a 1-yard run by Vinson with 11:44 remaining in the game.

Northwestern evened its record at 2-2 in the SLC and 4-4 overall. Nicholls improved to 3-1 in the league and 4-3 overall.

The Bobcats, meanwhile, took out their frustrations from the overtime loss to Nicholls with a 49-6 home beatdown of McNeese State.

Texas State's first four scoring drives began inside McNeese territory, including two because of Cowboy turnovers. As a result, the Bobcats went on to build a 35-0 halftime lead.

The Bobcats rushed for 296 yards and had six rushing touchdowns, including two each by Nealy and Brothers. Texas State's defense held McNeese to 75 yards rushing. Four Cowboys quarterbacks combined to complete only 5 of 23 passes for 54 yards with two interceptions.

A 1-yard run by Nealy and a 25-yard gallop by Brothers gave Texas State a 14-0 lead after one quarter. The duo each added a touchdown run in the second quarter and Nealy also tossed a 22-yard touchdown pass to Scott for a 35-0 halftime lead. McNeese's only score came on a 7-yard pass from Beau Lasseigne to Kyle Link with 5:21 left in the game.

Texas State stayed in Southland title contention at 3-1 while improving to 7-2 overall. McNeese dropped to 2-2 in the SLC and 4-3 overall.

With Southland Conference wins both at home and on the road, the next quest for Southeastern Louisiana was a shot at a three-game winning streak.

Things looked good early for Southeastern in its game at Sam Houston State when a Duke Adams interception of a Daugherty pass set up a 3-yard touchdown run by Willie to give the Lions a 7-0 lead. With the Bearkats' offense struggling early, Pate entered the game in relief of an ineffective Daugherty on Sam Houston's third possession of the game. Pate led his team to scores on three of the Bearkats' next four drives to give SHSU a 21-7 halftime lead.

The backup quarterback tied the game early in the second quarter on a 12-yard run. He then tossed touchdown passes of 63 yards to Smith and 17 yards to Perry for the 21-7 lead. The only time the Bearkats didn't score in the four drives was when Garner missed a field-goal attempt.

Pate was a factor in all five of Sam Houston's scores in the game. In the second half, he scored on a 23-yard scramble and hit Brian Christian with a 9-yard touchdown toss. SLU also scored twice in the second half, the last touchdown coming on the final play of the game on a 47-yard touchdown reception by Taylor to make the final 35-18.

The outcome left both teams 3-5 overall and 2-3 in the conference.

In Hammond, Nicholls State prepared to take on Southeastern Louisiana in football for the first time since SLU dropped the sport after the 1986 season, resuming what had been known as the Riverbell Classic. Southeastern Louisiana joined the Southland Conference in 1997 but didn't reinstate football until 2003, with the two long-time rivals going 19 years between games.

The teams traded scores throughout the first half before the Colonels took a seven-point advantage at intermission.

With 26 seconds remaining in the opening half and the score tied 21-21, the Lions called a timeout to force a Nicholls punt from the Colonels' 45. The deep snap went not to the Nicholls punter but to Harris, the upback. Harris scooted all the way down to the SLU 6-yard line. Harris scored on the next play as time expired in the opening half to give Nicholls a 28-21 lead.

"We did that quite a bit that year. We had the right personnel. If it presented itself and we had the opportunity to do it, we would try to do it. We knew because the way they were lining up potentially we could have it. Southeastern called timeout, wanted to get the ball back. We had the ball around midfield. It looked like they wanted to put their return team in and wanted to put pressure on our punter. We already knew we had the numbers we wanted to do it and it just came down to me making the decision to do it. We gambled a bit and the guys ran it perfectly," Thomas recalled.

A 44-yard field goal early in the fourth quarter gave Nicholls a 10-point cushion before the Lions attempted a late rally.

Willie, who threw for 403 yards and three touchdowns, connected with Taylor for 54 yards down to the Nicholls 6-yard line. Willie's 3-yard touchdown toss to Taylor moments later made the score 31-28 with 1:58 showing.

The Lions attempted an onside kick, with Tobias fielding the ball and racing to the SLU 24. Southeastern Louisiana allowed Tobias to score on a 9-yard run with 1:10 left in the game in order to get the ball back.

Trailing 38-28, the Lions reached the Nicholls 9-yard line before the drive ended with one second remaining in the contest as the Colonels moved to 4-1 in the Southland.

Southeastern Louisiana went on to close out the 2005 season with a 38-21 non-conference win against Mississippi Valley to end its first season in the Southland with a 4-6 record, including 2-4 in the conference.

Needing a win to remain in a first-place tie with Nicholls State in the Southland Conference, the Bobcats had a battle on their hands at Stephen F. Austin before eventually pulling away for a 38-21 victory.

SFA and Texas State were tied at the half before Nealy tossed a 22-yard pass to Jolly on the opening possession of the third quarter to give the Bobcats a 21-14 edge. Nealy tossed his third touchdown pass of the game later in the quarter to Markee White to put Texas State up by 14 points.

Runnels, who rushed for 149 yards in the game, scored on a 4-yard run to make it 28-21 at the end of three quarters but the Lumberjacks would not score again.

Jones added a 27-yard field goal and Nealy accounted for his fourth touchdown of the game on an 81-yard jaunt to give Texas State the 38-21 victory that allowed the Bobcats to reach eight wins in a season for the first time since the school became a Division I-AA program in 1984.

Nick Session scored on a 3-yard run to give Texas State the early lead before Dixon and Carl Price hooked up on scoring passes of 3 and 58 yards for a 14-7 edge for SFA. A 4-yard run by Jolly tied the game at halftime.

Texas State improved to 4-1 in the Southland Conference and 8-2 overall. SFA dropped to 1-4 in the league and 5-5 overall.

Playing their second, and final, home game of the 2005 season, the McNeese State Cowboys led throughout most of the Southland Conference encounter against Northwestern State before the Demons pulled ahead early in the fourth quarter.

Ricky Joe Meeks, starting at quarterback in place of an injured Vinson, tossed a 5-yard pass to A.J. Franklin to give Northwestern State a 17-16 lead at the 12:18 mark of the fourth quarter.

A poor punt gave McNeese the ball at midfield later in the fourth quarter. Following an 11-yard pass from Fontenot to Lawrence, the Cowboys gave the ball to Thomas. Thomas, who rushed for 106 yards in the game, ran for gains of 14, 9 and 16 yards. His 16-yard gainer with 5:30 left in the game gave McNeese a 22-17 victory and secured a winning season for the Cowboys.

Two Bercegeay field goals gave McNeese a 6-0 lead after one quarter. Northwestern's first score came on a safety when a John Cook punt was blocked and knocked out of the end zone. After a 56-yard touchdown pass from Fontenot to Lawrence, the Demons scored the final nine points of the quarter on a 3-yard run by Franklin and a 26-yard Marshal Burton field goal to trail 13-11 at halftime.

McNeese improved to 3-2 in the Southland Conference and 5-3 overall. Northwestern State fell to 2-3 in league play and 4-5 overall.

Closing the 2005 season on a Thursday night in Nacogdoches, Northwestern State's defense showed flashes of what had been missing in recent weeks.

Northwestern held the Lumberjacks to 69 yards rushing and scored two defensive touchdowns in a 41-21 win over SFA.

A defensive touchdown provided the first score and set the tone for the game. Linebacker Paul Mefford recovered a fumble and rambled 47 yards to give the Demons a 7-0 lead less than two minutes into the contest.

The first of two Sampson touchdown runs in the game, this one of 10 yards, was countered by a 1-yard Dixon dive as the Demons took a 14-7 halftime lead.

Sampson opened the second half with a 36-yard touchdown run and Bruce Woods recovered a fumble in the end zone as the Demons stretched their lead to 28-7 after three quarters.

Each team added a pair of touchdowns in the fourth quarter for the 41-21 final.

The Demons ended the season at .500 in both the Southland and overall. Northwestern finished 3-3 in the conference and 5-5 overall.

The season began for Nicholls with two hurricanes, two cancelled games and a 1-3 start. Going into the regular-season finale at home, a victory over McNeese State would secure at least a share of the Southland Conference title and the league's automatic bid to the Division I-AA playoffs.

Even with a win by Texas State in its season finale against Sam Houston State, a victory by Nicholls over the Cowboys would put the Colonels in the playoffs by virtue of their 32-29 overtime win over the Bobcats earlier in the season.

The Colonels took no chances against McNeese, riding their powerful ground game and an opportunistic defense to defeat the Cowboys 39-26 in advancing to the playoffs.

Nicholls, featuring the No. 2 rushing offense in the nation, amassed 458 yards on the ground with its triple-option offense against the Cowboys. Harris led the way with a career-high 149 yards.

The Colonels' defense, meanwhile, limited McNeese to 347 yards, including just 60 rushing. Nicholls intercepted three passes in the game.

With Nicholls leading 14-10, a second-quarter drive highlighted the Colonels' ground-game prowess. The Colonels used 16 plays and took 6:06 off the clock to travel 87 yards for a touchdown.

Facing a fourth-and-8 at its own 43, Nicholls snapped the ball to Harris, the upback in punt formation, who raced 29 yards down to the McNeese 28. Five plays later, the Colonels converted on fourth-and-1 at the McNeese 7. Harris took a pitch to his left for 4 yards and a first down. On the next play, Cole scored on a 3-yard run to give Nicholls a 21-10 lead with 2:34 left before halftime.

Cole's touchdown gave him 13 on the season, breaking the single-season school record previously set by Colt Colletti in 2003.

Nicholls built a lead of as much as 31-17 early in the fourth quarter before the Cowboys attempted to rally.

After a 28-yard field goal by Bercegeay made the score 31-20 on the first play of the fourth quarter, the Cowboys scored again slightly more than two minutes later.

Lawrence leaped high into the air to haul in a Jones pass and slipped a potential tackle and raced 46 yards to pull the Cowboys to within 31-26.

After a 3-yard run by Harris and a successful two-point conversion, the Colonels were up 39-26 with 8:36 left.

Two late drives by McNeese ended with interceptions by Colonels nickel back Chris Turner.

The Colonels' defense contributed mightily to the win as much as the offense. Nicholls, which finished 5-1 in conference play, held McNeese to minus-1 yard rushing in the first quarter and 21 yards at halftime. By contrast, the Colonels' offense already had amassed 225 yards on the ground by intermission.

McNeese ended the season 5-4 overall, including 3-3 in the Southland.

In Huntsville, the Bobcats captured a share of the Southland Conference title with a 26-23 win over Sam Houston State in the regular season finale, but Texas State had to go to overtime to do it.

Sam Houston forced overtime when Pate's 44-yard touchdown pass to Michael Malone tied the game 20-20 with 2:46 remaining in regulation.

SHSU got the ball first in overtime and had to settle for a 23-yard Garner field goal for a 23-20 lead.

Nealy, who rushed for 153 yards in the game, broke loose on a 20-yard run on Texas State's overtime possession to set up Sessions' 5-yard touchdown to give the Bobcats a 26-23 triumph.

After a scoreless opening quarter, Sessions scored on a 2-yard run while Garner and Jones exchanged field goals to give the Bobcats a 10-3 halftime edge.

Jones added another field goal in the third quarter and SHSU countered with a 30-yard pass from Pate to Dustin Dziuk as Texas State headed into the fourth quarter with a 13-10 advantage.

Garner tied the game on a 22-yard field goal before Texas State regained the lead with 9:29 left in the contest on a 7-yard run by Jolly, setting the stage for Malone's touchdown reception to force overtime.

Texas State concluded the regular season at 5-1 in the Southland and conference co-champions with Nicholls State. The Bobcats finished 9-2 overall. SHSU ended the season 2-4 in the SLC and 3-7 overall.

Competing in the postseason for the first time since 1996, the Colonels traveled to Greenville, South Carolina, to take on Furman of the powerful Southern Conference in the first round of the Division I-AA playoffs.

Nicholls advanced inside the Furman 20-yard line twice early in the game but had to settle for a pair of field goals.

After the Colonels went three-and-out on the opening possession of the game, Paladins fullback Jerome Felton fumbled on Furman's first play from scrimmage, with Stewart recovering for Nicholls at the Paladins' 23. The Colonels were unable to take full advantage, settling on a 34-yard Romero field goal and a 3-0 lead.

Taking over at their own 25 one possession later, a 40-yard pass from Vannoy to Michael Okoronkwo had the Colonels on the move. Nicholls drove down to the 2-yard line but once again had to settle on a Romeo field goal, this one from 20 yards out for a 6-0 advantage.

Furman drove 49 yards in the closing moments of the first half to take a 7-6 lead at the break. Quarterback Ingle Martin's 29-yard touchdown pass to Justin Stepp with 1:24 left in the second quarter put the Paladins on top by one point.

A 1-yard run by Martin, a Florida Gators transfer, midway in the third quarter extended the Furman lead at 14-6.

The Colonels came up with a gift touchdown late in the third quarter.

Nicholls was at the Furman 22-yard line when Wesley Bray, the Paladins' nose guard, appeared to jump into the neutral zone. Colonels center Cody Stogner snapped the ball as the Paladins let up on the play. Vannoy proceeded to toss the ball to Kenley Horton, who was wide open in the end zone. No whistle had been blown on the play and the touchdown stood up. A failed two-point conversion left the Colonels trailing 14-12 with 2:02 remaining in the third quarter.

The Paladins, who had experience defending the option in Southern Conference play, held the Colonels to their lowest offensive numbers of the season.

Nicholls finished with 199 yards rushing, 183 below its season average. Averaging almost 33 points per game, the 12 points scored against Furman was the fewest for Nicholls during the entire season as the Colonels concluded the year at 6-4.

"What a gut-wrenching game. It was a hard one to lose because we felt it was there for us to win."

Despite losing in the first round of the playoffs, the 2005 season has a special meeting for the Colonels.

"It was a testament to guys having a strong desire and strong commitment to one another," Thomas said. "We always talk about football being family but when you get tested that way, everybody finds out something different about one another. This team just bonded and was a very special group of guys.

"It was like one hurdle after another that just kept getting bigger. It was devastating with families losing their homes and property. Football was a savior for us. It gave us an opportunity to go out and kind of get away from the 'real world.' It gave us some relief."

Texas State, meanwhile, entered the 2005 postseason as the No. 4 seed. The Bobcats' stay in its first-ever Division I-AA playoff appeared as though it would be a short one as Texas State trailed at home against six-time champion Georgia Southern by 19 points late in the third quarter.

A 5-yard pass from Nealy to Chase Wasson with 1:13 remaining in the third quarter inched Texas State a bit closer at 35-23 heading into the fourth quarter.

The final quarter belonged to Nealy and the Texas State defense. Nealy fired touchdown passes of 26 and 11 yards to Dameon Williams. Williams' second scoring reception of the fourth quarter and a two-point conversion gave the Bobcats a 38-35 lead with 6:17 remaining in the game. Touchdown runs of 1 yard by Jolly and 9 yards by Sherman 35 seconds apart gave Texas State an improbable 50-35 comeback victory.

Nealy passed for 400 yards and four touchdowns in the game. Three of his scoring tosses came as part of 34 unanswered points to close the game. The Texas State defense was just as dominant as the Bobcats' offense in the final quarter. Texas State outgained the Eagles 196-0 in the deciding fourth quarter.

After a 1-yard touchdown run by Nealy to open the scoring, Georgia Southern countered with three scores to lead 21-7 after one quarter in a game played on a sunny day with temperatures hovering around 70 degrees despite heavy rain earlier in the day. Jayson Foster tossed a pair of touchdown passes to Teddy Craft, sandwiched around a 6-yard scoring run by Jermaine Austin.

Texas State scored the only points in the third quarter on a 23-yard Jones field goal.

Following the first of three touchdown connections between Nealy and Williams to open the third quarter, Foster scored on runs of 29 and 36 yards to give the Eagles their 35-16 lead.

Nealy became Texas State's all-time passing leader in the game, finishing the contest with 6,774 career yards.

The Bobcats found themselves in a completely different type of game from the Georgia Southern contest when Texas State played host to Cal Poly in the Division I-AA quarterfinals.

In 12 previous games in 2005, including the wild postseason win over Georgia Southern, the Bobcats had not scored less than 26 points in any game. Texas State managed only 14 against Cal Poly, but it proved to be enough for a 14-7 playoff-advancing triumph.

A 17-yard touchdown run by Nealy late in the second quarter provided the only scoring of the first half as Texas State led 7-0 at the break.

The Bobcats extended their lead to 14 points on a 5-yard run by Sherman with less than three minutes remaining in the third quarter. Sherman, who saw limited action late in the regular season and in the Georgia Southern game with an ankle injury, rushed for 125 yards against the Mustangs.

An 8-yard run by James Noble with 4:11 left in the game allowed Cal Poly to trail only 14-7. Clinging to its one-touchdown lead, Texas State was able to run out the clock after Nealy passed 8 yards to White on fourth-and-5 with less than one minute left in the contest.

Playing at home in the Division I-AA semifinals, Texas State coach David Baliff decided to take his chances in overtime against Northern Iowa.

The Bobcats held a 37-29 lead when Northern Iowa's David Horne scored on a 2-yard run and a two-point conversion pass from Eric Sanders to Justin Surrency tied the game with 1:27 remaining in the fourth quarter.

Texas State got the ball back at its own 25 with three timeouts remaining. Instead of taking a few shots down the field in an attempt to set up a potential game-winning score, Baliff opted to run out the clock and go to overtime.

Getting the ball first in overtime, Northern Iowa's Brian Wingert kicked a 25-yard field goal to give the Panthers a 40-37 lead. On third down on Texas State's overtime possession, pressure forced Nealy from the pocket. The quarterback's throw intended for Sherman was intercepted by defensive back Matt Tharp, eliminating the Bobcats from the playoffs.

Sanders tossed touchdown passes of 30 yards to Surrency and 12 yards to Brian Cutright to give Northern Iowa a 14-0 lead after one quarter. A pair of Nealy touchdown passes and a Jones field goal rallied Texas State to within three points at 20-17 before Wingert kicked a 41-yard field goal to give the Panthers a 23-17 halftime edge.

Texas State stretched a one-point edge after three quarters into a 37-29 lead with 5:01 left in the game on a 2-yard run by Jolly. Dominic Giametta's recovery of a Johnny Gray fumble at the Northern Iowa 6-yard line set up the Bobcats' touchdown.

Starting at the Northern Iowa 28 and no timeouts remaining, Sanders, who threw for 417 yards and four touchdowns, hit on 6 of 7 passes, the final being his 2-yard connection to Horne that eventually forced overtime.

Texas State ended the 2005 season 11-3.

MCNEESE'S MIDSEASON COACHING SWITCH

The majority of Southland Conference teams got off to bad starts to open the 2006 season. In non-conference play leading up to the league schedule, only two of the conference's teams managed .500 records. Four teams had one or fewer wins going into SLC play.

Sam Houston State and Northwestern State were the only two Southland teams with the distinction of reaching .500 going into conference play. The Bearkats did so by beating Arkansas-Monticello and Missouri State while losing to SMU and Texas. The Demons opened the year with losses to Kansas and Baylor, followed by wins over Delaware State and Arkansas-Monticello.

The two teams met each other to open Southland play when the Bearkats visited Northwestern State.

Three of Sam Houston State's touchdowns came from long range in a 30-20 victory over the Demons.

D.D. Terry set the tone only seconds into the game when he galloped 74 yards for a touchdown less than a minute into the contest. Leading 14-3, Brett Hicks hooked up with Brandon Perry with a 94-yard bomb for a 21-3 lead with 3:04 remaining before halftime. Early in the second half, Hicks spotted Perry, who broke several tackles on his way to a 69-yard touchdown and a 27-6 advantage.

The only time the Bearkats didn't score a touchdown from long range was on a 10-yard pass from Hicks to Brian Christian to cap a 71-yard drive that made the score 14-3.

Trailing 21-3, the Demons added three points on a 37-yard Robert Weeks field goal with less than a minute remaining before halftime. Northwestern State made the final score close with a 5-yard touchdown run by Byron Lawrence and a sneak by Ricky Joe Meeks.

The team with the distinction for the worst start among Southland teams was Stephen F. Austin, which went winless through five games going into conference action. SFA opened SLC play at a Texas State team that only had one win in four outings.

Looking for its first win of the season and seeking to snap a seven-game losing streak dating back to the 2005 season, things looked grim as Stephen F. Austin fell quickly behind 10-0 when Texas State scored on its first two possessions of the game.

A 27-yard Andrew Ireland field goal capped a 12-play opening drive for Texas State. After the defense forced a punt on Stephen F. Austin's next series, Stan Zwinggi, who rushed for 120 yards in the game, broke loose on a 41-yard scamper for a 10-0 lead for the Bobcats.

The Lumberjacks missed out on a chance to cut into the Bobcats' halftime lead. Kedric Holman's return of an errant Bradley George pass gave Stephen F. Austin the ball at the Texas State 15. On fourth down from inside the 1-yard line, Louie Runnels was stopped by Jonathan Lehmann and Shola Obafemi to end the threat.

The teams traded field goals early in the third quarter, leaving SFA behind 13-3. Danny Southall connected with Dominique Edison on a 44-yard strike to narrow the score to 13-10 going into the fourth quarter.

Stephen F. Austin could not cut into the Bobcats' lead until the late stages of the contest. Still down by three points, Southall went back to pass. After spotting an opening in the Texas State defense, the Lumberjacks quarterback galloped 59 yards for a touchdown to put SFA on top 17-13 at the 2:34 mark of the fourth quarter.

Holman came up big once again for SFA down the stretch. On the ensuing kickoff following Southall's touchdown run, Holman knocked the ball away from Bobcats return man Morris Crosby, with Bug Aymond recovering at the Texas State 30-yard line. SFA took advantage of Holman's effort this time when Runnels broke loose on a 30-yard gallop two plays later and the Lumberjacks earned their first victory of the season with a 24-13 triumph.

Also opening up Southland play that same day were rivals Nicholls State and Southeastern Louisiana. The Colonels went into their conference home opener 1-3. Among the defeats were losses to Nebraska and Louisiana Tech. Southeastern Louisiana's lone win in five games came against Jacksonville.

With fresh legs under them following a week off, the Colonels ran past Southeastern Louisiana 14-10. Broderick Cole rushed for 101 yards and quarterback Vincent Montgomery added 96 as Nicholls rushed for 331 yards.

Cole scored on a 2-yard run early in the game before Southeastern Louisiana countered with a 24-yard Jeff Turner field goal and a 22-yard touchdown run by Mario Gilbert to lead 10-7 at halftime.

The Lions appeared to tack onto their lead when Keylam Davis raced 94 yards with the second-half kickoff for a touchdown. During the return, a SLU player on the sideline bumped into one of the officials, nullifying the score. An offside penalty by the Colonels on the play led to a re-kick.

SLU mounted a drive after the second kickoff but came away with no points when Turner missed a 40-yard field goal.

The Colonels mounted a 58-yard drive on their second possession of the third quarter. A 30-yard keeper by Montgomery and a run of 23 yards by Michael McClendon advanced Nicholls to the SLU 5. McClendon scored two plays later on a 3-yard run for what proved to be the final score of the game in the Colonels' four-point victory.

McNeese State made its Southland debut a week later when the 2-3 Cowboys hosted Texas State.

The Cowboys faced midseason upheaval when Tommy Tate resigned at mid-week leading into the Southern Utah game after a 1-3 start and was replaced by offensive coordinator Matt Viator. Viator made his debut as the Cowboys' head coach in front of the home fans against Southern Utah as McNeese came away with a 30-27 triumph.

"You can have all the experience you want as a coach – and I had been a high school head coach for a long time – you have that experience. That (a midseason coaching change) doesn't happen very often," said Viator. "You take over a team on a Thursday during a week which was not an open week.

"Who do you call - even to get experience and ideas? It just doesn't happen very often and you are stuck with it and you are trying to figure out what the right things to do are. What do you do and how do you do it? There's just not a lot to lean on."

The Cowboys fell behind 14-3 after the first quarter against Texas State and McNeese State never was able to cut the margin to less than double digits in a 27-17 loss against the Bobcats in Viator's first Southland Conference game as head coach.

A pair of touchdowns from George to Chase Wasson gave Texas State its 14 first-quarter points. All McNeese could counter with in the opening quarter was a 25-yard Blake Bercegeay field goal.

Texas State extended its lead to 17-7 at halftime on an 18-yard Ireland field goal with 12 seconds remaining in the second quarter. George tossed a 20-yard touchdown pass to Crosby in the third quarter.

Derrick Fourroux, who threw three of the Cowboys' five interceptions in the game, tossed second-half touchdown passes to Quinten Lawrence and Wesley Mangan.

"We beat Southern Utah the first week and I felt we were fortunate to win that one. I think we were still in transition and there was a lot of uncertainty," Viator said of the Texas State defeat.

Unlike past years when Josh McCown and Dustin Long guided a pass-happy offense, the 2006 version of the Bearkats were powered by Terry, the Southland Conference's reigning 100-meter champion, and the running game.

Nicholls State found that out the hard way as Terry rushed for 176 yards and three touchdowns in Sam Houston State's 37-7 Southland Conference home win over the Colonels.

Terry's running and six Nicholls turnovers proved to be a deadly combination against the Colonels. Terry staked the Bearkats to an early 6-0 lead on a 3-yard run on a drive that was set up by a fumble by Montgomery.

After a 1-yard Terry touchdown run gave SHSU a 13-0 lead, the Colonels got their only points of the game on a drive set up by a Terry fumble. Chris Bunch, in at quarterback in place of Montgomery, scored from a yard out to make the score 13-7 with less than a minute remaining in the first half but Nicholls would not score again.

A 9-yard pass from Hicks to Michael Malone late in the third quarter increased the Bearkats' advantage to 20-7. Terry added his third touchdown of the game on a 36-yard run following a Bunch fumble. A 31-yard Taylor Wilkins field goal and a 7-yard run by Andrew Audelin allowed SHSU to win by a 30-point margin.

Sam Houston State became the first team to reach 2-0 in the SLC while improving to 4-2 overall. Nicholls dropped to 1-1 in the conference and 2-4 overall.

In Hammond, Southeastern Louisiana fell behind early against Northwestern State as Demons quarterback Roch Charpentier was red-hot to open the game. The freshman completed his first nine passes of the game for 136 yards. That set a school record for most completions to start a game while giving his team a 14-0 lead.

Charpentier's pin-point passing led to a 2-yard touchdown run by Patrick Earl to give the Demons a 7-0 lead. Three plays into the ensuing possession, Bradd Schlosser, making his first collegiate start, fumbled the snap from center, with

Russ Washington recovering for Northwestern at the SLU 36. Charpentier wasted little time, hitting Ben Bailey with a scoring strike on the first play following the turnover for a 14-0 advantage.

Southeastern pulled to within one point at halftime at 14-13 and led 24-21 late in the game. A low center snap on a punt from deep in Lions territory gave the Demons the ball at the SLU 48. Weeks hit a 26-yard field goal with 41 seconds remaining in the fourth quarter to force overtime.

The Lions scored four plays into the first overtime possession on a 1-yard run by Jay Lucas. Like on SLU's possession, a pass interference call put the Demons in excellent scoring position in overtime with a first-and-goal at the 3-yard line. On first down, Earl was thrown for a 2-yard loss. Charpentier then threw three-straight incomplete passes, allowing the Lions to escape with a 31-24 triumph that moved SLU to 2-5 overall while evening its Southland mark at 1-1.

A week later, Southeastern Louisiana broke a scoreless tie early in the second quarter in its game at Texas State on a 25-yard Turner field goal. That initial score seemed to wake up the Bobcats' offense as Texas State scored 28 unanswered points on its way to a 38-17 victory over the Lions.

Texas State countered on its next drive when George capped a 68-yard drive on a 9-yard touchdown toss to Crosby. The second of three touchdown passes by the redshirt freshman in the game, a 28-yard hookup with Luke, gave the Bobcats a 14-3 halftime lead. A 1-yard run by Alvin Canady in the third quarter and another Bradley-Luke connection in the fourth quarter extended the score to 28-3 with 14:52 left in the game.

SLU, which fell to 0-10 all-time against Texas State while dropping to 2-6 overall and 1-2 in conference, scored twice in the fourth quarter to make the final 38-17. The Bobcats improved to 3-4 overall and 2-1 in league action.

McNeese State broke open a 10-10 tie at halftime at Stephen F. Austin and then had to hold off a late Lumberjacks charge for a 20-17 Southland Conference win for the Cowboys.

A 40-yard field goal by Bercegeay and a 19-yard touchdown run by Jamie Leonard gave the Cowboys a 20-10 lead at the 6:35 mark of the third quarter.

Southall's 25-yard touchdown pass to Tyrell Williams closed the gap to three points with 3:06 remaining in the third quarter.

SFA missed out on a chance to force overtime twice in the closing minutes of the game. Cory Long missed a 40-yard field goal with 2:55 left in the game and misfired from 51 yards with 30 seconds left in the game as the Cowboys held on for the three-point triumph.

After a 7-yard touchdown run by Runnels, Bercegeay and Long traded field goals before Fourroux hit Mangan with a 3-yard touchdown pass for a 10-10 tie at halftime.

The outcome left both teams 1-1 in the Southland. McNeese improved to 3-4 while the Lumberjacks dropped to 1-6.

In Thibodaux, Northwestern State took care of one dilemma and overcame another to take a 9-0 win at Nicholls State for the Demons' first Southland Conference win of the season.

Demons coach Scott Stoker entered the game lamenting a minus-eight turnover differential by his team. Northwestern's defense more than compensated, forcing six turnovers in the win over Nicholls.

The other dilemma, the Demons' inability to score touchdowns in the red zone, surfaced once again. Despite the turnovers, all the Northwestern offense could manage were three Weeks field goals. In 35 red-zone opportunities through seven games, the Demons came up with only 10 touchdowns.

Touchdowns, however, wouldn't matter against the Colonels. Weeks kicked three field goals to give him 16 on the season to establish a new Northwestern State single-season record.

Two lost fumbles by Nicholls turned into only one field goal, a 38 yarder by Weeks in the first quarter to give the Demons a 3-0 lead at halftime.

The most the Demons could get out of a Bunch fumble at the Colonels' 20-yard line in the third quarter was a 23-yard field goal to make it 6-0.

Despite the mistakes, Nicholls was still in the game. A fifth fumble gave the Demons the ball at the Nicholls 23 with 5:05 remaining in the game. On third-and-7, Nicholls linebacker Cory Vavala dropped a potential interception at the goal line with an open field in front of him.

Weeks then kicked a 25-yard field goal to put the game out of reach.

Both teams played young quarterbacks. Bunch made his first start in place of an injured Montgomery for Nicholls. Charpentier took over as the starter at Northwestern following Meeks' departure from the team at midseason.

The result left both teams 1-2 in Southland play. Northwestern improved to 3-4 overall while Nicholls dropped to 2-5.

Coming off a 38-30 non-conference loss to Central Arkansas on a Thursday, Sam Houston State had a couple of extra days to prepare for McNeese State in the Bearkats' quest to become the only unbeaten team remaining in Southland Conference play.

Terry rushed for 253 yards – the most ever allowed by McNeese State – yet it still wasn't enough for Sam Houston State in the Bearkats' 31-18 Southland Conference home loss to the Cowboys.

The Bearkats' running back was a one-man show for SHSU. Wade Pate, making his first start after suffering an injury early in the season, was 0 for 5 passing. Hicks fared a bit better, connecting on 6 of his 16 attempts.

McNeese jumped out to a 14-0 lead on a 23-yard touchdown pass from Fourroux to Steven Whitehead, a 25-yard Bercegeay field goal and a 1-yard quarterback sneak by Mark Fontenot.

SHSU managed to make it 24-12 at halftime thanks to a 30-yard fumble return for a touchdown by Jeremy Wilson and a 12-yard run by Terry.

Each team scored once in the second half. Fourroux capped a 14-play drive with a 1-yard run for McNeese and Terry scored on a 26-yard scamper.

"I thought that was a turning point. Sam Houston was undefeated in the league and we already had lost to Texas State and couldn't afford to lose that game and still be in it," Viator said.

The outcome left McNeese and Sam Houston State atop the SLC standings at 2-1. Sam Houston State and McNeese both moved to 4-4 overall.

Stephen F. Austin held a slim 14-10 halftime lead at Southeastern Louisiana before the Lumberjacks pulled away in the second half for a 35-10 victory that allowed SFA to join McNeese and Sam Houston at 2-1 in the Southland Conference.

Runnels, who rushed for 205 yards, scored on a 1-yard run late in the third quarter for a 21-10 SFA advantage. Moments later, Lumberjacks linebacker Brian Ford returned an interception 39 yards for a touchdown to make the score 28-10.

The SFA defense played a large role in the victory. The Lumberjacks constantly harassed Schlosser, sacking the freshman quarterback five times. Except for two first downs on SLU's final possession of the game, the Lions earned only one other first down over the final two quarters.

An 18-yard pass from Southall to Nick Rhodes in the fourth quarter made the final score 35-10

Southall scored both of SFA's touchdowns in the first half on a 1-yard keeper in the first quarter and a 7-yard run with 17 seconds left in the second quarter. Southeastern Louisiana's points came on a safety and a 3-yard halfback pass from Lucas to Byron Ross and a two-point conversion.

SFA moved to 2-1 in the Southland Conference and 2-6 overall. Southeastern Louisiana slipped to 1-3 in the league and 2-7 overall.

Meanwhile, Northwestern State was involved in a 10-10 tie in its Southland home game against Texas State when the Demons opted to bring in Germayne

Edmond at quarterback. A true freshman, Edmond guided Northwestern on a 72-yard drive with tailback Greg Skidmore busting loose on a 37-yard touchdown run to give his team a 17-10 lead early in the fourth quarter.

The Demons put the game out of reach when George threw a desperation pass out of the end zone while trying to avoid a sack, resulting in a safety with 2:49 left to give Northwestern a 19-10 triumph.

A 29-yard pass from Charpentier to Bailey and a Weeks field goal, countered by a 21-yard pass from George to Tyrone Scott and an Ireland field goal led to a 10-10 tie at halftime.

Northwestern evened both its conference and overall record in moving to 2-2 in the SLC and 4-4 overall. Texas State moved to 2-2 in the league as well while falling to 3-5 overall.

Texas State was back in action five days later and leading Nicholls State when the Colonels came up with a big stop to preserve a 21-19 Southland victory on a Thursday night in San Marcos.

George's 30-yard touchdown pass to Alex Darley as time expired rallied the Bobcats to within 21-19. A two-point conversion attempt to force overtime was thwarted when Wasson was stopped at the goal line, allowing the Colonels to even their SLC record at 2-2 while moving to 4-5 overall. TSU fell to 2-3 in the league and 3-6 overall.

Texas State let a 13-0 halftime lead slip away. The Bobcats built their lead despite not scoring an offensive touchdown. Donovan King recovered a Colonels fumble in the end zone early in the second quarter. Texas State's other first-half points came on a pair of Ireland field goals.

Nicholls stormed back with a 21-point third quarter. A 1-yard run by Dwayne Jones, a 56-yard touchdown pass from Montgomery to McLendon and an 8-yard run by Zach Morgan put the Colonels on top 21-13 going into the fourth quarter.

Two days later, McNeese State trailed by 10 points at halftime but the Cowboys scored the first five times they got their hands on the ball in the second half to pull away for a 34-13 Southland Conference home win over Southeastern Louisiana.

Trailing 13-3, McNeese safety Jamelle Juneau returned a Schlosser interception to the Southeastern 16-yard line to set up a 30-yard Bercegeay field goal to pull the Lions to within seven points. Two plays into SLU's ensuing possession, Schlosser was unable to handle a snap over his head from shotgun formation, with Juneau recovering at the 2-yard line. Leonard scored one play later to tie the game 13-13.

On the next series, Schlosser again was unable to handle a snap, this time from under center. Kenneth Lundy's fumble recovery at the Southeastern 35 led to Fourroux's 8-yard touchdown pass to Carlese Franklin for a 20-13 McNeese lead with 6:45 still remaining in the third quarter.

Toddrick Pendland broke loose on a 72-yard gallop to close out the scoring in the third quarter and McNeese added the game's final score in the fourth quarter when Whitehead took the ball on an end-around before tossing to Frankin for a 27-yard touchdown.

After spotting the Cowboys a 3-0 lead on a Bercegeay field goal in the first quarter, Southeastern Louisiana scored on a 5-yard run by Lucas and a 5-yard pass from Schlosser to Crawford Kilpatrick in the second quarter for its 13-3 halftime advantage.

McNeese improved to 3-1 in the Southland and 5-4 overall. SLU slipped to 1-4 in the conference and 2-8 overall.

Needing a win to keep pace with McNeese, Sam Houston State bounced back from its loss to the Cowboys with a 21-17 win at Stephen F. Austin.

SFA jumped out to a 14-0 lead as both teams sought to reach 3-1 in conference play. Runnels and Southall had touchdown runs to put the Lumberjacks on top. Sam Houston State made it 14-6 at halftime on a 1-yard run by Terry late in the second quarter.

A 2-yard touchdown pass from Hicks to Perry and a two-point conversion tied the game early in the second half.

Audelin's 1-yard scoring run provided the only touchdown of the fourth quarter as the Bearkats took the lead for good on their way to the 21-17 triumph.

Sam Houston moved above .500 at 5-4 while SFA dropped to 2-7.

McNeese State, looking to move to 4-1 in the Southland, enjoyed a 23-14 halftime lead a week later at Northwestern State.

Lawrence scored on a 3-yard run for the only points of the third quarter to pull the Demons to within a field goal of McNeese. Edmond's 30-yard touchdown pass to Derrick Doyle with 5:59 left in the game gave Northwestern State a 26-20 lead.

Bercegeay forced overtime with a 39-yard field goal with 25 seconds remaining in regulation.

Four field goals by the kicker helped to keep McNeese in the game. Bercegeay proved to be the game's hero, connecting on a 29-yard attempt in overtime for a 29-26 Cowboys triumph.

McNeese moved into serious Southland title contention as the win over the Demons moved the Cowboys to 4-1 in the conference and 6-4 overall. Northwestern State fell to 2-3 in the league and 4-6 overall.

In Hammond, Sam Houston State needed to win once again to keep pace with McNeese State, but neither the Bearkats nor the Southeastern Louisiana Lions could produce much offense in SHSU's final road game of the season.

The only touchdown in the first half was a 15-yard pass from Hicks to Blake Martin. That capped a 26-yard drive that was set up by Tony Jones' block of a Jim Hall punt for SLU.

Southeastern Louisiana managed a 25-yard Jeff Tucker field goal on the final play of the first half to trail 7-3. The Lions' score was set up by Romaliz Mayo's interception of a Hicks pass that the safety returned to the SHSU 46.

The Bearkats turned to Terry in the second half. Terry's 41-yard gallop set up his 1-yard run three plays later for a 14-3 Sam Houston State lead less than three minutes into the third quarter.

After a 3-yard halfback pass for a touchdown from SLU's Lucas to Krishna Muhammad, Terry broke loose on a 51-yard sprint early in the fourth quarter for a 21-10 Bearkats lead.

Following a 12-yard touchdown run by Terry that made the score 28-17, Seth Babin tossed a 12-yard scoring pass to Kirkpatrick with 33 seconds left in the game. The Bearkats recovered the onside kick and ran out the clock for the 28-23 victory.

SHSU moved to 4-1 in the Southland and at 6-4, secured a winning season. Southeastern Louisiana ended its season 1-5 in the conference and 2-9 overall.

With both teams 2-2, Stephen F. Austin and Nicholls State met in Thibodaux with each team looking to move above .500 in the Southland Conference.

Stephen F. Austin trailed by a single point late in its game at Nicholls State before a 27-yard Alex Romero field goal gave the Colonels a 13-9 edge with 2:13 remaining in the game.

After being limited to three field goals in the game by the Nicholls defense, the Lumberjacks now needed a touchdown to pull out a victory.

Three completions by Southall and a 10-yard run allowed SFA to move from its 27 to the Colonels' 42 with 40 seconds left. Southall dropped the ball on the next play, picked it up and scrambled to the right sideline before heaving the ball into the end zone where Edison fought off Nicholls defensive back Lester Brooks for the touchdown and a 16-13 triumph for the Lumberjacks.

SFA, which moved to 3-2 in the Southland and 3-7 overall, sealed the win on Freddie Parish's interception of a Montgomery pass at the Lumberjacks' 2-yard line.

Nicholls, which fell to 2-3 in the SLC and 4-6 overall, led 10-0 until the Lumberjacks began to rally midway in the third quarter. Long connected on field goals of 32, 29 and 20 yards. The last of the three field goals pulled SFA to within one point with 9:46 left in the game.

The Colonels responded by using up 7:23 on a 15-play drive that forced the Lumberjacks to burn their last remaining timeout.

On third-and-2 from the SFA 8-yard line, Montgomery was dropped for a 2-yard loss. Facing fourth-and-4, Romero booted his 27-yard field goal to extend the Colonels' lead to 13-9.

Closing the season at home on a Thursday night, Stephen F. Austin did all of its scoring in the second quarter before holding off Northwestern State for a 20-11 victory.

Southall tossed a 19-yard touchdown to Edison and ran 11 yards for another for SFA's two touchdowns in the game. Long added field goals of 28 and 21 yards to give the Lumberjacks their 20-0 halftime lead.

Taking a page from the Lumberjacks, Northwestern State did all of the scoring in the second half. Weeks produced the Demons' first points with a 23-yard field goal late in the third quarter. Northwestern State's lone touchdown of the contest came on a 2-yard pass from Charpentier to Dudley Guice with 19 seconds left in the game.

The outcome left both teams with 4-7 records for the season. Stephen F. Austin concluded the year 4-2 in the SLC while Northwestern State ended 2-4.

Playing in the regular-season finale two days later, the McNeese State Cowboys were taking no chances at home against Nicholls State, jumping out to a 17-0 halftime lead on their way to a 26-10 win to capture the Southland Conference title.

McNeese State picked up league title No. 11 in a season in which the Cowboys started the year at 1-3 before Tate resigned as head coach and was replaced by Viator. Under Viator, McNeese won six of its final seven games on the way to claiming the conference crown.

A 27-yard Bercegeay field goal and a 19-yard touchdown pass from Fourroux to Franklin gave McNeese a 10-0 lead after one quarter. Frankin hauled in a 22-yard touchdown strike from Fontenot in the second quarter for McNeese's 17-0 lead at the break.

McNeese extended the score to 23-0 before Nicholls got its only points in the third quarter on a 1-yard run by Corey Buchanan and a 37-yard field goal by Romero. That made the score 23-10 before Bercegeay kicked a 34-yard field goal with 7:57 left in the game to make the final 26-10.

Cowboys' defensive end Bryan Smith picked up sack No. 12½ to set a new single-season record for McNeese.

McNeese sewed up the Southland title with a 5-1 record while finishing the regular season 7-4. Nicholls finished its season 4-7 overall, including 2-4 in the conference.

Playing for a share of the Southland Conference title at home against Texas State, the Bearkats jumped out to a 14-0 first-quarter lead over the Bobcats.

Terry factored in both touchdowns. He scored on a 7-yard run and added a 44-yard pass from Hicks.

Texas State countered with two touchdowns of its own in the second quarter to tie the game at halftime. Wasson tossed scoring passes of 4 yards to Blake Burton and 16 yards to Crosby to even the game.

Zwinggi came up big for the Bobcats in the second half. Zwiggi's 49-yard run early in the third quarter gave Texas State its first lead of the game at 21-14. Moments later, he raced 80 yards after hauling in a Wasson pass for a touchdown and a 28-14 Texas State advantage.

Derrick Harris gave the Bearkats one last bit of hope. With SHSU down by 14 points, he returned a punt 90 yards for touchdown with 20 seconds remaining. An onside kick attempt by the Bearkats failed and Texas State ran out the few remaining seconds on the season in a 28-21 triumph.

The playoff-denying loss ended Sam Houston State's season at 4-2 in the Southland and 6-5 overall. Texas State finished 3-3 in the conference and 5-6 overall.

McNeese State was unable to stop Josh Swogger, who threw four touchdown passes to give second-seeded Montana a 31-6 home win in the opening round of the Division I-AA playoffs.

Two Bercegeay field goals were sandwiched around Swogger's first touchdown pass, a 50-yard bomb to Dan Beaudin, as the Cowboys trailed only 7-6. Bercegeay's second field goal from 38 yards out came early in the second quarter as McNeese trailed by one point but the Cowboys would not score the remainder of the game.

Swogger, meanwhile, continued with his hot hand. His 14-yard touchdown strike to Eric Allen and a 22-yard Dan Carpenter field goal gave the Grizzlies a 17-6 halftime edge.

The Montana quarterback fired two touchdowns passes to Craig Chambers in the second half, one in the third quarter and the other in the final period, to give the Grizzlies a 31-6 win that eliminated the Cowboys from the playoffs.

"I felt like early in the game we had some chances. We had two long drives to start the game and only got three points out of them. We had to settle for field goals," Viator recalled.

McNeese ended the 2006 season at 7-5.

DIVISION I-AA TO THE FCS

The 2007 season brought a change in designation for the Southland Conference. Instead of being called Division I-AA, the Southland was now part of the Football Championship Subdivision. The major college programs went from being in Division I-A to the Football Bowl Subdivision. Other than a longer moniker and an awkward jumble of words, the new name meant no other changes in status.

What did change about the Southland Conference was its size. Central Arkansas joined the league, giving the SLC eight football-playing members. The expansion gave the conference a presence in the state of Arkansas for the first time since the days of Arkansas State. A founding member of the Southland, Arkansas State was in the conference from 1964-86.

Central Arkansas joined the Southland after making the transition from Division II. The Conway, Arkansas, school was a member of the Gulf South Conference from 1993-2005 and was a Division II independent in 2006.

The Bears were coached by Clint Conque. A former Nicholls State All-America, Conque sported a 52-29 record in seven seasons as Central Arkansas coach. His 2005 team was the Gulf South Conference champions.

Central Arkansas didn't have to wait long to make its conference debut, playing at Northwestern State only two games into the season. The Bears opened with a 28-7 loss to Louisiana Tech while Northwestern State was 1-0 after a win over Henderson State.

The Bears were in the SLC but not yet eligible for the conference title since Central Arkansas was transitioning from Division II. That didn't seem to matter to the Bears against Northwestern State as the Bears managed 14-point leads on the Demons twice in the game.

Central Arkansas' initial 14-point lead came to open the contest as the Bears scored the first two touchdowns of the game on a 23-yard run by quarterback

Nate Brown and a 33-yard gallop by Leonard Ceaser. The Demons rallied to trail 14-7 after one quarter on a 30-yard pass from Germayne Edmond to Dudley Guice.

A 35-yard pass from Brown to Marquez Branson in the second quarter gave Central Arkansas a 21-7 halftime lead.

Showing the upstart Bears they would not easily fade away, the Demons scored three touchdowns in the third quarter to take their first lead of the game at 28-21. Edmond scored on a 1-yard run and connected with Clayton Broyles on a 26-yard touchdown to tie the game. Byron Lawrence's 46-yard run with 1:55 left before halftime gave Northwestern the lead.

Central Arkansas mounted a 10-play, 69-yard drive to tie the game at the 7:40 mark of the fourth quarter on a 1-yard run by Brent Grimes.

Following an exchange of possessions, a 13-yard punt return by Jasper Edwards gave the Demons the ball at the Bears' 32 with 1:44 left in the game. After a 12-yard gain by Edmond, Northwestern let the clock run down before Robert Weeks kicked a 35-yard field goal as time expired to give the Demons a 31-28 triumph.

Along with the switch from Division I-AA to Football Championship Subdivision and the addition of Central Arkansas, the 2007 season also was a year of coaching changes in the Southland Conference.

Several weeks after Central Arkansas and Northwestern State opened league play, a pair of new coaches made their Southland debuts when Southeast Louisiana hosted Stephen F. Austin.

Mike Lucas officially was the new coach at Southeastern Louisiana. He had been serving as the Lions' defensive coordinator while then-head coach Dennis Roland was battling cancer. Roland died January 1, 2008, of non-Hodgkin lymphoma at the age of 51. Prior to being an assistant at SLU, Lucas was an assistant coach at Sam Houston State from 1987-2004. He was the Bearkats' assistant head coach and defensive coordinator from 1990-2004.

J.C. Harper was the new coach at Stephen F. Austin, replacing Robert McFarland. The Lumberjacks' defensive coordinator from 2005-06, Harper was a defensive line coach at McNeese State from 1999-2001. He was the assistant head coach and defensive coordinator at Northwestern State in 2002 before moving on as an assistant at Western Michigan from 2003-04.

Southeastern Louisiana and SFA went into the game with a combined one win. The Lions dominated Kentucky Wesleyan 79-7 for their only win through four games while the Lumberjacks were winless in four outings.

The open week prior to the SFA game seemed to work wonders for Southeastern Louisiana, especially for running back Jay Lucas. He rushed for 158 yards and scored two of the Lions' three touchdowns to lead SLU to a 21-3 victory over the Lumberjacks.

A 28-yard touchdown run by Lucas in the first quarter gave the Lions a 7-0 lead. Moments later, SLU safety Tommy Connors deflected a pitch by SFA backup quarterback Jeremy Claybon. Connors picked up the loose ball and scooted 9 yards for a touchdown to give Southeastern a 14-0 lead it would take to the locker room.

Conners' play was just one example of the performance by a stout SLU defense. The Lumberjacks threatened twice in the first half. On one occasion, an apparent 18-yard touchdown reception by Nick Rhodes was called back because Rhodes was ruled to have stepped out of bounds before making the catch. Stephen F. Austin came away with no points when Cory Long missed a 33-yard field goal attempt. SFA marched down to the Southeastern 23 late in the first half but a Mark Newbill sack of quarterback Danny Southall on third down forced a 47-yard field-goal attempt by Jamie Fernandez that was wide of the mark.

SFA, 0-5 overall after its conference opener, scored its only points of the game on a 30-yard field goal by Long midway in the third quarter. Lucas countered with a 78-yard touchdown run a few minutes later as SLU improved to 2-3 overall and 1-0 in league play.

Also making his Southland Conference coaching debut that day was Texas State's Brad Wright when the Bobcats hosted McNeese State. After the 2006 season, David Baliff left Texas State to become the new head coach at Rice. A former player at what was then called Southwest Texas, Wright was the running backs coach of the Bobcats from 2004-06 before being promoted to head coach.

Texas State was 1-3 on the season and sporting a three-game losing streak. Wright won his first game as head coach with the Bobcats' 38-35 victory over Cal Poly-San Luis Obispo.

McNeese was unbeaten through four games with victories over Portland State, Louisiana-Lafayette, Southern Utah and South Dakota.

Carlese Franklin and Quinten Lawrence each had more than 100 receiving yards as sixth-ranked McNeese State opened Southland play with a 41-20 win over Texas State.

The Cowboys led 20-10 at halftime before pulling away in the second half. When a 36-yard touchdown pass from Derrrick Fourroux to Frankin and a 2-yard run by Kris Bush were only countered by a 33-yard Andrew Ireland field goal, McNeese State built a 34-13 lead after three quarters. Franklin finished with 105 reception yards in the game.

A 1-yard run by Bush, a 37-yard dash by Fourroux and the quarterback's 51-yard strike to Lawrence gave McNeese its 20 first-half points. Lawrence finished with 104 reception yards.

Texas State led 10-7 after one quarter on a 31-yard Ireland field goal and a 2-yard pass from Bradley George to tight end Galen Dunk.

Central Arkansas, meanwhile, was seeking its first-ever Southland Conference win when the Bears visted Sam Houston State.

Following UCA's loss to Northwestern State, the Bears picked up their first win of the year over Tennessee-Martin before falling to Missouri State. Sam Houston State went into its Southland opener 2-2. The Bearkats won their first two games over Angelo State and Arkansas-Monticello before falling to North Dakota State and Oklahoma State.

UCA's Brown outgunned Sam Houston State quarterback Rhett Bomar, passing for 308 yards and two touchdowns. Brown spread the ball around as 14 different players had catches for the Bears.

Bomar passed for 241 yards with a touchdown and two interceptions. Continuing a trend of bringing in major college transfers to play quarterback for Sam Houston State, the Bearkats brought aboard Bomar for the 2007 season. Bomar actually arrived in Huntsville in 2006 and brought a lot of controversy with him. The former Oklahoma University quarterback was dismissed from the team shortly before the start of the Sooners' 2006 season after alleged NCAA rules violations. Bomar enrolled at Sam Houston State and sat out the 2006 season.

With the score tied 7-7 after one quarter, Spencer Hebert scored on a 1-yard run and Charles Twilley hauled in a 4-yard pass from Brown to open up a 21-7 halftime lead for Central Arkansas.

Bomar connected with Trey Payne for the only score of the third quarter as SHSU rallied to within 21-14 but the Bears scored the final two touchdowns of the game in the fourth quarter on a 17-yard Branson reception and a 1-yard Hebert run to hand the Bears their first Southland win with a 35-14 victory.

The result left both teams 2-3 overall. Central Arkansas evened its SLC mark at 1-1 while Sam Houston State fell to 0-1.

Also opening up Southland Conference play was Nicholls State. The Colonels went into their home game against Northwestern State 3-1 on the season. Nicholls spoiled the debut of Baliff at Rice by edging the Owls 16-14. Following a win over Southern Arkansas, the Colonels lost 52-17 to Nevada before escaping with a narrow 30-28 win over Azusa Pacific, a NAIA school.

After Northwestern State's win over Central Arkansas got the Demons off to a 2-0 start, they dropped their next two games to Northeastern and Texas Tech heading into the clash with Nicholls.

After Nicholls had a week off to forget the near upset loss to an NAIA school, Kareem Moore and Lardarius Webb demonstrated why both would be future NFL defensive backs in the Colonels' game against Northwestern State.

Moore and Webb each returned two interceptions for touchdowns as Nicholls routed the Demons 58-0. The two interception returns for touchdowns by the two Colonel safeties allowed Nicholls to tie the NCAA record for most interceptions returned for touchdowns in a game at four with three other teams.

Ironically, Northwestern State has been on both ends of the record. In 2003, the Demons returned four interceptions for touchdowns in an 87-27 win over Southeastern Louisiana.

The exploits of Moore, a future Washington Redskin, and Webb, a future Baltimore Raven, allowed the Colonels to build a 44-0 halftime lead. The interceptions were nothing new for Webb, a Southern Mississippi transfer. He picked off three in the season opener against Rice, returning one for a touchdown.

Nicholls ended up intercepting five Demon passes off of three Northwestern State quarterbacks. Drew Branch was picked off three times while Germayne Edmond and true freshman Adam Fayard tossed one interception each as Northwestern State fell to 1-1 in the Southland and 2-3 overall.

Playing on a Thursday night, Texas State grabbed an early lead at Southland Conference newcomer Central Arkansas but it was all Bears from that point on as the Bobcats lost their fifth-consecutive game of the season.

George tossed 26 yards to Alvin Canady for a 7-0 Texas State lead but the Bears countered with scores on five-straight possessions on their way to a 63-21 victory. Brown, who threw for 313 yards in the game, tossed six of his seven touchdown passes in the first half as Central Arkansas built a 42-14 lead at intermission.

Brown's backup, Robbie Park, threw a scoring pass in the second half as the Bears, who accumulated 662 total yards, finished with eight touchdown passes. Branson had four catches, three for touchdowns.

Central Arkansas improved to 2-1 in the Southland and 3-3 overall. Texas State fell to 0-2 in the conference and 1-5 overall.

Two days later, the Colonels moved to to 2-0 to open Southland Conference play for only the third time in school history and 5-1 overall for the first time since 2002 with a 17-16 victory at Stephen F. Austin.

An exchange of field goals by Long and Nicholls' Romero led to a 3-3 tie early in the second quarter. After the Lumberjacks pushed ahead 9-3 on a 5-yard touchdown pass from freshman quarterback Jeremy Moses to Dominique Edison, Nicholls scored the final two touchdowns of the second quarter for all the points the Colonels would need.

Broderick Cole's 1-yard run to cap a 58-yard drive gave Nicholls a 10-9 edge. With 12 seconds remaining before intermission, quarterback Vincent Montgomery hooked up with Grant Thorne from 14 yards out for a 17-9 halftime advantage.

The only score of the second half came on a 12-yard touchdown toss from Moses to Marcus Taylor midway in the third quarter as the Colonels won at Homer Bryce Stadium for the first time since 1986.

Being inserted into the game was a surprise for Moses, the freshman SFA quarterback.

"When I got there (at SFA) we had a fifth-year senior and a guy who was on the all-conference team the previous year. I didn't have a whole lot of high expectations of seeing the field. I was told I was going to redshirt up until the point I got thrown onto the field," said Moses. "It was unexpected, but exciting. I didn't get a whole lot of playing time that first year but just to see the field was a fantastic feeling."

"It was a matter of his ability and knowing what he could do. Also, obviously, we weren't doing very well," Harper said of playing Moses as a freshman. "I just felt like he was the future of the program. It was a chance for him to get an ability to play."

McNeese State joined Nicholls at 2-0 in the Southland with a 31-21 victory over visiting Sam Houston State. The Cowboys led 10-7 at halftime before coming up with two touchdowns in a span of less than 30 seconds in the third quarter in their win over the Bearkats.

Toddrick Pendland capped a 58-yard drive on a 14-yard touchdown run to give the Cowboys a 17-7 lead at the 10:33 mark of the the third quarter. One play after a Bearkats fumble, Pendland raced 24 yards for a touchdown and all of a sudden, McNeese led 24-7 with 10:16 still remaining in the third period.

The Cowboys' 10-7 halftime lead came on a 20-yard Blake Bercegeay field goal and a 9-yard Pendland run in the first quarter. The Beakats' only first-half points came on a 7-yard run by Chris Poullard in the second quarter.

McNeese's record remained unblemished at 2-0 in the Southland and 6-0 overall. SHSU fell to 0-2 in the league.

In Natchitoches, Branch, who saw action at quarterback in the interception debacle at Nicholls State, threw for a pair of touchdowns in the first quarter to give his team a 14-0 lead against Southeastern Louisiana. Those were gaudy numbers for the Demons who had been outscored by a combined 175-21 in their previous three games.

While Northwestern State came up with the early lead, it would be no easy going for the Demons in their attempt to snap a three-game losing streak. SLU rebounded from the early deficit, scoring three times in the second quarter on a 39-yard Jeff Turner field goal, a 38-yard pass from Brian Babin to Lucas and a 44-yard Lucas run to put the Lions on top 17-14 by halftime.

A Lee Scott 35-yard field goal in the third quarter and another from 30 yards out five seconds into the fourth quarter gave the lead back to Northwestern at 20-17.

Moments later, Babin hooked up with Byron Ross on a 72-yard pass play to put the Lions on top again, this time by a 24-20 margin.

Northwestern snapped its three-game losing streak when freshman Sterling Endsley scooted 18 yards for a touchdown with eight minutes left in the game for a 27-24 Demons triumph.

Northwestern improved to 2-1 in the Southland Conference and evened its overall record at 3-3. SLU fell to 1-1 in the league and 2-4 overall.

A week later, McNeese State started the second half at Nicholls State leading only by a touchdown but the Colonels had the ball to open the third quarter in a key Southland Conference showdown.

An opening second-half drive would allow Nicholls to tie sixth-ranked McNeese and gain the momentum. The Cowboys had other things in mind. Two plays into the possession, Colonels running back Cal Jones slipped trying to field a high pitch by Montgomery, giving McNeese the ball at the Nicholls 20.

Three plays later, a scrambling Fourroux spotted Bush on a 13-yard strike to give McNeese a 21-7 lead less than two minutes into the second half.

Two missed scoring opportunites following the turnover seemed to deflate the Colonels. Nicholls reached the McNeese 32 on its next possession but came away with no points when Romero missed a 50-yard field goal. Nicholls had another chance to get back in the game when a pass by Fourroux was tipped by Moore and intercepted by Jermaine Boggan. Boggan returned the interception to the McNeese 41 but the Cowboys eventually forced a Colonels punt.

After holding off the two scoring opportunities, the Cowboys marched 83 yards in 12 plays. Bush's 5-yard touchdown run with 2:30 remaining in the third quarter rounded out the scoring to give McNeese a 28-7 victory.

The win gave the Cowboys sole possession of first place in the Southland at 3-0 as McNeese moved to 7-0 overall. Nicholls dropped to 2-1 in the conference and 5-2 overall.

In Hammond, Lucas became the first Southeastern Louisiana running back to top 200 yards in a game since the Lions resumed football in 2003, but his 215-yard effort came up a bit short in SLU's 37-33 loss to newcomer Central Arkansas.

A pair of 2-yard touchdown runs by Lucas in the second quarter helped Southeastern take a narrow 16-14 lead at halftime. SLU held a 33-30 lead in the closing minutes of the game when the Lions faced a fourth-and-1 at the Central Arkansas 36. As it had done throughout the game, Southeastern handed the ball to Lucas. The prolific runner was stopped at the line of scrimmage, turning the ball over to the Bears with 2:06 left in the game. Brown guided his team down the field. A 17-yard pass from the UCA quarterback to Darius McNeal moved the ball down to the 1-yard line. Grimes, who managed only 15 yards rushing to that point, earned his biggest yard with 29 seconds remaining to give the Bears a 37-33 triumph.

UCA, 5-2 overall, 3-1 in the Southland, got a 343-yard, three-touchdown performance out of Brown, along with a pair of scores from its special teams. Following a safety early in the third quarter, Tristan Jackson returned a punt 86 yards for a touchdown. SLU, 2-5 overall and 1-2 in the conference, also got help from its special teams in the third quarter. Johnny Owen returned a blocked punt 18 yards for a touchdown to produce the first points of the second half.

Meanwhile, after Bomar's first pass of the game at home against Northwestern State was intercepted and returned for a touchdown by Blake Delcambre, Sam Houston State turned to the quarterback's feet instead of his arm. By the time the game was done, Bomar rushed for three touchdowns, including a 59-yard quarterback draw, to help Sam Houston State snap its four-game losing skid with a 42-20 victory over the Demons.

Poullard did most of the infantry work for the Bearkats, rushing for 186 yards and two touchdowns as SHSU piled up 301 yards on the ground.

After Delcambre's interception return for a touchdown, the Demons managed only two Weeks field goals the remainder of the half as Northwestern State trailed 28-13 after the game's first two quarters.

SHSU scored 28-consecutive points after falling behind 7-0. Poullard rushed for a pair of 6-yard runs in the first quarter. TyMagic Robinson raced 25 yards for a score in the second quarter before Bomar's quarterback draw for a touchdown.

Lawrence, who rushed for 110 yards, provided the first points of the second half on a 7-yard pass from Edmond early in the third quarter before Bomar added touchdowns runs in each of the final two quarters to hand Sam Houston State it's 42-20 victory.

The Bearkats improved to 1-2 in the Southland while Northwestern State dipped to 2-2. Both teams moved to 3-4 with the outcome.

Two teams with a combined one win and seeking their first Southland Conference victory of the season met when Texas State played host to Stephen F. Austin.

The Lumberjacks' highest-scoring output of the season, led by a 508-yard passing performance by Moses, was not enough to stave off their seventh loss of the season in a 52-29 defeat to the Bobcats.

Moses' 41 completions and 59 pass attempts were both school records but SFA could not match the Bobcats' balanced attack.

Cameron Luke had 152 reception yards and four touchdown passes, three from George. Karrington Bush rushed for 187 yards and Canady had 182 for the Bobcats. By contrast, Moses provided all of SFA's offense as the Lumberjacks were held to no yards rushing on 14 attempts.

Texas State improved to 1-2 in the SLC and 2-5 overall. The Lumberjacks dropped to 0-3 in the league.

McNeese appeared as though it might be in some trouble a week later when Fourroux was forced from the game in the Cowboys' second series against Southeastern Louisiana.

Connors, the SLU safety, grabbed the facemask of Fourroux and the quarterback was poked in the eye. Mark Fontenot, the seldom-used backup, entered the game. Five plays later, Fontenot connected with Lawrence on a 49-yard touchdown to give McNeese a 7-0 lead.

After SLU tied the game on a 26-yard pass from Babin to Ross, the Cowboys regained the lead on a short screen pass from Fontenot to Franklin.

Fourroux went back into the game but quickly gave way to Fontenot again. Fontenot capped another scoring drive on a 1-yard run for a 21-7 McNeese lead.

After a 32-yard Turner field goal for Southeastern, Fontenot tossed 3 yards to Wes Mangan with 54 seconds left in the second quarter to give the Cowboys a 28-7 halftime lead.

In less than a half of action, Fontenot was 15 of 16 passing for 261 yards. Fourroux returned in the second half and helped direct fifth-ranked McNeese to a 45-17 victory. The two quarterbacks guided the Cowboys to 570 yards of total offense.

"Mark had been with us for years. It wasn't like he was new to anything we were doing. Mark was a drop-back pass guy and could really throw it. I remember him coming in and being really hot," Viator said of Fontenot.

McNeese stayed perfect on the season at 4-0 in the SLC and 8-0 overall. The Lions fell to 1-3 in the league and 2-6 overall.

Although Southland Conference newcomer Central Arkansas was ineligible for the postseason with the school still in its transition period from Division II to FCS status, the Bears made a quick impression on Nicholls and the rest of the league.

In a game played at Conway, Grimes scored on a 1-yard run in overtime to hand the Colonels a costly 49-42 loss. With Nicholls unable to answer Grimes' score, the Colonels dropped to 2-2 in the league and 5-3 overall. UCA improved to 4-1 in the conference and 5-3 overall.

Nicholls forced overtime when Michael Okoronkwo hauled in a 20-yard touchdown pass from Montgomery with 34 seconds left in the game.

The teams used different styles to pile up yardage and points in the game. UCA's Brown tossed for 338 yards and four touchdowns to pace the Bears, while Cole rushed for 196 yards and four touchdowns to lead the Colonels' attack.

In Natchitoches, Texas State was tied 17-17 with Northwestern State with the Demons marching for a potential go-ahead score midway in the fourth quarter. Northwestern came away with no points, however, when an Edmond pass was intercepted at the goal line.

With regulation ticking away, the Bobcats faced fourth-and-7 from their own 44-yard line with 51 seconds remaining. A fake punt kept the drive alive, allowing Ireland to kick a 28-yard field goal as time expired to give Texas State a 20-17 victory.

Edmond had a pair of touchdown runs for the Demons. Lawrence rushed for 176 yards on 26 carries but was unable to score as Northwestern State fell to 2-3 in the SLC and 3-5 overall. Texas State's second-straight win improved the Bobcats to 2-2 in the league and 3-5 overall.

Meanwhile, a season of woe continued for the Stephen F. Austin Lumberjacks.

Running the football suddenly seemed to be the Bearkats' liking as Bomar scored twice on the ground and Poullard three times in Sam Houston State's 45-17 Southland Conference win at Stephen F. Austin that kept the Lumberjacks winless on the season.

Poullard scored the Bearkats' first two touchdowns and Bomar added a pair of 10-yard scoring runs to give SHSU a 28-3 halftime lead.

The Bearkats' defense factored in the scoring as well when Carlton Cobey returned an interception 56 yards for a touchdown.

SFA's lone bright spot was a 129-yard rushing effort by Louie Runnels.

Sam Houston State evened its record at 2-2 in the Southland and 4-4 overall. The Lumberjacks slumped to 0-4 in the conference and 0-8 overall.

Even opposing defenses and special teams seemed to be scoring more points than the Stephen F. Austin offense during the 2007 season. McNeese State scored three non-offensive touchdowns in the Cowboys' 49-20 win at struggling SFA.

Pendland had a 94-yard kickoff return in the second quarter that gave McNeese a 21-3 lead on the Cowboys' way to a 21-6 halftime edge. Bryan Smith sacked Southall to force a fumble and the defensive end ran 5 yards on the return to give McNeese a 28-6 advantage less than a minute in the third quarter. The final defensive score for the Cowboys came on a fumble return by linebacker Deron Minor.

Fourroux and Pendland each had 3-yard touchdown runs in the first quarter. After a 32-yard Fernandez field goal, Pendland raced 94 yards with the ensuing kickoff. Fernandez hit a 35 yarder to make the score 21-6 at halftime.

McNeese improved to 5-0 in the Southland and 9-0 overall. SFA remained winless on the season at 0-5 in the conference and 0-9 overall.

In Huntsville, Sam Houston State built a 13-0 lead against Nicholls State before losing Bomar with a knee injury.

Nicholls fought back on two Romero field goals and a 1-yard Joseph Tobias run to tie the game in the fourth quarter.

The big break of the game occurred in the middle of the fourth quarter when Cobey recovered a fumble by Montgomery. That set up Taylor Wilkins' third field goal of the game. His 18-yard attempt was good and the Bearkats held on to take the 16-13 triumph that extended SHSU's winning streak to three games.

Both teams moved to 5-4 with the outcome. Sam Houston State improved to 3-2 in the Southland Conference while Nicholls State slipped to 2-3.

Meanwhile, Texas State was content to trade touchdowns for field goals in the Bobcats' 45-31 home win over Southeastern Louisiana.

Turner kicked a Southland Conference-record six field goals in the game. Lucas rushed for 130 yards and two touchdowns for Southeastern. Meanwhile, George threw two touchdown passes, Bush rushed for 179 yards and a touchdown, while Luke hauled in five passes for 110 yards and a touchdown.

Stan Zwinggi scored the game's biggest touchdown when he scooted 46 yards to break a 31-31 tie with 5:26 left in the game. The Lions fumbled the ensuing kickoff, setting the stage for a game-icing 5-yard touchdown run by Texas State fullback Blake Burton with 1:37 left in the game for the 45-31 final.

Texas State moved to 4-3 overall and 3-2 in the SLC, while Southeastern fell to 2-7 overall and 1-4 in the league.

One more win would secure no worse than a share of the Southland Conference title for the Cowboys. McNeese State seemed well on the way to its goal with a 21-7 halftime lead at home against Northwestern State but the stubborn Demons hung tough in the second half.

Trailing by two touchdowns, the Demons tied the game on a touchdown run by Lawrence and a Clay Broyles fumble recovery. Lawrence, who rushed for 130 yards, scored on a 1-yard run for Northwestern's first score of the second half. Broyles recovered a fumble in the end zone to tie the game.

Pendland raced 64 yards for a touchdown with 5:35 remaining in the game for a 27-21 lead. Clinging to a six-point advantage, the Cowboys secured the victory when Jonathan Walker intercepted a Demons pass with 1:14 left in the contest.

Endsley's 1-yard run gave the Demons a 7-0 lead but McNeese scored the final three touchdowns of the opening half to lead by 14 points at halftime. Bush scored on a 2-yard run, Fontenot tossed a 4-yard touchdown pass to Mangan and Fourroux connected on a 47-yard strike to Frankin for a 21-7 Cowboys lead at halftime.

McNeese improved to 6-0 in the Southland and 10-0 overall. The Demons dropped to 3-7 with the loss.

Trying to avoid reaching double digits in the loss column, Stephen F. Austin jumped out to a 10-0 lead in its Southland Conference game at Central Arkansas.

A 26-yard Fernandez field goal and a 12-yard touchdown run by Jabar Williams gave Stephen F. Austin its 10-point advantage in the second quarter.

Looking to stay in Southland contention, Central Arkansas responded by scoring the next 28 points. A 2-yard touchdown run by Ceaser, a 3-yard sprint by Ross Brown and a 21-yard pass from Nate Brown to Cedric Logan gave the Bears a 21-10 halftime lead. Jackson's 69-yard punt return for a touchdown early in the third quarter made it 28-10.

SFA rallied to within five points at 28-23 on a 1-yard touchdown run by Southall and a 16-yard run by Taylor before Central Arkansas put the game away for good on Nate Brown's 71-yard touchdown pass to Preston Echols with 5:30 left in the contest to make the final 35-23.

Central Arkansas improved to 5-1 in the SLC and 6-4 overall. The Lumberjacks dropped to 0-6 in the conference and 0-10 overall.

Teams streaking in opposite directions met when Sam Houston State visited Southeastern Louisiana. The Bearkats entered the game riding a three-game winning streak while the Lions were trying to snap a four-game losing skid.

SLU's Turner and Wilkins traded field goals before several big plays helped the Bearkats to build a 17-6 advantage at the break.

A 31-yard pass from Brett Hicks to Blake Martin led to the quarterback's 35-yard strike to Catron Houston for the touchdown. After his fumble led to another Turner field goal, Hicks hit Poullard with a screen pass. Poullard scooted 65 yards before being brought down at the 2-yard line. Justin Wells scored on a short pass three plays later for Sam Houston State's 17-6 halftime lead.

Turner added his third field goal in the third quarter and Lucas, who rushed for 147 yards to top 1,000 on the season, scored on a 9-yard run to leave the Lions behind by only one point at 17-16.

SHSU answered by moving 53 yards to set up a 31-yard Wilkins field goal to stretch the Bearkats lead to four points at 20-16.

The Lions threatened down the stretch. Facing fourth-and-goal from inside the Bearkats' 1-yard line and down by four points with slightly more than eight minutes remaining in the game, SLU went for the touchdown. Bryan Richmond and Kevin Smith of Sam Houston State met Mario Gilbert behind the line of scrimmage for a short loss that allowed SHSU to take over on downs.

Sam Houston State continually fed the ball to the Poullard and the Bearkats were able to run out the clock.

The Bearkats improved to 4-2 in the Southland and clinched back-to-back winning seasons in moving to 6-4 overall. SLU's fifth-straight loss dropped the Lions to 1-5 in the conference and 2-8 overall.

Playing at home for the final time in 2007, Montgomery scored on two short touchdown runs and Webb returned a punt 96 yards for a touchdown as Nicholls built an early 21-7 lead on its way to a 52-28 win over Texas State.

The win snapped a three-game losing streak and moved Nicholls to 6-4 overall, securing a winning season for the Colonels. Nicholls evened its Southland Conference record at 3-3, while Texas State fell to 4-6 overall and 3-3 in the league.

Leading 7-0, Nicholls built a two-touchdown lead when Webb made an over-the-shoulder catch of a punt at his own 4-yard line and ran into one of his own blockers before cutting to the sideline on a record-setting punt return. The 96-yard effort was the longest punt return for a touchdown in school and SLC history. His return topped the Nicholls mark of 90 yards set in 1990 by Mark Carrier, who went on to play in the NFL for Tampa Bay, Cleveland and Carolina.

A 4-yard run by Zwinggi got Texas State on the scoreboard at 14-7 before Nicholls made it 21-7 on a 4-yard run by Montgomery with 2:08 remaining in the first quarter. The Colonels went on to lead 31-7 at the break.

Sam Houston State's quest to close the season with five-consecutive wins was in serious jeopardy at Texas State in a Thursday night game when Zwinggi's 3-yard touchdown run gave the Bobcats a 28-10 lead with 1:19 remaining in the third quarter of the Southland Conference tilt.

In a span of less than a minute in the middle of the fourth quarter, however, the Bearkats were back in business. Interceptions by George on back-to-back possessions led to a pair of 1-yard touchdown runs by Poullard, rallying Sam Houston State to within a touchdown at 28-22 with 7:44 remaining in the game.

The Bearkats got the ball back late in the game down by six points but needing to travel 80 yards for a touchdown. Sam Houston State raced down the field, striking paydirt when Chris Lucas hauled in a 5-yard pass from Hicks with 13 seconds remaining to give SHSU an improbable 29-28 triumph.

George factored in three of Texas State's four touchdowns as the Bobcats built their 28-10 lead. The Texas State quarterback tossed a pair of touchdowns to Luke and scored on a 1-yard run. Texas State's other touchdown came on Zwinggi's touchdown run.

The only points the Bearkats could muster in that time came on a 33-yard Wilkins field goal and a 3-yard run by Poullard.

Sam Houston State closed out the 2007 season with a 7-4 record, including 5-2 in the Southland after a 0-2 start in league play. Texas State finished 4-7 overall and 3-4 in the SLC.

Fourth-ranked McNeese State was about as proficient as a team could be in the Cowboys' home win in the final week of the regular season over league newcomer Central Arkansas to wrap up the Southland Conference championship.

McNeese scored all six times it advanced inside the red zone in a 41-14 victory for the Cowboys' 12th league title.

A 4-yard run by Bush and a 14-yard pass from Fourroux to Jordy Johnson gave McNeese a 14-0 lead after one quarter. A 27-yard Bercegeay field goal early in the second quarter gave the Cowboys a 17-point lead before Central Arkansas got its first points on an 11-yard run by Grimes. Johnson hauled in a 13-yard pass from Fontenot with 39 seconds left in the second quarter to make it 24-7 at halftime.

The only other points the Bears could generate came on a 5-yard pass from Brown to Charles Twilley early in the fourth quarter to make the score 34-14. A 1-yard run by Neely Hubbard made the final score 41-14.

McNeese finished unbeaten in the regular season for only the fourth time in school history. The Cowboys went 11-0, including 7-0 in the Southland Conference. Central Arkansas finished 6-5 on the season, including 5-2 in the SLC.

The Demons went into their season finale at home against Stephen F. Austin looking to avoid the ignominy of being the only team to lose to the Lumberjacks in 2007. Northwestern struggled to only three wins through 10 games. SFA dropped its first 10 games but had one last game to avoid a dubious 0-11 record.

Northwestern State was taking no chances. Scoring runs of 9 yards by Guice and 10 yards by Endsley gave the Demons a 14-0 lead after one quarter. Lawrence, who rushed for 231 yards to win the Southland Conference rushing title with 1,377 yards, scored on a 31-yard run early in the second quarter for a 21-0 Northwestern lead.

SFA's only points came on a 52-yard pass from Moses to Aaron Rhea late in the first half to make the score 21-6 going into intermission, and a 13-yard Claybon run early in the fourth quarter. Northwestern, meanwhile, added a 72-yard touchdown reception by Guice and a Weeks field goal in the second half to give the Demons a 31-12 victory.

Northwestern concluded the season 3-4 in the Southland and 4-7 overall. SFA finished 0-11 overall, including 0-7 in the conference.

In Hammond, the Lions were playing for pride in their season-ending game against rival Nicholls State. Southeastern was riding a five-game losing streak and with a 2-4 Southland Conference record, the Lions had long been eliminated from league contention. Nicholls State, meanwhile, entered the game 6-4 overall and 4-2 in conference play. While not playing for a league title, the Colonels already had secured a winning season and had a chance to finish with one of the better marks in the annals of Nicholls football.

Nicholls grabbed the upper hand, jumping out to a 13-0 halftime lead. A 1-yard run by reserve quarterback Zack Chauvin along with a 39-yard interception return by Lance Moore gave the Colonels their halftime advantage.

The Lions came to life, both offensively and defensively in the second half. Southeastern scored only seconds into the third quarter on a 62-yard gallop by Lucas. Lucas, who finished with 174 yards rushing in the game, set the SLU single-season rushing mark with 1,239 yards. He added a 4-yard run late in the third quarter to give the Lions a 14-13 edge.

It remained a one-point affair until the final few minutes of the game. Nicholls drove to the Southeastern 39 and faced fourth-and-2. A field goal attempt from that distance would have been from approximately 56 yards away. The Colonels elected to try and convert on fourth down. Connors, the SLU safety, forced a fumble that was recovered by Caleb St. Louis at the Southeastern 45. Turner kicked a 27-yard field goal with 3:13 left in the game for a 17-13 win that snapped the five-game losing streak and allowed the Lions to close the season on a winning note.

When Brant Linde returned a Matt Nichols interception for a touchdown less than three minutes into McNeese State's first-round Football Championship Subdivision playoff game at home against Eastern Washington, the Cowboys must have felt like it might be a day of easy pickings.

The Cowboys quickly learned that was not to be the case. Nichols shrugged off the early interception by going on to complete 34 of 44 throws for 434 yards and two touchdowns. Eastern Washington's sophomore quarterback guided his team to 626 yards, the most ever by an opponent at Cowboys Stadium.

McNeese, meanwhile, would score only one more time in the game on a 1-yard run by Fourroux in the third quarter as the Eagles eliminated the Cowboys 44-15.

"It was pouring down rain and (Nichols) was hot. It was cold and raining. It was the year before we got the turf and the field was sloppy and it looked like he was playing in 70 degree weather on turf the way he was throwing the football," Viator said.

After the opening interception, which came on a tipped pass, Eastern Washington scored the remaining points of the half to take a 16-7 halftime lead. The Eagles tied the game after one quarter on a 3-yard run by Dale Morris. A 24-yard Felipe Macias field goal and a 64-yard strike from Nichols to Tony Davis gave Eastern Washington its halftime edge.

Eastern Washington put the game away in the second half. Morris scored on two short touchdown runs in the third quarter and added another scoring run in the fourth period. Nichols, the Big Sky Conference Offensive Player of the Year, concluded the scoring on a 10-yard touchdown pass to Nathan Overbay with 6:57 remaining in the game.

McNeese ended its season at 11-1.

NO PLAYOFFS FOR CENTRAL ARKANSAS

Hurricanes are as much a part of life along the Gulf Coast as football tailgating, Louisiana gumbo and jambalaya, and Texas barbeque. For the second time since 2005 Southland Conference schools were affected by storms, this time hurricanes Gustav and Ike.

The most affected schools were McNeese State, Sam Houston State and Nicholls State.

McNeese managed to open the season with a loss at North Carolina and a win over Delta State before Hurricane Gustav and an open date gave the Cowboys a break of three weeks before hosting Southern Virginia.

After defeating East Central of Oklahoma in the 2008 season opener, a scheduled open date, followed by the cancellation of the Prairie View game because of Hurricane Ike caused a three-week gap between games for Sam Houston State. Because of power outages and other storm-related issues, the Bearkats spent the week leading up to the Kansas game sleeping in the school's field house.

Nicholls State felt the double-whammy of both Gustav and Ike. The storms caused the Colonels' first two games of the season to be canceled – a road game at New Mexico State and a home contest versus Bowie State.

The first teams to open up Southland Conference play in 2008 were Stephen F. Austin and Southeastern Louisiana when the teams met in Nacogdoches.

SFA opened the season with a 56-19 victory over Langston, snapping an 11-game losing streak and giving second-year coach J.C. Harper his first win as Lumberjacks coach. By the time the Southeastern Louisiana game rolled around, SFA was back on a three-game losing streak.

Southeastern Louisiana went into the Southland opener 1-4. The Lions' lone victory came against Jacksonville.

Things looked bleak in Stephen F. Austin's quest to end its three-game losing streak when the Lumberjacks fell behind 28-0 against Southeastern Louisiana.

Brian Babin was a factor in three of SLU's four first-quarter touchdowns. The Lions quarterback threw a pair of touchdown passes to Chris Wilson, including a 61-yard strike slightly more than two minutes into the game. He also scored on a 1-yard run. SLU also added a defensive touchdown in the opening quarter when Marquis Powell returned an interception 38 yards for a touchdown.

The Lumberjacks trailed by as much as 24 points at 45-21 following a 28-yard field goal by SLU's Jeff Turner at the 6:47 mark of the third quarter before Stephen F. Austin went on a rally for the ages.

A 1-yard run by Cornel Tarrant to close the third quarter and a safety 50 seconds into the final period still left the Lumberjacks behind by a count of 45-30.

Jeremy Moses, who connected with 10 different receivers while passing for 319 yards, hooked up on his fourth scoring toss of the game on a 31-yard pass to Roderick Warren. A 2-yard run by Tarrant and a two-point conversion pass from Moses to Dominique Edison tied the game at 45-45 with 3:45 remaining in the contest. Edison finished the game with 173 reception yards and two touchdowns.

The Lumberjacks ended the frantic rally when Cory Long kicked a 23-yard field goal with seven seconds left in the game to capture a 48-45 thriller for Stephen F. Austin to give SFA its first Southland Conference win since the final game of the 2006 season.

When Nicholls State opened Southland play a week later at Northwestern State, the Colonels only had two games of experience, a pair of road losses to Memphis and Northern Iowa. The Demons, by contrast, had played five games before facing the Colonels. Northwestern State alternated wins and losses on its way to a 3-2 start. A game against Grambling was moved back a day for a rare Sunday college game because of Hurricane Ike.

The Demons became the first-ever victims of Robert Griffin III. Making his first start as a Baylor freshman, the future Heisman Trophy winner and No. 1 NFL draft pick, tossed three touchdown passes to hand Northwestern State a 51-6 road loss.

With an open week to prepare for their Southland Conference opener against Nicholls State, the Demons seemed on their way to an easy victory after building a 21-6 lead early in the second quarter.

It was at that point the Colonels stormed back. Ross Schexnayder's third field goal of the game got the rally started. After a 63-yard pass from Chris Bunch to Antonio Robinson and a 1-yard run by Isa Hines, the Demons suddenly found themselves trailing 22-21 going to the locker room. Hines' touchdown came when he recovered an errant pitch from Bunch intended for A.J. Williams on fourth-and-goal.

The flurry to get back in the game seemed to take something out of the Colonels' offense, which was unable to score the remainder of the game.

Following a 48-yard field goal that allowed the Demons to regain the lead at 24-22, the Colonels managed to respond when Lardarious Webb returned the ensuing kickoff for a touchdown. Webb, who had 214 all-purpose yards in the game, gave the lead back to Nicholls at 28-24.

It would be the last points the Colonels would produce. A 43-yard Robert Weeks field goal left the Demons trailing 28-27 going into the final period.

Northwestern went up for good on a 10-yard run by Endsley five seconds into the fourth quarter and Weeks added an insurance field goal with 1:22 left in the game to give the Demons a 36-28 victory.

Four other teams also made their Southland Conference debut that same day with McNeese State hosting Texas State while Sam Houston State traveled to Central Arkansas.

McNeese State entered SLC play 3-1 on the season while Texas State was 3-2.

The Bobcats led visiting and third-ranked McNeese State 38-20 going into the fourth quarter before the Cowboys made a late rally.

Cowboys quarterback Derrick Fourroux factored in three fourth-quarter touchdowns for McNeese. He tossed touchdown passes of 16 yards to Steven Whitehead and 8 yards to Todd Pendland before scoring on a 2-yard run to give the Cowboys a total of 42 points.

Texas State scored in the fourth quarter on a 46-yard pass from Bradley George to Cameron Luke for a 45-42 triumph for the Bobcats.

Each starting quarterback accounted for four touchdowns. Fourroux passed for three and ran for another while George threw four scoring passes. Pendland rushed for 165 yards for McNeese and Karrington Bush 127 for Texas State. Luke had three touchdown catches for Texas State.

The game was tied 14-14 until the Bobcats scored the final 10 points of the first half on a 1-yard run by Blake Burton and a 36-yard Andrew Ireland field goal as time expired to give Texas State a 24-14 halftime edge.

In the Southland Conference opener at Central Arkansas, the Bearkats allowed a 49-yard touchdown pass from quarterback Nathan Brown to Marquez Branson to break a 27-27 tie with 1:30 remaining – in the first half.

Sam Houston State and Central Arkansas traded scores throughout the first half and there was nothing to suggest anything but a down-to-the-wire finish in a contest in which the teams combined for 917 yards of total offense.

In a game where neither team ever led by more than eight points, the Bearkats went from being seven down at the half to leading 37-34 heading into the final period by scoring the only points of the third quarter. A 9-yard touchdown pass from Rhett Bomar to Catron Houston tied the game for the fourth time less than five minutes into the third quarter. Taylor Wilkins' 37-yard field goal gave the Bearkats a 37-34 edge.

Brent Grimes scored on a 12-yard run early in the fourth quarter and the Bears were back on top at 41-37. Wilkins countered with a 30-yard field goal to make it 41-40.

The big play of the game came on a 60-yard strike from Brown to Willie Landers. The touchdown connection with 5:51 remaining put Central Arkansas on top 48-40. It marked the first time in the game a team led by more than seven points

Houston scored on a 3-yard run with 1:30 remaining in the fourth quarter to make the score 48-46. Needing a two-point conversion for a tie, Bomar went to the air. His pass was swatted away by Derrick Boyd, allowing the Bears to hold on for the win.

Bomar threw for 292 yards and three touchdowns as the Bearkats rolled up 503 yards of total offense. Brown, the returning conference player of the year, passed for 269 yards and three touchdowns as the Bears amassed 414 yards.

A week later, only Central Arkansas and Stephen F. Austin managed to be 2-0 in the Southland two games into the conference schedule. The Bears did so with a 31-24 win at Texas State while visiting SFA toppled Nicholls State 50-39.

The Bobcats cut into 14-point deficits three times against Central Arkansas but could get no closer than three points in Texas State's 31-24 loss to the Bears.

A 5-yard run by Leonard Ceaser provided the only scoring of the first quarter as Central Arkansas took an early 7-0 lead. After a 31-yard pass from Brown to Landers put the Bears on top by two touchdowns, the Bobcats responded on a 13-yard run by Stan Zwinggi.

Grimes, who rushed for 132 yards, scored on a 1-yard run to give Central Arkansas its second 14-point lead of the game before Texas State made it 21-14 at halftime on an 18-yard pass from George to Luke.

Neither team scored in the second half until Ireland kicked a 35-yard field goal eight seconds into the fourth quarter. Brown tossed a 1-yard touchdown pass to Nick Cowger and Eddie Carmona kicked a 35-yard field goal for a 31-17 UCA lead. George hooked up Daren Dillard with 52 seconds left in the game for the 31-24 final.

Central Arkansas moved to 2-0 the Southland and 6-1 overall. Texas State fell to 1-1 in the conference and 4-3 overall.

The Lumberjacks and Colonels could be excused for perhaps looking for cover in Stephen F. Austin's game at Nicholls State. The teams may have been fearful of lightning striking twice as SFA attempted to rally from another large deficit in Southland Conference play.

While not the 28-point margin of the Southeastern Louisiana game, the Lumberjacks found themselves down by as many as 19 points against the Colonels before attempting another big rally.

A 1-yard run by Nicholls quarterback Vincent Montgomery, a 62-yard touchdown reception by Robinson and a 75-yard Webb punt return staked the Colonels to a 19-0 lead in the first quarter. Another short Montgomery touchdown run and a Schexnayder field goal gave the Colonels a 29-14 halftime lead.

The Colonels' offense could hold the Lumberjacks and Moses down for only so long. Moses ended up hitting on 37 of 59 attempts for 416 yards and four touchdowns. His final touchdown toss, a 14 yarder to Marcus Taylor less than a minute into the fourth quarter, gave SFA a 33-32 lead.

Nicholls regained the lead at 39-36 with 5:26 left in the game on a 1-yard run by Montgomery before the Lumberjacks' defense took over down the stretch.

Leading by three, the Colonels got the ball back with 3:55 left in the game. On second down from the Nicholls 19, Montgomery was hit by SFA defensive end Tim Knicky as the senior quarterback attempted a pass. That caused an errant throw that sailed right into the hands of Lumberjacks linebacker Joe Savoie, who waltzed 24 yards to the end zone to give SFA a 43-39 lead with 3:44 left in the game.

Another interception return for a touchdown, this one by Cory Barlow of 63 yards with 2:28 left in the contest, sealed another remarkable win for the Lumberjacks.

SFA improved to 2-0 in the Southland Conference and 4-3 overall by extending its winning streak to three games.

McNeese State, meanwhile, picked up its first Southland Conference win of the season with a 28-17 victory at Sam Houston State.

Pendland, who rushed for 194 yards, scored two of his three rushing touchdowns in the first quarter to set the tone for McNeese. He scored on runs of 3 and 68 yards to give the Cowboys a 14-0 lead before the Bearkats made it 14-3 at halftime on a 40-yard Wilkins field goal in the second quarter.

McNeese added two second-half touchdowns on a 45-yard interception return for a touchdown by Jeremy Haynes in the third quarter and a 12-yard Pendland run in the fourth period.

Bomar tossed two second-half touchdowns. The Oklahoma transfer tossed an 80-yard bomb to Chris Lucas in the third quarter and a 14-yard strike to Trey Payne with 18 seconds left in the game.

McNeese improved to 1-1 in the Southland and 4-2 overall. SHSU fell to 0-2 in the conference and 2-3 overall.

Southeastern Louisiana also picked up its first SLC win of the year with a 26-21 victory over visiting Northwestern State.

SLU always seemed to have an answer for whenever Northwestern State inched closer as the Lions remained unbeaten at home with a 26-21 win. The Lions were playing without head coach Mike Lucas, who was recovering from a heart valve procedure. Tommy Condell, the team's offensive coordinator, was named acting head coach for the remainder of the season.

A 30-yard pass from Babin to Wilson and a 46-yard field goal by Turner gave Southeastern a 9-0 lead that lasted through halftime. The Demons drove 70 yards to open the second half, with Byron Lawrence's 10-yard run pulling Northwestern to within two points at 9-7. A 5-yard touchdown reception by Andre Cryer later in the third quarter gave the Lions a 16-7 advantage.

The Demons again made it a two-point game at 16-14 early in the fourth quarter on a 9-yard touchdown pass from Drew Branch to Darius Duffy. SLU quickly responded when a 49-yard toss from Babin to Wilson set up Babin's touchdown run from a yard out to make it 23-14. Turner added a 40-yard field goal to make it 26-14.

Northwestern scored on an 18-yard pass from Branch to James Swanson with 2:08 left in the game to pull to within five points at 26-21. The Demons recovered an onside kick, but Tommy Conners picked off a Branch pass three plays into the drive to preserve the win for the Lions.

Both teams moved to 4-3 overall and 1-1 in Southland Conference play with the result.

Grimes scored three touchdowns a week later, including two in a 21-point second quarter as Central Arkansas gained sole possession of first place in the Southland Conference with a 28-21 home victory over Southeastern Louisiana. The Bears moved to 3-0 in league play with the win and 7-1 overall. SLU fell to 4-4 overall and 1-2 in the conference.

Grimes scored on a 2-yard run and a 9-yard pass from Brown. The only other score in the second quarter came on a 34-yard pass from Brown to Branson as the Bears blanked the Lions in the opening 30 minutes to lead 21-0 at intermission.

A 14-yard run by Grimes in the third quarter made it 28-0 before Babin got a hot hand for Southeastern. Babin tossed a 25-yard touchdown pass to Wilson to make it 28-7 after three quarters. He then hit Simmie Yarbrough with an 8-yard strike and connected with Jay Lucas from 19 yards out to make it 28-21 with 3:12 left in the game. Following Lucas' touchdown, the Lions quickly stopped the Bears and got the ball back but Central Arkansas held Southeastern without a first down to halt the SLU rally attempt.

The Lumberjacks, the only other unbeaten team in the Southland, would have been better served not trying to stretch the limits of how big a deficit they could overcome in 2008. After rallying from deficits of 28 points against Southeastern Louisiana and 19 versus Nicholls State to get off to a 2-0 start in conference play, Stephen F. Austin ran out of luck in its game against Texas State.

It would have taken luck, and then some, with the Lumberjacks down by 48 points with 2:14 remaining in the game in SFA's humbling 62-21 loss to the Bobcats.

A 71-yard touchdown pass from George to Mishak Rivas on the Bobcats' first play from scrimmage normally might have caused a bit of alarm, but a quick 7-0 hole was nothing the Lumberjacks hadn't faced before. When the score grew to 41-14 at halftime, however, it was a different matter.

SFA trailed only 17-7 before Texas State began to pull away late in the first quarter. A 3-yard run by Clint Toon made it 24-7 after one quarter. After a 6-yard touchdown run by Tyrone Ross early in the second quarter, George and Luke hooked up on a pair of scoring tosses to give the Bobcats their 41-14 halftime lead.

George ended up throwing for 418 yards and four touchdowns for Texas State. Luke finished with 139 reception yards and Rivas 188, while the duo scored twice apiece. It wasn't all passing for the Bobcats, however, as Bush rushed for 121 yards as Texas State amassed 678 yards of total offense.

The teams really didn't need a fourth quarter as the only scoring of the second half came in the third period in Texas State's 62-21 domination of SFA.

Stephen F. Austin fell to 2-1 in the Southland and 4-4 overall as the Lumberjacks' three-game winning streak came to an end with a thud. Texas State also moved to 2-1 in the SLC while improving to 5-3 overall.

In Natchitoches, Northwestern State was clinging to 14-10 lead in its Southland Conference game against Sam Houston State when the Bearkats were driving early in the third quarter for a potential go-ahead touchdown.

A 38-yard pass by Bomar moved the ball down to the Northwestern 35. Two plays later, cornerback Kasey Brown picked off a Bomar pass at the 25 and returned the errant throw to the Demons' 42. The Demons marched downfield, with William Griffin eventually scoring on a 2-yard run to increase Northwestern's lead to 21-10.

Weeks added a 36-yard field goal before the Bearkats scored on the final play of the game to make the final 24-16.

Lawrence scored on a 3-yard run to cap the opening drive of the game and added a 9-yard run early in the second quarter to give the Demons a 14-0 lead. The Bearkats rallied to 14-10 on a second-quarter field goal by Wilkins and a 47-yard pass from Bomar to Lucas in the third quarter.

Northwestern improved to 2-1 in the SLC and 5-3 overall while the Bearkats dropped to 0-2 in the conference and 2-4 overall.

Bunch, the Nicholls State quarterback, proved to be an all-purpose signal caller against McNeese State, rushing for 38 yards and passing for 49 in a Southland Conference encounter in Lake Charles. While the numbers seemed meager, Bunch was quite effective, scoring rushing touchdowns on runs of 6 and 5 yards. He only was 3 of 4 passing but two of his completions were touchdown tosses to Robinson as the Colonels upset the Cowboys 38-35.

A high-scoring first half saw the Cowboys take a 24-22 lead at the break. Blake Bercegeay's 30-yard field goal early in the third quarter pushed McNeese's lead to 27-22. Bunch's first touchdown toss of the game to Robinson from 13 yards out later in the quarter gave Nicholls a 28-27 edge going into the final period.

Bunch's 58-yard touchdown connection with Robinson and a 37-yard Schexnayder field goal extended the Nicholls lead to 11 points at 38-27 with only 2:23 remaining.

Fourroux's 2-yard touchdown pass to Whithead and a two-point conversion pass cut the score to 38-35 with 1:01 left in the game.

The Colonels recovered the onside kick and ran out the clock for their first win of the season while McNeese fell to 1-2 in the Southland and 4-3 overall.

Nicholls State hosted a Central Arkansas team a week later that was in sole possession of first place in the Southland but the Bears still remained ineligible for the league's automatic bid to the playoffs since they still were transitioning from Division II. A win by the Colonels would move Nicholls to 2-2 in the SLC and into league contention.

The Colonels were leading most of the game until UCA tied it 17-17 on a 16-yard touchdown pass from Brown to Eric Ward and Brown's two-point conversion pass with 44 seconds left in the game.

Starting at the Nicholls 24-yard line, a 38-yard sideline pass from Bunch to Robinson advanced the ball to the UCA 38. Several plays later, a Bunch pass intended for Robinson in the end zone was intercepted by the Bears' Jerrel McKnight. Defensive holding was called on Central Arkansas, giving Nicholls a first down at the 28.

A 7-yard run by Corey Buchanan set up a 38-yard Schexnayder field goal as time expired to give the Colonels the three-point triumph.

"That was a tough loss," Conque said. "We kind of lived on the edge, beating Texas State in a close game and beating Sam Houston in a close game and coming from behind to beat Southeastern. We didn't play very well. Thibodaux is a very difficult place to play, having played and coached there. It's a tough environment. We kind of slept-walked through the game."

There was some good to come out of the game, according to Conque.

"I think it re-centered us and probably woke us up a little bit for the last several games of the year," he said.

Northwestern State took advantage of the Central Arkansas loss, defeating Texas State on the road 34-31 in dramatic fashion to match the Bears at 3-1 in the Southland Conference.

Trailing 28-21 late in the game, Lawrence, who rushed for 173 yards, scored on a 2-yard run with 3:55 remaining in regulation to force overtime.

Texas State got the ball to start overtime, with a 19-yard George pass quickly putting the Bobcats in a first-and-goal situation from the 6-yard line. After Bush was dropped for a 5-yard loss and two incomplete passes, Texas State settled for an 18-yard Ireland field goal and a 31-28 lead.

Lawrence gained 9 yards on Northwestern's first play of its overtime drive and followed with a 6-yard run to pick up a first down. On third-and-goal, Lawrence ran to his left for a 2-yard touchdown to give the Demons a 34-31 victory.

The game was close for all four quarters. Brown returned an interception for the only points of the first quarter as the Demons took a 7-0 lead. Down 14-7, a 10-yard pass from George to E.J. LeBlanc at the 3:05 mark of the second quarter tied the game at 14-14.

A 30-yard run by Lawrence was countered by a 2-yard Burton score for a 21-21 tie after three quarters.

Along with a first-place tie in the Southland at 3-1, the Demons moved to 6-3 overall. Texas State fell to 2-2 in the league and 5-4 overall.

In Hammond, McNeese State's defense shut down Southeastern Louisiana's running game in a 24-14 Southland Conference win for the Cowboys.

The Cowboys held SLU to 198 total yards, including just 49 rushing by Lucas, the Lions' star running back.

Southeastern took a 7-0 lead on a 14-yard pass from Babin to Cryer in the first quarter but McNeese scored three touchdowns to close the opening half for a 21-7 advantage at intermission. Fourroux tossed a 4-yard pass to Wes Mangan to tie the game before scoring on a 2-yard run for a 14-7 Cowboys lead after one quarter. Pendland's 11-yard run midway in the second quarter gave McNeese a two-touchdown lead at halftime.

The Lions rallied to within a touchdown on a 27-yard strike from Babin to Cryer in the third quarter before Bercegeay put the game away with a 31-yard field goal with 2:41 left in the game.

McNeese evened its Southland Conference mark at 2-2 while improving to 5-3 overall. SLU fell to 1-3 in league play and 4-5 overall.

Still seeking their first Southland Conference win, the Bearkats jumped out to a 24-7 lead at home against Stephen F. Austin.

Bomar tossed three touchdown passes to Houston, including a 64-yard bomb at the 13:52 mark of the third quarter for the Bearkats' 24-7 advantage. The other SHSU score in that span came on a 19-yard Wilkins field goal in the first quarter. SFA's only points came on Moses' 10-yard touchdown pass to Edison that tied the game 7-7.

In order to get back in the game, Moses needed to throw. So the Lumberjacks had the sophomore quarterback throw and throw, and throw some more. By the time he was done, Moses completed 57 passes in 85 attempts, both NCAA records. The 57 completions broke the record of 56 attempts by Wayne State's Jarrod DeGeorgia set in 1996. Moses topped the record for attempts by two. His 85 attempts broke the mark of Purdue's Drew Brees set in 1998.

Moses, who threw for 501 yards, passed for four touchdowns, three in the second half. His 21-yard toss to Duane Brooks tied the game at 24-24 with 18 seconds remaining in the fourth quarter to force overtime.

Sam Houston State got the ball first in overtime and scored on a 1-yard run by James Aston.

Moses tossed 15 yards to Edison to tie the game 31-31 and force a second overtime.

With SFA getting the ball first in the second overtime, Tarrant gained a yard on first down. Moses fumbled but recovered on second down for a 7-yard loss. He was sacked for an 8-yard loss, leaving the Lumberjacks facing fourth-and-24 from the 39-yard line. The last of Moses' 85 attempts fell incomplete.

Only needing a field goal to win, the Bearkats fed the ball to Aston. He gained 11 yards on first down. He got the ball on another three carries, leaving Sam Houston State with fourth-and-7 from the 11-yard line. Wilkins connected on his 28-yard attempt, giving the Bearkats a wild 34-31 triumph and SHSU's first conference win of the season.

By snapping a three-game losing streak, the Bearkats moved to 1-3 in the SLC and 3-4 overall. Stephen F. Austin dropped to 4-5 on the season.

Northwestern State didn't have to wait long for its showdown against Central Arkansas as the Demons hit the road to take on the Bears only a week after the Texas State win.

Considering the outcome, the Demons could have used more time to prepare. UCA's Brown threw four touchdown passes as the highly-motived Bears blasted Northwestern 42-6.

It was the understanding of Central Arkansas officials that the transitioning Bears would be eligible to win the Southland Conference. Words to the contrary the week of the Northwestern State game didn't sit too well in Conway.

"When we joined the league is 2006, which we announced in 2005, we knew the 2006 schedules were already done and we would play as an independent," Conque recounted. "We were under the assumption from the conversations we had with the conference office that we believed we could win the official conference title but we would be ineligible for the national playoffs. That turned out to not be true.

"That particular Monday, the commissioner (Tom Burnett) flew into Conway and notified us that we would lose our automatic qualifier status if they were to name us the official conference champion. Needless to say, that did not sit well with me; it did not sit well with our football team."

As a result of the announcement, the Demons still controlled their postseason destiny despite the loss.

Brown and the Bears, meanwhile, looked the part of the conference champion against the Demons. Brown, the reigning Offensive Player of the Year in the Southland, threw two of his touchdown passes to Branson. He also connected on scoring tosses of 71 yards to Ware and 50 yards to Grimes as the Bears' quarterback threw for 348 yards.

Northwestern actually scored first on a 41-yard Weeks field goal. Weeks provided the Demons with their only other points on a 45-yard field goal in the second quarter. Weeks' first kick gave him the record for career field goals at Northwestern, topping the mark of 37 by Keith Hodnett from 1985-88.

Brown's first touchdown pass of 18 yards to Branson and a 54-yard interception return by Pieri Feazel gave the Bears a 14-3 lead after one quarter on UCA's way to a commanding 28-6 halftime advantage.

Northwestern fell to 3-2 in the Southland and 6-4 overall. Central Arkansas moved to 4-1 in the conference and 8-2 overall.

In Lake Charles, the Cowboys saw Stephen F. Austin jump out to a 10-point lead before Pendland took over in McNeese State's 42-31 win over the Lumberjacks.

A 28-yard pass from Moses to Edison and a 29-yard Long field goal gave SFA the early lead. Pendland, who rushed for 242 yards in the game, scored three-consecutive touchdowns beginning late in the first quarter on runs of 1 and 39 yards, plus a 37-yard pass from Fourroux to give McNeese a 21-10 lead. The second of three touchdown passes from Moses to Edison made the score 21-17 at halftime.

The teams traded touchdowns in the third quarter as Moses tossed 20 yards to Brooks while Fourroux countered with a 1-yard run for a 28-24 Cowboys lead going into the fourth quarter.

Pendland added his fourth touchdown of the game on a 4-yard run less than two minutes into the final period before Moses and Edison hooked up for the third time. The 8-yard touchdown pulled the Lumberjacks to within four points at 35-31. Fourroux hit Immanuel Friddle with a 34-yard touchdown pass with 6:14 left in the contest for the 42-31 final.

McNeese improved to 3-2 in the SLC and 6-3 overall.

Meanwhile, Texas State did all of its scoring in the first half to cruise past Southeastern Louisiana 38-24 to hand the Lions back-to-back losses at home.

The Bobcats scored on their first play from scrimmage and never stopped for the remainder of the opening half. George's 68-yard touchdown strike to Luke gave Texas State a 7-0 lead less than 30 seconds into the game. A 20-yard run by Zwinggi, a 4-yard dash by Bush and another touchdown toss from George to Luke gave Texas State its 28 points in the first quarter.

The game still was relatively close at that point as the Lions countered with a 10-yard touchdown reception by Wilson and a 6-yard run by Jasper Ducksworth to make it 28-14.

Another 4-yard run by Bush and a 46-yard Ireland field goal made it 38-14 at halftime.

The only points in the second half came on a Turner field goal and a 16-yard reception by Yarbrough as SLU dropped its third-straight game to fall to 4-6 overall and 1-4 in the Southland.

Texas State improved to 6-4 overall and 3-2 in the conference.

Elsewhere, the Bearkats took advantage of four first-half turnovers in their Southland Conference game at Nicholls State to build a lead of as much as 31-3 on Sam Houston State's way to a 47-37 victory.

Sam Houston State was leading 3-0 before several Colonel miscues led to quick points for the Bearkats. Billy Skinner's interception of a Nicholls pass led to a 6-yard touchdown pass from Bomar to Payne. Fumbles on each of the Colonels' next two possessions netted SHSU a pair of short touchdown runs by Aston for a 24-0 lead.

Nicholls cut the deficit to 31-16 at halftime and inched even closer on the first play of the second half on a 66-yard touchdown pass from Bunch to Hines.

Just as the Colonels put themselves back in the game, another turnover helped to seal the Colonels' fate. Nicholls fumbled a punt, leading to another Aston scoring run. His 15-yard touchdown, one of four in the contest, extended SHSU's lead to 38-23 late in the third quarter.

Aston, who rushed for 142 yards, tied a school record with four rushing touchdowns in the game.

Sam Houston State built its lead back up to 47-23 before Nicholls added two late scores for the 47-37 final.

The outcome left both teams 2-3 in the SLC. The Bearkats evened their overall record at 4-4 while Nicholls slipped to 2-5.

A week later, Central Arkansas maintained its (now unofficial) lead in the Southland Conference with a 49-41 win at Stephen F. Austin.

Grimes rushed for five touchdowns to tie a school record as the Bears moved to 5-1 in the SLC and 9-2 overall. The Lumberjacks fell to 2-4 in the league and 4-7 overall.

Grimes rushed for 145 yards in the game while Brown passed for 335. Brown tossed two touchdown passes, both to Branson.

Unlike many other Lumberjacks games in 2008, this one remained close until the very end. SFA enjoyed the biggest lead twice at 10 points – the first time at 17-7 at the end of the first quarter and 24-14 in the second quarter.

Grimes' third touchdown of the game, a 4-yard run with 1:07 remaining in the second quarter, gave the Bears their first lead of the game at 28-27.

The teams traded touchdowns throughout the second half until Central Arkansas put the final two scores on the board.

A 12-yard pass from Moses to Taylor put SFA on top for the final time at 41-35 at the 4:07 mark of the third quarter.

Central Arkansas scored the only points of the fourth quarter. Grimes' fifth touchdown, this one from 2 yards out, gave the Bears a 42-41 lead. A 12-yard pass from Brown to Branson with 7:39 gave UCA a 49-41 lead it would not surrender.

The Bears maintained their lead down the stretch thanks to the defensive effort of Phillip Johnson. Despite playing with a cast because of a broken hand, he intercepted a pass early in the fourth quarter and tipped away a pass by SFA on fourth-and-goal in the end zone with 4:16 left in the game.

Central Arkansas maintained the best record in the Southland but several other teams were jockeying for the conference's automatic bid to the Football Championship Subdivision playoffs.

After spotting Nicholls State a 3-0 lead in the first quarter, Texas State exploded for 24 points in the second quarter to take a three-touchdown lead on its way to a 34-10 home victory.

A 19-yard Ireland field goal, two George touchdown passes and a 5-yard Zwinggi run gave the Bobcats their halftime lead. Texas State made it 31 unanswered points with George's third touchdown toss of the game to open the second half.

Other than Schexnayder's opening 40-yard field goal, the only other points Nicholls could produce came on a 13-yard touchdown pass from Montgomery to Robinson in the third quarter as the Colonels only managed 118 yards rushing on 44 attempts.

The Bobcats moved to 4-2 in the SLC and 7-4 overall while the Colonels fell to 2-4 in the conference and 2-6 overall.

Two other teams in control of their own postseason destiny met when the Demons played a second-consecutive Southland Conference road game, this time at McNeese State.

Northwestern State and McNeese State each entered the game 3-2 in the Southland standings.

Bercegeay's 32-yard field goal gave the Cowboys a 3-0 lead before the Demons countered with a 1-yard Hundley run at the 1:59 mark of the first quarter to give Northwestern a 7-3 edge at the end of one period of play.

Weeks came up with a 29-yard field goal in the second quarter and McNeese countered with a 1-yard Fourroux run for a 10-10 tie at halftime.

Following a scoreless third quarter, McNeese took a 17-10 lead with 9:55 remaining in the game on 4-yard Fourroux run to cap a 79-yard drive.

The big break of the game came on the next offensive play. Jamelle Juneau made a diving interception, giving the ball right back to the Cowboys. Fourroux led McNeese on a 69-yard drive, capping the march on a 14-yard scramble to increase his team's lead to 24-10.

Northwestern scored on a 28-yard pass from John Hundley to Dudley Guice with 39 seconds left in the game. An onside kick attempt glanced off one Cowboys player but Mangan ultimately recovered for McNeese, allowing MSU to hold on for the victory.

McNeese moved into a first-place tie with Texas State at 4-2 in the Southland while moving to 7-3 overall. Northwestern state dropped to 3-3 in the conference and 6-5 overall.

Although they were two teams out of the Southland race, Southeastern Louisiana and Sam Houston State provided late-game fireworks in their conference encounter in Huntsville.

The Lions trailed 10-0 and halftime before scoring 14 points in the third quarter to take the lead as the teams were starting to warm up offensively. Sam Houston State regained the lead by the end of the quarter on a 76-yard bomb from Bomar to Houston. Bomar ended up throwing for 506 yards in the game.

A 34-yard field goal by Turner was countered by a 16-yard run by Aston to give the Bearkats a 24-17 lead with 3:14 left in the game. Aston's touchdown was set up by a Babin fumble. Lucas helped Babin redeem himself three plays later when the SLU running back turned a screen pass into a 60-yard touchdown to tie the score at 24-24. The Bearkats had a chance to win the game in regulation but Connors, the big-play defensive back for the Lions, blocked a 32-yard field goal attempt by Taylor Wilkins.

SHSU got the ball first in the overtime period but had to settle for a 30-yard Wilkins field goal and a 27-24 lead. Cryer gained 10 yards on an end-around before Lucas carried for a yard. On the next play, Babin tossed the ball into the left corner of the end zone. Wilson hauled in Babin's throw to give Southeastern a 30-27 win and the Lions' first conference road win since 2005.

The win ended a three-game losing skid for SLU, which improved to 5-6 overall and 2-4 in the Southland. The Bearkats fell to 4-5 overall and 2-4 in the league.

Sam Houston State seemed poised to play spoiler in Texas State's quest for the Southland Conference title, jumping out to a 14-0 lead in the Bearkats' season finale at home.

A 4-yard touchdown run by Aston and a 25-yard pass from Bomar to Payne made it 14-0 after one quarter. Bomar hooked up with Jason Madkins on a 20-yard touchdown pass early in the second quarter to give the Bearkats a three-touchdown lead.

Texas State put itself back in the game, rallying for the final 13 points of the second quarter to trail 21-13 going to the break. A 14-yard touchdown pass from George to John Gilley and a pair of Ireland field goals tightened up the contest.

After Bomar's 14-yard touchdown run to open the scoring in the third quarter, the Bobcats went on another scoring spree. It started with Bush's 79-yard kickoff return for a touchdown following Bomar's score. A 91-yard bomb from George to Zwinggi and a 3-yard Bush run gave Texas State the lead at 35-28 going into the fourth quarter.

Alvin Canady's 2-yard touchdown run broke a 35-35 tie and gave the Bobcats a seven-point edge with only 1:08 remaining in the fourth quarter.

The Bearkats responded as Bomar tossed the final touchdown of his career, a 27-yard pass to a leaping Madkins in the end zone with four seconds left in regulation to force overtime.

SHSU got the ball first in overtime and had to settle for a 32-yard field goal and a 45-42 lead.

After a 6-yard pass on first down, Bush got the call on four-consecutive carries. His first three advanced the Bobcats to the 5-yard line. On third-and-2 from the 5, Bush ran wide on a pitch from George for the touchdown that gave the Bobcats a 48-45 triumph and the Southland Conference's automatic bid to the playoffs.

A 387-yard, three-touchdown performance by Bomar was not enough to stop the Bearkats from ending their season at 4-6 overall, 2-5 in the Southland.

Texas State finished 5-2 and 8-4 overall to advance to the playoffs.

McNeese went into the season finale at Central Arkansas with a chance to share the Southland Conference title with Texas State with a Bobcats loss while the Bears tried to prove who the best team was the conference, postseason berths notwithstanding. The Bears might not have been playoff bound but a win over the Cowboys would mean Central Arkansas finished the year with the best record in the conference.

The Bears led 20-14 at halftime when Whitehead raced 57 yards with a pass from Fourroux but the receiver fumbled before crossing the goal line when hit and the ball was recovered by Central Arkansas in the end zone.

Instead of a potential one-point McNeese lead, the Bears marched for a touchdown on the ensuing drive with Brown scoring on a 35-yard run to give Central Arkansas a 27-14 cushion.

"It was the play of the game. We had a young man that didn't give up on the play. Anthony Gambles, our backside corner, stripped (Whitehead) at the goal line," said Conque.

After McNeese scored on a 24-yard pass from Fourroux to Bernardo Henry for a touchdown, Brown hit Branson with an 18-yard strike to make the score 33-21.

The touchdown toss was No. 100 for Brown in a career that saw him throw for 10,000 yards.

Trailing 40-21 going into the fourth quarter, the Cowboys came up with a safety and a 15-yard interception return for a touchdown by Allen Nelson to rally within 10 points at 40-30 before Grimes scored on a 4-yard run with 7:34 left in the game to give Central Arkansas a 47-30 victory.

The result allowed Texas State to capture the Southland Conference's automatic bid to the playoffs. McNeese finished the season 7-4 overall, including

4-3 in league play. The Bears ended the year with a lot of satisfaction to go along with a 10-2 overall record and a conference-best 6-1 league mark.

"Officially, they gave it to Texas State, who we had beaten on the road earlier in the year. It was an unfortunate set of events for us down the stretch," Conque said.

Unofficially, the Bears proved their point.

"They fly a banner in Conway, Arkansas, the conference-championship team. They've got rings and it's noted in the media guide," said Conque.

Northwestern State went into its season finale at Stephen F. Austin with a chance to win the Southland Conference under a convoluted scenario. Northwestern could have shared the title with a win at SFA, a McNeese loss to Central Arkansas and a Texas State loss to Sam Houston State.

Had all that happened, the Demons would share the title and receive the automatic bid to the playoffs if Nicholls State also beat Southeastern Louisiana.

Things didn't go their way, but the Demons still played like they were trying to do their part against Stephen F. Austin. A 39-yard interception return by Gary Riggs less than two minutes into the game gave Northwestern a 7-0 lead. SFA tied the game moments later on a 1-yard run by Contrevious Parks but a 74-yard bomb from Calvin Stoker to Guice 15 seconds later gave the Demons a 14-7 lead after one quarter.

Northwestern extended the lead to 21-7 early in the second quarter on a 3-yard run by Hundley. After the Lumberjacks answered on a 60-yard Tarrent run, a 20-yard Weeks field goal on the final play of the period put the Demons on top 24-14 at intermission.

Following a trade of field goals in the third quarter, an 18-yard Endsley touchdown put Northwestern on top 34-17. Moses, who threw for 241 yards but with four interceptions, connected with Edison from 16 yards out with 2:12 left in the game to make the final 34-24. The catch allowed Edison to set a new conference record with 28 touchdown receptions.

The Demons did their job with the win, but not all the scenarios played out in Northwestern State's favor so there would be no playoffs as Northwestern finished the season 4-3 in the Southland and 7-5 overall. SFA ended the year 2-5 in the conference and 4-8 overall.

Meanwhile, teams playing out the string met when Southeastern Louisiana closed the 2008 season at Nicholls State.

The Lions found themselves behind 35-7 early in the fourth quarter before starting to rally. Nicholls led 21-7 at halftime on a pair of touchdown runs by Trey Hopson and 12-yard touchdown pass by Bunch.

Leading by 21 points, a 3-yard run by Bunch early in the fourth quarter gave the Colonels what seemed like an insurmountable 35-7 advantage. Lucas, who was held to 19 yards rushing, hauled in an 18-yard touchdown pass from Babin for the Lions' first points since the middle of the second quarter. A 20-yard fumble return for a touchdown by Quinten Pierre and a 3-yard touchdown pass from Mike Neville to Cole Wardell made it 35-28 with 5:08 left in the game.

SLU got the ball back with 3:07 left in the game and reached the Nicholls 40 before Babin was sacked on fourth down to end the Lions' comeback hopes.

The loss ended Southeastern's season at 5-7 overall and 2-5 in the Southland, while Nicholls finished 3-6 overall and 3-4 in the SLC.

Texas State earned a trip north to take on fourth-seeded Montana, a perennial Football Championship Subdivision power, in the opening round of the playoffs.

Texas State got off to a quick start in a game played in a steady drizzle, jumping out to a 10-0 lead in the first quarter. Ireland drilled a 47-yard field goal and George connected with Luke on a 16-yard touchdown strike to give the Bobcats the early advantage.

The Bobcats maintained their 10-point cushion until the closing moments of the first half. Montana marched 89 yards with quarterback Cole Bergquist hitting Marc Mariani with a 14-yard touchdown pass to make it 10-7 at intermission.

Montana scored on its first three drives of the second half to put the game away. Bergquist scored on a 21-yard run to put the Grizzlies on top for the first time. Chase Reynolds capped the next two drives on touchdown runs of 4 and 1 yard to stretch the Montana lead to 28-13. Reynolds finished with 233 yards, becoming the first Montana runner to top 200 yards in a playoff game.

The only points for Texas State in the second half came on a field goal as the Bobcats were eliminated 31-13. The 13 points were the fewest by Texas State all season and well below the Bobcats' seasonal average of 38.3, which was the fourth best in the nation.

Texas State concluded the 2008 season at 8-5.

Northwestern State brought back a familiar face in 2009.

Bradley Dale Peveto, the architect of some stout Northwestern State defenses during his tenure as the team's defensive coordinator from 1996-98, returned as the Demons' new head coach. Following his original tenure at Northwestern State, Peveto served as an assistant at Houston, Middle Tennessee and LSU. He was LSU's co-defensive coordinator in 2008.

Peveto and his Demons made their 2009 Southland Conference debut at home against Central Arkansas still seeking their first win of the season. The

Peveto era started with four-straight losses to Houston, Grambling, North Dakota and Baylor.

Central Arkansas entered the game with a 3-1 record.

The Bears set the tone early when Jackie Hinton scored on a 48-yard end-around for a 7-0 Bears lead slightly more than two minutes into the game. The score remained the same until Brent Grimes completed a 5-yard halfback pass to quarterback Robbie Park to cap a 68-yard drive with 4:59 remaining before halftime to give Central Arkansas a 14-0 lead at the break.

Two Eddie Carmona field goals in the third quarter made the score 20-0 before the Bears put the game away in the final period. Park connected on touchdown passes of 46 yards to Dominique Croom and 58 yards to Isaiah Jackson as the 34-0 UCA victory kept the Demons winless at 0-5.

Peveto's defense had a long way to go to match the unit he had during his initial tenure at Northwestern State. Giving up an average of 44.6 points per game through five outings, the 34 points surrendered to Central Arkansas represented the second-fewest points the Demons allowed in a game. The fewest points allowed came in a 27-20 loss to North Dakota.

Like Central Arkansas, Stephen F. Austin and McNeese State were off to 3-1 starts heading into Southland play at Nacogdoches.

The Lumberjacks did all the scoring in the first half with quarterback Jeremy Moses tossing a 19-yard touchdown pass to Gralyn Crawford in the first quarter and a 1-yard run by Williams early in the second quarter to give SFA a 14-0 halftime lead.

McNeese got back in the game by limiting the Lumberjacks to 58 total yards over the final two quarters. The only points SFA was able to manage in the second half was a safety early in the fourth quarter.

A 5-yard touchdown run by Champlain Babin, playing in place of an injured Toddrick Pendland, gave McNeese its first six points of the game with only 16 seconds remaining in the third quarter.

After a safety made the score 16-6, Babin scored again, this time on a 31-yard pass from Derrick Fourroux with six minutes left in the game as the Cowboys trailed 16-13.

Needing a field goal to force overtime, the Cowboys reached the Stephen F. Austin 43-yard line, only to lose the ball on a fumble with 50 seconds remaining in the contest.

"We punted and they had the ball at their 1-yard line that last drive," Harper remembered. "They drove it beyond the 50 and created a fumble defensively and got the ball back and won the game. That was kind of the start of everything we did at Stephen F. Austin."

Texas State and Southeastern Louisiana both were 2-2 when the two teams hooked up to open SLC play in San Marcos.

Taking advantage of a bit of creative scheduling, Southeast Louisiana opened the 2009 season with a 2-0 record for the first time in five years. The Lions dominated their competition, defeating Division II Texas A&M-Commerce 41-7 and Division III Union College 69-20 in a pair of home games. SLU lost its next two games to Ole Miss and South Dakota. The 52-6 defeat against the Rebels was particularly costly as the Lions lost ball-hawking safety Tommy Connors with a broken thumb.

Another lopsided loss seemed in the offing for the Lions as Southeastern Louisiana fell behind 38-20 going into the fourth quarter against Texas State. The Lions put themselves back in the game, however, with a 24-point fourth quarter.

Texas State put the first points on the board in the final quarter of regulation on a 6-yard run by Karrington Bush for a 44-20 lead. Brian Babin, who threw four touchdown passes in the game, tossed scoring strikes of 24 yards to Merrick Lanaux and 14 yards to Simmie Yarborough to make it 44-36 with 4:51 left in the game. The Lions defense held, giving the ball back to the offense at the Bobcats' 34. Facing fourth-and-15, Lanaux hauled in a pass from Babin while draped by two defenders at the 1-yard line. Jasper Ducksworth scored from a yard out one play later with 34 seconds left in the game. Yarborough scored on a pitch for the two-point conversion to force overtime.

Yarborough scored from 2 yards out on the opening possession of overtime to give the Lions a 51-44 lead. Texas State countered when quarterback Bradley George found Da'Marcus Griggs in the back of the end zone for a 12-yard touchdown. Justin Garelick missed the extra point, giving Southeastern an improbable 51-50 triumph.

Other than winless Northwestern State, Nicholls State was the only other team below .500 entering the opening weekend of Southland Conference play when the Colonels visited Sam Houston State. Nicholls was 1-3 on the season with its lone win against Duquesne. At Air Force, the Falcons showed their option attack was a lot more proficient than that of Nicholls in a 72-0 rout.

Sam Houston State, meanwhile, entered SLC play 2-2.

Against Nicholls, the Bearkats saw a 17-14 halftime lead turn into a 21-17 deficit when Colonels fullback Trey Hopson scored on a 1-yard run early in the third quarter.

Sam Houston State controlled the rest of the game, scoring the final 27 points to pull away. Blake Joseph factored in three of the Bearkats' final four touchdowns. He scored on runs of 6 and 17 yards in the third quarter as SHSU took a 31-21 lead heading into the fourth quarter. Joseph tossed an 11-yard touchdown pass to Chris Lucas before James Aston scored the last of his three touchdowns on a 20-yard run with slightly more than four minutes remaining in the contest.

After Aston's first touchdown gave Sam Houston State a 7-0 lead, Nicholls State's A.J. Williams raced 77 yards along the sideline before fumbling going into the end zone. An alert Antonio Robinson pounced on the ball in the end zone and the receiver's recovery tied the game.

Sam Houston State outscored the Colonels 10-7 in the second quarter on an 18-yard run by Aston and a Miguel Antonio field goal to lead 17-14 at the break. Robinson hauled in a 68-yard touchdown pass from LaQuintin Caston for Nicholls' lone score of the period.

Stephen F. Austin and Central Arkansas sported identical records of 4-1 overall and 1-0 in Southland Conference play when the teams met a week later in a key early league game on the Bears' home field.

The teams proved to be as evenly matched as their records with the game going down to the wire. Moses and Aaron Rhea got the best of Central Arkansas early in the game. The duo hooked up on touchdown passes of 14 and 12 yards while all the Bears could manage was a Carmona field goal as SFA built the biggest lead of the contest for either team at 14-3 early in the second quarter.

Before he was done, Moses tossed a total of three touchdown passes. The three scoring passes gave him 66 for his career, making him SFA's career leader by only the midway point of his junior season.

A 7-yard run by Grimes allowed Central Arkansas to make the score 14-10 at halftime and a 27-yard Carmona field goal early in the third quarter left the Bears behind by a single point.

From that point on, each team answered each others' scores but the Bears were never able to pull on top. UCA finally managed to tie the game when Park hit Preston Echols with a 44-yard touchdown strike with 59 seconds left in the game to even things up at 30-30.

Like the Lumberjacks had done throughout the game, they answered Central Arkansas' score. Evan Engwall connected on a 35-yard field goal with three seconds left in the game to eke out a 33-30 triumph for Stephen F. Austin.

If not for a distraction, the game might have gone into overtime instead of SFA winning in regulation.

"I had gotten into a discussion with the referee and before I really knew it, we already were moving the ball down the field," recalled Harper. "Jeremy had done a good job of pushing the ball down the field. We probably just would have gone into overtime if I hadn't been in discussion with that official. I was really kind of glad I had the discussion with the referee because when I finally looked up, we drove to midfield and Jeremy took a shot down the field and Aaron Rhea made an incredible one-handed catch and Evan Engwall, a true freshman, went out there and kicked the field goal and won the game."

In Hammond, whenever Sam Houston State's Joseph connected with Jason Madkins on a touchdown pass, Southeastern Louisiana answered with a flurry in the Lions' Southland Conference home opener against the Bearkats.

Joseph hit Madkins with a 16-yard touchdown pass to give the Bearkats a 7-0 lead. SLU responded by scoring the final 20 points of the first half on two Jeff Turner field goals and a pair of short touchdown passes from Babin to Yarborough. Joseph and Madkins drew first blood for SHSU in the second half on a 4-yard pass midway in the third quarter to make it 20-14. Southeastern followed with three scores, including a 52-yard touchdown reception by Yarborough. The Lions receiver finished the game with eight catches for 151 yards. Ashton returned the ensuing kickoff 89 yards for a touchdown to make the final 37-21.

SLU moved to 2-0 in conference play for the first time since 2005 and 4-2 overall with the win. Sam Houston State fell to 3-3 overall and 1-1 in the SLC.

Meanwhile, Babin helped McNeese State get off to a quick start in the Cowboys' 51-23 win over visiting Northwestern State.

The freshman tailback capped the Cowboys' opening drive of the game with a 30-yard touchdown run. He added a 10-yard run minutes later as McNeese went on to build a 16-3 lead in the opening quarter. A 19-yard run by Jaravaris Murry and a 45-yard toss from Fourroux to Chad Davis made it 30-3 at halftime.

"Babin came in and had a really good game. We went through a little stretch without Pendland but I remember being real proud of Champlain. Champlain and Jaravaris Murray kind of ended up being the two backs. They were both freshmen and did really good," recalled McNeese coach Matt Viator.

Fourroux added two more touchdown passes in the second half, including a 19-yard strike to Babin.

The defense got into the scoring act for the Cowboys when Desmund Lighten returned a fumble 29 yards for a touchdown early in the fourth quarter.

Northwestern State's lone score in the first half came on a 30-yard John Shaughnessy field goal in the first quarter. Demons quarterback John Hundley accounted for two touchdowns, one on a 14-yard pass to Bradley Brown and the other on an 11-yard run.

McNeese improved to 1-1 in the SLC and 4-2 overall while the Demons dropped their sixth-straight game.

An opportunistic Texas State team, meanwhile, converted three first-half miscues by Nicholls State into a 24-7 lead on the Bobcats' way to a 34-28 road win.

Texas State turned a Nicholls fumble on the Colonels' opening possession into a quick 3-0 lead on a Garelick field goal. Leading 10-7, the Bobcats converted the Colonels' next turnover into a 4-yard Bush touchdown to push their advantage to 10 points.

The Colonels fumbled the ball on the ensuing kickoff, giving possession back to Texas State at the Nicholls 11. A 10-yard touchdown strike from George to Woody McClendon made it 24-3.

Trailing 24-14 at halftime, the Colonels got right back in the game at the start of the second half. Williams broke loose on a 70-yard scamper down to the Texas State 1-yard line on the second play of the third quarter. Caston followed with a touchdown run to pull Nicholls to within three points at 24-21.

Texas State answered on the next drive, using 13 plays to set up a 26-yard Garelick field goal and a 27-21 advantage. A 6-yard touchdown pass by George less than minute into the fourth quarter made it 34-21 before Nicholls scored on a 10-yard run by Williams with less than three minutes remaining to account for the final margin.

The Bobcats improved to 2-0 in the Southland and 3-3 overall. Nicholls dropped to 0-2 in the conference with the loss and 1-5 overall.

Stephen F. Austin continued to roll with a one-sided 42-3 home win over Sam Houston State a week later for the Lumberjacks' sixth-consecutive victory.

Moses passed for 372 yards and five touchdowns as SFA routed the Bearkats. The Lumberjacks' quarterback tossed a pair of touchdown passes to Rhea while also hooking up with Brandon Scott, Contrevious Parks and Duane Brooks for scores.

The big numbers for Moses were becoming routine but the Lumberjacks quarterback took it all in stride.

"The statistics was always something that was mentioned around here, especially with the media department," said Moses. "It was something I never put too much weight in throughout my playing career. I was more focused on trying to the the 'W' and get a conference championship for my team. Whatever stats I had to do to put us in that position is what I had to do. I never paid attention with the numbers that went along with it."

Sam Houston State, which had a five-game winning streak over the Lumberjacks snapped, got its only points on a 23-yard Antonio field goal.

SFA moved to 3-0 in the Southland Conference and 6-1 overall. The Bearkats dropped to 1-2 in the league and 3-4 overall.

Southeast Louisiana's quest to make it three-in-a-row in Southland Conference play looked grim when the Lions fell behind 24-7 in the first half of their game at McNeese State. SLU managed to make it 24-14 at the break on a 4-yard touchdown pass from Babin to Chris Wilson.

The Lions picked up where they left off at the end of the opening half, scoring 21 third-quarter points. A 1-yard sneak by Babin made it 24-21 less than three minutes into the second half. Special teams set up the next score when Wes Ladner blocked a punt that was returned by Clint Coleman to the McNeese 1-yard line. Zeke Jones scored on the first play from scrimmage to give the Lions their first lead of the game at 28-24. Ladner was the man on the spot once again, this time recovering a muffed punt to set up a 3-yard touchdown reception by Wilson and a 35-24 lead.

Javaris Murray's 2-yard touchdown run moved the Cowboys to within a touchdown at 35-30 early in the fourth quarter. SLU had a chance to extend the lead to eight points but Turner missed a 38-yard field goal with 3:18 left in the game. That opened the door for the Cowboys, who used receptions of 17 yards to Davis and 20 yards to Immanual Friddle to advance to the Lions' 41. A personal foul call against Southeastern and a 17-yard Fourroux run set the stage for the quarterback's 5-yard touchdown toss to Richard Conner in the back of the end zone with 39 seconds left in the game for a 36-35 McNeese victory.

Both teams moved to 2-1 in the Southland Conference with the outcome, while McNeese improved to 5-2 overall and Southeastern fell to 4-3.

In Conway, Nicholls State was unable to contain Grimes in a 42-13 loss to Central Arkansas.

Grimes rushed for 142 yards and three touchdowns. His 36-yard score in the first quarter and an 18-yard run in the second helped the Bears take a 35-6 halftime lead. Grimes added a 42-yard gallop in the third quarter.

Robinson scored both touchdowns for Nicholls on a 41-yard touchdown reception in the second quarter and a 42-yard run in the fourth.

UCA improved to 2-1 in the Southland and 5-2 overall with the win. Nicholls fell to 0-3 in the conference and 1-6 overall.

When William Griffin scored on a 28-yard touchdown run to give Northwestern State a 17-14 lead at home against Texas State in Southland Conference play, the Demons were only 11:49 away from their first win of the season.

Garelick's 29-yard field goal for Texas State tied the game at 17-17 but at least the Demons were 7:26 away from going to overtime. Not even that was to happen when the snakebit Demons saw Garelick boot a 21-yard field goal with 1:55 left in the game for a 20-17 Bobcats victory.

The Demons trailed 14-3 early in the third quarter before a 14-yard run by Phil Harris pulled Northwestern State to within four points going into the fourth quarter before Griffin's touchdown early in the final period gave Northwestern its momentary lead.

Northwestern fell for the seventh-consecutive game while Texas State improved to 2-1 in the Southland and 4-3 overall.

Stephen F. Austin's potent offense met its match in the Lumberjacks' Southland Conference encounter at Texas State.

The Lumberjacks were held to a single score while Texas State's George was a passing fancy as Stephen F. Austin suffered its first SLC loss of the season in a 28-7 defeat.

A 9-yard touchdown pass from George to Mischak Rivas accounted for the only score in the first half. Like Texas State, the Lumberjacks were stout on defense in the early going. That allowed SFA to hang around and tie the game 7-7 on an 11-yard pass from Moses to Duane Brooks midway in the third quarter.

Texas State regained the lead at 14-7 with 16 seconds remaining in the third quarter on an 8-yard touchdown pass from George to Alvaro Garcia.

George, who passed for 324 yards and set a new Texas State record with 31 completions, tossed touchdown passes of 17 yards to Griggs and 32 yards to Rivas in the final four minutes of the game to make the final 28-7.

The outcome left both teams 3-1 in the SLC. Stephen F. Austin dropped to 6-2 overall as its six-game winning streak came to an end. Texas State improved to 5-3 overall.

"We were 3-0 and lost to Texas State, but really, it was good to be able to look ourselves in the mirror and know what we really are as a football team and what we really have to do to get a 'W,'" said Moses.

A pair of teams took advantage of SFA's loss to Texas State to force a four-way tie for first place in the Southland Conference.

One of those teams was McNeese State, which jumped out to a 24-10 halftime lead and cruised to a 38-27 win at Nicholls State.

A pair of short Pendland runs gave the Cowboys a 14-0 lead after one quarter. Following an 8-yard run by Williams early in the second quarter for the Colonels' first points of the game, McNeese closed the period with a 7-yard pass from Fourroux to Murray and a 32-yard Josh Lewis field goal for a two-touchdown advantage.

McNeese took advantage of excellent field position, scoring on five of seven possessions that began inside Colonels territory.

Nicholls fullback Marlin Meeks, who scored the game's final touchdown on a 2-yard run with 5:26 remaining in the contest, led all rushers with 143 yards on the ground.

McNeese improved to 3-1 in the SLC and 6-2 overall. Nicholls remained winless in conference play at 0-4 while dropping to 1-7 overall.

Southeastern Louisiana also had a chance to force its way into a first-place tie with a home win over Central Arkansas. That assignment, however, seemed a tough one as SLU had to play the game without several key players. Babin was ruled out only moments before the game because of a shoulder injury. Injures also caused the Lions to play without Yarborough and Lanaux, the team's top two receivers. Throw in a strong north wind and a quarterback making his first start since his high school days four years earlier and the task seemed daunting, indeed.

None of that seemed to matter to quarterback Tyler Beatty. Subbing for Babin, he took advantage of the wind to produce 10 first-quarter points for the Lions. Beatty helped guide SLU to a 48-yard field goal and his 61-yard touchdown strike to Chris Wilson gave Southeastern its 10-point advantage.

When the wind favored the Bears in the second quarter, Central Arkansas responded with three of Carmona's four field goals in the game. Beatty tossed his second touchdown of the game when he hooked up with Kory Theodore on a 13-yard toss to give the Lions a 17-9 halftime edge.

Central Arkansas produced the only points of the third quarter on a 6-yard Grimes touchdown run and another Carmona field goal to give the Bears their first lead of the game at 19-17.

The big break of the game came midway in the fourth quarter when Lions defender Re'Keem Wilson returned a Park interception down to the Central Arkansas 28. Beatty, who threw for 297 yards in the game, found Chris Wilson in the corner of the end zone from 16 yards out for the go-ahead touchdown. A two-point conversion pass put Southeastern Louisiana on top 25-19 with 8:18 left in the game. The Bears managed to reach the SLU 9 in the closing moments, but another Re'Keem Wilson interception, this one in the end zone, ended the threat. A safety with 18 seconds remaining accounted for the 25-21 final.

SLU joined McNeese State, Stephen F. Austin and Texas State atop the Southland standings at 3-1 as the Lions moved to 5-3 overall.

While just about everyone else seemed to be in first place in the Southland, Northwestern State's quest for its first victory continued. If Northwestern was going to fall to 0-8 with a loss at Sam Houston State, at least the Demons were going to go down fighting.

In an affair that featured eight lead changes, Harris' 8-yard touchdown pass to Griffin with 1:35 remaining in the third quarter provided the seventh lead change. The fourth touchdown pass for the Demons quarterback gave Northwestern State a 30-27 edge.

The Bearkats regained the lead one more time when Madkins turned a pass from Joseph into a 39-yard score for a 34-30 SHSU advantage with 5:37 left in the game.

Facing third-and-11 with less than four minutes left in the game, Harris scrambled for the needed first-down yardage but fumbled when hit from behind with 3:19 showing on the clock. With 1:30 left in the contest, Harris heaved a pass that was intercepted by Darnell Taylor near midfield to preserve the four-point Bearkats victory.

A low-scoring first quarter gave way to a second quarter that featured a combined 34 points. Northwestern led 7-3 after one quarter before the teams traded field goals to open the second period. The teams traded two touchdowns each the remainder of the quarter.

The Bearkats scored on a 65-yard run by Joseph and the quarterback's 13-yard pass to Madkins. Harris countered with touchdown throws of 20 and 32 yards to Justin Aldredge, leaving the Demons with a 23-20 halftime edge.

Northwestern fell to 0-8 while Sam Houston State evened its Southland mark at 2-2 and its overall record at 4-4.

All four teams tied for first place in the Southland won the following week, meaning the weaning-down process to determine the 2009 conference champion would go down to the final two weeks of the season.

Stephen F. Austin, which allowed everyone else back in the Southland race with its costly loss to Texas State, had to fight off a pesky Nicholls State squad to get back to its winning ways.

The Colonels played a rare turnover-free game and amassed 434 yards but it still wasn't enough to hold off the Lumberjacks in SFA's 31-27 victory.

Nicholls and SFA traded scores in the opening quarter as the Colonels took a 21-14 lead after one period of play. Caston, Williams and Meeks had rushing touchdowns in the first quarter. Meeks, who rushed for 143 yards against McNeese a week earlier, followed up his effort with 144 against the Lumberjacks. Meeks rushed for 117 of his yards in the opening quarter.

A 9-yard pass from Caston to Robinson with 19 seconds left in the third quarter gave Nicholls a 27-21 lead.

The Colonels forced four turnovers but were unable to stop a Lumberjacks rally. Engwall's 27-yard field goal pulled SFA to within three points at 27-24.

Moses, who threw for 366 yards and four touchdowns, saved his best for last. His 6-yard strike to Brooks with 2:45 left in the game gave the Lumberjacks the 31-27 victory.

The Lumberjacks improved to 4-1 in the SLC and 7-2 overall while Nicholls dropped to 0-5 in the conference and 1-8 through nine games.

Southeastern Louisiana also took advantage of another winless team in SLC play with a 27-0 blanking of Northwestern State. The shutout by the Lions' defense was the first for Southeastern since the school brought back football in 2003.

With Babin back in control of the SLU offense, the Lions exploded for 24 first-half points. Babin, who threw three touchdowns in the game, fired two in the final 30 seconds of the half to turn a 10-0 lead into a 24-0 blowout by intermission. The first of the two late touchdown passes in the second quarter was a 48-yard bomb to Theodore with 30 seconds left before intermission. Jamaal White fumbled the ensuing kickoff after a jarring hit by linebacker Kendrick Jackson, with Ryan Godare recovering at the Northwestern State 21. A 10-yard screen pass to Ducksworth with five seconds remaining made it 24-0. The only points in the second half came on a 36-yard Turner field goal late in the third quarter.

While the Demons remained winless, SLU stayed in the Southland race at 4-1 while improving to 6-3 overall.

Texas State, the team that created the logjam atop the Southland with its win a week earlier over SFA, needed a 24-yard touchdown pass from George to Darius Bolden with 27 seconds left in the game to keep pace in the conference with a 27-24 triumph at Central Arkansas.

In a game that featured six lead changes, the Bears took their final lead with 1:40 left in the contest on a 2-yard run by Grimes as Central Arkansas edged ahead 24-20. Needing a touchdown for the win, the Bobcats drove 50 yards, culminating in Bolden's touchdown reception.

Texas State led 6-3 after one quarter in a game in which neither team led by more than six points. A 6-yard touchdown run by Park gave the Bears their first lead of the game at 10-6 before the Bobcats gained a three-point halftime edge of 13-10 on a 15-yard pass from George to Rivas.

The Bobcats moved to 4-1 in the SLC and 6-3 overall. Central Arkansas dropped to 2-3 in the conference and 5-4 overall.

Also keeping pace was McNeese State with a 63-42 victory over visiting Sam Houston State.

Back in top form after being hobbled with injuries the previous two games, Pendland rushed for 171 yards and four touchdowns. As it turned out, the Cowboys needed all of the running back's touchdowns and then some in McNeese State's high-scoring affair against Sam Houston State.

The combined 105 points was the highest-scoring game in McNeese history.

Pendland scored on runs of 31 and 14 yards in the first quarter and added an 8-yard trot in the second to give McNeese a 28-14 halftime lead. The Bearkats matched Pendland's two first-quarter touchdowns on a 1-yard run by Chris Poullard and a 23-yard pass from Joseph to Lucas in the first quarter before being blanked the remainder of the half.

The McNeese runner added a 23-yard score in the third quarter as the Cowboys led 42-28 going into the fourth quarter. The two teams combined for 35 fourth-quarter points with the biggest play being a 76-yard run by Babin.

McNeese improved to 4-1 in the Southland and 7-2 overall. SHSU dropped to 2-3 in the conference and 4-5 overall.

All four teams atop the Southland Conference were in action against one another a week later, meaning the tie at the top of the SLC would be pared down to two contenders.

Playing at home against Stephen F. Austin, Southeastern Louisiana was looking to remain in the hunt for a first conference title since 1961.

SFA, meanwhile, showed it meant business on the opening drive, using 12 plays to travel 77 yards. The drive was capped on a 13-yard pass from Moses to Rhea. A 2-yard run by Vincent Pervis late in the first quarter and a 32-yard touchdown reception by Brandon Scott early in the second quarter gave the Lumberjacks a 21-0 lead.

For the second time in three weeks, Beatty got the start in place of an ailing Babin. Unlike the Central Arkansas game, there would be no magic performance by the backup quarterback. When SFA built its 21-0 lead, the Lions were still without their initial first down and Beatty was replaced by Babin. The only points SLU could produce in the first half was a Turner field goal as the Lions trailed 28-3 at the break.

Babin had little success as well, being sacked six times and losing three fumbles. The only touchdown Southeastern produced in the game occurred when receiver Greg Johnson tossed a 27-yard touchdown to Yarborough on a reverse in the fourth quarter as the Lumberjacks went on to take a 41-10 victory.

Stephen F. Austin improved to 5-1 in the SLC and 8-2 overall. Southeastern Louisiana fell to 4-2 in the conference and 6-4 overall.

Texas State and No. 10 McNeese State entered their encounter both needing a win to keep pace with Stephen F. Austin in the conference race.

The score was tied 20-20 at halftime as Pendland, who rushed for 187 yards, and Texas State's Alvin Canady each rushed for two touchdowns in the opening half of play.

Pendland broke the tie on a 5-yard run, his third touchdown of the game, with 4:03 remaining in the third quarter. Canady countered with his third score of the contest to tie things up again at 27-27 less than a minute later.

Lewis provided the game-winning points when he kicked a 28-yard field goal with 1:30 left in the game to give the Cowboys a 30-27 triumph.

It was a milestone game for Fourroux. He was 17 of 23 passing for 222 yards and a touchdown. His 7,951 passing yards, 583 completions, 1,931 yards rushing and 91 combined rushing and passing touchdowns all established new McNeese career marks for quarterbacks.

McNeese's fifth-consecutive win improved the Cowboys to 8-2 on the season. Texas State fell to 4-2 in the conference and 6-4 overall.

Among non-contenders, Sam Houston State edged visiting Central Arkansas 17-14 to improve to 3-3 in the Southland. The Bears slipped to 2-4 in the SLC as the result left both teams 5-5 overall.

After allowing more than 600 yards and 63 points a week earlier against McNeese State, the Bearkats' defense was out for redemption in Sam Houston State's home finale against Central Arkansas.

The Bearkats needed a good defensive effort in light of the fact the Sam Houston State offense also was not as efficient as it was a week earlier. After scoring 42 points in a losing effort to McNeese, all SHSU could produce in the first half against the Bears was a mere field goal to trail 7-3 at the break.

With the offense struggling and the defense tying its hardest, the Bearkats special teams decided to lend a helping hand. SHSU forced Central Arkansas to punt from the Bearkats' 49 early in the third quarter. Vincent Dotson blocked Jonathan Beard's punt and scooted 36 yards for a touchdown to give Sam Houston State a 10-7 advantage.

Finally able to mount one of the few drives of the game, the Bearkats marched 54 yards. Poullard went wide on an option pitch for 11 yards down to the 1-yard line. He scored on the following play to give SHSU a 17-7 lead.

Central Arkansas countered with a 3-yard touchdown run by Grimes to leave the Bears behind by three points.

The Bears managed to get the ball back in the closing moments. Park, the Central Arkansas quarterback, needing to make a play with less than a minute remaining, tossed downfield, only to have his pass picked off by SHSU's Jarvis Pippins, allowing the Bearkats to defeat the Bears for the first time ever.

Someone was finally going to win a Southland Conference game when Northwestern State visited an equally-struggling Nicholls State team. It was the Colonels who came out on top when Nicholls turned to its passing game to snap a seven-game losing streak with a 28-21 victory over the Demons.

Caston tossed a touchdown strike of 82 yards to Robinson and connected with Mike Barba on two other scores. Caston hooked up with Barba on touchdowns of 12 and 64 yards as Nicholls passed for 197 yards.

Along with the offense's performance, Nicholls also got one of its better efforts of the season from the Colonels' defense. The outcome marked only the second time all season the Nicholls defense allowed an opponent less than 30 points in a game. Going into the Northwestern State game, the Colonels were allowing an average of 41.7 points per game.

Mistakes hurt the Demons in their comeback bid.

An apparent touchdown pass from Harris to Aldredge to tie the game 21-21 was called back because of a holding penalty with 12 minutes left in the game.

Instead of a tied game, it became a 14-point lead for Nicholls six minutes later on a 65-yard run by Williams.

An 8-yard touchdown run by Harris pulled Northwestern State to within a touchdown at 28-21 with 4:48 remaining in the game but a final rally attempt for the Demons ended on a Dominic Daniels interception at the Nicholls 15 in the closing moments.

Nicholls improved to 1-5 in the Southland and 2-8 overall. Northwestern remained winless through 10 games, including 0-6 in the SLC.

The main focus of the final weekend of the regular season was McNeese State and Stephen F. Austin both being 6-1 in the Southland with the conference championship on the line.

Before that took place, Nicholls State and Southeastern Louisiana met on Thursday night in a contest that had intrigue beyond the final game of the season. Although nothing was official, word leaked out that the Colonels' game at Southeastern Louisiana would be the last for coach Jay Thomas as Nicholls officials decided to make an offseason coaching change.

Other than trying to send their popular coach out with one final victory, if the Colonels had anything else going for them in closing out a trying season, it was that Nicholls would take on the Lions on a Thursday night. The Colonels seemed to have a special affinity for playing on Thursdays, having won eight of their last 10 such games going into the SLU contest.

Nicholls' running game managed to out-duel SLU's pass-happy offense in a 45-30 victory for the Colonels.

The Colonels rushed for 322 yards and rolled up 447 total yards. Meeks led the Nicholls ground attack with 119 yards. It marked the third time in final four games of his career that the senior topped the 100-yard mark.

SLU's yards came through the air, as usual. Despite nursing a sore shoulder, Babin threw for a career-high 382 yards in his final game in a Southeastern Louisiana uniform.

With SLU leading 13-7, Nicholls defensive back Bobby Felder returned an errant Babin throw 63 yards for a touchdown to put the Colonels on top by a point.

Short touchdown runs by Earvin Moore and Caston could only be countered by a 33-yard Turner field goal as Nicholls increased its lead to 28-16. Felder returned a second interception 44 yards to set up a 32-yard Ross Schexnayder field goal to give the Colonels a 31-16 lead at the break.

Meeks and Caston added touchdown runs in the second half while Babin and Andre Cryer hooked up on a pair of touchdown passes for the 45-30 final.

Nicholls won its final two games of the season to finish 2-5 in the Southland and 3-8 overall. SLU dropped its final two games to close at 4-3 in the conference and 6-5 overall.

Playing with the Southland Conference's automatic bid to the Football Championship Subdivision playoffs on the line, Stephen F. Austin discovered winless Northwestern State still had some fight left in the 2009 regular-season finale.

SFA and Northwestern State were tied 10-10 at halftime before the Lumberjacks nudged ahead 13-10 on a 33-yard Engwall field goal early in the second half. The game remained a three-point affair until Moses hooked up with Cordell Roberson on a 57-yard scoring strike 59 seconds into the second half to give Stephen F. Austin a 19-10 triumph.

The win earned the Lumberjacks a share of the Southland Conference title as SFA posted its first winning season since 2004. Stephen F. Austin finished the season 9-2 overall, including 6-1 in the SLC. Northwestern State ended the year 0-11, including 0-7 in the league.

McNeese State won its final regular-season game against visiting Central Arkansas 21-17 to share the Southland title but the Cowboys missed out on the conference's automatic bid by virtue of their 16-13 head-to-head loss with Stephen F. Austin earlier in the season.

Central Arkansas took a 3-0 lead with a 28-yard Carmona field goal late in the first quarter. An 8-yard run by Fourroux and a 4-yard sprint by Pendland gave McNeese its 14-3 halftime advantage.

Grimes scored on short touchdown runs in the second half while Bernardo Henry broke loose on a 64-yard scamper as the Cowboys went on to capture a share of their 13th conference title.

Pendland scored his 46th touchdown for a school record and increased his points total to 118, a single-single school mark. Fourroux threw for 83 yards and rushed for an additional 50 to give him 10,038 for his career to become the first player in Cowboy history to top 10,000 yards. He also became only the third player in Southland history to reach that milestone.

McNeese finished the 2009 regular at 9-2 overall while Central Arkansas moved to 5-6 overall, while ending 2-5 in the Southland.

In San Marcos, Sam Houston State, needing a win in the final game of the season against Texas State in order to finish the year with a winning record, held a 17-14 halftime lead against the Bobcats.

The teams traded touchdowns until Antonio kicked a 31-yard field goal with slightly more than two minutes remaining in the second quarter for a three-point advantage for Sam Houston State. Prior to Antonio's kick, the Bearkats scored on a 1-yard Poullard run and a 22-yard pass from Joseph to Lucas. Texas State countered with a 48-yard Canady run and a 19-yard pass from George to Daren Dillard.

Antonio kicked a 36-yard field goal early in the third quarter to push the SHSU lead to six points but the Bearkats would not score again.

George hooked up with Griggs on a pair of 13-yard touchdown passes. The first, with 2:41 remaining in the third quarter put Texas State on top 21-20. The second connection, with 8:06 left for a 28-21 Bobcats lead, put the game out of reach.

George, who passed for 322 yards and three touchdowns, closed out his career as Texas State's all-time passer. He finished with 9,556 yards and 76 touchdowns. Griggs set a new school reception record with 80 catches and 969 yards.

The loss cost the Bearkats a winning season. Sam Houston ended the season 5-6 overall and 3-4 in the Southland. Texas State finished 7-4 overall, 5-2 in the SLC.

The Southland Conference co-championship earned McNeese a home game against New Hampshire in the opening round of the Football Championship Subdivision playoffs.

New Hampshire traded a pair of touchdowns with two McNeese field goals to give the Wildcats a 14-6 lead after one quarter. New Hampshire's scores came on a 9-yard pass from quarterback R.J. Toman to Scott Sicko and a 1-yard Toman run. The Cowboys countered with Lewis field goals of 31 and 40 yards. The teams traded touchdowns in the second quarter for a 21-13 Wildcats edge at halftime.

The game turned into a rout in the third quarter. After Toman and Sicko hooked up again on a 9-yard touchdown pass, Terrence Klein returned an errant Fourroux pass 79 yards for a touchdown to give New Hampshire a 35-13 lead going into the fourth quarter.

New Hampshire held the Cowboys scoreless for the remainder of the game while adding two fourth-quarter touchdowns to take a 49-13 win that ended McNeese's season at 9-3.

"The game got out of hand in the second half," said Viator. "The thing I remember is the interception for a touchdown. We had got it to a one-touchdown game again and we are going in to score. Instead of being a one-touchdown game it became a three-touchdown game and that was it."

Stephen F. Austin's 9-2 record earned the Lumberjacks a home game to open the Football Championship Subdivision playoffs against Eastern Washington.

In a game in which the teams combined for 893 passing yards, Moses put on a clinic in the third quarter.

SFA was leading 23-12 early in the third quarter when Moses went to work. He hooked up with Scott on a 4-yard touchdown pass less than four minutes into the second half. Moses and Scott connected later in the quarter on a 19-yard score. After a 20-yard touchdown pass from Eastern Washington quarterback Matt Nichols to Brandon Kaufman, Moses tossed his third touchdown pass of the period to give the Lumberjacks a 44-19 lead on their way to a 44-26 advantage after three quarters.

Moses simply picked part the Eastern Washington defense, completing 20 passes in 24 attempts in the third quarter alone on his way to a 432-yard passing performance.

Nichols, who passed for 461 yards, tossed a 5-yard pass to Nathan Overbay with 9:38 left in the game to make the final 44-33 as the Lumberjacks picked up win No. 10 on the season.

It was Nichols who had the hot hand in the first quarter, completing all but three of his 15 attempts in the opening 15 minutes of play. Unlike Moses' effort in the third quarter, the best Nichols' heroics could do for the Eagles in the opening quarter was a 10-10 tie.

The only points Eastern Washington could produce in the second quarter was a safety. Meanwhile, Moses tossed his first touchdown pass of the game – a 24-yard strike to Roberson – and Engall added a pair of 34-yard field goals in the final three minutes to give SFA a 23-12 halftime lead.

"That was probably the most exciting game I was involved with in my entire coaching career," said Harper. "We had them at our place and Jeremy went toe-to-toe with their quarterback and he came out on top."

Stephen F. Austin had to consider itself lucky after the first quarter of its quarterfinal playoff game at frigid Montana. Moses was intercepted on the opening possession of the game but the Grizzlies failed to produce any points off of the turnover. On the Lumberjacks' next drive, Montana defensive lineman Austin Mullins intercepted a screen pass to set up a 34-yard Brody McKnight field goal. A muffed punt by Brooks at his own 22 set up 3-yard touchdown run by Chase Reynolds to make the score 10-0.

Despite all the early mistakes, the Lumberjacks were only down by 10 points. That was about the only thing that could pass as a bright spot for Stephen F. Austin. By the time the game was over, SFA was guilty of five interceptions and five lost fumbles in a 51-0 blowout loss to the Grizzlies.

The Montana defense continued to play takeaway the entire game and the Grizzles' offense constantly turned Lumberjacks miscues into points.

Going into the game, Montana's pass defense was No. 106 in the nation and a tough task seemed to lie ahead against Moses, the most prolific passer in the FCS who had thrown for slightly less than 4,000 yards and 40 touchdowns. Along with four interceptions, the Grizzles held Moses to 214 yards passing and shut out the nation's top-scoring offense.

The Lumberjacks seemed poised to get back in the game early in the second quarter. SFA marched to the Grizzlies' 2-yard line before Ramont Hampton fumbled. Montana drove 98 yards, capping the drive on a 4-yard run by quarterback Andrew Selle. Selle fired touchdown passes of 14 yards to Marc Mariani, 13 yards to Jabin Sambrano and 11 yards to Steve Pfahler to give the Grizzlies a 38-0 halftime lead and the rout was one.

The intimidating Montana venue claimed yet another victim.

"You hear about it, but getting up there and experiencing it is a totally different deal," said Moses. "They have the greatest home-field advantage, in my mind, within the FCS programs. Game day there is different from anything I've ever seen. It presents a tough environment."

SFA ended the 2009 season 10-3.

SFA'S MOSES WINS WALTER PAYTON AWARD

An unusual occurence took place in the Southland in 2010. Two of the schools in the conference filled head coaching positions by hiring a head coach and assistant from the same school from outside the league in the same year.

Willie Fritz was named the new coach at Sam Houston State. A former Bearkats graduate assistant, Fritz served as head coach at Blinn College and Central Missouri before being named the Sam Houston State coach. Fritiz coached Central Missouri from 1997 to 2009, leading the Mules to their first postseason appearance in 32 years with a victory over Minnesota-Deluth in the 2001 Mineral Water Bowl. His 2002 team won the Mid-America Athletic Association title.

Charlie Stubbs, Fritz's assistant at Central Missouri, was named the new coach at Nicholls State. The Nicholls job was his first as a collegiate head coach. Stubbs had an extensive background as an assistant coach in college. His stops as an assistant coach included Oregon State, Memphis, Tennessee-Martin, Nevada-Las Vegas, Alabama, Tulsa, Louisville and Central Missouri. Stubbs served as offensive coordinator at Central Missouri 2008-09.

McNeese State and Northwestern State kicked off Southland play when the teams met in Natchitoches. Starting the season 1-2, the Cowboys' lone victory came in the season opener against Lamar. McNeese spoiled the return of Lamar, a founding member of the SLC, with a 30-27 victory. It was the first game back for the Cardinals after dropping the program following the 1989 season.

Northwestern State was off to a 1-3 start. After opening the season with losses to Air Force and Samford, the Demons defeated Tarleton State before falling to North Dakota. The victory over Tarleton was the first ever for second-year Northwestern State coach Bradley Dale Peveto. The Demons snapped a 13-game losing streak stretching back to the start of the 2009 season with the victory.

McNeese trailed 7-0 against Northwestern State with the Demons threatening to add another score midway in the second quarter before the Cowboys' defense changed the momentum of the game.

Kentrel Butler's interception of a Tyler Wolfe pass at the McNeese 19-yard line eventually led to a game-tying 1-yard run by Jacob Bower midway in the second quarter. From that point on, the game belonged to the Cowboys in a 24-7 victory.

Josh Lewis broke the 7-7 tie on a 23-yard field goal for the only points of the third quarter. The Cowboys put the game away on a pair of fourth-quarter touchdown runs of 21 and 5 yards by Marcus Wiltz.

Northwestern had taken a 7-0 lead on a 15-yard pass from Wolfe to Adrian Reese less than four minutes into the game.

In an ironic twist, Fritz and Stubbs made their Southland coaching debuts a week later against each other in Thibodaux. Sam Houston entered the encounter 2-2 on the season. The Bearkats opened the year with losses to Baylor and Western Illinois before giving Fritz his first win as coach with a 30-14 victory over Gardner-Webb. SHSU followed up that game with a victory over Lamar.

Nicholls State opened the year with three-consecutive road losses to San Diego State, Western Michigan and South Alabama. A 44-28 home victory over Bacone gave Stubbs his first win as a collegiate head coach going into the tilt against Sam Houston State.

The Bearkats' defense came up big against Nicholls, limiting the Colonels to less than 100 yards of total offense in Sam Houston State's 26-7 triumph.

Sam Houston State set a school record with 12 sacks, including four by linebacker Will Henry. Kenneth Jenkins had two interceptions for the Bearkats.

SHSU's special teams chipped in as well. With Nicholls leading 7-3, Robert Shaw blocked a Colonels punt and recovered the ball in the end zone late in the second quarter to give the Bearkats a 10-7 halftime edge.

Freshman running back Tim Flanders, who finished with 105 yards, topped the 100-yard mark for the fourth-consecutive game. He scored the game's final touchdown on a 4-yard run in the fourth quarter.

Nicholls State's only points came on a 13-yard run by LaQuintin Caston to give the Colonels their 7-3 lead.

The SHSU-Nicholls encounter was just one of a full slate of games to open Southland play that day.

Two other teams playing their initial conference game that day were Southeastern Louisiana and Texas State. SLU went into its game against the visiting Bobcats 1-3 on the season while the Bobcats were 3-1.

Southeastern Louisiana's Tyler Beatty passed for 368 yards and five touchdowns in the Lions' 49-24 victory but despite the quarterback's big numbers, the Lions were unable to put the game away until the fourth quarter.

SLU held a slim 28-21 lead going into the second half. A 28-yard pass from Beatty to Simmie Yarborough was countered by a 27-yard Justin Garelick field goal to extend the Lions' lead to 35-24 after three quarters. Yarborough had three touchdown catches in the game to give him 24 in his career to establish a new SLU career record.

A fumble recovery in the end zone by Kevin Hughes and a 10-yard touchdown pass from Beatty to Zeke Jones allowed SLU to pull away for a 49-24 victory.

After Dexter Imade and Jones exchanged short touchdown runs in the first quarter, Beatty tossed a touchdown pass to Brandon Collins and two to Yarborough in the second quarter as the Lions built their 28-21 halftime advantage.

Stephen F. Austin was off to a 3-1 start heading into its Southland opener at McNeese State, with the Lumberjacks' only blemish being a 48-7 loss at Texas A&M.

The final 5:10 of the game between SFA and McNeese made for a nail-biter. Cowboys quarterback Cody Stroud tossed 27 yards to Wes Briscoe to give McNeese a 27-26 lead.

Stephen F. Austin moved into field goal range but a blocked kick with 3:45 remaining in the game allowed McNeese to cling to its one-point edge. SFA forced a Cowboys punt, giving the Lumberjacks one last chance. Jeremy Moses, who threw four touchdown passes in the game, made his biggest throw with 55 seconds left in the contest, hitting Cordell Roberson with a 15-yard strike to give the Lumberjacks a 32-27 triumph. Moses was coming off the Lamar game in which he passed for 353 yards to bring his career total to 10,596 to become the all-time passing leader in the Southland Conference.

"That was one of the most memorable games of my career," Moses said. "It was a fantastic football game on both sides. I always loved playing against McNeese. Even when you had to travel to McNeese, it's a different atmosphere within the Southland Conference. I always loved going there. They will play you tough every snap."

Moses' start to the season, to go along with an already stellar career, made the senior quarterback a serious candidate of the Walter Payton Award, given to the best player on the Football Championship Subdivision level.

"I enjoyed it because it gave the university publicity and it gave our football program publicity but as a personal achievement, I didn't think about it much,"

Moses said of the Payton Award campaign. "My mindset was when I had the award in my hands, then I would celebrate."

Although there was a lot of hype involved with the award, it was never a distraction for the team, according to Lumberjacks coach J.C. Harper.

"Jeremy is a competitor and loves to play the game. He was a chosen guy for that because he was deserving," Harper said.

McNeese scored all 10 of its first-half points in the opening quarter. A 4-yard run by Wiltz and a 46-yard Lewis field goal accounted for the scoring. SFA countered with 12 points in the second quarter to lead by two points at the break. Moses tossed his first touchdown of the game on a 34-yard strike to Ayron Morgan. A Logan Barrett field goal with 1:50 left in the half tied the game. The Lumberjacks took their first lead of the contest on a safety with 27 seconds remaining in the second quarter.

Central Arkansas also was playing its initial Southland Conference game of the season when the Bears faced off against visiting Northwestern State. UCA opened the year with wins over Elizabeth City State, Eastern Illinois and Murray State before suffering a 41-14 loss at Tulsa going into the game against the Demons.

Northwestern State held the Bears scoreless through the first quarter but fell behind 10-0 early in the second quarter on a 31-yard Eddie Carmona field goal and a 5-yard pass from Nathan Dick to Dominique Croom.

The Demons tied the game on a 23-yard John Shaughnessy field goal and a 34-yard run by Phil Harris but a Carmona field goal with 31 seconds remaining before halftime gave UCA a 13-10 edge at intermission.

Northwestern gained its first lead when Rumeall Morris, who rushed for 122 yards in the game, broke loose on a 58-yard scamper for a touchdown in the third quarter to put the Demons on top 17-13.

The Demons extended their lead to 11 points at 24-13 on a 3-yard pass from Harris to Bradley Brown with 12:11 remaining in the game.

Terence Bobo scored on a 2-yard run with 8:36 left in the game but when a two-point conversion attempt failed, the Bears continued to trail by five points. UCA never seriously threatened the remainder of the game as the Demons held on for a 24-19 victory.

The win was the first Southland Conference victory for the Demons under Peveto as coach. Northwestern State improved to 1-1 in the SLC and 2-4 overall. Central Arkansas dropped to 3-2 overall in the league opener for the Bears.

Central Arkansas dropped it second Southland game in a row, falling 30-7 at Stephen F. Austin to allow the Lumberjacks to reach 2-0 in conference action.

Moses connected with Roberson for two touchdown passes; the first from a yard out gave the Lumberjacks a 6-0 lead early in the first quarter.

SFA added to its lead when Octavious Hypolite blocked a Bears punt that was scooped up and returned 23 yards for a touchdown by Romeo Robinson.

Central Arkansas suffered two blocked punts in the game to go along with two lost fumbles and an interception.

The Bears got their only points of the game on a 1-yard pass from Dick to Terence Bobo with 48 seconds left in the first quarter to make the score 13-7.

Stephen F. Austin put the game away in second half. Moses hooked up with Jeremy Barnes on a 6-yard touchdown pass and Henshaw added a 21-yard field goal to give the Lumberjacks a 23-7 lead after three quarters.

Moses, who passed for 333 yards in the game, hooked up with Roberson on a 33-yard toss in the fourth quarter for the 30-7 final.

SFA moved to 2-0 in the Southland and 5-1 overall. Central Arkansas slipped to 1-1 in the league and 4-2 overall.

Joining SFA at 2-0 in the Southland was Sam Houston State with a dominating 57-7 win over Southeastern Louisiana in Huntsville.

Sam Houston State's defense held an opponent to 10 points or less for the third-consecutive week and added offensive firepower to the mix in the Bearkats' 57-7 domination of Southeastern Louisiana.

The only points for the Lions came on a 95-yard bomb from Brian Young to Yarborough in the third quarter with SLU already trailing by 34 points.

Flanders topped the 100-yard mark again, rushing for 141 yards. His two touchdown runs in the first quarter, along with Robert Shaw's 24-yard return of a blocked punt for a touchdown gave the Bearkats a 21-0 lead after one quarter. The ever-alert Shaw also returned an interception 54 yards for a touchdown in the third quarter.

SHSU improved to 2-0 in the Southland and 4-2 overall. Southeastern Louisiana dropped to 1-1 in the league and 2-4 overall.

Meanwhile, Nicholls State picked up its first Southland Conference victory under Stubbs with a wild 47-45 shootout at Texas State.

Trying to win on the road for the first time all season, Caston hit Kenyad Blair with a 13-yard touchdown pass with 13 seconds left in regulation to tie the game 21-21 and force overtime at Texas State. The game-tying touchdown came on fourth down on a drive set up by a punt return to the Bobcats' 37 by Bobby Felder with 3:14 remaining in the game.

A 5-yard run by Caston was matched by a 10-yard pass from Texas State quarterback Tyler Arndt to Daren Dillard to force a second overtime. The teams traded field goals in the second extra period to force a third overtime.

Jesse Turner scored on a 10-yard run to open the third overtime. Now forced to go for a two-point conversion as mandated by overtime rules, Caston tossed to Marcus Washington to give Nicholls a 39-31 lead. A 4-yard run by Imade and a two-point conversion pass sent the game to a fourth overtime.

Imade scored on a 1-yard run to open the fourth overtime but a two-point conversion pass attempt was intercepted by Aldaro Roussell, leaving the Bobcats with a 45-39 lead.

Caston hit Joshua Warren with a 2-yard touchdown pass to tie the game. The quarterback connected with Chucky Nichols on the two-point conversion to give the Colonels a dramatic 47-45 triumph.

Nicholls evened its Southland mark at 1-1 while improving to 2-4 overall. Texas State fell to 0-2 in the conference and 3-3 overall.

The long rivalry between Sam Houston State and Stephen F. Austin found a bigger stage in 2010. For the 85th meeting of the Battle of the Piney Woods, the two teams, both unbeaten in SLC play, met in Houston's Reliant Stadium before a series-record crowd of 24,685.

Fourth-ranked Stephen F. Austin built leads of 14 points, the last time at 28-14 early in the third quarter on a 30-yard touchdown pass from Moses to Kris Lott. Moses passed for 418 yards and four touchdowns in the game.

The Bearkats answered late in the third period on a 1-yard touchdown run by Flanders. Flanders, who finished with an even 100 yards, reached the century mark in rushing for the sixth-consecutive game.

Just as Sam Houston State put itself back in the game, a special teams mistake put a damper on the Bearkats' rally attempt. A snap over the head of Matt Foster, forced the Bearkats' punter to run down the ball. He managed to get the kick off, but his effort went for minus-17 yards, giving Stephen F. Austin the ball at the SHSU 30. Thomas Henshaw kicked a 34-yard field goal to give the Lumberjacks a 31-21 lead with 13:19 remaining in the fourth quarter.

The Bearkats made it 31-28 on a 7-yard touchdown pass from Brian Bell to D.J. Morrow with seven minutes left in the contest.

Sam Houston State had two chances down the stretch. The first ended with a turnover on downs on fourth-and-4 at the Bearkats' 31. SHSU got the ball back at its own 26 with less than a minute remaining in the game. The Bearkats reached their own 46 but an incomplete pass by Bell on fourth-and-4 turned the ball over on downs with eight seconds left in the contest.

"There was a huge crowd and I'm a Houston-based kid so a lot of my friends and family were able to watch it," Moses recalled of playing at Reliant Stadium. "I was a big Houston Texans fan so to be able to step on that field and play at their house was a big deal for me."

Stephen F. Austin's sixth-consecutive win moved the Lumberjacks into sole possession of first place in the Southland at 3-0 and 6-1 overall. SHSU fell to 2-1 in the conference and 4-3 overall.

Following a 32-10 loss at LSU, the sixth-ranked team in the Football Bowl Subdivision, McNeese State had to wait until the final play of the game at Southeastern Louisiana to get back on the winning track with a 13-10 triumph over the Lions.

With the score tied 10-10, the Cowboys were pinned back at their own 3-yard line with 1:51 left in the game following a 61-yard punt by the Lions' Beau Mothe. McNeese quickly moved into Southeastern territory, with a 13-yard pass from Stroud to Briscoe sending Lewis onto the field. The kicker's effort from 52 yards away as time expired lifted the Cowboys to a 13-10 victory.

A 3-yard run by Andre Anderson gave McNeese a 7-0 lead before SLU tied the game at halftime on a 1-yard run by Jones with 2:54 left in the second quarter. Lewis put the Cowboys up by three points early in the third quarter on a 38-yard field goal before Seth Sebastain tied the game 10-10 on a 20-yard field goal with 5:58 remaining in the fourth period.

McNeese improved to 2-1 in the Southland and 3-4 overall. SLU fell to 1-2 in the league and 2-5 overall.

An off week allowed a well-rested Northwestern State team to do something it had never done before under Peveto as coach – win consecutive games. The Demons did just that with a 16-3 victory at Texas State.

The Demons led 7-3 at halftime when a 4-yard run by Sterling Endsley in the first quarter was countered by a 42-yard field goal by Garelick in the second quarter.

Neither team would score an offensive touchdown the remainder of the game. The Bobcats, who were limited to 57 yards rushing, were shut out in the final two quarters.

Northwestern, meanwhile, added a 50-yard Shaughnessy field goal in the third quarter and Kedon Franklin recovered a blocked punt in the end zone with 8:05 remaining in the contest to secure the win for the Demons.

The result left both teams 3-4 overall. The Demons improved to 2-1 in the Southland Conference while Texas State dropped to 0-3.

A week after recording their first Southland Conference victory, the Colonels handed Central Arkansas its initial league win in Nicholls State's 31-7 home loss to the Bears.

On the second play of the game, Caston fumbled when sacked by UCA's Jermayne Lett, with Seth Allison scooping up the ball and racing 10 yards for a touchdown. It was the first of 10 sacks allowed by the Colonels after giving up 12 two weeks earlier against Sam Houston State.

The lone touchdown held up until the closing moments of the first half when Dick tossed 15 yards to Kenneth Robey to give Central Arkansas a 14-0 halftime lead. The conference's leading receiver, Robey finished with eight catches for 124 yards.

Any hopes for a Colonels comeback ended early in the second half when the Bears marched 74 yards on their opening possession of the third quarter. Carmona's 27-yard field goal gave UCA a 17-0 lead.

The Bears tacked on 17 more points the remainder of the game, including a 98-yard interception return for a touchdown by Jestin Love.

Trailing 31-0, Nicholls avoided the shutout when Turner scored on a 6-yard run five seconds into the fourth quarter.

The outcome left both teams 1-2 in the SLC. Nicholls dropped to 2-5 overall while Central Arkansas improved to 4-3.

Like it had done a year earlier, front-running Stephen F. Austin lost after a 3-0 start to let numerous teams back into the Southland Conference race. Just as the previous season, the loss came at the hands of Texas State.

Things couldn't have looked much better for Stephen F. Austin in the Lumberjacks' encounter with Texas State. Third-ranked SFA was on top of the Bobcats 24-0 and less than 10 minutes away from moving to 4-0 in the Southland Conference.

Texas State finally got on the scoreboard with 9:21 left in the game when sophomore quarterback Tim Hawkins, subbing for injured starter Arndt, tossed his first touchdown pass of the year to Darius Bolden.

Ron Jackson's recovery of a Lumberjacks fumble on Stephen F. Austin's next possession gave the ball back to the Bobcats at the SFA 20-yard line. Four plays later, Hawkins scored from a yard out to make the score 24-14.

Texas State continued to trail by 10 points until DaMarcus Griggs returned a punt 73 yards for a touchdown as the Bobcats rallied to within three points at 24-21 with 6:21 left in the fourth quarter.

SFA, which hadn't scored since early in the third quarter on a Henshaw field goal, marched into Texas State territory with the intent of finally putting the game away. T.P. Miller kept that from happening when he recovered a Lumberjacks fumble at the Bobcats' 34-yard line.

The Bobcats took 10 plays to march down the field. Hawkins, who passed for 194 yards and rushed for 121, drilled Dillard with a 28-yard strike with 1:10 left in the game to give Texas State a 27-24 lead.

A last-gasp effort by the Lumberjacks failed when Henshaw was wide left on a 47-yard field goal on the final play of the game.

"It was a snapshot of the previous year," said Moses. "I think it might have been a situation where it's halftime and we're looking ahead to the next week instead of taking care of business in the third and fourth quarters. Again, it was a good opportunity for us to look in the mirror and figure out who we are as a football team and regroup and go out with a different head of steam the next week."

Stephen F. Austin had built its 24-0 lead on three Moses touchdown passes in the first half and Henshaw's third-quarter field goal. Moses tossed a pair of 8-yard touchdown passes to Gralyn Crawford and Lott and hooked up with Roberson from 7 yards out for a 21-0 halftime lead.

The loss, which snapped a five-game winning streak for Stephen F. Austin, left the Lumberjacks 3-1 in the Southland and 6-2 overall. Texas State, which ended a three-game losing skid, improved to 1-3 in the conference and 4-4 overall.

Looking to take advantage of the SFA loss, McNeese State jumped out to a 21-0 lead at home against Nicholls State but had to hold on for a 24-14 win to move to 3-1 in Southland Conference play.

McNeese led by three touchdowns before the Colonels made it 21-7 at halftime on 1-yard run by quarterback Landry Klann with 56 seconds remaining in the second quarter. Nicholls rallied to within a touchdown early in the third quarter on a 35-yard pass from Klann to Blair.

After Lewis kicked a 21-yard field goal less than a minute into the fourth quarter for a 24-14 McNeese lead, the Colonels could get no closer than the McNeese 34-yard line the remainder of the game.

McNeese, which evened its record at 4-4, built its 21-0 lead on an 8-yard run by Bower and a 1-yard run by Champlain Babin in the first quarter and a 1-yard pass from Bower to Corday Clark in the second quarter.

Northwestern State and Sam Houston State each were looking to match SFA and McNeese at 3-1 in the Southland when the teams met in Natchitoches.

A third-straight win appeared as though it might be slipping away for the Demons against Sam Houston State. The game had been tied 10-10 since the third quarter and the Bearkats moved into Northwestern State territory to attempt a 36-yard field goal with three seconds left in regulation. The Demons called three timeouts and the strategy to freeze the SHSU kicker worked when Miguel Antonio missed his attempt to force overtime.

Northwestern got the ball first in overtime and scored on a 20-yard pass from Harris to Louis Hollier. The Bearkats forced a second overtime when Seth Patterson hauled in a 26-yard pass from Bryan Randolph.

The Bearkats got the ball first in the second overtime and were held to a 31-yard Antonio field goal for a 20-17 SHSU lead. Facing third-and-goal from the 1-yard line, Harris rolled out and scored on a quarterback keeper to give the Demons a 23-20 victory.

The result left both the Demons and Bearkats 4-4 overall while SHSU dropped to 2-2 in conference action.

Interceptions played a huge role in Central Arkansas' 30-23 victory over visiting Southeastern Louisiana. Following a 29-yard Sebastian field goal to rally the Lions to 23-16 with 8:01 left in the game, UCA's Dominique Brown returned an interception 33 yards for a touchdown to extend the Bears' advantage to 30-16.

After a 54-yard touchdown pass from Beatty to Collins made it 30-23 with 2:17 left in the game, Love picked off a Lions pass with 1:49 left in the game to preserve the win for Central Arkansas. It was Love's second interception of the game. He returned the first 25 yards for a touchdown in the first quarter to give the Bears a 7-0 lead on their way to a 13-10 edge at halftime.

Central Arkansas improved to 2-2 in the SLC and 5-3 overall. The Lions dropped to 1-3 in the conference and 2-6 overall.

All of the 3-1 teams in the Southland won the following week, leaving a three-way logjam atop the conference going in the season's final two weeks.

Stephen F. Austin, now ranked No. 10 following its loss, built a 34-0 lead and was never threatened in the Lumberjacks' 48-13 win at Nicholls State.

Moses tossed three touchdown passes in the opening half. He had touchdown passes of 1 and 4 yards to Jeremy Barnes in the first quarter. Barnes also rushed for a 6-yard touchdown in the quarter.

Moses, who threw for 280 yards in less than three quarters of action, connected with Roberson on a 73-yard bomb in the second quarter. SFA opened the second quarter with a 9-yard touchdown run by Keith Lawson.

Nicholls managed to get on the scoreboard just before halftime on a 32-yard Andrew Dolan field goal with three seconds left in the second quarter to make the score 35-3 at intermission.

Dolan added a third-quarter field goal before the Colonels scored their only touchdown of the game on a 6-yard pass from Caston to Brandon Johnson with 3:20 left in the game for the 48-13 final. Caston came off the bench in place of Klann. Klann, who earned the start after his play the previous week against McNeese, was 7 of 15 passing for 44 yards against SFA. Caston ended 12 of 19 passing for 78 yards.

The Lumberjacks improved to 4-1 in the Southland Conference and 7-2 overall. Nicholls fell to 1-4 in the league and 2-7 overall.

In Hammond, Harris picked apart the Southeastern Louisiana secondary in Northwestern State's 35-16 win as the Demons moved above the .500 mark for the first time in Peveto's two seasons as coach.

The sophomore quarterback fired three touchdown passes in the first period to stake the Demons to a 21-0 lead after one quarter. Harris hooked up on scoring tosses to Tucker Nims, Jake Bryan and Brown – none from more than 4 yards out.

Justin Aldredge hauled in a 33-yard touchdown strike from Harris with 27 seconds left before halftime to give the Demons a 28-9 halftime lead.

All of SLU's first-half scoring came on three Sebastian field goals. The Lions' only other score came on a 58-yard pass from Young to Collins with 6:59 remaining in the game.

Northwestern State improved to 4-1 in the Southland and 5-4 overall. Southeastern Louisiana fell to 1-4 in the conference and 2-7 overall.

McNeese State's win at Sam Houston State, on the other hand, was more difficult for the Cowboys than either of the SFA or Northwestern State games.

With McNeese leading 33-22, Bell tossed a 64-yard bomb to Melvis Pride with 3:02 left in the game. A two-point conversion attempt failed, leaving the Cowboys with a 33-28 lead.

The Bearkats recovered an onside-kick attempt to keep their hopes of a last-minute win alive. SHSU advanced to the McNeese 20-yard line but a final pass attempt into the end zone was knocked away by Cowboys defender Seth Thomas.

SHSU grabbed a quick 7-0 lead less than a minute into the game when Richard Sincere broke loose on a 67-yard gallop. The teams traded scores the remainder of the half, with a 26-yard field goal by Lewis with six seconds remaining in the second quarter giving McNeese a 19-17 halftime edge.

The Bearkats came up with a safety and a 40-yard Antonio field goal before McNeese countered with a 9-yard pass from Bower to Babin for a 26-22 advantage after three quarters.

McNeese improved to 4-1 in the SLC and 5-4 overall. The Bearkats dropped to 2-3 in the conference and 4-5 overall.

In San Marcos, a well-balanced Central Arkansas offensive machine put on a dominant performance in the Bears' 49-17 win over Texas State.

The Bears passed for 252 yards and rushed for 248 in the rout. The method for entering the end zone wasn't nearly as balanced as six of Central Arkansas' seven touchdowns came on short runs, none longer than 6 yards. The only passing touchdown for UCA came with less than 10 minutes left in the game on a 20-yard pass from Dick to T.J. Adams for the final score.

Four of the Bears' six rushing touchdowns came in the second quarter as Central Arkansas turned a 14-3 lead after one quarter into a 42-3 blowout by halftime. Two of the touchdowns in the quarter came on runs of 2 and 5 yards by Bobo. Bobo finished with three rushing touchdowns in the game. The other two scores in the quarter came on a 1-yard run by Jackie Hinton and a 6-yard run by Dick with 18 seconds remaining in the half.

Texas State managed two touchdowns in the third quarter on Hawkins scoring passes to Dillard and Griggs before Dick hooked up with Adams in the fourth quarter.

Central Arkansas improved to 3-2 in the Southland Conference and 6-3 overall while Texas State fell to 1-4 in the SLC and 4-5 overall.

About the only difference between Stephen F. Austin's home game against Southeastern Louisiana and its game a week earlier versus Nicholls State was the fact the Lions managed to take a brief, early lead.

The Lions led 7-0 less than five minutes into the contest on a 19-yard touchdown pass from Beatty to Kory Theodore, but SFA went on to score the next 51 points on its way to a resounding 51-14 victory. Other than SLU's opening touchdown, the only other score for the Lions came with 2:24 left in the game on an 11-yard pass from Young to Yarborough.

Everything in between belonged to the Lumberjacks. After the Lions' initial score, five of the next six touchdowns for SFA came on passes from Moses. His first two to Roberson, along with a 9-yard toss to Anthony Foster, gave Stephen F. Austin a 21-7 lead after one quarter.

A 7-yard run by Romante Hampton was sandwiched between touchdown passes to Lott and Roberson as SFA built a 42-7 halftime lead. The Lumberjacks rounded out their scoring with a safety and an 80-yard kickoff return by Crawford in the third quarter.

SFA improved to 5-1 in the Southland Conference and 8-2 overall. Southeastern Louisiana dropped to 1-5 in the league and 2-8 overall.

Meanwhile, a pair of big plays late in the second quarter sparked McNeese State in the Cowboys' 36-6 Southland Conference home win against Texas State.

With McNeese leading 9-0, the Bobcats scored on a 6-yard pass from Hawkins to Dillard to trail by three points following a missed extra-point attempt with 7:15 remaining in the first half.

Bernardo Henry returned the ensuing kick 87 yards for a touchdown and McNeese ended the scoring in the first half on a 74-yard interception return for a touchdown by Malcolm Bronson as the Cowboys took a 22-6 lead at the break on their way to the 30-point victory.

The win left McNeese in a first-place tie in the SLC with Stephen F. Austin at 5-1. The Cowboys improved to 6-4 overall with the victory. Texas State fell to 1-5 in the conference and 4-6 overall.

Northwestern State was unable to keep pace as Nicholls State played the role of classic spoiler against the Demons.

Caston scored the first three touchdowns of the game over a surprised Demons squad in Natchitoches. A 39-yard run by Caston gave the Colonels a 7-0 lead in the first quarter. His 2-yard score following an interception by Jordan Hanberry made it 14-0. Caston scored on a 22-yard run in the second quarter to give Nicholls a three-touchdown lead.

The Demons made it 21-7 at halftime on a 20-yard touchdown pass from Harris to Justin Aldredge.

Northwestern, held to 59 yards rushing and 195 passing, was unable to score in the second half. Nicholls, meanwhile, added a 7-yard pass from Caston to Blair in the third quarter before recording a safety and a 12-yard touchdown run by Dalton Hilliard Jr. to give the Colonels a 37-7 victory.

The costly loss for Northwestern State dropped the Demons to 4-2 in the Southland and 5-5 overall. Nicholls improved to 2-4 in the conference and 3-7 overall.

Elsewhere, Sam Houston State snapped a three-game losing streak with a 20-13 win over Central Arkansas in the Bearkats' final road game of the season.

Sincere scored on touchdown runs of 9 and 5 yards and Antonio kicked a pair of field goals for Sam Houston State.

Dominique Croom had 11 catches for 116 yards for the Bears.

Central Arkansas threatened twice down the stretch. SHSU intercepted a Bears' pass in the end zone to end one scoring bid. The Bears reached the Bearkats' 29 late in the game but turned the ball over on downs.

The outcome left both teams 3-3 in the Southland. Sam Houston State improved to 5-5 overall while Central Arkansas fell to 6-4.

Coming off a game in which he accounted for four touchdowns, Caston had another big game against rival Southeastern Louisiana in a game played on a Thursday night to close out the 2010 season.

Caston scored three rushing touchdowns against the Lions, none bigger than his score late in the fourth quarter.

With Nicholls clinging to a 20-19 lead, Caston broke loose on a 43-yard run with 4:23 left in the game to give the Colonels an eight-point cushion.

SLU responded by marching 78 yards for a touchdown. A 1-yard sneak by Beatty made the score 27-25 with 2:19 left in the game. Beatty's pass on a two-point conversion attempt was knocked down by Nicholls defender Jordan Piper.

The Colonels recovered the onside kick and were able to run out the clock on the two-point victory. By winning its final two games, Nicholls topped its win total from each of the previous two years in Stubbs' first season as Colonels coach.

Caston, who rushed for 139 yards, scored on runs of 7 yards in the first quarter and 1 yard in the second to give Nicholls a 14-0 halftime lead.

Southeastern cut the margin in half to start the third quarter on a 24-yard touchdown pass from Beatty to Yarborough. Yarborough, who had six catches in the game, finished as the school's all-time leading receiver with 168 career receptions.

Following Yarborough's touchdown reception, Dolan and SLU's Sebastian exchanged field goals before Jones scored on an 11-yard run to pull the Lions to within one point at 17-16 heading into the fourth quarter.

The kickers again exchanged field goals in the fourth quarter for the Colonels' 20-19 edge to set the stage for Caston's 43-yard run.

Nicholls ended the 2010 season 4-7 overall, including 3-4 in the SLC. Southeastern Louisiana finished 2-9 overall, including 1-6 in the conference.

If McNeese State was going to qualify for the playoffs, the Cowboys were going to earn it the hard way. The Cowboys dug themselves a deep hole, falling behind 21-0 in the first quarter at Central Arkansas in the final game of the 2010 season.

The Cowboys fought off the bad start, coming up with a 2-yard run by Babin and a 12-yard pass from Bower to Damion Dixon late in the first quarter to rally to within a touchdown.

Central Arkansas' 21-14 lead held up until late in the third quarter. A 42-yard field goal by Lewis with 4:44 remaining in the third period allowed the Cowboys to rally within four points at 21-17.

McNeese gained the lead for the first time in the contest when Bower hooked up with Briscoe on a 10-yard touchdown strike to put the Cowboys on top 24-21 at the seven-minute mark of the fourth quarter.

After holding the Bears scoreless since midway in the first quarter, the McNeese defense finally cracked when Dick hit Kenneth Robey with a 10-yard touchdown toss with 3:20 left in the game for a 28-24 lead to cap a 76-yard drive.

The Cowboys advanced deep in Central Arkansas territory twice in the closing minutes. The first drive concluded with an interception at the 5-yard line. The final drive ended when the Cowboys ran out of downs inside the 5.

Central Arkansas built its early three-touchdown lead on a 6-yard run by Dick to cap a 70-yard drive with the opening kickoff, a 69-yard pass from Dick to Isaiah Jackson and a 36-yard fumble return by Markell Carter for a touchdown.

The loss ended McNeese's season at 6-5 overall, including 5-2 in the Southland. Central Arkansas finished 7-4 overall, including 4-3 in conference play.

The fifth-ranked Lumberjacks, meanwhile, held a slight 12-7 lead at halftime of their 2010 regular season finale at home against Northwestern State before taking control in the third quarter.

Leading by five points, Moses tossed a 17-yard touchdown pass to Foster. Henshaw kicked a 26-yard field goal and Hampton scored on a 2-yard run to up the lead to 29-7 on the Lumberjacks' way to a 36-13 victory. The win, coupled with Central Arkansas' victory over McNeese State, made SFA the outright champions of the Southland Conference.

Moses, who threw for 489 yards, tossed his final touchdown of the game on a 17-yard strike to Crawford seven seconds into the fourth quarter. Wolfe, subbing for Harris, the injured starter at quarterback for Northwestern State, hit James Swanson with a 28-yard touchdown pass on the final play of the game. Harris left the game in the second quarter after a blow to the head in the opening period of play.

SFA claimed the Southland crown and automatic bid to the playoffs with a 6-1 conference mark. The Lumberjacks concluded the regular season 9-2 overall. Northwestern State finished 4-3 in the league and 5-6 overall.

Needing a win in their last game of the year against visiting Texas State to finish with a winning season, the Bearkats jumped out to a 21-3 lead early in the second quarter.

The game marked the final time Sam Houston State and Texas State would meet on the field as Southland Conference rivals. Texas State elected to move up to Football Bowl Subdivision status and although the two teams were slated to meet again in 2011, the Bobcats would be Football Championship Subdivision independents.

After Texas State narrowed the deficit to 21-9 at halftime, the Bearkats scored on the opening drive of the third quarter on a 1-yard run by Flanders.

The Bobcats closed to within five points at 28-23 on a 15-yard touchdown pass from Hawkins to Griggs with 12:52 left in the game.

A 46-yard Antonio field goal pushed SHSU's lead to 31-23.

The Bobcats responded by marching 74 yards. Karrington Bush's 4-yard touchdown run made it 31-29. A two-point conversion pass attempt from Hawkins intended for Bolden was incomplete, leaving Texas State behind by two points with 2:31 left in the game.

Sam Houston State was able to run out the clock to secure a winning season.

A 21-yard Zac Ammar field goal gave Texas State a 3-0 lead before the Bearkats scored the next 21 points to create some distance between the teams heading into halftime. Touchdown runs of 8 yards by Torrance Williams, 13 yards by Flanders and 19 yards by Frank Ridgeway made it 21-3 before the Bobcats cut the margin to 21-9 at the half on 41-yard touchdown reception by Bush.

Sam Houston State ended the season 6-5 overall and 4-3 in the Southland. Texas State bowed out of the SLC at 1-6 while finishing the season 4-7 overall.

An opening-round playoff bye gave the Stephen F. Austin Lumberjacks an extra week to get ready before hosting Villanova, the defending national champion.

Moses came out throwing to open the game, passing for 140 yards in the first quarter. His throwing led to three touchdown runs by Lawson, all from a yard out, to give Stephen F. Austin a 21-7 lead after one quarter. The only score for the Wildcats in the opening quarter came on a 16-yard pass from Chris Whitney to Norman White.

The Lumberjacks started to make mistakes at that point and Whitney and company made SFA pay dearly.

A muffed punt by Crawford set up an 11-yard hookup between Whitney and White early in the second quarter. SFA got three of the points back when Henshaw kicked a 35-yard field goal to make the score 24-14.

The Lumberjacks would not be so fortunate the rest of the game.

Three plays after Mark Hamilton kicked a 37-yard field goal, another turnover gave the ball back to the Wildcats. John Dempsey picked off an errant Moses throw and raced 24 yards to the SFA 18. Three plays picked up a total of 1 yard, sending in the Villanova field goal unit. Holder Marlon Calbi took the snap and tossed to his right. White was wide open and the 17-yard touchdown allowed the Wildcats to tie the game 24-24 with two minutes left in the half.

"I thought the key of the game was they were lining up to kick a field goal and they faked it. They executed and scored a touchdown and that was one that really hurt and we had a hard time coming back from that," said Harper.

Two minutes was just enough time for Villanova to score twice more. A short punt by SFA traveled only 18 yards before going out of bounds, giving the Wildcats the ball at the Lumberjacks' 45-yard line. Four plays later, Whitney tossed to Mikey Reynolds for a 4-yard touchdown for a 31-24 Villanova lead with 34 seconds remaining in the second quarter. Crawford fumbled the kickoff return, allowing Hamilton to kick a 38-yard field goal as time expired for a 34-24 lead at the break.

"We came out hot right out of the gate, which is exactly what we wanted to do," said Moses. "I believe they made a few adjustments and we weren't able to get that rhythm back. The turnovers were huge."

Villanova added another 20 points in the second half, including two Hamilton field goals and Whitney's fourth touchdown pass of the game for a 54-24 victory that eliminated the Lumberjacks from the playoffs.

Moses passed for 340 yards but failed to throw a touchdown pass while suffering three interceptions in his final collegiate game. He left Stephen F. Austin as the all-time passer in the Southland Conference and the career completions leader among Football Championship Subdivision quarterbacks as SFA concluded the season with a 9-3 record.

After the season, Moses indeed became the first-ever player from the Southland Conference to win the Walter Payton Award.

"For me to get to that point, obviously, I had to have an outstanding supporting cast," Moses said. "That includes teammates and coaches, of course, but family, my wife, who was my girlfriend at the time, her parents, the (university) president, athletic director, the supporting staff around here. For me to get to that stage to accept that award, all those people had to be present in my life to get to that point."

The award, said Harper, was certainly deserved.

"They ought to hang up a statue for him so he can be there (at Stephen F. Austin) forever," Harper said. "It's amazing to think no one else has won the Walter Payton Award (in the Southland). I just can't say enough for what Jeremy Moses has done for SFA, the program and himself. I was very lucky to be able to coach him."

TEXAS STATE EXITS, LAMAR RETURNS

The departure of Texas State in 2011 was offset by the return of Lamar, a charter member of the Southland Conference. Lamar left the SLC after the 1986 season and dropped football following the 1989 season. Football returned to Lamar in 2010.

Sam Houston State and Central Arkansas opened up Southland play in 2011 when the Bearkats hosted Central Arkansas. SHSU went into the game 1-0 on the season with a 20-6 victory over Western Illinois. Central Arkansas was 1-1 after a season-opening win over Henderson State and a loss to Louisiana Tech.

After opening the season on a Thursday night, Sam Houston State had an open date, giving the Bearkats a gap of 16 days before facing Central Arkansas in the conference opener.

Sam Houston State was leading 7-0 when Central Arkansas receiver Isaiah Jackson raced 73 yards on a pass reception for the Bears' first threat of the game. A missed 24-yard field-goal attempt by Eddie Camara seemed to put the Bears in funk they were never able to recover from.

Following Camara's miss, Miguel Antonio connected on a 42-yard field goal for a 10-0 lead. Looking to make something happen, the Bears attempted a fake punt. The Bearkats spoiled the gambit, taking over at the Central Arkansas 35. SHSU took advantage of the field position when Ryan Wilson scored on an 8-yard run for a 17-0 lead early in the second quarter.

A rally by the Bears would have to come without Nathan Dick. The senior quarterback had to leave the field after taking a blow to the head in the second quarter.

Trailing by 21 points, Central Arkansas scored on a 9-yard run by Jackie Hinton to make the score 24-10 but the Bears would not score again in a 31-10 loss.

Four teams opened up Southland Conference play a week later when McNeese State hosted Southeastern Louisiana and Northwestern State visited Nicholls State.

McNeese went into its initial conference game 1-1 on the season, opening with a loss at Kansas followed by a win over Sioux Falls. SLU was 1-2 on the young season. After opening with a loss to Tulane, the Lions defeated Savannah State before falling to Southern Mississippi.

A three-touchdown spurt in the third quarter propelled McNeese State to a 48-27 win over Southeastern Louisiana.

After the Lions scored to trail 24-20 in the third quarter, Jaravis Murray returned the ensuing kickoff to midfield for McNeese. Marcus Wiltz, who rushed for 104 yards, scored five plays later on a 4-yard run for a 31-20 Cowboys lead late in the third period.

Andre Anderson, who ran for 114 yards, broke loose on a 55-yard gallop for a touchdown early in the fourth quarter. A 6-yard touchdown pass from Cody Stroud to Murray following Malcolm Bronson's interception of a Brian Young pass, put McNeese on top 45-20 on the Cowboys' way to the 48-27 victory.

McNeese led 24-10 at halftime before SLU rallied to within four points on a 64-yard pass from Young to Brandon Collins and a 33-yard Seth Sebastian field goal.

Northwestern State went into its Southland opener 1-2 on the season. After struggling in a 24-23 win over Division II Delta State, the Demons lost 49-2 at LSU, the second-ranked team in the FBS. A 40-7 loss to SMU ruined Northwestern State coach Bradley Dale Peveto's return to his alma mater.

Nicholls State also was 1-2 on the season. After a season-opening 42-0 win over Evangel College, the Colonels lost a pair or road games to Western Michigan and Louisiana-Lafayette.

The Demons showed in their regionally-televised Southland Conference opener at Nicholls State that nothing was going to stop them from their destiny.

Northwestern State jumped out to a 21-0 lead in the first quarter on the Demons' way to a 34-0 victory for win No. 500 in school history. The Demons, who started football in 1907, saw their record improve to 500-418-22 all-time.

All three of the Demons' touchdowns in the first quarter came on touchdown tosses by Brad Henderson. He tossed 9 yards to JaMarcus Williams to open the scoring less than five minutes into the game before adding strikes of 2 yards to Tucker Nims and 48 yards to T.C. Henry to give Northwestern State its quick three-touchdown advantage. Henderson finished with 187 yards passing.

The score remained the same until the third quarter. A 21-yard John Shaughnessy field goal and a 1-yard run by D.J. Palmer gave the Demons a 31-0 lead after three periods.

Nicholls was held to 104 total yards, 69 coming on one drive. A serious Colonel scoring threat ended when backup quarterback Beaux Hebert, the son of former Demons quarterback Bobby Hebert, was stopped short on fourth-and-1 from the Northwestern 3-yard line.

The win was the first shutout victory for the Demons in 53 games.

Lamar played its first Southland Conference game since 1986 a week later when the Cardinals visited Southeastern Louisiana. Lamar went into the game 2-1 on the season with wins over Texas College and Incarnate Word and a loss to South Alabama.

The Cardinals were coached by Ray Woodard. A head coach at Navarro Junior College in 2007, Woodward was hired by Lamar in 2008 to resurrect the football program. In Lamar's first season back in competition in 2010, Woodard guided the Cardinals to a 5-6 record.

The odds of Lamar capturing a win in its first game back in Southland Conference competition didn't appear too promising with the Cardinals trailing Southeastern Louisiana 24-13 midway in the third quarter.

A 2-yard touchdown pass from quarterback Andre Bevil to Payden McVey to cap an 80-yard drive inched Lamar a bit closer. Late in the third quarter, Bevil lateralled to receiver Marcus Jackson. Jackson, who had five catches for 123 yards and two touchdowns, tossed to a wide-open J.J. Hayes for a 62-yard scoring strike to put the Cardinals on top 27-24.

Bevil, who passed for 270 yards and four touchdowns in the contest, added scoring tosses of 32 yards to Mike Venson and 29 yards to Jackson on Lamar's way to a 48-38 victory and a successful return to the SLC for the Cardinals.

Also opening up Southland play that same day was Stephen F. Austin when the Lumberjacks visited Central Arkansas. SFA won its season opener against McMurry before suffering defeats to Northern Iowa, Baylor and former conference foe Texas State heading into the encounter with the Bears on UCA's new purple and gray turf.

In the Baylor game, the Bears, behind the play of future Heisman Trophy winner Robert Griffin III, scored on every drive when the game was halted with Baylor leading 31-0. After a 41-minute delay, it was decided that halftime would be skipped and a shortened second half would take place. When lightning struck late in the third quarter and Baylor on top 48-0, the game was stopped once again and the clock was allowed to run down so the contest could be declared official.

The Lumberjacks used a pair of Jordan Wiggs field goals to rally to within one point at the midway mark of the second quarter in Stephen F. Austin's game against Central Arkansas.

Wiggs kicked field goals in the first and second quarter to narrow the gap to 7-6 against the Bears, who had taken the lead on a second-quarter touchdown pass from Dick to Dezmin Lewis.

After Wiggs' 26-yard kick in the second quarter, the Bears began to put together quick scores in each of the second and third quarters to pull away for an eventual 38-28 victory.

Following Wiggs' field goal, Jackson returned the ensuing kickoff 91 yards for a touchdown to stretch Central Arkansas' lead to 14-6. Moments later, Seth Allison returned an interception 34 yards to put the Bears on top 21-6 at the break.

Dick opened the third quarter with a 58-yard scoring strike to Jesse Grandy. Less than two minutes later, it was 35-6 when Marcus Peters returned a fumble 55 yards for a touchdown.

Brady Attaway, faced with the task of trying to replace Jeremy Moses, tossed three touchdown passes in the fourth quarter, include two to Kris Lott to make the final 38-28.

In a tightly-contested game for four quarters, McNeese State gained the early upper hand in the Southland Conference race with a narrow 20-18 victory at Northwestern State.

McNeese's Josh Lewis and Shaughnessy traded field goals for a 3-3 tie after one quarter. Following a 22-yard Lewis field goal less than a minute into the second quarter, a 4-yard pass from Henderson to Louis Hollier put Northwestern State on top 9-6 following a failed two-point conversion.

An interception by Demons defensive tackle Anthony Gilbert at the McNeese 9-yard line set up a 26-yard Shaughnessy field goal for a 12-6 Northwestern advantage. Stroud's 8-yard touchdown pass to Darius Carey with 16 seconds left in the second quarter gave the Cowboys a 13-12 edge at halftime.

Following a scoreless third quarter, Joe Narcisse returned an interception 18 yards for a touchdown to stretch McNeese's lead to eight points at 20-12. The McNeese linebacker tipped the ball near the line of scrimmage before hauling it in and racing for the touchdown.

The Demons responded with 11:42 remaining in the game on a 5-yard touchdown run by Sidney Riley but another failed two-point conversion left Northwestern State trailing by 20-18.

A desperation throw by the Demons into the end zone from 47 yards away fell to the turf as the game ended.

The outcome left McNeese as the only 2-0 team in the SLC as the Cowboys improved to 3-1 overall. Northwestern fell to 1-1 in the conference and 2-3 overall.

A week later, Sam Houston State and Stephen F. Austin set a new series attendance record again in 2011 with a crowd of 25,038 at Houston's Reliant Stadium as the Bearkats put on a dominating performance with a 45-10 victory. The win allowed SHSU to get off to a 5-0 start for the first time since the 1994 season. After the Bearkats' win over Central Arkansas, SHSU defeated New Mexico and first-year program Texas-San Antonio on its way to an undefeated start to the season.

The Bearkats' halftime lead against SFA was only 10-3 following a 49-yard touchdown pass from Brian Bell to Torrance Williams and a 30-yard Antonio field goal.

SHSU quickly extended the lead to 17-3 on a 55-yard touchdown pass to Keith Blanton to open the second half. Andrew Weaver's interception of an Attaway pass later in the third quarter led to a 9-yard Flanders touchdown to suddenly make the margin 21 points at 24-3 with more than seven minutes still remaining in the third quarter.

After giving up a field goal for a 3-0 deficit, the Bearkats scored the next 45 points in the game.

Bell passed for two touchdowns in the game while Flanders and Richard Sincere had two rushing touchdowns apiece. The SHSU defense, meanwhile, forced five turnovers and held the Lumberjacks to 23 yards rushing.

Sam Houston State moved to 2-0 in the Southland. SFA dropped to 0-2 in the conference and 1-5 overall.

"Whenever we went down to Reliant Stadium, that was a huge game for both teams. It's a great atmosphere," Sam Houston State coach Willie Fritz said.

Northwestern State bounced back from its loss to McNeese State with a 37-17 win at Lamar as Henderson and Riley each accounted for two first-half touchdowns.

A 1-yard run by Riley and an 8-yard pass from Bevil to Jackson led to a 7-7 tie after one quarter before the Demons gained a bit of separation with a 20-point second quarter.

Henderson tossed touchdown passes of 5 yards to Trevor Goodie and 19 yards to Phillip Harvey while Riley scored on a 5-yard run to give Northwestern a 27-7 halftime lead.

Trailing 30-10, Bevil hooked up with Hayes on a 40-yard touchdown strike to make it a 13-point game with 4:25 left in the fourth quarter but Palmer made sure the game stayed out of reach when he turned a screen pass from Henderson into a 54-yard touchdown reception.

Northwestern State improved to 2-1 in the SLC and 3-3 overall. Lamar dropped to 1-1 in the league and 3-2 overall.

Playing their most competitive game of the season in weeks, the Colonels came up with a big defensive stand late while trailing 37-31 at home against Central Arkansas to give the Nicholls offense one last shot to rally.

Nicholls forced the Bears into a fourth-and-1 situation at the Central Arkansas 33-yard line with 4:31 remaining in the game. Seeking a fourth-down conversion, Dick was stopped by Colonels linebacker Jordan Piper on a quarterback sneak, handing the ball over to the Nicholls offense.

With the offense facing fourth-and-goal from the 7-yard line, Nicholls quarterback Landry Klann, who passed for a career-high 237 yards, tossed to Nick Scelfo. As the Colonels tight end tried to stretch his way to the goal line, he was knocked out of bounds by two Central Arkansas defenders at the 1-yard line, allowing the Bears to hold on for the six-point triumph.

"I had a poor coaching decision. We had fourth and less than a foot at the 33-yard line and went for it and didn't make it," Central Arkansas coach Clint Conque recalled. "Frank Newsome made a tackle at the 1-yard line. The kids overcame coaching that day because I put them in a bad situation."

Nicholls led 7-3 after one quarter before the teams combined for 30 points in the second quarter.

Klann, making his first start of the season, scored on a 1-yard run to get things started in the second quarter. Dick countered with a 1-yard run of his own for the Bears. Marcus Washington, who rushed for a career-high 101 yards for Nicholls, came up with his second touchdown of the game on a 5-yard run. UCA's Anthony Blackmon followed with a 49-yard scoring gallop but the extra point was blocked. Dolan booted a 39-yard field goal with 11 seconds remaining in the first half for a 24-16 Nicholls lead at the break.

T.J. Adams' recovery of a Colonels fumble in the end zone, along with a two-point conversion, tied the game at the seven-minute mark of the third quarter. After a 47-yard pass from Klann to Kenyad Blair, Dick hit Lewis with a 20-yard touchdown pass with seven seconds left in the quarter to tie the game 31-31.

Dick connected with Dominique Croom on a 16-yard touchdown pass for what proved to be the game-winning score with 10:06 remaining in the fourth quarter.

Nicholls fell to 0-2 in the SLC and 1-5 overall. Central Arkansas improved to 2-1 in the league and 3-3 overall.

Central Arkansas faced another 2-1 Southland Conference team a week later when the Bears hosted McNeese State.

The Cowboys scored on their opening possession of the game on an 8-yard run by Murray. Central Arkansas led 14-7 after the first quarter on a pair of touchdown passes by Dick. The UCA quarterback hooked up with Croom on an 81-yard strike and tossed to Brett Soft to give the Bears the lead. The go-ahead pass to Soft was set up by a McNeese fumble, one of five turnovers for the Cowboys.

McNeese appeared poised to tie the game in the second quarter but the momentum completely changed when a Wiltz fumble was returned 98 yards for a touchdown by Frank Newsome. Instead of a potential tie game at intermission, the Bears were up 21-7.

The Cowboys tightened things up on a 27-yard field goal by Lewis in the third quarter and a 4-yard pass from Stroud to Devionte Edmonson with 3:43 remaining in game. Anderson's two-point conversion following Edmonson's touchdown catch rallied McNeese to within three points.

McNeese got the ball back in the closing seconds with a pass to Murray advancing the ball to the Cowboys' 39. Jestin Love intercepted a McNeese pass and Central Arkansas was able to run out the clock.

The Cowboys dropped to 2-1 in the SLC and 3-3 overall. Central Arkansas improved to 3-1 in the conference and 4-3 overall.

Northwestern State also moved to 3-1 in the Southland as Lamont Simmons' 24-yard fumble return for a touchdown only 15 seconds into the game set the tone in the Demons' 51-17 home win over Southeastern Louisiana.

The Demons put the game away early by scoring the first 17 points of the contest. Following Simmons' fumble return, Northwestern pulled off a successful onside kick to get the ball right back to set up a 44-yard Shaughnessy field goal. When Palmer broke loose on an 82-yard gallop, the Demons had their 17-point advantage.

Sebastian momentarily broke Northwestern's momentum with a 42-yard field goal, but the Demons added 10 more points before the opening quarter was over on a 28-yard pass from Henderson to Rumeall Morris and a 24-yard Shaughnessy field goal for a 27-3 lead.

If the Lions, who were coming off an open date, held any hope of rallying after a scoreless second quarter, it came to a sudden halt when Harvey returned the second-half kickoff 99 yards for a touchdown.

SLU managed a pair of third-quarter touchdown passes by Young but the Lions never seriously threatened the Demons in the contest.

Along with moving to 3-1 in the Southland, the Demons improved to 4-3 overall. The Lions remained winless in conference play at 0-3 and moved to 1-5 overall.

While Southeastern Louisiana stayed winless in the Southland, Sam Houston State remained the only unbeaten team in conference play with a 47-7 domination of visiting Nicholls State.

Robert Shaw, the Bearkats' longtime ball hawk, returned an interception 61 yards for the game's first touchdown in Sam Houston State's rout of Nicholls State. As it turned out, the SHSU offense hardly needed the help as the unbeaten Bearkats went on to score the game's next 40 points.

An 8-yard touchdown pass from Bell to Williams, a 1-yard run by Flanders and a 41-yard Antonio field goal as time expired in the second quarter gave the Bearkats a 24-0 halftime lead.

Flanders and Sincere added short touchdown runs in the third quarter to make it 38-0 after three quarters. A safety and a 50-yard pass from Greg Sprowls to Keyshawn Hill made it 47-0 before the Colonels managed to avoid the shutout on a 12-yard touchdown pass from LaQuintin Caston to Jesse Turner with 1:01 remaining in the game.

SHSU improved to 3-0 in the Southland and 6-0 overall. Nicholls dropped to 0-3 in the conference and 1-6 overall.

A test of just how good the Bearkats might be in 2011 was Sam Houston State's Southland Conference encounter at McNeese State. Going into the contest, the Bearkats had beaten the Cowboys in Lake Charles only once in 12 tries.

SHSU passed the test with flying colors – in the second half. At halftime, the seventh-ranked Bearkats were not so sure, clinging to a 14-7 edge.

After forcing the Cowboys to punt on the opening possession of the second half, the Bearkats struck on their first play from scrimmage when Flanders, who rushed for 168 yards in the game, scooted right through the heart of the McNeese defense for a 55-yard touchdown.

McNeese was forced to punt from near its own goal line later in the third quarter. Williams virtually took the ball off the foot of Cowboys punter Ben Bourgeois. Shaw hauled in the loose ball for a touchdown for a 28-7 Sam Houston State lead.

A 41-yard touchdown pass from Bell to Trey Diller gave the Bearkats a 21-point third quarter and a 35-7 lead on Sam Houston State's way to the 38-14 victory.

The streaking Bearkats moved to 7-0 overall and 4-0 in the SLC. McNeese fell to 2-2 in the conference and 3-4 overall.

"That was a big win for us. We started getting people traveling with us and we had a real large contingent of fans that came over to Lake Charles," Fritz said.

Central Arkansas, meanwhile, kept the pressure on Sam Houston State with a 38-24 victory at Lamar to move to 4-1 in the Southland Conference.

The Bears broke a 17-17 tie at halftime on a 12-yard pass from Dick to Jesse Grandy. Lamar tied the game again on a 55-yard run by Jeremy Johnson. Dick's 35-yard touchdown pass to Al Lasker late in the third quarter gave Central Arkansas a 31-24 lead and the Bears put the game away when Love, UCA's ball-hawking defender, returned an interception 31 yards for a touchdown with slight more than two minutes left in the game for the 38-24 final.

Along with moving to 4-1 in the SLC, Central Arkansas improved to 5-3 overall. Lamar fell to 1-2 in the conference and 3-4 overall.

On the same day Sam Houston State and Central Arkansas were earning their fourth Southland victories of the season, a pair of teams seeking their initial conference win met when Nicholls State visited Stephen F. Austin.

It can still be quite warm in Thibodaux in late October but no one was hotter than Attaway in the Lumberjacks' game against Nicholls State in 2011.

Attaway scorched the Colonels' secondary for seven touchdown passes in the Lumberjacks' 57-21 romp over Nicholls. It was the second-highest single-game total in Southland history. The effort was topped only by another SFA quarterback, Todd Hammel, who pitched eight touchdown passes against Northeast Louisiana in 1989.

The current SFA quarterback, who was 30 of 49 passing for 264 yards against the Colonels, hooked up with Cordell Roberson for three of the touchdown strikes. Roberson finished with eight catches for 115 yards.

Attaway's other touchdown tosses went to Ryan Gambel, Grayln Crawford, Tyler Boyd and Brandon Scott.

While Attaway's eye-popping performance didn't set a new conference record, his exploits overshadowed a Nicholls record setter.

Chiki Madu established new Southland and Nicholls records by returning two kickoffs for touchdowns. He needed 22 yards going into the game to surpass the previous Nicholls career mark of Darryl Pounds. Madu shattered the mark on his first return, racing 91 yards for a touchdown in the first quarter.

He returned another kick 94 yards for a touchdown in the third quarter. Madu finished the game with 304 kick-return yards in the contest. That gave him 1,555 yards in his career. His two returns for touchdowns also set single-game conference and school marks.

Madu's first touchdown return came after Attaway's initial touchdown pass, a 10-yard toss to Gambel. SFA went on to score the game's next 45 points.

Following Attaway's final touchdown pass of the game, a 27-yard strike to Scott, Madu raced 94 yards for a touchdown that made the score 51-14.

The only score the Colonels could muster other than Madu's returns came on a 2-yard pass from Caston to Washington in the fourth quarter. Beside Attaway's seven touchdown passes SFA's other scores came on three Wiggs field goals.

SFA improved to 1-2 in the Southland and 2-5 overall in snapping its five-game losing streak. Nicholls fell to 0-4 in the conference and 1-7 overall.

Sam Houston State went from test to no contest in the course of a week after a 66-0 home drubbing of Lamar.

Four different players for SHSU scored a total of seven rushing touchdowns for the Bearkats. Flanders scored three times, Wilson, Hill and Sincere once each. Sincere also had a 77-yard scoring reception.

Hill and Sincere each topped 100 yards rushing in the game while the SHSU defense held the Cardinals to 98 total yards.

Sam Houston State moved to 8-0 overall and 5-0 in the SLC. Lamar dropped to 1-3 in the league and 3-5 overall.

"Our defensive guys had really grown up," Fritz said. "They had taken their lumps in 2009. We played a lot better defensively in 2010. In 2011 and 2012, we really played well defensively and were really able to dominate people defensively."

Central Arkansas stayed on the heels of Sam Houston State as the Bears took advantage of a school-record nine turnovers by Southeastern Louisiana in UCA's 55-29 rout of the visiting Lions.

Dick tossed five touchdown passes to five different receivers in passing for 299 yards. Gandy hauled in four catches for 93 yards and a touchdown. Not all of the Bears' damage came through the air as Hinton rushed for 106 yards and a touchdown.

Southeastern Louisiana led 10-7 in the first quarter following a 3-yard touchdown pass from Young to Antoine Duplessis. Central Arkansas countered with a 5-yard scoring run by Bobo as the Bears began to pull away.

Jordan Wells of Southeastern Louisiana set two Southland records in the game. He had nine returns for a total of 265 yards, breaking the single-game mark of 233 by McNeese State's Flip Johnson versus Northern Iowa in 1986. His season total of 1,171 yards topped the record of Texas State's Karrington Bush, who had 1,055 yards in 2008.

The loss overshadowed the career-best 409 yards passing by SLU's Young.

Central Arkansas improved to 5-1 in the Southland and 6-3 overall while the Lions remained winless in the conference at 0-4 in falling to 2-6 overall.

In Nacogdoches, McNeese State's slide continued with a 37-17 Southland Conference loss against Stephen F. Austin for the Cowboys' fourth-consecutive defeat.

Like a week earlier, a poor second half doomed the Cowboys.

McNeese led 17-14 at halftime before the Lumberjacks scored 24 unanswered points. Wiggs' third field goal of the game opened the second-half scoring before a 9-yard pass from Attaway to Roberson gave SFA a 23-17 lead going into the fourth quarter.

A pass interception in the end zone for a touchdown by SFA's Willie Jefferson when McNeese faced a third-and-20 deep in its own territory and a 1-yard run by Fred Ford rounded out the scoring for the Lumberjacks.

Turnovers helped to give the Cowboys their 17-14 halftime edge. Following a 5-yard run by Champlain Babin to tie the score, Bronson's recovery of a SFA fumble set up a 27-yard Lewis field goal to give McNeese a 10-7 lead after one quarter. Bronson returned an interception 67 yards to set up a 2-yard pass from Stroud to Harold Turnage less than a minute into the second quarter. The reception was the first touchdown catch for the tight end in his McNeese career.

McNeese fell to 2-3 in the SLC while the Lumberjacks evened their league mark at 2-2. The result left both teams 3-5 overall.

The two teams atop the Southland continued to win. Unbeaten Sam Houston State moved to 6-0 in the conference with a 38-9 victory at Southeastern Louisiana while Central Arkansas won 45-20 at home against Northwestern State to improve to 6-1 in the SLC.

The Lions scored first against Sam Houston State on a Sebastian field goal. SHSU grabbed the lead for good when Flanders scampered 39 yards on a shovel pass to set up his own 9-yard touchdown. After a 1-yard touchdown run by Bell, Preston Sanders blocked a Southeastern Louisiana punt with Mike Littleton recovering for the Bearkats at the SLU 38. That set up a 4-yard run by Bell for a 21-3 halftime lead.

SLU's only touchdown came on a 19-yard pass from Young to Kory Theodore with less than five minutes remaining in the game.

The Bearkats remained unbeaten in the Southland while moving to 9-0 overall.

Southeastern Louisiana remained winless in conference play at 0-5 while dipping to 2-7 overall.

Central Arkansas and Northwestern State, each with one Southland Conference loss, were in a fight for second place in the league when the teams met on the Demons' home turf.

The Demons built a 20-14 halftime lead on an 18-yard touchdown run by Morris, a 12-yard pass from Henderson to Hollier and a pair of Shaughnessy field goals. Central Arkansas' points came on an 8-yard run by Bobo for the game's first score and a 29-yard pass from Dick to Soft in the second quarter.

Northwestern led by six points at halftime and received the ball to open the second half. Jeremy Lane, the Demons' return man, fumbled when hit by a host of Bears defenders and Lasker raced 20 yards with the recovery to give Central Arkansas a 21-20 lead.

Lasker's touchdown was just the start of total domination for the Bears in the second half, particularly the third quarter. Central Arkansas outgained the Demons 134-3 in the period while adding two more scores on Dick touchdown passes of 25 yards to Croom and 1 yard to Thomas Hart for a 35-20 Bears lead through three quarters.

Camara kicked a 25-yard field goal early in the fourth quarter and Peters returned an interception 55 yards for a touchdown with 42 seconds left in the game to give Central Arkansas a 45-20 victory.

While UCA picked up another win, the Southland's automatic bid to the FCS playoffs was sealed. Sam Houston State's win over Southeastern Louisiana left the Bearkats with a one-game lead over the Bears. Even with a loss by SHSU the following week against Northwestern State, Sam Houston State would own the tiebreaker over Central Arkansas because of the Bearkats' 31-10 win in head-to-head competition.

Still, the Bears improved to 6-1 in the Southland and 7-3 overall. Northwestern fell to 3-2 in the conference and 5-4 overall.

Meanwhile, two struggling teams met when McNeese State played host to Nicholls State. The Cowboys entered the game with a four-game losing streak while the Colonels had lost seven in a row.

McNeese struck first on a 4-yard run by Anderson in the first quarter. Nicholls countered with a 39-yard Dolan field goal in the first quarter and a 1-yard run by Caston in the second quarter for a 10-7 Colonels lead at halftime.

For a third-straight week, a poor third quarter doomed Nicholls. Anderson scored on a 3-yard run, Lewis booted a 42-yard field goal and Stroud tossed a 4-yard touchdown pass to Kegan Myers as the Cowboys' took a 24-10 lead after three quarters.

Nicholls scored on a 10-yard pass from Caston to Demon Bolt in the fourth quarter. Caston was sacked in the end zone for a safety with less than two minutes remaining to make the final 26-17.

McNeese improved to 3-3 in the SLC and 4-5 overall. Nicholls remained winless in league play at 0-5 while falling to 1-8 overall.

In Beaumont, Stephen F. Austin seemed to really want to make quick work of the Lamar Cardinals. The Lumberjacks scored three touchdowns in a span of 1:11 in the first quarter for a quick 20-0 lead on their way to a 69-10 rout of Lamar. Attaway tossed a 20-yard touchdown pass to Roberson to start the scoring. Jackson fumbled the ensuing kickoff, with Devin Ducote recovering for SFA to set up a 23-yard touchdown run by Keith Lawson. Three plays into the ensuing drive, Ben Wells returned a Doug Prewitt interception for a touchdown for the 20-0 lead.

Lamar's only points in the first half came on a 40-yard pass from Prewitt to Kevin Smith to make the score 20-7. SFA scored the final 35 points of the first half to lead 55-7 at halftime. Among the scores were a 29-yard return of a blocked punt for a touchdown by Jordan Aubrey and three Attaway scoring passes.

Attaway added another touchdown pass in the third quarter as the SFA quarterback finished with 359 yards passing and five scoring tosses. The only points for Lamar in the second half came on a 29-yard Justin Stout field goal with four minutes remaining in the third quarter.

The Cardinals played without their top two quarterbacks. Bevil, the starter, and Johnson, both missed the game after suffering injuries a week earlier.

SFA improved to 3-2 in the Southland and 4-5 overall. Lamar dropped to 2-4 in the conference and 3-6 overall.

Now ranked No. 3 in the nation, Sam Houston State was on a mission to capture its first outright Southland Conference title in front of the home folks with a 43-17 victory over Northwestern State.

Sam Houston State took control early by scoring in a variety of fashions.

Sincere scored on a 31-yard pass from Bell on the opening possession of the game. Flanders, who rushed for 145 yards to top 1,000 on the season, scored on a 15-yard run. After a 38-yard Craig Alaniz field goal, Darnell Taylor returned an interception 23 yards for a touchdown and a 23-0 lead.

Northwestern State avoided a first-half shutout when a direct snap to Sincere was off the mark and Anthony Gilbert recovered the ball in the end zone for a touchdown.

The Bearkats made sure there would be no Northwestern State rally in the second half. Flanders raced 35 yards after a catch for a touchdown while Sincere added touchdowns through the air and on the ground to give SHSU a 43-10 lead on its way to the 43-17 victory.

Sam Houston State finished a perfect 7-0 in the SLC while moving to 10-0 overall. The Bearkats closed out the regular season a week later with a 36-14 victory at Texas State for an unbeaten regular season. A bye in the opening round of the FCS playoffs gave SHSU a week of rest to prepare for the postseason.

Meanwhile, Central Arkansas edged Texas State 23-22 to finish 8-3, good enough to earn an at-large playoff berth. With no game scheduled in the final week of the regular season for most teams, the Bears, like Sam Houston State, had an extra week to prepare for the postseason.

"It was Texas State's transition to the FBS and they really didn't want to play that game and the conference kind of held their feet to the fire that they would play a conference schedule," Conque recounted.

Among non-contenders, Stephen F. Austin's points didn't come quite as quickly or as often against Lamar from a week earlier, but an early lead allowed the Lumberjacks to hold on for a 28-20 victory over Southeastern Louisiana in SFA's final home game of the 2011 season.

A 2-yard pass from Attaway to Marquis Mosley gave SFA a 7-0 lead at the 5:26 mark of the first quarter. Slightly more than two minutes later, it was 14-0 following a 12-yard run by Gus Johnson on a drive set up by a 51-yard punt return by Crawford.

SLU rallied back when Frank Bryant returned an errant Attaway throw 78 yards to set up a 1-yard touchdown run by Zeke Jones to close out the first quarter and a 33-yard Seth Sebastian field goal late in the second quarter to trail 14-10 before Stephen F. Austin closed out the first half on a 3-yard pass from Attaway to Crawford.

Sebastian provided the only scoring of the third quarter with a 32-yard field goal. A 45-yard touchdown toss from Attaway to Gambel early in the fourth quarter was countered by a 29-yard scoring strike from Young to Theodore to make the score 28-20.

Needing a touchdown and two-point conversion to force overtime, the Lions reached the SFA 10-yard line in the closing moments of the game. Three-consecutive incomplete passes by Young allowed the Lumberjacks to hold on for the victory.

SFA improved to 4-2 in the Southland and 5-4 overall. Southeastern Louisiana dropped to 0-6 in the conference and 2-8 overall.

In Thibodaux, Caston and Bolt hooked up on a 9-yard touchdown pass less than three minutes into Nicholls State's home finale against Lamar but the lead would not last in a 34-26 loss for the Colonels.

By the time halftime rolled around, the Colonels trailed 14-10. Lamar increased its advantage to 11 points midway in the third quarter when Adrian Guillory returned a blocked punt 29 yards for a touchdown.

Nicholls got back in the game on a 27-yard Dolan field goal and a 21-yard run by Caston to trail 21-19 after three quarters.

The Cardinals put the game away in the fourth quarter on Bevil touchdown passes of 14 yards to Jackson and 32 yards to Hayes.

Caston and Bolt hooked up on another 9-yard touchdown pass with five seconds left in the game to account for the final margin.

Nicholls fell to 0-6 in the SLC and 1-9 overall. Lamar improved to 2-4 in the conference and 4-6 overall.

Teams with a combined 0-12 Southland Conference record met less than a week later when Nicholls State visited Southeastern Louisiana to close out the 2011 season on a Thursday night.

The Colonels never seriously challenged Southeastern although the game remained close going into the second half. A 21-yard Sebastian field goal on the opening possession of the game gave the Lions a 3-0 lead. SLU made it 10-0 at halftime on a touchdown pass from Young to Theodore with two seconds remaining before intermission.

Nicholls missed out on a pair of scoring opportunities in the first half. Dolan missed a 39-yard field goal attempt and Caston fumbled near the goal line on fourth-and-1 from the Lions' 1-yard line.

SLU pulled away with a 21-point third quarter. A 1-yard run by LaTruan Weary, a 6-yard sprint by Zeke Jones and a Dean Johnson score from 8 yards out gave the Lions a 31-0 lead.

Lions' receiver Simmie Yarborough had three catches for 67 yards in the game. He concluded his career as SLU's all-time receiver with 229 receptions, 2,780 receiving yards and 30 touchdown catches.

Nicholls, which started the season with a victory for a three-game win streak over two seasons, scored the last two touchdowns of the contest on a 2-yard run by Klann and the quarterback's 3-yard pass to Blair to make the final 31-14.

SLU ended the year 3-8 overall and 1-6 in the Southland. The Colonels, who closed the season with 10-consecutive losses, finished the season 1-10 overall and 0-7 in the conference.

Meanwhile, Stephen F. Austin used a strong second quarter in a 33-0 victory at Northwestern State to end the 2011 season and secure a winning campaign for the Lumberjacks.

Attaway connected with Roberson on a 42-yard touchdown pass early in the second quarter for the only score of the first half. A 2-yard run by Johnson, a 7-yard touchdown catch by Crawford and a 22-yard Wiggs field goal allowed SFA to pull away for a 24-0 lead after three quarters. Wiggs added another field goal and Dalton Williams tossed to Gambel for a touchdown to make the final 33-0.

The Lumberjacks recorded eight sacks in the game and limited the Demons to 100 yards of total offense.

SFA concluded the season 6-5 overall and 5-2 in the Southland. Northwestern State ended 5-6 overall and 3-4 in the conference.

In Beaumont, McNeese State secured its seventh-consecutive winning season with a 45-17 thrashing of Lamar to close out the 2011 season.

A pair of big defensive plays helped McNeese to pull away in the Southland Conference tilt. Holding only a 17-10 lead, Bronson returned an interception 44 yards to put the Cowboys up by two touchdowns. Janzen Jackson returned another errant Cardinals throw 84 yards for a touchdown in the final minute of the game.

Lamar held an early 10-3 lead on a 24-yard pass from Bevil to Hayes before McNeese tied the game at the end of one quarter on a 34-yard run by Carey. An 11-yard run by Anderson with 1:15 showing in the second quarter gave the Cowboys a 17-10 lead at the break.

Following Bronson's interception return for the only score in the third quarter, Lamar countered with a 12-yard touchdown pass from Caleb Berry to Jesse Sparks less than a minute into the fourth quarter. McNeese scored the final 21 points of the game. Dontae Spencer scored on a 67-yard gallop and Anderson added a 2-yard touchdown before Jackson came up with his 84-yard interception return.

Bevil and Berry combined to pass for 336 yards but were picked off a total of four times. The Cardinals were held to 39 yards rushing on 26 attempts.

McNeese concluded the season 6-5 overall and 4-3 in the Southland. Lamar ended the year 4-7 overall, including 2-5 in conference play.

Making the Football Championship Subdivision playoffs in only its second year of eligibility, Central Arkansas decided to hang around for a little while. Dick passed for 319 yards and accounted for three touchdowns as the Bears won at Tennessee Tech 34-14 in the opening round of the playoffs.

A 1-yard run by Bobo in the first quarter and a 25-yard Camara field goal four seconds into the second quarter staked the Bears to a 10-0 lead. Leading 10-7, Dick came up with his first touchdown of the game on a 1-yard run to cap a 97-yard drive at the 1:55 mark of the second quarter for a 17-7 halftime edge for UCA

After another Camara field goal in the third quarter, Dick fired touchdown passes of 42 yards to Gandy in the second quarter and 30 yards to Hart in the fourth.

Tennessee Tech, which was held to 58 yards rushing, including only 10 at halftime, got its points on touchdown passes by quarterback Tre Lamb in the second and fourth quarters.

"It was probably our most complete game all season, to go on the road and beat a good Ohio Valley Conference team," said Conque.

As the No. 1 seed in the playoffs and with an opening-round bye, Sam Houston State had home-field advantage through the semifinals. If the Bearkats reached the championship game, they would not have to travel out of the state since the site for the finals was in Frisco, Texas.

So, the Bearkats found themselves in familiar surroundings against Stony Brook but facing unusual circumstances. Sam Houston State's high-scoring offense was held to only a 28-yard Alaniz field goal and less than 100 yards of total offense to trail 10-3 at halftime. For the first time all season, SHSU trailed going into the second half.

Sam Houston State did all the scoring in the third quarter to pull ahead 17-10 going into the final 15 minutes of play. Bell tossed a 5-yard touchdown pass to Sincere to tie the game and the quarterback scored on a 5-yard run to give his team the advantage.

Seawolves kicker Wesley Skiffington and Alaniz traded field goals to open the fourth quarter before a 3-yard touchdown pass from Kyle Essington to Kevin Norrell tied the game 20-20 with 8:56 remaining in the game.

Bell tossed an 80-yard bomb to Diller on the first play from scrimmage after Norrell's touchdown to again give SHSU the lead but Stony Brook tied the game at 27-27 with 6:37 showing on a 2-yard run by Brock Jackolski.

Taking over at their own 17-yard line, the Bearkats mounted a time-consuming, 10-play drive. Flanders picked up 36 yards on the drive and Bell had two runs that provided timely conversions to keep the possession alive. With 1:01 left in the game, Flanders raced for a 7-yard touchdown to give Sam Houston State a 34-27 triumph.

"That was the second-best team we played that season behind North Dakota State," Fritz said of Stoney Brook. "They were an excellent team. They were a real hard-nosed team on offense, defense and the kicking game."

Central Arkansas couldn't make it past the second round of the playoffs, falling 41-14 at perennial national contender Montana.

The fifth-ranked Grizzlies turned three first-quarter Central Arkansas turnovers into 17 points on their way to a 31-0 halftime lead. A 31-yard Brody McKnight field goal, an 8-yard pass from Jordan Johnson to Jabin Sambrano and a 2-yard run by Peter Nguyen gave Montana its 17-0 edge

Central Arkansas, which was held to 25 yards rushing, didn't score until the Bears were down 38-0. Dick tossed a 44-yard pass to Gandy in the third quarter for UCA's initial score. Dick hooked up with Lasker from 8 yards out with 1:58 left in the game to make the final 41-14.

"It's one of the great environments in the country to play college football on any level. It was like 18 degrees at kickoff," Conque recalled.

The Bears ended their season 9-4.

"It was a great run and a great year," said Conque.

Sam Houston State was looking to avoid the slow start of the Stony Brook game but the Bearkats nevertheless found themselves with a scant 7-6 edge early in the second quarter against Montana State in the FCS quarterfinals.

A 54-yard touchdown run by Bell and the quarterback's 40-yard touchdown strike to Sincere gave SHSU a 21-6 lead but the Bobcats were looking to cut into the deficit with a field goal to close out the first half. Instead, Sanders blocked Jason Cunningham's 39-yard attempt and the Bearkats kept their 15-point lead and the momentum.

The Bobcats seemed to shrug off the blocked field goal, coming up with a 7-yard touchdown pass from DeNarius McGhee to Everett Gilbert to open up the third quarter and pull Montana State to within eight points at 21-13.

Sam Houston State's special teams again snatched the momentum for the Bearkats when Brandon Closner returned the ensuing kickoff 82 yards for a touchdown. It was never a contest from that point as SHSU added three more touchdowns for a 49-13 final that advanced the Bearkats to the FCS semifinals.

The Bearkats won the game by rushing for a season-best 428 yards while holding Montana State's normally-strong ground attack to 77 yards. Sincere produced 203 all-purpose yards, including a career-high 160 yards rushing.

"We really did a good job of stacking the box and playing a lot of man coverage," Fritz said of the Bearkats' defensive effort.

Up next for the Bearkats was 11-2 Montana, a nemesis to both Southland Conference teams and Sam Houston State in particular. SHSU seemed to continually run into the Grizzlies in the playoffs, including the 2004 semifinals when Montana eliminated the Bearkats 34-13 at home.

Unlike Sam Houston State's first two games of the playoffs, the Bearkats jumped out to big advantage, leading 21-0 after one quarter.

An 11-yard touchdown run by Bell gave SHSU a 7-0 lead. Shortly after Montana's McKnight missed a 48-yard field goal attempt, Flanders broke loose on a tackle-breaking 69-yard run for a 14-0 lead. The run was the longest of Flanders' career and came in a game in which he rushed for a school-record 287 yards. A 20-yard pass from Bell to Grant Merritt made it 21-0.

A 30-yard touchdown pass from Johnson to Sambrano and a 61-yard interception return for a touchdown by Calebe McSurdy allowed the Grizzlies to make it a 14-point game at halftime at 28-14.

Alamoz kicked a 25-yard field goal in the third quarter for a 31-14 SHSU lead but that would be the last time the Bearkats would score in the game.

Meanwhile, the Grizzlies fought back. A 3-yard run by Jordan Canada late in the third quarter made it 31-21. Johnson's 54-yard run with 11:26 remaining in the game made it a three-point contest at 31-28.

Clinging to their three-point lead in the closing minutes, the Bearkats faced fourth-and-1 from their own 47. Instead of punting the ball away, Sam Houston State elected to go for the first down in the hopes of running out the clock. Flanders broke loose on a 22-yard run and the Bearkats advanced to the national championship game with a 31-28 triumph.

"Flanders was really hot that ball game. They were having a hard time stopping him on that particular drive. We felt like we wanted to keep it in our hands and not put it in their hands for the outcome of the game. He (Flanders) made a great run and actually had the wherewithal to stay in bounds and that ended the ball game," Fritz said.

Sam Houston State was not exactly playing in its own back yard for the national championship, but the Bearkats knew the neighborhood. The title game was held at Pizza Hut Park in Frisco, Texas, a suburb of Dallas. The professional soccer stadium was only about 200 miles north of Huntsville, with the Southland serving as the host conference for the event.

North Dakota State may have had a much longer journey, but the Bison felt at home before a sellout crowd of 20,586, especially while clinging to a scant 3-0 lead in the first half.

For most of the first half, the only points produced in the defensive-oriented contest was a 19-yard Ryan Jastram field goal.

Sam Houston State managed to tie the game with 2:18 remaining in the first half on a 24-yard Alaniz field goal. The Bearkats forced a three-and-out to get the ball back. Alaniz connected on a 31-yard field goal with 40 seconds remaining in the first half to give SHSU a 6-3 halftime edge.

The Bearkats managed to gain the lead by shutting down the Bison after North Dakota State's initial field goal. Sam Houston State looked to do the same at the start of the second half.

North Dakota State faced fourth-and-4 from its own 34 when Matt Voigtlander went into punt formation. Voigtlander, a former running back, took off on a 27-yard sprint for a first down past the surprised Bearkats. On the next play, Bison quarterback Brock Jensen tossed a screen pass to D.J. McNorton. McNorton raced 39 yards for a touchdown and a 10-6 Bison lead at the 12:47 mark of the third quarter.

"That was a big turning point in the game," Fritz said of the fake punt. "We had played so well defensively. They did a good job of taking a chance and we didn't have it defended very well."

Like the first half, yards and points were tough to come by for both teams in the final two quarters.

An errant throw by Bell was picked off by North Dakota State's Travis Beck. The Bison linebacker rambled down to the 1-yard line before being brought down by Bell. Jensen dove in for the touchdown on the next play for a 17-6 North Dakota State lead with 8:45 left in the fourth quarter that would hold up the remainder of the game to deny the Bearkats a national championship.

North Dakota State won the national championship despite being limited to 235 yards of total offense. Meanwhile, the Bison defense did a masterful job of shutting down a Sam Houston State offense that boasted the highest-scoring offense in the country. North Dakota State held the Bearkats to 210 total yards and 33 points below their seasonal average.

"They had a great plan for us defensively. The big deal is they did a great job of not allowing us to run the ball," said Fritz.

Sam Houston State's most successful season ended at 14-1. The loss in the national championship game snapped a 16-game winning streak stretching back to the 2010 season.

BEARKATS RETURN TO FRISCO

Southeastern Louisiana made a coaching change for the 2012 season, replacing Mike Lucas with Ron Roberts. The head coach at Delta State from 2007-2011, Roberts was familiar with the Southland Conference, having served as defensive coordinator at Texas State in 2003.

Roberts made his Southland debut when the Lions hosted McNeese State. Southeastern Louisiana went into the game still seeking its first win of the season after opening with losses to Missouri, South Dakota State and Tennessee-Martin. McNeese was unbeaten through three games with victories over Middle Tennessee State, McMurry and Weber State.

McNeese seemed to be headed to a 4-0 start on the season before the Lions began to rally late in the third quarter.

A 2-yard touchdown run by Michael Chaney rallied Southeastern Louisiana to within 24-17 with less than four minutes remaining in the third quarter. Nathan Stanley's 3-yard touchdown pass to Taylor Jenkins with less than three minutes left in the game made the score 24-23. Electing to go for a two-point conversion, Chaney scored on a run to put the Lions on top 25-24.

On the first play of the ensuing drive, Robert Alford intercepted a pass by McNeese quarterback Cody Stroud and the Lions ran out the clock to give Roberts his initial win as Southeastern Louisiana's coach.

Also opening Southland Conference play was Sam Houston State and Central Arkansas when the teams met Conway. Sam Houston State went into the game 1-1 while UCA was 2-1.

Tim Flanders, who rushed for 96 of his 125 yards in the first quarter, gave the third-ranked Bearkats an early lead on a 39-yard touchdown run against Central Arkansas. After Flanders added an 11-yard touchdown run in the fourth quarter and Miguel Antonio kicked a 26-yard field goal, the Bearkats enjoyed a 20-10 lead late in the final period.

A 17-yard run by Central Arkansas quarterback Wynrick Smothers rallied the Bears to within three points. After forcing a SHSU punt, Smothers hooked up with Dominique Croom on a 41-yard connection to the Bearkats' 26. Smothers fired to Croom in the end zone to give the Bears their first lead of the game at 24-20.

Trey Diller hauled in three passes from Bearkats quarterback Brian Bell to help Sam Houston State reach the Bears' 24 in the closing seconds. Bell threw in the direction of Diller in the end zone with three seconds left. Diller was unable to make the catch, with the deflected ball being intercepted by safety Karl Brady to give Central Arkansas a 24-20 upset victory.

The loss snapped a 13-game regular-season winning streak for SHSU and was the Bearkats' first Southland Conference loss since the 2010 season.

"It was one of the great games I was a part of," Central Arkansas coach Clint Conque said. "You had two really good football teams going at it. It was probably the hottest game. It was a 3 p.m. TV game in September. I can remember the temperature down on the field being in the 125-130 degree range. It was extremely hot."

Central Arkansas wasn't quite so fortunate a week later, falling 42-37 at Stephen F. Austin. The Lumberjacks went into the contest 1-3 on the season. After opening with a win over Southwestern Oklahoma State, SFA lost its next three games going into the UCA encounter.

Despite heavy rain that led to a slick artificial turf field and a combined eight lost fumbles, the Lumberjacks proved to be better handling the conditions in Stephen F. Austin's 42-37 win over Central Arkansas.

Gus Johnson rushed for 215 yards and four touchdowns for the Lumberjacks. The SFA passing game was effective as well. Brady Attaway passed for 296 yards and two touchdowns, while Cordell Roberson hauled in nine passes for 149 yards. Roberson was coming off a Texas State game in which he caught two touchdown passes to give him 32 for his career, setting new SFA and Southland Conference career marks.

Central Arkansas, meanwhile, was limited to 217 total yards. One of the game's many fumbles was returned 72 yards for a touchdown by Jonathan Woodard with 4:29 remaining in the game to pull the Bears to within a touchdown of Stephen F. Austin at 42-35. A late safety made the final 42-37.

Along with Woodard's return for a touchdown, UCA scored two other touchdowns in the game off of Lumberjacks turnovers. Trailing 6-0, Woodward forced a fumble that was recovered by Rojae Jackson at the SFA 46. Four plays later, Terence Bobo scored on a 4-yard run to give the Bears a 7-6 edge. On the first play following the ensuing kickoff, Attaway was dropped for a 7-yard loss on a running attempt and fumbled. The ball scooted into the end zone with Markeit Gaines recovering for a Central Arkansas touchdown and a 14-6 lead for the Bears.

"It was estimated there was 12 inches of rain between Satuday and Sunday morning. It was played in a constant monsoon. At times, you couldn't see the opposite side of the field," Conque said. "There was so much rain, the artificial turf field bubbled up and Stephen F. Austin had to get a new playing surface after that season."

The loss, Conque said, refocused his football team.

"It was one of those years where we had a very good football team, similar to 2008 when we went to Thibodaux and got beat in a close game. I think it re-centered our football team. We were real driven and focused from then on," he said.

Southeastern Louisiana moved to 2-0 in the Southland Conference for the first time since 2009 and snapped a 14-game road losing streak with a 31-21 victory at Lamar.

The Cardinals went into their league opener against SLU 2-1 on the season with wins over Texas College and Incarnate Word and a loss to South Alabama.

Against SLU, Lamar rallied to within three points at 17-14 on a 10-yard touchdown pass from quarterback Ryan Mossakowski to Payden McVey with 7:40 remaining in the third quarter. A 75-yard punt return moments later by Alford increased the Lions' advantage to 24-14. Stanley hooked up with Blaine LeBlanc on a 3-yard touchdown pass four seconds into the fourth quarter to provide added cushion for the Lions.

Southeastern Louisiana's defense held Lamar to 244 yards total offense and intercepted Mossakowski four times.

Northwestern State went into its Southland opener at McNeese State sporting a 2-2 record. The Demons split their first four games with wins over Arkansas-Monticello and Mississippi Valley, with losses to Texas Tech and Nevada.

Touchdown passes from Stroud to Josh Jordan and Diontae Spencer, plus a 17-yard Josh Lewis field goal saw the Demons fall behind 17-0 at halftime.

Down 30-14, Northwestern State quarterback Brad Henderson connected with Jovhan Jilbert on a 58-yard touchdown pass with less than six minutes left in the game. The Demons marched deep into McNeese territory on their next possession but Ford Smesny's interception of a Henderson pass ended the threat as Northwestern State went on to lose by eight points.

Nicholls State opened Southland Conference play a week later with a 34-14 loss at Central Arkansas. The Colonels went into the game coming off a 73-17 whipping of Evangel. The victory over the Crusaders was the first of the year for Nicholls and snapped a 12-game losing streak for the Colonels. The last win for

Nicholls came over the NAIA Crusaders in the 2011 season opener. Prior to the victory over Evangel, the Colonels lost their first two games of 2012 to South Alabama and Tulsa.

A pair of Central Arkansas field goals and a 1-yard touchdown run by Jackie Hinton were countered by a 4-yard run by Marcus Washington and a 79-yard touchdown strike from Nicholls quarterback Landry Klann to Erik Buchanan to give the Colonels a 14-13 halftime edge.

Central Arkansas put the game away by scoring 21-unanswered points in the second half. An 18-yard run by Bobo capped the Bears' opening drive of the third quarter to put UCA on top 20-14. The Bears added a 13-yard touchdown reception by Croom and a Jacoby Walker touchdown to pull away.

Sam Houston State and Stephen F. Austin continued to put on a show in the Battle of the Piney Woods rivalry and the fans continued to show up in record numbers for the event at Houston's Reliant Stadium. The schools set a new attendance record of 26,185 for the event when the teams squared off in 2012.

The Bearkats looked like a team on their way to a blowout victory, building leads of 23-14 at halftime and 44-21 late in the third quarter.

It didn't start off or conclude that way. Attaway tossed two of his six touchdowns in the early going to give the Lumberjacks an early 14-3 edge. Following an Antonio field goal slightly more than two minutes into the game, Attaway hooked up with Ryan Gambel on a 30-yard touchdown toss in the closing seconds of the first quarter and 27 yards to DeVante Lacy six seconds into the second quarter to give SFA its lead.

Sam Houston State countered by scoring the final 20 points of the half to lead 23-14 at the break. Bell threw a touchdown pass, Bookie Sneed returned an interception a school-record 92 yards for a touchdown and Antonio kicked two field goals to spark the Bearkats.

Attaway's third touchdown of the game, a 77-yard bomb to D.J. Ward less than 30 seconds into the second half, rallied SFA to within two points at 23-21 but the Bearkats went on another run, scoring three touchdowns for their 44-21 lead. Bell tossed two touchdown passes and ran for another as SHSU took a 23-point lead at the 5:10 mark of the third quarter.

After Attaway closed out the quarter with a 70-yard strike to Roberson, Bell scored Sam Houston State's final touchdown of the game on a 9-yard run for a 51-28 SHSU lead with 13:05 left in the contest. Bell finished the game with three touchdown passes and two scoring runs.

The Lumberbacks, however, were not done. Moments after Bell's run, Brady hit Roberson with a 3-yard scoring pass and added a two-point conversion toss to Ward to make it 51-36. Brady's third touchdown of the game to Roberson from 8 yards out with 5:43 showing brought the score to 51-43.

SFA marched downfield one last time but an Attaway pass on fourth down fell incomplete near the goal line, enabling the Bearkats to hang on for the eight-point triumph.

The result left both teams 1-1 in the Southland while Sam Houston State improved to 3-2 overall and SFA dropped to 2-4.

"At the end, Attaway got really hot. They spread it out and they have talented receivers. It was a tough game. We did just enough to run out the clock," said Bearkats coach Willie Fritz.

Northwestern State and Lamar went into their contest seeking their first Southland wins of the season when the teams squared off in Natchitoches.

The Demons built a 10-0 lead on a 41-yard John Shaughnessy field goal and a 26-yard touchdown run by receiver Phillip Harvey out of the wildcat formation for a 10-0 lead after one quarter. Northwestern State was looking for more when Lamar's James Washington scooped up a Demons fumble and scampered 62 yards for a touchdown with less than five minutes remaining in the second quarter to make the score 10-7. The Demons responded with a 4-yard touchdown pass from Henderson to Tucker Nims to lead 17-7 at halftime.

With the Demons clinging to a 20-17 lead going into the fourth quarter, Northwestern State's Leslie Deamer forced a fumble on a sack and came up with the loose ball at the Lamar 5-yard line. Robert Walker scored on a 3-yard run to extend the Demons' lead to 27-17 with 6:46 left in the game.

Northwestern State added a 20-yard Shaughnessy field goal and an 8-yard touchdown pass from Lamar's Caleb Berry to Jordan Edwards with 36 seconds left in the game made the final 30-23.

The Demons evened their record at 1-1 in the SLC and 3-3 overall. Lamar dropped to 0-2 in the conference and 2-4 overall.

Southeastern Louisiana moved to 3-0 in the Southland Conference a week later with a 27-22 victory over visiting Northwestern State.

The Lions built a lead of 14-3 and when Northwestern State attempted the rally, Southeastern Louisiana seemed to have an answer. A 4-yard touchdown pass from Henderson to Corey Simmons made the score 14-9 before the Lions countered with a pair of Seth Sebastian field goals. Henderson's 30-yard strike to Daniel Taylor made it 20-15 but an 11-yard touchdown run by Xavier Roberson stretched the Lions' advantage on SLU's way to the 27-22 triumph.

The result left both teams 3-4 overall while Northwestern State dropped to 1-2 in SLC action.

Central Arkansas, meanwhile, moved to 3-1 in the Southland by nipping McNeese State 27-26 in Lake Charles.

Things didn't look good for the Bears late in the game as Central Arkansas trailed by nine points with less than four minutes remaining in the contest. Needing to score quickly, the Bears moved 72 yards in 2:18, capping the drive on a 19-yard touchdown pass from Smothers to Dezmin Lewis to make the score 26-24 with slightly more than a minute left in the game.

Central Arkansas recovered an onside kick, enabling the Bears to get the ball back at the McNeese State 38. Three running plays set up a 47-yard Eddie Camara field goal with 23 seconds left in the game to give UCA its 27-26 victory.

McNeese, which fell to 1-2 in the Southland and 4-2 overall, seemingly had command of the game when Marcus Wiltz scored on a 29-yard run with 3:28 left in the game to put the Cowboys on top 26-17.

Along with moving to 3-1 in the SLC, the Bears improved to 5-2 overall with the come-from-behind triumph.

Playing on the road for the fifth-consecutive week didn't seem to bother the ninth-ranked Bearkats as Sam Houston blanked Nicholls State 41-0.

Nicholls missed out on an early scoring opportunity when Andrew Dolan missed a 32-yard field-goal attempt in a scoreless opening quarter. The first of three touchdown runs by Flanders and a 5-yard pass from Bell to Melvis Pride gave the Bearkats a 14-0 lead at halftime.

Flanders, whose three touchdowns gave him 270 points to become SHSU' all-time scoring leader, scored twice in the second quarter and Bell tossed a touchdown pass as the Bearkats put the game away by halftime with a 34-0 lead.

"If you look at it statistically, Tim might be the most dominant player in the history of the Southland Conference," Fritz said of the Bearkats running back. "By far, he has the (conference's all-time) rushing record. By far, he has the touchdown record. And there was a ton of games where he played very little in the second half or didn't play at all in the fourth quarter. There was one season, if you added up the quarters he didn't play, it was almost four games. That's how dominating he really was."

SHSU rushed for 261 yards in the game while Nicholls was limited to 258 total yards. Playing without Washington, the team's starting tailback, the Colonels were held to 20 yards rushing.

Sam Houston State improved to 2-1 in the Southland Conference and 4-2 overall, while Nicholls dropped to 0-2 in the league and 1-4 on the year.

"To me, this was the beginning of us playing really well. From that point forward, we really dominated in the Southland Conference," said Fritz.

With all the recent success Sam Houston State enjoyed while playing on the road for five weeks, the Bearkats might have experienced a few anxious moments after falling behind 10-7 in the second quarter at home against McNeese State.

A 32-yard pass from Stroud to Kelvin Bennett and a 44-yard Lewis field goal gave the Cowboys the lead with slightly less than 10 minutes remaining in the first half. SHSU countered with touchdown runs of 44 yards by Sincere and 12 yards by Flanders to close out the first half with the Bearkats on top 21-10.

Sincere and Flanders combined to rush for 225 of Sam Houston State's 336 yards on the ground. Meanwhile, the Bearkats' defense began to clamp down on the McNeese offense. After surrendering 119 yards in the first quarter, the SHSU defense held the Cowboys to 73 total yards over the remaining three quarters.

Starting with Sincere's touchdown run in the second quarter, the Bearkats scored the final 38 points of the game to take a 45-10 victory. Sincere, who rushed for 132 yards, added a 65-yard touchdown run in the fourth quarter.

The Bearkats' four-game winning streak moved SHSU to 3-1 in the Southland Conference and 5-2 overall. McNeese fell to 1-3 in the league and 4-3 overall.

Central Arkansas, meanwhile, made sure it remained near the top of the Southland Conference standings with a 24-14 victory over visiting Lamar.

Although never seriously threatened, the Bears put the game away with 10 minutes left in the contest on a 75-yard touchdown pass from Smothers to Jesse Gandy to build a 24-7 advantage. Lamar tightened the score on a 4-yard run by DePaul Garrett with less than two minutes left in the game. The only other score for the Cardinals came on a 7-yard run by Berry in the third quarter.

UCA moved to 4-1 in the Southland and 6-2 overall. Lamar remained winless in the conference at 0-3 while dropping to 3-5 overall.

In Nacogdoches, Stephen F. Austin scored the game's first 31 points as the Lumberjacks had little trouble disposing of Nicholls State with a 44-10 domination of the Colonels.

Attaway tossed four of his five touchdown passes in the first half. Two of the scoring passes went to Aaron Thomas, the first one giving the Lumberjacks a 10-0 lead after one quarter.

Nicholls cracked the scoreboard early in the third quarter when a Darvin Butler interception set up a 40-yard Dolan field goal to make the score 31-3. The only touchdown for the Colonels came with 4:08 left in the contest on a fake field goal when Ben Landry tossed to Nick Scelfo for a 20-yard score.

Attaway finished with 474 yards passing and five touchdowns.

Nicholls struggled offensively, finishing with 13 yards rushing. Klann, who got the start at quarterback for the Colonels, passed for only 91 yards. Beaux Hebert was 11 of 18 passing for 163 yards in relief of Klann.

SFA improved to 2-1 in the Southland Conference and 3-4 overall. Nicholls fell to 0-3 in the league and 1-5 overall.

Smothers fired three touchdown passes a week later as Central Arkansas won at Southeastern Louisiana 34-14 in a critical Southland Conference encounter. The Bears went into the game 4-1 in the SLC while Southeastern was undefeated at 3-0.

The Bears jumped out to a 21-0 lead, with two of the scores coming on Smothers touchdown passes of 7 yards to Chase Dixon and 60 yards to Gandy. SLU put itself right back in the contest on touchdown tosses to Tony McCrea and Roberson in the third quarter.

A 26-yard field goal by Eddie Camara and a 48-yard touchdown pass to Gandy in the fourth quarter allowed the Bears to pull away.

UCA moved to 5-1 in the Southland and 7-2 overall. The Lions' first SLC loss of the year dropped Southeastern Louisiana to 3-1 in the league and 3-5 overall.

Meanwhile, one-sided victories continued for Sam Houston State with a 56-7 road domination of Lamar.

Touchdown runs by Flanders in each of the first two quarters plus a 48-yard pass from Bell to Diller gave Sam Houston State a 21-0 halftime lead over the Cardinals. Flanders ran for four touchdowns in a game in which the Bearkats rushed for slightly less than 300 yards.

After Keshawn Hill's 6-yard touchdown run gave SHSU a 42-0 lead, Lamar came up with its only points of the game when Kevin Johnson returned the ensuing kickoff 89 yards for a touchdown at the 4:38 mark of the third quarter.

Sam Houston State improved to 4-1 in the Southland and 6-2 overall. Lamar remained winless in the league at 0-4 while dropping to 3-6 overall.

In Lake Charles, Stephen F. Austin trailed by a touchdown at halftime but stormed out of the gate early in the third quarter to take the lead over McNeese State. A 1-yard run by Doug Gentry two minutes into the third quarter tied the game 21-21. Jordan Wiggs kicked a 20-yard field goal at the 7:41 mark of the third period to give SFA its first lead of the game at 24-21.

McNeese countered moments later when Stroud tossed 15 yards to Kenny Brown to put the Cowboys back on top at 28-24 heading into the fourth quarter. Marcus Wiltz, who rushed for 111 yards, scored on a 35-yard touchdown run with three minutes left in the game to secure a 35-24 victory for McNeese.

The Cowboys jumped out to a 14-0 lead on an 11-yard pass from Stroud to Wes Briscoe and a 4-yard run by Darius Carey in the first quarter.

SFA tied the game on a couple of Attaway touchdown passes. Attaway, who had a Cowboys Stadium-record 68 pass attempts, hooked up with Roberson on a 3-yard touchdown and Ward from 9 yards out to tie the game in the second quarter. Stroud hit Jordan with a 20-yard strike with 1:06 remaining in the second quarter to give McNeese its 21-14 edge at the break.

McNeese improved to 2-3 in the SLC and 5-3 overall. The Lumberjacks fell to 2-2 in the conference and 3-5 overall.

A missed extra point after Nicholls State's opening touchdown of the game came back to haunt the Colonels at Northwestern State.

Washington's 2-yard run produced the game's first points but Jamaal White's block of the conversion attempt left the Colonels with a 6-0 lead. Touchdown runs of 3 yards by Henderson and 55 yards by Taylor sandwiched a 28-yard Dolan field goal to give the Demons a 14-9 halftime lead.

Trailing 21-9, the Colonels rallied to take the lead at 26-21 on a 22-yard Dolan field goal, along with Klann touchdown passes of 29 yards to Aldaro Russell and 9 yards to Jesse Turner early in the fourth quarter.

Shaughnessy's 42-yard field goal with 11:30 left in the game inched Northwestern State to within two points at 26-24. The Demons kicker connected again from 42 yards out with 8:57 left in the game to make it 27-26.

Nicholls got the ball back with 1:21 left in the contest but a sack of Klann on second down and two incomplete passes by the Colonels quarterback gave the ball back to the Demons, who were able to run out the clock for the one-point triumph.

Northwestern State evened its record at 2-2 in the Southland and 4-4 overall. Nicholls joined Lamar at the bottom of the SLC at 0-4 while falling to 1-6 overall.

Smothers accounted for five touchdowns as Central Arkansas defeated visiting Northwestern State 35-14 to capture the Southland Conference's automatic bid to the FCS playoffs.

The win allowed the Bears to finish SLC play 6-1. Even if Central Arkansas ended up finishing in a tie with either of the two remaining one-loss teams in the conference, Sam Houston State or Southeastern Louisiana, the Bears would end up with the league automatic bid by virtue of UCA's head-to-head wins over both the Bearkats and Lions.

Smothers passed for 225 yards and four scores, with two of his touchdown tosses going to Croom. The Central Arkansas quarterback also rushed for 97 yards and a touchdown.

Finished with Southland Conference play, UCA had an open date before defeating Eastern Illinois 48-30 to head into the playoffs 9-2 and on a six-game winning streak.

While there would be no automatic bid to the playoffs in the offing for Sam Houston State, the Bearkats put themselves in position to claim a share of the Southland Conference title with a whopping 70-0 home victory over Southeastern Louisiana.

Flanders scored on a 14-yard run six minutes into the game to give fourth-ranked Sam Houston State a 7-0 lead against Southeastern Louisiana. The other 63 points really weren't necessary as the SHSU defense blanked the Lions.

The Bearkats recorded their second shutout in four weeks. Over that four-game span, Sam Houston State outscored its opponents 212-17.

Flanders' score was the start of five touchdowns in five possessions for the Bearkats to give Sam Houston State a 35-0 lead. A 23-yard pass from Bell to Torrance Williams with 24 seconds remaining in the second quarter gave SHSU a 42-0 halftime lead.

Sam Houston State improved to 5-1 in the Southland and 7-2 overall. Southeastern Louisiana fell to 3-2 in the SLC and 3-6 overall.

In Nacogdoches, a weather delay may have seemed a bit longer for Lamar than it did for Stephen F. Austin. Bad weather caused a two-and-a-half hour delay and once play began, the Cardinals found themselves behind 7-6 after one quarter.

Gentry started things off for Stephen F. Austin with a touchdown before Justin Stout countered with a pair of field goals for Lamar.

The Lumberjacks played like they wanted to put the game away by halftime, just in case more bad weather appeared. SFA scored four times in the second quarter to give the Lumberjacks a 27-6 halftime lead. Wiggs kicked two field goals while Attaway tossed touchdown passes of 11 yards to Ward and 12 to Kris Lott to put the Lumberjacks up by 21 points at the break.

Mossakowski did his best to keep the Cardinals in the game in the second half. The Lamar quarterback tossed all three of his touchdown passes in the final two quarters. All three scores went to Edwards. The duo hooked up twice in the third quarter on scoring passes of 60 and 39 yards. Mossakowski connected with Edwards from 56 yards out for the game's last touchdown to make the final 40-26.

Despite the effort of Mossakowski and Edwards, the closest the Cardinals could get in the second half was 14 points on three different occasions as SFA continually answered a Lamar touchdown with one of its own.

Wiggs finished with four field goals in the game, adding a kick of 27 yards late in the third quarter and another from 21 yards out in the fourth period.

SFA improved to 3-2 in the Southland and 4-5 overall. Lamar remained winless in the conference at 0-5 while dropping to 3-7 overall.

A 50-yard toss from Stroud to Carey on McNeese State's opening play of the game set up the quarterback's 5-yard touchdown pass to Javaris Murray two plays later to give the Cowboys a quick 7-0 lead on their way to a 42-10 victory at Nicholls State.

Wiltz's 1-yard run and an 8-yard touchdown pass from Stroud to Ernest Celestie gave McNeese a 21-0 halftime lead. The only points in the first half for Nicholls came on a 27-yard Dolan field goal in the second quarter.

McNeese improved to 3-3 in the Southland and 6-3 overall. Nicholls joined Lamar at 0-5 in the conference while dropping to 1-8 overall.

A week later, Northwestern State became the latest team to witness a Sam Houston State offensive onslaught as the Bearkats scored 31-consecutive points to break a 7-7 tie on their way to a 52-17 road win to conclude Southland Conference play.

Sam Houston State won its seventh-consecutive game to finish 6-1 in the Southland and 8-2 overall. The Bearkats failed to score fewer than 41 points in any game during the streak.

The Bearkats' 31-point run came after Northwestern State's Ed Eagan returned a kickoff 82 yards for a touchdown to tie the game.

Bell tossed three touchdowns in the span, Antonio kicked a field goal and Snead returned an interception for a touchdown. The spree ended on a Shaughnessy field goal as time ran out in the first half to make the score 38-10 at the break.

The Bearkats built their lead to 52-10 before the Northwestern State offense scored its only touchdown of the game on a 4-yard pass from Henderson to Louis Hollier with 5:47 remaining in the contest for the 52-17 final.

Northwestern State slipped to 2-4 in the Southland and 4-6 overall.

As dominant as the Bearkats had been since the fourth week of the season, Sam Houston State was no match a week later for Texas A&M and the Aggies' future Heisman Trophy winner, freshman quarterback Johnny Manziel, to close out the regular season. Manziel threw for 267 yards, rushed for 100 and had a total of five touchdowns to snap the Bearkats' winning streak at seven games with a 47-28 home win over Sam Houston State as SHSU finished the regular season 8-3 heading into the playoffs.

"Manzel was the difference in the game," said Fritz. "We didn't have an answer for him."

In Hammond, the Lions may have been honoring 16 seniors in Southeastern Louisiana's final home game of the 2012 season against Stephen F. Austin, but youth was definitely served in SLU's 42-27 victory.

Roberson and Rasheed Harrell, a pair of freshmen running backs, each topped 100 yards in the game to ignite the Lions. Roberson rushed for 117 yards and Harrell 151.

Roberson had a 30-yard touchdown run and McCrea, a junior, returned a punt 54 yards for a score to give the Lions a 14-0 lead after one quarter.

Johnson almost single-handedly gave SFA the lead. Johnson, who rushed for 124 yards, scored on touchdown runs of 13, 4 and 19 yards to put the Lumberjacks on top 21-14. After Johnson's 19-yard score, Roberson raced 96 yards with the ensuing kickoff for a touchdown. A missed extra point caused the Lions to trail 21-20 at halftime.

Another Johnson touchdown run, this one from 11 yards out in the third quarter, extended the Lumberjacks' lead to seven points at 27-20 but the rest of the game belonged to Southeastern Louisiana.

Sophomore tight end Jeremy Meyers helped tie the score at 27-27 when he hauled in a 26-yard touchdown pass from Stanley. Stanley was 13 of 20 passing for 188 yards in his final home game.

Harrell and Roberson capped the scoring for the Lions. Harrell scored on a 28-yard run late in the third quarter while Roberson raced in from 8 yards out for the only points of the fourth quarter to give SLU the 42-27 triumph.

Stephen F. Austin fell to 3-3 in the Southland and 4-6 overall, guaranteeing the Lumberjacks a losing season. Southeastern Louisiana moved to 4-2 in the league, giving the Lions their first winning season in conference play since 2009. The outcome also left SLU 4-6 overall.

Someone was finally going to win a Southland game when Lamar and Nicholls State, both 0-5 in the conference, met in Thibodaux.

Lamar built a 20-3 halftime lead on Mossaskowski touchdown passes of 15 yards to Johnson, 20 yards to Ford and 8 yards to Begelton. The only points for the Colonels came on a 25-yard Dolan field goal in the first quarter.

Touchdowns runs of 1 yard by Washington and 4 yards by LaQuintin Caston in the third quarter rallied the Colonels to within 20-17. Caston's touchdown was set up by Toren Joseph's interception of a Mossaskowski pass.

Nicholls would get no closer as the Cardinals answered with a 15-play, 90-yard drive that used up more than eight minutes on the clock, culminating in a 18-yard run by Berry to extend the lead to 27-17 on Lamar's way to a 34-24 victory.

Lamar improved to 1-5 in the Southland and 4-7 overall. Nicholls fell to 0-6 in the conference and 1-8 overall.

Nicholls State had one last chance to avoid a winless Southland Conference record five days later in a Thursday night affair against visiting Southeastern Louisiana.

The Colonels literally fumbled away their chance early in the game when Devan Walker lost control of the ball, setting up SLU's first score of the game on a 3-yard run by Harrell. It didn't get any better for Nicholls when Todd Washington's interception of a Klann pass set up a 4-yard touchdown run by Harrell for a 14-0 lead on the Colonels' way to a 35-16 loss.

Southeastern Louisiana closed out the season 5-6, including 5-2 in the Southland.

Nicholls ended conference play winless for the second year in a row. While other FCS teams were starting the playoffs a week later, the Colonels played their final regular-season game at Oregon State. Originally scheduled as the season opener, the game was postponed because of Hurricane Isaac. The Beavers' 77-3 rout ended Nicholls' season at 1-10 and on an eight-game losing streak.

Two days after the Nicholls-Southeastern Louisiana game, Stephen F. Austin and Northwestern State both went into their 2012 season finale in Nacogdoches with losing records, so playing for Chief Caddo was about all that was left for the teams.

Pride obviously meant something as the teams went into the fourth quarter tied 17-17.

The game went into the fourth quarter tied following a 7-yard pass from Attaway to Lott with 34 seconds remaining in the third quarter. A fumble by Eagan on the ensuing kickoff led to Johnson's 8-yard touchdown run on the first play of the fourth quarter to give SFA its first lead since the opening quarter. Johnson finished the game with 211 yards rushing.

Attaway found Roberson on a 38-yard touchdown pass minutes later to extend the Lumberjacks' lead to 31-17. For Roberson, the touchdown was No. 39 of his career. The senior, who already had established himself as the career leader in touchdown receptions both at SFA and the Southland Conference, went out in style by making a diving catch for the final score of his career.

Wiggs added a 22-yard field goal with slightly more than two minutes left in the game to make the final 34-17.

A 3-yard pass from Attaway to Thomas and a 19-yard Wiggs field goal gave SFA a 10-0 lead before the Demons made it 10-3 after one quarter on a 27-yard Shaughnessy field goal. Northwestern State tied the game 10-10 at halftime on a 52-yard pass from Henderson to Clifton Brown with 4:38 left in the second quarter.

Stephen F. Austin concluded the season 5-6 overall, including 4-3 in the Southland. Northwestern State ended 4-7 overall, 2-5 in the SLC.

In Lake Charles, Bennett's 93-yard touchdown run hightlighted McNeese State's 35-0 blanking of Lamar to close out the regular season.

Stroud passed for 158 yards and two touchdowns in the contest. Garrett rushed for 100 of his 112 yards in the first half for Lamar.

McNeese conclude the year 7-4, its eighth-consecutive winning season. The Cowboys finished 4-3 in the Southland. Lamar ended 4-8 overall, including 1-6 in the SLC.

Central Arkansas was unable to contain Georgia Southern's offense, especially Georgia Southern quarterback Jerick McKinnon, in the Bears' 24-16 road loss to the Eagles in the FCS playoffs.

McKinnon rushed for 316 yards and accounted for three touchdowns. He had two touchdown runs and passed for another.

Central Arkansas, which had the ball for less than nine minutes in the second half, was only 3 of 12 in third-down conversions against the Georgia Southern defense.

Smothers passed for 251 yards and ran for 79 while Camara kicked three field goals as the Bears ended their season at 9-2.

"We had two open dates in a three-week time period. As sharp as we were against Eastern Illinois, the second open date hurt us and we lost a bit of our edge," said Conque.

Opening the playoffs at home for the second-consecutive year, Sam Houston State was held to a season-low 241 yards, so the Bearkats had to turn to their defense and special teams against Cal Poly-San Luis Obispo.

Following a scoreless first quarter, a safety and a pair of Antonio field goals gave the Bearkats an 8-0 halftime edge.

Bobby Zalud hit on two field goals for Cal Poly in the third quarter to narrow the gap to 8-6 before SHSU scored its only offensive touchdown of the game on an 18-yard pass from Bell to Hill in the closing seconds of the third quarter to make the score 15-6.

The Mustangs entered the contest averaging 333 yards per game on the ground. Cal Poly was held to a season-low 224 yards rushing, and like Sam Houston

State, had to turn to its kicker to produce points on offense. Zalud's third field goal of the game, from 48 yards out with 9:25 left in the contest, made the score 15-9.

SHSU moved 66 yards to set up Antonio's third field goal with 3:23 left in the game. Antonio's 26-yard kick put the Bearkats on top by nine points at 18-9.

Cal Poly answered with its only touchdown of the game. Getting the ball on a reverse, Ryan Taylor tossed 50 yards to fellow receiver Willie Tucker to make the score 18-16 with 1:34 left in the fourth quarter.

The Mustangs' onside kick attempt was recovered by Diller. Sam Houston State was able to run out the clock to advance to the quarterfinals with its two-point triumph.

"We were off for two weeks and we had been on a big-time roll. They (the Mustangs) were hard-nosed and physical and ran the ball extremely well with the triple option. We made just enough plays to win the game," said Fritz.

Sam Houston State faced a playoff rematch against Montana State, only this time the Bearkats had to play on the road after winning 49-13 the previous year at home.

After an exchange of field goals in the opening quarter, the Bearkats scored the only 17 points of the second quarter to lead 20-3 at the break. Sincere scored on a 12-yard run, Bell tossed a 56-yard touchdown pass to Diller and Antonio kicked an 18-yard field goal to give Sam Houston State the lead.

The Bobcats put themselves back in the game at 20-9 by scoring on their opening possession of the second half. An 8-yard run by DeNarius McGhee gave Montana State its first touchdown of the game.

Looking for more on Montana State's next possession, Jon Ellis hauled in a first-down reception, only to fumble on the play. SHSU made the Bobcats pay dearly for the mistake when Bell connected with Chance Nelson on a 16-yard touchdown pass to extend the Bearkats' lead to 27-9.

The duo hooked up again on a 45-yard scoring strike in the fourth quarter before Ellis hauled in a 12-yard pass touchdown pass from McGhee to make the final 34-16.

"We really threw the ball well. They were kind of stacking the box against us," Fritz explained. "I was really proud of our guys. We had to fly all the way out to Montana and they had a huge, hostile crowd. It was really, really cold that day."

Sam Houston State faced a third-consecutive Big Sky opponent when the Bearkats played at Eastern Washington in the FCS semifinals.

Using a powerful ground game that amassed 418 yards, the Bearkats built a 35-0 halftime lead.

A 6-yard touchdown run by Bell and a 37-yard interception return for a touchdown by Robert Shaw gave Sam Houston State a 14-0 lead after one quarter. Bell added a 72-yard run in the second quarter while Hill and Sincere both rushed for touchdowns as the Bearkats built their 35-0 halftime lead.

In the second half, the Eagles just decided to let Vernon Adams fling the ball. The Eastern Washington quarterback tied a school record with six touchdown passes as the Eagles scored on seven possessions to miraculously get back in the game.

Adams tossed touchdown passes of 31 yards to Greg Herd, 22 yards to Brandon Kaufman and 43 yards to Ashton Clark to make the score 35-21 after three quarters.

Adams and Kaufman hooked up on a 43-yard touchdown early in the fourth quarter to make it a seven-point game at 35-28.

The Bearkats finally ended their scoring drought when Bell tossed a 4-yard touchdown pass to Shane Young to make the score 42-28 with 10:49 remaining in the game.

After a 7-yard touchdown pass from Adams to Nicholas Edwards, Sam Houston State countered with a 42-yard Antonio field goal that left the Bearkats with a 45-35 lead with 5:33 remaining in the contest.

Adams and Kaufman hooked up on a third touchdown strike, this one from 33 yards out with 3:04 left in the game to make the score 45-43. The Bearkats picked up two first downs on the ensuing drive to run down the clock and advance to the national championship game for the second year in a row.

The teams did their damage in opposite fashion. Although Flanders failed to score, he did rush for 231 yards as the Bearkats produced 503 yards of total offense. Adams passed for 361 yards. Of the Eagles' 523 total yards, 481 came through the air.

"We had to fly out there and it might have been colder than the week before," said Fritz. "Our guys came out the box and played extremely well. They got hot and we kind of played not to lose instead of playing to win. We got that corrected midway through the fourth quarter."

Sam Houston State faced North Dakota State again in Frisco, Texas, in a rematch of the 2011 national championship game.

In the 2011 title contest, the Bearkats held a 6-3 halftime edge before North Dakota State scored early in the second half on its way to a 17-6 win and the FCS national championship.

This time around, Sam Houston State and North Dakota State were tied 10-10 at halftime when Flanders broke loose on a 40-yard touchdown run on the opening possession of the second half.

The play was called back because of a holding penalty. On the next play, Bell was intercepted by Bison defender Carlton Littlejohn. That ended up leading to a 1-yard touchdown run by Brock Jensen. Instead of a seven-point advantage, the Bearkats were suddenly down 17-10.

"That was a huge, huge play in the game. I still haven't seen the hold yet," said Fritz. "If we had been able to get that (score), it might have given us some momentum and confidence."

Later in the third quarter, Sam Ojuri scored on a 2-yard run. In a sign that it would not be the Bearkats' day, the Bison mishandled the snap from center on the extra point attempt but kicker Adam Keller threw up a prayer that was answered by Mike Hardie's catch and a 25-10 North Dakota State lead.

All the Bearkats could muster after that was a 32-yard Antonio field goal with 13:20 remaining in the game. Jensen added his third touchdown run of the game and Ojuri scored on an 11-yard run to make the final 39-13 and deny Sam Houston State a national championship for the second year in a row.

"We got down and we are not a passing team and they really started to play with confidence and we were doing things we normally don't do. From that point on, we did not play very well. They had a great game plan and they out-executed us," Fritz said.

Antonio kicked a 38-yard field goal early in the second quarter to answer Keller's 32-yard kick in the opening quarter to tie the game. Jensen's first touchdown run from 20 yards out put the Bison on top. SHSU scored its only touchdown in two championship games on a 1-yard pass from Bell to K.J. Williams with 33 seconds remaining in the first half for a 10-10 tie at intermission.

Flanders, Sam Houston State's all-time rusher, was limited to 53 yards against North Dakota State.

SHSU ended its season 11-4.

50TH YEAR: THREE SLC TEAMS MAKE PLAYOFFS

A familiar face returned to the Southland in 2013 when Jay Thomas was named the new coach at Northwestern State in what was the 50th year of competition in the conference.

The head coach at Nicholls State from 2004-2009, Thomas replaced Bradley Dale Peveto, who had a 14-30 record in four years as coach of the Demons. Thomas guided Nicholls State to a 27-35 mark in six years, including a Division I-AA playoff appearance in 2005.

After being dismissed from Nicholls, Thomas served as defensive line coach under Peveto for two years at Northwestern State before becoming defensive coordinator at Missouri Southern in 2012.

Ironically, Thomas made his Southland debut as Northwestern State coach against Nicholls. The Demons were off to a 3-2 start under Thomas with wins over Missouri State, Southern University and Langston. Northwestern State's two losses were to Cincinnati and Alabama-Birmingham.

Nicholls State went into the Northwestern State game 3-2 as well. A 66-3 loss at third-ranked Oregon of the FBS to open the 2013 season extended the Colonels' losing streak to nine games. Nicholls snapped the losing skid with a 27-23 victory over Western Michigan. The triumph over the FBS Broncos was the first win other than victories over NAIA Evangel in three years. Following a 70-7 rout by Louisiana-Lafayette, the Colonels defeated Langston and Arkansas Tech to move Nicholls above .500 through the first five games for the first time since a 4-1 start in 2007 under Thomas.

Returning to Thibodaux, Thomas and his Demons were never really in the game. Nicholls controlled time of possession on its way to a 33-21 triumph. The Colonels, who rolled up 404 yards of total offense, held onto the ball for almost 42 minutes in the contest.

A 2-yard run by Marcus Washington, the first of three touchdowns on the ground for the Nicholls running back, gave the Colonels a 6-0 lead after one quarter. A 30-yard pass from Tuskani Figaro to Demon Bolt, a 1-yard run by Washington and a 55-yard toss from Figaro to Erik Buchanan gave Nicholls a 27-0 halftime lead.

Northwestern State's first score came less than a minute into the second half on a 3-yard run by Garrett Atzenweiler.

The victory snapped a 14-game Southland Conference losing streak for Nicholls and was the Colonels' first SLC-opening win since a 58-0 beatdown of Northwestern State in 2007 under Thomas.

A week earlier, McNeese State and Central Arkansas were the first two teams to kick off Southland Conference play when the teams met in Conway. The Cowboys went into the game 4-1, with the only loss coming against Northern Iowa. The Bears were off to a 2-2 start. UCA's season-opening win came against Incarnate Word, which was playing its first-ever Division I game.

The Cowboys seemed to have a particular hunger for red beans and rice. Trailing Central Arkansas 14-7, McNeese scored a school-record 35 points in the second quarter on its way to a 59-28 victory over the Bears to regain the Red Beans & Rice Bowl trophy for the first time in four years.

McNeese outscored Central Arkansas 35-14 in the second quarter to lead 42-21 at halftime. Marcus Wiltz, who rushed for a career-best 181 yards, got the scoring spree going for the Cowboys with a 3-yard run. Ryan Bronson returned an interception 98 yards for a touchdown. Other scores for McNeese in the quarter came on a pass from receiver Diontae Spencer to Jereon McGilvery, a 12-yard run by Javaris Murray and a 40-yard touchdown toss from quarterback Cody Stroud to Spencer. The scoring spree was briefly interrupted by a 39-yard pass from Bears quarterback Wynrick Smothers to Damien Watts following Bronson's interception return.

On the same day Nicholls State and Northwestern State were playing their initial Southland games of the season four other teams also were making their conference debuts.

Southeastern Louisiana opened league play against visiting Stephen F. Austin while Sam Houston State hosted Lamar.

The Lions went into their SLC opener 3-2 on the season. Stephen F. Austin was off to a 2-3 start. One of the wins was over third-ranked Montana State. SFA lost 56-48 to Prairie View despite 827 yards of total offense. Lumberjacks quarterback Brady Attaway set single-game team and Southland Conference records with 662 yards passing and 655 yards of total offense.

Against Stephen F. Austin, Southeastern Louisiana quarterback Bryan Bennett fired four touchdown passes in the second quarter as the Lions cruised to a 56-14 victory over the Lumberjacks. Bennett, an Oregon transfer, accounted for a total of five touchdowns.

Bennett, who rushed for 72 yards, scored on a 63-yard run to give SLU a 7-0 lead. A 4-yard run by Rasheed Harrell made it 14-0.

SFA cut the deficit in half with a 3-yard run by Gus Johnson and was on the move again when Marice Sutton returned an Attaway interception 45 yards for a touchdown.

After Bennett, who passed for 337 yards, tossed his four touchdowns in the second quarter, he opened the second half with an 85-yard touchdown strike to Chris Malot.

Sam Houston State went into its game against Lamar 4-1 on the season. In one of the wins, a 55-17 pasting of Texas Southern, Tim Flanders rushed for two touchdowns to give him 61 in his career to set a new Southland Conference mark. Flanders topped the record of 59 set by Central Arkansas' Brent Grimes from 2006-09. In SHSU's 52-21 win over Incarnate Word, Flanders rushed for 157 yards to become the all-timer rusher in the Southland with 4,720 yards. Southwest Texas State's Claude Mathis established the previous mark of 4,694 from 1994-97.

The Bearkats were no match for Johnny Manzel and Texas A&M, the seven-ranked team among Football Bowl Subdivision teams. The Heisman Trophy winner passed for 426 yards and three touchdowns and ran for another score in the Aggies' 65-28 rout of Sam Houston State.

Lamar went into the SHSU encounter 3-2 on the season. The Cardinals defeated Panhandle State, Bacone College and Grambling. Lamar's losses were to a pair of FBS teams, Louisiana Tech and Oklahoma State.

Sam Houston State quarterback Brian Bell accounted for both of the Bearkats' touchdowns in a 14-3 triumph over Lamar.

Bell's 45-yard run in the second quarter provided the first score of the contest. A 47-yard Alex Ball field goal late in the first half rallied Lamar to within 7-3. Bell's 18-yard touchdown strike to Stephen Williams accounted for the only scoring of the second half.

It was a sub-par performance for the Bearkats' offense. Sam Houston State went into the game averaging 51.6 points per game. Flanders, who was coming off a 280-yard performance against Eastern Washington, was held to 83 yards rushing.

Sam Houston State was unable to make it two-in-a-row to open Southland play, falling 31-23 a week later at McNeese State. Both teams went into the game with identical records of 1-0 in the SLC and 5-1 overall.

A pair or touchdown passes by Stroud, including a 29-yard strike to Ernest Celestie with 59 seconds remaining in the first half, gave McNeese a 17-6 halftime edge. The Bearkats' first-half points came on field goals by Luc Swimberghe.

After Swimberghe's third field goal of the game, Wiltz scored on a 4-yard run in the third quarter to make it 21-9. McNeese's biggest lead came at 31-16 on a Ryan Rome field goal before SHSU came up with the game's final score on a touchdown toss from Bell to Williams with one minute left for the final eight-point margin.

Southeastern Louisiana joined McNeese at 2-0 in the Southland with a 37-22 victory at Northwestern State.

A 30-yard field goal by Moore with 8:55 remaining in the third quarter gave Northwestern State a 16-7 lead before Southeastern Louisiana rallied with a pair of quick scores.

Following Chris Moore's field goal, Xavier Roberson's 92-yard kickoff return left the Lions down by two points. On the ensuing possession, a fumble by Demons quarterback Zack Adkins in the end zone was recovered for a safety to tie the game 16-16.

SLU took its first lead of the contest on a 4-yard run by Kody Sutton but Northwestern State quickly answered on a 43-yard pass from Adkins to Bryant Mitchell but a missed extra point left the Demons trailing 23-22.

Short touchdown runs by Bennett and Harrell in the fourth quarter allowed the Lions to pull away.

In Beaumont, Ryan Howard tossed a 23-yard touchdown pass with less than three minutes remaining in the game to give Central Arkansas its first Southland victory of the season with a 26-24 triumph over Lamar.

Howard was making his first start of the year at quarterback after Smothers, the SLC's Player of the Year in 2013, was lost for the season in the Bears' 31-0 win over Nebraska-Kearney a week earlier. Facing third-and-20, Howard connected with Courtney Whitehead on the game-winning touchdown strike.

Lamar quarterback Caleb Berry, who tossed three touchdowns in the game, hooked up with Reggie Begelton to give the Cardinals a 24-20 edge before Central Arkansas rallied.

The win improved the Bears to 1-1 in the SLC and 4-3 overall. Lamar dropped to 0-2 in the conference and 3-4 overall.

In a high-scoring game in Nacogdoches, Stephen F. Austin broke a 14-14 tie by outscoring Nicholls State 28-7 the remainder of the first half to lead 42-21 on the Lumberjacks' way to a 55-41 victory and SFA's initial Southland win of the season.

After pulling to within 42-28, the Colonels recovered an onside kick at their own 47-yard line. Five plays later, Figaro scored on a 12-yard run with 9:25 left in the game to make the score 42-35 but that was as close as Nicholls would get the remainder of the contest.

SFA rolled up 687 yards of total offense as Attaway passed for 317 yards and six touchdowns. Joshawa West rushed for 175 yards. West replaced Johnson, the starter, who ran for 99 yards before leaving the game with an ankle injury. Mike Brooks, Aaron Thomas and D.J. Ward each hauled in two of Attaway's touchdown tosses.

Nicholls piled up 518 total yards, including 249 rushing. Figaro had 145 yards on the ground while Dalton Hilliard Jr. rushed for 93.

The result left both teams 1-1 in the Southland as SFA improved to 3-4 overall while Nicholls slipped to 4-3.

Nicholls State ended up on the losing end of another high-scoring game the following week, falling 55-30 against visiting McNeese State as the Cowboys improved to 3-0 in Southland Conference play.

The Colonels fell behind 27-10 at halftime. Stroud tossed a touchdown pass to Spencer and Dylan Long added a pair of short scoring runs. Nicholls countered with an Andrew Dolan field goal and a 42-yard touchdown pass from Kalen Henderson to Erik Buchanan. The Cowboys led 21-10 before Rome booted a pair of field goals, including a 43 yarder with 30 seconds left in the half for the 17-point margin at the break.

Along with moving to 3-0 in SLC play, McNeese improved to 7-1. Nicholls dropped to 1-2 in the league and 4-4 overall.

Southeastern Louisiana scored 42-straight points to overcome an early 14-0 deficit in a 56-34 win over visiting Lamar that allowed the Lions to remain in a tie with McNeese State at 3-0 and to set up a key Southland Conference showdown a week later.

A pair of touchdown passes by Berry gave Lamar its early lead before SLU went on its scoring spree. Highlighting the run were two touchdown passes by Bennett and a pair of scoring runs by Harrell.

Off to its best start since 1981, Southeastern improved to 6-2 overall. Lamar dropped to 3-5 overall, including 0-3 in the Southland.

At Huntsville, Sam Houston State stretched its home winning streak to 20 games with a 44-10 win over Northwestern State.

The Bearkats managed only one field goal in their first four possessions of the game for a 3-3 tie before SHSU scored on its next six drives to blow away the Demons.

A touchdown run by Flanders gave Sam Houston State a 10-3 lead before Bell followed with scoring passes to Richard Sincere, Torrance Williams and Chance Nelson. The Bearkats quarterback scored on an 18-yard run and Steven Hicks contributed a short touchdown run.

The win improved SHSU to 2-1 in the Southland and 6-2 overall. Northwestern State remained winless through three conference games while falling to 3-5 overall.

Meanwhile, big plays dominated in Central Arkansas' 66-31 victory over visiting Stephen F. Austin.

Howard continued to have a hot hand, tossing for 403 yards and four touchdowns. Three of his scoring tosses were from 40 yards or more.

The first big play of the game belonged to SFA when Tyler Boyd hooked up with Ward on a 73-yard touchdown play to pull the Lumberjacks to within 14-10 early in the second quarter. Howard followed with a 45-yard strike to Dezmin Lewis less than a minute later to give the Bears a 21-10 halftime lead.

Central Arkansas quickly extended its lead when Jatavious Wilson raced 85 yards with the second-half kickoff. Attaway, who passed for 442 yards, tossed a 10-yard pass to Boyd to narrow the SFA deficit to 35-24, but the remainder of the big plays belonged to Central Arkansas as the Bears pulled away late in the third quarter.

Howard tossed touchdown passes of 64 yards to Jose Moore and 41 yards to Watts. Following Marvin Mitchell's 98-yard interception for a touchdown and a 29-yard Jace Denker field goal, Kelton Warren's 81-yard run made the score 66-24.

Central Arkansas improved to 2-1 in the Southland and 5-3 overall while SFA dropped to 1-2 in the conference and 3-5 overall.

The showdown between the only two unbeaten Southland Conference teams was surprisingly one-sided in Lake Charles as Bennett accounted for four touchdowns in Southeastern Louisiana's 41-7 rout of McNeese State.

SLU jumped out to a 20-0 lead on a 30-yard field goal by Seth Sebastian less than three minutes into the game, a 12-yard pass from Bennett to Juwaan Rogers, a 44-yard Sebastian field goal and a 1-yard run by Bennett. McNeese State's lone score of the game came on a 24-yard pass from Stroud to Spencer to make the score 20-7 at halftime.

Bennett added a touchdown pass to Jeff Smiley and a 9-yard run to account for his four scores as the Lions improved to 4-0 in the Southland and McNeese slipped to 3-1. The outcome left both teams 7-2 overall.

At Reliant Stadium in Houston, Sam Houston State and Stephen F. Austin were one yard shy of 1,300 yards of combined offense as the Bearkats claimed The Battle of the Piney Woods with a 56-49 shootout over the Lumberjacks.

The win allowed SHSU to stay in the Southland Conference hunt at 3-1 as the Bearkats improved to 7-2 overall. The Lumberjacks fell to 1-3 in the league and 3-6 overall.

The game was tied four times until the Bearkats broke away in the fourth quarter.

A 38-yard pass from Bell to Torrance Williams broke a 28-28 tie seven seconds into the fourth quarter. Williams' reception was the first of four touchdowns scored by the Bearkats in a span of 2:26 seconds. A 31-yard run by Keshawn Hill, a 16-yard pass from Bell to Ragan Henderson and a 45-yard interception for a touchown by DeAntrey Loche gave the Bearkats a 56-28 lead.

SFA scored the game's final three touchdowns. Attaway, who passed for 505 yards and five touchdowns, had scoring tosses of 59 and 2 yards to Brooks and 75 yards to Boyd for the final seven-point margin.

Johnson rushed for 136 yards and a touchdown for SFA. Four runners had at least 61 yards rushing for the Bearkats, with Hill leading the way with 72 yards and two touchdowns. Boyd had 11 catches for 206 yards to lead all receivers while Torrance Williams had four catches for 175 yards to pace SHSU.

Meanwhile, Adkins accounted for four touchdowns and Northwestern State held on to defeat visiting Central Arkansas 31-28. The victory was the first Southland Conference win for Thomas as Demons coach while the loss dropped the Bears to 2-2 in the league and kept UCA from matching McNeese State and Sam Houston State atop the SLC.

Northwestern State built a 14-3 lead on touchdown passes of 25 yards to Shakeir Ryan and 33 yards to Tuff McClain from Adkins.

A pair of 11-yard touchdown runs by Willie Matthews gave Central Arkansas it first lead of the game at 17-14 before the Demons quickly countered on a 38-yard touchdown pass from Adkins to Daniel Taylor to put Northwestern back on top 21-17 with eight minutes remaining in the third quarter.

Leading 24-20, the Demons stretched their advantage to 11 points at 31-20 on a 6-yard run by Adkins with 8:05 left in the contest.

A 2-yard touchdown pass from Howard to Whitehead and a two-point conversion made it 31-28 with 1:25 left in the game but the Demons recovered an onside kick attempt by Central Arkansas to run out the clock.

Lamar also picked up its first Southland Conference victory of the season with a 56-34 home triumph over Nicholls State.

The Cardinals and Colonels traded scores in a wild 45-point second quarter that saw Lamar take a 35-17 halftime lead. Berry passed for four of his five touchdown passes in the big second quarter. Two of Berry's touchdown tosses in the quarter went to Kade Harrington while Carey Fortson had a 94-yard kickoff return for the Colonels.

A 23-yard Dolan field goal and a 2-yard run by Hilliard rallied the Colonels to within 35-27 heading into the fourth quarter. Hilliard rushed for a career-high 111 yards in the game.

Lamar took advantage of two Colonel fumbles and an interception return for a touchdown to score 21 points in a span of less than four minutes to pull away. The Cardinals turned the fumbles into a 9-yard touchdown run by Harrington and an 18-yard scoring toss from Berry to Michael Handy. A 56-yard Tyrus McGlothen interception return made it 56-27.

A 29-yard pass from Henderson to Xavier Marcus with 21 seconds left in the game accounted for the final margin as the result left both teams 1-3 in the SLC and 4-5 overall.

Roberson returned the opening kickoff 90 yards for a touchdown a week later as Southeastern Louisiana's special teams and defense played a big role in the Lions remaining the only undefeated team in Southland Conference play with a 58-31 win at Central Arkansas.

Even with Roberson's return, the Lions only could manage a narrow 24-17 edge at halftime.

That all changed in the third quarter.

A 48-yard interception return for a touchdown by Harlan Miller extended SLU's lead to 31-17 less than two minutes into the second half. After a block field goal, Marquis Hayes sprinted 46 yards one play later for a 38-17 Lions advantage. A fumble by Howard led to a 4-yard touchdown run by Bennett to make the score 45-17.

Bennett accounted for four touchdowns in the game. Along with two rushing touchdowns in the second half, he had scoring tosses of 53 yards to Jeremy Meyers and 14 yards to Marquis Fruge to help Southeastern build a 21-14 lead early in the second quarter.

Trailing 24-14, UCA's Eddie Camara kicked a 45-yard field goal with less than five minutes left in the second quarter to narrow the score to 24-17 at halftime.

The win improved Southeastern Louisiana to 5-0 in the Southland and 8-2 overall. Central Arkansas dropped to 2-3 in the conference and 5-5 overall.

Meanwhile, Spencer returned three kicks for scores and amassed five touchdowns as McNeese State bounced back from the Southeastern Louisiana loss and moved to 4-1 in the Southland Conference with a 69-38 win at Stephen F. Austin.

Spencer tied a Football Championship Subdivision record with the three touchdown returns, scoring on kickoffs of 93 and 87 yards, while returning a punt 35 yards for a touchdown. Spencer accounted for five touchdowns and his 365 all-purpose yards set a McNeese record.

"Spencer had a really good career here and that was kind of the icing on it for that game to have that type of performance," McNeese coach Matt Viator said.

Despite Spencer's heroics, SFA led 24-14 before the Cowboys scored 27-straight points. Stroud, who passed for 333 yards, tossed three of his four touchdown passes during the scoring spree.

Attaway, who passed for 255 yards, connected on two touchdown passes to Boyd.

Along with improving to 4-1 in the Southland, the Cowboys moved to 8-2 overall. The Lumberjacks fell to 1-4 in the SLC and 3-7 overall.

Sam Houston State matched McNeese at 4-1 in the SLC with a 49-24 home win over Nicholls State.

Hill and Bell each accounted for two touchdowns in the win. Hill had scoring runs of 16 and 1 yard while Bell contributed a 45-yard run and a 56-yard pass to Torrance Williams.

Nicholls State's three touchdowns came in the fourth quarter on a 2-yard run by Michael Henry and two touchdown passes by quarterback Beaux Hebert.

Along with moving to 4-1 in the Southland, Sam Houston State improved to 8-2 overall. Nicholls fell to 1-4 in the SLC and 4-6 overall.

The outcome marked the seventh time in eight games that the Bearkats scored at least 44 points. By contrast, Nicholls allowed 49 or more points in its six losses.

Teams coming off their first Southland Conference victories of the season a week earlier met in Natchitoches when Northwestern State hosted Lamar.

A pair of Adkins touchdown passes in the second half turned a Northwestern State halftime deficit of 21-17 into a 30-21 Demons lead early in the fourth quarter.

The quarterback's 26-yard toss to Taylor in the third quarter put the Demons on top before Adkins extended the advantage to nine points on a 4-yard strike to Louis Hollier Jr.

After Lamar cut the margin to two points on a 1-yard run by Payton Ploch with less than 10 minutes remaining in the game, Northwestern State's De'Mard Llorens put the game away with a 55-yard touchdown run with 1:16 remaining in the contest.

The Demons improved to 2-3 in the Southland and 5-5 overall. Lamar, held to 5 yards rushing, dropped to 1-4 in the league and 4-6 overall.

A showdown took place a week later when Sam Houston State visited Southeastern Louisiana. The Bearkats, who had won or shared the Southland Conference title each of the previous two years, went into the game with the Lions 4-1 and looking for a win to force a tie atop the SLC. Southeastern Louisiana, meanwhile, stood at 5-0 and was seeking a victory over the Bearkats to clinch at least a share of its first Southland title.

The teams traded scores throughout the first half, leaving Southeastern Louisiana with a 21-17 halftime edge.

Bell tossed three touchdowns in the first half for SHSU, hooking up on scoring throws of 6 yards to Sincere, 21 yards to Gerald Thomas and 7 yards to Torrance Williams. Bell's connection to Williams gave the Bearkats a 21-10 lead with 1:31 remaining in the the opening half.

SLU countered with a 36-yard Sebastian field goal and a pair of touchdown passes from Bennett to Fruge. The second Bennett-to-Fruge connection with 15 seconds left in the first half made the score 21-17 at the break.

The second half belonged to the Lions. Bennett hooked up with Roberson on a 62-yard touchdown pass slightly more than a minute into the second half to put Southeastern on top 24-21. An 18-yard run by Hayes late in the third quarter stretched the Lions' lead to 31-21.

The only score of the fourth quarter came on a Sebastian field goal and the Lions blanked the Bearkats over the final 30 minutes for a 34-21 Southeastern Louisiana triumph.

Along with moving to 6-0 in Southland play, the Lions improved to 9-2 overall. The Bearkats fell to 4-2 in the SLC and 8-3 overall.

Southeastern Louisiana's victory over Sam Houston State meant McNeese State needed a win at home over Northwestern State to stay within one game of the Lions.

The Cowboys faced a few anxious moments early in the game when Moore kicked a 19-yard field goal to give Northwestern State a 10-7 lead in the middle of the second quarter. Any jitters for McNeese fans quickly disappeared when Stroud tossed short touchdown passes to Nic Jacobs and David Bush to give the Cowboys a 21-10 halftime edge.

Stroud's touchdown passes to close the first half were part of 36-straight points for the Cowboys, who concluded the scoring spree on a 1-yard run by Murray with seven minutes left in the game for a 43-10 lead. A 25-yard pass from Adkins to Ed Egan with 4:45 left in the game accounted for the 43-17 final.

The result lifted McNeese to 5-1 in the Southland and 9-2 overall. Northwestern State dropped to 2-4 in the league and 5-6 overall.

The other two games that weekend all involved non-contenders in the Southland.

Central Arkansas managed to even its SLC record at 3-3 with a 17-10 win at Nicholls State.

A 40-yard Dolan field goal gave Nicholls an early 3-0 lead before Central Arkansas rallied for a 17-3 halftime lead on a 7-yard touchdown pass from Howard to Clay Murphy, a 28-yard Camara field goal and a 48-yard scoring reception by Desmond Smith. Smith, a freshman, finished with 140 receiving yards.

The only points of the second half came on an 11-yard touchdown pass from Hebert to Buchanan with 46 seconds left in the game as Nicholls dropped to 1-5 in the SLC and 4-7 overall. Central Arkansas improved to 6-5 overall with the win.

Meanwhile, a pair of teams with only one conference win each, met when Lamar hosted Stephen F. Austin.

Trailing 7-0, an 11-yard pass from Berry to Mark Roberts tied the game midway in the first quarter. Lamar pulled off a successful onside kick and scored seven plays later on a 1-yard run by Harrington for a 14-7 Cardinals lead.

SFA scored the final 14 points of the second half on short touchdown runs by Johnson and Keith Lawson to lead 28-24 at halftime.

After a 1-yard touchdown run by West with 4:59 left in the game, Lamar countered with a 20-yard scoring strike from Berry to Begelton to rally the Cardinals to within two points at 45-43. Begelton, who had 167 yards receiving, set a new single-game school mark with 18 receptions. Berry opened the game by completing 19-straight passes.

Lamar failed to recover an onside-kick attempt but the defense managed to get the ball back to the Cardinals.

Ball connected on a field goal with 20 seconds left in the game but the play was blown dead because of a penalty against the Lamar band. That backed up the Cardinals but the freshman kicker was true on his next attempt from 41 yards out as Lamar eked out a 46-45 triumph.

The result left Lamar 5-6 on the season and SFA 3-8.

Playing on a Thursday night to close the 2013 regular season, a win by Southeastern Louisiana at home against Nicholls State would allow the Lions to finish a perfect 7-0 in conference play for SLU's first-ever Southland championship.

The home fans were a bit on edge at halftime when a pair of touchdown runs by Figaro helped to give Nicholls a 14-13 advantage over the Lions.

Any anxiety on the part of Southeastern fans quickly disappeared as the Lions scored 39 second-half points. A 46-yard Sebastian field goal slightly more than two minutes in the third quarter put SLU on top 16-14. Before the third quarter was done, Southeastern added touchdowns runs by Devante Scott, Miller, Sutton and Bennett, along with a 54-yard pass from Bennett to Hayes. A 3-yard run by Roberson gave the Lions a 52-20 lead at the 10:40 mark of the fourth quarter.

Southeastern Louisiana, which amassed 702 yards of total offense, finished the regular season 10-2. Nicholls closed the 2013 season 1-6 in the Southland and 4-8 overall.

SLU's win over Nicholls meant there would be no chance for McNeese State to capture a share of the Southland Conference title two days later, but a Cowboys' victory at Lamar would enable McNeese to finish with 10 regular-season wins for the first time since 2007.

Lamar wasn't ready to just hand a 10-win season to the Cowboys as four touchdown passes by Berry allowed the Cardinals to build a 38-26 lead by the middle of the fourth quarter.

McNeese began to rally when Stroud connected with Spencer on a 50-yard strike to make the score 38-33 with 6:24 left in the third quarter. A 39-yard Rome field goal cut the Cowboys' deficit to two points at 38-36 heading into the fourth quarter.

The Cowboys turned the ball over on downs when failing to convert on fourth-and-1 in the fourth quarter but McNeese drove 89 yards in nine plays in the closing moments to set up Spencer's 16-yard touchdown run with 58 seconds left in the game to pull out a 42-38 triumph for McNeese.

Along with closing the regular season 10-2 overall, McNeese improved to 6-1 in the SLC with the victory. Lamar ended the year 2-5 in the conference and 5-7 overall.

Elsewhere, Central Arkansas defeated visiting Sam Houston State 49-31, allowing both teams to finish 4-3 in the Southland Conference. The Bears ended the season 8-4 overall and the Bearkats 7-5. SHSU won seven home games but failed to win a game away from Huntsville in 2013.

Howard tossed four touchdown passes for Central Arkansas, two each to Matthews and Lewis.

Although Bell did not start the game for Sam Houston State because of a shoulder injury suffered a week earlier against Southeastern Louisiana, the senior came off the bench to pass for 327 yards and four touchdowns. He finished his career as the Bearkats' all-time leader in passing and total yards.

In Natchitoches, Stephen F. Austin closed the 2013 season on a five-game losing streak with a 40-27 loss to Northwestern State in what would be J.C. Hatcher's final game as Lumberjacks coach. Hatcher was dismissed following the season in which SFA finished 3-9 overall, including 1-6 in the Southland Conference.

The Demons scored the game's first 16 points and added a 21-point second quarter to lead 37-24 at halftime.

Imoan Claiborne's 48-yard interception return for a touchdown and a safety gave the Demons a 9-0 lead less than three minutes into the game before Northwestern State came up with its first offensive touchdown on a 2-yard pass from Adkins to Mitchell.

Adkins tossed two touchdown passes to Hollier in the second quarter, the second giving the Demons a 37-17 lead. Lawson scored on a 2-yard run with 19 seconds remaining before halftime to inch the Lumberjacks a bit loser at 37-24. The teams traded field goals in the third quarter for the only points of the second half.

The victory allowed Northwestern State to finish with a .500 overall mark at 6-6, including a 3-4 record in Southland Conference play.

Despite losing its final two games of the regular season, Sam Houston State, which had reached the Football Championship Subdivision title game the previous two years, qualified for the 24-team field in 2013. Even with an 8-4 record, the Bearkats managed to host an opening-round game against Southern Utah.

A 42-yard Colton Cook field goal and a 38-yard pass from Aaron Cantu to Anthony Norris gave the Thunderbirds a 10-0 lead as the Bearkats' normally-potent running game was held to a total of 4 yards after their first three drives.

Sticking with the running game paid dividends for Sam Houston State. After the Bearkats pulled with within 10-7 on a 32-yard pass from Bell to Nelson, SHSU came up with scoring runs of 3 yards by Hill and 1 yard by Bell before Swimberghe connected on a 24-yard field goal on the final play of the first half to give the Bearkats a 23-10 halftime lead.

Trailing 30-10 in the third quarter, Southern Utah countered with a 38-yard Cook field goal and a 39-yard Robert Torgerson fumble return to cut the deficit to 10 points at 30-20 heading into the final period.

The fourth quarter belonged to the Bearkats as Flanders scored on a pair of short touchdown runs and Hill added a 2-yard scoring run as SHSU pulled away for the 51-20 victory.

Despite the slow start from the Bearkats' running game, Flanders managed to finish with 176 yards on the ground and Hill 101.

Sam Houston State's win over Southern Utah set up a rematch with Southland Conference champion Southeastern Louisiana in the second round of the playoffs. During the regular season, the Beakats lost 34-21 to the Lions.

Along with playing at home, the fourth-seeded Lions had the extra advantage of an additional week to prepare for the rematch with Sam Houston State. Despite that, it was the Bearkats who jumped out to a 14-0 lead on an 11-yard run by Torrance Williams and a 12-yard interception return for a touchdown by Loche. Loche's interception return came only moments after Williams' touchdown as SHSU took a two-touchdown lead less than five minutes into the contest.

When a 5-yard touchdown run by Bennett was answered by a 3-yard run by Flanders to give Sam Houston State a 21-7 lead after one quarter, the playoff encounter had a familiar feel to the regular-season battle between the teams.

In the regular-season tilt, the Lions had to battle back from a 21-10 halftime deficit. This time around, however, Southeastern Louisiana didn't wait around until the second half. A 25-yard Sebastian field goal, a 45-yard run by Harrell and a 16-yard touchdown pass from Bennett to Fruge put SLU on top 24-21 at halftime.

The only points in the third quarter came on Eric Fieilo's sack of Bennett in the end zone for a safety to inch the Bearkats to within a single point at 24-23.

Sam Houston State regained the lead at 29-24 on a 2-yard run by Bell with 10:58 left in the game.

Trailing by five points, the Lions got the ball back at their own 15-yard line with 1:29 left in the game. Bennett completed four-straight passes, advancing the ball to the Sam Houston State 26. After off-setting penalties, Bennett hooked up with Fruge on a 25-yard toss down to the 1-yard line. On first-and-goal, Bennett tossed to Smiley with 36 seconds left in the game to give the Lions a hard-earned 30-29 triumph over their conference rivals.

The loss ended Sam Houston State's season at 9-5.

On the same day of the Southeastern Louisiana-Sam Houston State rematch, McNeese State was playing its postseason opener as the sixth-seeded Cowboys hosted Jacksonville State. McNeese went into the game seeking its first postseason win since 2002.

On McNeese's first possession of the game, Ketrick Wolfe picked off a Stroud pass. A personal-foul penalty against the Cowboys during Wolfe's return helped to advance the ball to the McNeese 19-yard line. On Jacksonville State's first offensive play of the game, quarterback Eli Jenkins hooked up with Josh Barge on a touchdown toss to give the Gamecocks a 7-0 lead.

A pair of 1-yard touchdown runs by DaMarcus James in the second quarter gave Jacksonville State a 21-0 halftime lead. James' final touchdown run of the half came following a second Stroud interception.

The Gamecocks, a former Southland Football League rival of McNeese, continually harassed Stroud. The Cowboys quarterback was sacked 11 times and threw two interceptions. In 12 regular-season games, Stroud had been sacked a total of only 14 times and tossed only five interceptions. Stround ended the game 18 of 40 passing for 255 yards.

"We had done a great job all year not getting behind like that. We just got behind and pretty much had to throw it and they knew it. It (throwing the ball) really wasn't what we did," said Viator.

The Cowboys' running attack fared poorly as well. When taking all the sacks into account, McNeese was held to 46 yards rushing.

McNeese never was able to get its offense going. The Cowboys were 0 of 9 on third down conversions in the first half and 1 of 16 for the game.

Jacksonville State's Griffin Thomas and McNeese's Rome traded field goals for the only points of the third quarter.

The Cowboys' only touchdown came on a 10-yard pass from Stroud to Celestie with 10:11 left in the game to make the score 24-10. A 3-yard run by James with 4:35 left in the game accounted for the 31-10 final as McNeese ended its season 10-3.

The Southland Conference's only team still alive in the FCS playoffs; Southeastern Louisiana hosted New Hampshire in the quarterfinals a week later.

Southeastern scored on its opening drive of the game on a 2-yard run by Bennett. New Hampshire countered on a 32-yard run by Wildcats quarterback Sean Goldrich to tie the game after one quarter.

The only score of the second quarter came on a 1-yard run by Goldrich to give New Hampshire a 14-7 halftime lead. The only score of the third quarter was a 22-yard Sebastian field goal to make it a four-point contest going into the final period.

Continuing to trail by four points, Bennett and the Lions marched midway in the fourth quarter. Starting at the SLU 20, the Lions advanced to the New Hampshire 5-yard line in 13 plays. Facing fourth-and-goal, Bennett rolled to his right to avoid two Wildcat defenders before spotting Fruge in the end zone to give Southeastern Louisiana a 17-14 lead with 5:17 remaining in the game.

Following Fruge's touchdown catch, the Wildcats got the ball back at their own 20-yard line. Converting on a fourth-and-1 and third-and-5 to keep the drive alive, Goldrich eventually scored on a 2-yard run with 47 seconds left for a 20-17 New Hampshire victory to eliminate the Lions from the playoffs.

The Lions stayed in the game by blocking two field goals and intercepting a pass to halt another New Hampshire drive. Conversely, Southeastern Louisiana twice missed out on taking advantage of favorable field position inside the Wildcats' 30-yard line created by the Lions' special teams. On one occasion, a kickoff return to the New Hampshire 29 led to no points when SLU turned the ball over on downs. A punt return to the Wildcats' 28 also yielded no points when Sebastian missed a 37-yard field goal attempt.

The loss snapped Southeastern's school-record 10-game winning streak as the Lions concluded the 2013 season at 11-3.

LEGACY

For those involved in the Southland Conference, one theme seems to be a constant when referring to the success of the league for 50 years.

"The great thing about the Southland is it was so competitive year after year," said Ron Randleman, Sam Houston State's coach from 1982-04. "You could be on the bottom one year and on top the next year.

"You better be ready to play every week. If you didn't, you weren't going to win. It was never boring. It was always exciting."

"I really thought it was one of the best and most competitive leagues in the country on any level. Anybody, on just about any week, can win a game or upset somebody," said Larry Blakeney, whose Troy State team was in the Southland from 1996-00.

"Every time you played a football game against a Southland Conference opponent in those days, it was a battle. It was the kind of game a man would love to buy a ticket to see," said Pat Collins, who coached Northeast Louisiana from 1981-88.

"We played the Texas schools and Louisiana Tech and Southwestern Louisiana. When you went down there to play, you better tighten your jock strap. Those guys would hit you. The Texas schools were great, too," said Chet Douthit, a receiver at Arkansas State from 1969-70.

A key factor in the competive play of the Southland, many agree, is because of the recruiting footprint of the conference.

"The recruiting footprint gives us access and the opportunity to recruit some of the finest talent from some of the finest states in the country. It's predominately a Louisiana and Texas footprint and I think where we are located, we have access to tremendous high school football players," said Clint Conque, who has served as head coach at both Central Arkansas and Stephen F. Austin.

"One of the things I loved about coaching at Sam Houston was you can draw a circle four hours around us and you don't have to go any farther," said

Randleman. "If you can't find good football players in that four-hour circle, you can't find good football players."

"There are a lot of really good (high school) football schools between Houston and New Orleans and all of east Texas. There are a lot of good high school coaches and a lot of good high school programs," said Tommy Tate, a player at McNeese State in the 1970s who later served as the Cowboys' coach from 2000-06.

"You go along Interstate 20 into east Texas and right into Shreveport, Ruston and Monroe, there's just wonderful football players in that area," said Roger Carr, a receiver on Louisiana Tech's 1973 national championship team who went on to a successful NFL career.

"We basically just recruited the state of Texas," said Willie Fritz, an assistant coach at Sam Houston under Randleman who later led the Bearkats to the Football Championship Subdivision finals in 2011 and 2012.

Along with outstanding players, the Southland has produced its share of top-notch coaches over the years.

"The coaches are all tremendous coaches. I think it's a real coaching league," said J.C. Harper, Stephen F. Austin's coach from 2007-13. "You have to really be able to put it together coaching-wise in order to win a championship. All of the players are pretty much the same. If you can get a couple of difference makers like Jeremy Moses (the SFA quarterback who went on to win the Walter Payton Award as the best player on the FCS level), it puts you in front."

With so much high school talent to draw from in the Southland's footprint, there are a lot of good players to go around - even after the power conference schools get the cream of the crop.

One thing the Southland have done well over the years is project players coming out of high school that might not measure up to the standards of Football Bowl Subdivision programs, but with the right coaching, turn out ot be good college players.

"A lot of these small schools have a diamond in the rough," Tate said of some of the high schools in the SLC's footprint. "That's something McNeese has kind of made a living on – being able to project offensive linemen and being able to really get good skilled kids from some of those smaller schools that really end up being outstanding football players."

"It has some good football coaches and coaches that believe they had to recruit different kind of kids," said Stan Humphries, who quarterbacked Northeast Louisiana to a national championship in 1987 and later led the San Diego Chargers to the Super Bowl. "The Power-5 (conferences) would get everybody they wanted but (the SLC) had to recruit kids that could pass block, throw the ball a little bit more and a few more receivers and things like that and turn it into a good football team."

Even going back to the early days of the conference, the league was a bit of a trend setter. For example, Trinity University, a founding member of the Southland in 1964, was recruiting African-American athletes before programs from the larger Southwestern and Southeastern conferences.

One of the early African-American stars in the Southland was Trinity's Marvin Upshaw. A linebacker and kicker at Trinity from 1964-67 and the brother of Pro Football Hall of Famer Gene Upshaw, Marvin was a first-round pick in the NFL draft and enjoyed a successful professional career of his own.

Another early star was Trinity running back Earl Costley, who played from 1970-73 and is still second on the school's all-time rushing list.

"It was exciting to be in the Southland," said Costley. "It was a great conference to be in. You knew you were playing against top-notch football players."

Trinity wasn't the only school recruiting African-American athletes in the early days of the Southland.

"We had a few more African-American players on our team than any of the Southwest Conference teams in the early days," said Danny Griffin, a fullback at Texas-Arlington in the late 1960s. "There were very few African-American players in the Southwest Conference, two or three, maybe. We had a least that on our team each year and they were outstanding players."

The membership has changed over the years, but the quality and competitiveness have remained. With the league now in its second half-century, the Southland continues to grow and even has come full circle with the return of Abilene Christian, a founding member of the conference in 1964.

For those who have been involved in the conference, the future looks bright for the Southland.

"The structure of the NCAA is changing. With the Football Championship Subdivision still expanding the number of teams in the playoffs, there's a lot of excitement," said Tate. "You like to see more teams involved in the playoffs and giving more teams a chance to actually have a chance to win a national championship. I see nothing but good things ahead."

"I have no doubt the conference will continue to thrive and make its mark, not just regionally, but nationally," said Conque.

Southland Conference 50th Anniversary All-Time Football team

First Team Offense

Player	Pos.	School	SLC Career	Superlatives
Jeremy Moses	QB	Stephen F. Austin	2007-10	2010 Walter Payton Award
Tim Flanders	RB	Sam Houston State	2010-13	SLC career rushing leader
Buford Jordan	RB	McNeese State	1980-83	SLC's first 4,000-yard rusher
Bruce Collie	OL	Texas-Arlington	1981-84	1984 All-American
Marcus Spears	OL	Northwestern State	1991-93	1993 Outland Trophy semifinalist
Reggie Nelson	OL	McNeese State	1995-98	1997, 1998 All-American
Ray Brown	OL	Arkansas State	1983-85	1985 All-American
Randy Barnhill	OL	Arkansas State	1984-86	1986 All-American
Mike Barber	TE	Louisiana Tech	1972-75	1974, 1975 All-American
Roger Carr	WR	Louisiana Tech	1971-73	1972, 1973 All-American
Matt Dominquez	WR	Sam Houston State	1997-00	SLC career receiving leader
Shonz LaFrenz	K	McNeese State	1996-99	1997, 1998, 1999 All-American

First Team Defense

Player	Pos.	School	SLC Career	Superlatives
Fred Dean	DL	Louisiana Tech	1971-74	College Football Hall of Famer
Kavika Pittman	DL	McNeese State	1993-95	1995 All-American
Walter Johnson	DL	Louisiana Tech	1983-86	1986 All-American
Al Lucas	DL	Troy State	1996-99	1999 Buck Buchanan Award Winner
Jeremiah Trotter	LB	Stephen F. Austin	1995-97	1996 All-American
Bill Bergey	LB	Arkansas State	1965-68	1968 All-American
Terry Irving	LB	McNeese State	1990-93	1992, 1993 All-American
Lardarius Webb	DB	Nicholls State	2007-08	2007, 2008 All-American
Darryl Pounds	DB	Nicholls State	1991-94	1994 All-American
Zack Bronson	DB	McNeese State	1993-96	1996 All-American
Leonard Smith	DB	McNeese State	1980-82	1982 All-American
Chad Stanley	P	Stephen F. Austin	1996-98	1998 All-American
Gralyn Crawford	RS	Stephen F. Austin	2009-12	2010, 2011 American

All-Time Head Coach

Coach	School	Southland Tenure
Maxie Lambright	Louisiana Tech	1971-78

Second Team Offense

Player	Pos.	School	SLC Career	Superlatives
Jim Lindsey	QB	Abilene Christian	1967-70	1970 All-American
Claude Mathis	RB	Texas State	1994-97	1996, 1997 All-American
Larry Centers	RB	Stephen F. Austin	1987-89	14-year NFL career
Kerry Jenkins	OL	Troy State	1995-96	1996 All-American

Demetress Bell	OL	Jacksonville State	2006-07	2007 All-American
Bill Phillips	OL	Arkansas State	1968-71	1970 All-American
Mark Cannon	OL	Texas-Arlington	1980-83	7-year NFL career
Murphy Yates	OL	Sam Houston State	1988-91	1991 All-American
Jackie Harris	TE	Northeast Louisiana	1986-89	1989 All-American
Pat Tilley	WR	Louisiana Tech	1972-75	11-year NFL career
Cordell Roberson	WR	Stephen F. Austin	2009-12	SLC Career touchdown catches leader
Rafael Septien	K	SW Louisiana	1974-76	10-year NFL career

Second Team Defense				
Player	*Pos.*	*School*	*SLC Career*	*Superlatives*
Michael Bankston	DL	Sam Houston State	1988-91	9-year NFL career
Marvin Upshaw	DL	Trinity	1964-67	1967 All-American
Bryan Smith	DL	McNeese State	2005-07	2006, 2007 All-American
Clovis Swinney	DL	Arkansas State	1967-69	1969 All-American
Doug Landry	LB	Louisiana Tech	1982-85	1985 All-American
Andre Carron	LB	Northwestern State	1988-91	1991 All-American
Eugene Seale	LB	Lamar	1983-85	1983 All-American
Tim McKyer	DB	Texas-Arlington	1982-85	12-year NFL career
Terrence McGee	DB	Northwestern State	1999-02	2000 All-American
Mike Green	DB	Northwestern State	1997-99	1999 All-American
Jermaine Jones	DB	Northwestern State	1995-98	1998 All-American
Cory Elolf	P	Texas State	2003-05	2004 All-American
Toby Zeigler	RS	Northwestern State	2002-05	SLC career punt return leader

Total Offensive Yards							
Player	*School*	*Years*	*Plays*	*Rush*	*Pass*	*Yards*
Jeremy Moses	Stephen F. Austin	2007-2010	2,034	-200	13,401	13,201
Brady Attaway	Stephen F. Austin	2010-2013	1,738	-242	11,433	11,191
Nathan Brown*	Central Arkansas	2005-2008	1,474	435	10,558	10,993
Derrick Fourroux	McNeese State	2006-2009	1,517	2,037	8,226	10,263
Brian Bell	Sam Houston State	2010-2013	1,439	1,526	8,655	10,181
Bradley George	Texas State	2006-2009	1,479	230	9,556	9,786
Kerry Joseph	McNeese State	1992-1995	1,649	1,802	7,874	9,676
Mitch Maher	North Texas	1991-1994	1,471	487	8,519	9,006
Barrick Nealy	Texas State	2003-2005	1,383	1,727	7,206	8,933
Todd Hammel*	Stephen F. Austin	1987-1989	1,359	184	8,631	8,815
*Entire career not played as Southland member						

Passing Yards							
Player	*School*	*Years*	*Att.*	*Comp.*	*Int.*	*TDs*	*Yards*
Jeremy Moses	Stephen F. Austin	2007-2010	1,893	1,184	55	121	13,401
Brady Attaway	Stephen F. Austin	2010-2013	1,688	1,004	66	89	11,433
Nathan Brown*	Central Arkansas	2005-2008	1,267	856	32	100	10,558
Bradley George	Texas State	2006-2009	1,277	753	35	76	9,556
Brian Bell	Sam Houston State	2010-2013	1,077	621	31	84	8,655
Todd Hammel*	Stephen F. Austin	1986-1989	1,060	544	51	65	8,631
Jim Lindsey	Abilene Christian	1967-1970	1,237	642	69	61	8,521
Mitch Maher	North Texas	1991-1994	1,149	640	50	67	8,519
Derrick Fourroux	McNeese State	2006-2009	1,034	618	24	64	8,226
Kerry Joseph	McNeese State	1992-1995	1,114	565	47	67	7,874
*Entire career not played as Southland member							

Rushing Yards						
Player	*School*	*Years*	*Att.*	*Avg.*	*TDs*	*Yards*
Timothy Flanders	Sam Houston State	2010-2012	999	5.6	66	5,664
Claude Mathis	Texas State	1994-1997	882	5.3	45	4,694
Henry Fields	McNeese State	1992-1995	839	5.2	30	4,358
Buford Jordan	McNeese State	1980-1983	750	5.5	43	4,106
Leonard Harris	Stephen F. Austin	1992-1995	741	5.1	28	3,771
Tony Taylor	Northwestern State	1998-2000	688	5.4	32	3,720
Derrick Jensen	Texas-Arlington	1974-1977	676	4.9	14	3,346
Tony Citizen	McNeese State	1986-1988	713	4.6	28	3,284
Scotty Caldwell	Texas-Arlington	1981-1984	652	5.0	31	3,267
Karrington Bush	Texas State	2007-2010	477	6.7	24	3,193

Receiving Yards			
Player	*School*	*Years*	*Yards*
Matt Dominquez	Sam Houston State	1997-2000	3,273
Cordell Roberson	Stephen F. Austin	2009-2012	3,191
Joey Hamilton	Jacksonville State	1996-1999	2,903
Simmie Yarborough	Southeastern Louisiana	2008-2011	2,780
Roger Carr	Louisiana Tech	1970-1973	2,717
Dominique Edison	Stephen F. Austin	2005-2008	2,696
Jermaine Martin	McNeese State	1999-2002	2,636
Jonathon Cooper	Sam Houston State	1998-2001	2,617
Chris Jefferson	Stephen F. Austin	1993-1995	2,571
Gralyn Crawford	Stephen F. Austin	2009-2012	2,623

Field Goals made			
Player	*School*	*Years*	*FGM*
Shonz LaFrenz	McNeese State	1996-1999	66
Jose Larios	McNeese State	1992-1995	66
Chuck Rawlinson	Stephen F. Austin	1988-1991	57
Teddy Garcia	Northeast Louisiana	1984-1987	56
Miquel Antonio	Sam Houston State	2009-2012	51
Jeff Turner	Southeastern Louisiana	2006-2009	50
Keith Chapman	North Texas	1985-1989	49
Blake Bercegeay	McNeese State	2005-2008	48
Billy Hayes	Sam Houston State	1985-1988	47
Lawrence Tynes	Troy State	1997-2000	47

Punting Average				
Player	*School*	*Years*	*No.*	*Avg.*
Chad Stanley	Stephen F. Austin	1996-1998	178	43.3
Patrick Dolan	Nicholls State	2007-2010	165	43.1
Ryan Klaus	Sam Houston State	1995-1998	225	42.1
Cory Elolf	Texas State	2003-2005	147	41.9
Don Stump	McNeese State	1978-1981	236	41.5
Drew Nelson	Stephen F. Austin	2008-2011	203	41.3
Kollin Kahler	Lamar University	2010-2013	265	41.3
Bruce Gartman	Arkansas State	1980-1982	210	41.2
Bart Bradley	Sam Houston State	1986-1989	264	41.2
Matt Allen	Troy State	1997-2000	219	41.0
*Minimum 100 punts, two seasons to qualify				

Total Tackles			
Player	*School*	*Years*	*Tackles*
Andre Carron	Northwestern State	1988-1991	521
Doug Landry	Louisiana Tech	1982-1985	509
Jerry Muckensturm	Arkansas State	1972-1975	493
David Temple	Stephen F. Austin	1988-1991	492
Charles Ayro	McNeese State	1995-1998	486
Terry Irving	McNeese State	1990-1993	461
Greg Pitts	Texas State	1999-2002	447
Brad Fulks	Texas State	1985-1988	441
Bill Bergey	Arkansas State	1965-1968	436
Ron Smith	Arkansas State	1976-1979	422

Interceptions			
Player	*School*	*Years*	*No.*
Dennis Meyer	Arkansas State	1968-1971	27
Billy Blakeman	McNeese State	1970-1973	25
Cedric Walker	Stephen F. Austin	1990-1993	25
Dick Ritchey	Arkansas State	1964-1967	19
Charles Jefferson	McNeese State	1975-1978	19
Ron Irving	Southwestern Louisiana	1976-1978	19
Zack Bronson	McNeese State	1993-1996	19
Terry Whiting	Arkansas State	1968-1971	16
Doyle Adams	Louisiana Tech	1982-1985	16
*Four tied with 15			

Quarterback Sacks			
Player	*School*	*Years*	*Sacks*
Walter Johnson	Louisiana Tech	1983-1986	38.0
Andre Finley	Sam Houston State	1986-1989	36.0
Tim Knicky	Stephen F. Austin	2006-2009	32.5
C.J. Carroll	Texas State	1997-2000	32.0
Bryan Smith	McNeese State	2005-2007	31.0
Greg Necaise	Northwestern State	1989-1990	28.5
Marvin Neloms	Arkansas State	1983-1986	28.0
Reggie Lowe	Troy State	1994-1997	28.0
James Folston	Northeast Louisiana	1990-1993	27.0
Anthony Williams	Northeast Louisiana	1987-1990	26.0

1964								
	Conference				All Games			
School	W	L	T	Pct	W	L	T	Pct
Lamar Tech*	3	0	1	.875	6	2	1	.723
Arkansas State	2	0	2	.750	7	0	2	.889
Trinity University	2	2	0	.500	3	7	0	.300
Abilene Christian	1	3	0	.250	5	5	0	.500
Arlington State	0	3	1	.125	3	6	1	.350
*Includes win in Pecan Bowl								

1967								
	Conference				All Games			
School	W	L	T	Pct	W	L	T	Pct
Texas Arlington*	4	0	0	1.000	10	1	0	.909
Lamar Tech	3	1	0	.750	7	3	0	.700
Arkansas State	2	2	0	.500	4	5	0	.444
Trinity University	1	3	0	.250	3	7	0	.300
Abilene Christian	0	4	0	.000	4	6	0	.400
*Includes win in Pecan Bowl								

1965								
	Conference				All Games			
School	W	L	T	Pct.	W	L	T	Pct.
Lamar Tech	3	1	0	.750	6	4	0	.600
Arlington State	2	2	0	.500	6	3	0	.667
Trinity University	2	2	0	.500	4	5	1	.450
Abilene Christian	2	2	0	.500	4	5	0	.444
Arkansas State	1	3	0	.250	6	3	0	.667

1968								
	Conference				All Games			
School	W	L	T	Pct	W	L	T	Pct
Arkansas State*	3	0	1	.875	7	3	1	.682
Texas Arlington	3	1	0	.750	6	4	0	.600
Trinity University	2	2	0	.500	5	4	0	.556
Abilene Christian	1	2	1	.375	4	5	1	.421
Lamar Tech	0	4	0	.000	0	10	0	.000
*Includes win in Pecan Bowl								

1966								
	Conference				All Games			
School	W	L	T	Pct.	W	L	T	Pct.
Arlington State	3	1	0	.750	6	4	0	.600
Lamar Tech	3	1	0	.750	6	4	0	.600
Arkansas State	2	2	0	.500	7	2	0	.778
Trinity University	2	2	0	.500	5	4	0	.556
Abilene Christian	0	4	0	.000	4	6	0	.400

1969								
	Conference				All Games			
School	W	L	T	Pct	W	L	T	Pct
Arkansas State*	4	0	0	1.000	8	1	0	.850
Abilene Christian	2	2	0	.500	8	2	1	.800
Texas Arlington	2	2	0	.500	5	5	0	.500
Trinity University	2	2	0	.500	4	6	0	.400
Lamar Tech	0	4	0	.000	3	7	0	.300
*Includes win in Pecan Bowl								

1970

School	Conference				All Games			
	W	L	T	Pct	W	L	T	Pct
Arkansas State*	4	0	0	1.000	11	0	0	1.000
Abilene Christian	3	1	0	.750	9	2	0	.818
Trinity University	2	2	0	.500	5	6	0	.455
Lamar Tech	1	3	0	.250	3	7	0	.300
Texas Arlington	0	4	0	.000	0	10	0	.000

*Includes win in Pecan Bowl

1971

School	Conference				All Games			
	W	L	T	Pct	W	L	T	Pct
Louisiana Tech*	4	1	0	.800	9	2	0	.818
Trinity University	4	1	0	.800	8	2	0	.800
Lamar University	4	1	0	.800	5	6	0	.455
Southwestern Louisiana	2	2	1	.500	5	4	1	.550
Arkansas State	1	3	1	.300	4	4	1	.500
Abilene Christian	1	4	0	.200	5	5	0	.500
Texas Arlington	1	4	0	.200	2	9	0	.182

*Includes win in Pioneer Bowl

1972

School	Conference				All Games			
	W	L	T	Pct	W	L	T	Pct
Louisiana Tech*	5	0	0	1.000	12	0	0	1.000
Texas Arlington	4	1	0	.800	5	6	0	.455
McNeese State	3	2	0	.600	8	3	0	.728
Lamar University	3	2	0	.600	8	3	0	.728
Southwestern Louisiana	1	4	0	.200	5	6	0	.455
Arkansas State	1	4	0	.200	4	7	0	.364
Abilene Christian	1	4	0	.200	3	8	0	.273

*Includes win in Grantland Rice Bowl

1973

School	Conference				All Games			
	W	L	T	Pct	W	L	T	Pct
Louisiana Tech*	5	0	0	1.000	12	1	0	.923
Arkansas State	3	2	0	.600	7	3	0	.700
Lamar University	3	2	0	.600	5	5	0	.500
McNeese State	2	3	0	.400	7	3	0	.700
Texas Arlington	2	3	0	.400	4	6	0	.400
Southwestern Louisiana	0	5	0	.000	0	10	0	.000

*Includes 3-0 record in Division II playoffs

1974

School	Conference				All Games			
	W	L	T	Pct	W	L	T	Pct
Louisiana Tech*	5	0	0	1.000	11	1	0	.971
Lamar University	4	1	0	.800	8	2	0	.800
Arkansas State	3	2	0	.600	7	3	0	.700
McNeese State	2	3	0	.400	6	4	1	.591
Texas Arlington	1	4	0	.200	1	10	0	.091
Southwestern Louisiana	0	5	0	.000	2	9	0	.182

*Includes 1-1 record in Division II playoffs

1975

School	Conference				All Games			
	W	L	T	Pct	W	L	T	Pct
Arkansas State	5	0	0	1.000	11	0	0	1.000
Louisiana Tech	4	1	0	.800	8	2	0	.800
McNeese State	3	2	0	.600	7	4	0	.740
Southwestern Louisiana	2	3	0	.400	6	5	0	.545
Texas Arlington	1	4	0	.200	4	7	0	.364
Lamar University	0	5	0	.000	1	10	0	.091

1976

School	Conference				All Games			
	W	L	T	Pct	W	L	T	Pct
McNeese State	4	1	0	.800	10	2	0	.833
Southwestern Louisiana&	4	1	0	.800	7	4	0	.636
Texas Arlington	3	2	0	.600	5	6	0	.455
Louisiana Tech	2	3	0	.400	6	5	0	.545
Arkansas State	2	3	0	.400	5	6	0	.455
Lamar University	0	5	0	.000	2	9	0	.182

*Includes 1-1 record in Division II playoffs
&Forfeited two regular-season wins

1979

School	Conference				All Games			
	W	L	T	Pct	W	L	T	Pct
McNeese State*	5	0	0	1.000	11	1	0	.917
Texas Arlington	4	1	0	.800	9	2	0	.818
Lamar University	3	2	0	.600	6	3	2	.636
Southwestern Louisiana	1	4	0	.200	4	7	0	.364
Arkansas State	1	4	0	.200	4	7	0	.364
Louisiana Tech&	1	4	0	.200	3	8	0	.273

*Includes loss in Independence Bowl
&Includes one win by forfeit

1977

School	Conference				All Games			
	W	L	T	Pct	W	L	T	Pct
Louisiana Tech*	4	0	1	.900	9	1	2	.833
Southwestern Louisiana	2	1	2	,600	6	4	2	.582
Texas Arlington	3	2	0	.600	5	6	0	.455
Arkansas State	2	3	0	.400	7	4	0	.636
McNeese State	1	3	1	.300	5	5	1	.500
Lamar University	1	4	0	.200	2	9	0	.182

*Includes win in Independence Bowl

1980

School	Conference				All Games			
	W	L	T	Pct	W	L	T	Pct
McNeese State*	5	0	0	1.000	10	2	0	.833
Southwestern Louisiana	4	1	0	.800	7	4	0	.636
Texas Arlington	3	2	0	.600	3	8	0	.273
Louisiana Tech	2	3	0	.400	5	6	0	.455
Lamar University	1	4	0	.200	3	8	0	.273
Arkansas State	0	5	0	.000	2	9	0	.182

*Includes loss in Independence Bowl

1978

School	Conference				All Games			
	W	L	T	Pct	W	L	T	Pct
Louisiana Tech*	4	0	1	.800	6	5	0	.545
Arkansas State	4	1	0	.800	7	4	0	.636
Texas Arlington	3	2	0	.600	5	6	0	.455
McNeese State	2	3	0	.400	7	4	0	.636
Southwestern Louisiana	2	3	0	.400	3	8	0	.273
Lamar University	0	5	0	.000	2	8	1	.227

*Includes loss in Independence Bowl

1981

School	Conference				All Games			
	W	L	T	Pct	W	L	T	Pct
Texas Arlington	4	1	0	.800	6	5	0	.545
McNeese State	3	1	1	.700	7	3	1	.682
Arkansas State	3	2	0	.600	6	5	0	.545
Louisiana Tech	2	1	1	.500	4	6	1	.409
Lamar University	1	3	1	.300	4	6	1	.409
Southwestern Louisiana	0	4	1	.100	1	9	1	.136

1982							
	Conference				All Games			
School	W	L	T	Pct	W	L	T	Pct
Louisiana Tech*	5	0	0	1.000	10	3	0	.769
Northeast Louisiana	4	1	0	.800	8	3	0	.727
Arkansas State	2	3	0	.400	5	6	0	.455
McNeese State	2	3	0	.400	4	6	1	.409
Lamar University	1	4	0	.200	4	7	0	.364
Texas Arlington	1	4	0	.200	3	8	0	.273
North Texas	0	0	0	.000	2	9	0	.182
*Includes 1-1 record in I-AA playoffs								

1984							
	Conference				All Games			
School	W	L	T	Pct	W	L	T	Pct
Louisiana Tech*	5	1	0	.833	10	5	0	.667
Arkansas State&	4	1	1	.750	8	4	1	.654
Texas Arlington	4	2	0	.667	7	4	0	.636
Northeast Louisiana	3	3	0	.500	7	4	0	.636
McNeese State	2	3	1	.417	7	3	1	.682
Lamar University	1	5	0	.167	2	9	0	.182
North Texas	1	5	0	.167	2	9	0	.182
*Includes 3-1 record in I-AA playoffs								
&Includes 1-1 record in I-AA playoffs								

1983							
	Conference				All Games			
School	W	L	T	Pct	W	L	T	Pct
North Texas*	5	1	0	.833	8	4	0	.667
Northeast Louisiana	5	1	0	.833	8	3	0	.727
McNeese State	3	3	0	.500	6	5	0	.545
Arkansas State	3	3	0	.500	5	5	1	.500
Texas Arlington	2	4	0	.333	5	6	0	.455
Louisiana Tech	2	4	0	.333	4	7	0	,364
Lamar University	1	5	0	.183	2	9	0	.182
*Includes 0-1 record in I-AA playoffs								

1985							
	Conference				All Games			
School	W	L	T	Pct	W	L	T	Pct
Arkansas State*	5	1	0	.833	9	4	0	,692
Louisiana Tech	4	2	0	.667	8	3	0	.727
McNeese State	3	1	2	.667	6	3	2	.636
Northeast Louisiana	3	3	0	.500	6	5	0	.545
North Texas	2	3	1	.417	4	6	1	.409
Texas Arlington	2	3	1	.417	4	6	1	.409
Lamar University	0	6	0	.000	3	8	0	.273
*Includes 1-1 record in I-AA playoffs								

1986								
	Conference				All Games			
School	W	L	T	Pct	W	L	T	Pct
Arkansas State*	5	0	0	1.000	12	2	1	.833
North Texas	3	2	0	.600	6	4	0	.600
Louisiana Tech	3	2	0	.600	6	4	1	.591
Northeast Louisiana	3	2	0	.600	5	6	0	.455
McNeese State	1	4	0	.200	2	9	0	.222
Lamar University	0	5	0	.000	2	9	0	.222
*Includes 3-1 record in I-AA playoffs								

1987								
	Conference				All Games			
School	W	L	T	Pct	W	L	T	Pct
Northeast Louisiana*	6	0	0	1.000	13	2	0	.867
Sam Houston State	5	1	0	.833	8	3	0	.727
North Texas&	5	1	0	.833	7	5	0	.583
Northwestern State	3	3	0	.500	6	5	0	.545
Southwest Texas	2	4	0	.333	4	7	0	.364
Stephen F. Austin	1	5	0	.167	3	7	1	.318
McNeese State	1	5	0	.167	2	9	0	.182
*Includes 4-0 record in I-AA playoffs								
&Includes 0-1 record in I-AA playoffs								

1988								
	Conference				All Games			
School	W	L	T	Pct	W	L	T	Pct
Northwestern State*	6	0	0	1.000	10	3	0	.769
Stephen F. Austin*	5	1	0	.833	10	3	0	.769
North Texas&	4	2	0	.667	8	4	0	.667
McNeese State	3	3	0	.500	6	5	0	.545
Northeast Louisiana	2	4	0	.333	5	6	0	.455
Southwest Texas	1	5	0	.167	4	7	0	.364
Sam Houston State	0	6	0	.000	3	8	0	.273
*Includes 1-1 record in I-AA playoffs								
&Includes 0-1 record in I-AA playoffs								

1989								
	Conference				All Games			
School	W	L	T	Pct	W	L	T	Pct
Stephen F. Austin*	5	0	1	.917	12	2	1	.833
Northwestern State	3	1	2	,667	4	5	2	.455
Southwest Texas	3	3	0	.500	5	6	0	.454
Northeast Louisiana	2	3	1	.416	4	6	1	.409
McNeese State	2	4	0	.333	5	6	0	.455
North Texas	2	4	0	.333	5	6	0	.455
Sam Houston State	2	4	0	.333	3	8	0	.273
*Includes 3-1 record in I-AA playoffs								

1990							
	Conference				All Games		
School	W	L	T	Pct	W	L	T	Pct
Northeast Louisiana*	5	1	0	.833	7	5	0	.583
McNeese State	4	2	0	.667	5	6	0	.455
Southwest Texas	3	3	0	.500	6	5	0	.545
Northwestern State	3	3	0	.500	5	6	0	.455
Sam Houston State	3	3	0	.500	4	7	0	.364
North Texas	2	4	0	.333	6	5	0	.545
Stephen F. Austin&	1	5	0	.167	1	10	0	.091

*Includes 0-1 record in I-AA playoffs
&Includes forfeit of one regular-season game

1991							
	Conference				All Games		
School	W	L	T	Pct	W	L	T	Pct
McNeese State*	4	1	2	.714	6	4	2	.583
Sam Houston State*	5	2	0	.714	8	3	1	.708
Northeast Louisiana	4	2	1	.643	7	3	1	.682
Southwest Texas	4	3	0	.571	7	4	0	.636
Northwestern State	4	3	0	.571	6	5	0	.545
Nicholls State	2	5	0	.286	4	7	0	.364
North Texas	2	5	0	.286	3	7	1	.318
Stephen F. Austin	1	5	1	.214	2	8	1	.227

*Includes 0-1 record in I-AA playoffs

1992							
	Conference				All Games		
School	W	L	T	Pct	W	L	T	Pct
Northeast Louisiana*	7	0	0	1.000	10	3	0	.769
McNeese State*	6	1	0	.857	9	4	0	.692
Northwestern State	4	3	0	.571	7	4	0	.636
Sam Houston State	3	2	2	.571	6	3	2	.636
North Texas	3	4	0	.428	4	7	0	.363
Southwest Texas	2	4	1	.357	5	5	1	.500
Stephen F. Austin	1	6	0	.142	3	8	0	.273
Nicholls State	0	6	1	.071	1	9	1	.136

*Includes 1-1 record in I-AA playoffs

1993							
	Conference				All Games		
School	W	L	T	Pct	W	L	T	Pct
McNeese State*	7	0	0	1.000	10	3	0	.769
Northeast Louisiana&	6	1	0	.857	9	3	0	.750
Stephen F. Austin&	5	2	0	714	8	4	0	.667
Northwestern State	3	4	0	.429	5	6	0	.455
Sam Houston State	2	5	0	.286	4	7	0	.364
North Texas	2	5	0	.286	4	7	0	.364
Nicholls State	2	5	0	.286	3	8	0	.273
Southwest Texas	1	6	0	.143	2	9	0	.182

*Includes 1-1 record in I-AA playoffs
&Includes 0-1 record in I-AA playoffs

1994								
	Conference				All Games			
School	W	L	T	Pct	W	L	T	Pct
North Texas*	5	0	1	.917	7	4	1	.625
McNeese State&	5	1	0	.833	10	3	0	.769
Stephen F. Austin	4	1	1	.750	6	3	2	.636
Northwestern State	3	3	0	.500	5	6	0	.455
Sam Houston State	1	5	0	.167	6	5	0	.545
Nicholls State	1	5	0	.167	5	6	0	.455
Southwest Texas	1	5	0	.167	4	7	0	.364

*Includes 0-1 record in I-AA playoffs
&Includes 1-1 record in I-AA playoffs

1996								
	Conference				All Games			
School	W	L	T	Pct	W	L	T	Pct
Troy State*	5	1	0	.833	12	2	0	.857
Nicholls State&	4	2	0	.667	8	4	0	.667
Stephen F. Austin	3	3	0	.500	7	4	0	.636
Northwestern State	3	3	0	.500	6	5	0	.545
Sam Houston State	3	3	0	.500	4	7	0	.364
Southwest Texas	2	4	0	.333	5	6	0	.455
McNeese State	1	5	0	.167	3	8	0	.273

*Includes 2-1 record in I-AA playoffs
&Includes 0-1 record in I-AA playoffs

1995								
	Conference				All Games			
School	W	L	T	Pct	W	L	T	Pct
McNeese State*	5	0	0	1.000	13	1	0	.928
Stephen F. Austin*	4	1	0	.800	11	2	0	.846
Northwestern State	2	3	0	.400	6	5	0	.545
Sam Houston State	2	3	0	.400	5	5	0	.500
Southwest Texas	2	3	0	.400	4	7	0	.364
Nicholls State	0	5	0	.000	0	11	0	.000

*Includes 2-1 record in I-AA playoffs

1997								
	Conference				All Games			
School	W	L	T	Pct	W	L	T	Pct
McNeese State*	6	1	0	.857	13	2	0	.867
Northwestern State&	6	1	0	.857	8	4	0	.667
Stephen F. Austin	5	2	0	.714	8	3	0	.727
Sam Houston State	3	4	0	.429	5	6	0	.455
Nicholls State	3	4	0	.429	5	6	0	.455
Southwest Texas	2	5	0	.286	5	6	0	.455
Troy State	2	5	0	.286	5	6	0	.455
Jacksonville State	1	6	0	.143	1	10	0	.091

*Includes 3-1 record in I-AA playoffs
&Includes 0-1 record in I-AA playoffs

1998							
	Conference				All Games		
School	W	L	T	Pct	W	L	T	Pct
Northwestern State*	6	1	0	.857	11	3	0	.786
McNeese State&	5	2	0	.714	9	3	0	.750
Troy State&	5	2	0	.714	8	4	0	.667
Jacksonville State	4	3	0	.571	7	4	0	.636
Nicholls State	3	4	0	.429	4	7	0	.364
Southwest Texas	2	5	0	.286	4	7	0	.364
Stephen F. Austin	2	5	0	.286	3	8	0	.273
Sam Houston State	1	6	0	.143	3	8	0	.273

*Includes 2-1 record in I-AA playoffs
&Includes 0-1 record in I-AA playoffs

2000							
	Conference				All Games		
School	W	L	T	Pct	W	L	T	Pct
Troy State*	7	0	0	1.000	10	2	0	.833
McNeese State*	5	2	0	.714	8	4	0	.667
Southwest Texas	5	2	0	.714	7	4	0	.636
Sam Houston State	4	3	0	.571	7	4	0	.636
Stephen F. Austin	3	4	0	.429	6	5	0	.545
Jacksonville State	2	5	0	.286	4	6	0	.400
Northwestern State	1	6	0	.143	4	7	0	.364
Nicholls State	1	6	0	.143	2	9	0	.182

*Includes 0-1 record in I-AA playoffs; Note: Northwestern State forfeited conference wins against Troy State and Nicholls State as the result of the use of an ineligible player. The standing reflect the forfeitures.

1999							
	Conference				All Games		
School	W	L	T	Pct	W	L	T	Pct
Troy State*	6	1	0	.857	11	2	0	.846
Stephen F. Austin	6	1	0	.857	8	3	0	.727
McNeese State	5	2	0	.714	6	5	0	.545
Sam Houston State	4	3	0	.571	6	5	0	..545
Nicholls State	3	4	0	.429	4	7	0	.364
Southwest Texas	2	5	0	.286	3	8	0	.273
Jacksonville State	1	6	0	.143	2	9	0	.182
Nicholls State	1	6	0	.143	1	10	0	.091

*Includes 1-1 record in I-AA playoffs

2001							
	Conference				All Games		
School	W	L	T	Pct	W	L	T	Pct
Sam Houston State*	5	1	0	.833	10	3	0	.769
McNeese State&	5	1	0	.833	8	4	0	.667
Northwestern State&	4	2	0	.667	8	4	0	.667
Stephen F. Austin	4	2	0	.667	6	5	0	.545
Jacksonville State	2	4	0	.333	5	6	0	.455
Nicholls State	1	5	0	.167	3	8	0	.273
Southwest Texas	0	6	0	.000	4	7	0	.364

*Includes 1-1 record in I-AA playoffs
&Includes 0-1 record in I-AA playoffs

2002								
	Conference				All Games			
School	W	L	T	Pct	W	L	T	Pct
McNeese State*	6	0	0	1.000	13	2	0	.967
Northwestern State&	4	2	0	.667	9	4	0	.692
Nicholls State	3	3	0	.500	7	4	0	.636
Stephen F. Austin	3	3	0	.500	6	5	0	.545
Jacksonville State	2	4	0	.333	5	5	0	.500
Sam Houston State	2	4	0	.333	4	7	0	.364
Southwest Texas	1	5	0	.167	4	7	0	.364

*Includes 3-1 record in I-AA playoffs
&Includes 0-1 record in I-AA playoffs

2003								
	Conference				All Games			
School	W	L	T	Pct	W	L	T	Pct
McNeese State*	5	0	0	1.000	10	2	0	.833
Stephen F. Austin	4	1	0	.800	7	4	0	.636
Northwestern State	2	3	0	.400	7	5	0	.583
Texas State	2	3	0	.400	5	7	0	.417
Sam Houston State	2	3	0	.400	3	8	0	.272
Nicholls State	0	5	0	.000	0	11	0	.000

*Includes 0-1 record in I-AA playoffs; Note: Nicholls State forfeited league wins to Northwestern State, Sam Houston State and Texas State and two non-conference wins for use of ineligible players. The standing reflect the forfeitures.

2004								
	Conference				All Games			
School	W	L	T	Pct	W	L	T	Pct
Sam Houston State*	4	1	0	.800	11	3	0	.786
Northwestern State&	4	1	0	.800	8	4	0	.667
Texas State	3	2	0	.600	5	6	0	.454
Nicholls State	2	3	0	.400	5	5	0	.500
McNeese State	1	4	0	.200	4	7	0	.364
Stephen F. Austin	1	4	0	.200	6	5	0	.545

*Includes 2-1 record in I-AA playoffs
&Includes 0-1 record in I-AA playoffs

2005								
	Conference				All Games			
School	W	L	T	Pct	W	L	T	Pct
Texas State*	5	1	0	.833	11	3	0	.786
Nicholls State&	5	1	0	.833	6	4	0	,600
McNeese State	3	3	0	.500	5	4	0	.556
Northwestern State	3	3	0	.500	5	5	0	.500
Southeastern Louisiana	2	4	0	.333	4	6	0	.400
Sam Houston State	2	4	0	.333	3	7	0	.300
Stephen F. Austin	1	5	0	.167	5	6	0	.455

*Includes 2-1 record in I-AA playoffs
&Includes 0-1 record in I-AA playoffs

2006							
	Conference				All Games		
School	W	L	T	Pct	W	L	T	Pct
McNeese State*	5	1	0	.833	7	5	0	.583
Sam Houston State	4	2	0	.667	6	5	0	.545
Stephen F. Austin	4	2	0	.667	4	7	0	.364
Texas State	3	3	0	.500	5	6	0	.455
Nicholls State	2	4	0	.333	4	7	0	.364
Northwestern State	2	4	0	.333	4	7	0	.364
Southeastern Louisiana	1	5	0	.167	2	9	0	.182

*Includes 0-1 record in FCS playoffs

2007							
	Conference				All Games		
School	W	L	T	Pct	W	L	T	Pct
McNeese State*	7	0	0	1.000	11	1	0	.917
Sam Houston State	5	2	0	.714	7	4	0	.636
Central Arkansas	5	2	0	.714	6	5	0	.545
Nicholls State	3	4	0	.429	6	5	0	.545
Texas State	3	4	0	.429	4	7	0	.364
Northwestern State	3	4	0	.429	4	7	0	.364
Southeastern Louisiana	2	5	0	.286	3	8	0	.273
Stephen F. Austin	0	7	0	.000	0	11	0	.000

*Includes 0-1 record in FCS playoffs

2008							
	Conference				All Games		
School	W	L	T	Pct	W	L	T	Pct
Central Arkansas*	6	1	0	.857	10	2	0	.833
Texas State&	5	2	0	.714	8	5	0	.615
McNeese State	4	3	0	.571	7	4	0	.636
Northwestern State	4	3	0	.571	7	5	0	.583
Nicholls State	3	4	0	.429	3	6	0	.333
Southeastern Louisiana	2	5	0	.286	5	7	0	.417
Sam Houston State	2	5	0	.286	4	6	0	.400
Stephen F. Austin	2	5	0	.286	4	8	0	.333

*Ineligible for Southland Conference championship and postseason play during transition to NCAA Division I.
&Includes 0-1 record in FCS playoffs.

2009							
	Conference				All Games		
School	W	L	T	Pct	W	L	T	Pct
Stephen F. Austin*	6	1	0	.857	10	3	0	.769
McNeese State&	6	1	0	.857	9	3	0	.750
Texas State	5	2	0	.714	7	4	0	.636
Southeastern Louisiana	4	3	0	.571	6	5	0	.545
Sam Houston State	3	4	0	.429	5	6	0	.455
Central Arkansas	2	5	0	.286	5	7	0	.417
Nicholls State	2	5	0	.286	4	8	0	.273
Northwestern State	0	7	0	.000	0	11	0	.000

*Includes 1-1 in FCS playoffs
&Includes 0-1 in FCS in playoffs

2010								
	Conference				All Games			
School	W	L	T	Pct	W	L	T	Pct
Stephen F. Austin*	6	1	0	.857	9	3	0	.750
McNeese State	5	2	0	.714	6	5	0	.545
Central Arkansas	4	3	0	.571	7	4	0	.636
Sam Houston State	4	3	0	.571	6	5	0	.545
Northwestern State	4	3	0	.571	5	6	0	.455
Nicholls State	3	4	0	.429	4	7	0	.364
Texas State	1	6	0	.143	4	7	0	.364
Southeastern Louisiana	1	6	0	.143	2	9	0	.182
*Includes 0-1 in FCS playoffs								

2012								
	Conference				All Games			
School	W	L	T	Pct	W	L	T	Pct
Central Arkansas*	6	1	0	.857	9	3	0	.750
Sam Houston State&	6	1	0	.857	11	4	0	.733
Southeastern Louisiana	5	2	0	.714	5	6	0	.454
McNeese State	4	3	0	.571	7	4	0	.636
Stephen F. Austin	4	3	0	.571	5	6	0	.454
Northwestern State	2	5	0	.286	4	7	0	.364
Lamar University	1	6	0	.143	4	8	0	.333
Nicholls State	0	7	0	.000	1	10	0	.091
*Includes 0-1 in FCS playoffs								
&Includes 3-1 in FCS playoffs								

2011								
	Conference				All Games			
School	W	L	T	Pct	W	L	T	Pct
Sam Houston State*	7	0	0	1.000	14	1	0	.933
Central Arkansas&	6	1	0	.857	9	4	0	.692
Stephen F. Austin	5	2	0	.714	6	5	0	.545
McNeese State	4	3	0	.571	6	5	0	.545
Northwestern State	4	3	0	.571	6	5	0	.545
Lamar University	2	5	0	.286	4	7	0	.364
Southeastern Louisiana	1	6	0	.143	3	8	0	.273
Nicholls State	0	7	0	.000	1	10	0	.091
*Includes 3-1 in FCS playoffs								
&Includes 1-1 in FCS playoffs								

2013								
	Conference				All Games			
School	W	L	T	Pct	W	L	T	Pct
Southeastern Louisiana*	7	0	0	1.000	11	3	0	.786
McNeese State&	6	1	0	.857	10	3	0	.769
Sam Houston State	4	3	0	.571	9	5	0	.643
Central Arkansas	4	3	0	.571	7	5	0	.583
Northwestern State	3	4	0	.364	6	6	0	.500
Lamar University	2	5	0	.286	5	7	0	.500
Nicholls State	1	6	0	.143	4	8	0	.333
Stephen F. Austin	1	6	0	.143	3	9	0	.250
*Includes 1-1 in FCS playoffs								
&Includes 0-1 in FCS playoffs								

Printed in the United States
By Bookmasters

Printed in the United States
By Bookmasters